Introduction to
STRUCTURALISM

Introduction to
STRUCTURALISM

EDITED AND INTRODUCED BY

MICHAEL LANE

BASIC BOOKS, Inc., Publishers   New York

Introduction and compilation © 1970 by Michael Lane
Library of Congress Catalog Card Number: 71-135624
SBN 465-09508-9

The Editor is grateful to the following for permission to
reproduce copyright material:
Peter Owen, London and Philosophical Library, New
York; M.I.T. Press, Cambridge, Massachusetts; Indiana
University Press; Linguistic Circle of New York; Social
Science Information; *L'Esprit*; Mouton & Co., The Hague;
L'Homme; *Les Temps Modernes*; *Yale French Review*;
European Journal of Sociology; Cambridge University Press;
Sociology; *The Times Literary Supplement*; M. Roland
Barthes, Professor Roman Jakobson, Professor Claude
Lévi-Strauss, Dr Edmund Leach.

Published in Great Britain under the title:
Structuralism: A Reader

check
Foucault

Printed in the United States of America

10 9 8 7 6 5 4 3

CONTENTS

Contents

ACKNOWLEDGMENTS

The author of any book such as this, which attempts to pursue a method through fields and across disciplines, is inevitably indebted to the advice and assistance of many, unless he be polymath, which I am not.

My initial debt, though it is the most distant in time, is far from being the least important. More than anyone else Raymond Williams made me aware of the fruitfulness of ignoring the strict, traditional, academic boundaries. At the time I was disconcerted by it: I have been grateful ever since. More directly I am indebted to the work of Edmund Leach and Rodney Needham who have done more than any others to make available and accessible the ideas of the structuralists. There is no doubt that without their pioneering work this book would not have existed.

My largest general debt, though, is that which I owe to my colleagues at the University of Essex, whose company is a constant source of stimulation, if not comfort. In particular I have had several useful discussions on structuralism with Alasdair MacIntyre, though we are by no means in agreement. Nevertheless, he has sharpened my own thinking on the subject. Peter Abell of the Department of Sociology and Roger Purves of the University of California at Berkeley were invaluable for the aid they gave me in understanding the notion of structure in mathematics. I made considerable use of Katie Furness-Lane's knowledge of French, apart from its application to the translation of one of the most difficult pieces. Alan Ryan, of New College, Oxford, gave me the benefit of his philosophical knowledge, and Professor Meyer Fortes of the Department of Anthropology at the University of Cambridge allowed me to test out some of my ideas on his students. I must acknowledge the work done by Christine Troughton, who was my research assistant for much of the time while I was working on the book. Her voluminous knowledge of publishing and her gift for ferreting out material from the most unlikely corners of libraries, and then organizing it in a way that was easy for me to handle, were, quite literally, invaluable. We are jointly responsible for the Bibliography at the end of the volume. Joan Busfield, who read the many manuscript drafts of my introduction with enormous care, made many useful suggestions. Where it is intelligible most of the credit is hers. Any blame, needless to say, remains my own.

Acknowledgments

Finally, Ed Victor, of Jonathan Cape, was all and more than I could ask for in a publisher, as much for his patience and tolerance as for his skill and knowledge.

MICHAEL LANE

TO MY PARENTS

INTRODUCTION

I. THE STRUCTURALIST METHOD

Intellectual movements are seldom easy to describe, and structuralism presents more difficulties than most. In the first place, it is a mode of thought common to disciplines as widely separated as mathematics and literary criticism. Next, its debts to the past and its relations to the present are highly eclectic. Again, none of those who call themselves or are called 'structuralist' has explicitly formulated the fundamentals of structuralism, except in the most allusive or partial way. Finally, the literature of structuralism is very widely dispersed and very often inaccessible, not only in terms of place of publication but also linguistically. This collection sets out to remedy that defect by bringing together in one volume a selection of articles from learned journals and extracts from books which is, as far as possible, representative of the range and depth of structuralist activity.

In editing and introducing this collection I am conscious of two audiences and a double duty. On the one hand there is the specialist reader or scholar who is well informed concerning the literature of his own subject, but who would like to know how the application of structuralism in his own particular field relates to its application in others. On the other hand there are those readers, students and the body of what are often called educated laymen, who wish to extend their knowledge of contemporary intellectual currents. These two audiences differ not only in their attributes but also in their demands. The former, for example, rightly expects a full critical apparatus with references and footnotes, whilst the latter, equally rightly, finds these a hindrance to comprehension. There are various ways in which an editor can respond to this conflict, ranging from an outright refusal to recognize that it exists, to writing two separate versions, one for his colleagues, the other for the public at large. My own choice tends somewhat to the latter. This book has in effect two introductions. In Part I, I have tried to provide as straightforward a guide as the complexities of the subject will permit, uncluttered by references or details that are not central to the thread of the argument. In Part II, 'Structure and Structuralism', I have gone more deeply into some of the more purely scholarly problems that structuralism involves: there I have felt free to employ a conventional critical apparatus. The two are essentially complementary, rather than versions of the same material at differing levels of difficulty. The student or non-academic reader may prefer to go directly to the examples of structuralist writing after reading the first introduction; the specialist, on the other hand, may find some advantage in first going on to 'Structure and Structuralism'.

In that strange and attractive book, *Tristes Tropiques*, part autobiography, part traveller's tale, part anthropologist's fieldwork diary, Claude Lévi-Strauss has described how he studied philosophy and law, and came to give them up in favour of sociology and ethnology. Then, in 1935, he left France to go and teach at the University of São Paulo in Brazil, and found himself in a position to carry out fieldwork amongst idigenous tribes. In particular he was able to organize an expedition to the hinterland of central Brazil to study the Nambikwara Indians, a group which until that time had had no contact with the civilized world for over thirty years. By comparison with the other tribes that he studied, themselves primitive, its material condition led Lévi-Strauss to the impression, in his own words, that he was in the presence of 'the childhood of humanity'. From this encounter and the cross-fertilizing experience of war-time meetings in America with the structural linguist Roman Jakobson developed what is (with the possible exception of Jakobson's own work) the most extended and systematic application of structuralist methods and the structuralist vision to human phenomena. None would deny Lévi-Strauss the stature of a figure of major intellectual importance, though he is neither the inventor of structuralism nor its only practitioner (as witness, for example, Barthes in literary criticism, Leach in anthropology and Althusser in political science). Much, though by no means all, of what follows derives from what he has said, or is inferred from what he has practised. (Some of the more important differences within structuralism are discussed in 'Structure and Structuralism'.)

The problems which confront all anthropologists, Lévi-Strauss included, can best be expressed as a series of questions. First, how can the social behaviour of any human group be most exactly, meaningfully and intelligibly described? Next, how can these social phenomena be accounted for or explained? More important, how do the different sets of social phenomena within a single group – its myths, its system of kinship and marriage and so on – relate one to another, and to the totality? Finally, what are the interrelations, if any, that exist between social groups as wholes, whether they be primitive tribes, feudal states or advanced industrial societies? What have they in common that might provide a basis for meaningful comparison? These are all questions for which sociology and social anthropology have traditionally sought answers. Structuralism, in the eyes of its practitioners, constitutes essentially a *method* for handling these questions and ordering the raw material of observed fact in order to answer them.

I have emphasized the word 'method'. Man believes his world to be orderly and we can, somewhat artificially, but nevertheless usefully, divide the means that men employ to order their universe into two categories: theories and methods. By the former I mean any more or less consistent system of beliefs and values which describes and accounts for the relations of men to one another, and to the material, and not infrequently the immaterial, universe. This category includes religions, philosophies and sometimes political ideologies, which may be basically conscious, or basically unconscious and simply taken for granted. By the latter I mean any set of rules or regulations which describes and prescribes the operations to be performed upon any matter (in the case of Lévi-Strauss, the social behaviour of primitive peoples) with the purpose of ordering it and understanding its workings. The most obvious example of this category is the 'scientific method', which lays down rules for ordering, on the basis of empirical observation and experiment. Now, this distinction, as I have said, is clearly artificial, in that we would nowhere find *only* a system of beliefs, or *only* a system of methods. Any example of the former will tend to have attached certain methods for verifying its truth; any example of the latter depends ultimately upon certain theoretical assumptions. That they are, nevertheless, separate can be easily demonstrated. Astronomers share a common method in their work, yet one group holds to a 'steady state' theory of the universe, another to a 'big bang' theory. Structuralism belongs clearly to the category of methods in that it prescribes certain operations and ways of working upon data, though in so doing it makes certain theoretical assumptions.

What, then, are the distinctive properties of structuralism? In the first place it is presented as a method whose scope includes all human social phenomena, no matter what their form, thus embracing not only the social sciences proper (anthropology, sociology, politics, economics and psychology) but also the humanities (literature, history and linguistics) and the fine arts. This is made possible by the belief that all manifestations of social activity, whether it be the clothes that are worn, the books that are written or the systems of kinship and marriage that are practised in

assumpt.?

any society, constitute languages, in a formal sense. Hence their regularities may be reduced to the same set of abstract rules that define and govern what we normally think of as language. In an attempt to reduce terminological confusion the word 'code' is sometimes used, notably by Roland Barthes, to cover all types of socially employed systems of communication. All these social codes are seen to have, like natural languages, a lexicon, or 'vocabulary'. If we take as an example the code of kinship and marriage, as Lévi-Strauss did in his first major book, *Les Structures élémentaires de la parenté* (*Elementary Structures of Kinship*), we see that all those members of a society who stand in a kinship relation (or kinship relations) to other members constitute the lexicon, or repertory, of permissible terms. The rules about who may, and who may not, marry whom, constitute the syntax, or grammar, which determines what elements may be legitimately (or 'meaningfully') strung together. Roland Barthes has similarly attempted (in *Système de la mode*) to construct a lexicon and syntax for fashion.

Probably the most distinctive feature of the structuralist method is the emphasis it gives to wholes, to totalities. Traditionally, in Anglo-American social science, structure has been used as an analytical concept to break down sets into their constituent elements, an essentially atomistic exercise. As structuralists understand and employ the term, a new importance has been given to the logical priority of the whole over its parts. They insist that the whole and the parts can be properly explained only in terms of the *relations* that exist between the parts. The essential quality of the structuralist method, and its fundamental tenet, lies in its attempt to study not the elements of a whole, but the complex network of relationships that link and unite those elements. Hence in the three volumes entitled *Mythologiques* which Lévi-Strauss has written about the myths of Amerindia we are given not the traditional explanation of a series of myths, or even of the recurrent episodes and figures that occur in them, but rather an account of the relations of myths to one another, and the relations of episodes to wholes. These three volumes show moreover the exhaustive quality of the structuralist method.

Next, structuralism seeks its structures not on the surface, at the level of the observed, but below or behind empirical reality. Lévi-Strauss, in the Overture to *Le Cru et le cuit* (*The Raw and the Cooked*), both states this most forcibly and gives the rationale for it. 'We should not exclude the possibility that the men themselves, who produce and pass on these myths, *could* be aware of their structure and mode of operation, though this would not be usual, but rather partial and intermittent.' He compares the situation to that of men using their own language. Though they consistently and constantly apply its phonological and grammatical laws (its structure, in other words) in their speech, they will not, unless they are versed in linguistics, be consciously aware of them. Nor, if asked, would they be able to supply these laws. The same is true, the structuralists argue, of all social activity. What the observer sees is not the structure, but simply

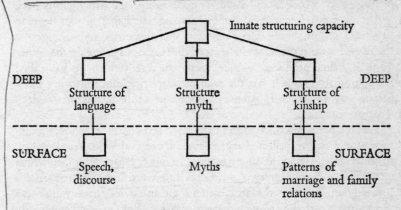

the evidence and product of the structure. On the other hand, though the structure of any activity is not itself what can be seen, it can only be derived from what is seen. It is beyond the scope of this Introduction to discuss the nature of this 'deep' structure (as it has been called by the American linguist Noam Chomsky, in opposition to the 'surface' structure – what we actually see or hear). Nevertheless, there seems to be general, if implicit, agreement among certain structuralists, notably Lévi-Strauss in anthropology, Roman Jakobson in linguistics, Jean Piaget in psychology and François Jacob in biology, that there is in man an innate, genetically transmitted and determined mechanism that acts as a structuring force. Moreover, this inherent quality or capacity is so designed as to limit the possible range of ways of structuring. It has been pointed out, for example, that the structures of natural languages (that is, those that actually exist) represent only a very restricted spectrum of the possible structures of language. If this is the case (and it is still being vigorously debated by scholars in the various disciplines), then we can imagine a hierarchy in which the innate structure generates a specialized structure for a particular type of activity – language, myth or kinship systems, say – which in turn produces the observable pattern of speech, story or marriage.

This model makes more clear, perhaps, the reasons for the structuralist emphasis on the essential indivisibility of all the social phenomena emanating from any given society. If phenomena are simultaneously created and circumscribed in the way this diagram suggests, then we would expect to find the homologies, or correspondences in structure, between one aspect of a society and another, upon which the structuralists have laid such stress. Again, Lévi-Strauss has suggested that groups develop structural means of resolving conflicts, inconsistencies and ambiguities that arise between different elements of the surface structure, in the course of their being produced by the deep structure (which he has called 'mediating structures'). For the sake of simplicity, and following Lévi-Strauss's own practice, I shall use the word 'structure' to refer to this deep structure alone.

The 'relations' described earlier exist at the level of the structure, though they are, of course, reflected at the level of observable empirical reality. In abstract these relations can be reduced to one of *binary opposition*, which term tends to be used in two somewhat different senses. The first sense is precisely analogous to that in which a logician ascribes truth values to a propositional variable '*p*', such that it is either true or false, and conversely such that 'not *p*' ($\sim p$, in logicians' notation) is either false or true. This sense is further exemplified in the logical calculus of classes when the universe of discourse is said to be divided into the class α and its complement $\sim\alpha$ ('not α'), two mutually exclusive and exhaustive categories. In this sense a structural anthropologist might divide the members of a group into the categories 'married' and 'not married', which would constitute a binary opposition. The second sense in which the concept is used is far less rigorous in terms of formal logic, and includes the bulk of the binary oppositions found in structuralist analyses. The title of the first volume of Lévi-Strauss's *Mythologiques, Le Cru et le cuit*, is an instance of this sense, as are the bulk of the oppositions he employs in it: for example, fire/water, Sun/Moon, ant-eater/jaguar. These are not logically pairs of complementary, exhaustive, mutually exclusive categories in the sense in which 'α', '$\sim\alpha$' is, but are shown by the author to be perceived as such, within *specific contexts*, by the groups who employ the terms in their myths.

Further, structuralist analysis is centrally concerned with synchronic as opposed to diachronic structures; its focus is upon relations across a moment in time, rather than through time. For the structuralist time as a dimension is no less, but also no more important than any other that might be used in analysis. History is seen as the specific mode of development of a particular system, whose present, or synchronic nature must be fully known before any account can be given of its evolution, or diachronic nature. Moreover, the synchronic structure is seen as being constituted or determined not by any historical process, but by the network of existing structural relations. Hence structuralism is rather atemporal than strictly ahistorical.

Partly as a result of this, structuralism is effectively anti-causal. The language of structuralist analysis in its pure form makes no use of the notions of cause and effect: rather, it rejects this conceptualization of the world in favour of 'laws of transformation'. By these are meant the law-like regularities that can be observed, or derived from observation, by which one particular structural configuration changes into another. What the structuralists are saying is essentially this: if we compare two patterns of social relations (once again they may be myths, or kinship relations, or patterns of power and authority, or any other such), separated by time or space (in other words the same society at two different points in history, or two societies at the same point in history), we observe differences in their respective structural configuration, the order and nature of the patterning of relations. Traditionally we should argue that a particular factor or factors *caused* the one to differ from the other. The structuralist would argue, instead, that we can only say that a certain structure is seen to be *transformed* into another structure, and that repeated observations permit us to say that a given structure is always transformed in a particular way, thus giving us not causal laws (since that concept has not been invoked) but laws of transformation.

No single one of these properties is by itself a distinguishing characteristic of structuralism. Most have separately been held as items of belief or rules of procedure in other philosophies and methods. What is distinctive is this particular combination of them.

Various objections have been voiced against structuralism which must be noted. In many cases the battle rages on, and final answers (if such things exist) are still far off. I have described structuralism as a method, a definition with which most who are called structuralist would emphatically agree. Nevertheless, as I have also suggested, the divorce between theory and method can never be complete. Structuralism is taxed by its critics with two failings in this respect. First, it has been accused of making an excessive number of theoretical assumptions which are both important and untested. These are, briefly:

1. All patterns of human social behaviour are codes, with the characteristics of languages.
2. Man has an innate structuring capacity which determines the limits within which the structure of all types of social phenomena can be formed.
3. Relations can be reduced to binary oppositions. (Though this may be logically true, the critics argue – in that any universe, as we have seen, can be divided into classes α and ∼α – this type of opposition is trivial and sterile and has been replaced by another, which is not logically sound, *and* imposes false, distorting categories upon social reality.)

Second, it has been accused of modulating from a method into a full-fledged theory, or ideology even, without admitting the fact or recognizing its implications. The latter criticism I leave to the reader of my selections to judge. As for the former, I have listed the theoretical assumptions that are attacked and must again leave a final decision to the reader.

Next, structuralism has been attacked for effectively ignoring history. By setting time as a dimension on a par with any other it has ignored the particular and vital quality of movement through time, that it is irreversible. Again, it is suggested that structuralist models of man and society are simply an heuristic device, a help to understanding. Society, the sceptics say, is not actually at all like the structuralists' description of it, though it may help to make society intelligible to behave as if it were. Laws of transformation have been attacked: conventionally scientific *explanation* as opposed to *description* has always dealt with causes. By eliminating them the structuralists, it is said, have eliminated the possibility of satisfactory, adequate explanation. Finally, it is said that structuralism simply does not work: it is nothing more than an intellectual castle in the air that has proved quite ineffectual in handling the earthy stuff of social reality. The reader will find some of these doubts and criticisms discussed at greater length in 'Structure and Structuralism'. All of them stand or fall by what the structuralists themselves, rather than those who comment upon them, have written.

My aim has been to provide a selection of structuralist writing that represents not only the breadth of the fields covered but also some of the variation in approach that may be found within a single field. Beyond that I can only echo the words of generations of editors: the perfect, complete anthology is a mythical beast, pursued with a mixture of vigour and despair, but never caught. There are always authors or pieces whose omission one regrets wholeheartedly but whose absence is, for some reason or another, inevitable. Here, for example, I have included no Dumézil or Lacan. The taste of the former is, I hope, conveyed by Einar Haugen's 'The Mythical Structure of the Ancient Scandinavians'. The latter, like Michel Foucault, is almost impossible to do justice to in a short extract, and with a single exception I have adopted a policy of including only whole articles or papers, in fairness to the authors. The selection from Lévi-Strauss is unusual in that it includes two very little-known items: I have included these because they are too good and too representative to remain inaccessible and unknown in the English-speaking world. In the end, though, this remains a personal choice, yet, I hope, one that will give some of the pleasure I have derived from compiling it to those who read it.

II. STRUCTURE AND STRUCTURALISM

No description of structuralism is possible without a prior consideration of the underlying notion of 'structure'. Of the eight definitions that the *Oxford English Dictionary* provides, four deal with the act of building, arising out of the etymological basis of the word (from the Latin *struere*, to build). However, as the other four definitions and the examples used to illustrate them show, the word has from an early date been used with other significations: thus 'the mutual relation of the constituents, parts or elements of a whole, as determining its peculiar nature or character' and 'the coexistence in a whole of distinct parts having a definite manner of arrangement' and 'an organized body or combination of mutually connected and dependent parts or elements. Chiefly in Biology applied to component parts of an animal or vegetable organism.'

Hence 'structure' entered other fields originally as a metaphor derived from building; though clearly its usage long ago converted it from a figure of speech into a term proper to the disciplines which employ it. The first question is: What do its users understand by this term?[1] This is far from being as simple as it appears at first sight; if we ignore for the time being the self-styled (and I do not mean this pejoratively) structuralists who may have a special notion of what constitutes structures which is radically different from some other general non-structuralist usage, we have, nevertheless, two difficulties to face. First, that even in disciplines where relatively rigorous definitions are usual – in mathematics, for example – concepts may vary from context to context; second, that much of the popularity of the term, particularly in the social sciences and the humanities, springs from the flexibility with which it can be employed. It seems that it is at least partly its inherent imprecision which enhances its utility. Some who employ it in an imprecise and ill-defined way do so, moreover, wittingly, and would argue very strongly against any attempt at greater definitional rigour on the following grounds. First, that the material from which their structures are derived or to which they are applied is of such a nature as to defy methodological over-niceness; second, that any hard-edged definition would have to be at such a high level of generality as to be, of necessity, trivial. Some have argued against this that it is, rather, contingent factors – the relative newness of the subjects as academic disciplines, the lack of technical skills and the anti-pathy of scholars in these disciplines to precise and 'scientific' modes of thought – than any intrinsic intractability in the material studied, that give rise to this looseness, which could in principle be avoided. This is only partly true, at least in the present state of knowledge. For those in the social siences and humanities who themselves use the word (as opposed to anyone who, as I am doing, comments on its usage), one further major obstacle remains which I can do no more than indicate as a problem here, though its implications should be clear.

The disciplines employing the notion 'structure' can be ordered along a continuum, ranging from mathematics through the physical sciences, the life sciences, the social sciences, to the humanities. (This is not a perfect or exhaustive ordering: certain disciplines, linguistics for example, as will be seen below, occupy a somewhat anomalous position.) Mathematics, first, possesses structure *by definition*. Even so, as Pouillon[2] points out, the Bourbaki (the pseudonym of a group of French structuralist mathematicians) tend to define it implicitly rather than explicitly. Nevertheless, any relation or any operation on a set of objects – which is what mathematics consists of – constitutes 'putting structure' on that set. Though mathematics may from choice concern itself with structures which represent features of the empirical world it does not of necessity do so. In this way it is distinguished from all other disciplines (if we define mathematics sufficiently loosely to include certain logical calculuses).[3] The relationship between the natural sciences and the social sciences has been extensively discussed[4] and there is no virtue in rehearsing these arguments again here. Three generally acknowledged points of difference between the two groups of disciplines are relevant to the present discussion: first, that 'in no area of social inquiry has a body of general laws been established, comparable with outstanding theories in the natural sciences in scope of explanatory power or in capacity to yield precise and reliable predictions';[5] second, that 'in the social sciences there is nothing like the almost complete unanimity commonly found among competent workers in the natural sciences as to what are matters of established fact'[6] and hence little or no sense among social scientists of working in an area in which knowledge is in any way cumulative; and third, that there is still extensive debate over what has been called 'the supposed consequences of the fact that the study of society is part of its own subject-matter'.[7] The impact of phenomeno-logical thinkers such as Schutz[8] and Merleau-Ponty[9] has only served to heighten the debate over the respective merits and meanings of 'inter-subjectivity' and 'objectivity'.

The consequences for the notion of structure are immediately apparent; in asserting that the structure of the helium atom is *this* rather than *that*, the physicist has available to him a corpus of accepted knowledge and explanatory laws which may be used to verify whether or not the given elements of his structure (sub-atomic particles, say) are present, and whether or not the relationship between those elements that he posits holds. Whether or not his fellow-scientists would accept the utility or virtue of thinking in such terms is not at issue here.[10] On the other hand, the social anthropologist's assertion that such a group has such a structure of exchange, or the sociologist's assertion that such a society has such a structure of stratification and mobility, tends to beg more questions than it answers and arouse more objections than it satisfies, since, as we have seen, neither has available to him for purposes of verification the re-sources of a body of more or less unquestioned facts, or generally accepted laws of relation. This means, in effect, that though the possibility of using a notion of structure is in principle not entirely ruled out, the probability is, in practice, very high that any given example will be rejected.[11]

Some of these objections and difficulties can be more clearly seen if we look at the use of 'structure' in specific contexts. It may also be easier to see ways in which the objections might be overcome. Psychology pro-vides a good example of this. The long-standing links between psychology and biology have given rise to a natural propensity among psychologists to conceive of psychic structure along the lines of an organic model. However, the most explicit and obvious recourse to a notion of structure is to be seen not so much among physiological psychologists as in gestalt theory. (Indeed, the word *Gestalt* is usually, when translated, rendered either as 'structure' or 'configuration'.) According to gestalt theorists complex perceptions cannot adequately be accounted for simply as the sum of the sensations that go to make up those perceptions. The mind acts to organize or structure perception and behaviour in such a way that the resultant structure of parts in relation has characteristic properties which are not subsumed in its constituent elements. Defined very simply, structure designated, for the early gestaltists such as Köhler, the configurations of the perceptual or behavioural field, wholes articulated by lines of force (analogous to the operations of current in an electromagnetic field), which gave every phenomenon its local value. Hence no part could alter or be altered without its affecting everything held within that net of relationships. According to Piaget,[12] we may locate the origin of these structures in one of three possible sources. First, we may see them as the result of some kind of preformation, whether it be by predestination or biological determinism. Second, they may be the result of what he called 'contingent creation', as in Foucault's notion of an *archéologie* of ideas.[13] Finally, they may arise from acts of construction, out of experience, for example.

The initial inspiration that physics gave to psychologists such as Köhler (most evident in the concept 'field') has remained strongly evident in the work of his largely social-psychological successors, notably Kurt Lewin,[14] where it has been cross-fertilized with the developments of Moreno's sociometric analyses. However, the failure of this rather mechanical concept of structure has been, first, in its inability to account for certain observed phenomena,[15] and second, in the way in which it has more generally left no room for the actor's or perceiver's intentionality, his individual capacity for structuring perception and behaviour.

In contrast to the confusions and uncertainties that attend the use of the word 'structure' in psychology, mathematical usage presents a model of clarity and elegance. One of the most familiar mathematical structures is the group, discovered by Galois. In part, a group is a set of elements (for example, the positive and negative whole numbers), together with a binary operation (for example, addition) such that when it is applied to a pair of elements of the set it returns an element of the set.[16] To complete the definition of a group it is necessary to specify certain conditions which the binary operation must satisfy. These are:

(i) The operation must be closed. That is, if a, b are any elements of the group then $a \otimes b$[17] must also be an element of the group.

(ii) The operation must be associative. That is, if a, b, c are any elements of the group, then $(a \otimes b) \otimes c = a \otimes (b \otimes c)$.

(iii) There must be a unit element, e, in the group – that is, an element which satisfies the equations $e \otimes a = a \otimes e = a$ for every member a.

(iv) There must be inverse elements. That is, for each member a of the group there must be a member a^{-1} such that $a \otimes a^{-1} = e$.

In general, an algebraic structure is a set, together with one or more binary operations which typically meet conditions similar to those mentioned in the case of the group. Other commonly studied algebraic structures are the groupoid, the semi-group, the ring, the field and the vector space.

Sets may also possess structure by virtue of the presence of one or more *relations*.[18] A basic type of binary relation is the equivalence relation. An equivalence relation ($\sim$) is one which satisfies three conditions:

(i) Reflexivity: for every element a in the domain of the relation, $a \sim a$.

(ii) Symmetry: for every a, b if $a \sim b$ then $b \sim a$.

(iii) Transitivity: for every a, b, c if $a \sim b$ and $b \sim c$ then $a \sim c$.

Structures such as partial orders, linear orders and lattices consist of a set together with a binary relation which meets conditions similar to those given in the case of an equivalence relation.

The most general type of mathematical structure would consist of a set together with a number of operations and relations. Though the preceding discussion has been in terms of binary relations and binary operations they are not of necessity so; they may be unary, ternary or n-ary.

The Bourbaki have attempted to abstract the most basic structures under which all others can be subsumed. By retrospection (and not by any a priori process) they arrived at three 'mother structures' (*mère structures*). First, there are algebraic structures (prototypically the group), which are characterized by the presence of operations. Second, there are structures of order, which have to do with relations, and whose prototype is the lattice, which assigns to each pair of its elements a successor and a predecessor of the pair. Third, and last, there are topological structures which are based on notions of neighbourhood, continuity and limit.[19]

From the foregoing we can generalize a definition of structure as follows (though it is, as Granger says, 'en un langage intuitif et qui abrège beaucoup les démarches logiques d'une définition axiomatique complète'):[20]

A structure is a set of any elements between which, or between certain sub-sets of which, relations[21] *are defined.*

Both the elements and the relations are conceived of as abstract, and hence logically independent of any eventual intuitive content. The essential point to be noted is that the quality of the objects that have been 'structured' in this way is completely *extrinsic*. They are expressed wholly in the relations constituted between them.

It would not be difficult to devote a whole book to a discussion of the notion of structure in the social sciences. This section is intended to provide no more than a brief, and perhaps somewhat over-simplified prospect of the field. Like causality, social structures cannot be directly observed but must be deductively constituted: they stand in relation to the observable as causality does to laws. For the sociologist structure is what the analysis of a totality supplies – the elements, the links between these elements and the arrangement of these links. To return to the etymological root of the word we might say that for the social scientist a structure is like a plan which he devises to find his way round a building. Though this structure is not itself observable, nevertheless it is derived from observation alone. A view of structure which is simultaneously direct and restricted is expressed by the English social anthropologist Radcliffe-Brown: 'But direct observation does reveal to us that these human beings are connected by a complex network of human relations. I use the term "social structure" to denote this network of actually existing relations.'[22] Structure used in this sense is virtually synonymous with organization, ordering or arrangement, and it is in this sense, perhaps, that we should take Kroeber's comment that anything, no matter what, on condition only that it be not completely amorphous, possesses structure.[23] This conception of structure has certain characteristics which mark it off rather radically from the definition with which I concluded the preceding section on structure in mathematics. First, for any single given set of elements of social reality which are said to possess structure the internal organization of that set and the structure are not differentiated. Next, the elements are not considered abstractly, for the quality of the objects that have been structured is still seen as being intrinsic. (This can perhaps be clarified if we consider a specific example. When sociologists discuss the structure of a small group the roles of the leader and his lieutenant are defined partly by relation to the other elements in the group – its members – but also in terms of certain inherent qualities in those roles.) So the objects, or elements, are not delineated wholly in terms of the relations constituted between them.

Comparison of so-called 'social structures' usually proceeds by the construction of a model in which the recurrent characteristics of a number of groups are subsumed, whilst differences are eliminated as being inessential. Various procedures may be adopted to reach this 'basic structure' (of industrial society, say, or kinship systems, or social stratification). I shall do no more here than sketch out three commonly used ways in which a more generalized notion of structure is abstracted from empirical reality.[24] The first is by means of the notion of the *ideal type* advocated by Max Weber, which he saw as being analogous to the 'synthetic constructs' of contemporary economic theorists. Though not intended as a description of social reality it aimed, at least in part, at permitting unambiguous description. He stated, further, that it was neither a stereotype, nor an average, nor an abstract concept. 'An ideal type is formed by the one-sided *accentuation* of one or more points of view and by the synthesis of a great many diffuse, discrete, more or less present and occasionally absent concrete individual phenomena, which are arranged accordingly to those one-sidedly emphasized viewpoints into a unified *analytical* construct. In its conceptual purity this mental construct cannot be found anywhere in reality.'[25] The classic example of the type of structure produced by this procedure is Weber's own ideal-type rational bureaucracy.[26]

The second means of reaching a more abstract notion of structure is by way of what Hempel[27] has called 'classificatory types'. Here a group of objects for which an underlying structure is sought are classified according to their position on one or more dimensions of evaluation or measurement and gathered together into classes, each class possessing a 'characteristic' or 'typical' structure.[28] Though no single member of that class may possess precisely that structure they all, in theory, approximate more closely to it than to any other. Each member of the class of neurotics, for example, will have a personality-structure more akin to that of other members of that class than to members of the class of psychotics. Physiological theories of personality-structure similarly depend upon a prior classification into ectomorphs, endomorphs and mesomorphs. Discussions of the structure of 'the average this' or 'the average that' (in so far as they have more than an intuitive basis) may be seen as a sub-category of this means, using more or less sophisticated statistical devices. The literature of sociology abounds with studies – 'The structure of the small business', 'The structure of the working class family' – which usually turn out to be based on an artefact of this kind.[29] The final means which I intend to consider here might be called the structure of the extreme type.[30] In this case the trait or traits characterizing the structure do not, or at least are believed not to, exist empirically without there being present to a greater or lesser extent traces of some quality which is seen as their opposite. The economists' concept of pure competition (or pure monopoly, for that matter) is an example of this type, since competition appears empirically to be always less than perfect. Marx's characterization of the structure of feudal and capitalist society might also be seen as falling into this category.[31]

Is the idea of structure, then, no more than an heuristic device? One of the primary functions of each of the three ways of approaching structure that I have considered is clearly to aid the observer, either in making coherent sense of what he sees, or in allowing him to compare diverse phenomena or complexes of phenomena which he has reason to believe are in some important sense similar. (Whether this belief springs from his intuition or from some known measure – that is, whether he seeks a common structure for industrial societies because he 'feels' that they somehow *ought* to be alike in important respects, or because he sees that the Gross National Products of industrial societies resemble each other more than they do the Gross National Products of non-industrial societies – is not an issue here.) But the question remains as to what status over and above this the notion of structure has for any sociologist who employs the term. A cursory examination of any random selection of sociological texts suggests that it signifies rather more for its users. For the majority structure does not serve as an initial organizing principle that can be discarded as the phenomena come to be coherently arranged: on the contrary, it is the conclusion, the ultimate form in which the phenomena are presented. But are these structures inherent in social reality (as Kroeber seems to suggest) or are they imposed upon it as an artefact of the observer? More particularly we should ask why, if structure is inherent in social reality, it is possible for one and the same area of social reality to have, apparently, as many structures as observers?

The other question that is clearly raised concerns not so much structure itself as *structuralism*. If this latter is to be justified as a worth-while intellectual endeavour, rather than a fashionable invocation, it is necessary to show not only that it uses a notion of structure that is more rigorous than those used in the social sciences that I have been discussing, but also that this notion either intrinsically does overcome, or can be employed in such a way as to overcome, these earlier difficulties and ambiguities. This I propose to do by considering first the use of the structuralist method in linguistics, then its use in the humanities and social sciences which have drawn very heavily on work in the former.

Modern proponents of structuralism all acknowledge allegiance to Ferdinand de Saussure as the founding father of the method. When, in 1878, he wrote his *Mémoire sur le système primitif des voyelles dans les langues Indo-européennes*, linguistics was dominated by the two traditions of comparative grammar and etymology. His innovatory vision of language as a collective institution demanded equally innovatory ways of studying it, which we can find expounded in his *Cours de linguistique générale*. This was not originally written as a book, but was reconstructed from his notes together with notes made by students at his lecture courses in Geneva in the years 1906–7, 1908–9 and 1910–11. The problems that this provenance has given rise to are discussed by Rulon S. Wells in 'De Saussure's System of Linguistics'.[32] The modern linguist or structuralist who refers to de Saussure does so not because de Saussure was right in this or that detail – which would, besides, hardly account for the reverence in which he is held by scholars in other fields than his own – but because of his contribution of 'a whole mode of thought, a whole structure of interests and values'.[33] If we distinguish between authoritative and seminal thinkers, de Saussure falls clearly in the latter category. Four of his ideas are specially relevant here. First, he saw language as a social system that was coherent, orderly and susceptible to understanding and explanation as a whole. Syntax and semantics together constitute a group of rules imposed on individuals, and to which individual thought must be submitted if it seeks expression. Second, he pointed the arbitrariness of the verbal sign, the *signifier*, which being conventional supposes neither an intrinsic rapport with the concept which constitutes its signification, the *signified*, nor in consequence any inherent stability with it.[34] Third, de Saussure made a cardinal distinction between, on the one hand, *langue*, the institution of language, 'l'ensemble des habitudes linguistiques qui permet à un sujet de comprendre et de se faire comprendre'; and, on the other hand, *parole*, or the particular and individual acts of linguistic expression. Both together make up *le langage*. Finally, he is important for what he saw as the key principle of the structure of language, that it forms a system that is fundamentally one of contrasts, distinctions and ultimately oppositions, since the elements of language never exist in isolation but always in relation to one another. It follows, moreover, from this that the structure is synchronic, since these relations are relations of mutual and simultaneous interdependence. De Saussure's most direct intellectual descendants have tended to move from this position to the view that structures are entirely independent of history, though he himself did not hold this. Hence the most important recent contribution to the study of structural linguistics has been the renewed recognition of the place of diachronic structuring, notably through the transformational perspective of Noam Chomsky[35] and Zellig Harris.[36]

In the period between de Saussure and these latter the explorations of the schools of Prague and Copenhagen deserve note. Roman Jakobson was a central figure in the formalist school of literary criticism in Moscow before he went to Prague, where the Linguistic Circle (whose battle-cries were 'Structuralism!' and 'Formalism!') was established in 1926. His whole life and work – from his early elaborations of the linguistic model worked out by de Saussure, through his contributions to the field of Slav studies (which were much indebted to Vladimir Propp's seminal *Morphology of the Folktale*[37] and which are exemplified here by 'On Russian Fairy Tales'[38]), to his present endeavour to establish the inherent distinctive features found in all the languages of the world, which 'underlie their entire lexical and morphological stock' – exemplify the reorientations of linguistic feeling and its tremendous expansion.

Troubetzkoy's structuralism with its system of phonological opposi-tions, in which a phoneme is defined as a function of these, is closely related to Jakobson's system of differential elements. In the glossematics of Hjelmslev and the school of Copenhagen structure becomes an autono-mous entity of internal dependences. Hjelmslev further predicates a type of 'sublogic' which constitutes a common source both for linguistic and logical structures. Nevertheless, his structuralism remains essentially static, with the emphasis upon the 'dependences' and not the transforma-tions.

With Chomsky and Harris linguistic structuralism has come to con-centrate on the structure of syntaxes. Chomsky himself has elucidated the distinction between the 'deep structure' of the semantically interpretable and the 'surface structure' of the phonetically interpretable.[39] There appear to be two major sources of this shift of emphasis. In the first place the work of Harris and Halle has tended to bring out the creative aspect of language – in Saussurean terms it has tended to study *parole* rather than *langue*. Further, the growth of psycholinguistics has led Chomsky himself towards the notion of a sort of innate grammaticality, a genetic code 'which in its turn determines the semantic interpretation of an undefined group of real phrases, expressed or understood. Everything happens, in other words, as if a man has at his disposition a "generative grammar" of his own language.'[40] In pursuing the notion that grammar has its roots not only in the reason, but moreover in an *innate* reason, Chomsky is essentially looking for the postulates of a grammatical theory which is sufficient both to characterize the structure common to all languages and to differentiate them according to their particular qualities. By the use of a combination of logico-mathematical formalization (for example, algorithms and recursive functions), general linguistics and psycholinguistics, Chomsky has shown the following. First, that it is possible recursively to obtain a set of rules for rewriting in the form $A \rightarrow Z$ (where A is a symbol for categories – for example, phrases – and Z is a string of one or more symbols). Second, that by applying transformational operations to the strings of non-terminal symbols we obtain derived statements; and it is the set of these transformations which constitutes the rules of generative grammar.[41] (Some of what this means both in terms of human practice and research orientations is to be seen in Susan Ervin's paper 'Imitation and Structural Change in Children's Language'.[42]) As Chomsky himself puts it: 'If it is really true that the grammars of natural languages are not only complex and abstract, but also very limited in their variety ... we must again put in question the problem of knowing whether they are actually the product of culture, which seems generally to be believed ... '[43] In short, it is possible that though we have started by asking questions about language we may be involved in asking about the human organism, since it may be that genes transmit not only the capacity to acquire a language from outside, as it were, but also a formative, fixed schema, the mould in which language itself is cast.

Though for Bastide structuralism in the social sciences begins with the publication, in 1930, of Freyer's *Soziologie als Wirklichkeitswissenschaft* (Teubner, Leipzig and Berlin), which event was, he says 'l'envahissement, presque explosif, de toutes les sciences sociales par la préoccupation structuraliste', I would hold to the more conventional view that it is in the work of Claude Lévi-Strauss that structuralism 'invades' first social

anthropology, then the neighbouring disciplines. Consequently I intend /
here to discuss the work of Claude Lévi-Strauss, its findings and the problems it raises, at some length. This is not because I aim at the exegesis of the writings of one man – much less a hagiography – but rather because I see his intellectual career as offering us what is, in many respects, a paradigm of the structuralist endeavour.

Certain questions must be answered before we can go on to any consideration of the method itself. First, how is the discipline of anthropology conceived; second, what is the aim or objective of the structuralist method; finally, what are the links between this aim or objective and the concept of the discipline. Lévi-Strauss himself provides a partial, and somewhat Delphic answer, in his introduction to the works of Marcel Mauss,[44] in whose 'Essai sur le don'[45] he sees a perfect example of the operation of the structuralist method. He says the following of Mauss's work: 'For the first time in the history of ethnological thought an effort to transcend empirical observation and to achieve a deeper reality (*des réalités plus profondes*) was made.'[46] What, then, is this 'deeper reality'? Georges Balandier, discussing *Tristes Tropiques*,[47] sees the anthropologist's aim as being that of 'rediscovering unity and permanence beneath the diversity that our journeys through space and time reveal',[48] whilst Jean Viet has spoken of Lévi-Strauss's 'taste for an architectural equilibrium which guarantees stability, and against which the flux of time cannot prevail'.[49] This unity and permanence, this stable architectural equilibrium, is founded on the discovery of 'certain general properties of social life'.[50] But, as Viet has pointed out, this would seem to be diametrically opposed to the general orientation of social anthropology which has as its end the analysis of the *particularity* of human groups.[51] Rather as Lévi-Strauss sees myths as mediating the contradictions, uncertainties and ambivalences that arise between and within sets of beliefs and actual behaviour,[52] so we might see the structuralist method itself as providing a way out of this impasse. If 'certain general properties of social life' are the thesis and the particularizing end of social anthropology the antithesis, then structuralism is the synthesis that both contains and transcends them. Nor in saying this are we imposing an alien mode of thought: Lévi-Strauss himself has spoken of Marxism, geology and psycho-analysis as his *'trois maîtresses'*[53] and the dialectic mode runs throughout his work.

He begins with the assumption – a not unreasonable one – that social life is characterized by a quality of systematic organization. He believes, moreover, that the variety of systematic organizations is limited: 'I am persuaded that these systems do not exist in limitless numbers, and that human societies, like individuals ... do not create in any absolute way, but are limited to a choice of certain combinations from an ideal repertory, which it should be possible to reconstruct.' This is the case because social structures are the product of a reason (*esprit*) that is innate in all men. That is, it is genetically rather than socially or culturally determined. Further, this reason operates unconsciously, and we can have access to it only through the systems that it forms, myths, kinship systems, systems of exchange, linguistic structures, cultural artefacts and so on.

> If, as we believe, the unconscious activity of the reason[54] consists in imposing forms upon content, and if these forms are fundamentally the same for all who possess this faculty, ancient and modern, primitive and civilized – as the study of symbolic functions, such as is expressed by language, so strikingly demonstrates – it is both necessary and sufficient to grasp the unconscious structure which underlies each institution or each custom in order to obtain a principle of interpretation which is valid for other institutions and other customs, that is, provided the analysis is pursued sufficiently far.[55]

When Lévi-Strauss writes of 'social structures', meaning both the 'systems' formed by customs and the 'unconscious structures' underlying institutions, he is very directly taking issue with the Radcliffe-Brown position.[56] In an article in the *Bulletin de Psychologie* he describes them explicitly as the investigator's models: 'The terms of social structure are not concerned with empirical reality, but with the models constructed upon it ... Social relations [in the Radcliffe-Brown sense] are the basic material from which the models that constitute social structure are built ... '[57] However, these structures are not achieved by the reduction of the real to forms. Lévi-Strauss is seeking by means of them to grasp 'des réalités plus profondes' and is emphatic that structuralism is not formalism. On the contrary it challenges the distinction between form and matter: '*Form* is defined by opposition to a *content* which is foreign to it; but *structure* has no distinct content. It *is* the content itself apprehended in a logical organization, conceived as a property of the real.'[58]

Structuralism, then, is a method whose primary intention is to permit the investigator to go beyond a pure description of what he perceives or experiences (*le vécu*), in the direction of the quality of rationality which underlies the social phenomena in which he is concerned. As Lévi-Strauss says in the Overture to *Le Cru et le cuit*: 'We are engaged in researching for the conditions under which *systems of truths* become mutually convertible.'[59] Further, 'types of societies become definable by their intrinsic characteristics; and mutually comparable because these characteristics are no longer located in a qualitative order but in the number and arrangement of elements which are themselves constant in all types of society.'[60] Following the example of structural linguistics, structural anthropology shifts its consideration away from conscious relations and on to unconscious ones, hoping to find there a system from which general laws may be derived. Just as the native speakers of a language have no need of a knowledge of the structure of their own tongue in order to be able to use it, let alone a knowledge of the structure of language in general, so we should not expect the members of a society to be conscious of its structures, but only to be aware of the concrete manifestations of that structure – ways of behaving, myths and so on. 'Without our actually excluding the possibility that those who produce and pass on myths could be conscious of their structure and mode of operation, this could not be normal, but could only occur partially and intermittently.'[61] On the other hand, myths themselves together with other normative systems do constitute what Lévi-Strauss has called 'conscious models' for the societies in which they are found. They are, however, amongst the most 'impoverished' of models since their function is to perpetuate beliefs and practices, rather than to expose the 'mainsprings' ('*les ressorts*').[62]

Structures, as we have seen, are characterized by relations, which for Lévi-Strauss are all ultimately reducible to binary oppositions. The structuralist method, then, is a means whereby social reality may be expressed as binary oppositions, each element, whether it be an event in a myth, an item of behaviour or the naming and classification of natural phenomena, being given its value in society by its relative position in a matrix of oppositions, their mediations and resolutions. In Hawaii, for example, one of the manifestations of mourning at the death of a chief was the wearing of the loin-cloth round the neck rather than the loins. This can be expressed as a binary opposition 'high–low' which is reflected in many aspects of Hawaiian society.[63] The Osage Indians characterize the two tribal moieties by the oppositions 'right–left', 'north–south', 'winter–summer'. These moieties are both quantitatively and qualitatively asymmetrical: quantitatively since the 'sky' moiety is single, the 'land' moiety divided into 'dry land' and 'water'; qualitatively, since one is responsible in war, the other in peace. On the basis of this initial logical structure of opposition is built up, equally logically, a whole system which embraces the range of social relations and the range of natural phenomena.[64] The three volumes of *Mythologiques* that have so far appeared[65] examine the ramifications of binary oppositions that are to be found in the myths of the Bororo and neighbouring tribes. These, as I have indicated earlier, Lévi-Strauss sees as codes which transmit information; they express beliefs, they are the ritual explanation of certain patterns of behaviour, and at the same time they mediate the paradoxes which social life, in all its expressions, inevitably creates. He starts from the opposition of the cooked to the raw, of culture to nature, and from this constructs models which allow the whole corpus of myth, apparently confused, diverse and discrete, to be intelligibly ordered, both internally and in relation to one another. The following analysis, based on Chaco and Tukuna myths on the origin of tobacco and the jaguar, gives an example of the method:

$$\text{A mother} \brace \text{A wife} \text{ changed into a jaguar, and whose} {\text{son} \brace \text{husband}}$$

$$\text{climbed a tree} {\text{in order to hunt} \brace \text{in order to dislodge}} \text{birds} {\text{toucans} \brace \text{parrakeets}},$$

$$\text{eats the birds which have fallen} {\text{dead} \brace \text{alive}}. \text{ The woman kills}$$

$$\text{the man and takes} {\text{the liver to her grandsons} \brace \text{the head to her sons}} \text{who recognize}$$

its origin. The jaguar-woman is destroyed by fire.[66]

However, not only can the content of myth be analysed in this way but also the form. Hence, Lévi-Strauss suggests, among the Chaco at the rhetorical level proper meaning is transformed into figurative meaning as, on the sociological level, the seduction of a woman by a man is transformed into the seduction of a man by a woman.[67] It is impossible to give anything more than a brief flavour of this technique in describing it; both Lévi-Strauss's own 'The Sex of the Heavenly Bodies'[68] and Edmund Leach's 'The Legitimacy of Solomon: Some Structural Aspects of Old Testament History'[69] (which employs the technique on a somewhat unusual type of material) should be consulted to see its operation in practice.

One further aspect of Lévi-Strauss's own work concerns us, that is, his insistence upon the importance of the 'mathematization' of structuralist social anthropology. He is not unique in this. In their different ways social scientists as diverse as Paul Lazarsfeld,[70] Hubert Blalock[71] and F. Harary[72] have insisted on at least the development of adequate means of quantifying the matter of social research, but only the last of these has moved in a direction which would be generally regarded as both mathematically adequate *and* structuralist. The tradition of which he is a part is represented in this volume by Peter Abell's 'Some Problems in the Theory of Structural Balance',[73] which sets out to handle the binary opposition of relations of hostility and friendship both formally and rigorously, yet not at a level which precludes the application of his theorem to actual empirical material. Precisely what this mathematization means and the implications that it has have been much misunderstood.[74] Above all, mathematical formulation of structures neither constitutes nor implies the mathematization of empirical social facts themselves, but is simply an instrument, a means of advancing structural analysis, and of reaching a better knowledge of social reality.[75]

Since Lévi-Strauss's own pioneering formalizations in *Les Structures élémentaires de la parente*,[76] notably of the Murngin system of kinship, there have been an increasing number of studies that have used logico-mathematical techniques and expressions to further the understanding of complex social phenomena. G. T. Guilbaud, for example, has used algebraic means in his study of the kinship system of Ambrym,[77] whilst H. Hoffman has applied symbolic logic to the analysis of Pawnee organization.[78] At the Paris colloquium on structure[79] Lévi-Strauss took the position that the most important line of future advance, the development of laws of transformation, ultimately depended upon the ability of anthropologists to formulate their structures algebraically. But despite this intense concern with formal expression his feeling for the 'lived reality' remains pre-eminent. 'None of us has ever thought to substitute a type or a fixed structure for this exciting reality. The search for structures comes in at the second stage when, after we have observed what exists, we try to pick out from those stable elements – which are always only a part – that which will permit us to compare and classify.'[80]

The final goal of structuralism is the realization of the whole inventory of social relations that the unconscious reason both makes posssible and restricts (just as 'innate grammaticality' both makes language possible and circumscribes the structures it may take): I have touched, however briefly, on the tools it utilizes to realize this inventory. At this point my task must be to attempt to recapitulate the qualities and concerns that characterize the endeavours of the structuralist method. First, it is shaped by '*l'attitude totalisante*',[81] an idea which it is extremely difficult to express directly in English since it encompasses both the notions of the all-embracing, and the summation of parts. This expresses itself in a rejection of any atomistic tendency, notably in its insistence that the meaning of the individual elements which are structured arises out of *and only out of* the relations of the elements to one another and their mutual interdependence. Next, it is centrally concerned with the search for certain general properties of social life; with, if we may extend Lévi-Strauss's own metaphor, the discovery and scientific description of the mainsprings that are the moving force behind the multiplicity and diversity of observable social systems. This it seeks to do in two ways. On the one hand it attempts to produce analyses that will expose the underlying formal relations of any given structure: on the other hand it attempts to deduce laws of transformation such that structures as wholes may be compared.

In part this is, of course, the aim of much conventional sociology, and the following example may help to clarify some of the important differences between the two. As we saw above, traditional notions of structure in the social sciences draw much of their utility from various ways of generalizing that allow comparisons to be made. Prototypically these ways of generalizing involve eliminating differences and emphasizing similarities. Structuralism proper, on the other hand, begins when it is recognized that differing structures can be brought together not despite, but in virtue of, differences, for which an order is then sought. The linguist, for example, orders phonemic and morphemic oppositions, rather than regroups differences. For the structuralist there is no such thing as a 'basic' or 'ideal type' of structure for each group, whose members are all variants of it. Instead, structure should be seen essentially as a syntax of transformations. Consider the following simple example:

$$\text{(i)} \quad a : b :: c : d$$
$$\text{(ii)} \quad a : x :: c : d$$
$$\text{(iii)} \quad a : b :: c : y$$

(where $: \ldots :: \ldots$ means 'is to ... as ... ')

Presented with these three structures the traditional sociologist would look for a basic structure. This might take various forms. Given the constant repetition of the elements a and c it might consist of these alone, with b, d, x and y seen simply as variants of differing statistical probability. Alternatively, a, b, c and d might all be retained, with only x and y seen as variant, or deviant, forms. But whichever way the sociologist took he would no longer be able to define the elements purely in relation to one another, since a number of them would have been eliminated. The structuralist method, on the other hand, would see these three structures not as in any sense hierarchically arranged, but as equal to one another, and capable of mutual comparison by virtue of laws of transformation of a type such as:

$$a : b \Rightarrow a : x$$
$$c : d \Rightarrow c : \gamma$$

(where $\Rightarrow$ means 'is transformed into')

In conclusion I would say only this: that structure consists in elements, and in law-like relations between those elements. Any 'structure' which disregards those laws, or discards any of them or any of the elements for the purpose of comparing or generalizing between sets of elements, is not, by definition, a structure at all. Instead it is a device of the investigator which may or may not resemble the actual structure of the social reality he is purporting to describe or explain by it. Hence I believe what I have described as the usual, traditional sociological procedures to be neither concerned with structure in any meaningful sense of the word, nor ultimately to be faithful to social reality.

The application of the structuralist method to ethnological material sprang from the recognition that language was a social system and, conversely, that other social systems might be considered in the same terms as language. It is, then, almost inevitable that the same method should be applied to languages that use language: that is, that there should be a structuralist school of literary criticism. As Roman Jakobson and Claude Lévi-Strauss observe: 'The linguist discerns structures in works of poetry which are strikingly analogous to those which the analysis of myths reveals to the ethnologist. For his part, the latter cannot fail to recognize that myths do not simply consist of arrangements of concepts but that they are also works of art which arouse in those who hear them (and in the ethnologist himself when he reads them in transcription) profound aesthetic emotions.'[82] Literary criticism has traditionally sought to discover and reveal 'the truth' about an author or his work.[83] Structuralist criticism rejects this search, rather as structuralist anthropology rejects the search for the 'basic' structure. Roland Barthes, both the most outstanding and the most original of the structuralist school, has this to say of the critic's role: 'The world exists and the writer speaks – there is literature. The subject of criticism is very different; it is not "the world", but discourse: criticism is discourse about discourse; it is a *secondary* or *meta-language* which operates on a primary language (or *language-object*) ... If criticism is solely a meta-language that means that its task is certainly not to discover what is "truth" but only what is "valid". In itself a language is neither true nor false, but valid or not valid; by valid I mean constituting a coherent system of signs.'[84] Of the works that are the subject of the critic's consideration he states: 'Literature is simply a language, a system of signs. Its being (être) is not in its message, but in this "system". Similarly, it is not for criticism to reconstitute the message of a work, but only its system, exactly as the linguist does not decipher the meaning of a sentence, but establishes the formal structure which allows the meaning to be conveyed.'[85] Criticism, then, can no longer be the analysis of content but the enumeration of forms and their organization, the exposition of signifying structures (*structures signifiantes*) and their mode of functioning. In what is probably Barthes's most widely known work – and certainly in France his most violently controversial – *Sur Racine*,[86] he divides his analysis into two parts. The first is a study of what he calls *jeux de figures*, which are conceptually equivalent to the models of Lévi-Strauss. The second is the establishment of a *combinatoire*, or calculus of combinations, analogous to the laws of transformation discussed earlier, which account for the particular set of *jeux de figures* that are found in any given play. 'What I have tried to reconstitute is a sort of Racinian anthropology, which is simultaneously structural and analytic: at base structural, because tragedy is treated here as a system of unities (the "figures") and of functions ...'[87] Barthes sees the plays of Racine as being founded on a complex of binary oppositions, the most fundamental of which is between the outdoor and the indoor. The former, the place of death, flight and action, the sun makes 'pure, clear, unpeopled': the latter, shadowy and peopled, divides into another binary opposition of Chambre and Anti-Chambre, the one the place of silence, the redoubt of Power, the other the mediator between silence and action, where language holds sway and where tragic man 'lost between the letter and the meaning of things, speaks his reasons (parle ses raisons)'.[88] Within this space we see the working out of the basic relation of power, which is so general that it can be expressed, for Barthes, in the double equation:

A has complete power over B;
A loves B, who does not love him/her.[89]

Sur Racine is, I would argue, the most significant and directly rewarding of all the pieces of structuralist criticism. As in Jacques Ehrmann's 'The

Structures of Exchange in *Cinna*'[90] the method is not only applied to some particular body of writing, but also to writing which is generally highly valued. As T. Todorov has pointed out, there has been very much more criticism and exposition of structuralist criticism than there has been actual structuralist criticism.[91] I would add a further objection, that much of the criticism that has employed the method has taken ephemera for its subject. Barthes himself has written an extended analysis comparing Ian Fleming's *Goldfinger* as book and film,[92] whilst Umberto Eco has dealt with Superman and Steve Canyon,[93] and J. K. Seglov with Sherlock Holmes.[94] There seem to me to be several reasons why it should be the case that there has been so much that is exciting and illuminating written about the tools of structuralist criticism,[95] and so little application of those tools to classic literature. In the first place structuralist methods offer little or no help in the evaluation of literary works, an exercise that is as fundamental to criticism as explanation. Hence in the Foreword to *Sur Racine* Barthes avers that 'without doubt Racine is the greatest French writer', but supports this assertion with arguments that are in no sense structuralist. If criticism can do no more than test for a validity that is defined by a work's possession of a 'coherent system of signs', then the situation could hardly be other. There is no a priori reason to believe that the system of signs in *Superman* is any less coherent than that in *King Lear*. Values are a function of ideologies, not methods.

In the second place, structuralism hovers uneasily between treating literary works as *objects* and as *things*. In the former case the risk is always that the criticism becomes a giant tautology;[96] in the latter that it ignores the fact that each aesthetic object is 'the expression of a structuring consciousness'.[97] Doubrovsky has stated the problem very directly.

> In my opinion the error arises from seeing literary works as objects, and, arising from that, from wishing to control one's understanding of them by the modes of objective thought. For it must be repeated that the work of art is a false object, an object-subject, the objective support of a subjective intention, by whose means alone it is possible to grasp the real meaning ... The technical machinery is simply the vehicle of a vision. The 'organization of the signifiers' ... has no autonomous reality; the signifier can never be separated from the signified, nor the literary from the existential.[98]

As possible solutions to the dilemma Doubrovsky offers phenomenology and the dialectic, whose respective merits are no concern of ours here.

For, despite these undoubted objections, my own feelings about structuralist literary criticism, no less than about the structuralist method in general, agree with those of Todorov.

'By its original research, by its exploration of fresh ways, by its unceasing rejuvenation, structuralism bears witness ... to an enviable vitality and fruitfulness.'[99]

MICHAEL LANE

Introduction to
STRUCTURALISM

ON THE NATURE OF LANGUAGE*

Ferdinand de Saussure

NATURE OF THE LINGUISTIC SIGN

1. Sign, Signified, Signifier

Some people regard language, when reduced to its elements, as a naming-process only – a list of words, each corresponding to the thing that it names. For example:

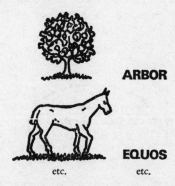

ARBOR

EQUOS

etc.　　　　etc.

This conception is open to criticism at several points. It assumes that ready-made ideas exist before words; it does not tell us whether a name is vocal or psychological in nature (*arbor*, for instance, can be considered from either viewpoint); finally, it lets us assume that the linking of a name and a thing is a very simple operation – an assumption that is anything but true. But this rather naïve approach can bring us near the truth by showing us that the linguistic unit is a double entity, one formed by the associating of two terms.

We have seen in considering the speaking-circuit that both terms involved in the linguistic sign are psychological and are united in the brain by an associative bond. This point must be emphasized.

* Extracts from *Course in General Linguistics* by Ferdinand de Saussure (first published in 1916); translated from the French by Wade Baskin (Philosophical Library, New York, 1959; Peter Owen, London, 1960).

The linguistic sign unites, not a thing and a name, but a concept and a sound-image. The latter is not the material sound, a purely physical thing, but the psychological imprint of the sound, the impression that it makes on our senses. The sound-image is sensory, and if I happen to call it 'material', it is only in that sense, and by way of opposing it to the other term of the association, the concept, which is generally more abstract.

The psychological character of our sound-images becomes apparent when we observe our own speech. Without moving our lips or tongue, we can talk to ourselves or recite mentally a selection of verse. Because we regard the words of our language as sound-images, we must avoid speaking of the 'phonemes' that make up the words. This term, which suggests vocal activity, is applicable to the spoken word only, to the realization of the inner image in discourse. We can avoid that misunderstanding by speaking of the *sounds* and *syllables* of a word provided we remember that the names refer to the sound-image.

The linguistic sign is then a two-sided psychological entity that can be represented by the drawing:

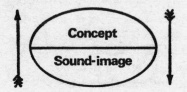

The two elements are intimately united, and each recalls the other. Whether we try to find the meaning of the Latin word *arbor* or the word that Latin uses to designate the concept 'tree', it is clear that only the associations sanctioned by that language appear to us to conform to reality, and we disregard whatever others might be imagined.

Our definition of the linguistic sign poses an important question of terminology. I call the combination of a concept and a sound-image a *sign*, but in current usage the term generally designates only a sound-

image, a word, for example (*arbor*, etc.). One tends to forget that *arbor* is called a sign only because it carries the concept 'tree', with the result that the idea of the sensory part implies the idea of the whole.

Ambiguity would disappear if the three notions involved here were designated by three names, each suggesting and opposing the others. I propose to retain the word *sign* (*signe*) to designate the whole and to replace *concept* and *sound-image* respectively by *signified* (*signifié*) and *signifier* (*signifiant*); the last two terms have the advantage of indicating the opposition that separates them from each other and from the whole of which they are parts. As regards *sign*, if I am satisfied with it, this is simply because I do not know of any word to replace it, the ordinary language suggesting no other.

The linguistic sign, as defined, has two primordial characteristics. In enunciating them I am also positing the basic principles of any study of this type.

2. Principle I: The Arbitrary Nature of the Sign

The bond between the signifier and the signified is arbitrary. Since I mean by sign the whole that results from the associating of the signifier with the signified, I can simply say: *the linguistic sign is arbitrary*.

The idea of 'sister' is not linked by any inner relationship to the succession of sounds *s-ö-r* which serves as its signifier in French; that it could be represented equally by just any other sequence is proved by differences among languages and by the very existence of different languages: the signified 'ox' has as its signifier *b-ö-f* on one side of the border and *o-k-s* (*Ochs*) on the other.

No one disputes the principle of the arbitrary nature of the sign, but it is often easier to discover a truth than to assign to it its proper place. Principle I dominates all the linguistics of language; its consequences are numberless. It is true that not all of them are equally obvious at first glance; only after many detours does one discover them, and with them the primordial importance of the principle.

One remark in passing: when semiology becomes organized as a science, the question will arise whether or not it properly includes modes of expression based on completely natural signs, such as pantomime. Supposing that the new science welcomes them, its main concern will still be the whole group of systems grounded on the arbitrariness of the sign. In fact, every means of expression used in society is based, in principle, on collective behaviour or – what amounts to the same thing – on convention. Polite formulas, for instance, though often imbued with a certain natural expressiveness (as in the case of a Chinese who greets his emperor by bowing down to the ground nine times), are none the less fixed by rule; it is this rule and not the intrinsic value of the gestures that obliges one to use them. Signs that are wholly arbitrary realize better than the others the ideal of the semiological process; that is why language, the most complex and universal of all systems of expression, is also the most characteristic; in this sense linguistics can become the master-pattern for all branches of semiology although language is only one particular semiological system.

The word *symbol* has been used to designate the linguistic sign, or, more specifically, what is here called the signifier. Principle I in particular weighs against the use of this term. One characteristic of the symbol is that it is never wholly arbitrary; it is not empty, for there is the rudiment of a natural bond between the signifier and the signified. The symbol of justice, a pair of scales, could not be replaced by just any other symbol, such as a chariot.

The word *arbitrary* also calls for comment. The term should not imply that the choice of the signifier is left entirely to the speaker; I mean that it is unmotivated, i.e. arbitrary in that it actually has no natural connection with the signified.

3. Principle II: The Linear Nature of the Signifier

The signifier, being auditory, is unfolded solely in time from which it gets the following characteristics: (a) it represents a span, and (b) the span is measurable in a single dimension; it is a line.

While Principle II is obvious, apparently linguists have always neglected to state it, doubtless because they found it too simple; nevertheless, it is fundamental, and its consequences are incalculable. Its importance equals that of Principle I; the whole mechanism of language depends upon it. In contrast to visual signifiers (nautical signals, etc.) which can offer simultaneous groupings in several dimensions, auditory signifiers have at their command only the dimension of time. Their elements are presented in succession; they form a chain. This feature becomes readily apparent when they are represented in writing and the spatial line of graphic marks is substituted for succession in time.

Sometimes the linear nature of the signifier is not obvious. When I accent a syllable, for instance, it seems that I am concentrating more than one significant element on the same point. But this is an illusion; the syllable and its accent constitute only one phonational act. There is no duality within the act but only different oppositions to what precedes and what follows.

IMMUTABILITY AND MUTABILITY OF THE SIGN

I. Immutability

The signifier, though to all appearances freely chosen with respect to the idea that it represents, is fixed, not free, with respect to the linguistic community that uses it. The masses have no voice in the matter, and the signifier chosen by language could be replaced by no other. This fact, which seems to embody a contradiction, might be called colloquially 'the stacked deck'. We say to language: 'Choose!' but we add: 'It must be this sign and no other.' No individual, even if he willed it, could modify in any way at all the choice that has been made; and what is more, the community itself cannot control so much as a single word; it is bound to the existing language.

No longer can language be identified with a contract pure and simple, and it is precisely from this viewpoint that the linguistic sign is a particularly interesting object of study; for language furnishes the best proof that a law accepted by a community is a thing that is tolerated and not a rule to which all freely consent.

Let us first see why we cannot control the linguistic sign and then draw together the important consequences that issue from the phenomenon.

No matter what period we choose or how far back we go, language always appears as a heritage of the preceding period. We might conceive of an act by which, at a given moment, names were assigned to things and a contract was formed between concepts and sound-images; but such an act has never been recorded. The notion that things might have happened like that was prompted by our acute awareness of the arbitrary nature of the sign.

No society, in fact, knows or has ever known language other than as a product inherited from preceding generations, and one to be accepted as such. That is why the question of the origin of speech is not so important as it is generally assumed to be. The question is not even worth asking; the only real object of linguistics is the normal, regular life of an existing idiom. A particular language-state is always the product of historical forces, and these forces explain why the sign is unchange-able, i.e. why it resists any arbitrary substitution.

Nothing is explained by saying that language is something inherited and leaving it at that. Cannot existing and inherited laws be modified from one moment to the next?

To meet that objection, we must put language into its social setting and frame the question just as we would for any other social institution. How are other social institutions transmitted? This more general question includes the question of immutability. We must first determine the greater or lesser amounts of freedom that the other institutions enjoy; in each instance it will be seen that a different proportion exists between fixed tradition and the free action of society. The next step is to discover why, in a given category, the forces of the first type carry more weight or less weight than those of the second. Finally, coming back to language, we must ask why the historical factor of transmission dominates it entirely and prohibits any sudden widespread change.

There are many possible answers to the question. For example, one might point to the fact that succeeding generations are not superimposed on one another like the drawers of a piece of furniture, but fuse and interpenetrate, each generation embracing individuals of all ages – with the result that modifications of language are not tied to the succession of generations. One might also recall the sum of the efforts required for learning the mother language and conclude that a general change would be impossible. Again, it might be added that reflection does not enter into the active use of an idiom – speakers are largely unconscious of the laws of language; and if they are unaware of them, how can they modify them? Even if they were aware of these laws, we may be sure that their awareness would seldom lead to criticism, for people are generally satisfied with the language they have received.

The foregoing considerations are important but not topical. The following are more basic and direct, and all the others depend on them.

(i) *The arbitrary nature of the sign.* Above, we had to accept the theoretical possibility of change; further reflection suggests that the arbitrary nature of the sign is really what protects language from any attempt to modify it. Even if people were more conscious of language than they are, they would still not know how to discuss it. The reason is simply that any subject in order to be discussed must have a reasonable basis. It is possible, for instance, to discuss whether the monogamous form of marriage is more reasonable than the polygamous form and to advance arguments to support either side. One could also argue about a system of symbols, for the symbol has a rational relationship with the thing signified; but language is a system of arbitrary signs and lacks the necessary basis, the solid ground for discussion. There is no reason for preferring *sœur* to *sister*, *Ochs* to *bœuf*, etc.

(ii) *The multiplicity of signs necessary to form any language.* Another important deterrent to linguistic change is the great number of signs that must go into the making of any language. A system of writing comprising twenty to forty letters can in case of need be replaced by another system. The same would be true of language if it contained a limited number of elements; but linguistic signs are numberless.

(iii) *The over-complexity of the system.* A language constitutes a system. In this one respect language is not completely arbitrary but is ruled to some extent by logic; it is here also, however, that the inability of the masses to transform it becomes apparent. The system is a complex mechanism that can be grasped only through reflection; the very ones who use it daily are ignorant of it. We can conceive of a change only through the intervention of specialists, grammarians, logicians, etc.; but experience shows us that all such meddlings have failed.

(iv) *Collective inertia towards innovation.* Language – and this consideration surpasses all the others – is at every moment everybody's concern; spread throughout society and manipulated by it, language is something used daily by all. Here we are unable to set up any comparison between it and other institutions. The prescriptions of codes, religious rites, nautical signals, etc., involve only a certain number of individuals simultaneously and then only during a limited period of time; in language, on the contrary, everyone participates at all times, and that is why it is constantly being influenced by all. This capital fact suffices to show the impossibility of revolution. Of all social institutions, language is least amenable to initiative. It blends with the life of society, and the latter, inert by nature, is a prime conservative force.

But to say that language is a product of social forces does not suffice to show clearly that it is unfree; remembering that it is always the heritage of the preceding period, we must add that these social forces are linked with time. Language is checked not only by the weight of the collectivity but also by time. These two are inseparable. At every moment solidarity with the past checks freedom of choice. We say *man* and *dog*. This does not prevent the existence in the total phenomenon of a bond between the two antithetical forces – arbitrary convention, by virtue of which choice is free, and time, which causes choice to be fixed. Because the sign is arbitrary, it follows no law other than that of tradition, and because it is based on tradition, it is arbitrary.

2. Mutability

Time, which insures the continuity of language, wields another influence apparently contradictory to the first: the more or less rapid change of linguistic signs. In a certain sense, therefore, we can speak of both the immutability and the mutability of the sign.

In the last analysis, the two facts are interdependent: the sign is exposed to alteration because it perpetuates itself. What predominates in all change is the persistence of the old substance; disregard for the past is only relative. That is why the principle of change is based on the principle of continuity.

Change in time takes many forms, on any one of which an important chapter in linguistics might be written. Without entering into detail, let us see what things need to be delineated.

First, let there be no mistake about the meaning that we attach to the word 'change'. One might think that it deals especially with phonetic changes undergone by the signifier, or perhaps changes in meaning which affect the signified concept. That view would be inadequate. Regardless of what the forces of change are, whether in isolation or in combination, they always result in *a shift in the relationship between the signified and the signifier*.

Here are some examples. Latin *necāre* 'kill' became *noyer* 'drown' in French. Both the sound-image and the concept changed; but it is useless to separate the two parts of the phenomenon; it is sufficient to state with respect to the whole that the bond between the idea and the sign was loosened, and that there was a shift in their relationship. If, instead of comparing Classical Latin *necāre* with French *noyer*, we contrast the former term with *necare* of Vulgar Latin of the fourth or fifth century meaning 'drown', the case is a little different; but here again, although there is no appreciable change in the signifier, there is a shift in the relationship between the idea and the sign.

Old German *dritteil* 'one-third' became *Drittel* in Modern German. Here, although the concept remained the same, the relationship was changed in two ways: the signifier was changed not only in its material aspect but also in its grammatical form; the idea of *Teil* 'part' is no longer implied; *Drittel* is a simple word. In one way or another there is always a shift in the relationship.

In Anglo-Saxon the pre-literary form *fot* 'foot' remained while its plural **fōti* became *fēt* (Modern English *feet*). Regardless of the other changes that are implied, one thing is certain: there was a shift in their relationship; other correspondences between the phonetic substance and the idea emerged.

Language is radically powerless to defend itself against the forces which from one moment to the next are shifting the relationship between the signified and the signifier. This is one of the consequences of the arbitrary nature of the sign.

Unlike language, other human institutions – customs, laws, etc. – are all based in varying degrees on the natural relations of things; all have of necessity adapted the means employed to the ends pursued. Even fashion in dress is not entirely arbitrary; we can deviate only slightly from the conditions dictated by the human body. Language is limited by nothing in the choice of means, for apparently nothing would prevent the associating of any idea whatsoever with just any sequence of sounds.

To emphasize the fact that language is a genuine institution, Whitney quite justly insisted upon the arbitrary nature of signs; and, by so doing, he placed linguistics on its true axis. But he did not follow through and see that the arbitrariness of language radically separates it from all other institutions. This is apparent from the way in which language evolves. Nothing could be more complex. As it is a product of both the social force and time, no one can change anything in it, and, on the other hand, the arbitrariness of its signs theoretically entails the freedom of establishing just any relationship between phonetic substance and ideas. The result is that each of the two elements united in the sign maintains its own life to a degree unknown elsewhere, and that language changes, or rather evolves, under the influence of all the forces which can affect either sounds or meanings. The evolution is inevitable; there is no example of a single language that resists it. After a certain period of time, some obvious shifts can always be recorded.

Mutability is so inescapable that it even holds true for artificial languages. Whoever creates a language controls it only so long as it is not in circulation; from the moment when it fulfils its mission and becomes the property of everyone, control is lost. Take Esperanto as an example; if it succeeds, will it escape the inexorable law? Once launched, it is quite likely that Esperanto will enter upon a fully semiological life; it will be transmitted according to laws which have nothing in common with those of its logical creation, and there will be no turning back. A man proposing a fixed language that posterity would have to accept for what it was would be like a hen hatching a duck's egg: the language created by him would be borne along, willy-nilly, by the current that engulfs all languages.

Signs are governed by a principle of general semiology: continuity in time is coupled to change in time; this is confirmed by orthographic systems, the speech of deaf-mutes, etc.

But what supports the necessity for change? I might be reproached for not having been as explicit on this point as on the principle of immutability. This is because I failed to distinguish between the different forces of change. We must consider their great variety in order to understand the extent to which they are necessary.

The causes of continuity are a priori within the scope of the observer, but the causes of change in time are not. It is better not to attempt giving an exact account at this point, but to restrict discussion to the shifting of relationships in general. Time changes all things; there is no reason why language should escape this universal law.

Let us review the main points of our discussion and relate them to the principles set up in the Introduction.*

(1) Avoiding sterile word definitions, within the total phenomenon represented by speech we first singled out two parts: 'langue' and 'parole'. Langue is speech less speaking. It is the whole set of linguistic habits which allow an individual to understand and to be understood.

(2) But this definition still leaves language outside its social context; it makes language something artificial, since it includes only the individual

* See Introduction, pp. 1–37, to *Course in General Linguistics*, not reprinted here.

part of reality; for the realization of language, a community of speakers (*masse parlante*) is necessary. Contrary to all appearances, language never exists apart from the social fact, for it is a semiological phenomenon. Its social nature is one of its inner characteristics. Its complete definition confronts us with two inseparable entities, as shown in the drawing on p. 52

But under the conditions described language is not living – it has only potential life; we have considered only the social, not the historical, fact.

(3) The linguistic sign is arbitrary; language, as defined, would therefore seem to be a system which, because it depends solely on a rational principle, is free and can be organized at will. Its social nature, considered independently, does not definitely rule out this viewpoint. Doubtless it is not on a purely logical basis that group psychology operates; one must consider everything that deflects reason in actual contacts between individuals. But the thing which keeps language from being a simple convention that can be modified at the whim of interested parties is not its social nature; it is rather the action of time combined with the social force. If time is left out, the linguistic facts are incomplete and no conclusion is possible.

If we considered language in time, without the community of speakers – imagine an isolated individual living for several centuries – we should probably notice no change; time would not influence language. Conversely, if we considered the community of the social forces that influence language. To represent the actual facts, we must then add to our first drawing a sign to indicate the passage of time:

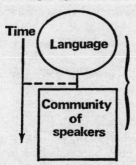

Language is no longer free, for time will allow the social forces at work on it to carry out their effects. This brings us back to the principle of continuity, which cancels freedom. But continuity necessarily implies change, varying degrees of shifts in the relationship between the signified and the signifier.

STATIC AND EVOLUTIONARY LINGUISTICS

Inner Duality of All Sciences Concerned with Values

Very few linguists suspect that the intervention of the factor of time creates difficulties peculiar to linguistics and opens to their science two completely divergent paths.

Most other sciences are unaffected by this radical duality; time produces no special effects in them. Astronomy has found that the stars undergo considerable changes but has not been obliged on this account to split itself into two disciplines. Geology is concerned with successions at almost every instant, but its study of strata does not thereby become a radically distinct discipline. Law has its descriptive science and its historical science; no one opposes one to the other. The political history of states is unfolded solely in time, but an historian depicting a particular period does not work apart from history. Conversely, the science of political institutions is essentially descriptive, but if the need arises it can easily deal with an historical question without disturbing its unity.

On the other hand, that duality is already forcing itself upon the economic sciences. Here, in contrast to the other sciences, political economy and economic history constitute two clearly separated disciplines within a single science; the works that have recently appeared on these subjects point up the distinction. Proceeding as they have, economists are – without being well aware of it – obeying an inner necessity. A similar necessity obliges us to divide linguistics into two parts, each with its own principle. Here as in political economy we are confronted with the notion of *value*; both sciences are concerned with *a system for equating things of different orders* – labour and wages in one and a signified and a signifier in the other.

Certainly all sciences would profit by indicating more precisely the co-ordinates along which their subject-matter is aligned. Everywhere distinctions should be made, according to the following illustration, between (1) *the axis of simultaneities* (*AB*), which stands for the relations of coexisting things and from which the intervention of time is excluded; and (2) *the axis of successions* (*CD*), on which only one thing can be considered at a time but upon which are located all things on the first axis together with their changes.

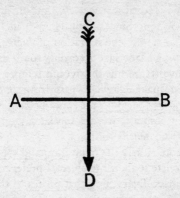

For a science concerned with values the distinction is a practical necessity and sometimes an absolute one. In these fields scholars cannot organize their research rigorously without considering both co-ordinates and making a distinction between the system of values *per se* and the same values as they relate to time.

This distinction has to be heeded by the linguist above all others, for language is a system of pure values which are determined by nothing except the momentary arrangement of its terms. A value – so long as it is somehow rooted in things and in their natural relations, as happens with economics (the value of a plot of ground, for instance, is related to its productivity) – can to some extent be traced in time if we remember that it depends at each moment upon a system of coexisting values. Its link with things gives it, perforce, a natural basis, and the judgments that we base on such values are therefore never completely arbitrary; their variability is limited. But we have just seen that natural data have no place in linguistics.

Again, the more complex and rigorously organized a system of values is, the more it is necessary, because of its very complexity, to study it according to both co-ordinates. No other system embodies this feature to the same extent as language. Nowhere else do we find such precise values at stake and such a great number and diversity of terms, all so rigidly interdependent. The multiplicity of signs, which we have already used to explain the continuity of language, makes it absolutely impossible to study simultaneously relations in time and relations within the system.

The reasons for distinguishing two sciences of language are clear. How should the sciences be designated? Available terms do not all bring out the distinction with equal sharpness. 'Linguistic history' and 'Historical linguistics' are too vague. Since political history includes the description of different periods as well as the narration of events, the student might think that he is studying a language according to the axis of time when he describes its successive states, but this would require a separate study of the phenomena that make language pass from one state to another. *Evolution* and *evolutionary linguistics* are more precise, and I shall use these expressions often; in contrast, we can speak of the science of *language-states* (*états de langue*) or *static linguistics*.

But to indicate more clearly the opposition and crossing of two orders of phenomena that relate to the same object, I prefer to speak of *synchronic* and *diachronic* linguistics. Everything that relates to the static side of our science is synchronic; everything that has to do with evolution is diachronic. Similarly, *synchrony* and *diachrony* designate respectively a language-state and an evolutionary phase.

IMITATION AND STRUCTURAL CHANGE IN CHILDREN'S LANGUAGE[*]

Susan M. Ervin

We all know that children's grammar converges on the norm of the community in which they live. How does this happen? One source might be through adult correction of errors and through operant conditioning reinforced by the responses of others. This is probably a relatively weak source of change in first-language learning. We know, for instance, that children learn certain grammatical structures which nobody taught them explicitly, and we also know that often teachers try hard to eradicate some of them. All over the world children learn grammatical patterns whether or not anyone corrects their speech, and there have been cases in which children who were believed for years to be mute have been found employing relatively mature grammatical patterns. A second source of change is maturation. Young children cannot learn grammatical and semantic concepts of a certain degree of complexity, and they produce sentences limited in length. Gvozdev,[1] in a book on child language development in Russian, has presented evidence that, when grammatical complexity is held constant, semantic difficulty is related to the age of acquisition of certain grammatical patterns. For instance, the conditional is learned late. Recent work by Roger W. Brown and his group supports this view. But maturation cannot account for the content of language nor for the particular structures acquired. A third factor affecting language development might be comprehension. We know that, typically, recognition precedes production. We know that people can understand many more words than they ever use. The number of cues for recognition is less than the information needed for accurate production, and in recognition we can often profit from redundancy.

Fraser, Bellugi and Brown[2] have recently found that children's imitation of grammatical contrasts regularly surpassed their comprehension, which in turn was superior to their freely generated speech. For instance, they would choose the right picture, or repeat 'The sheep are jumping',

* Reprinted from Eric H. Lenneberg (ed.), *New Directions in the Study of Language* (M.I.T. Press, Cambridge, Massachusetts, 1964).

or 'The sheep is jumping', more often than they could speak the right name when a picture was pointed out.

The children in this study were asked to imitate. The real test as to whether imitation is significant as a source of progress in grammar should be based on spontaneous imitations, for children may imitate selectively.

The material to be reported here is merely suggestive. It consists of a study of only five children.[3] It is unique in that I have the advantage of working from careful descriptive grammars for each of the children about whom I shall report. The crucial test is this: Are imitated utterances grammatically different from free utterances? If they are different, are they more advanced grammatically?

Ideally, one would write independent grammars for the imitated sentences and for the freely generated sentences and compare the grammatical rules. Since the number of imitations was far too small, grammatical rules were written only for the free sentences, and then the imitations were tested for their consistency with these rules. This method loads the dice against the similarity of the imitations to the free sentences.

TABLE I   Sentence-generating Rule for Donnie, Age 2:2

Optional Classes[a]						Required Class
1	2	3	4	5	6	7
goodness					bead	bead(s)
oh	here(s)				blanket	blanket
oh oh	there(s)	go[b]			bow-wow	bow-wow
oh dear	where(s)		a		car	car(s)
				big	choochoo	choochoo
see			the		Daddy	Daddy
whee	this				kiddy-car	kiddy-car
	that(s)				ring	ring
					truck	truck(s)
					water	water
					etc.	etc.

[a] Classes 1 to 6, selected in that order, may precede 7.

[b] 'This' and 'that(s)' never precede 'go'.

I shall first describe what I mean by a grammar, then define what I mean by imitation, and finally test the hypothesis of similarity.

We collected 250 sentences of two words or more from Donnie (Table 1). At this time, when he was two years and two months old, his mother reported that he had just begun to put words together. The rule described here accounts for 198 of Donnie's sentences.

Another 16 sentences followed another rule, producing 'what's that' and 'what's this'. There were 35 sentences which could be described by neither rule.

Three months later, Donnie's grammar had changed (Table 2). Some of the sentences that we could not account for at the earlier stage have now become more frequent and stable. We now find it necessary to set up a phrase rule for a nominal phrase, which you see in Table 2. Although

TABLE 2   Nominal Phrase-generating Rule for Donnie, Age 2:5

	Optional Classes[a]			Required Class
	1	2	3	4
NOMINAL	a	red	all-gone	all-gone
	the	big	ball	ball
		more	bead	bead(s)
			broken	broken
			bye-bye	bye-bye
			choochoo	choochoo
			green	green
			monkey	monkey
			truck	truck
			yellow	yellow
			etc.	etc.

[a] Classes 1 to 3, in that order, may precede 4.

all the regular sentences at the younger age contained at least one nominal, there are now more frequent sentences without a nominal phrase (Table 3). We can conveniently divide Donnie's sentences into four types at this age. The largest number, 173, were declarative sentences like 'there's a bus', 'there's a green', 'here's a broken', and 'there's all-gone'. Ninety-six were nominal sentences like 'big yellow', 'oh, broken', 'yellow broken', or 'monkey broken'. Another 76 contained 'go' or 'goes' as in 'car go broken', 'goes the bubbles', and 'there's it go'. There were 20 sentences with 'have-it', meaning 'I want it'. For example, 'there beads, have-it' and 'where the choo-choo, have-it'.

TABLE 3   Sentence-generating Rule for Donnie, Age 2:5

1	2	3[a]	4	5	6
oh boy	there(s)	it			
hi	where(s)	all	go	NOMINAL	have-it[c]
no	here(s)		goes		
don't	that(s)[b]				
etc.	this is[b]	NOMINAL			

[a] Multiword sentences contain at least one item from columns 3 to 6, with order as in the sequence of columns.

[b] That(s) and this (is) never precede columns 4 to 6.

[c] Columns 4 and 6 are mutually exclusive.

These are inductive or descriptive rules or grammars. Alternative descriptions might do as well: our criteria were brevity and completeness. We can test a grammar of an adult language by asking speakers if test sentences are acceptable; with so-called dead, literary languages we can cross-check different sources. With children, our descriptions must be more tentative. For these two-year-olds we found that between 77 and 80 per cent of the sentences could be described by our grammars.

Now we turn to the central issue. Are the spontaneous imitations of these children governed by the same rules as their freely generated sentences? To illustrate, here are some examples of Donnie's imitations at two years five months. You will find that the first three are consistent, the last two are not. The first column is the model, the second the imitation.

'This is a round ring.'	'This ring.'
'Where does it go?'	'Where's it go?'
'Is Donnie all-gone?'	'Donnie all-gone?'
'Is it a bus?'	'It a bus.'
'Is it broken?'	'Is broken?'

We have confined this study only to overt, immediate repetitions. We have excluded imitations in which there were changes, as in 'Liz is naughty', 'He's naughty'. We found that adult conversations are heavily threaded with such partial imitations and also that they are hard to separate from answers to questions. Judges might easily disagree in judging which were imitations. We kept the clear-cut cases, including exact repetitions, which were few, echoes of the final few words in sentences, repetitions with words omitted, and the few instances of repetitions with changes in word-order. Omissions bulked large in our cases of imitation. These tended to be concentrated on the unstressed segments of sentences, on articles, prepositions, auxiliaries, pronouns and suffixes. For instance: 'I'll make a cup for her to drink' produced 'cup drink'; 'Mr Miller will try', 'Miller try'; 'Put the strap under her chin', 'strap chin'. Thus the imitations had three characteristics: they selected the most recent and most emphasized words, and they preserved the word-order.

When the imitations have been isolated, the next step is to identify the grammatically consistent sentences. These were of two types. Some used vocabulary that we had included in describing the grammars. As I have said, our rules included lists of words according to classes, or by positions that they could occupy. Some of the imitated sentences included new words that were not on these lists. Any speech-sample is selective in vocabulary, and since we were interested in structure and not vocabulary, we arbitrarily included as grammatical any sentences containing a single new word by treating these words as 'deuces wild'. That is to say, any new word could be assigned to a class so as to make a grammatical sentence. The same rule was used on the residual sentences which were freely generated. Some of these sentences were called ungrammatical simply because they included grammatically ambiguous words.

We used exactly the same rule of procedure for the imitated sentences and for the free sentences in deciding whether the sentence fitted the structural rules or not. We made liberal, but equally liberal, provision for accepting new vocabulary in both samples. Thus we can see whether the rules of word-arrangement were the same in the two samples (Table 4).

For all the children except one, Holly, the sentences in both samples were equally predictable from both rules. Donnie was studied at three ages, and there was no change with age in the consistency of his imitated sentences.

But what about Holly? We must move to our second question with her: Were the imitated sentences grammatically more advanced than the free ones, or simply more inconsistent? We shall use three criteria in judging the grammatical maturity of these sentences. These criteria are based on the changes that characterized the children's speech in the months following those we are considering. First, sentence-length increased

TABLE 4   Grammatical Novelty of Imitations

	Percentage Imitated	Percentage Grammatically Consistent	
		Freely Generated	Imitated
Susan (1·10)	7	88	79
Christy (2·0)	5	91	92
Donnie (2·2)	6	93	100
Lisa (2·3)	15	83	65
Holly (2·4)	20	88	68[a]
Donnie (2·5)	8	91	94
Donnie (2·10)	7	92	91

[a] $X^2 = 9.4$

with age. Donnie's sentences at the three ages considered had an average length of 2·2, 2·4, and 2·7 words. Secondly, there is an increase in certain grammatical markers with age, including an increase in the use of articles and pronouns. Finally, there is an increase in adult-like sentence constructions consisting of imperative-plus-object, or subject-verb-object, or subject-verb-adjective, or subject-verb-particle. Examples are 'hold it', 'he took it', 'that's hot', and 'they came over'.

Using these three criteria, we examined all Holly's residual sentences, both imitated and free, that did *not* fit the rules of arrangement we had called her grammar. The average length of the free sentences was three words, of the imitated sentences two words. There were grammatical markers such as articles and pronouns in 62 per cent of the free sentences, and in 28 per cent of the imitated sentences. Half of the free sentences and a third of the imitated sentences were structurally complete, from an adult standpoint. There were no subject-verb-object imitated sentences, but there were six subject-verb-object free sentences, such as 'I want play game' and 'I don't see Heather car', Heather being Holly's sister.

We are left with a question about why Holly was so different from the other children. It was something of a tour de force to write a grammar for Holly. One class, identified as a class by the fact that its members occupied initial position in sentences, included 'this-one', 'see', 'want' and 'there'. Another heterogeneous class, identified only by the fact that it followed the words just described, include 'around', 'pull', 'raining', 'book' and 'two'. No other child had such a bizarre system, if system it was. Probably Holly's imitations did not fit this system because these were not in fact rules governing her speech. Donnie's rules were far more simple, consistent, and pervasive. It is possible that the high percentage of imitations produced by Holly is related to the fluidity of her grammar. But if it is so, then her imitations were a disturbing rather than a productive factor in her grammatical development.

If we can rely at all on this sample of five children, there is an inescapable conclusion. Imitations under the optimal conditions, those of immediate recall, are not grammatically progressive. We cannot look to overt imitation as a source of the rapid progress children make in grammatical skill in these early years.

A word of caution. I have *not* said that imitation is never important in language-learning. In comprehension covert imitation may be important. Possibly imitation aids in the acquisition of vocabulary or of phonetic mastery. Perhaps overt imitation is indispensable in the special conditions of classroom language-learning. All I have said is that there is not a shred of evidence supporting a view that progress towards adult norms of grammar arises merely from practice in overt imitation of adult sentences.

Fitting Theories to Facts

One may take several different approaches in accounting for child language development. We have already touched on one: the imitative view. According to this conceptualization the child makes errors and introduces abbreviations in his effort to approximate sentences he hears. Development is thought to consist of gradual elimination of such random errors.

This point of view is implied in the studies of grammatical development which have counted grammatical errors, omissions, and sentence length as criteria for development level. A second view assumes that children have sets of rules like those of adults, since they can understand adults, but that in speaking they have a combination of editing rules and random production errors. Development consists in eliminating the omissions and redundancies arising from these editing rules. A third view would assume that development can be described as the evolution of a series of linguistic systems increasing in complexity, with changes in behaviour reflecting changes in the child's syntactical rules.

The data reported below have been collected in a collaborative study with Wick Miller, in which frequent texts were collected from seven monolingual oldest children, and monthly systematic tests were conducted on twenty-four children, during a period approximately from age two to four.

In English plural inflection, the contrast *dogs* – *dog* might be learned as if the two words were unrelated, separate items of vocabulary. Each would be learned by imitation and by association with the appropriate semantic discrimination. Yet imitation will not account for the behaviour of adults speaking English. If an adult hears a new word, say, the name of a new tool, such as a *mindon*, he will surely call two of them *mindons*, a word he has never heard. We might say that he has formed a new word by analogy. Such analogic extensions are not explainable by simple generalization, because they occur when both the referent and the word itself are new and clearly distinguishable from previously known words. We found that children formed new plurals in this way when they were between two and three years old.

We tested children systematically by showing them objects, first singly and then in pairs, and asking for a description. These tests were conducted at monthly intervals. Some of the things we asked about were familiar, such as 'boys' and 'oranges'. Others were new objects, called such things as a *bik*, *pud*, or *bunge*.

If a child learns the plural first in terms of separate items of vocabulary, we should expect him to employ the plural suffix with some consistency with familiar words before he generalized to new words. In fact, this is just what happened. For nearly all the children, there was a time-gap between the time when a familiar plural was used and the time when an analogous new word was given a plural. Thus, between the time when the child contrasted *block* and *blocks* and the time when he said that two things called *bik* were *biks*, there was a small but reliable gap of about two weeks. For *car* and *boy* and the analogous *kie*, the gap was about six weeks. For other words the gap was greater. In all cases – *pud*, *bik*, *kie*, *tass* and *bunge* – the new contrast appeared later than the contrasts the children had heard.

We would expect that this extension to new forms also would occur for the irregular plurals. All the children, over the period we studied them, regularized the plural for *foot* and *man*. They said *man–mans*, and *foot–foots* or *feet–feets*. Most preferred *foot–foots*. Very few of the children fluctuated between *foot* and *feet*, so although the word *feet* must have been heard by the children, we can clearly see a regularizing influence. If imitation alone were at work, we would have expected fluctuation between *foot* and *feet*.

There was a difference in the time of acquisition depending on form. The English plural form is quite regular and has few exceptions. Its form is governed by certain sound-rules. Thus we had *mat* and *mats*, but *match* and *matches*. We can describe this difference by saying that words ending in sibilants, such as *horse*, *buzz*, *match*, *judge*, *marsh* or *rouge*, add a vowel plus *s*. Children at this age frequently do not distinguish these sounds phonetically – orange may be pronounced unpredictably as *orinch*, *orinz*, *orints*, *orins*, *orinsh* by the same child. The children all shared the problem of adding *s* to words ending in sibilant sounds. What they did was omit a plural contrast for these words. The usual pattern in the earlier grammars was distinction of singular and plural except for words ending in sibilants, which had the same forms for singular and plural. Occasionally we would have analogies which removed the sibilant, as in singular *bun* plural *buns* for *bunges*, and singular *bok* plural *boks* for *boxes*.

At some point each child produced the regular plural for one of these sibilant words. Quite often, when this happened, the plural for other earlier forms changed. Thus when *box–boxes* first was given, we found such forms as *foot–footses*, or *hand–handses*. Another pattern sometimes appeared. When *tass–tasses* came in, we found *foot–footiz* or *bik–bikiz*.

These changes occurred with children who had previously used the –*s* plural regularly, for *foot*, *bik* and *hand*. Why did these words change? If we examine the whole range of plurals employed at one of these points in time, we might describe the system as involving two plural forms vacillating unpredictably from –*s* to –*iz*. Alternatively, –*s* or *siz* were both in unpredictable variation. Surely, at this point, it is clear that the child is employing some common response, whatever you may call it, in using all of these plural forms. A linguist would say that the child had a plural morpheme with two allomorphs in free variation. How can a psychologist translate this behaviour into terms familiar to him? This is most certainly not behaviour learned by accumulated imitation. It is transitory, lasting at most two months, and is then resolved into a system of conditioned variation like that of adults.

There are two pieces of evidence here which will not fit a theory that inflection develops through imitation of familiar forms and extension by generalization to new items. One is the fact that *foot* and *feet* do not fluctuate as much as imitation of adults would lead us to expect. The other is that even highly practised, familiar plurals may be temporarily changed in form by overgeneralization of new patterns. Both these data suggest that analogy in the production of sentences is a very important process and may outweigh the imitation of familiar forms.

Analogy is a familiar process to linguists. Formal similarity is the basis for the construct that they call a morpheme. Yet overlaid on the child's systematic analogic forms, or morphemic patterns, we have a gradual accumulation of successful imitations which do not fit the stabilized pattern of the child, in such instances as *oranges* and *boxes*. Eventually these result in a change in the system, which becomes evident in the errors, from the adult standpoint, and in the analogic extensions to nonsense words. The conditioned allomorphs in the adult system – the different plurals in *mats* and *matches* – were imitated one by one at first. Then they produced random fluctuation between the two forms, and later stable responses conditioned by the same features in the phonetic environment as the adult plurals.

Now let us turn to past-tense inflection. Our best data are from the group of seven children from whom we collected extensive texts in interviews over a period of time. It is, of course, much harder to elicit a contrast in tense than one in plurality. The semantic cues are less controllable. For this reason we relied on less systematic methods of testing. Now it happens that the English tense system has analogies to the system of plurals. Like the plurals, it has both a regular pattern and irregular forms. There is *walk–walked*, and there is *go–went*. As with the plurals, the specific phonemic pattern depends on the particular final phoneme of the simple verb – we have *pack–packed* and *pat–patted*, when a vowel is added in the suffix. As with plurals, the children used forms that indicated the difficulty of the pattern of adding a vowel – forms such as *toasteded*.

The major formal difference in English between plural inflection of nouns and tense inflection of verbs is the great frequency of irregular (or strong) verbs, whereas irregular nouns are relatively few. It was a surprise to me, in examining verb frequency tables for the children we studied, to find that verbs with regular inflection were few and infrequent in our earliest texts. Therefore, tense inflection begins with the *irregular* forms.

I looked for the first case of extension of the regular past-tense suffix which could not have been imitated – for instance *buyed, comed, doed*. The odd, and to me astonishing thing is that these extensions occurred in some cases before the child had produced any other regular past-tense forms according to our sample. In some cases the other past-tense forms consisted of only one or two words of dubious significance as past-tense signals.

Relatively rare was the extension of irregular patterns – though we did find *tooken*. With plurals we had found that extension to new instances followed considerable practice with the regular pattern. Of course, our texts must underestimate the frequency of regular verbs, since they are small samples, but the regularity with which we found such extensions occurring quite early suggests that it takes relatively few instances and little practice to produce analogic extension. Another interpretation is that such extensions can occur with little or no actual contrasts in the child's speech; he may base them on the variety of types employing the regular contrast in the language of the adult. That is, if he can comprehend the contrast in the adult language he may on that basis be led to produce analogous forms.

With plurals, the regular patterns were learned and extended first; children did not waver between *foot–feet* and *foot–foots* but employed *foot–foots* normally. With the irregular past-tense forms, the children learned the unique, irregular contrasts as separate items of vocabulary first. Sometimes they were separate even contextually, as in the child who said *it came off* and *it came unfastened*, but *come over here* and *come right back*. Next, the children produced analogic past-tense forms for these highly frequent words. At the same period in which a child said *did*, he might say *doed*; at the same age at which he said *broke*, he might say *breaked*, and so on. We do not know if there were correlated linguistic or semantic differences between these two versions of the past-tense forms. At any event, these productive analogies occurred before we had evidence of practice on the familiar forms from which the analogies presumably stemmed. Whatever its basis in practice, it seems clear that the regularizing or analogizing tendency is very strong.

The learning of syntax is even more difficult to explain. Let us go back to before the age of two. In the earliest examples we have obtained, we find that there are consistencies of order between words. A very simple system might be one that produced sentences like *all-gone candy*, *candy up-there, all-gone book, read book*, and *book read*. Another said *snap on*, *snap off, fix on.* Notice that these sentences could not all be produced by simple abbreviation of adult sentences. Many of the children's sentences are such imitations, but some have a word-order that cannot be explained by simple imitation. Children talk a great deal and they hear a great deal. It is improbable that they could produce the great variety of sentences they do produce from memorized strings of words.

When we introduced words to a child in controlled sentences, he put them into new and appropriate sentences. When told of a nonsense object *that's a po,* or *there is a po,* the child said *here's a po, where's a po, there's a po, the po go up there,* and *poz go up there.* When told *I'm gonna sib the toy,* he later said *I sib 'em,* indicating the appropriate gesture. Yet the form *wem,* in *this is a wem bead,* was not extended. Thus a noun-form was productively utilized in many new contexts, a verb-form in one, and an adjective-form in none. However slight, at least here is an indication of an analogic extension at the syntactic level.

One explanation which has been offered by several different observers of young children, for instance, Braine,[4] Brown and Fraser,[5] and Miller and Ervin,[6] is that these early systems indicate the beginnings of syntactic classes.

How do such classes develop? Two features of classes have been noted to account for the development of regularities. In children's language, there is greater semantic consistency than in adult language. Brown[7] has shown that by nursery school age children identify verbs with action, nouns with things. Perhaps groupings into classes of words that can occur in the same place in sentences rest at least partly on semantic similarities. Another feature is that in all these grammars there are some positions where only a few words can occur, but that these words are very frequent. Thus one child started many of her sentences with *thats.* Another ended many of her sentences with *on* or *off.* The words that can occur following *thats* constitute a class, in the same sense that nouns are identified as following *the* for adults. This is not the only way we recognize nouns, but it is almost as useful as a suffix in marking the class. How do we know that these words 'go together' in a class for the child? We find that the recorded bedtime monologues of a child described by Weir[8] were filled with instances of words substituting for each other: *what colour blanket, what colour mop, what colour glass; there is the light; here is the light; where is the light.* Such practice, like the second-language drill in the classroom, could make some words equivalent counters in the game rearrangement we call language. Thus, both meaning and high frequency of certain linguistic environments seem important in the evolution of syntactic classes.

Clearly, we have evidence that children are creative at the very beginnings of sentence formation. They imitate a great deal, but they also produce sentences which have both regularity and systematic difference from adult patterns. At the same time, within these classes there are always statistical tendencies towards finer differentiations.

As my last example, I will take the grammatical features called transformations by Chomsky.[9] A good instance is the rule for the purely syntactical use of *do* in English. This word appears in a variety of sentence-types: in elliptical forms, such as *yes, they do*, in emphatic forms such as *they do like it*, in questions such as *do they like it?* and in negatives as in *they don't like it*. According to Chomsky's analysis, these uses of *do* are analogous and can be described by a single set of related rules in the grammar of adult English.

Let us see how children employ *do*. In the negative, a simple rule for the contrast of affirmative and negative would be simply to add *no* or *not* in a specified place. *He's going* v. *he's not going; he has shoes* v. *he has no shoes*. Another procedure would be to contrast *is* with *isn't, can* with *can't*, and so on. In both cases, the contrast of affirmative and negative rests on a simple addition or change, analogous to the morphological change for tense or for the plural. Neither rule presents new problems.

Some children had several coexisting negative signals. During the time-period, one child had the following: (1) *any* in possession sentences, such as *Joe has any sock* and *all the children has any shirt on;* (2) *not* in descriptions and declaratives, such as *not Polly;* (3) *don't* in most verb sentences, such as *don't eat that*, and *I don't like that*. Note that all these utterances can be described in very simple terms without the use of more complex constructs than those needed to account for inflection, or simply syntactic classes.

But as the child acquires verb inflection, more complex rules develop. We say *he goes*, but we do not usually say *he goes not*. Simple addition of *not* is inadequate. We say *he doesn't go*. In the contrast *he can go* v. *he can't go* there is only one difference. In the contrast *he goes* v. *he doesn't go* there are two: the addition of the word *don't* in appropriate number and tense, and the difference between *go* and *goes*.

Usually children use *don't* quite early as a negative signal, but as inflections began we found sentences like *Joe doesn't likes it* and *it doesn't fits in there*. In these sentences inflections appeared, but in two places. In an analogous development, *do* appeared early in elliptical sentences as a verb–substitute. Thus we find, in response to the remark *there aren't any blocks in this book*, the reply *there do*, and when Wick Miller said *I'm Joe*, the child said *no you don't, you're Wick*. Thus the child had not differentiated subclasses of words used in elliptical constructions, just as the subclasses of inflections of *do* with different number and tense did not appear until later. By age three, this child said *it goes right here, doesn't it?* and *you're named 'she' aren't you?*, employing complex constructions which cannot be explained in terms of the simple semantic signals we found in *Joe has any sock*.

Chomsky has described the various uses of *do* in adult English as economically based on the same rule. Does the use of *do* appear concurrently in negatives, interrogatives, ellipsis and emphasis? Quite clearly this is not the case. As we have seen, *don't* appears early in negatives. It is often the only negative signal. In interrogatives, the question is signalled by question words or by a rising pitch, and *do* is typically not present until months after it appears in negatives or in ellipsis. Thus we cannot infer the process of acquisition from an analysis of the structure of the adult language. Sentences that are described as generated through transformation rules in the adult grammar may be based on different, and simpler, rules in the early stages of the child's grammar. And a rule that may apply to a variety of types of sentences in the adult grammar may develop through quite separate and independent rules in the early stages of the children's grammars.

I have mentioned the development of tense and number inflection, simple syntax, and more complex syntactical processes called transformations. These have all raised certain similar problems of explanation.

In adult language, it has been found necessary to postulate such constructs as morpheme classes, syntactic classes, and grammatical rules. It is not inevitable that similar constructs need be employed in accounting for the earliest stages of language acquisition.

Three different theories of child language development were described earlier. The imitation view assumed that the child imitates adult sentences and gradually eliminates abbreviations and errors as he grows older. A second view assumes that children comprehend adult rules but make random errors in speaking. A third view sees language in children as involving successive systems, with increasing complexity.

In their simplest forms all these positions seem wrong. Let us review the evidence. We found that spontaneous imitations were syntactically similar to or simpler than non-imitations. In examining plural inflection, we saw that indiscriminate imitation would lead us to predict free variation of *foot* and *feet*, but, in fact, one form was usually preferred, and the plural contrast was based on analogic extension. We found it necessary to postulate a plural morpheme to account for the sudden and transitory appearance of forms like *bockis* and *feetsiz*. With verbs, mere frequency of use of a contrast was less important than the variety of types employing it, suggesting again the need for conditions giving rise to a past-tense morpheme, with varied environments for a particular form, before analogic extension can occur.

In children's early syntax, the data are still ambiguous, for it is hard to elicit and identify extensions to new cases. On the one hand, sentences like *fix on*, *all-gone puzzle*, *I not got red hair*, and *once I made a nothing pie* clearly involve processes of analogic extension. Here we see at least rudimentary classes. On the other hand, in any system we devised there were indications of incipient subdivision, of statistical irregularities in the direction of the adult model, prior to shifts in the system.

In the use of *do* we found that the adult rule applies equally to the negative, interrogative, elliptical and emphatic sentence. But among children *do* did not appear at the same time in these types of sentences. The pattern of development, and the rules that might describe usage at a particular point in time, differed for these different sentence types and differed for different children. Yet there were rules; errors were not random.

In all these cases, we find that children seem to be disposed to create linguistic systems. We have not examined the speech of twins, but it seems likely that we should find there a rich source of systematic creation of constructions. It is hard to conceive that children could, by the age of four, produce the extraordinarily complex and original sentences we hear from them if they were not actively, by analogic extensions, forming classes and rules.

At the same time we cannot wholly accept the third position presented – that of idiosyncratic systems. In every instance of systematic change I have examined there has been some evidence of fluctuation, some evidence of greater similarity to adult speech than one would expect on the basis of the system alone. In addition, in the early stages of some complex rules – such as the use of *do* – we found that there were phases that seemed to rest on rudimentary acquisition of vocabulary. The use of *don't* as an undifferentiated negative signal could be so described.

The shift from one system to another may be initiated from several sources. One is the comprehension of adult speech, another is imitation. The relation of imitation to comprehension has barely been faced in discussions of child language, yet these two must account for the accretion of instances which eventuate in systematic changes.

In language, unlike other intellectual processes, the child can monitor his output through the same channel by which he receives the speech of others. If he knows how – if he can make discriminations and remember models – he can compare his own speech to that of others. Thus, language development involves at least three processes.

It is obvious that there is continual expansion in the comprehension of adult speech. Perhaps comprehension requires some ability to anticipate and hence, at a covert level, involves some of the same behaviour that occurs in speech production. But this practice in comprehension alone is not sufficient to bring overt speech into conformity with understood speech. Consider again the phenomenon of so-called twin languages, for instance, or the language skills of second-generation immigrants who have never spoken the parents' first language but understand it, or of second-language learners who persistently make certain errors of syntax after years of second-language dominance, or of some children of immigrants who understand their age peers but speak the English of their parents. More than comprehension is involved.

Another process is the imitation of particular instances by children. What is entailed in hearing and imitation we do not know at this point. The fact that phrases may be uttered long after they are heard, without overt practice, suggests that our study of immediate, spontaneous imitation concerns only a fraction of actual imitation-derived utterances. Yet unless these utterances constitute a systematically simpler sample of all imitated utterances, it is obvious from our analysis of them that syntactical development at least cannot rest on imitation.

The third process is the building by analogy of classes and rules, a process which we infer from the child's consistent production of sentences he could not have heard. Of the three approaches which I offered earlier, I would suggest that the third is closest to the truth, but that the accrual of gradual changes under the influence of listening to adults lies at the base of the generalizations and analogies formed by the child. Any system of analysis which omits either the idiosyncratically structured and rule-governed features of children's language or the gradual changes within these rules is contradicted by evidence from all levels of the linguistic behaviour of children.

PRAGUE STRUCTURAL LINGUISTICS*

B. Trnka and others

The starting-point of linguistic work as done by the Prague linguists is the assumption that its true objective is the analysis of speech-utterances of all kinds, both spoken and written. This subject-matter of linguistics, as any other raw material of physical, psychological and other phenomena, can be grasped and comprehended only in terms of the verifiable laws which govern them. In contradistinction to the *nomothetic*, mechanical operation of natural laws, the validity of linguistic laws is *normothetic*, restricted to definite periods of time and to definite bodies of utterances. If formulated and presented in grammar, they may exert a stabilizing influence upon the speech of the community by strengthening the stability and uniformity of its linguistic norms, as prescribed by the grammarians. The normothetic character of linguistic laws does not exclude, of course, the validity of some of them for several languages or even for all languages of the world in all their historically accessible periods of development. Despite many differences all languages must have some laws in common (e.g., the general law of minimal phonological contrast, according to which some consonantal clusters and vocalic combinations are excluded from all languages of the world), and one of the true goals of linguistics is to discover and formulate them.

Structuralism may be defined as the trend of linguistics which is concerned with analysing relationships between the segments of a language, conceived as a hierarchically arranged whole. The question may be asked whether the segments or the relationships are primary, but this problem cannot be solved at the present stage of our knowledge, at least not by linguists alone. It is clear, however, that both relators and relations are coexisting and correlated entities which cannot appear separately from each other. The relationships of a segment are recognized by its properties, and as every segment is constituted by its properties, the elimination of these results in the elimination of the segment itself, not in the discovery of a 'substratum' – a concept which modern science

* Reprinted from J. Vachek (ed.), *A Prague School Reader in Linguistics* (Indiana University Press, 1964).

makes superfluous. In other words, the structural linguist conceives of linguistic reality as a system of sign events, i.e., as a system of linguistic correlates to extra-linguistic reality.

The word 'structuralism' is used to designate various trends in modern linguistics which came into existence between the two world wars, but, apart from the school of Geneva, those associated with the Cercle Linguistique de Prague, the Cercle Linguistique de Copenhagen and the name of Leonard Bloomfield are regarded as the most typical. From the historical viewpoint, these three currents of structural linguistics have at least two features in common: divergence from the Neo-grammarian methods which tended to the psychologization and atomization of linguistic reality; and a tendency to establish linguistics, looked upon by the older school as a conglomerate of psychology, physiology, sociology and other disciplines, as an independent science based on the concept of linguistic sign. Otherwise they differ considerably from one another in their principles and procedures, and it is therefore advisable to use a special designation for each of them, viz. *functional linguistics* (V. Mathesius's term) for the linguistic school of Prague, *glossematics* for Hjelmslevian linguistics and *descriptive linguistics* for the Bloomfieldian trends. We cannot devote our attention here to other outstanding currents of structural linguistics deviating from the above-mentioned schools in different ways, and the following remarks will thus be mainly restricted to these three.

Hjelmslev's glossematics introduces into linguistics the deductive method of the algebraic calculus and declares itself to be independent of any linguistic reality. His theory does not purport to be a system of hypotheses which would be found true or untrue by reference to factual linguistic evidence, but it tends to serve in analysing a given 'text' by means of a strategy of assumptions which should be as few and as general as possible in order to fulfil conditions of applicability to the greatest number of linguistic data. Let us quote his own words. 'This calculus, which is deduced from the established definition independently of all experience, provides the tools for describing or comprehending a given text and the language on which it is constructed. Linguistic theory cannot be verified (confirmed or invalidated) by reference to such existing texts and languages. It can be controlled only by tests to show whether the calculation is self-consistent and exhaustive.' It must be pointed out that the correctness of such a linguistic theory rests not only on the truth of calculation, but also on the veracity of the general linguistic assumptions which enter into the calculus. The latter in Hjelmslev's calculus are, however, neither self-evident nor acceptable to all structural linguists (cf. his sharply-drawn dichotomy text–system, contents–expression, the forms of contents–the forms of expression; his views of *sign* as representing both 'contents' and 'expression'), and his logically consistent and conceptually well-arranged theory appears to be divorced from, and inadequate for, linguistic reality. The Prague linguists have not been influenced by Hjelmslev's glossematics, and especially strong reservations are made by them concerning his theory of the phoneme as a mere 'taxeme', the identity of which is thought by Hjelmslev as consisting only in the identity of its distribution in words. Hjelmslev seems to regard both relevant (or distinctive) and irrelevant features of a phoneme as a 'substance', and while mixing the functional features of a phoneme with its functionless elements, he builds up an artificial wall between the sound and the phoneme. The Prague school takes into consideration not only the distribution of phonemes in words, but also their relevant features, the superposition of which determines the identity of a particular phoneme. Thus the English sounds *ph* and *p* in *paper* are phonetic implementations of the phoneme *P*, because both of them consist of the superposition of the same relevant (distinctive) features, i.e. bilabiality, plosion, oralness and voicelessness, aspiration being an irrelevant phenomenon determined mechanically by stress. On the other hand, Old Indian *ph* is a phoneme, not a positional variant of *p*, because its aspiration is not determined by its environment or its position. If two phonemes (e.g., *b* and *ŋ* in English) are in complementary distribution with each other and there is no environment in which both of them occur, their ever-present and potential capacity for differentiating words (cf. *pen–ſen–ten–den*) remains unutilized, so that the *only* test of their phonemic status is their differences of make-up in terms of relevant features. Strictly speaking, the true function of phonemes is not keeping the meanings of words (or morphemes) from each other (cf. [*nait*] night–knight, [*frendz*] friend's–friends), but only distinguishing phonemes between each other.

Various trends of *descriptive linguistics* appear to be in agreement with the linguistic theory of the Prague group on some points, but owing to their behaviouristic basis they differ from the latter in terminology, definitions and details of the procedure of linguistic analysis. Both schools agree in rejecting the psychological approach to phonology and in regarding the phoneme as a unit of the phonological plane of language, but while the Prague group stresses the analysis of the phoneme into the relevant features which constitute it, the Bloomfieldians (Bloch, Trager,

Harris, Hockett) seem to lay the emphasis on its distributional features in words or in utterances. As to the semantic criteria, which most American linguists exclude from their definitions of the phoneme, Prague phonologists lay stress on the capacity of phonemes to distinguish words and morphemes (cf. *točka–dočka, burit'–buril*) and consequently on the morpheme and word boundaries as important factors, the disregard of which might lead to unwarrantable conclusions, e.g., in the phonological evaluation of affricates, in the formulations of neutralization rules and in ascertaining phonological foreignisms adopted by a given language. On the other hand, Prague linguists are aware of the fact that phonemes as such have no meaning – the word *hand* is something different from the mere sequence of the phonemes *h, ae, n, d* – and that their capacity of differentiating words need not actually be utilized in a linguistic system (cf. the zero functional load of the opposition *b–ŋ* in English cited above). Nor are phonemes the only exponents of the word and morphemic dia-crisis: homonyms, which may be defined as two (or more) words possessing identical phonemic implementation, are distinguished from each other only in that their respective meanings have no semantic elements in common. It is clear that the phoneme, as conceived by the Prague school, *is* an abstraction, but such a one as is made, consciously or unconsciously, by all speakers of a language, and as necessary for description of the sound-level of a language as the concepts of 'morpheme', 'word' and 'sentence' are for that of its higher levels. Only this abstraction allows us to reduce a great number of sounds, acoustically or (and) articulatorily different, to a comparatively small number of units capable of being represented by letters.

There are some other divergences between the linguistic theory of the Prague school on the one hand and that of the American schools of descriptive linguistics on the other. In fact, there are some minor divergences even between the views of the individual adherents of Prague functionalism. Linguistic theory is not viewed by Prague structuralists as an a priori discipline independent of all experience, but as a theoretical framework derived from concrete linguistic materials and liable to verification, development and improvement by the use of further material and by further research work. Another characteristic of the Prague school, its structural conception of linguistic historical development, may be mentioned. At the very outset of their activity, Prague linguists emphasized the view contrary to the Saussurean theory that language is a system where 'tout se tient' not only from the synchronic viewpoint, but

also in its diachronic aspect. In fact, at any stage of its historical development language never ceases to be a system, as Time constantly affects all
its levels and all its components.

In the recent history of linguistics the structuralist movement represents a reaction to the atomism of the Neo-grammarians, and a tendency
to grasp linguistic reality without any contradiction, more fully and more
simply than current methods permitted. Some elements of linguistic
structuralism can be found much earlier, in the grammar of Panini, in
some works of Italian and other grammarians of the Renaissance, and
later on in the writings of some modern linguists, but no consistent theory
of structural analysis had been undertaken before Ferdinand de Saussure
and N. Troubetzkoy. A growing opposition to the neo-grammarian
principles of linguistic analysis was, of course, manifest as early as the
'eighties of the nineteenth century, and took on different forms in different
countries. Thus some germs of structuralism had developed in some
countries independently from each other. Some linguists (as Baudouin
de Courtenay, Ščerba, and others) sought to deepen the mechanistic
conception of linguistic development by emphasizing the psychological
correlates of linguistic phenomena, others (as Winteler, Sweet, Jespersen)
accentuated differentiation between the functionally relevant and
functionally irrelevant features of speech, or insisted on the fact of interrelationship of all components of language. The methods of the so-called
relative chronology, as developed by Meyer-Lübke and Karl Luick in
Austria, M. Křepinský in Czechoslovakia and Šachmatov in Russia in
their respective fields of philology, also contributed – partly at least – to
this conception. It must be pointed out that the rise of linguistic structuralism was encouraged and influenced to some extent by similar trends,
taking place at the same time, in logic, mathematics, psychology, ethnology, natural sciences and philosophy. Its growth and development,
however, is chiefly due to the progress of linguistic thought itself. As
regards Prague structuralism, its development was prepared partly by
Josef Zubatý (1855–1932), whose anti-mechanistic views were shared by
his younger students (B. Havránek and J. M. Kořínek, among others),
partly by Vilém Mathesius (1882–1945) and his pupils (B. Trnka and
J. Vachek), who were interested in establishing new or more precise
methods in both synchronic and diachronic linguistics. The Russian
members of the Cercle Linguistique de Prague (R. Jakobson, N. S.
Troubetzkoy, and S. Karčevskij) were influenced by Šachmatov and
Ščerba, as well as by de Saussure, while their study of ethology and of

some Caucasian languages enlarged their scope of linguistic vision and strengthened them in their efforts to find a more adequate approach to linguistic materials than the traditional one, used in Indo-European comparative philology. It must be mentioned here that the extensive study of Indian languages and folklore in the United States of America was also instrumental in bringing fresh ideas to linguistics and in contributing a good deal to the development of American structuralism. As to the further progress of structural linguistics, the Prague school expects the best results of this study, provided that it will never lose sight of its true purpose to analyse linguistic reality without imposing any preconceived limitations on its materials and without excluding a study of linguistic correlates to cultural and other extra-linguistic realities. It is understandable, of course, that owing to the present state of structural linguistics and to the immense tasks with which it is faced, no complete structural analysis of any language has so far been achieved by any linguist. The relatively best descriptions of a number of languages have been accomplished in the field of phonology.

Whereas the phonological level of a language is based on the phoneme and its relevant constituents, the morphological level is constituted by the word and the morpheme. The word may be defined as a minimal meaningful unit implemented by phonemes and capable of transposition in sentences. The morphemes are minimal meaningful segments of a word (e.g. *hand-s, hand-y, might-i-er; ruk-á, ruč-n-ój,* in Russian). Leaving aside the formation of words, the role of structural morphology is (1) to state morphological oppositions (e.g., that of the number of substantives, that of common case–adnominal case, etc., in English) and their neutralizations (e.g., the neutralization of the opposition genitive-accusative of masculines denoting living beings in Russian and Slovak, the neutralization of grammatical genders in plural in German, the neutralization of number in the third person in Lithuanian verbs, etc.); (2) to state the phonemic means (often homonymous) implementing the morphological oppositions of a language, such as prefixes, suffixes and alternations of phonemes (so-called *morphonemics*). The Prague functionalists underline the necessity of describing the morphological structure, as any other, of a given language as it really is, without forcing it into the traditional categories of Latin grammar. A common basis for the morphological, phonological and syntactical comparison of languages under study cannot be created by a mechanical application of the grammatical rules of any language or any state of the same language, but only by adopting the same principles as tools for functional analysis. Thus the so-called parts of speech (*partes orationis*) of Latin grammar cannot be viewed as a priori classes of words which must have their parallels in every language, but as word-classes characterized, in a given language, by taking part in different bundles of morphological oppositions. E.g., the class of substantives in Russian includes all words that are able to participate (i) in the opposition of cases, (ii) in the opposition of number (singular–plural), and (iii) in the oppositions of gender, irrespective of whether they are used to denote a 'substance' (*stol*, *voda*), quality (*len'*, *zlo*, *dobrota*) or action (*bd'en'e*, *chod*, *chožd'en'ije*). It is clear that the number of interrelational functions of parts of speech varies considerably from one language to another, as the classification of words into classes rests upon differences in the bundles of morphological oppositions in which they take part. Other criteria, either purely phonemic or purely semantic, cannot be applied to a linguistic analysis of *partes orationis*. Another point of deviation of Prague functionalism from the grammatical tradition is its conception of the function of morphological analogy. Whereas the Neo-grammarians looked upon analogy as a disturbing factor in the phonetic development of language, the Prague functionalists regard it as a realizer of morphological oppositions which can never suspend the validity of the phonemic laws of any stage of the historical development of a language. There is no denying the fact that the phonological plane co-operates with other planes of the linguistic system in order to achieve its purpose, namely intersubjective understanding, but the roles allotted to it are accomplished on the basis of its own specific laws. In consequence, neither new phonemes nor new combinations of phonemes can ever come into existence by the agency of morphological analogy in the historical development of a language.

As to the relationship of morphology to syntax, both disciplines are viewed – apart from Hjelmslev's theory – either as 'paradigmatics' and 'syntagmatics' respectively (by the followers of the Genevan school, Karčevskij, Bröndal, and Gardiner) or as two different levels of structural analysis (by American and Prague structuralists). According to the latter, morphology is concerned with the analysis of the word, whereas syntax is mainly the analysis of the sentence into its constituent relationships (e.g. subject–predicate, etc.). In contradistinction to the views of the former linguists, the Prague school holds that morphology and syntax cannot be linguistically contrasted to each other as two disciplines concerned with *parole* and *langue* respectively, because even syntax deals not only with parole, but also with langue, in attempting to discover normothetic laws, whose individual actualizations take place in utterances. In consequence, the line of division between morphology and syntax cannot be drawn as between paradigmatics (conceived as belonging to *langue*) and syntagmatics (as belonging to *parole*), and must be sought in the units in which they are concerned, i.e., the word and the sentence. In fact morphology and syntax represent two different levels of grammatical abstraction necessary for the analysis of linguistic material. The segmentation of a sentence (e.g. *father is ill*) never results in the elements of the morphological level (i.e. in the words *father* + *is* + *ill*), and vice versa; the summation of morphological units can never make up a sentence, because the latter is fundamentally something different from the total of the isolated words or groups of words by which it is implemented. Of course, both morphology and syntax, as well as phonology, *include* both paradigmatics and syntagmatics, in correspondence to the logical relationships 'either–or' and 'both–and'. Thus phonology treats not only of the inventory of phonemes and their relevant features (phonological paradigmatics), but also of their combinations in words and sentences (phonological syntagmatics) without mixing its own units with those of the higher ranks. In a parallel way, morphology deals both with words (morphological paradigmatics) and the combination of words in sentences (morphological syntagmatics) without infringing on the domain of syntax and its higher units. The chief business of the latter is, on the one hand, the analysis of sentences into the constituent syntactic oppositions, as well as the implementation of these by morphological oppositions (syntactic paradigmatics), and the analysis of the combination of sentences (syntactic syntagmatics) on the other. The doctrine of 'immediate constituents', derived by some American linguists from de Saussure's conception of 'syntagma', is not shared by the Prague school, since it may lead to a mechanistic analysis of speech-units disregarding the basic distinction between the morphological units on the one hand and the syntactical units on the other. In fact, the Saussurean conception of 'syntagma' has never become a starting-point for any scientific inquiry of the Prague linguists, if we leave aside the studies of Karčevskij, who was associated with the school of Geneva rather than with that of Prague. As another point of the Genevan syntagmatics questioned by the Prague school may be mentioned the reduction of *all* speech-elements, including the relation subject–predicate, to the relation determinant–determined.

It is clear from the foregoing exposition that the sharp Saussurean dichotomy langue–parole is no longer held to be a realistic basis of linguistic investigation by the Prague school. What de Saussure describes as 'parole' is regarded by the Prague linguists as utterances (or parts of utterances) in which a code of inherent structural rules is to be detected.

The lexical structure of a language is its legitimate and very important part. Its connection with morphology and syntax is clear from the fact that every morpheme (i.e. every minimal significative part of a sentence) must needs have a meaning in order to be identified as a morpheme and that this meaning acquires many shades and variations in combination with other words. At the present stage of linguistics the lexicon of a language is merely a more or less exhaustive and alphabetically arranged store of phonological, morphological, syntactic and stylistic facts, explained by means of approximate definitions and (or) approximate equivalents of the same or some other language. An investigation of the structural features of meaning is one of the most urgent tasks of modern linguistics.

By the application of structural principles the present-day historical grammar of a language may be converted into a description of the whole linguistic system, including features which, from the viewpoint of the Neo-grammarians, seem to have been unaffected by any changes. In reconstructing any particular feature of a language, the investigator must consider the whole linguistic system and seek to synchronize its other components as far as they are ascertainable by the diachronic comparison of the written evidence. In this way he may arrive at more realistic results and at a more critical view of its possibilities than previous research workers. Both synchronic and diachronic linguistics have the final aim in common: the discovery of linguistic laws. The formulation of diachronic laws differs from that of synchronic only by stating the period of time of their validity in terms of relative chronology. E.g., the validity of Verner's law – the neutralization of voice in the spirants f, θ, x and the rise of the variant z, if not preceded by stress – extended from the period of time in which p, t, k changed into f, θ, x to the dephonologization of Indo-European stress, in Old Germanic.

As to the study of the relationship between the relevant features of language and those of society, it must be admitted that all schools of structural linguistics – with the exception of that of Edward Sapir and his followers – have failed to develop it in a satisfactory way. The Copenhagen school has been prevented by its own particular theory of language from the systematic investigation of the problems involved, and the American descriptive linguists, who often refer to Sapir as to their precursor, neither advanced to grasp the whole body of problems nor developed adequate methods for their solution, owing to non-historical trends in their linguistic thinking. As for the Cercle Linguistique de Prague, a penchant for immanentism was shared by some of its members and manifested itself in their stressing the basically correct view of the therapeutic character of many phonological and other changes. Other members of the Cercle (V. Mathesius and others), however, emphasized the functional role of language as a system serving to satisfy the communicative and expressive needs of the community and liable to changes in order to meet new needs. The reflection of social factors in language has been never denied by the Prague linguists (cf. Havránek's theory of development of the Czech literary language), although the chief interest of the Cercle was devoted to the elaboration of phonology and morphology. In the words of K. Horálek, the deficiency of the scientific inquiries of some Prague structuralists was that they were not structural enough. It must be pointed out, however, that not every level of language is affected by features of extra-linguistic structures in the same measure. Whereas the strongest influence of these factors is exerted on the lexical plane of language, it is less manifest in syntax and morphology (cf. the ousting of ME *hie, hi* by Scand. *theirr; thou* by *you*) and much less still in phonology and phonetics. The function of this plane is almost restricted to providing the linguistic community with a number of mutually distinct and combinative units (i.e. phonemes) as implements of the higher planes of language, so that its correspondence with the social needs of the community is only indirect. This subservient, though very important, role of the phonological plane is relatively constant for all linguistic systems and helps us to account for the fact that most results of the research work of the Cercle Linguistique de Prague still remain useful contributions to structural linguistics. It would be a mistake, of course, to believe that the sound-level of the language has absolutely nothing to do with the social history of the speech community. Interesting examples of the influence of extra-linguistic factors on the sound level of languages may be found, e.g. in phonological changes which were suggested or at least promoted by a widespread use of loan-words containing phonological features foreign to the language of adoption. Thus the phonologization of voice distinction between f and v, s and z, θ and δ, which took place in Middle English in consequence of the loss of final $-e$, the change of x to f, and the dephonologization of consonantal quantity, was doubtless facilitated by such words as *basin*, *mason*, adopted from French, in which both voiced and voiceless spirants *f* and *v*, *s* and *z* were phonemes.

It may be seen from the above remarks that a study of culture–language correlation is one of the major tasks of linguistics and that structural methods should be extended to the problems involved, as far as the character of a particular linguistic level admits. It is especially necessary to substitute loose formulations relating to the subject by precise structural laws. This task cannot be carried through to completion, of course, without a deeper analysis of the semantic aspects of language.

A complete knowledge of linguistic reality cannot be achieved without combining the *qualitative* analysis of its constituents with that of their *quantitative* relationships. E.g., a statement as to the various formations of the plural in English would be incomplete and inadequate if it were not complemented by data relating to their productivity and frequency.

It is important to state that the quantitative approach to linguistic materials has no useful purpose if the mathematically minded research worker does not set out to solve a concrete linguistic problem or if he does not furnish at least some raw material for further qualitative evaluation. It is used in linguistics, as in other social sciences, for analysing a complicated and heterogeneous reality or for verifying the results of an analysis already obtained. The heuristic value of the quantitative analysis of a linguistic feature in terms of its productivity, contextual frequency and periodicity consists in detecting a contradiction between its anticipated quantitative relationships and the quantitative results actually arrived at. E.g., it has been ascertained that voiceless 'paired' consonants *p*, *t*, *t'*, *s*, *š* in Czech and Slovak are more productive (functionally loaded) and more frequent than their voiced counterparts *b*, *d*, *d'*, *z*, *ž*, whereas the voiceless back fricative *ch* (x) is less productive and less frequent than the voiced glottal spirant *h*, which is in the same phonological relationship with *ch* as *s* is with *z*. This striking exception to the rule of quantitative relationship between voiced and voiceless consonants in both languages is to be explained in terms of qualitative linguistics. It is doubtless in connection with the fact that (x) owes its phonemic status to the phonologization of a positional variant of *s* in Primitive Slavonic and does not belong to the older stock of the phonemes *p/b*, *t/d* and *s*. Since it formed voice correlation with *h* after the change of Old Czech *g* to *h*, i.e. as late as the eleventh or twelfth century, its peculiar quantitative feature in present-day Czech or Slovak must be interpreted as an interesting reflection of its earlier uncorrelated character.

The field of quantitative linguistics is very extensive. So-called *linguistic typology* may be regarded as one of its branches, and likewise *linguistic characterology*, which V. Mathesius sought to establish on the basis of the comparison of structural features between a number of European languages, cannot do without an appeal to statistics.

DE SAUSSURE'S SYSTEM OF LINGUISTICS[*]

Rulon S. Wells

1. Though the *Cours de linguistique générale*[1] is justly credited with providing 'a theoretic foundation to the newer trend of linguistics study',[2] it strikes the reader as very often obscure in intention, not seldom inconsistent with itself, and in the main too barren of detail to be satisfying. In short, it needs exegesis. The present study takes a cue from de Saussure's treatment of language, by treating his thought as a synchronic self-contained system. It is our thesis that the solutions to most of the unclarities in the *Cours* can be resolved by careful internal collation of the *Cours* itself. Often a problem presented by a certain statement is cleared up by one or more slightly different expressions of the same idea to be found elsewhere in the book. Much of our work consists in bringing such scattered passages together. Beyond this, analysis shows how the various doctrines that de Saussure maintains are related to fundamental principles. In stating his ideas as sharply as possible, we bring to bear insights that have been gained since his day. Occasionally our interpretation leads us to venture a guess about how de Saussure would have dealt with facts or viewpoints that do not come up in the *Cours*.

Naturally, many of the ambiguities and inadequacies of exposition in the *Cours* must be attributed to the circumstances under which the work was prepared. The editors' task of integrating students' notes (not their own) on courses given in the three years 1906-7, 1908-9 and 1910-11 must have called for a good deal of adjustment in the wording and the manner of exposition. However, the main theses are expressed over and over, giving confidence that they are amply attested in the notes. Moreover, the editors occasionally indicate in footnotes points which they do not understand, or feel impelled to comment upon. This suggests that most of what they wrote had a clear basis in the notes or in their memory of discussions with de Saussure.

After the difficulties due to de Saussure's or his editor's exposition have been resolved there remain the ones inherent in the thought itself. Two

[*] Reprinted from *Word*, journal of the Linguistic Circle of New York, no. 3 (1947), pp. 1-31.

evidently untenable notions we probe into at some length: the idea that the formal systematic properties of phonemes are independent of their specific quality, and the idea that a change suffered by a system (a particular language at a particular time) is never engendered by that system itself.

Our treatment falls into six sections, as follows: Phonetics, Phonemics, Historical Phonetics; Language as a Synchronic System; Langue and Parole; Linguistic Change; Critique; de Saussure as Methodologist.

PHONETICS, PHONEMICS, HISTORICAL PHONETICS

2. De Saussure distinguishes three different points of view from which speech may be studied. First, it may be studied as a set of physical-physiological events with correlated psychic events: phonation, sound-waves, audition. Second, it may be studied from the point of view of native speakers and hearers of the language to which it belongs. And third, one may study the sound-changes which a language undergoes in the course of time. Since 'bien loin que l'objet précède le point de vue, on dirait que c'est le point de vue qui crée l'objet' (23b), we may recognize three sciences, each of which studies speech in its own way: phonetics, phonemics (see §5), historical phonetics.

3. The phonational act (*acte phonatoire* 69a, c, 83b, 103c; cf. 65b) gives rise, in the hearer, to an acoustic image which is distinct from the physical sound (29a). Viewed as physical sounds, many words, phrases, and even whole sentences are continuous; but the acoustic images to which they give rise are not continuous but beaded, segmented, sequences of units (32b, 64a).

La délimitation des sons de la chaîne parlée ne peut donc reposer que sur l'impression acoustique; mais pour leur description, il en va autrement. Elle ne saurait être faite que sur le base de l'acte articulatoire; car les unités acoustiques prises dans leur propre chaîne sont inanalysables. Il faut recourir à la chaîne des mouvements de phonation; on remarque alors qu'au même son correspond le même acte: *b* (temps acoustique) = *b'* (temps articulatoire). Les premières unités qu'on obtient en découpant la chaîne parlée seront composées de *b* et *b'*; on les appelle *phonèmes*; le phonème est la somme des impressions acoustiques et des mouvements articulatoires, de l'unité entendue et de l'unité parlée, l'une conditionnant l'autre: ainsi c'est déjà une unité complexe, qui a un pied dans chaque chaîne (65b).

As for the length of these phonèmes, 'la chaîne acoustique ne se divise pas en temps égaux, mais en temps homogènes, charactérisés par l'unité d'impression' (64a).

To paraphrase: phonetics (*phonologie*[3]) does not treat sounds in the raw, but as broken up into segments. It must consider acoustic images as well as phonation (63b), and the reason is that only the images can yield the segments. But (and de Saussure's doctrine presumably reflects the conspicious failure on the part of phoneticians to produce a workable analysis of *sounds* as such) it must return to phonation for a means of distinguishing one sound from another. This procedure will work because 'un phonème est identifié quand on a déterminé l'acte phonatoire' (69c).

4. 'La phonologie [phonetics] est en dehors du temps [cf. 135, 194b end, 202c–3c], puisque le mécanisme de l'articulation reste toujours semblable à lui-même' (56a). This differentiates it from historical phonetics, which 'se meut dans le temps' (ibid.). Moreover, 'il peut être intéressant de rechercher les causes de ces changements, et l'étude des sons nous y aidera; mais cela n'est pas essentiel: pour la science de la langue, il suffira toujours de constater les transformations de sons et de calculer leurs effets' (37a).

5. The third science that deals with sound is linguistics in the narrow sense, that is, linguistics of langue.[4] It is distinct from phonetics. 'Quand on a expliqué tous les mouvements de l'appareil vocal nécessaires pour produire chaque impression acoustique, on n'a éclairé en rien le problème de la langue. Celle-ci est un système basé sur l'opposition psychique de ces impressions acoustiques' (56b).

De Saussure nowhere differentiates a specific sub-branch of linguistics dealing with phonemes, as is usual nowadays. However, he shows (see §§20, 23, 27) that langue is made up of phonemes and morphemes, both of which form systems. Hence it is easy to abstract the materials in the *Cours* which fall under phonemics, and it is convenient to do so for the purposes of exposition and comparison. But it is necessary to warn the reader that no such concept and no such term are to be found in de Saussure.

6. The trichotomy of speech-sciences into phonetics, phonemics and historical phonetics fits neatly into the structure of de Saussure's classification. Phonetics has to do with parole (56b), phonemics with langue, and historical phonetics with the diachronic aspect. The how and why will be shown in §§23, 36, 37. Let it suffice for now to remark that, according to de Saussure, phonemics is irrelevant to historical studies.

7. Before comparing de Saussure's conception of phonemes with that of the present day, we must eliminate from consideration the superficially similar notion of phonetic species (*espèce phonologique*).

The Appendix to the Introduction (63–95), *Principes de phonologie*, is an excursus dealing, not with langue like the rest of the book, but with phonetics. It incorporates material not only from the lectures of 1906–7 and 1910–11, but also from three lectures of 1897 on the theory of the syllable (63a). Regardless of what de Saussure may have said about the independence of linguistics from phonetics, he devised an original phonetic theory with the aim of making intelligible the Indo-European semi-vowels (79b); the excursus expounds this theory of what constitutes a syllabic, the core of a syllable.

The fundamental classification of speech-sounds is by their degree of aperture (70c); this yields seven classes: stops; spirants, nasals; liquids; i, u, ü (the semivowels 75b); e, o, ö, a. (Only the main sounds are reckoned with, 71c, 73 fn, 80d, 85b.) Sounds of all classes except the a-class (80a, 81b) exist in pairs: an implosive or *fermant* (symbolized p̂, î, etc.) and an explosive or *ouvrant* variety (p̌, ǐ, etc.) (80b, 81c; 93a). A syllabic (*point vocalique*) is now very simply defined as an implosion not immediately preceded by another implosion (87c; cf. the ed. note of 94b); when a second implosion follows immediately without interruption, the two implosions together form a diphthong (92b). It follows that every sound except *a* is capable of functioning either as syllabic or as non-syllabic; in practice, the ambivalence is mainly limited to nasals, liquids and semi-vowels (88a).

8. Now when we consider any minimal segment of speech, e.g. t, 'Le fragment irréductible t, pris à part, peut être considéré *in abstracto*, en dehors du temps. On peut parler de t en général, comme de l'espèce T (nous désignerons les espèces par des majuscules), de i comme de l'espèce I, en ne s'attachant qu'au caractère distinctif, sans se préoccuper de tout ce qui dépend de la succession dans le temps' (66a). This sounds as if species were phonemes, whose allophones we are being invited to neglect. The impression seems to be supported by the statement: 'on parle de P [the species of p-sounds] comme on parlerait d'une espèce zoologique; il y a des exemplaires mâles et femelles, mais pas d'exemplaire idéal de l'espèce' (82b). But what can we make of it, then, when he (ibid.) calls species abstractions? We shall see (§56) how strongly he insists that phonemes are not abstract but concrete.

9. The answer is that 'phonetic species' is primarily a phonetic, not a

phonemic notion. For instance, i and y are of the same phonetic species (presumably regardless of the language where they occur), and so are u and w (87d–8a, 88d–9, 92a, 93). The whole point of de Saussure's theory of the syllable is that one cannot tell just from knowing the phonetic species of a sound whether it will be syllabic or not (89c). Another matter on which the theory throws light is length by position: only an implosive consonant, not an explosive one, can make length by position (91a, b). So for phonetic purposes it is vital to distinguish implosive and explosive; and hence 'on peut dire que P n'était rien sinon une unité abstraite réunissant les caractères communs de p̄ et de p̣, qui seuls se rencontrent dans la réalité' (82b). The great mistake of phonetics was to consider only these abstractions (82c), that is, not to consider separately implosive allophones and explosive allophones. Otherwise put, its mistake was to neglect what Sweet calls synthesis, the fact 'qu'il y a dans la langue non seulement des sons, mais des étendues de sons parlés' (77c). Therefore, 'à côté de la phonologie des espèces, il y a donc place pour une science qui prend pour point de départ les groupes binaires et les consécutions de phonèmes, et c'est tout autre chose' (78b; cf. 79). We hereinafter call these two studies analytic and synthetic phonetics respectively.

10. Several unclarities remain. If phonetic species are purely phonetic, what does de Saussure mean by their 'caractère distinctif'? Actually, de Saussure's term refers only to the kind of units that phoneticians have hitherto talked about. Now phoneticians do not distinguish sounds to the limit of discriminability; they deal with types of sounds that they call 'the s-sound', 'the front unrounded a-sound', etc. Each type includes a range of sounds, whose limits are left vague. In practice the limits are often decided by the phonemics of the languages best known to the phoneticians, particularly their native tongues. This practice accounts for many a resemblance between phonetic species and phonemes, in respect of their range of membership. De Saussure does not say this, but we, having hindsight, can see that 'phonetic species' was a mixture of phonetics and phonemics; and de Saussure does say in effect that in limiting their attention to phonetic species, phoneticians do a halfway job. Qua phonetician, de Saussure has no interest in making precise the notion of species, but only in distinguishing between implosives and explosives. And hence, pursuant to his policy of simplification (see references in §7), he does not raise such questions as 'In a language where i and y contrast and so are phonemically distinct, do they belong to the same species?' and, conversely, 'In a language where a stop and a spirant or a voiced and a voiceless

stop belong to the same phoneme, do they belong to the same species?' The implication (see 71b, 84d; 87c is carelessly worded) is that one species falls wholly within one degree of aperture. But the fact that languages differ markedly in the phonetic varieties of sounds that they unite under one phoneme is not brought out by de Saussure. Occasional individual examples (e.g. 72b) may illustrate it, but the reader of the *Cours* would not emerge with an appreciation of it as a sweeping, general truth. Pointing it out was Franz Boas's contribution; de Saussure approached phonemics by a different route, namely by drawing the parallel between morphemic and phonemic systems.

11. De Saussure does speak (68–9) of the distinctive character of species: 'énumérer ces facteurs de production du son, ce n'est pas encore déterminer les éléments différentiels des phonèmes. Pour classer ces derniers, il importe bien moins de savoir en quoi ils consistent que ce qui les distingue les uns des autres.' But the context shows that the viewpoint is not specifically phonemic; he means merely that 'par exemple l'expiration, élément positif, mais qui intervient dans toute acte phonatoire, n'a pas de valeur différentiatrice; tandis que l'absence de résonance nasale, facteur négatif, servira, aussi bien que sa présence, à caractériser des phonèmes' (ibid.). It would do so in any language. The English *a* is as much characterized by the absence of nasalization as the French *a*, although in French but not in English there is an opposing *ã*. French š, ž, ɲ are phonetically differentiated from the other French sounds not merely by being 'back' (which is their phonemic position), but by being palatal. At least there is no denial in de Saussure, explicit or implicit, of the above interpretation; and it is sounder method to lean over backward than to read too much into him.

Outside the Appendix, there is just one other passage where de Saussure speaks of species; this is apropos of sound-changes: 'Les exemples précédents montrent déjà que les phénomènes phonétiques, loin d'être toujours absolus, sont le plus souvent liés à des conditions déterminées; autrement dit, ce n'est pas l'espèce phonologique qui se transforme, mais le phonème tel qu'il se présente dans certaines conditions d'entourage, d'accentuation, etc.' (199b). Not analytic but only synthetic phonetics (see §9 end) can help historical phonetics.

12. It has been necessary to devote a very elaborate discussion to de Saussure's notion of phonetic species, in order to disentangle it from his genuine contribution to phonemics. *Phonème*, in the passages where we have encountered it so far, has meant simply an acoustically minimal and

homogeneous segment of speech. Now de Saussure never lays down the necessary and sufficient conditions under which two sounds are the same phoneme; therefore we cannot ascertain in what degree his sense of phoneme is similar to ours, except by squeezing what information we can from his few examples.

In the first place, the number of phonemes, unlike the number of sounds, is sharply definite (32b, 164c). In the second place, we are invited (83b, 84c) to disregard, even in phonetics, 'furtive' transitional sounds which are not perceivable by the ear [of native speakers? of trained phoneticians?]. In the third place, the existence of voiceless m and l is noted in French (72e, 74d 1), 'mais les sujets parlants n'y voient pas un élément différentiel' – differential, presumably, from the voiced varieties. In other words, we are told to consider voiceless m, l as belonging in French to the m and l phonemes respectively. In the fourth place, the existence of free and individual variations is noted, apropos of French '*r grasseyé*' and '*r roulé*' (164d–5a). In the fifth place, speaking about synthetic phonetics (see §9 end), de Saussure says (78–9): 'Dès qu'il s'agit de prononcer deux sons combinés ... on est obligé de tenir compte de la discordance possible entre l'effet cherché et l'effet produit; il n'est pas toujours en notre pouvoir de prononcer ce que nous avons voulu. La liberté de lier des espèces phonologiques est limitée par la possibilité de lier les mouvements articulatoires.'

All these stray hints do not tell us the necessary and sufficient conditions for two distinguishable sounds to be assigned to the same phoneme. The concept of complementary distribution is nowhere stated, and only remotely implied. The drift of de Saussure's remarks is that two sounds (of the same dialect, let us add) belong to one phoneme if they do not convey to native hearers distinct acoustic impressions. But this means that an implosive and its corresponding explosive, being acoustically different (65 fn, 79c–80), are different phonemes, a conclusion proclaimed by de Saussure (81c). But perhaps we ought to regard the following amazing statement as a lapse: When the early Greeks distinguished between kappa and koppa, 'Il s'agissait de noter deux nuances réelles de la prononciation, le k étant tantôt palatal, tantôt vélaire; *d'ailleurs le koppa a disparu dans la suite*' (65 fn; italics ours).

13. If de Saussure has not told us definitely whether and when two segments belong to one phoneme, at least he plainly answers the converse question: one segment can never belong to two phonemes at once. Thus the accent of a syllabic cannot be considered a separate phoneme. His

stated reason is that 'la syllabe [rather *le point vocalique* since a syllable may be more than one segment 65a, 66a] et son accent ne constituent qu'un acte phonatoire; il n'y a pas dualité à l'intérieur de cet acte, mais seulement des oppositions diverses avec ce qui est à côté' (103c). It is surprising to find unity ascribed here to the phonational act rather than to the acoustic image (65b, '*l'unité parlée*', is not to be taken seriously, since de Saussure has told us that *la chaîne parlée* is broken up into units only by its correspondence with the acoustic image); but the import is the same.

14. The upshot of all the previous discussion is that a number of passages which might seem, to a hindsighted reader, adumbrations of phonemics cannot be so regarded after careful study. Yet de Saussure does make a major contribution to phonemics, greater than any of his predecessors. For his whole system is the contribution. In this system, phonemics occupies a clear place; it belongs to the system only because of its analogies with grammar. The discussion of phonemics is generally a simple transfer, *mutatis mutandis*, of principles of grammar proper, that is, of the relations between morphemes, and this schematizing and abstract theory, rather than any specific and particular analysis, is de Saussure's contribution to phonemics. We are thus led to an *abrégé* of his entire system.

LANGUAGE AS SYNCHRONIC SYSTEM

15. Speech (*la parole*) is made up (146c; cf. 167a) of two linear sequences, each of which is articulated (26b, 156c), that is, discrete. The members of the one sequence are *tranches de sonorité* (146a, 150b) which are in turn sequences of one or more phonemes (180b); and (103, 170c) two phonemes cannot occur at once (cf. §13). Now phonemes are defined as sums of acoustic images and articulatory movements; but in the synchronic study of langue (see §§33, 37), the acoustic image alone is relevant (98c). So much so that in one place de Saussure proposes, on etymological grounds, to discard the term 'phoneme'. 'C'est parce que les mots de la langue sont pour nous des images acoustiques qu'il faut éviter de parler des "phonèmes" dont ils sont composés. Ce terme, impliquant une idée d'action vocale, ne peut convenir qu'au mot parlé, à la réalisation de l'image intérieur dans le discours. En parlant des *sons* et des *syllabes* d'un mot, on évite ce malentendu, pourvu qu'on se souvienne qu'il s'agit de l'image acoustique' (98d). In practice he retains the term; but we must remember that in the passages quoted from now on, it has a more limited sense; the phoneme no longer 'has a foot in each chain' (cf. §3).

16. The other sequence composing speech is a sequence of meanings. A meaning is not a physical thing but a concept (98c). The boundaries of a *tranche de sonorité* are not marked phonemically, but only by the fact that just this much of the stream of speech is correlated with a certain meaning and the next *tranche* is correlated with another meaning (145d–6a; cf. 135a).

A *tranche de sonorité* consisting of one (180b) or more phonemes which is associated with a concept de Saussure calls a *signifiant*; the concept with which it is correlated, a *signifié*; and 'nous appelons *signe* la combinaison du concept et de l'image acoustique' (99c), 'le total résultant de l'association d'un signifiant à un signifié' (100c; cf. 32a, 99d, 144c–5). However, de Saussure does not always adhere strictly to this definition. Now and then (e.g. 159b) he applies the term sign to 'le rapport qui relie ses deux éléments'; more often (e.g. 26b, 33c, 109d twice; 208c; also 98d, 99c, 160a, 162b, where *mots*, which are elsewhere called signs, are treated as *signifiants*) he lapses into 'l'usage courant' according to which 'ce terme désigne généralement l'image acoustique seule' (99c). But a definition that conforms better to de Saussure's regular usage in practice is that a sign is neither a relation nor a combination of *signifiant* and of *signifié*, but the *signifiant* itself qua *signifiant*. In adding 'qua *signifiant*' we are taking note of the caution that 'si *arbor* est appelé signe, ce n'est qu en tant qu'il porte le concept "arbre" ' (99c), which means two facts: (1) every sign is a *tranche de sonorité* but not vice versa (135, 146–7); (2) if one *tranche de sonorité* is associated with two distinct *signifiés*, it constitutes two distinct, though homonymous, signs (147a, 255c; cf. 150b–1). Needless to say, the converse is also true: if one *signifié* is expressed by two (therefore synonymous) *signifiants*, these *signifiants* are still different signs (147c–8); this applies even to what would nowadays be regarded as morpheme alternants. See also §23. The *signifié* is also, for its part, sometimes called '*la signification*' (158e, 159c, 160a, 162b). Our proposed emendation harmonizes with the definition (146a) of a linguistic unit (which is a linguistic entity 145c, this in turn being, 144a, a sign): 'une tranche de sonorité qui est, à l'exclusion de ce qui précède et de ce qui suit dans la chaîne parlée, le signifiant d'un certain concept' (italicized in the text).

17. Signs are the primary objects of linguistic study. Words, word-groups, and sentences are all signs – *signifiants* linked with *signifiés* (177c); but they are, in general, further analysable into component signs. Those that are simple (not further analysable) are the units par excellence of linguistics (145 ff.).

The term 'units' ('*unités*') is de Saussure's own; it is obvious from their definition that the simple units are essentially the same as the morphemes of Baudouin de Courtenay and of modern linguistics, except that what we today regard as morpheme alternants de Saussure subsumes under his broader concept of alternance (cf. §§22, 45). The term *morphème* was current in de Saussure's day, but with a specialized significance: the 'formative' elements of a word (affixes, endings, etc.) as opposed to the root. For clarity's sake, let us define a simple unit (= simple sign) more rigorously than he did but probably in accord with his intentions, as a sign meeting the following conditions: (1) it is an uninterrupted linear sequence of phonemes; (2) it has a meaning; (3) it is not divisible into two sequences meeting conditions (1) and (2) and such that its meaning is derived from their meanings. Thus there are two signs haiə in Southern British English: one, spelled *higher*, is composed of hai and -ə; the other, spelled *hire*, cannot be divided into parts which meet the required conditions and it is therefore a simple sign. A compound sign, i.e. an uninterrupted sequence of morphemes (no two of which occur simultaneously) is called a syntagm (170c).

18. De Saussure ascribes (100b, 103b) to linguistic signs two fundamental properties; they are arbitrary and they are arranged in a line. But he neglects to mention in this place another essential trait which figures far more prominently in his theory than linearity, to wit that linguistic signs are systematic. The characterization of langue as a deposit of signs 'passivement enregistrés' (see §31) does not mean that these signs are disordered, and simply a nomenclature (34c, 97a, 158d; cf. 162b); on the contrary, they form a very tightly knit system (26b, 29g, 32a, 43b, 107c, 124c, 149d, 154a, 157e). 'Arbitrary' and 'systematic' are the two fundamental properties of signs. A further discussion of the arbitrariness of the sign will be deferred to §§28, 44; it will suffice here to say that signs are arbitrary, according to de Saussure, in the sense that they are unmotivated (101c, 102b, 180–4): there is no natural, inherent connection between a *signifiant* and its *signifié*; any *signifié* could be expressed by any *signifiant*. This is proved a posteriori by the existence of different languages and by the fact that languages change. The same concept is equally well expressed by *bœuf* (which in turn came from a former *bov-em*) and by *Ochs* (100). The element of onomatopy in language is too slight to invalidate the general principle (101–2). Linguistic signs are not aptly called symbols, since 'symbol' ordinarily connotes a more or less natural non-arbitrary sign (101b).

19. Simple signs (e.g. Fr. *neuf, dix, vingt*) are wholly arbitrary (unmoti-

vated), but syntagms (e.g. *dix-neuf*) are relatively motivated (180–4). Their motivation consists in the fact that each is related syntagmatically to its components and associatively to the other syntagms having the same pattern (182b). But this is a poor explanation of what de Saussure is driving at, since simple signs also stand both in syntagmatic and in associative relations. A better statement, we suggest, would be as follows. Let us call a class of similar syntagms a *pattern*. Given a syntagm S_1 consisting of morphemes M_1, M_2, ... M_n, then any syntagm belongs to the same pattern as S_1 if its first morpheme belongs to the same morpheme-class as M_1, its second to the same class as M_2, and so on to M_n. Now patterns have meanings, and the meaning of a syntagm is a function of the meaning of the morphemes contained in it and of the pattern to which it belongs. From a small number of morphemes and a smaller number of patterns a very large number of sentences can be constructed; this is how we understand sentences that we have never heard before. (Cf. Bertrand Russell, *An Inquiry into Meaning and Truth* (1940), pp. 11a, 34a, 238b, 306f, 386–7.) French *deux-cents* and *cent-deux* contain the same morphemes, but the pattern-meanings are different: since *deux-cents* means 'two hundred', the meaning of the pattern is 'multiplied by', and since *cent-deux* means 'one hundred and two', the meaning of its pattern is 'added to'. The meaning of a pattern is not determined simply by the order of the morphemes, because one pattern (as defined above) may have very different meanings – e.g. *old men and women* means either 'old men and old women' or 'women and old men'. It is important to realize that the meaning of a pattern is as arbitrary, as unmotivated as the meaning of a morpheme; the meaning of a syntagm on the other hand is motivated in that it is a function of the meanings of the morphemes and the patterns entering into it. Moreover, not every mathematically possible combination of morphemes occurs; there is the syntagm *désireux* but no *eux-désir* (190c). For these two reasons, although 'une unité telle que *désireux* se décompose en deux sous-unités (*désir-eux*) ... ce ne sont pas deux parties indépendentes ajoutées simplement l'une à l'autre (*désir + eux*). C'est un produit, une combinaison de deux éléments solidaires, qui n'ont de valeur que par leur action réciproque dans une unité supérieure (*désir × eux*)' (176c; cf. 182a).

20. As we have shown (§18), a fundamental property of linguistic signs is that they are systematic. Now, de Saussure does not hold that every linguistic fact fits into a system. He holds that, as we narrow our attention from language as a whole (*langage*) to that part of it which is a socially acquired and passive repository in the minds of native speakers (langue),

we find that langue, thus defined, is a system. What de Saussure calls parole embraces the non-systematic elements of language. Precisely what is the difference between langue and parole, and why langue should engage the primary attention of the linguist, are points dealt with in §§30-2, 36, 37, 56.

De Saussure says, 'En déterminant ... les éléments qu'elle manie, notre science remplirait sa tâche tout entière' (154c). By continued and very clear implication, the elements of langue are of two kinds: signs, divided into morphemes and syntagms, and *tranches de sonorité* – phonemes and sequences of phonemes. In order to understand de Saussure's views about the properties and relations of phonemes, it is well to examine first his notions on the relations of signs.

21. In linguistics, 'comme en économie politique, on est en face de la notion de *valeur*; dans les deux sciences, il s'agit d'un *système d'équivalences entre des choses d'ordres différents*: dans l'une un travail et un salaire, dans l'autre un signifié et un signifiant' (115a; cf. 116b, 160a, and 164b). The linguistic analogue of economic value consists (158-60) in the relations of a sign (1) to its *signifié*, and (2) to other signs. (160a weighed against 159b and the diagram of 159c proves again the conclusion of §16 that in practice *signe* means for de Saussure '*signifiant* qua *signifiant*'.) Since value includes relations to other signs, it can change without either the sign itself changing or its relation to its *signifié* (166b, 179d), and different languages can have signs that have the same *signifié* but different values (160b-c).

Relations of a sign to other signs are again of two types (170-5): associative and syntagmatic. The relations of a sign to signs that may precede, follow or include it, and also to those included in it if it is a syntagm, are its syntagmatic relations. All these result from the fact that the signs constituting an utterance are arranged in a line; and it may be that de Saussure's insistence upon the linearity both of phonemes and of signs was for the sake of preserving the picture of language as articulated (§15). Of an entirely different type are the associative relations; a sign can recall other signs which are grammatically like it, or semantically affiliated with it, or even connected by nothing more than similarity of sound (e.g. *enseignement*, *justement*). 'Le rapport syntagmatique est *in praesentia*: il repose sur deux ou plusieurs termes également présents dans une série effective. Au contraire le rapport associatif unit des termes *in absentia* dans une série mnémonique virtuelle' (171). The two types of relation support each other (177-80); de Saussure's meaning, restated in modern terms, is that each syntagm (e.g. French *défaire*, Latin *quadruplex*) is capable of associatively recalling all the other syntagms that have the same pattern (e.g. Fr: *décoller, déplacer, ... refaire, contrefaire*), and that each morpheme is associatively connected with all the other signs which may replace it to form syntagms having the same pattern.

22. The want of detail in de Saussure's classification is deliberate; it is scarcely necessary to point out that a sign stands in much more intimate relations with some signs than with others. For example, there is the special kind of associative relation called by de Saussure (as also in his *Mémoire* of 1878, and by Baudouin de Courtenay as a borrowing therefrom) *alternance* (215–20; cf. §45). Again (174b–5) a sign stands in associative relations sometimes with a definite, sometimes with an indefinite number of other signs. But quite apart from this lack of detail, it would seem that there is no room in de Saussure's scheme for frequency-relations, much emphasized nowadays. Perhaps he would have held that relative frequency pertains to parole, not to langue. But the bearing of frequency on linguistic change (§50) seems to oppose such an explanation.

23. The crux of de Saussure's theory, for the statement of which all the preceding exposition has been preparatory, is the role of relations in a system. Signs are constituted partly, and phonemes wholly, by their relations, that is by belonging to a system. (But cf. §53.) For them, to be is to be related.

A langue is a system of signs. Signs, therefore, are its elements. And yet, in some sense phonemes and their sequences are also elements (cf. §§20, 27). How so? 'Une suite de sons', we are told in 144c, 'n'est linguistique que si elle est le support d'une idée; prise en elle-même, elle n'est plus que la matière d'une étude physiologique.' Ambiguous passage; for it might mean that a phonetic sequence is the object of linguistics only if it is a *signifiant*; or it might mean that only psychic sounds (phonemes) and their sequences (including *signifiants*) are linguistic because only they are supports of ideas: *signifiants* directly, and phonemes indirectly in that *signifiants* are built out of them. The former interpretation seems to be borne out by the context; yet cf. 180b: 'Un phonème joue par lui-même un rôle dans le système d'un état de langue.'

24. The important concept of opposition is treated by de Saussure in several passages:

(i) '[le] signifiant linguistique ... n'est aucunement phonique, il est incorporel, constitué, non par sa substance matérielle, mais uniquement par les différences qui séparent son image acoustique de toutes les autres' (164b; cf. 163a–b).

(ii) 'Ce principe est si essentiel qu'il s'applique à tous les éléments matériels de la langue, y compris les phonèmes … Ce qui les caractérise, ce n'est pas, comme on pourrait le croire, leur qualité propre et positive, mais simplement le fait qu'ils ne se confondent pas entre eux. Les phonèmes sont avant tout des entités oppositives, relatives et négatives' (164c).

(iii) The same is true of *signifiés* considered in themselves: concepts 'sont purement différentiels, définis non pas positivement par leur contenu, mais négativement par leurs rapports avec les autres termes du système. Leur plus exacte caractéristique est d'être ce que les autres ne sont pas' (162a). Troubetzkoy, 'La phonologie actuelle', *Jour. de Psych.* (1933) p. 233 fn. 1, quotes this passage as though it applies to phonemes, but since de Saussure's view of *signifiants* and *signifiés* was the same in this respect, no misrepresentation results.

(iv) 'Tout ce qui précède revient à dire que *dans la langue il n'y a que des différences … sans termes positifs*' (166b).

(v) But this is true only of *signifiés* and *signifiants* considered apart from each other; 'bien que le signifié et le signifiant soient, chacun pris à part, purement différentiels et négatifs, leur combinaison est un fait positif; c'est même la seule espèce de faits que comporte la langue, puisque le propre de l'institution linguistique est justement de maintenir le parallélisme entre ces deux ordres de différences' (166–7; cf. 146c, cited in §15).

(vi) In short, 'Dès que l'on compare entre eux les signes – termes positifs – on ne peut plus parler de différence; l'expression serait impropre …; deux signes … ne sont pas différents, ils sont seulement distincts. Entre eux il n'y a qu'*opposition*' (167c).

25. Let us try to find out exactly what de Saussure means by opposition. 'En grec éphēn est un imparfait et éstēn un aoriste, bien qu'ils soient formés de façon identique; c'est que le premier appartient au système de l'indicatif présent phēmí 'je dis', tandis qu'il n'y a point de présent *stémí; or c'est justement le rapport phēmí–éphēn qui correspond au rapport entre le présent et l'imparfait (cf. deíknūmi–edeíknūn), etc. Ces signes agissent donc, non par leur valeur intrinsèque, mais par leur position relative' (163–4). To quote an example from Bally, 'Ferdinand de Saussure et l'état actuel des études linguistiques' (Lecture delivered October 27th, 1913), p. 14: 'Dans *chevaux* la finale -ô … a la valeur d'un pluriel parce que notre esprit l'oppose au signe -al du singulier *cheval*, tandis que dans *tuyaux* [phonemically the same as the singular *tuyau*] le *même* son -ô est dépourvu de valeur, parce que notre esprit ne l'oppose à rien.' Similarly, in the *Cours*, 'Le fait de synchronie est toujours significatif; il fait toujours

appel à deux termes simultanés; ce n'est pas *Gäste* qui exprime le pluriel, mais l'opposition *Gast–Gäste*' (122b). And so, since 'la valeur de l'un [terme] ne résulte que de la présence simultanée des autres' (159c),

ce qu'on appelle communément un 'fait de grammaire' répond en dernière analyse à la définition de l'unité, car il exprime toujours une opposition de termes; seulement cette opposition se trouve être particulièrement significative, par exemple la formation du pluriel allemand du type Nacht: Nächte. Chacun des termes mis en présence dans le fait grammatical (le singulier sans umlaut et sans e final, opposé au pluriel avec umlaut et -e) est constitué lui-même par tout un jeu d'oppositions au sein du système; pris isolément, ni Nacht ni Nächte ne sont rien ... Cela est si vrai qu'on pourrait fort bien aborder le problème des unités en commençant par les faits de grammaire. Posant une opposition telle que Nacht–Nächte, on se demanderait quelles sont les unités mises en jeu dans cette opposition (168b).

The oppositions of a sign are its relations, syntagmatic and associative, with other signs (180b, apropos of phonemes), and are therefore part of its value.

De Saussure goes so far as to say (vii) 'les caractères de l'unité se confondent avec l'unité elle-même. Dans la langue, comme dans tout système sémiologique, ce qui distingue un signe, voilà tout ce qui le constitue. C'est la différence qui fait le caractère, comme elle fait la valeur et l'unité' (168a).

26. We have now come to the genuine crux of de Saussure's theory. Passage i tells us that *signifiants* are characterized by their differences. Now what is the difference between, say, English *hit* and *hits, hid, hot, bit,* etc.? That they are composed of different phonemes, no doubt. But ii tells us that phonemes are characterized – not by their differences – but by the fact that they are different, 'le fait qu'ils ne se confondent entre eux.' If phonemes are characterized only by being different, it does not matter *how* they differ; pushed to its extreme this means that only the number of distinct phonemes matters. If any or all of the elements should be respectively replaced by materially different ones, provided that the same number be preserved, the system would be the same (43b, 153d–4). There could not be two distinct systems of phonemes whose number of phonemes was the same, for if so they could differ only in some property or relation of the phonemes other than that of being different, which violates the hypothesis.

On the other hand if the phonemes are characterized by their differences, then they are like *signifiants* as described in passage i. It is yet a third thing to say as de Saussure says of signs (vii) that they are characterized by those of their properties that are distinct, i.e. not common to all the signs, phonemes, or whatever one makes the statement about. A distinctive feature or property, a difference or distinction, and the property of being different or distinct are all three entirely distinct properties, and it is far from hyper-subtle to say this. It is not clear, even from the larger context of the whole *Cours*, whether ii is meant simply as a restatement of i (a rather careless one, if so), or whether it is intended to say something different about phonemes than has been said about *signifiants*. In 163b, we read (viii) that 'puisqu'il n'y a point d'image vocale qui réponde plus qu'une autre à ce qu'elle est chargée de dire, il est évident, même a priori, que jamais un fragment de langue ne pourra être fondé, en dernière analyse, sur autre chose que sur sa non-coincidence avec le reste. *Arbitraire* et *différentiel* sont deux qualités corrélatives.' This lends colour to the view that ii is meant to apply to *signifiants* as well as to phonemes, and that i is simply a preliminary version of it. The next paragraph says: 'la conscience … n'aperçoit perpétuellement que la différence a/b' (163c); but the following example and comment show that 'la différence a/b' means 'the fact that a differs from b'. The total impression conveyed by all the statements is that de Saussure means to say that phonemes, *signifiants* and *signifiés* are all alike in being characterized not by their differential properties – nor by their differences – but by their being different; but that to be different is only part of the characterization of signs. This is what he means in saying that signs are distinct, not merely different.

27. De Saussure does not consistently maintain the terminological separation between difference and distinction, nor his restriction of opposition to signs (to the exclusion of phonemes and *signifiants*); phonemes as well as signs enter into oppositions, and of the same two types:

Un phonème joue par lui-même un rôle dans le système d'un état de langue. Si par exemple en grec m, p, t, etc., ne peuvent jamais figurer à la fin d'un mot, cela revient à dire que leur présence ou leur absence à telle place compte dans la structure du mot et dans celle de la phrase. [For other anticipations of Troubetzkoy's concept of Grenzsignale, cf. 256c, 316b.] Or dans tous les cas de ce genre, le son isolé, comme toutes les autres unités, sera choisi à la suite d'une opposition mentale double: ainsi dans la groupe imaginaire *anma*, le son m est en opposition syntagmatique avec ceux qui l'entourent et en opposition associative avec tous ceux que l'esprit peut suggérer, soit a n m a (180b).

v
d

Let the reader thoroughly absorb this passage, for it is all that de Saussure has to say about the system of phonemes. And with this quotation we have concluded our exposition of de Saussure's direct contribution to phonemics. His greater contribution is indirect, his linguistic theory in general and his concept of synchronic systems in particular. All he has to say about phonemes is that what is true of morphemes is true *mutatis mutandis* of them also; but he does not indicate what the *mutanda* are. From the standpoint of present-day phonemics, we can see the analogues: the syntagmatic relations of phonemes are what we call their positions of occurrence, and the phonemes with which a given phoneme is associatively related are the phonemes involved in the same morphophonemes as it, and the phonemes which occur in the same position; also those which undergo similar morphophonemic changes. But of all this there is no hint in de Saussure.

28. What are the relations between the two fundamental properties of signs, their arbitrary and their systematic nature (see §18)?

'Une langue constitue un système ... C'est le côté par lequel elle n'est pas complètement arbitraire et où il règne une raison relative' (107c, cf. 180–4, esp. 182b). We have discussed this contrast between the absolutely arbitrary and the relatively motivated in §19.

A sentence of 157c, 'Les valeurs restent entièrement relatives, et voilà pourquoi le lien de l'idée et du son est radicalement arbitraire,' makes it sound as if arbitrariness resulted from the nature of value; but this contravenes de Saussure's whole teaching, and is merely careless wording. His basic teaching may be stated as follows: (1) Signs stand in systematic relations to one another. (2) Simple signs are completely arbitrary; all that matters is that they be distinct from one another. (3) Therefore, *only* the relations of signs, i.e. their values, are relevant to the system; the systematic (relational) properties and the non-relational properties are independent of each other, they do not involve or affect each other. Signs are distinct, not merely different; this means, we take it, that not only their relations to each other but their relations to their respective *signifiés* are relevant and in fact essential. And all that is relevant to *signifiants* and to the phonemes of which they are composed is that they are different from each other. This follows from the arbitrariness of the sign (cf. 165e).

This framework of ideas is strikingly similar to the doctrine known in anthropology as functionalism, to which de Saussure comes closest in his discussion (150–4) of synchronic identity: two materially different entities are the same as far as the system goes if and only if they have the same value (154a), that is, are characterized by the same relations.

29. By the comparative method linguists have reconstructed large parts of the vocabulary of Proto-Indo-European. This method lets us ascertain the number of phonetic elements and their combinations. Its validity, according to de Saussure, is not contingent upon our demonstration of the precise or even the rough phonetic properties, articulatory or acoustic, of these elements, though we are often in a position to do so; it is sufficient to establish the number and distinctness of these elements (302–3).

Offhand one might think that this example shows the relevance of phonemics to historical linguistics. But actually it is not part of history in the strict sense, according to de Saussure's conception. For, though no doubt linguists have ascribed to PIE features that were not in fact contemporaneous, so that our reconstruction of it does not represent a language spoken by one particular community in one particular year or even decade or century, still PIE is roughly and in the main a single language-state.

And in fact, de Saussure does not apply phonemics to problems of historical change. This is no accidentally omitted detail; it reflects his general doctrine of linguistic change: every linguistic change is isolated. A system does not engender changes within itself.

By Sapir, Bloomfield and the Prague school phonemics is thought to be just as relevant to problems of linguistic change as to the descriptions of languages in their momentary states. It is part of our job, therefore, to show why de Saussure holds the opposite view. This requires that we penetrate still more deeply into the groundwork of his system of thought.

LANGUE AND PAROLE

30. Language (*le langage*), like any social phenomenon, is subject to perpetual change, and so may be analysed at any one time into an inherited or institutional element and an element of innovation. The institutional element de Saussure calls *la langue* and the innovational element *la parole*; by definition the two together exhaust *le langage* (36a, 37c, 112c).

31. Langue is (30f, 32b; cf. §18) a deposit of signs that each individual

has received from other members of the same speech-community, 'l'ensemble des habitudes linguistiques qui permettent à un sujet de comprendre et de se faire comprendre' (112c; cf. 100f); in other words, it is a passively accumulated repository in relation to which each person is a hearer, not a speaker (30f, 31d). Parole, by contrast, is both active and individual (30–1); it consists of particular speech-utterances. It is (24, 30e) *le côté individuel* as opposed to *le côté social* of language. A sentence is the typical unit of parole (148c, 172c), for 'le propre de la parole, c'est la liberté des combinaisons'. More comprehensively stated (38c; 30g–1a), 'la parole ... est la somme de ce que les gens disent, et elle comprend: (a) des combinaisons individuelles, dépendant de la volonté de ceux qui parlent, (b) des actes de phonation également volontaires, nécessaires pour l'exécution de ces combinaisons.'

32. Langue, though described as a repository, is not to be thought of simply as a pile of words (cf. §18); the previous sections have shown clearly how it is essentially a system, to which belong not only the signs with their values but what we defined as patterns. Native speakers (excluding scholars) are ignorant of the history of their own language, which means that the history is irrelevant to the system as they know it: 'La parole n'opère jamais que sur un état de langue, et les changements qui interviennent entre les états n'y ont eux-mêmes aucune place' (127a). And 'la première chose qui frappe quand on étudie les faits de langue, c'est que pour le sujet parlant leur succession dans le temps est inexistante: il est devant un état' (117c). It follows (ibid.) that 'aussi le linguiste qui veut comprendre cet état doit-il faire table rase de tout ce qui l'a produit'. It is the business of the linguist, in describing a system, to describe just those relations of which the native speakers are aware (128c, 136a, 140c, 189b, 251b–2), though in precision and explicitness the linguist's comprehension of the system will far exceed the speaker's. There are syntagms of whose analysis the speakers are doubtful (234a, 258c), and even signs such that the speakers are doubtful whether to regard them as syntagms or as simple signs (181c). 'Autre chose est de sentir ce jeu rapide et délicat des unités, autre chose d'en rendre compte par une analyse méthodique' (148b; cf. 106b, d, 107c, 256b). This methodical analysis is grammar (141).

33. The point of view so far described is what de Saussure calls (117, 12c) synchronic linguistics, whose essence is that it considers langues one by one. In discussing it, de Saussure speaks as though it were opposed only to historical or diachronic linguistics, but actually the *Cours* recognizes

two or possibly three non-synchronic studies, each of which considers langues two or more at a time.

34. The first such study is diachronic linguistics, which differs from the synchronic branch in taking change into account. But an immediate elucidation is needed. On the one hand, synchronic linguistics abstracts from time and change not by treating facts of different times as though they were simultaneous – doing so has been a common mistake (137b–8, 202a), sometimes deliberate (251a, 252b); but by considering a langue during a span of time too short to show any appreciable change (142b). In short, synchronic linguistics describes language-*states* (117a). And on the other hand, diachronic linguistics does not directly capture the process of change. De Saussure seems to have adopted the physicists' conception that change may be described as a succession of states (117a only apparently contradicts this); diachronic linguistics, taking as its data synchronic descriptions of different states of cognate languages, infers the changes that led from the earlier states to the later ones (128a, 140d). To do this one must have ascertained the diachronic identities (249; cf. §53) – e.g. that Latin *passum* is diachronically identical with French *pas*. Diachronic identity does not imply synchronic identity, nor vice versa; *pas* 'step' and *pas* 'not' are diachronically but not synchronically identical (129b, 150b, 250a); whereas *décrépi* < Latin *de* + *crispus* and *décrépit* < Latin *decrepitus* are synchronically identical (119d; 160c; 167b, 136a). Thus diachronic linguistics arrives inferentially at the phenomena which are its special province, viz. events (117a, 129b).

35. Diachronic linguistics is achieved by two different techniques (128c, 291–4), according to the character of the data on which it operates. The *prospective* method requires as data records of two or more states of the same language, that is, such that each state is either an ancestor or a descendant of each other state; this is the method mainly used in Romance linguistics. The *regressive* (better known as the comparative) method is primarily inferential, and requires – to continue the metaphor of family-terms – that they be brothers, cousins, uncles and nephews etc. of each other; in other words, that they be only collaterally, not linearly, related. From these data it infers so far as possible the state which was the last common ancestor of all these known states. In practice, the data are usually such as to admit and require the application of both prospective and retrospective methods.

36. The langue–parole distinction entails (37c, 38e) a corresponding dichotomy of linguistics (cf. §§37, 56). Of the two branches, linguistics

of langue is primary, and the main object of the *Cours* (39b, 317c); as we have seen, it is in turn bifurcated into synchronic and diachronic linguistics. Now by definition, langue and parole stand in a chicken-and-egg relation to each other. On the one hand, parole is based on langue (227a–b); we might restate de Saussure's idea in Aristotelian terms and say that langue is the active potentiality of producing parole. And on the other hand 'c'est la parole qui fait évoluer la langue' (37d; cf. 127a, 138c–9, 231a). More specifically, 'un fait d'évolution est toujours précédé d'un fait, ou plutôt d'une multitude de faits similaires dans la sphère de la parole; cela n'infirme en rien la distinction établie ci-dessus, elle s'en trouve même confirmée, puisque dans l'histoire de toute innovation on rencontre toujours deux moments distincts: 1⁰ celui où elle surgit chez les individus; 2⁰ celui où elle est devenue un fait de langue, identique extérieurement, mais adopté par la collectivité' (139a). Now since parole is the source, the *situs* of linguistic change, how does linguistics of parole differ from diachronic linguistics (of langue)? Are they not the same province under different names? De Saussure does not anticipate this question, but the answer is clearly implied. There is no necessary passage from the first of the two moments mentioned above to the second; 'toutes les innovations de la parole n'ont pas le même succès' (138c, cf. 232b). Diachronic linguistics does not take parole as its subject matter; by a comparison of earlier and later states it ascertains the changes from one to the other; and though these changes arose in parole, its concern is with the changes and not with their source. We have already (§§4, 6) pointed out how historical phonetics (which is part of diachronic linguistics) is wholly separate from the study of 'la parole y compris la phonation' (37c), which includes phonetics.

37. From the characterization of diachronic linguistics, it is clear that it rests upon synchronic descriptions (128a) – a doctrine which is the polar reversal of Hermann Paul.[5] And yet diachronic and synchronic linguistics are two radically separate enterprises.

According to de Saussure, synchronic linguistics is grammar (cf. §32 end), and (as we shall see in §§43, 44), diachronic linguistics is historical phonetics (137a, 194c, 209c, 226c, 228a, 317a). 'Qui dit grammatical dit synchronique et significatif, et comme aucun système n'est à cheval sur plusieurs époques à la fois [cf. 140d, 122b], il n'y a pour nous de "grammaire historique" …' (185b). What, then, says Jespersen (*Linguistica* 109–115; originally written 1916), have people like myself been writing about all these years, if not historical grammar? De Saussure has anticipated the question: 'Il faut s'en souvenir pour ne pas affirmer à la légère qu'on fait de la grammaire historique quand, en réalité, on se meut successivement dans la domaine diachronique, en étudiant le changement phonétique, et dans le domaine synchronique en examinant les conséquences qui en découlent' (195d; cf. §62).

38. So much for the delineation of diachronic linguistics. There is a second non-synchronic study which may belong with it, and that is dialect-geography. De Saussure distinguishes (40–3) between internal and external linguistics, by the latter term understanding in particular (40a, 41d, cf. Bally, 'L'état actuel', 21b) the type of studies upon 'words and things' undertaken by Meringer. The significance of the distinction is evidently methodological: 'La séparation des deux points de vue s'impose ... La meilleure preuve en est que chacun d'eux crée une méthode distincte' (42–3). The following formulation, we think, expresses de Saussure's basic thought more incisively than his own characterizations do: That is internal which lets systems be studied autonomously, whether one by one or two or more at a time, without reference to anything except other linguistic systems; in short, internal linguistics of langue is *pure* linguistics of langue (cf. 143a).

Now de Saussure relegates dialect geography to external linguistics (41c, 261a), presumably on the ground that it studies correlations between langues and something else. However, could we not consider that dialect geography is the spatial analogue of diachronic linguistics in that it considers contemporaneous cognate systems as they are arrayed in space rather than in time? There would be two significant differences: the array would have to be two-dimensional rather than one-dimensional (because isoglosses cross over each other), and there would be no *direction* to the array – nothing corresponding to the earlier and later of time. Of two contemporaneous dialects, one could not be singled out as cause and the other as effect. Still, inter-dialect identities could be established; this is done in phonemics by Daniel Jones's notion of diaphone. It is true that dialect geography as ordinarily conceived includes more than the pure comparison of the spatial relations of linguistic states; these other topics are truly external and would have to be separated in order that dialect geography might be regarded as part of the internal linguistics of langue. There would of course be combinations of the dialectual and the diachronic mode of comparison. We are content to have suggested this viewpoint without insisting upon it.

39. The third non-synchronic study of language is the comparison of

two or more non-cognate languages (263–4; cf. 183–4), a branch of study to which de Saussure barely alludes.

LINGUISTIC CHANGE

40. According to the neo-grammarian picture, linguistic change consists of (1) sound-change, (2) analogy, (3) borrowing, and (4) miscellaneous minor processes, such as coinage, blending, folk-etymology, syncope, obsolescence (or, as we would put it today in more general terms, change of frequency), semantic change, syntactic change (distribution of morphemes), and perhaps sundry others. De Saussure's discussion leaves out of account the third and fourth groups of changes except for brief examples and adventitious chapters, and states (194b) that linguistic change is, in the main, phonetic change. Moreover (198a), that every linguistic change is isolated.

By the latter statement de Saussure appears to mean two things: (1) linguistic changes are not general, and (2) they are not systematic.

41. The *Cours* says:

> Les faits diachroniques sont particuliers; le déplacement d'un système se fait sous l'action d'événements qui non seulement lui sont étrangers … mais qui sont isolés et ne forment pas système entre eux (134b). [This is as true when the change is semantic as when it is phonetic.] A une certaine époque presque toutes les formes de l'ancien cas sujet ont disparu en français; n'y a–t–il pas là un ensemble de faits obéissant à la même loi? Non, car tous ne sont que les manifestations multiples d'un seul et même fait isolé. C'est la notion particulière de cas sujet qui a été atteinte et sa disparition a entraîné naturellement celle de toute une série de formes (132c).

Clearly, in so far as it applies to *phonetic* change, this is simply the neo-grammarian proposition 'sound-changes have no exceptions'.

When a certain phoneme or cluster of phonemes in a certain environment undergoes a certain change no matter in what words it is contained, it is easy to say that the change in the words is secondary, stemming from the primary change of the phoneme. When all the words having a certain meaning become obsolete, it is easy to say that it is primarily the meaning and only secondarily the individual words which have perished. But certain apparent embarrassments come to mind.

The *Cours* (130) mentions four phonetic laws concerning the passage from Indo-European to Greek: (1) voiced aspirates become voiceless aspirates; (2) initial prevocalic s becomes h; (3) final m becomes n; (4) final stops are dropped. Now (2) and (3) concern one phoneme each; but (1) concerns bh, dh, ĝh, gh, gʷh, and (4) concerns p, t, k̂ and q. Are not then (1) and (4) general? De Saussure's only answer seems to squarely avoid the issue (133b; cf. 248c):

> La vraie question est de savoir si les changements phonétiques atteignent les mots ou seulement les sons; la réponse n'est pas douteuse: dans néphos, méthu, ankhō, etc. [instances of (1)], c'est un certain phonème, une sonore aspirée indo-européenne qui se change en sourde aspirée, c'est l's initial du grec primitif qui se change en h, etc. et chacun de ces faits est isolé, indépendant des autres événements du même ordre, indépendant aussi des mots où il se produit.

But (1) and (4) are not isolated in the same sense as (2) and (3), since each of them concerns not one phoneme but a class – of five and of four phonemes respectively. One could of course go a step further and, seeking a property common to all the voiced aspirates or all the stops, say it is this which has changed. This obvious suggestion is made by the editors, 133 fn., and seems to be implicit in 203c also. Another response, in the vein of the dismissal (102) of onomatopy, would be that even though whole classes of phonemes sometimes undergo a common change, such cases are the exceptions, or at least are not the only kind, and that it is the existence of changes like (2) and (3), rather than like (1) and (4), that is noteworthy. But de Saussure's own answer is right in the quotation above. He would not have hesitated to admit that (1) and (4) are general in a sense – only not in the sense which he had in mind. In his sense, to ask whether phonetic changes are general or particular is to ask whether they 'atteignent les mots ou seulement les sons'. Phonetic changes are specific in that 'le déplacement d'un système se fait sous l'action d'événements qui … lui sont étrangers' (134b; cf. 133c). The point would have been much clearer if de Saussure had given some examples of what he would be prepared to call a general change, but we shall undertake to construct one. A change is particular if there is common to all the entities which exhibit this change some part or else some property which changes. But if all members of a certain class change, not by change of their common part or common property but by changes in their respectively peculiar features, the change is called general. Thus suppose that in a certain language all nouns are single morphemes and that they end in a consonant, and that the names of plants have no common feature of phonemic structure that differentiates them from other nouns; in particular that for every consonant in the language there is at least one plant-name and also at least one other noun ending in that consonant. Now suppose that in the course of time every plant-name loses its final consonant, but every other morpheme retains it. The change cannot be ascribed to the common feature of plant-names, which is semantic only; it is therefore general, and if our interpretation is correct it is this sort of change whose occurrence de Saussure denies. On the other hand, if all feminine nouns become neuter, this could be regarded as a particular (even though not a phonetic) change like the French loss of the Latin nominative or (122-3) the loss of the post-tonic syllables of Latin words.

42. De Saussure's meaning is clear when he says that linguistic changes are non-systematic, for we know what it is that he is denying. Changes do not depend on each other, they do not have value; they are brute facts. The change of bh to ph would in no wise have been affected had dh and the others remained as they were. Nor does a later change depend *directly* on an earlier one; the earlier one results in a certain state, and the later one then affects this state. 'La parole n'opère jamais que sur un état de langue, et les changements qui interviennent entre les états n'y ont eux-mêmes aucune place' (127a).

In 125b, de Saussure compares synchronic description with the description of a transverse cross-section of a plant-stalk, and diachronic description with the description of an axial (longitudinal) section. He tells us that the study of the transverse section 'fait constater entre les fibres certains rapports qu'on ne pourrait jamais saisir sur un plan longitudinal'. True; but the converse is also true: the tissues are as 'solidaire' in the longitudinal section as in the transverse. The analogy of the plant-section is ill-chosen to illustrate de Saussure's teaching that in studying the 'axis of successivities' 'on ne peut jamais considérer qu'une chose à la fois, mais où sont situées toutes les choses du premier axe [the 'axis of simultaneities'] avec leurs changements' (115b).

43. De Saussure admits difficulties in his thesis that all linguistic change is phonetic. Quite apart from the tremendous role of analogy (of which more anon, §§47-51), there are purely syntactical changes like the one mentioned on p. 247: the Indo-European verbal modifiers, still fairly freely placed in early Greek (e.g. óreos baínō káta 'I descend from the mountain'), came to be fastened to the verb (katabaínō óreos). 'Si donc la phonétique intervient le plus souvent par un côté quelconque dans l'évolution, elle ne peut pas l'expliquer tout entière; le facteur phonétique

une fois éliminé, on trouve un résidu qui semble justifier l'idée d'une "histoire de la grammaire"; c'est là qu'est la véritable difficulté; la distinction – qui doit être maintenue – entre le diachronique et le synchronique demanderait des explications délicates, incompatibles avec le cadre de ce cours' (196–7; cf. 194c–d and 248a).

44. The concession does not imperil de Saussure's argument; for the important point is that every linguistic change is external to the synchronic system which it affects. In the first place, it is not deliberated nor motivated by the system; the arbitrariness of the sign excludes deliberateness (106b–d, 107c, 110d, 116b). 'La langue ne prémédite rien' (127b; cf. 30f). Though one sometimes speaks of langue as a convention (25c) or a contract (31d), it is not really either of these, because 'à tout instant, la solidarité avec le passé met en échec la liberté de choisir' (108b). Thus 'on arrive au principe de continuité, qui annule la liberté' (113c; cf. 34e, 101c, 102b, 104, 110d, 113c). The question about the origin of langue is meaningless, because (111c) 'aucune sociète ne connaît et n'a jamais connue la langue autrement que comme un produit hérité des générations précédentes et à prendre tel quel' (105b). *Langue* is not only social but bound to time (108b, 112f–3). On the other hand, when a change arises from without, 'une langue est radicalement impuissante à se défendre contre les facteurs qui déplacent d'instant en instant le rapport du signifié et du signifiant. C'est une des conséquences de l'arbitraire du signe' (110c). And such factors are constantly arising (111e–2); hence 'la continuité du signe dans le temps, liée à l'altération dans le temps, est un principe de la sémiologie générale.'

45. In the second place, a linguistic change is not telic: it does not work for the benefit of the system (121c); on the contrary it disrupts it (211–13, 219d, 221a). Or, at best, by creating alternances, it merely supports a grammatical difference which already existed (219d–20). Thus, there is a French alternance eu/ou; but *neuv-* comes from L. *nóv* (accented, of *novum*) and *nouv-* from *nov* (accentless, of *novellum*); there was already a phonetic difference in Latin and it expressed a grammatical relation (216–217; cf. 215a). (By alternance de Saussure means (216c) a regular alternation, that is, one occurring in many pairs of morphemes of a certain category, not one confined to isolated pairs like French *moi/me*.) So 'la langue est un mécanisme qui continue à fonctionner malgré les détériorations qu'on lui fait subir' (124a).

46. In the third place, a linguistic system is never modified all at once; 'ce qui domine dans toute altération, c'est la persistance de la matière ancienne; l'infidélité au passé n'est que relative. Voilà pourquoi le principe

d'altération se fonde sur le principe de continuité' (109a). Specifically, only certain units, certain signs of a system are violently changed; and, by definition of value and system, their change involves a change in the values of all the other signs.

> Jamais le système n'est modifié directement; en lui-même il est immuable; seuls certains éléments sont altérés sans égard à la solidarité qui les lie au tout. C'est comme si une des planètes qui gravitent autour du soleil changeait de dimensions et de poids: ce fait isolé entraînerait des conséquences générales et déplacerait l'équilibre du système solaire tout entier (121e; cf. 37a, 124d, 126c–d, 134b).

CRITIQUE

47. Of the varieties of linguistic change, only phonetic change receives extended consideration. Although de Saussure regards semantic change as being fundamentally like it in that each is 'un déplacement du rapport entre le signifié et le signifiant' (109c), it is dealt with only in passing (cf. 33 fn. 1), perhaps for that very reason.

But analogy cannot be neglected so easily. Does it not contradict everything that de Saussure has said about linguistic change? He has taught that system limits the arbitrariness of signs, and also (226c, 227b) that speakers manifest their understanding of the system by analogical creation. Then isn't analogy a change of the system which is inspired by the system itself?

48. De Saussure undercuts all these objections with one bold sweep. Analogy is not change at all, but a synchronic fact. 'L'analogie est d'ordre grammatical: elle suppose la conscience et la compréhension d'un rapport unissant les formes entre elles' (226c; cf. 226e, 227d–8). But how can he say this, especially when he notes explicitly that 'la création qui en est l'aboutissement ne peut appartenir d'abord qu'à la parole' (227a; cf. §36)? The answer is short. 'Il faut y distinguer deux choses: 1⁰ la compréhension du rapport qui relie entre elles les formes génératrices; 2⁰ le résultat suggéré par la comparaison, la forme improvisée par le sujet parlant pour l'expression de sa pensée. Seul ce résultat appartient à la parole' (ibid.). This result of analogy is never a simple sign, but always a syntagm which is, most often, nothing but a new arrangement of old simple signs (235c–6) 'et sa réalisation dans la parole est un fait insignifiant en comparaison de la possibilité de le former' (227c).

49. Here is another reason why analogy is not regarded as a change.

When rhotacism had changed Latin honōsem to honōrem but left honōs untouched, and when honor had come into general currency alongside of honōs, on the pattern ōrātor : ōrātōrem, etc., 'au moment où naît honor, rien n'est changé puisqu'il ne remplace rien; la disparition de honōs n'est pas davantage un changement, puisque ce phénomène est indépendant du premier. Partout où l'on peut suivre la marche des événements linguistiques, on voit que l'innovation analogique et l'élimination de la forme ancienne sont deux choses distinctes et que nulle part on ne surprend une transformation' (224d–5). It is in this sense that the disappearance of the older syntagm is independent of the instituting of the new one; 'tandis que le changement phonétique n'introduit rien de nouveau sans annuler ce qui a précédé (honōrem remplace honōsem), la forme analogique n'entraîne pas nécessairement la disparition de celle qu'elle vient doubler' (224d).

50. It is true that neither honōs nor honor has been 'changed' if one declines to call generation and obsolescence change (cf. 225b–6a); the fact remains that the *system* has been changed, once when honor entered it and again when honōs left it (cf. 232c, 235a). Moreover, the patterns have been changed (cf. 235c, also 227b). And we see how de Saussure neglects change of frequency, just as he neglected relative frequency as a synchronic relation (cf. §22). An analogical creation, like the other innovations of parole, more often than not fails to take hold (231–2); but whether it or its older rival wins, the loser is likely to disappear (unless it is saved in a special meaning), since 'la langue répugne à maintenir deux signifiants pour une seule idée' (224d; a concomitant principle is stated 167b). Thus casually is mentioned one of the fundamental principles governing changes in relative frequency.

51. Even if analogy is synchronic, it is nevertheless clear that the system itself inspires certain innovations of parole, some of which succeed in changing the system by leading to the currency of some new terms and the obsolescence of some old ones. One can readily grant that analogical change is different in the ways named by de Saussure from phonetic change, and still contend that it is a type of change whose ultimate cause may be external to the system, but whose immediate cause is the system itself.

The fact is that de Saussure's idea of system is radically vitiated by an ambiguity. *In his parlance, 'système' has two meanings: (1) state and (2) stable state, that is, equilibrium.* His argument that linguistic changes always arise externally is wholly dependent upon the switch from one of these senses to another. Every language during a sufficiently short span of time is necessarily a system in the first sense; but when de Saussure says that a system never originates a change, he can only mean an equilibrium, as he himself calls it (126c, f, 154a, 169a). In a passage already quoted, he compares a language with the solar system, but as usual he does not follow his simile through. At each instant the solar system is a state, but at no time is it an equilibrium. It is at all times changing, but the changes from any prior state to a following state are caused immediately by the prior state, and can even be computed if one knows three data: the general laws of dynamics, the prior state, and either the direction of change or a sufficient number of earlier states. The original impetus was doubtless external (one of the fundamental ideas of science is that all change may be ultimately traced to an external cause), yet one change inaugurates a chain of others lasting for a shorter or longer time. Another way of expressing de Saussure's ambiguity is that in effect he assumed the effects of every linguistic change to be instantaneous. His idea seems to have been that linguistic change is like a car going uphill: it stops as soon as it is no longer actively propelled. It is quite true that he declares linguistic change to be unlimited (126e, 208–10; cf. 121c, 124d); but he simply means that one diachronically identical sign may become vastly changed by a series of phonetic changes (e.g. German *je* stemming from PIE *aiwom*), and also that phonetic change of certain signs indirectly affects other signs.

52. Can one, by an inductive study of antecedent and consequent states, establish that given states lead to given changes, regardless of the external buffets or supports to which they are subjected? Or can one make such predictions by taking into account the prior history of the system? If so, one will have founded, alongside of retrospective and of what de Saussure inaptly calls prospective linguistics, a third branch of diachronics, a truly prospective branch – predictive, let us call it, for it would enable one, given a set of linguistic states as data, to infer another state which is *later* than all of them. When it becomes predictive not only of the past but also of the future, linguistics will have attained the inner circle of science. In admitting that 'on ne peut pas dire d'avance jusqu'où s'étendra l'imitation d'un modèle, ni quels sont les types destinés à la provoquer' (222d), de Saussure shows that linguistics has not yet achieved this triumph. The Prague school believes that it has been able to make the beginning steps; and it is mainly because their efforts were formulated as a refutation of de Saussure's opposite view that we have analysed the latter so carefully.

53. De Saussure teaches in effect that signs have two independent sets

of properties: their values or relations (with their *signifiés* and with other signs) and their content or 'material envelope'. This thesis is true in a sense and in another sense not, and calls for some remarks of elucidation.

The distinction between synchronic and diachronic linguistics is methodological (115b): '[La] différence de nature entre termes successifs et termes coexistants, entre faits partiels et faits touchant le système, interdit de faire des uns et des autres la matière d'une seule science' (124d). But diachronic linguistics cannot ignore synchronic relations, for a diachronic identity (cf. §34) between a sign of state S_1 and a sign of a later state S_2 can be established only by considering both the phonemic make-up of the signs and their relations to other contemporary signs.

Furthermore, as de Saussure has pointed out at great length, a change in the content of a sign generally entails a change in its synchronic relations. This could not be so if the relations were completely independent of the 'material envelope'. However, de Saussure has nowhere implied that the independence is complete. He has only implied, by his doctrine that phonemes and *signifiants* are differential in function, that if one were to replace the material envelopes of all the signs of a system by any others whatsoever which would keep all those same signs phonemically distinct from each other, the relations of the signs and therefore the system would be preserved intact (see esp. 43b and 153d–4, and cf. §26).

Finally, the material envelope is relevant to the synchronic system in yet another respect. Though de Saussure points out 'la latitude dont les sujets jouissent pour la prononciation dans la limite où les sons restent distincts les uns des autres' (164d; cf. all of 164b–6a), there are limits to this latitude, much narrower limits than mere preservation of the system would require. This is because of the continuity with the past which de Saussure has pointed out. In short, his own discussion (104–8) of the 'immutability' of the sign indicates a sense in which material envelopes as well as relations constitute the system.

DE SAUSSURE AS METHODOLOGIST

54. If there is one feature of the *Cours de linguistique générale* which is more stiking than all others, it is that it holds true to its name by dealing strictly with principles. It is clear that de Saussure was a meticulous thinker. He re-examined methodically and painstakingly the doctrines which lay at the basis of current thinking, ferreting out the tacit and hidden ones as well as testing the propositions which were daily mouthed by

everyone. His conclusions he sought to weave into a coherent and almost deductive system.

55. The propositions involved in any field of inquiry are of three sorts: First, delimitations of the *aims* of the inquiry, characterizing the objects which it studies. Second, the description of *methods*. And third, the *results*, the statements of fact which emerge from the inquiry.

Those ideas of the *Cours* which we have discussed up to this point, as well as the contributions of the *Mémoire* and the other papers which de Saussure published in his lifetime, deal with the results of linguistics, the matters of fact. But these do not begin to exhaust the content of the *Cours*. For an appraisal of de Saussure's thought, the keen interest which he manifests in aims and methods has a twofold importance. In the first place, the discussions of aims and the strictures about methods that are dispersed throughout the *Cours* add up to a considerable portion of it; they are not intrusive, but integral, and they have influenced other thinkers. In the second place, de Saussure's method of thinking was systematic. He did not merely track down premises and consequences; he did not merely try to segregate truths of linguistics into basic principles and derived propositions. He strove to contract the group of basic principles still more and exhibit the relations between those that remained irreducible. We do not mean to say that he anticipated modern logistic method or that, like Newton and Spinoza, he emulated Euclid by casting his treatise into axioms, theorems, corollaries and lemmas. But in 100e, 103b, 104c, and other passages he signalizes propositions (that signs are arbitrary, linearly arrayed, and independent of individual volition) from which many consequences follow; and it is a good guess – though one which the pitiful meagreness of biographical data prevents us from testing – that this patient weaving of the general facts of linguistics into a fabric of premises and consequences was for de Saussure an actual method of discovery which led to many of his aperçus and to his grappling with problems not faced, and for the most part not even sensed, by previous thinkers (see Bally, 'L'état actuel', 8d–9 and 12b).

56. De Saussure lists (20) three tasks for linguistics: to describe all languages and their histories as far as possible; to seek universal laws and forces; and 'de se délimiter et de se définir elle-même'. The brand of linguistics pursued by his predecessors from Bopp onward, he says, 'ne sait pas exactement vers quel but elle tend' (118c; cf. 16c, 18c, 20e item c, and all of 118–9b). The reason for this confusion is that the phenomena of language can be studied from different points of view. Dozens of sciences

can study linguistic phenomena (20–1, 24e–5, 40–3) from as many points of view – each one putting these phenomena into relation with phenomena of some other sort. What aspect of the phenomena, if any, is left to linguistics as its exclusive property? How can language be studied not in relation to other phenomena but as the self-contained object of an autonomous science? As de Saussure himself puts it, 'Quel est l'objet à la fois intégral et concret de la linguistique?' (23). The sequel makes it clear that *signs* are the integral and concrete objects of linguistic study; and that by concentrating first on the synchronic systems which they form (langues), then on the diachronic relations between these systems, and lastly upon parole, linguistics will have found a rational and unifying order (23–30, esp. 25b, d; 36a, 37b; 38e, 139b), an ideal order, whether or not it prove practicable (139c–40).

Now what is the methodological significance of the quest for objects that are both integral and concrete?

57. By calling a class of phenomena or of objects 'integral' (though the word itself is not used after 24e), de Saussure means that the phenomena are all of one kind and are sufficiently unified that they may be studied by one science, that they are 'classable parmi les faits humains' (33a, 25c). Now 'tandis que le langage est hétérogène [cf. 24e, 25c, 31d, 38e], la langue ainsi délimitée est de nature homogène: c'est un système de signes où il n'y a d'essentiel que l'union du sens et de l'image acoustique, et où les deux parties du signe sont également psychiques' (32d; cf. 29a, 37c, 98b–c). It is true that the study of langue is subdivided into synchronic and diachronic linguistics; moreover, within the class of psychic entities, images are different from concepts (98c, 115a). But these diversities are nothing like the diversity within la parole 'y compris la phonation' (37c), the study of which is, therefore, psychophysical (ibid.).

58. De Saussure's idea of concreteness is less easy to establish. He uses the term 'concret' in several senses.

(1) Phonetic species are abstract whereas allophones are concrete (82b); words (e.g. the word *mois* 'month') are abstract whereas their alternant forms (e.g. the two liaison forms, phonetically *mwa* and *mwaz*) are concrete (147c–8; cf. 188b); form-classes, such as the genitive case, are abstract (190b, 191b) whereas the forms that belong to them are concrete. The sense in question is explicitly stated in 148c–9 of sentences: the class of sentences is abstract because there is no property common to all sentences. Consonantly, the sign is so defined that the *signifiant* must be just one sequence of phonemes, just as the *signifié* must be just one concept, one

meaning. Slight variation in the shades of meaning is allowed (151a, 152b), but (255c) if one *signifiant* is correlated with two distinct *signifiés*, we must consider that there are two distinct signs. This saves the concreteness of the sign.

(2) An entity is concrete in the second sense in so far as it has instances (173b), a material realization (151b–2b). This implies, though de Saussure does not point it out, that there is a gradation from greatest concreteness to greatest abstractness. Thus, the 8.45 train from Geneva is a concrete entity, even though the material realization of it on different days need not be the same train in the physical sense. The analogues in linguistics are obvious: a phoneme is concrete because many sounds are instances of it; a *signifiant* is concrete because many *tranches de sonorité* belong to it, and so on. Langue and the signs that compose it are concrete in the second sense; '[ils] ont leur siège dans le cerveau' (32b). People sometimes use 'abstract' as synonymous with 'universal' and 'concrete' as synonymous with 'particular', but in the present usage both abstractness and concreteness are predicated only of universals.

(3) Signs are concrete, whereas *signifiants* and *signifiés* are abstract (144; 153c, 157a); it is presumably in this sense that words are said to be concrete (158b), implying no contradiction of the other sense, in which some words are abstract. To emphasize his point, de Saussure compares the sign to a chemical compound, such as of water out of hydrogen and oxygen (145), an inapt analogy since both hydrogen and oxygen can exist separately with properties distinct from the compound. The point seems to be that wholes are concrete whereas each of their parts, considered by itself, is abstract, and apparently de Saussure's intention is the same as when he says (162a, 166b–7) that both *signifiants* and *signifiés* are, by themselves, purely negative, differential entities whose positive qualities do not matter in the least whereas (167c; though cf. 168a) signs are positive entities which are not merely different but distinct. If one carried out this viewpoint fully, one would expect that a whole system would be concrete but its parts, the component signs, would not.

59. It is plain that in these different passages de Saussure speaks of 'concreteness' in different senses. When he says (32b) that 'la langue n'est pas moins que la parole un objet de nature concrète', I think he means simply that it admits of being studied by itself: that is concrete (to put it paradoxically) which can be successfully studied *in abstracto*. His insistence that the objects of study must be concrete is in effect a critique of the Neo-grammarians, as is evident from the following passage. Remarking that

'l'ancienne école [Bopp etc.] partageait les mots en racines, thèmes, suffixes etc. et donnait à ces distinctions une valeur absolue', he continues:

On devait nécessairement réagir contre ces aberrations, et le mot d'ordre, très juste, fut: observez ce qui se passe dans les langues d'aujourd'hui, dans le langage de tous les jours, et n'attribuez aux périodes anciennes de la langue aucun processus, aucun phénomène qui ne soit pas constatable actuellement. [Lyell's principle of uniformitarianism, enunciated 1830 in his *Principles of Geology*, which had a great influence upon Darwin and others.] Et comme le plus souvent la langue vivante ne permet pas de surprendre des analyses comme en faisait Bopp, les néo-grammariens, forts de leur principe, déclarent que racines, thèmes, suffixes, etc. sont de pures abstractions de notre esprit et que, si l'on en fait usage, c'est uniquement pour la commodité de l'exposition. Mais s'il n'y a pas de justification à l'établissement de ces catégories, pourquoi les établir? Et quand on le fait, au nom de quoi déclare-t-on qu'une coupure comme hípp-o-s, par exemple, est préférable à une autre comme hípp-os?

L'école nouvelle, après avoir reconnu les défauts de l'ancienne doctrine, ce qui était facile, s'est contentée de la rejeter en théorie, tandis qu'en pratique elle restait comme embarrassée dans un appareil scientifique dont, malgré tout, elle ne pouvait se passer. Dès qu'on raisonne ces 'abstractions', on voit la part de réalité qu'elles représentent, et un correctif très simple suffit pour donner à ces artifices du grammarien un sens légitime et exact (252).

In short, roots etc. are concrete after all, not abstract: but they are relevant units primarily in diachronic, and only occasionally and accidently in synchronic descriptions.

60. Whichever sense of concreteness he meant, there remains the task of deciding which of the various entities (morphemes, syntagms, words, phrases, sentences) are concrete. De Saussure puzzles over this task (148a–b, 149d–e, 153c, 154c, 158b) without making the ground of his perplexity clear. Is it because there are signs of which we are uncertain whether they are morphemes or syntagms (181c)? Only in part; but mainly, I think, because of difficulties in accurately defining the 'word'. On the one hand, 'le mot, malgré la difficulté qu'on a à le définir, est une unité qui s'impose à l'esprit, quelque chose de central dans le mécanisme de la langue' (154c); on the other, it does not exactly fit the definition of linguistic unit (158b) – presumably because of the existence (147c–8) of alternant forms of what

we want to call one word and which, not differing in a regular manner, cannot be subsumed under de Saussure's concept (215–20) of alternation. However, he makes an attempt to characterize words: 'Un mot représente toujours une idée relativement déterminée, ou moins au point de vue grammatical' (255c); and moreover, 'tout mot qui n'est pas une unité simple et irréductible ne se distingue pas essentiellement d'un membre de phrase, d'un fait de syntaxe; l'agencement des sous-unités qui le composent obéit aux mêmes principes fondamentaux que la formation des groupes de mots' (187b; cf. 172a). This is perhaps why 'en matière de langue on s'est toujours contenté d'opérer sur des unités mal définies' (154c).

There is another problem of concreteness. Language is a social phenomenon which requires 'une masse parlante' (112–3). 'C'est un trésor déposé par la pratique de la parole dans les sujets appartenant à une même communauté, un système grammatical existant virtuellement dans chaque cerveau, ou plus exactement dans les cerveaux d'un ensemble d'individus; *car la langue n'est complète dans aucun, elle n'existe parfaitement que dans la masse*' (30d, emphasis ours). More specifically: 'Tous les individus ainsi reliés par le langage ... reproduiront, – *non exactement sans doute, mais approximativement* – les mêmes signes unis aux mêmes concepts' (29 bottom, emphasis ours). Can langue be concrete when it does not repose complete in any one individual?

Speaking of linguistic change de Saussure says it is incessant and gradual, and (296a) for this very reason there is no sense in speaking of 'mother-languages' and 'daughter-languages'. 'D'ailleurs la délimitation dans le temps n'est pas la seule difficulté que nous rencontrons dans la définition d'un état de langue; le même problème se pose à propos de l'espace' (143). That many dialects shade off into one another is set forth (275–80), but the most striking fact is not mentioned: there can be an area divided into a series of sub-areas such that people of any two adjacent sub-areas understand each other readily, but people from the two extreme sub-areas scarcely understand each other at all. What this proves is that the concept of langue is an idealized one. There are degrees of intelligibility; every one can understand some speakers better than others. Can a langue be concrete when it does not even have fixed limits? It is a montage, a composite photograph. It is not enough to admit the indefinite subdivisibility of a language into distinguishable dialects (128d; cf. 264b, 278–80). The only real solution is to admit that 'one language', like a perfectly pure chemical or a cause without any interfering complications whatsoever, is nowhere to be met with in experience, but is an idealized construct designed to make explanation practicable; and to boldly embrace what seems to be, for de Saussure, a reluctantly wrung admission: 'La notion d'état de langue ne peut être qu'approximative. *En linguistique statique, comme dans la plupart des sciences, aucune démonstration n'est possible sans une simplification conventionelle des données*' (143, emphasis ours).

61. The notion of langue is the first step in making linguistics a science. It not only orders the problems of language among themselves, but it gives linguistics a place among the sciences (33d–4a): there is a science of semiology, hitherto unrecognized, (34b) 'qui étudie la vie des signes au sein de la vie sociale; elle formerait une partie de la psychologie sociale, et par conséquent de la psychologie générale ... Elle nous apprendrait en quoi consistent les signes, quelles lois les régissent' (33d). This semiology is differentiated by definition from semantics, 'qui étudie les changements de la *signification*' (33 fn. 1, editorial note). Sign-systems are necessarily social (34d; 112d–3, 157d), but they have their own differentia: 'la signe échappe toujours en une certaine mesure à la volonté individuelle ou sociale, c'est là son caractère essentiel' (34e). The reason is that a system of signs is strictly bound to the past (104–8, 113), as a heritage. There are constant laws of semiology (135 lines 4–5, referring to 126b); one of these is (111c) 'la continuité du signe dans le temps, liée à l'altération dans le temps'. According to de Saussure (34), semiology has never been recognized as a science, first because langue has rarely been treated as a self-contained object of study, second because people think of langue as a nomenclature, third because they study it in relation to the individual, and fourth because even when it is studied as social, the distinctive feature of sign-systems – their arbitrariness – is not sufficiently recognized.

Even if semiology includes the study of symbols, 'les signes entièrement arbitraires réalisent mieux que les autres l'idéal du procédé sémiologique; c'est pourquoi la langue, le plus complexe et le plus répandu des systèmes d'expression, est aussi le plus caractéristique de tous' (101a). To differentiate langue from other sign-systems is the business of the linguist (33e).

62. The second step in making linguistics a science is the clear-cut discrimination in principle, even when it is difficult in practice (139c) between the synchronic and diachronic branches. In attaining to this discrimination, linguistics has passed through an interesting triad of stages (118–9). *Grammaire raisonnée* was synchronic but normative. The nineteenth century inaugurated a phase that abandoned the prescription of norms (a last shred of prescription was the temptation to brand analogy as 'false'), but was preponderantly historical. The latest phase is to study

both synchronic and diachronic linguistics, but to study both of them factually and in conscious contrast with each other.

63. Nevertheless, neither synchronic nor diachronic linguistics is able to arrive at true laws, says de Saussure. The word law is commonly used in two senses: juridical and natural (134e). A juridical or social law is imperative and general (130a); by contrast (134c) 'les faits synchroniques, quels qu'ils soient, présentent une certain régularité, mais ils n'ont aucun caractère impératif; les faits diachroniques, au contraire, s'imposent à la langue, mais ils n'ont rien de général'. Are there natural, i.e. panchronic laws 'qui se vérifient partout et toujours' (134e)? 'En linguistique comme dans le jeu d'échecs ... il y a des règles qui survivent à tous les événements [the constant laws of semiology are instances, see §61]. Mais ce sont là des principes généraux existant indépendemment des faits concrets; dès qu'on parle de faits particuliers et tangibles, il n'y a pas de point de vue panchronique' (135).

This critique is remarkable in its oversights. We have seen de Saussure's reason for saying that diachronic facts are particular, not general. Now 'on pourra objecter que dans le fonctionnement de la parole, la loi synchronique est obligatoire, en ce sens qu'elle s'impose aux individus par la contrainte de l'usage collectif ... sans doute; mais [emphasis ours] *nous n'entendons pas le mot d'impératif dans le sens d'une obligation relative aux sujets parlants*; il signifie que [emphasis de Saussure's] *dans la langue* aucune force ne garantit le maintien de la régularité quand elle règne sur quelque point' (131d). It is curious that de Saussure failed to think of a very simple retort which renders his critique nugatory: a juridical law itself is not imperative in this sense, for dictators, legislators, and even common consent may change laws and statutes. And as for natural laws, in no empirical science do they exist strictly 'indépendemment des faits concrets'. It is true that the statement 'intervocalic s is replaced by r' differs from the chemical proposition 'vaporized hydrochloric acid and vaporized ammonia mixed together produce a white cloud' in not being panchronic. But the other sciences of life and mind (or behaviour) are in pretty much the same state. Moreover, de Saussure has said nothing to show that this deficiency is inherent in linguistics; he has adduced no reason to believe that no possible future progress will ever be able, by specifying the conditions more fully, to state panchronic laws of sound-change or of other linguistic phenomena.

64. De Saussure's critique of law brings out a general trait of his methodological viewpoint that is worth noting because it lets us draw an

inference about his background. He habitually exaggerates the unique features of linguistic phenomena and the concomitant peculiar difficulties of linguistics. For example, he tells us that 'en zoologie, c'est l'animal qui s'offre dès le premier instant' whereas 'la langue présente donc ce caractère étrange et frappant de ne pas offrir d'entités perceptibles de prime abord' (149). But if the linguist is offered a multiplicity of objects – languages, utterances, words, morphemes, sounds – equally the zoologist has to contend with species, individuals, systems (the vascular system), organs (the heart), tissues, cells and the parts of cells. The *Cours* (114) tells us that astronomy, geology and even political history (cf. 116d–7) do not need to be divided into a synchronic and a diachronic part, and presumably de Saussure would have said the same of zoology; but in fact zoology is divided into a synchronic and a diachronic part; indeed, into two parts each. Each species can be studied synchronically, as a fixed type, and diachronically, as a product of evolution. The diachronic study is called· phylogeny. Then again, anatomy studies the members of each species in one stage of their lives (e.g. the mature adult stage), embryology their development from inception onward.

Further, de Saussure approves (25, 110e) Whitney's conception of language as a social institution, but insists upon a differentia: language is *purely* conventional and traditional, unlike manners, ethical institutions, economic set-ups and so on; there is no rational norm to regulate its changes either by arresting or by hastening and guiding them (105d, 106d, 110d, 116b). Later, to be sure, this broadly sweeping statement is, if not retracted, at least reinterpreted: there is no rational norm to stay or encourage the changes of simple signs (morphemes), nor the concomitant changes in syntagms, but there is a norm which can lead to further changes. And analogical remodelling is precisely the result of applying this norm.

So language is not so different from other institutions after all. And it may be asked whether de Saussure has not exaggerated the extent to which institutions other than sign systems are shaped by rational criticism, and subject to the deliberate volition of the community; and whether on the other hand, quite apart from analogy, he has not underplayed the element of natural symbolism, i.e. of onomatopy, in language.

In fine, language (*le langage*), the immediately given object of linguistics, is as complex as the immediately given object of zoology or of any other science, but no more so. Its complexity begets the problem of finding an object at once integral and concrete, but at the same time it also furnishes the solution. For language is an assemblage of facts some of which can be considered apart from others; this is why langue, although in one sense an abstraction, is also concrete. For it is self-contained. And it is in this sense that, to repeat a passage that we have already quoted at the beginning of our paper (§2), 'bien loin que l'objet précède le point de vue, on dirait que c'est le point de vue qui crée l'objet'.

THE SEMANTICS OF STYLE*

Seymour Chatman

In an encyclopedia article on the subject, E. A. Tenney has written: 'Because of the ambiguity latent in the term style, careful critics set it in an unmistakable context or eschew its use. For style in the Platonic sense, they use the terms mind or soul or spirit; and for style in the Aristotelian sense, they use manner or fashion. Our critical vocabulary would be strengthened if we had not one but two words to name and differentiate the two concepts. Until someone invents these words, style will remain an equivocal term.'[1] Tenney echoes a common complaint in modern discussion of style, as did John Middleton Murry[2] before him. It is surely one of the keener pleasures of scholarly activity to define terms, even if no one, finally, pays any attention to your definitions. Many have responded to what they conceive to be the need to 'find out' finally what style is. But our terms are what we make of them; we divide up – or, better, construct – the world through our vocabulary, in the last analysis, and the only real criteria are consistency and adequacy, not some discoverable jewel called 'truth'. Still, the word has a history that is worth looking into.

It is clear that many different things are often referred to by 'style'; indeed, it is as if its favour were being courted, as if applying 'style' to one's particular distinction adds prestige to it. In this state of affairs, the term can only be precise for those who are constantly aware of its trickiness. 'Style' derives from Latin *stilus*, an instrument for writing upon waxed tablets; in England, the term was generalized to refer to other sorts of sharp instruments – markers on a sun-dial (1577), weapons (1669), engraving tools (1662), surgical probes (1631), and, recently, gramophone needles.[3] The first transference in Latin seems to have been to penmanship – 'he who manipulated this instrument firmly and incisively to make a clear, sharp impression was deemed praiseworthy (*stilus exercitatus*); his opposite, worthy of blame (*tardus, rudis, et confusus*)'.[4] It was easy to extend the term to contexts relating to the composition itself, a use

* Reprinted from *Social Science Information* (International Social Science Council), vol. VI, no. 4 (August, 1967).

current in Late Latin, and thence Old French and Middle English: thus, 'manner of expression characteristic of a given writer' (*Shorter Oxford English Dictionary*, II, 2) is the second transference.[5] The earliest uses of the term were both normative and descriptive, and today the term is still essentially ambivalent in that way.[6] Let us call the normative sense of 'style', that is, 'good writing', Definition A.

It is easy to see why the purely descriptive sense arose along with the normative sense: just as faces, bodies and personalities, so handwritings and the messages they impart differ from individual to individual. These differences serve to identify individuals and groups. Good Aristotelian dualists would inevitably find these identifying differences to be one half of a dichotomy, 'manner', or the 'how', the other half being 'matter' or the 'what'. Aristotle himself said in the *Rhetoric*: 'It is not sufficient to know what one ought to say, but one must also know how to say it.' Only later would Platonist, monist, organicist theories be developed to question whether matter and manner can in fact be separated. Let us refer to 'individual manner' as Definition B. This sense has generalized to the arts and many other activities of life: we speak of styles of cooking, painting, horseback-riding, diving, etc.

Both of the senses must have suggested the usefulness of isolating parts of writing for inspection, for comparison of writers, and for the determination and collection of excellencies for emulation. So Definition C arose: 'Those features of literary composition which belong to form and expression rather than to the substance of the thought or matter expressed ...' (*S.O.E.D.*, II, 3).[7] According to *S.O.E.D.*, this sense of style became current in English around 1577. With it an additional source of confusion developed, since 'style' was now partly synonymous with 'form'.[8] It is often forgotten how profound the change is from 'style' as individual manner (B) to 'style' as a general property of writing itself (C). Having separated the term from the usage of individuals, it became possible to write about style C in the abstract, to enumerate details in handbooks.[9] The items in these handbooks tended to fall into language categories already established by Greek and Latin writers in the various disciplines – grammar, prosody, rhetoric. The full list of rhetorical figures and tropes, in particular, was garnered from antiquity and discussed at great length. Indeed, Ramus and his school argued that the schemes and tropes were 'the whole of elocution [style] from which even considerations of grammar were excluded'.[10] These features were 'ornaments', and it was the assumption that literature was created by *superadding* such ornaments to the 'plain content', making the content graceful and beauteous. The ornaments were really not part of the ordinary language. To the English critic George Puttenham, they were a 'noveltie of language' and in other contexts could even be called, with Isidore, 'vices of speech'.[11]

During the sixteenth century arose still another sense in English (definition D), namely 'A manner of discourse, or tone of speaking, adopted in addressing others or in ordinary conversation' (*S.O.E.D.*, II, 4). This sense is the one referred to in expressions like 'colloquial style', 'formal style', and so forth, and thus is related to or perhaps even derived from the classical 'levels of style' – high, medium and low. Style D is the verbal reflection of decorum, set by the social situation or audience before whom a speaker finds himself. The sense is still used today, even in sophisticated circles, for example, by the modern British school of linguistics.[12] It is clear that the basis for style in this sense is social-class-structure itself. Selection is essentially of words to 'match' the element of society one is depicting or wishing to communicate with.

These then are four senses of the word 'style' that we inherit from antiquity and the Renaissance: as noted, they are all Aristotelian, presupposing an essential dualism between form and content. We shall come to the Platonic view in a moment.

Many of the bewildering array of modern usages of 'style' can be seen as variants of one or another of these definitions. I shall not undertake anything like a complete survey, since my main business is to work out the semantic ramifications of only one of the definitions, namely B. However, since part of the problem is to separate B from the other definitions, it is worth examining a few modern statements that consider 'style' in different terms. My categorization resembles that of Nils Enkvist, but is less extensive than his, and I refer the reader interested in further details to his essay.[13]

Little need be remarked about definition A – style as good writing – except its ubiquity. Randomly picking up articles with 'style' in their titles in the popular and semi-popular literary journals, one is very likely to find such observations as these: ' ... the word "style" is being used here to refer simply to the felicity of an author's choice and arrangement of words ... '[14] Indeed, 'style' in this sense has come more and more into vogue as a prestigious word to use in books on 'composition' or expository writing, a subject everlastingly and largely unsuccessfully taught to American college freshmen.[15]

The alternative to conceiving of good writing as the successful introduction of ornaments into the plain sense of an argument is a Platonic monism in which 'the achievement of the proper form *is* the content: when a thought is invested with its essential form, style results'. Some of the headier definitions of 'style' fall into this category. For one who 'has' style, like Wordsworth, writes Matthew Arnold, 'Nature herself seems ... to take the pen out of his hand, and to write for him with her own bare, sheer, penetrating power.'[16] And Havelock Ellis: 'Style, indeed, is not really a mere invisible transparent medium, it is not really a garment but, as Gourmont said, the very thought itself. It is the miraculous transubstantiation of a spiritual body, given to us in the only form in which we may receive and absorb that body ... '[17] These are not the kinds of pronouncements about which there is much to say. They raise only one – and a very troublesome – question, namely: If style is in fact only thought or content itself, why bother using a separate term? It is clear that writers like Arnold and Ellis cannot provide a satisfying answer. Even if style is, as Murry has it, 'not the clothes but the flesh and blood', it still can be separated from the 'what' in analysis, it still can be understood to consist of distinct *features*.

Let us turn to Style C – 'aspects of form' separated from content, that is, as local textual (i.e., 'textural') detail. This sense, too, can be interpreted from either the dualistic or monistic point of view. For the dualist, as Enkvist neatly states it, style is, 'a shell surrounding a pre-existing core of thought or expression'.[18] Renaissance Aristotelians equated style with *elocutio*, the expression of thoughts in language, the third division of rhetoric, and particularly that subdivision translated as 'Dignity' – 'adornment of the thoughts with rhetorical flowers'.[19] Thus, for Puttenham, the figure, the central stylistic device 'is a certaine lively or good grace set upon wordes, speaches and sentences to some purpose and not in vaine, giving them ornament and efficacie by many maner of alterations in shape, in sounde, and also in sense'.[20] This position could be maintained in virtually its pristine form into the nineteenth century, when the famed literary historian George Saintsbury wrote: 'Style is the choice and arrangement of language with only a subordinate regard to the meaning to be conveyed.'[21]

In later centuries the baldness of such a dichotomy came to be questioned.[22] By the turn of the present century, Benedetto Croce and the English critic-philosopher A. C. Bradley attacked the separation of content and style (C) in forceful terms. Croce urged the identity of language and style as simply overt aesthetic manifestations of inner psychological forms. Less categorically, but more persuasively, Bradley wrote:

> There is no such thing as mere form in poetry. All form is expression. Style may have indeed a certain aesthetic worth in partial abstraction from the particular matter it conveys, as in a well-built sentence you may take pleasure in the build almost apart from the meaning. Even so, style is expressive – presents to sense, for example, the order, ease, and rapidity with which ideas move in the writer's mind – but it is not expressive of the meaning of that particular sentence. And it is possible, interrupting poetic experience, to decompose it and abstract for comparatively separate consideration this nearly formal element of style. But the aesthetic value of style so taken is not considerable; you could not read with pleasure for an hour a composition which had no other merit. And in poetic experience you never apprehend this value by itself; the style is here expressive also of a particular meaning, or rather is one aspect of that unity whose other aspect is meaning.[23]

By 1939, the demise of the Aristotelian dualism – style as 'a kind of scum' overlaying meaning – seemed so certain that W. K. Wimsatt, one of the most acute of American literary theorists, could write: 'It is hardly necessary to adduce proof that the doctrine of identity of style and meaning is today firmly established. This doctrine is, I take it, one from which a modern theorist hardly can escape, or hardly wishes to.'[24] Even the expression 'stylistic device' was to be eschewed:

> It might be better if the term 'device' were never used, for its use leads almost immediately to the carelessness of thinking of words as separable practicably from meaning. That is, we think of a given meaning as if it may be weakly expressed in one way but more forcefully in another. The latter is the device – the language applied, like a jack or clamp, or any dead thing, to the meaning, which itself remains static and unchanged, whether or not the device succeeds in expressing it. There is some convenience in this way of thinking, but more philosophy in steadily realizing that each change of words changes the meaning actually expressed. It is better to think of the 'weak' expression and the 'strong' expression as two quite different expressions, or, elliptically, two different meanings, of which one is farther from, one nearer to, what the author ought to say, or what he intends to say.[25]

Wimsatt formally defines style as 'one plane or level of the organization of meaning ... the furthest elaboration of the one concept that is the centre'.[26] Essentially the same idea forms part of the definition of Monroe Beardsley, an aesthetician and collaborator of Wimsatt's. (The second part of Beardsley's definition – 'general purport' – will be discussed below.) Beardsley speaks of this as the 'semantic definition' of style, and relates it to a general theory of artistic construction. It is worth while to explicate his theory in some detail.[27] For Beardsley, every aesthetic unity – a painting, a symphony, a poem – can be divided into two basic aspects, its global aspect – or *structure* – and its local aspect – or *texture*. Structural meanings are meanings 'that depend upon, or are a function of the whole discourse, or a large section of it', for example that summarized by the statement: 'Raskolnikov murdered and confessed.' Textural meanings are details of meaning or small-scale meanings – this is style. Like Bradley and Wimsatt, Beardsley illustrates the nature of these semantic details by comparing minimally different utterances. The utterances must be neither too divergent nor too similar: in the first case, the resultant semantic difference would be too 'basic': 'The baby is a boy' v. 'The baby is a girl'; in the second, the semantic difference would be so slight as to be 'not even' stylistic: 'She sells cakes and pies' v. 'She sells pies and cakes'. An example of stylistic difference would be 'I am here' v. 'Here I am', the latter suggesting, according to Beardsley, 'that I have been long awaited or searched for'. A second is 'Go home' v. 'Return to your abode', where 'go' and 'return' are obviously divergent: 'return' means not just 'go' but 'go *back*'; and 'abode' differs from 'home' in that 'abode' may be a temporary refuge. A third is 'I will meet you at Church on Sunday' v. 'I will meet thee at the Meeting House on First-Day', which will be discussed below.

Now one is struck by several difficulties in this formulation, despite the fact that the semantic definition of style C is obviously superior to the simple ornamental view. First of all, as Beardsley points out, not *all* small-scale semantic differences are stylistic: some are too small and some too big ('basic'). But if the matter is simply quantitative, how does one decide? What sort of measuring-stick does one use? The two *here*s in the first example, it could be argued, differ as radically as 'boy' and 'girl' in the non-style example: the first is locative and the second presentative, a lexical distinction which French expresses by different words: 'Je suis ici' v. 'Me voici'. Would Beardsley say that in French too the difference is only stylistic? The two utterances seem different in meaning and nothing more, yet it is precisely the case that stylistic differences are 'something more'. The second example is different. Here also are the small-scale meaning differences, between 'go' and 'return', and between 'home' and 'abode', and those differences taken alone amount to nothing more than the differences between the two *heres*. Yet there is an additional *dimension* of difference in these utterances, conveying distinctions which are qualitative rather than quantitative – the fact that, unlike the two *heres*, they tell us something else about the speaker (Style B) and/or the general social setting (Style D). 'Abode' has quite other implications than 'home' – it sounds mock-late-Victorian-melodramatic, pseudo-poetic, and so on. This is not merely a matter of connotation, although connotation does enter into it,[28] there are not only added suggestions about the *word* 'abode' but also about the speaker (he's playing the melodramatic Victorian, either really or facetiously) and the situation (it's a mid-Victorian scene; it's a light-hearted modern encounter). The same thing is true of the third example. What seems to be stylistically relevant is not the meaning differences between the *words* 'thee' and 'you', nor imputed differences between the person to whom they refer, but rather what the choice of 'thee' over 'you' tells us about the speaker (he's a Quaker) or the situation (it's a situation in which Quaker forms are appropriate). It is not accurate to call style texture of meaning[29] if that amounts to saying that any critic who 'talks about the meanings of certain paragraphs, sentences, phrases, or words [therefore] is talking about its texture of meaning' and therefore about its style. A critic who says that 'in his first speech (a blank verse paragraph) King Lear attempts to extract effusive protestations of love from his daughters' is surely talking about the meaning of a local passage of the play, but he is not talking about its style. Nor is it very helpful to assert that 'style is nothing but meaning'.[30] We can say that a stylistic choice is a formal choice *and also* that it entails differences in meaning; in other words, one can be Aristotelian without being a simple-minded ornamentalist.

The same distinction seems to apply to syntactic differences. Compare Beardsley's example of a sentence written in a highly balanced, parallel syntax by Samuel Johnson:

> As this practice is a commodious subject of raillery to the gay, and of declamation to the serious, it has been ridiculed with all the pleasantry of wit, and exaggerated with all the amplifications of rhetoric,

with its non-balanced, 'skewed' counterpart:

> As this practice is a commodious subject of raillery to the gay, and serious people declaim upon it as well, it has been ridiculed with all the pleasantry of wit, and furthermore the amplifications of rhetoric have been used to exaggerate it.

Here there are few differences between words, and meaning differences corresponding to different syntactic structures are difficult precisely to articulate. But, again, what seems to be stylistically important is what the balanced-syntax version tells us about the *author*; to use Beardsley's own words, balanced 'sentences like these give ... an air of judiciousness, of having considered things from both sides'.[31]

A. C. Bradley recognized the issue in the quotation cited above: ' ... style is expressive – presents to sense, for example, the order, ease, and rapidity with which ideas move in the writer's mind – but it is not expressive of the meaning of that particular sentence.'[32] 'Order', 'ease', and 'rapidity' are attributes of the minds of authors, not of sentences – that point is quite clear. As far as style is concerned, the semantic arrow points toward the author, not towards the detail of the message. In later papers,[33] Wimsatt, too, withdraws from an extreme 'monist expressionism': 'I believe,' he writes, 'in the integration of literary-meaning [i.e. style and content] but at the same time in different kinds and levels of meaning.' Style occurs at a particularly 'formal' and implicit level. The study of style

> ought to cut in between a Platonic or Crocean monism, where meaning either as inspired dialectic or as intuition-expression is simply and severely one meaning, and the various forms of practical affective rhetoric, Aristotelian or modern, where stylistic meaning bears to substantial meaning a relation of *how* to *what* or of *means* to *end*.

How exactly one 'cuts in between' these two positions is not, however, entirely clear; verbal style

> must be supposed to refer to some verbal quality which is somehow structurally united to or fused with *what* is being said by words, but is also somehow to be distinguished from *what* is being said. A study of verbal style, though it ought to deal only with meaning, ought to distinguish at least two interrelated levels of meaning, a substantial level and another more like a shadow or echo or gesture.

So not only is the level of meaning at which one finds style formal and implicit, but it is also shadowy, echoic, gestural – those are slippery terms, indeed; and there is a danger that 'meaning' as the criterion will vanish through our fingers. What is important in Wimsatt's later work, however, is the clear distinction between ordinary semantic and stylistic meaning differences. In Pope's 'pseudopoetic' version of 'close the door', namely, 'The wooden guardian of our privacy/Quick on its axle turn', 'more things are being said and intimated about the door', and *therefore* these two sentences differ far more than in style in its 'strict conception'. Isolating stylistic meaning 'is made difficult by the fact that substantial meaning itself has various strata, some of which are readily confused with the level of strictly verbal style ... ' More things are being said about 'the door' in 'the wooden guardian of our privacy' than about 'door' alone, about 'abode' than about 'home', about 'thee' than about 'you'. But what these other things are – what this 'pure style' is – is tantalizing in its tenuity: it is depicted as a 'thin solid line of white' on top of a semantic cake whose basis is 'a solid red stratum of stated meaning' itself 'shading into an even thicker ground of mixed red and white, the levels of all the complex kinds of epithetic, metaphoric, and intimated meaning which one may conceive as in some broad sense stylistic.' Wimsatt has retreated from monism, but his 'monism and a half' seems as murky as the middle ground of his cake. How do these complex kinds of 'epithetic, metaphoric and intimated meanings' relate to better established terms like 'designation', 'denotation', 'connotation', etc.?

Beardsley's concession was not to attenuate his definition but to tack on an amendment, and the amendment seems, to me, more interesting than the original proposal. To understand it, we have to add to our sketch an account of his general theory of meaning.[34] Beardsley's definitions are in the behaviourist semiological tradition; they are concerned with effects of linguistic acts upon perceivers. The central concept is that of 'import', 'the capacity of a message to affect' a perceiver. The message may affect the perceiver's *beliefs* or his *feelings* – the first he calls 'cognitive import' or 'purport', the second 'emotive purport' (as when 'home' or 'mother' mean more than 'domicile' and 'mater'). 'Purport' is itself of three types – 'cognitive purport' (for Beardsley 'meaning' *tout court*), that is, the 'capacity to convey information about the speaker's beliefs'; 'emotive purport', the 'capacity to convey information about the speaker's feelings' ('alas', and 'oh, dear'), and finally, 'general purport', the capacity to convey information about other characteristics of the speaker. The concept of general purport, is, to my knowledge, the first semiological formulation of Definition B. I only object to the name, which I find insufficiently descriptive. I shall substitute the term 'identificational purport' instead, and shall mean by this 'purport which serves to identify the speaker as such and such a person'. Beardsley lists several aspects of personality that general purportive features can communicate. I add illustrative examples: nationality (e.g., British 'lorry' v. American 'truck'), provenance (Northern U.S. /ai/ v. Southern U.S. /a/, as in 'five'), religious affiliation (Quaker 'thee' v. non-Quaker 'you'), social class or level (vulgar 'ain't' v. standard 'aren't'), vocation (use of technical terms, particularly where the context is non-technical: the engineer's 'feedback', the psychologist's 'bind'), avocation (ditto: the amateur sailor's 'tacking', the skier's 'powder'), state, status, condition (a category I'm less clear about – perhaps physical condition, as when one slurs his speech when he is drunk or has suffered a paralytic stroke?). In addition to these, other categories obviously suggest themselves – age, sex, social sensitivity, i.e., decorum, etc. Notice that there is a difference in kind between the social aspects or decorum of the communicative act per se (Definition D), and the identificational functions of such features. In identificational purport, Definition B, the choice of a given feature (say, referring to a man as 'this gentleman' rather than 'this guy') is taken as a datum which serves to characterize the speaker. It is *the fact* that he uses that feature rather than another that is stylistic (B), not the feature itself (which is 'stylistic' only in sense D). In other words, when a man uses a formal rather than slang term, there are two kinds of 'stylistic' information conveyed: one is 'formality' itself (Definition D), and the other is 'the fact that he can be formal' (for it is a fact that some people, by reasons of education or temperament, *cannot* be formal). 'Formality', or any feature in Style D, is about the *message*; 'the fact that X is now and can be formal (or whatever)' is about the speaker, hence Style B.

Phenomena of Style B can be conveniently displayed in terms of a matrix or table in which the columns refer to the aspects of personality which are characterized and the rows to divisions of the communicative act; a few examples are shown on the next page.

By this chart it is clear that some sorts of generally purportive features are more subject to conscious control than others. The use of parallelism and balance is a highly conscious artifice; the use of /a/ for /ai/ is an automatic and unalterable feature of one's speech. It is useful to bear this distinction in mind; it might be said, perhaps, that every speaker has

	Nationality	Provenance	Religious affiliation	Social class, etc.
Phonology		/a/ in 'five' = Southern American		
Morphology				
Syntax			'thee' for 'you'	
Vocabulary	British 'lorry' v. American 'truck'			'ain't' for 'aren't' = vulgar

an unconscious style, but that only professional writers and speakers have developed conscious styles, that is, sets of regularly recurrent features which clearly characterize them in the universe of authors. At least in terms of literary criticism conscious features are obviously of greater interest than unconscious.[35] The fundamental assumption is that the style of a writer is an idiosyncratic selection of the resources of the language more or less forced on him by the combination of individual differences summarized under the term 'personality'. This selection might be called a set of preferences except that this term suggests that the process is mainly conscious and willed. Although it is doubtless true that some part of the process of composition is deliberate and conscious, especially at the level of meaning, much of it is not fully conscious and it is this part which is of greater interest to the student of style. The reason is obvious: the unconscious stylistic decisions are less likely to be affected by the occasional and temporary character of a given composition (its subject matter) and are more likely to reveal something that the writer might deliberately wish to conceal (p. 82).

There is another sort of distinction that can be made in this connection. It seems useful to distinguish between two sorts of literary stylistic inquiry: one in which the guiding purpose is to discover any and all sorts of features that serve to identify an author, and the other in which only features having significance for larger aspects of the work are of interest. The first sort of inquiry – which we may call 'stylometric' – is essentially bibliographical, rather than critical: a common goal is the identification of authorship of anonymous or disputed texts.[36] It proceeds by counting *everything*; if it discovers, for example, that a document has a certain specific percentage of *and*s or *of*s which exactly corresponds to the statistics of other of an author's works, it ascribes the document to him and its task is complete.[37] The second kind of inquiry – more genuinely stylistic in the usual sense – is concerned with features in so far as they shed light on the personality and art of an author. The writings of Leo Spitzer are perhaps the best example of stylistics in search of literarily *relevant* features, although it is true that Spitzer sometimes went too far in extrapolating from minute features, or in relating them to larger themes of works and authors.

Or looking at the matter in reverse perspective:

> the personality of a writer is an inferential structure built upon what we know or can guess about his subjects of interest, his reasoning, his feelings, his linguistic decisions, his attitudes ... Personality may thus be thought of as the reverse of humanity: it is the identity of a human unit as an individual, not his identification with the race in general. Personality, therefore, and one of its literary reflections, style, is the combination of drives to break away from the uniformity of the human mass and to establish, by expressing, one's particular indefinable uniqueness.[38]

It is clearly possible to think of style as manner without giving way to temptations to 'mere ornamentalism'. Formulations like the following indicate the possibility of a responsible and literarily useful Aristotelian dualism. Note, however, that the 'what' is not only local or textural meaning but global or structural meaning as well:

> The very many decisions that add up to a style are decisions about what to say, as well as how to say it. They reflect the writer's organization of experience, his sense of life, so that the most general of his attitudes and ideas find expression just as characteristically in his style as in his matter, though less overtly. Style, in this view, far from being intellectually peripheral ornament, is what I have called 'epistemic choice', and the study of style can lead to an insight into the writer's most confirmed epistemic stances.[39]

Here surely is the voice of Buffon in its modern manifestation.

Naturally, in the search for relevancies, one need not naively conclude that every identificational feature corresponds to a personality trait of the author himself. That many people are not always what they would like to be, or even thought to be, is so obvious as not to need comment, and in speech, as in other traits, a selected role may not correspond at all points to the real 'facts' of personality (whatever *they* are). Dr Johnson's frequent petulance is too amply documented for us to assume that he was always capable of that 'air of judiciousness, of having considered things from both sides' imputed to his balanced syntax. But, as modern critics have shown us, the literary context is different from the ordinary speech situation: the *persona*, the literary speaking voice is not necessarily the author's although it may be close to his. But the author we only know by extra-literary, hence irrelevant, information anyway. And since, in literature, we are concerned with roles, not with realities, we need not trouble ourselves with questions of discrepancy between the two. This is as true of essays as it is of narrative poems. The *persona*'s voice may be so close to the author's as to be virtually identical, or it may veer so far off as to be clearly that of a separate character. In that case, of course, one can speak of two styles – the style of the character and the style of the author, not excluding the way in which he depicts characters!

Another point needs to be made about the interpretation or semantic effect of general purport. It is clear that in many cases general purport is not fully interpretable by itself but only in close combination with the other two kinds of purport. A given stylisticum – say, the frequent use of antithesis – may have different repercussions according to the express content which is being related. Though antithesis may sound 'judicious' when combined with Johnsonian content, it has quite another effect when combined with other kinds of content: in Swift's style, antithesis or 'pointing' has been said to make 'for a style aesthetically suited to matter of argument', it 'gives an impression of wit or intelligence even when it is not there, and keeps the attention lively, ready for when it is'; the effect is one combining 'lively intellection with strict relevance'.[40]

And the combination may be more of a conflict than a co-operation; this fact has been cleverly pointed out by R. P. Draper in an article on 'Style and Matter'.[41] Draper discovers in Yeats's 'An Irish Airman Foresees His Death' a considerable number of rhetorical figures: antithesis, parison, traductio, zeugma, anaphora, and so on, which give the poem 'an air of terseness and forceful economy'. Yet this impression conflicts with the sense of the *persona* which we infer from the immediate para-phraseable content of the poem:

> What the airman says amounts to the expression of a highly romantic individualism ... the only thing that the airman admits as valid for him is the spirit of adventure and the romantic death wish:
>
> > A lonely impulse of delight
> > Drove to this tumult in the clouds.
>
> But the style of the poem, the impression of terse economy created by those rhetorical devices ... suggests the non-romantic qualities of weight, judgment and restraint. Against the romanticism and individualism of the matter is set the responsibility suggested by the manner. Detailed analysis of the language reveals that the style oper-ates *as* style, not as the mere icon of the matter ...

Is this an instance where the poet's style has obscured a character's style? That would suggest that the poem was a failure if one demands homo-geneity of style and content. But, as Draper points out, 'a resolution, explaining the fact that the poem does not fall to pieces despite this contradiction, might be found in Yeats's notion of an aristocratic elite which combines splendid individualism with support for a mellowed and traditionally sanctioned order'.[42] But note that the airman is not *of* this elite – 'his countrymen [are] Kiltartan's poor'. So the source of conflict is that the aristocratic poet *projects* on to the character of the airman a nobility and tradition not actually his. Perhaps the rhetorical language itself is a kind of metaphor which treats the airman's romantic individualism *as if* it could be articulated in classical terms. The effect is not unlike that of Henry James's endowing the heroine of *What Maisie Knew* with the most sophisticated of social dialects at the very moment of exhibiting her child's ignorance of what is happening around her.

Let us return to Beardsley's definition of style, which we now quote in its final version: 'Style is detail, or texture of secondary meaning plus general purport.'[43] But the status of the word 'plus' is thrown into some doubt by the immediately succeeding sentence: 'Or in another way, two discourses differ in style when they differ either in their details of meaning or in their general purport.' 'Plus' implies 'both ... and'; 'or', at best, can mean 'and/or'. Doubtless Beardsley means that two utterances differ in style C or Style B or both. An instance of style C alone would be the same man uttering what amounts cognitively to the same thing in two different sets of words: 'Go home' v. 'Return to your abode', 'He's an important guy' v. 'He's a distinguished gentleman', etc. An instance of Style B would be two different men uttering the same words, yet revealing their different personalities by a variety of vocal features, phoneme selections, syntactic preferences, etc. An instance of the combination of style B and style C would be two different men uttering slightly different versions of the same basic message. So Beardsley's argument might run. But now we must repeat a question which we posed before in different terms: is it really possible to exclude style B? In other words, isn't every utterance somehow illustrative of identificational purport? Take the case of 'He's an important guy' v. 'He's a distinguished gentleman' uttered by the same man in the same intonation and so on: disregarding the fact that these are appropriate to two different speech-contexts, two different audiences, two different occasions (style D), isn't it precisely indicative of the *manner* of some speakers that they can have both 'important guy' and 'distinguished gentleman' in their speech repertoire? For others do not have this double capacity and that's part of *their* styles.

In his discussion of style in painting, Beardsley writes:

> ... what sort of thing do critics refer to when they talk about style? For one thing, they speak about the style of a particular painting: the brushstrokes are short and close together; or there is much impasto; or the work is a pointillist painting. And these are statements about recurrent features of the texture of the painting. In other words, if certain textural characteristics are repeated within the work, these are singled out and regarded as traits of style. And this can be done without any reference to the artist at all.[44]

The notion of recurrence seems important for literary style, too. Strangely enough, though the word appears in Beardsley's preliminary definition – ' "Style" can be defined, tentatively, in some such way as this: the style of a literary work consists of the recurrent features of its texture of meaning'[45] – it does not appear in the final definition, quoted above: 'Style is detail, or texture, of secondary meaning plus general purport.' Assuming that there are no profound theoretical reasons for omitting recurrence from the definition, we might ask ourselves what recurrence means in respect to literary style. In the above discussion of painting style, Beardsley seems to limit recurrence to features upon a single canvas. But there doesn't seem to be any reason to make so sharp a limitation in literature: Johnson's use of parallelism and balance is characteristic both of individual works by him and of his writing in general. Furthermore, recurrence must not be taken in too crude a sense. For one thing, measures must always be made against the language as a whole. Secondly, a style feature is highlighted not only by its sheer prevalence but also by its relative position in the work. Some features may be infrequent, yet may occur in very crucial spots and hence receive a heavy 'weighting' as stylistica. In Milic's observation that 'unless the stylistic characteristics recur consistently, they are not really characteristic',[46] the word 'consistently' has to be very narrowly defined to account for qualitative as well as quantitative highlighting.

It should be noted, finally, that taking style as individual manner does not require us to insist upon the uniqueness of each of its components. The fact that a feature characteristic of an author's style was generally popular in his period or school does not make it any less characterizing of him. It is added to other features to make up his unique pattern or configuration. Because of its complex nature, the recognition of a writer's style is not a mere act of perception, as that term is generally defined (for example, 'whenever we "perceive" what we name "a chair", we are interpreting a certain group of data (modifications of the sense-organs), and treating them as signs of a referent.'[47]) Perception entails the recognition of a thing as an instance of a *class* of things, whereas style-recognition, as the recognition of a personality, is something more, namely the recognition of an individual as a unique complex or pattern of perceived features. That is why perception tends to be virtually instantaneous whereas the ability to recognize an author's style takes time to acquire.

Beardsley's trichotomy of functions reveals the inadequacies of expressivist theories of style, like that of Bally:

> ... all the resources of vocabulary and of sound, form, auxiliaries, and order, in so far as they do not constitute a system of neutral references, are available for affective or emotional ends. This is the domain of *stylistics*, independent of grammar, and reaching out from certain specific devices at the service of all speakers towards highly effective personal uses of language which can only be estimated intuitively.[48]

Clearly, signals with 'affective or emotional ends' are better handled under emotive purport, as are references to ·'judgments of value' (Marouzeau) and so on.

There is sometimes confusion between the concept of style and the means by which style is achieved. Recall Saintsbury's definition: 'Style is the choice and arrangement of language with only a subordinate regard to the meaning to be conveyed ... ' And Marouzeau: 'Répertoire des possibilités, fonds commun mis à la disposition des usagers, qu'ils utilisent selon leurs besoins d'expressions en pratiquant le choix, c'est-à-dire le style, dans la mesure où le leur permettent les lois du langage.'[49] But surely that is to confound cause and effect: one makes his choices and the *result* is style, not the act of choosing. Marouzeau makes this clear in another place: style is 'Qualité de l'énoncé, *résultant* du choix ...'[50] (my italics). The evidence is the fact that choice can be conceived of as the mechanism of *any* of the four senses of 'style' distinguished above.

The same point could be made about 'deviation from norm' defini-tions: 'style is defined as an individual's deviation from norms for the situations in which he is encoding ... '[51] But, again, style is not the act of deviating but rather the product of deviating. Deviation itself, of course, is simply another way of viewing the mechanism – not merely choice but choice seen as a special departure from some set of averaged choices of others in the linguistic community at large. Ohmann puts it more accurately: '... a writer's characteristic style is largely the product of relatively few idiosyncratic variations from the norm, out of the vast number possible'.[52]

Many have argued that style is not the product of deviation from some norm but rather the norm itself. 'Norm' is obviously being used in a different sense here than that used by the deviationists. Compare

> ... style involves the totality of a writer's use of language; it cannot be limited to isolated deviations, and even what is apparently ordi-nary or normal may be significant.[53]

and

> A style may be said to be characterized by a pattern of recurrent selection from the inventory of optimal features of a language.[54]

In so far as it refers to a holistic conception – the *set* of choices where choice is possible – this definition is acceptable enough and less likely to mislead than the choice or deviation definitions. But it too needs to be completed by a clear semantic reference, namely, the totality of features in their function of meaning or identifying the author in the universe of authors.[55]

So far this paper has been essentially a critique of other people's theories. It would be less than fair to end without venturing one of my own. I shall present it as a diagram with commentary on divisions and subdivisions (see page 142 for chart). Two things will be noted immediately: (1) this analysis is essentially of Style B, 'individual manner' (where manner does not exclude the semantic ramifications or entailments of the modified Wimsatt–Beardsley Platonic monism), particularly as an expansion of Beardsley's concept of 'general purport'; and (2) it attempts to replace 'style' by other terms wherever they exist, and to qualify 'style' by explanatory epithets wherever possible. Several terms need to be defined. 'Register' is used to refer to the general purport of casual discourse, so that style may be reserved for non-casual discourse. The distinction 'casual' v. 'non-casual', taken from C. F. Voegelin,[56] although differing from his account in detail, is based on a single criterion: any discourse which is planned and executed in terms of standard modes of discourse (poems, novels, plays, legal briefs, sermons, etc.) is non-casual; anything else is casual. Casual utterances are extempore and completely dependent upon the immediate social context; they reflect the speaker in his non-professional aspects. Whereas the register of a casual utterance has a more or less natural relation to the speaker – that is to say, he reveals himself as such and such a person more or less automatically – all the complex possibilities of artifice flourish in non-casual utterances. An author may have a literary style very different from his personal register. (For example, I have not found an extensive number of balanced or parallel sentences in Johnson's oral remarks as noted down by Boswell.)

It is to be observed further that the chart allows for the common practice of referring to the style of the *work* (the register of the *message*) as well as that of the author. This is, perhaps, a shorthand way of saying 'the style of the author *in* the work' (the register of the speaker *in* the message), and to that extent boxes 3 and 6 may be superfluous. But the dichotomy seems to be useful for recognizing the distinction between, say, 'formality' itself (style D), which is a property of the message, and 'the fact that Mr X can be formal' which is a property of the speaker (style B). The personal register or style is always more extensive and long-lasting than the register of the message or the style of the work; otherwise we could not say things like: 'His formality on that occasion was really quite unlike him,' and so forth.

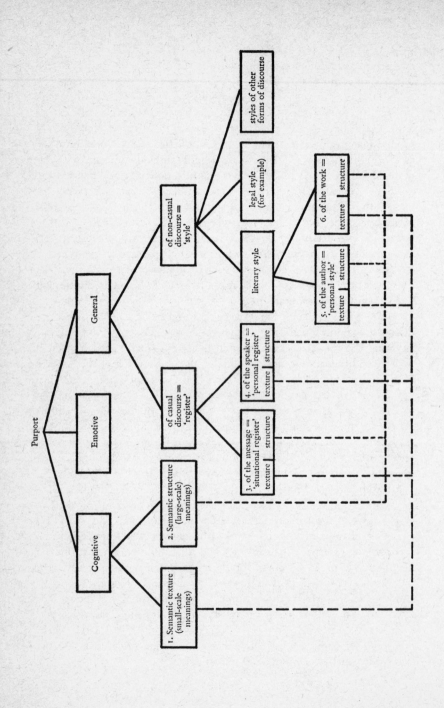

Finally, it is to be noted that the meaning ramifications or entailments of register and style features are accounted for in boxes 3 to 6 by the fact that not only semantic texture is subject to individual treatment but also semantic *structure*. A man is characterized as much by the larger patterns of what he says as by the smaller; he is disjointed or logical, he sticks always to the point or admits many diversions, and so on. Beardsley recognized painting criticism:

> Suppose a historian says that the Baroque 'style' is characterized by open, rather than closed, forms, by extreme contrasts of light and dark, by compositions built upon the diagonal receding into space. Some of these are recurrent features of texture, some are recurrent features of structure. It is a little odd, if a painter is fond of using spiral compositions, to say that this is a feature of his style, but perhaps it is not too odd, and the habit is deeply rooted in art history.[57]

But it is only 'odd' to one who is trying to reconcile or even identify the two different senses of style which we have labelled 'B' and 'C'; if style is general purport (B), why should it be so strange that one idiosyncratically varies his larger design as much as his details of writing? It is only superimposing style C on style B that makes a restriction to texture necessary. Recognizing a stylistic repercussion in structural selection seems particularly important for literary stylistics since otherwise one would have to deny that matters like choice of genre or overall organization are stylistic. Yet surely the fact that Milton chose to write an epic and that Shakespeare did not, that Henry James was successful in novels but not in plays, is relevant to the stylistic analysis of these authors. Surely it is not odd to speak of choices made in the architectonics of novels or the argumentative structures of lyric poems as characteristic of their creators' styles. The fact that every choice in register or style has meaning ramifications or entailments is indicated in the diagram by drawing broken lines in all cases back to cognitive purport.[58]

Box 6 is created to allow us to distinguish between aspects of the work and aspects of the author (or, more precisely, *persona*). The choice of a particular rhyme-scheme or stanza-pattern, of a particular point of view or manner of handling fictional time, does not serve to identify the author or *persona* in human terms, but it does tell us something of interest about the work which we are disposed to call 'stylistic'. Notice here another distinction between casual and non-casual utterances: it is characteristic of non-casual utterances to contain special features of this sort, superimposed upon and restricting the choices provided by the language as a whole. In literature, the rhetorical figures and tropes, metre and rhyme provide additional restrictions upon vocabulary and syntactic choice. Other sorts of restrictions are traditional in other forms of discourse – legal, religious, etc. These are matters of choice and are stylistic, although not 'linguistically' stylistic in the strict sense. Category 6 also permits us to speak clearly of the style of a character, which may be poles apart from the style of the author himself.

HISTORICAL DISCOURSE*

Roland Barthes

The formal description of units longer than the sentence (i.e. of *discourse*) is no new thing. From Gorgias to the nineteenth century it was the main concern of classical rhetoric. Recent developments in linguistic science have however led to a revival of interest in the subject and to novel techniques for handling it. A linguistics of discourse may now be said to lie within the realm of possibility. The implications this would have for literary analysis – and for the educational procedures in which literary analysis plays so large a part – make this one of the major current tasks of semiology.

The target of this second-level linguistics must be not only to look for universals of discourse (if such exist) and the units and combinatorial rules which express them, but also to decide whether structural analysis confirms the traditional typology of discourse-genres – whether, for example, we are always justified in contrasting poetic and novelistic discourse, fictional and historical narrative. It is the second of these distinctions which is the subject of the following reflections: is there in fact any specific difference between factual and imaginary narrative, any linguistic feature by which we may distinguish on the one hand the mode appropriate to the relation of historical events – a matter traditionally subject, in our culture, to the prescriptions of historical 'science', to be judged only by the criteria of conformity to 'what really happened' and by the principles of 'rational' exposition – and on the other hand the mode appropriate to the epic, novel or drama? And if such distinctive features exist, what parts of the discourse do they affect, at what point in the language-act do they operate? A tentative answer to this question will be sought here through an informal (and by no means exhaustive) survey of the discourse of certain classical historians such as Herodotus, Machiavelli, Bossuet and Michelet.

* Reprinted from *Social Science Information* (International Social Science Council), vol. VI, no. 4 (August, 1967); translated from the French by Peter Wexler.

I

Under what circumstances, firstly, is the classical historian led (or permitted) to refer, within his own discourse, to the act by which it is uttered? What are the forms taken in discourse by what Jakobson (who is, however, concerned to analyse language, not discourse) calls the *shifters*,[1] which mark the transitions into and out of the sui-referential mode?

Historical discourse seems to have two standard types of shifter. The first marks what might be called the *monitorial* mode, corresponding to what Jakobson calls (again at the level of language) the *evidential* category, which combines a message (the event reported), a code-statement (the informer's contribution) and a message about the code-statement (the author's evaluation of his source). The category therefore covers any mention of sources and witnesses' accounts and any reference to the reportorial act of this historian adducing *another text*, explicitly. The choice of this mode is an open one – the historian may very well make tacit use of his source; but if he does choose it he comes close to the status of the ethnographer, who is conventionally required to give details about his informant; the monitorial mode is therefore common in ethnographer-historians like Herodotus. It may take many forms of expression: asides like *as I have heard, as far as can be ascertained*; the use of the present tense to mark an intervention by the historian; or any reference to the historian's personal experience. Michelet, for example, 'monitors' the history of France through the filter of a subjective illumination (the 1830 revolution) and mentions this explicitly. But the monitorial mode is not of course confined to historical discourse. It is common in conversation and in certain devices of exposition in the novel (anecdotes attributed to fictitious informants and the like).

The second type of shifter covers all those devices by which the writer declares a departure from or return to his itinerary, any explicit signpost to the organization of his own discourse. This is an important category, with many possible exponents; they can, however, all be reduced to an indication of some displacement of the discourse with reference to the matter, or more exactly in the same dimension as the matter, rather in the manner of the temporal and locative deictics *voici* and *voilà*. The possible relationships to the narrative dimension include immobility (*as stated above*), regression (*altius repetere, replicare da più alto luogo*), resumption (*ma ritornando all' ordine nostro, dico come ...*), finality (*on this subject I need say no more*), announcement (*further memorable deeds of this reign may be mentioned*). The organization-shifter poses one noteworthy problem which can only be briefly indicated here, namely the difficulty which arises from the coexistence of or rather friction between two time-scales – history's and the history book's. This friction gives rise to a number of interesting features in the discourse, of which three may be mentioned here. The first concerns all the phenomena of acceleration: the same number of pages (if this can be taken as a crude measure of the history book's own time-scale) covers quite different periods of historical time. In Machiavelli's *Florentine History* the same measure (one chapter) may cover twenty years or several centuries. The nearer the historian gets to his own time, the greater the pressure of the act of utterance, and the slower the time-scale: the two scales are not isochronic.

But this is to imply that discourse is not linear, and to suggest the possibility of 'paragrammatism' in historical statement.[2] The second feature to be noted reminds us that even in the purely material sense in which the discourse must of necessity remain linear its function seems to be to add depth to historical time, by contrast with its own zigzag progress. Thus when Herodotus first mentions a new character, he goes back to give an account of his ancestry, then returns to his starting-point and a little beyond, until the next new character appears, when the whole process is repeated. The third feature, an important one, illustrates how the even chronological sequence of historical time may be disrupted by the organizational shifters which mark the onset of historical discourse, the point at which the beginning of the historical event coincides with the exordium of the historiographic event.[3] This onset may take one of two forms: the first might be called the performative opening, where the utterance is in the fullest sense a formal inauguration; the model here is the *I sing* of the epic poets. Thus Joinville begins his history with a religious invocation (*In the name of God the omnipotent, I, Jehan, sire of Joinville, do here set forth the life of our saintly king Louis*); and even the socialist Louis Blanc does not disdain the purificatory introit;[4] for there is always something daunting – one might almost say sacrosanct – in the initiation of any act of language. The second form of onset, the Preface, is much commoner; it is the typical specimen of meta-statement, and may be prospective (when the work is announced) or retrospective (when it is judged, as with the Preface which Michelet added to his *Histoire de France* after the text had been entirely composed and published).

These examples suggest that transposition into the mode of sui-referential meta-statement serves not so much to enable the historian to express his subjectivity, as is commonly supposed, but rather to 'de-simplify' the chronological Time of history by contrasting it with the different time-scale of the discourse itself (document-time, as we may for brevity call it); to 'dechronologize' the historical thread and restore, if only by way of reminiscence or nostalgia, a Time at once complex, parametric, and non-linear, resembling in the richness of its dimensionality the mythical Time of ancient cosmogonies, inseparable from the word of the poet or seer. The organization-shifters reveal (though the fact is sometimes disguised by various rationalistic devices) that the historian's function is a predictive one: it is because he *knows* what has not yet been related that the historian, like the myth-bearer, needs a two-layered Time, braiding the chronology of the subject-matter with that of the language-act which reports it.

The signs or shifters discussed above concern only the language-act itself. There are others which express what Jakobson calls the protagonists – the receiver and the sender. It is a remarkable and rather odd fact that literary discourse rarely carries any mark acknowledging the reader's presence; one might even characterize it as (apparently) a discourse without *Thou* – though in fact its whole structure implies a reader as 'subject'. In historical discourse destination-signs are normally absent; they are found only when the history is offered as a lesson, as with Bossuet's *Histoire universelle*, explicitly addressed by the preceptor to his royal pupil; and even then the framework is in a sense possible only because Bossuet's discourse is taken to be a homological reproduction of God's own discourse to mankind – that is, of the history he sends for their meditation. It is because the history of man is God's Writ that Bossuet can in turn write in a mode which establishes the destination-relationship between the young prince and himself.

Marks of the writer's presence are, of course, much more common. They include all those fragments of discourse by which the historian, of whom initially we know nothing more than the mere fact of his authorship, gradually fills in all the attributes which will establish him as a *person*, a psychological solid. A special case of this 'filling-in', and one more directly a matter for the literary critic, is that where the author seeks to stand aside from his own discourse by systematically omitting any direct allusion to the originator of the text: the history seems to write itself. This approach is very widely used, since it fits the so-called 'objective' mode of historical discourse, in which the historian never appears himself. What really happens is that the author discards the human persona but replaces it by an 'objective' one; the authorial subject is as evident as ever, but it has become an objective subject. This is the process that Fustel de Coulanges revealingly and rather naively calls the 'chastity of history'. At the level of discourse, objectivity, or the absence of any clues to the narrator, turns out to be a particular form of fiction, the result of what might be called the referential illusion, where the historian tries to give the impression that the referent is speaking for itself. This illusion is not confined to historical discourse: novelists galore, in the days of realism, considered themselves 'objective' because they had suppressed all traces of the *I* in their text. Nowadays linguistics and psychoanalysis unite to make us much more lucid towards such ascetic modes of utterance: we know that the absence of a sign can be significant too.

One last aspect of the language-act must be briefly mentioned, and that is the special case – recognized by Jakobson (again at the level of language, not of discourse) as one of the possible set of shifters – where the utterer of the discourse is at the same time a participant in the events described, i.e. where the protagonist of the language-act is the same person as the protagonist of the historical event – where, in short, the actor turns historian, as with Xenophon and the retreat of the Ten Thousand. The most illustrious example of this conjunction of the historical *I* and the historiographical *I* is the well-known use of *he* in Julius Caesar; this is confined to the historical mode, corresponding to *we* in the historiographical mode (*ut supra demonstravimus*). At first sight this Caesarean *he* seems to be indistinguishable from the other actors, and it has for this reason been taken to be the supreme sign of objectivity; it can, however, be formally differentiated from the others on collocational grounds, being confined to a few syntagms, which might be called the syntagms of leadership (*give orders, hold assizes, inspect, congratulate, explain, think*), all of which are in fact close to being performatives, in which speech and action are identical. There are other examples of this use of *he* as past actor and present narrator (particularly in Clausewitz): they show that the choice of the apersonal pronoun is only a rhetorical alibi, and that the true situation of the narrator is manifest in the syntagms he chooses to express his past acts.

II

It must in the nature of the case be possible to break down the historian's message into content-analytical units amenable to classification in various ways. These units represent what the history book is about; they have the status of significata, not to be equated with the complete discourse nor yet with the pure referent, but rather with the referent divided, named and intelligible, but not yet captured by any syntax. It would be premature to attempt a thorough analysis of these units; the following remarks are in the nature of preliminaries only.

The historical statement, like any other, can be divided into 'existents' (entities or themes) and 'occurrents' (predicates or themes). It seems on preliminary examination that each of these may be a relatively closed (and therefore controllable) list, or *collection*, whose items eventually recur, though of course in varying combinations. In Herodotus, for example, the list of existents is confined to dynasties, princes, generals, soldiers, peoples and places, and the occurrents to actions like devastate, enslave, make an alliance, undertake an expedition, consult the oracle, etc. Since these collections are (relatively) closed, they must lend themselves to rules of substitution and transformation, and it must be possible to assign a structure to them – a task which will of course be easier with some historians than with others. In Herodotus the units will mostly depend on the vocabulary of warfare; it would be worth inquiring how far modern historians would need more complex combinations of vocabularies, and, even if this proved to be the case, whether historical discourse is not always based, in the last analysis, on some well-structured *collection* (not *vocabulary*, since we are working at the level of content). Machiavelli seems to have had an intuition of some such structure, for at the beginning of his *Florentine History* he presents his own 'collection', i.e. the entities which are to be mobilized and combined in his narrative.

In the case of more fluid collections (from historians less archaic than Herodotus), the content-units may nevertheless receive a high degree of structuration not from the vocabulary but from the author's own private obsessions. Recurrent themes of this kind are frequent in romantic historians like Michelet; but they are also found in authors of a reputedly more intellectual stamp – *fama* is a personal unit for Tacitus, and Machiavelli bases his history on a thematic contrast between *mantenere* (alluding to the fundamental energy of the man of government) and *ruinare* (implying a logic of the decadence of things).[5]

To the extent that a thematic unit is regularly expressed by the same lexical item, it serves as an indicator not only of units of content but also of units of discourse; and this brings us to the problem of the nominalization of historical entities, whereby a single word may save specifying a whole situation or succession of actions; this encourages structurization to the extent that its reflex on the content plane is itself a small-scale structure. Thus Machiavelli uses the term *conspiracy* as shorthand for a whole complex datum, to convey the only form of struggle which remains when a government is victorious over all those who oppose it openly. A nominal style encourages a clear-cut articulation of the discourse and so reinforces its structure. All highly-structured histories proceed by substantives; Bossuet, for whom the history of mankind is structured by God, frequently uses whole strings of such single-noun shorthand notations.[6]

These remarks apply as much to occurrents as to existents. Here an interesting problem arises concerning the status of historiographical processes (independently of the history of the names for them). In general a statement may be assertive, negative or interrogative. In historical discourse, however, it is never anything but assertive – the historical fact is ontologically privileged in its linguistic expression; we relate what happened, not what didn't happen, or what might or might not have happened. In short, historical discourse has no negative (or only very rarely and eccentrically). It is curious but significant to note that the same is true of the psychotic patient who is unable to give the negative transposition of a sentence.[7] We may say that, in a sense, 'objective' discourse (as in positivist history) resembles schizophrenic discourse; in both cases there is a radical censorship of the utterance, in which negativity cannot be expressed (though it can be felt), and there is a massive reversion of discourse away from any form of sui-reference, or even (in the case of the historian) a reversion towards the level of pure referent – the utterance for which no one is responsible.

Mention must be made of one other essential aspect of the historical utterance, where the content-units enter into higher-level classes and class-sequences. Preliminary investigation suggests that those classes are the same as in fictional narrative.[8] One such class covers all those segments of discourse which refer metaphorically to an implicit meaning. For example, Michelet describes the motley clothes, the vulgarization of heraldry and the mixture of architectural styles in the early fifteenth century as equivalent expressions of a single meaning – the moral break-up of the end of the middle ages; the members of this class are therefore indexes (in Pierce's sense) or more specifically signs; they are frequent in the classical novel. Another class comprises those items of discourse which mark rational steps in a syllogism (or rather in an enthymeme, since they are nearly always imperfect approximations to a syllogism).[9]

Enthymemes are not exclusive to historical discourse either: they are common in the novel, where a switch in the story-line is generally justified in the reader's eyes by pseudo-reasonings of a syllogistic type. The interest of the enthymeme in historical discourse is that it combines the intelligible with the non-symbolic; does this hold true for recent histories, which try to break with the classical Aristotelian model? Last but not least, a third class carries what we may call, after Propp, the 'functions' of the narrative, i.e. the crucial turning-points in the story; these 'functions' occur in groups which syntactically speaking are closed lists and logically speaking are exhaustive sequences. In Herodotus, for example, there are several occurrences of the sequence *Oracle*; this sequence consists of three terms, each of them a binary choice (to consult or not to consult, to reply or not to reply, to follow or not to follow), which may be separated by other units not part of the sequence – either terms in another imbricated sequence or minor developments which operate catalytically, filling in the gaps between the nodes of the sequence.

Generalizing (perhaps rashly) from these remarks on the structure of the message, one may suppose that historical discourse oscillates between two poles according to the proportion of indexes to functions. When units of the index type predominate (with continual reference to an implicit meaning), history falls into metaphorical form and tends to become lyrical and symbolic; a representative example is Michelet. In the opposite case, when functional units predominate, history takes the form of a metonymy, and tends to become epic; the representative example is Augustin Thierry. There is a third alternative, where the structure of the discourse attempts to reproduce the structure of the dilemmas actually faced by the protagonists. In this case reasoned argument predominates and the history is of a reflexive – one might say strategic – style. Machiavelli is an excellent example of this variety.

III

For a history to be totally without meaning, its discourse would have to be nothing but an unstructured catalogue of isolated observations, as with chronologies and annals (in the strict sense of the term). In fully-constituted 'flowing' discourse the facts function irresistibly either as indexes or as links in an indexical sequence; even an anarchic presentation of the facts will at least convey the meaning 'anarchy' and suggest a particular philosophy of history of a negative kind.

Historical discourse can be meaningful on at least two levels. At the first of these the meaning is inherent in the historical content – the historian offers an interpretation (e.g. Michelet on the motley costumes of the fifteenth century, or Thucydides on certain particularly 'significant' encounters) or draws a lesson, either moral or political (e.g. Machiavelli or Bossuet). If the lesson is pervasive, we enter the second category, where the meaning is independent of the historical discourse as such and is expressed by the pattern of the historian's private obsessions; for example, the very imperfection of the narrative-structure in Herodotus (due to the open-endedness of certain *series* of events) expresses in the last analysis a particular philosophy of history – that men propose and the gods dispose; or in Michelet, where the meaningful items are highly structured in pairs of polar opposites, contrasted both conceptually and morphologically, the effect is to imply a Manichean view of life and death. In our civilization there is permanent pressure to increase the meaningfulness of history; the historian assembles not so much facts as *signifiants*; and these he connects and organizes in such a way as to replace the vacuousness of the pure catalogue with positive meaning.

As can be seen, by its structures alone, without recourse to its content, historical discourse is essentially a product of ideology, or rather of imagination, if we accept the view that it is via the language of imagination that responsibility for an utterance passes from a purely linguistic entity to a psychological or ideological one. It is for this reason that the very notion of historical 'fact' has at various times seemed suspect. 'There are no facts in themselves,' says Nietzsche. 'For a fact to exist, we must first introduce meaning.' As soon as language intervenes (as it always does), the fact can only be defined tautologically: we take note of what is notable; but the notable (and already for Herodotus the word had lost its mythical meaning) is nothing more than the noteworthy. It turns out that the only feature which distinguishes historical discourse from other kinds is a paradox: the 'fact' can only exist linguistically, as a term in a discourse, yet we behave as if it were a simple reproduction of something on another plane of existence altogether, some extra-structural 'reality'. Historical discourse is presumably the only kind which aims at a referent 'outside' itself that can in fact never be reached. We must therefore ask ourselves again: What is the place of 'reality' in the structure of discourse?

Historical discourse presupposes a complex, twofold operation. At the first stage (speaking of course metaphorically) the referent is detached from the discourse and becomes primordial to it; this is the period of the *res gestae*, where the discourse appears as no more than *historia rerum gestarum*; but then the very idea that history can have a meaning (*signifié*) other than referential is rejected. The referent and its expression (*signifiant*) are seen as directly related; the function of discourse is confined to the mere expression of reality; and meaning, the fundamental term of imaginary structures, becomes superfluous. Like all discourse with pretensions to 'realism', historical discourse believes it need recognize no more than two terms, referent and expression, in its semantic model. This (illusory) confusion of referent and meaning is of course characteristic of sui-referential discourse like the performatives; we can say that historical discourse is a fake performative, in which what claims to be the descriptive element is in fact merely the expression of the authoritarian nature of that particular speech-act.[10]

In other words, in 'objective' history 'reality' is always an unformulated meaning sheltering behind the apparent omnipotence of the referent. This situation defines what we may call the *reality effect*. Elimination of meaning from 'objective' discourse only produces a new meaning; confirming once again that the absence of an element in a system is just as significant as its presence. This new significance extends to the whole discourse, and in the last analysis constitutes what distinguishes historical discourse from all others; it is reality, but surreptitiously changed into shamefaced meaning: historical discourse does not follow reality, it only signifies it; it asserts at every moment: *this happened*, but the meaning conveyed is only that someone is making that assertion.

The prestige of *this happened* is of truly historical importance and magnitude. Our whole civilization is drawn to the reality effect, as witness the development of genres like the realist novel, the diary, the documentary, the *fait divers*, the historical museum, the exhibition of ancient objects and above all the massive development of photography, which differs from drawing only in conveying the additional meaning that the event portrayed *really* happened.[11] This is our secularized reliquary; it has lost all trace of sacred meaning, except that which is inseparable from something which once existed, no longer exists, but presents itself as a present sign of a dead thing. Conversely, the profanation of these relics is tantamount to the destruction of reality itself, once we achieve the insight that reality is nothing but a meaning, and so can be changed to meet the needs of history, when history demands the subversion of the foundations of civilization 'as we know it'.[12]

By denying this, by refusing to separate the referent from the simple assertion of it, history could not do otherwise – at that privileged moment in the nineteenth century when it was trying to establish itself as a genre in its own right – than take the 'pure and simple' narration of the facts as the best proof that they were true, and thus promote narrative into a privileged form for the expression of reality. The theoretician of this view is Augustin Thierry, who sought his guarantees of 'truth' in the care he took over his narrative, in the elegance of his plan and the abundance of 'concrete details'[13] he provided. The paradox comes full circle: narrative structure was evolved in the crucible of fiction (via myth and the first epics), yet it has become at once the sign and the proof of reality. It is clear that the attenuation (if not disappearance) of narrative in contemporary historians, who deal in structures rather than chronologies, implies much more than a change of school; it represents in fact a fundamental ideological transformation: historical narrative is dying: from now on the touchstone of history is not so much reality as intelligibility.

STRUCTURAL ANTHROPOLOGY AND HISTORY*

Marc Gaboriau

In his inaugural lecture at the Collège de France, Claude Lévi-Strauss praises history briefly and then concludes: 'This historian's profession of faith may come as a surprise since I have sometimes been criticized for being uninterested in history ... I hardly practise it, but I am determined that its rights should be preserved.'[1] In speaking of history, here as in his other works, Lévi-Strauss holds to the anthropologist's point of view, and this is the one we wish to analyse: how can anthropology, the science of organizations and social performances, which studies the structure rather than the origins, the results rather than the gradual development, how can it explain the impact of certain events upon societies?

These few lines echo the discussion which the work of Lévi-Strauss has aroused; discussions about this concept of history, or rather, of the word 'history' itself. 'It is difficult to know whether it is the history which man makes unknowingly, or the history of men written by historians who know it, or finally the philosopher's interpretation of man's history or of the historians' history.'[2] The term 'history' fluctuates between these three meanings; this is the origin of the discussions or the misunderstandings which we shall try and clarify, so that we may gradually see what Lévi-Strauss's attitude is, and what reasons he has for it.

ANTHROPOLOGY AND THE PHILOSOPHY OF HISTORY

The last chapter in *La Pensée sauvage* tries to clear up a misinterpretation which Lévi-Strauss has always contended with, especially in *Les Structures élémentaires de la parenté* and in *Race et histoire*: this is the confusion which the three meanings of the word history arouse. By claiming to take one's stand on 'real' history, one is really using a certain 'interpretation', which is a 'philosophy of history'. The confusion is even more serious if one wishes to found anthropology on this sense of 'history', that is to say,

* First appeared in *L'Esprit*, no. 322 (1963); translated from the French by Natalia Court.

upon philosophic presuppositions which are debatable. What is this philosophy of history which Lévi-Strauss criticizes? And what place does he give history in his own concept of anthropology?

In order that we may answer these questions, let us briefly examine the field of research and the problems posed by anthropology. It studies all forms of social life, past and present; but these are not always given in the same form: each society, and in particular the one to which the anthropologist belongs, can divide culture into three categories from its own point of view: 'Contemporary cultures found in another world; cultures which have developed in the same area as the society in question but at an earlier period; and finally, those earlier in time and occupying a different area in space.'[3] This triple diversity (in time, in space, and in space and time) characterizes the subject matter of anthropology and shows the extent of the problems presented by this science. 'It is a discipline whose first if not its only objective is to analyse and to explain differences.'[4] To avoid falling into these diversities, a unity of reference must be found to explain the differences without dispersing them. This is the fundamental problem of anthropology.

From this point of view, anthropology bears some analogy with history: both of these 'study societies other than those we live in'.[5] They are sciences of change and diversity. There is, however, this important distinction, that history studies only one of the dimensions of diversity which we listed, variety in time. Could one not take it a step further, and pass from partial analogy to identity, and so make history, expressed thus as the unity of diversity in time, the model and foundation of anthropology, in other words, 'grant it the dimension of time'? This in reality is what has been attempted since the nineteenth century.

To bring about this identification of history with anthropology, we shall take as unity of reference the unity of our history, the history of 'western civilization' which we postulate to be 'the most advanced expression of human evolution'.[6] In such a perspective we are both committed in history and situated at such a point of view that we have not to look at ourselves objectively in order to understand other societies. In fact, ever since Hegel, history has been thought of as cumulative: our society keeps within its institutions, or in its memory, all that others have been able to bring into being; all societies complement each other, and are neither incompatible nor exclusive. So, without leaving our own society, we know a priori that we can understand others, by bringing them within the unity of our gradual development.

This takes place through a double reduction; other societies in the globe are assimilated to anterior stages of our development. 'The primitive groups [will seem] like survivals of previous types, whose logical classification will at the same time complete the order of appearance in time.'[7] The diversity in space is in this way reduced to diversity in time. A second reduction will be a corollary of the first: the history which other societies have lived will be assimilated to a fragment of our past history. The three dimensions of diversity from which we started out are reduced to a single one. The only diversity between past and present societies is that of the stages of a genesis, where all aspects of social life (technical, intellectual, artistic) are simultaneously developed by 'approximations' and progressive complication; as we find in Hegel, each society which illustrates a 'degree' of history is animated by the same 'Idea'. The gradual development of humanity, unified according to these assumptions, would then be subject to a logic (the word was used earlier on) which would guarantee the intelligibility of the passing from one kind of society to another. The subject matter of anthropology would then be only the genetic development of humanity: in such a perspective, anthropology and history would intermingle.

Such are the assumptions to which Lévi-Strauss is referring when he criticizes a certain 'philosophy of history'. No name is quoted but in *Race et histoire* he affirms that it is a 'unique prescription', that is to say, it seems, a certain number of presuppositions carried by our culture for more than a century: from this it is not difficult to recognize the fundamental tenets of Hegel's philosophy and history. Lévi-Strauss, when he speaks of pseudo-evolutionism, criticizes most particularly its sociological or psychological applications (e.g. *Les Structures élémentaires de la parenté*, chap. VII, 'L'Illusion archaïque'). Sartre takes up more or less explicitly these assumptions, since he is open to the same kind of criticism.

In fact, for Lévi-Strauss, these are philosophic assumptions, which neither methodology nor facts can confirm. This 'history' remains purely 'conjectural',[8] the genetic relationship which is established among societies is not based on any document. Indeed, what grounds has one to say with Hegel that such a form of civilization has preceded another, or with Durkheim that a certain religion is more 'primitive', that a certain system of relationships preceded another, other than on a priori classification, a certain form of logic? Finally, what concerns us is what Husserl called a 'history without documents', whose validity is guaranteed by a sequence of concepts, not by facts. What value has such a guarantee? For Hegel, the coincidence of logic and historical account posed no problem since he based himself in fact on a dialectic logic which included a discipline of unique deduction: the number and arrangement of the stages in the future were determined there unequivocally. On the other hand, Lévi-Strauss's anthropology makes use of an analytic logic where several orders of deduction are possible. 'An unlimited choice of criteria would enable us to build an unlimited number of different series.'[9]

From amongst these possible origins, only the facts themselves can decide: however, we have no document which allows us to place in genetical order the different types of societies; and if we sometimes have certain fragmentary information, it seems to point to there being a multitude of real geneses for attaining a certain system of relationships, or a certain type of caste organization. This leads us to dispute the second reduction; the history of other societies cannot be reduced to fragments of our own, there are 'many ways of reacting to history'. There is not only *one* history, that is in the sense of a genetic unity of human societies, but many histories.

But that is not the only weakness of the great historic syntheses. The first reduction is debatable. If one considers the special aspects of a given society, one can assimilate them to anterior 'stages' of our development: as for the techniques, the systems of relationships, etc., if they are taken in isolation, a partial analogy may be valid. But on the strength of a partial analogy, can one arrive at identity? 'The method consists in taking the part for the whole; in concluding, because certain aspects of two civilizations (one present, the other past) bear resemblances, that there is analogy from all points of view. Now, not only is this reasoning logically unsound, but in a fair number of cases it is refuted by the facts.'[10] Here, Lévi-Strauss dissociates what one had been used to associate after Hegel: all the aspects of the same society do not evolve simultaneously, they are not all in accord; it follows that analogy on the one hand can go hand in hand with very great differences on the other. It is never possible to compare two societies fully; each becomes clear by a multitude of determinations, which makes it a unique individual in space or time. Here again the diversity reappears.

What arises from this argument? We must reassert the triple diversity from which we started, against a certain 'philosophy of history' which shows itself as 'attempting to suppress the diversity of culture, at the same time claiming to acknowledge it fully'.[11] Thus anthropology cannot be founded upon 'history' in the sense of the genetic unity of all human societies. What methods then will anthropology use, and what place will history hold?

If we abandon unity through history do we not run the risk of falling into pure diversity? Lévi-Strauss avoids this danger, and seeks unity at a more radical level, that of the conditions of the possibilities of all social organizations. When the different systems making up a society and their articulations are analysed, it is found that they apply a certain number of logical laws which are found in all societies. These are the 'constants' which provide the necessary unity on which anthropology is based. Lévi-Strauss applies this method for the first time in *Les Structures élémentaires de la parenté*: he proposes extending it to all the fields of anthropological research. These 'constants', presented at first as 'imaginary truths', are assigned an existence of fact in the subconscious: 'If, as we believe, the mind's subconscious activity consists of imposing form to content, and if this form is fundamentally the same for all, ancient and modern, primitive and civilized, one must, and it is sufficient, reach the subconscious structure underlying each institution or content, to attain a principle of interpretation which is valid for other institutions and other contents.'[12] The conditions of possibility affirm the homogeneity and intelligibility of the subject matter of anthropology.

They also solve, at least theoretically, the problem of the observer: thanks to my subconscious, and in so far as I can objectivize it in certain models, I am in a way the absolute spectator.

'The subconscious is the intermediary between myself and others ... it unites us with forms of activity which are both ours and others', conditions of all the thinking lives of mankind of all time.'[13]

In what sense are they 'ours and others'? In other words, what is Lévi-Strauss's opinion on the diversity of societies? All forms of social life are 'ours' in that we have the same subconscious and that they are all within our reach. The unity of one's subconscious is the unity of possibility and not of reality; it is the unity of the formal laws which order all possible combinations of elements: 'Societies, like individuals in their games or fantasies, never entirely create, but limit themselves to choosing certain combinations in an ideal list, which it would be impossible to recreate.'[14] Change, by its very process, creates a mythology or a system of relationships which are different because they convert a certain combination into one reality rather than another. 'The structures are exclusive. Each one of them can only combine with certain of the elements which are offered.'[15] The only totality is that of potential: while for Hegel, or

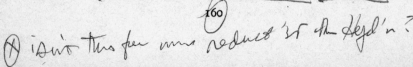

(A) isn't this far *more* reduced 'n the Hegel'n?

for Sartre, the most advanced society contains all the others within itself, here the whole has no present existence; each society, even our own, is a complex of partial and exclusive applications. The diversity of societies is defined by these limitations in the current situation. We must leave our present-day situation, go back to our potentials so that we can understand other societies. In Lévi-Strauss's eyes, it is only this distinction of potential and the present which enables us to respect the diversity of societies.

What place then does history occupy? Firstly, anthropology suggests that we list the possible or real combinations, and make laws from them, before we discuss origins, as in the *Leçon inaugurale*. Or rather, origins pose no problem; if the conditions of the possibilities are identical 'for all men and for all time' 'there are no young races'. The sequence of the structures created by a society, that is to say, its history, would only be particularly understandable if there were a question of genesis, that is to say, a succession of 'approximations' directed towards more perfect structures. But there is no origin, so one should not overestimate the role of history. The fact that different systems of relationships are affected successively by one society, or simultaneously by different societies, makes no essential difference to anthropology. The diversity of the states of a society in time is only a special case of diversity coexisting in space. 'The spreading out in space, and the succession in time provide equivalent perspectives.'[16] With reference to this, Chapter IV of *La Pensée sauvage*, 'Totem and Caste', is very enlightening. Here Lévi-Strauss studies all the intermediary states between a society known as totemic and a society made up of castes. This provides a table of real or possible variants, often converted into reality by different societies. The work of the anthropologist is first to establish such a table where the sequences are affirmed by the facts. The particular historic development will only be completely understood if it is then replaced in the table of possibilities. History from an anthropological point of view is always subordinate. From the very first, Lévi-Strauss lays stress upon this; it is an indispensable source for material, to indicate variants and to locate different types; in short, it is an auxiliary science. In the long run, it only has any meaning, only becomes comprehensible, if it is confronted with the list of possibilities.

Basing anthropology upon history was only possible if one attached to this term a certain number of philosophic presuppositions, which we have seen to be unacceptable. It would be best to put aside the third of the senses which we selected at the beginning; structural anthropology is an autonomous science, which must deal with transformations in societies without assuming a priori that they have a meaning, or a direction; the only evidence it has is that 'all societies change'; it must respect the diversity of its aim: the diversities of societies and of their gradual development.

SYNCHRONY AND DIACHRONY

We now have to ask ourselves how anthropology can interpret history in the first two senses of the word – how does a society change in the course of time? How can one describe and explain these changes? To avoid any ambiguity, let us use the linguistic term and substitute for the term 'history', as used in this narrow sense, the term diachrony. So our problem is the following one: a society, during a given period of time, passes through a series of states; how does structural anthropology propose to study it? Can it analyse these changes and explain them? Firstly let us try and find out any information in the statements of fundamentals. On many occasions Lévi-Strauss affirms, contrary to what people have made him out to say, that there is no antinomy between synchrony and diachrony. In studying gradual development, it should be possible to apply structural analysis: this is stated in *Le Totémisme aujourd'hui* in opposition to Durkheim and, in the *Leçon inaugurale*, in opposition to de Saussure, for whom the diachronic is non-structural as opposed to the synchronic. It should be possible to study in terms of structure the passage from one state to another in any system or society. But how can structural anthropology lead up to this study? What the *Leçon inaugurale* sets out is both promising and vague at the same time: 'The idea of a structural history contains nothing which could shock historians ... It is not contradictory that a history of symbols and signs engenders unforeseeable developments, even though it brings into play a limited number of structural combinations. In a kaleidoscope, each combination of identical elements yields new results.'[17] The text only affirms that the changes are describable in terms of structure, and anthropology, which has made an inventory of possibilities, is better equipped for this analysis. So much for the positive contents of these statements of principle. But there is still an obscurity: in this text, the order of gradual development seems left to chance: is a structural analysis able to explain it? Is it only descriptive? I believe that this text is too vague and it should be corrected by other quotations. 'Structural dialectic is not inconsistent with historical determinism; it calls on it and gives it a new implement.'[18] Here structural analysis seems to be ready to provide explanations, and it is in this sense that most of the texts use it.

What kind of explanations are these? One must not expect conclusive answers, but put the questions in order and proceed to methodological abstractions in order patiently to discover the factors of change. It is in this way that Lévi-Strauss poses the 'theoretical hypothesis' of a society without an exterior, eliminating by thought the existence of any other societies and of a natural environment. In this field of research, the most simple method seems to be the one adopted by the phonologist: that is, to limit oneself to one of the many systems which make up a society (system of relationships, mythology, rituals) and to try and find out whether there is an internal lack of balance which turns it towards this or that state. The analysis is then strictly a structural one. Lévi-Strauss analyses in this way a system of relationships and concludes: 'Either the particular society succumbs to its contradictions, or its transitive and non-cyclic system must be transformed into an intransitive and cyclic system.'[19]

This analysis, based on only one system, is obviously mandatory for those studies bearing only a certain aspect of society. But if one questions the changes which may affect this society as a whole, it soon proves itself insufficient. In fact, any system, taken in isolation, is more characterized by its withstanding change than by its dynamism; the analyses in *La Pensée sauvage* bear witness to this; especially those pages dedicated to the Aranda people, amongst whom the system of relationship is perfectly balanced, and whose mythology develops cyclically, always identical to itself. 'There is a sort of fundamental aversion between history and the system.'[20] Reduced to these means, structural anthropology would be incapable of explaining most of the changes in societies, and many of the criticisms directed at Lévi-Strauss have not considered this aspect of his thought. Now, if one reads the texts very carefully, one realizes that he goes much further in his analysis. 'New elements ought to be brought into the theoretical model, and the interventions of these will explain the diachronic changes, and at the same time will account for the reasons why a social structure is never reduced to a system of relationships.'[21] Lévi-Strauss, in what follows, tries to find explanations for 'diachronic changes' in the relationship which different systems making up a society have amongst each other. In fact, 'all culture can be considered as a unity of symbolic systems, and on the top level can be placed language, matrimonial rules, economic relationships, art, science and religion.'[22] These systems 'express themselves' in the same way in which Marx says law is a 'systematic expression' of civil society.

How can we explain the diachrony by the simple fact of superimposing these systems? Theoretically, one could imagine this mutual expression of systems to be a strict correspondence, a homology: the society being studied, granted its stability at a given moment, could remain indefinitely identical to itself; however, according to Lévi-Strauss, this homology is impossible; by their 'working conditions', these systems remain 'incommensurable', in the sense that no satisfactory interpretation is possible. Each system cannot exactly express the other; there is therefore, first of all, an inadequacy of principle, which is the source of disequilibrium and of the transformations.

The divergence does not stop there: as we pass from one system to another, we find not only those imperfections due to the very nature of the codes, but also to operations: the expression can be varied or even inverted. It is possible 'to characterize different types of society by a law of transformation: this is a formula showing the number, the power, direction and order of the transformations necessary, to cancel the operations and rediscover the relationship of ideal homology.'[23] It is within this internal lack of harmony that one must look for the crux of the change: it is this which prevents any society from remaining stable; Lévi-Strauss analyses it at all levels: those of the myth and social reality, myth and ritual ... The oft-quoted example is that of the 'dialectic' between the system of attitudes and that of terminology. 'The rules governing behaviour between relations, in a certain society, try to resolve contradictions which arise from the terminological system of the rules of alliance. In so far as the first ones have a tendency to make up a system, new contradictions appear, which bring about a reorganization of the terminology, which has repercussions in the attitudes, and so on.'[24]

Inadequacies and operations between the systems, these are the 'new elements' introduced in the theoretical models. These explain why the dynamic properties are linked with the superposition of the systems. But they set the question further away: society is here made into a sort of subject which generates divergencies between the systems, and tries to reabsorb them. What can these 'anthropomorphic expressions' mean?

Before replying to this question, let us rapidly run through the occurrence of 'external factors', raising the theoretical hypothesis of a society with no exterior. 'A society is always placed in space and in time, therefore it is subject to what happens in other societies.'[25] The diachronic study of language makes us see changes due not solely to purely internal factors, nor to extra-linguistic ones, but to the introduction of borrowed traits from neighbouring languages. Such is Jakobson's theory of 'affinities' which Lévi-Strauss applies, for example, to the diffusion of myths in a given area, according to a subtle thought-process. 'The affinity consists not only in the diffusion of certain structural characteristics outside their origin, or of the repulsion which opposes its propagation; the affinity may come from the antithesis, and engender structures which provide the following characteristics ... replies, remedies, excuses or guilt.'[26]

But these 'allogeneous' elements are not the only ones 'which determine the gradual attraction of one society towards another'. It would certainly narrow the field of analysis if one were to limit it here and to neglect the influence of extra-social factors, in the same sense as we speak of extra-linguistic factors. A whole section of *La Pensée sauvage* is devoted to the occurrence of these factors (demographic variations, alterations of natural environment) which introduce unshakeable changes. The theoretical importance of these analyses may seem minor: what are they but the development of evident banalities? To appreciate their just worth, one must see the meaning they have for Lévi-Strauss – they reveal a primary foundation of experience, underlying all societies and perpetually altering. If we define the different systems which go to make up a society as 'denotators' and the reality to which they adapt themselves as 'connotators', even here, static equilibrium is impossible for reasons of principle. 'Even in our civilization, there remains constant a fundamental situation which is a response to the human condition ... There is always inadequacy (between denotation and connotation), which results from the existence of a superabundance of denotations in comparison with the connotation on which it can rest.'[27] It is, Lévi-Strauss tells us, 'the condition of the exercise of symbolic thought' and of the functioning of any and all societies. As in the case of the relationship between symbolic systems, it is an inadequacy of principle which affords the model these dynamic properties.

In accordance with this inquiry, is the 'structural history' talked about in the *Leçon inaugurale*, that is, the diachronic study of a society, is it a clearly defined and organized seance? In actual fact, all we have found are subjects for research: internal factors of disequilibrium, many exterior influences, etc., and some glimpses on the methods of analysing these different factors. Here, as in linguistics, one must always bring into play a very large number of factors. But it still remains to co-ordinate them into a theory which can establish their respective values. What are perhaps to be discovered, and Lévi-Strauss often alludes to them, are 'diachronic structures' which would release the recurrent characteristics of a certain type of society. In short, in the present state of anthropology, and in this it differs from linguistics, this structural history is as yet only a plan, a research programme.

This investigation, at least, helps us to specify the way Lévi-Strauss sees the impact of events upon societies. He has recently been considered in opposition to Merleau-Ponty: he has been called a person of fixed and crystallized systems, against a philosophy of ambiguities and indefinite senses. However, all the works we have read suggest nothing of the sort: balance and clarity are in principle impossible in Lévi-Strauss's conception of a society, since the connotation and denotation are never exactly suitable, and the different systems can never express themselves adequately amongst themselves. The shifting of the connotation upon the denotation, and especially the continual effort of the connotations' readjusting between themselves, carry the societies along in perpetual transformations. The *Leçon inaugurale* briefly sets forth this obscure principle which results from a 'multiplicity of the subconscious systems, each of which affects an aspect or a level of social reality. (These systems) are as if diffracted over temporal dimensions whose breadth gives consistence to synchrony, and in the absence of which it would dissolve into an intangible and tenuous essence, a ghost of reality.'[28]

HISTORY AND SUBJECTIVITY

So far, the articulation of the systems has been taken as a fact: no doubt this simple formal definition is sufficient for an objective study of diachrony. Nevertheless, perhaps it would be possible to go further in our analysis, to try and interpret this fact. In certain texts, as we have already seen, Society is presented as a kind of subject which chooses and breeds divergencies, and seeks remedies for its inadequacies. Is this just a way of speaking? It is rather a case of one of Lévi-Strauss's interpretations of Society which is brilliantly developed in the *Préface à Mauss*. 'All these systems are trying to express certain aspects of physical and social reality; and even more the relationships which these two kinds of reality maintain with each other and which symbolic systems themselves maintain.'[29]

In this text, Lévi-Strauss defines the articulations of these systems between each other: they are not of the same type.

Certain systems are in keeping with expression and law 'expresses social relationships'; others are a kind of reflection: the second-degree expression of the connection between the expresser and object expressed, in the sense of a mythology which defines the relationships between nature ('object expressed') and culture ('expresser').

Here Lévi-Strauss seems to grant society a kind of objective reflection which does not coincide with the individual's conscience, for it only ever attains a dialectical mean between all these systems. Society is seen as a subject reacting to exterior influences, and correcting its own failings. We could see here a kind of psychoanalytic model of society. In opposition, other texts, earlier or later chronologically, no longer interpret society as a subject but as a machine. To this end *La Pensée sauvage* is very explicit. 'Let us imagine an initial moment (this is a completely theoretical notion) where all the systems are exactly adjusted, this whole will react to all changes affecting first of all one of its parts like a feed-back.'[30] These two interpretations are not in contradiction with the initial definitions. But how can they coexist in the work of one author? If we could answer this question, perhaps we should be able to reveal those philosophic preferences which would clarify what Lévi-Strauss means by history.

Lévi-Strauss's main idea, both in his reflections on history and elsewhere, is the elimination of illusions of subjectivity. 'The being must be understood in relationship to itself and not to me.'[31] But the being does not reveal itself completely and straight away; the phenomena can be approached on different levels before reading 'the master sense, doubtless obscure, but of which each of the others is the partial or deformed transposition'.[31] This theory of levels of sense is reaffirmed in the last chapter of *La Pensée sauvage*; in the light of it, one can understand why the texts hesitate between different interpretations of society. No one doubts that the mechanical interpretations of *La Pensée sauvage* represent the level where the interpretation of Society would coincide with 'its very being'. But as our knowledge is not extensive enough to finish this 'reduction', the psychoanalytical 'interpretation' represents a strategic level which is completely appropriate to anthropology: since with it one can pursue an objective analysis of the systems of signs and their articulations. Most of Lévi-Strauss's texts are at this level.

But if we go lower down, we cannot fail to be more or less victims of the illusions of subjectivity: that is to say, to be bound to the conscious interpretations of individuals, biased and incomplete, because of their belonging to a certain society or a certain social class. Here we come across the problem of history again; at whatever level we analyse the gradual development, it surprises us by the multiplicity of changes which lie within. In the confrontation of Society with its exterior, in the articulation of the different systems, in the multiplicity of factors which come into play, something always happens so that complete knowledge is beyond human power. Here, where choice is a necessity if we are to attain a true perspective, the dangers of subjectivity reappear. In a sense, anthropology is saved, since it works back from the many facts to their possible conditions; it seeks for the master sense beyond, to transpositions. But what about structural history? Even at this level, the necessity for choice is imperative, and if as we have seen, this theory is not perfected, it is because Lévi-Strauss has not defined his criteria of the selection which one must apply to it – doubtless he would say that diachronic studies in anthropology select the 'truest' aspects, 'preserve a meaning which is more valid than that which one has the wisdom to reject'.

That is why the *Leçon inaugurale* opposes structural history to the history of historians. This is set forth by a perspective similar to the actor's situation in his conscious apprehension of facts; the ideology is opposed to the 'truth', the 'for me' to 'the person in relationship to himself'. Lévi-Strauss seems here to play upon the slightly facile opposition between the person and appearances. In fact, his arguments are more subtle; in *La Pensée sauvage* especially, he resorts to the *et alia* argument: the one-sidedness of a perspective can always be refuted by presenting another equally possible perspective. In this work as in *Tristes Tropiques*, such is the dialectic function, in the Aristotelian sense of the word, of the Anti-histories, sequences of history rewritten in a way which differs from that which we are accustomed to. Following this argument, his 'philosophy of history' is no longer valid, it is not only intrinsic but also 'ideological'.[32]

Nevertheless, is it not dangerous to play in this way with the different interpretations? Lévi-Strauss's attitude towards history has a different motivation. Firstly it puts forth the attitude of an anthropologist who wishes to safeguard his subject matter. The difference between the civilizations, his method: the analysis of the essential differences as opposed to the abusive simplifications of a certain 'philosophy of history'. It is also a scientific man's attitude, that of one who wishes to sacrifice nothing to choice and to the onesidedness of a society or an ideology.

Lévi-Strauss's interpretation of what anthropology is all about seems thus tied to the demands of this subject. What is the meaning of this connection? Can we say that Lévi-Strauss's views on society 'reflect' this society objectively? Are they the significant system of the highest degree, which tries to explain all meaningful reality?

If this is the case, Lévi-Strauss's philosophy will be homogeneous with its objective, it will speak the same language as him, it will show him these strategic gaps, these constant changes which appear in the subject matter of anthropology. It will be like the psychoanalyst who must have in his language the means of communicating with the patient. Are the fluctuations which we have discovered in Lévi-Strauss's interpretation of this kind? The reply is not an easy one. In so far as Lévi-Strauss does not in his theory go over the problems posed by his very objective, and especially when he has recourse to 'psychoanalytical models' which bring to light in a privileged way the methodological importance of the inadequacy and structural changes, the fluctuations and differences of interpretation have an importance which is fundamentally positive.

But this free interplay of difference, which goes to make up research, is disturbed by the presence of a theoretical horizon bound to a system of personal preference, and which arbitrarily determines the 'leaving out', the psycho-chemical objectivity as absolute system on which all the other systems fall back.

The necessity for objectivity of description tends then towards the strategy used by western positivism: by wanting to 'loop the loop' and base all the differences on the identity of Nature in itself, Lévi-Strauss endangers the depth and richness of his analyses, whose essential theme is, paradoxically, inadequacy.

THE MYTHICAL STRUCTURE OF
THE ANCIENT SCANDINAVIANS:
SOME THOUGHTS ON READING DUMÉZIL*

Einar Haugen

It is gradually being recognized that in Professor Georges Dumézil of the Collège de France we have, in the words of C. Scott Littleton, 'one of the most remarkable figures to appear in the field of comparative Indo-European mythology since the turn of the century'.[1] Writers of standard works in the subfield of Scandinavian and Germanic mythology have increasingly been won over to the strikingly original points of view presented by Dumézil in his numerous publications. Much of the difference between Jan de Vries's first (1935–7) and second (1956–7) edition of his *Altgermanische Religionsgeschichte* is a result of his having profited from Dumézil's work in the intervening years. The survey of *Die altgermanische Religion* by Werner Betz (1957) acknowledges fully the importance of Dumézil's studies. Cautious acceptance of Dumézil's general framework is also characteristic of two recent English surveys of Scandinavian and Germanic myths, the anthropologically oriented *Gods and Myths of Northern Europe* by H. R. Ellis Davidson (1964) and the philologically oriented *Myth and Religion of the North* by E. O. G. Turville-Petre (1964). Only an English version of his scientific contributions is now lacking to give Dumézil's name its proper position among students of myth and folklore in the English-speaking world. This would make it easier also to assess the merits of his system and of the criticisms which have been raised against it.[2]

To a linguist like the present writer, whose connection with mythology is only that he has from time to time taught a course in Scandinavian mythology,[3] it is something of a revelation to come across the work of this brilliant contemporary. It is at once evident that he has applied to the myths the comparative method developed by linguists of the nineteenth century, which established once and for all the basic, historical identity of the Indo-European language family. While attempts were made a century ago to apply this method to Indo-European myths, Dumézil has

* Reprinted from *To Honour Roman Jakobson* (Mouton, The Hague, 1956).

introduced certain refinements which make his work original and pro-vocative. His writings have restored to Scandinavian and other Indo-European mythologies their backward perspective, revealing them as indigenous products with roots going back into the parent society of the Indo-Europeans. One is not surprised to learn that he is a pupil of Antoine Meillet, and one's respect is further confirmed on learning of his extensive contributions to the linguistic exploration of the languages of the Caucasus.[4]

A far from exhaustive reading of Dumézil's contributions to mytho-graphy has stimulated certain thoughts in this writer about the structure of Scandinavian myth, which he would like to present for the considera-tion of scholars in the field. He is particularly concerned with Dumézil's claim to have made a structural analysis of mythology, and his insistent argumentation against what he calls the evolutionary approach which his own is supposed to supersede. Dumézil argues repeatedly against 'historicism', as if this were incompatible with structuralism. While the same battle has raged in linguistics over the past generation, it now appears to have been reasonably solved. Another problem is whether Dumézil has in fact found the correct structure of the daughter mytho-logies. Here it is tempting to apply some of the principles developed in structural linguistics, in so far as the material permits. One finds oneself unconsciously sorting out the ideas of the ancient Scandinavians along lines that are suggested by the treatment of linguistic categories, for example in the phonological work of the Prague school, as exemplified by Roman Jakobson and his followers. There is room here for such con-cepts as minimal oppositions, distinctive features, and neutralization of contrasts.[5]

Without going into the subject too deeply, the writer would like to offer a few suggestions along these lines. His conclusions turn out to coincide with and confirm some of the ideas advanced by Claude Lévi-Strauss in his studies of mythical structure.[6]

(2) Dumézil's comparative reconstruction of Indo-European mythology is based on his doctrine of a tripartite ideology, which he finds repeated in a number of the mythologies preserved in the Indo-European daughter languages. Basing himself primarily on Indic and Iranian mythology, he finds a prevalent structure embodying three functions, with one or more gods specialized to perform each of these. He numbers the functions first,

second, and third, and sums them up in the catchwords of SOVEREIGNTY, FORCE and FECUNDITY. The full import of these terms does not become clear without extensive reading of his text. For Scandinavian myth the three functions are primarily associated with the gods Óðinn, Thor and Frey, respectively. The comparable Indic gods are Varuna, Indra and the twin Nasatyas. Each god or group of gods performs a function which is useful to society and its preservation and is complementary to the other functions. But the several functions are of special interest to each one of the three classes into which Dumézil finds that most Indo-European peoples are divided. In India these are the *brahmaṇa* or priestly class, the *kṣatriya* or warrior class, and the *vaiśya* or farming class. In Scandinavia this is reflected in the division into kings, earls, and farmers, for example in the poem *Rígsthula* of the Elder Edda. To anyone who would contend that these functions and social classes are not peculiar to the Indo-Europeans, Dumézil replies that he has investigated a wide selection of class structures and mythologies among other peoples without finding anything precisely comparable. The similarities between the daughter mythologies are hence too great to be due to chance and too different to be due to borrowing.

Dumézil's arguments in favour of this thesis are often coupled with vigorous attacks on the 'evolutionary' school, as he calls it, which dominated the scene up to his appearance. The work of many excellent scholars has gone into a painstaking effort to show that Scandinavian mythology as presented in the writings of Snorri Sturluson (1178–1241) is a mosaic of native and borrowed elements, many of them not even pagan in origin. The culmination of this view is represented by the work of Eugen Mogk, who went so far as to ascribe to Snorri a 'mythological school' in which myths were invented out of whole cloth on the basis of a small amount of traditional lore. Mogk is therefore Dumézil's particular *bête noire*, against whom he polemicizes with Gallic gusto. Mogk and others used the information available from older sources, including archaeology, place-names, and outside observers, to build up a picture of gradual evolution in Germanic and Scandinavian mythology. Gods of agriculture like Frey were thought of as representing an older society, on which were superposed such deities as Thor and Óðinn by a gradual change in social structure and the spread of cults from one part of the Germanic area to the rest.

The peculiar thing about Dumézil's position here, and a point on which it is difficult to follow his reasoning, is that he seems to think that his '*thèse structuraliste*' excludes the possibility of historical development. Yet the very essence of the comparative method which he applies to the functions of the Indo-European gods is that it aims at a reconstruction of an earlier structure from which later structures may be derived by historical change. When we compare Latin *pater* and Sanskrit *pitā* with English *father*, it is for the purpose of constructing an Indo-European ancestor from which it will be possible to derive these forms by a set of historical formulas known as sound laws. The indispensable condition is that there be a correspondence of phonological and grammatical form and a sufficient similarity of meaning to identify the words involved. The parallel requirement for the gods would be that their names correspond linguistically and their functions with a degree of approximation comparable to that of word meanings. This requirement is not fulfilled by Dumézil's material. With one possible exception, to which we shall return, not one of the Germanic gods has a linguistically comparable name and also a similar function. His comparisons refer to the functions alone: it is as if the mythology consisted wholly of slots ('functions') which could be filled by a variety of gods. However similar Indra and Thor may be in function, their identity as gods is dependent on their having the same name. Two successive village priests do not become identical even though they may perform precisely the same function.

The difference between Dumézil and many of his predecessors lies in his concentration on the functions, the slots in the structure, while they have concentrated on the gods themselves, who filled the slots.[7] It is perhaps his greatest contribution that he has separated the gods from their functions and shown that the latter can be analysed independently of the former. Even in Dumézil's thinking there is room for an historical change in the functions; as he puts it in discussing the Germanic gods, 'les frontières des fonctions y sont simplement, parfois, un peu déplacées'.[8] But what is equally striking is that the gods themselves have not only been 'un peu déplacées', they have quite simply been replaced by others. This is what the evolutionists had been saying all along, and there is no apparent way of denying their findings or to maintain that their efforts 'n'ont pas réussi, ne pouvaient pas réussir'.[9] So long as the names of the trinities in each of the daughter languages are demonstrably different, there is room for a study of the changes that led to the gradual displacement of one god by another. Anyone who should undertake to reconcile the Dumézil structure with the findings of the historians would probably discover that some parts of each might have to be discarded. But each has its place, just as structural-descriptive linguistics can be shown to be inseparable in fact from historical-comparative linguistics. This has been made explicit in recent linguistic work, for example, by Dumézil's countryman André Martinet, and others.[10]

Even the one god who has appeared to constitute an exception to the discontinuity from Indo-European times, Germanic *Tiwaz* (ON *Týr*, OE *Tīw*, OHG *Ziu*), cannot be reliably connected with the Indic sky god Dyāus. As De Vries admits, 'die Rechnung stimmt nicht genau', since the form *Tiwas* from earlier *Teiwas* corresponds to IE *deiw*, from which we also have Latin *deus* (plural *dii*) and a host of other words meaning simply 'god'.[11] *Dyāus* (and Greek *Zeus*, Latin *Juppiter*) come from *djēw*, the ancestor also of Latin *dies*. That the two roots may have a common IE ancestor *dejew* 'shining' is only the same as can be said about a number of the gods' names: that they are IE words, which at some point in their development were applied as descriptive terms to gods and later came to be taken as their names.

(3) We turn now to the second question suggested by Dumézil's insights, that of the structure itself. Any tripartite structure or trinity raises the question of whether its members are in fact equal, or whether perhaps they are not actually grouped 2–1. The presence of three members in a classification makes one ask by what criteria (in linguistics: distinctive features) they are distinguished. It is more likely that the three arise by the application of two criteria successively than simultaneously, or in other words, that they are related as a tree with two successive branchings (A) rather than as a tree with three simultaneous ones (B):

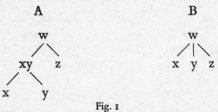

Fig. 1

In order to determine which of these alternatives applies, we ask for minimal contrasts and try to determine the distinctive feature that establishes each one.

It is not difficult to see that Dumézil's trinity is like A above rather than B. If w represents the class of gods (*goð*), x is Óðinn, y is Thor, and z is

Frey. It is easy to show that xy are closer to one another than either is to z. Óðinn is represented as Thor's father, and they belong to a subgrouping of the gods called *æsir* (**ansuz*). Frey is said to be unrelated to the other two and to belong to another subgrouping called *vanir* (**waniz*). If we ask for the distinctive feature, we find that the *vanir* are characterized (as Dumézil quite accurately has pointed out) by fecundity, of man, beast, and soil. The *æsir* are not similarly delimited; they have no distinctive feature in common, and in some situations they even share in the concern about fecundity. We may therefore describe the *vanir* as the marked member of this opposition. The myths account for this situation quite explicitly by telling the story of how the *vanir* became a part of the society of gods. After an inconclusive war they were given as hostages to the *æsir* and accepted as full members of their company (oddly enough, we never hear of any other *vanir* than the ones who were given as hostages). They had curious customs which were not common among the *æsir*, such as incestual marriage: Frey and his sister Freya were the children of a union between Njǫrð and an unnamed sister. Mythographers have suspected that the sister was the lost goddess Nerthus, whose name is identical with Njǫrð's and who is reported to us by Tacitus. Frey is accused in the poem *Lokasenna* of the Elder Edda of having slept with his sister. These three (or four) divinities constitute the entire *vanir* group, unless we include also their servants Skirnir, Byggvir, and Beyla.

Dumézil is not unaware of this primacy of the division of the gods; he speaks at one point of 'la coupure initiale qui sépare les représentants des deux premières fonctions et ceux de la troisième' and even traces it back to IE times.[12] There can certainly be no objection to interpreting this structural contrast historically: the *vanir* are an earlier group of gods, some of whose functions were usurped by the *æsir*. The truce between them is a mythical way of describing that higher unity into which they have entered, in which the opposition is neutralized. The symbol of the neutralization itself is the man Kvasir, who came into being from the combined spittle of the *æsir* and *vanir*, and who is therefore neither one nor the other, but something of both. Symbolically, he became the chief ingredient in the mead of poetry. We are reminded of a word of Lévi-Strauss: 'Mythical thought always works from the awareness of oppositions towards their progressive mediation.'[13] It is a further aspect of this that the *vanir*, individually, are often referred to as *æsir*, while the reverse is never true. This means, in effect, that the marked member of the opposition is submerged in the higher unity of the unmarked whenever the opposition is not contextually important. The structure can be diagrammed as in Fig. 2, with the distinctive feature on the side of the marked member, and the neutralization between the members of the contrast.

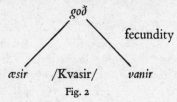

Fig. 2

The opposition of Thor to Óðinn is on quite a different level, as the diagram above suggests. There is abundant material to show that there was an opposition between them; although they were both *æsir*, they were rivals for power and position. In the mythology of the Eddas Óðinn was the patriarchal ruler of the gods: 'They all serve him as children do their fathers.'[14] But the evidence of outside observers, placenames, and the weekday names is sufficient to show that in many times and places Thor was supreme: in eleventh century Uppsala he was the central one of three figures, with Óðinn and Frey on either side. This is confirmed most vividly in the Elder Edda, where a whole poem is devoted to a taunting match of the two gods, the *Hárbarðsljóð*. The taunts and boasts reveal clearly the opposing natures of the two gods: Óðinn prides himself on skill in the magic arts, which he uses in devious ways; Thor is the straightforward battler, whose sole activity is to defend the gods against the ever-threatening giants. Óðinn is also a god of war, but he is the general, the strategist, who never fights himself. He has many faculties, including the gift of poetry, and insight into the future. Clearly, Thor is the marked member of the opposition: he is defined by the feature of force, applied to the defence of gods and men, not against each other, but against the nature around them. But on a higher level the opposition is neutralized, Óðinn and Thor becoming father and son, who stand together as the leading lights of the *æsir* kin. Our diagram of this structure will look as follows:

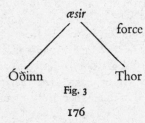

Fig. 3

Just as the term *æsir* can double as a word for 'god', so Óðinn, the un-marked member, is the father of all the *æsir* and their chief representative.

Is there any neutralization between Óðinn and Thor, other than the kinship that is posited for them? If we look at the profusion of other deities that inhabit the Nordic pantheon, we will soon find that they are either mere names of divine qualities, usually attached to Óðinn and his wife Frigg, or else emanations of Óðinn. Thor has only a small aura around him: his mother Jǫrð ('Earth'), his wife Sif ('Kin'), and his sons Magni ('Strength') and Móði ('Courage'). Contrary to Dumézil I am inclined to place Týr alongside Thor, rather than as a companion of Óðinn corresponding to Mitra, the Indic god of justice. Týr's partici-pation in the binding of Fenrir is not an act of justice; it is part of a trick played on Fenrir by the gods, an episode in their war against the giants, and therefore part of Thor's sphere of activity. Týr accompanies Thor to the giant Hýmir; in *Lokasenna* Loki taunts both him and Thor with having seduced their wives; and his role as a god of war is confirmed by the use of his name to replace that of Mars in the weekday names. On Óðinn's side stand Bragi, god of poetry, Baldr, Óðinn's much-mourned son, Forseti, Baldr's son, Hǫðr, Baldr's brother and killer, Vili and Vé, Óðinn's shadowy brothers, Viðarr and Váli, his equally shadowy sons, his companions Hønir and Lóðurr, and of course his wife Frigg with her large entourage of poetically conceived goddesses. The rest of the women in the pantheon, the Norns and the Valkyries, are even more directly attached to Óðinn.

Two enigmatic gods are left, without clear attachment to any of the preceding groupings: Ull and Heimdall. Place-names testify to a worship of Ull that associates him with the fertility gods. His traits in the literary tradition are ambiguous: archer, skier, patron of single combat, son of Sif (and possibly Thor). In Saxo's euhemerized story he takes Óðinn's place for a time. His name means 'glory', which could be applied to all the chief gods. The opposition is clearly neutralized in his case: he is just a god; historically this would mean a confirmation of De Vries's hypo-thesis that he belongs to an earlier stratum of gods than the rest, that he may even have been the original sky god.[15] Heimdall is wise like Óðinn, white like Baldr, guards the gods like Thor, and (in the *Thrymskviða*) looks into the future 'like the other Vanir'. Like Óðinn he is associated with the world tree Yggdrasill, like Thor he fights giants (in his case Loki: they kill each other in the end) and like the *vanir* he is specially associated with procreation. He is himself born of nine mothers and according to the poem *Rígsthula* he is the procreator of the social classes of men. He is like Freya in being characterized by gold and in having a name ending in -*dall* 'bright' (she is called Mardǫll). De Vries wants to attribute him to the second function, but Dumézil recognizes in him a parallel to Janus, associated with the beginnings and ends of things. Although, like Ull, he is reckoned among the *æsir*, his wide-ranging traits and the meaning of 'world-bright' (which may be the correct interpretation of his name) place him rather in an ambiguous and therefore earlier, undifferentiated stratum.

(4) The gods are far from being the only inhabitants of the invisible world. In clear and unquestioned opposition to them stand the giants, as we shall here traditionally translate the term *jǫtnar* (virtually synonymous with *risar*, *pursar*, and *troll*). The central concern of Norse mythology is the unceasing combat of these opposing hosts, from the day of creation when the first gods carved up the first giant, Ymir, and made the earth from his body, to the end of the world, when gods and giants mutually annihilate one another. The surprising fact about this opposition is that it is not as absolute as one would suppose in looking at it from a modern point of view. As Turville-Petre points out, 'the differences between gods and giants were not fundamental', though we should not from this draw his conclusion, that therefore 'the dualist system, according to which gods were good and giants were bad, developed late in Norse heathendom'.[16] The opposition must have existed for a long time, for the very terms are meaningless unless they reflect a basic philosophical dichotomy: the gods are the forces on our side, the giants are the forces that are against us. In the myths the giants are similar in constitution and powers to the gods, they form a foil for them and give their lives significance. If the battle were not between evenly matched contenders, it would not have been so absorbingly interesting.

For one thing, these two races are like neighbouring tribes in being sexually compatible (a biologist's definition of membership in the same species). They have a common ancestry: Óðinn himself is a son of the giantess Bestla. Thor has a son by the giantess Jarnsaxa, while Njǫrð and Frey are both married to giantesses; Frey's wife Gerð is even described as the most beautiful woman in the world. The giants on their side are always on the look-out for goddesses, and almost succeed in capturing Freya and Iðunn. Skaði aspires to marry Baldr, but gets ancient Njǫrð instead. There are numerous social calls, during which Norse courtesy imposes a cessation of hostilities: for example, Thor's visits to Jǫtunheim, his fishing trip with the giant Hýmir, and Ægir's banquet for the gods. The giants also serve the gods as workmen: one of them builds Ásgarð and the closely related dwarfs produce many of the gods' finest treasures.

In most of these neutralizations of the prevailing opposition, Loki, the arch-mediator and central figure of Norse mythology, is involved. Snorri lists him as one of the *æsir*, but hastens to add that he was 'the mischief-monger of the *æsir* and the father of falsehoods and the blemish of all gods and men'.[17] He is a giant by ancestry, but a god by adoption, having blended blood with Óðinn in a ceremony that in Norse tradition meant an undying pact of brotherhood. He brings subversion right into the camp of the gods and makes their lives a good deal more dramatic than they like. Loki is in many ways a negative replica of Óðinn, his foster-brother, just as he is a companion of the giant-like Thor, and sexually more than a match for the *vanir*. He caricatures and subverts all the divine functions, alternately hindering and helping the gods in their beneficent purposes. He is the necessary antagonist in the divine drama.

The solidarity of gods and giants is expressed in the word *vættir* 'creatures', which may be applied to both. We may express this relationship in the diagram shown in Figure 4.

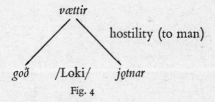

Fig. 4

In *Lokasenna* Thor calls Loki *rǫg vættr* (unmanly creature) four times in bidding him hold his peace after having taunted the gods. In another poem of the Elder Edda, *Oddrúnargrátr*, Oddrún calls on the *hollar vættir, Frigg ok Freyia ok fleiri goð* (friendly creatures, Frigg and Freya and the other gods) to help her friend in childbirth. Within this solidarity the giants are the marked member, being characterized by hostility to man. Loki, together with the dwarfs, who are a race of diminutive giants (*sit venia verbo*), neutralize the opposition by being both friendly (when they have to be) and hostile (when they can). Loki is thus the mediator between gods and giants. The inclusion of Loki among the gods repeats a pattern we have seen before, whereby the unmarked member of an opposition (here 'goð') can on occasion be extended to both members. Characters like Skaði, Gerð, Ægir and others acquire a status among the gods by being allied in one way or other with them. There is one further group of supernatural creatures known as elves (*alfar*). Snorri tells us that there are both light and dark elves, i.e. good and bad. As De Vries and Holtsmark have noted, the dark and light elves are not known from any other source; in general the elves were friendly creatures, honoured by sacrifices and closely allied to the gods.[18] They had their own world known as *Alfheimr*, where Frey also lives; in the *Lokasenna* Ægir's guests are said to include both *æsir* and *alfar*. We may quite simply regard them as diminutive gods, just as the dwarfs are diminutive giants.

While the effects of the battle between gods and giants were crucial in the life of men, the battle itself and its combatants were not usually visible. The world in which the struggle was won or lost was a spiritual one, populated by the spirits or *vættir*, who thus in this respect were significantly different from the living men and women of the natural world. As in English, the term *menn* 'men' could be applied to both men and women, but in addition it was often applied to include the supernatural spirits. In the story of Loki and the giant Geirrøðr, Loki was caught in the shape of a bird. But when the giant examined him and 'saw his eyes, he suspected that he was a *maðr* (man)', i.e. human. Yet Loki was, as we have seen, a spirit.[19] When the context demands that human beings be distinguished from non-human, the adjective *mennskr* is added to the word *maðr*. In *Grímnismál* 31 the third root of Yggdrasill reaches down to *mennskir menn*, the others to Hel and the frost giants. In *Sigrdrífumál* 18 the runes are said to be found among the *æsir*, the *alfar*, the *vanir*, and among *mennskir menn*. In *Egils Saga*, chapter 25, it is said that 'men have come here, if one can call them men, who are more like *þursar* (giants) in size and appearance than like *mennskir menn*'.[20] These passages show that the term *menn* could apply either to the visible or the invisible creatures of the universe, including both the (*mennskir*) *menn* and the *vættir*. This suggests that the *vættir* were the marked members of the opposition, characterized by invisibility.

If we look for a neutralization between the visible and the invisible, we can find it primarily in the category of the legendary heroes. These were part god and part man, men like Sigurðr, Helgi, Starkaðr, Haddingr. They were kings and chieftains, descended in many cases from Óðinn, but the sons of earthly women. They lived in a world where the opposition of visible and invisible was not relevant, the mythical past. In this world dragons, dwarfs, talking birds, and werewolves were part of everyday experience. At the same time many of the heroes can be identified with real-world people, like Gunnar with Gundiharius, king of the Burgundians, and his sister Guðrún, daughter of Giúki or Gibicha. As Turville-Petre has pointed out concerning Sigurð, 'he has as much to do with the mythical as he has to do with our world.'[21] Even kings were in this position, for (as Turville-Petre puts it) 'they were commonly thought to form a bridge between the worlds of gods and of men.'[22] The hero was the essence of the potency implied in the word *man* itself, borrowing from the visible as well as the invisible world. We may see the relation of these concepts in Figure 5.

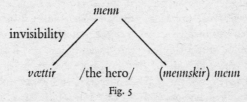

Fig. 5

The world of men was in opposition to the world of animals, and in this case men appear to constitute the marked member. There is no single word that marked off all non-human animals in Old Norse: the word *dýr* did not usually include birds or reptiles, as we see from Snorri's expression in the preface to his Edda: *dýrin ok fuglarnir* 'the animals and the birds'. The word *kvikvendi* 'living things' was used in the same way, but also more broadly: the earth, says Snorri, 'bore all *kvikvendi* and received everything that died'. In the poem *Reginsmál* of the Elder Edda it is said of the serpentine monster Fafnir that 'he had a helm of terror which all *kvikvendi* feared'.[23] Here it is clear that men and animals, gods and giants are all included in the term. The instance of Fafnir, who was originally a human being, before he began brooding over the gold in the shape of a dragon (*í orms líki*), shows how the opposition of man and animal could be neutralized. The *berserkir* or *ulfheðnir* were men who could take on the shape of bears and wolves as readily as other men could change their garments. The birds who warned Sigurð of Regin's evil intent represent another instance of neutralization: just as men can assume the shape of animals, so animals can assume man's prerogative of speech. In the world of myth there is a truly Hegelian synthesis of opposites, as we see in Figure 6.

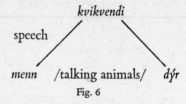

Fig. 6

The opposition of the quick and the dead was clear enough to the Norsemen, as we see from the passage about the earth quoted from Snorri in the previous paragraph. In trying to account for the pagan thinking of his ancestors, Snorri attributes a natural religion to their spiritually unenlightened minds: 'They wondered how it might be that the earth and the animals and the birds had the same nature in some respects and yet were unlike in others.'[24] The capacity of an apparently dead nature to produce life was a subject matter of their religious thinking: 'They understood that the earth was quick and had life in some way.'[25] The story of creation, as told in both Eddas, involved the emergence of the first man, the giant Ymir, by a spontaneous union of heat and cold in the primeval chaos. If we take immobility to be the distinctive feature of death, this becomes irrelevant on the level of the whole universe. Life and death are neutralized in the figure of the world tree Yggdrasill, which is for ever both living and dying, sustained by the gods and gnawed at by the giants. According to Snorri, its limbs 'extend throughout the whole universe (*um heim allan*)'.[26] Although not strictly a *kvikvendi*, it mysteriously interpenetrates the nine worlds of the universe, and when it trembles, the end of the world is near. It symbolizes the eternal unity of the living and the dead (see Figure 7).[27]

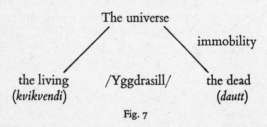

Fig. 7

Without wishing to impose a particular scheme of analysis on the mythical thinking of the Norsemen, we have here tried to put the gods into relation with each other and with the universe in which they lived.

We have seen that each contrast has its own distinctive feature, that each contrast can be neutralized where the distinctive feature is irrelevant, and that this irrelevance leads to a higher level on which another feature is relevant. At no point is a tripartite division necessary, although any succession of dichotomies can of course be so interpreted. In the following diagram the contrasts are summed up in a tree, which is at the same time a definition of the entities contained within it:

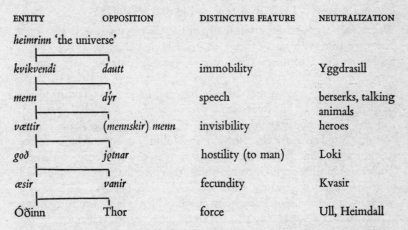

ENTITY	OPPOSITION	DISTINCTIVE FEATURE	NEUTRALIZATION
heimrinn 'the universe'			
kvikvendi	*dautt*	immobility	Yggdrasill
menn	*dýr*	speech	berserks, talking animals
vættir	*(mennskir) menn*	invisibility	heroes
goð	*jǫtnar*	hostility (to man)	Loki
æsir	*vanir*	fecundity	Kvasir
Óðinn	Thor	force	Ull, Heimdall

From this structure it would not be difficult to derive the entire Weltanschauung of the pagan Norsemen.

ON RUSSIAN FAIRY TALES*

Roman Jakobson

1. THEIR LIFE – THEIR STUDY

'When *Juan* went his progress, many of the Commons as well as Gentry presented him with fine Presents: A good honest Bask-shoemaker, who made shoes of Bask for a kopek a pair, consults with his wife what to present his Majesty; says she, a pair of fine *Lopkyes*,[1] or shoes of Bask; that is no rarity (quoth he); but we have an huge great Turnip in the Garden, we'll give him that, and a pair of *Lopkyes* also. Thus they did; and the Emperour took the present so kindly, that he made all his Nobility buy *Lopkyes* of the fellow at five shillings a pair, and he wore one pair himself. This put the man in stock, whereby he began to drive a Trade, and in time grew so considerable, that he left a great estate behind him. His family are now Gentlemen, and call'd *Lopotsky's*. There is a tree standing near his *quondam* house, upon which it is a custom to throw all their old *Lopkyes* as they pass by, in memory of this Gallant.

A Gentleman seeing him so well paid for his Turnep, made account by the rule of proportion to get a greater Reward for a brave Horse; but the Emperour suspecting his design, gave him nothing but the great Turnep, for which he was both abash'd and laugh'd at.'

This story about Ivan the Terrible is among some ten Russian folk tales recorded by an Oxford doctor of medicine, Samuel Collins (1619–1670). In the 'sixties he lived in Moscow as physician to the Tsar Aleksej Mixajlovič, father of Peter the Great, and brought back to England a sable coat, presented to him by the Russian sovereign, and some curious data on the Muscovite empire. Shortly after Collins's death his notes were published under the title *The Present State of Russia* (London, 1671). The tales mentioned above are entered in this booklet.

The classic collection of Russian folk tales was gathered by the outstanding ethnographer Afanas'ev, who first brought it out, in serial form, between 1855 and 1864. Almost two hundred years separate this

* Reprinted from *Selected Writings* (Mouton, The Hague, 1967), vol. IV.

edition from the modest debut of Samuel Collins. It is worthy of remembrance that Russian folk tales were first recorded and first published, not in their homeland and not in their mother tongue, but in England, in English translation. Similarly, Russian secular folk songs were first recorded under the initiative of an Oxford graduate, Richard James, who had been in Moscow as chaplain to an English diplomatic mission and returned to Oxford in 1620 with these invaluable texts. Not in Russia, but in England, there appeared at the end of the same century a first and brilliant attempt at a grammar of spoken Russian from the pen of H. W. Ludolf.

Such beginnings of an active attention to oral Russian speech and poetry are, of course, characteristic of the territorial and scientific breadth of British interests in the seventeenth century. On the other hand, there arises the not unimportant question as to why, in the land of its birth, the Russian spoken language and oral tradition, and in particular the Russian folk tale, remained so long unrecorded in writing. Here we are confronted with one of the most peculiar features of Russian cultural life, which sharply distinguishes it from that of the occidental world. For many centuries Russian written literature was almost entirely subordinated to the Church: with all its wealth and high artistry, the Old Russian literary heritage is almost wholly concerned with the lives of saints and pious men, with devotional legends, prayers, sermons, ecclesiastical discourses, and chronicles in a monastic vein. The Old Russian laity, however, possessed a copious, original, manifold, and highly artistic fiction, but the only medium for its diffusion was oral transmission. The idea of using the written word for secular poetry was thoroughly alien to Russian tradition, and the expressive means of this poetry were inseparable from its oral execution and transmission.

Deviations from this dichotomous principle in the history of Old Russian literary art (ecclesiastical writings – secular oral poetry) are relatively rare. Thus, under the influence of hagiography and apocrypha, there slowly emerged new offshoots of folklore – oral legends and spiritual songs. On the other hand, in the oldest epoch of Russian history, before the Tatar invasion of the thirteenth century, secular elements had infiltrated from the oral tradition into the written literature, and some precious fragments of ancient written epos intimately linked with oral poetry fortunately survived in the Russian manuscript heritage. Later, echoes of this heroic epopee appeared in connection with the centuries-long struggle against the Tatar yoke. But on the whole the knights' tales are drowned in the tens of thousands of old Russian religious texts, and even in the few exceptions the ecclesiastic mould obtrudes more and more.

In general, the laymen – from the courtiers and boyars down to the lowest ranks – continued to seek amusement and satisfaction for their aesthetic cravings, above all, in the oral tradition and in oral creation. Therefore it would be erroneous to interpret this tradition and creativeness as a specific property of the lower classes. The oral literature of Russia, in the era before Peter, was at the service of all the layers of the social hierarchy, and this multiform, inter-class, national character of Old Russian folklore left its indelible stamp. In the Old Russian milieu the difference between the written and the oral literature was a matter of function and not at all of social allocation.

The manifold functions of secular fiction were performed by folklore, and the language of these works was close to the usual colloquial Russian. Written literature was reserved for ecclesiastical tasks and used Church Slavonic, a somewhat renovated and Russified version of the language in which, at the dawn of Slavic Christianity, the church books were written in Great Moravia and Bulgaria.

Unprecedented social upheavals, with shifts and revaluations of traditional values – such are the characteristic marks of the seventeenth century in Russia. The boundaries between the ecclesiastical and the secular, between letters and folklore, between the written and the spoken language, begin to be effaced. The traditional disunion is replaced by a fertile interpenetration. A laicization of the written literature begins; for the first time in the history of Muscovy written attempts at secular fiction are made. And as the only native tradition upon which these attempts could lean was the oral one, there appears in Russian literature of the seventeenth century a vigorous influence of folklore. In its turn, the book – especially the translated book – had a much stronger effect than before on oral poetry. When Russian literature ceased to segregate itself from secular elements, translations of foreign fiction naturally became frequent. Then, in line with old habits, the oral tale, susceptible to profane elements, easily assimilated this new material. Russian literature of the seventeenth century is particularly rich in works standing on the border line between written and oral tradition. The capricious fusion of both these elements created such peculiar, inimitable masterpieces as, for instance, the tales of Woe-Misfortune (*Gore-Zločastie*), of Savva Grudcyn, of a Lad and a Lass. But precisely such hybrid formations show with particular clarity how tenacious in the Russian consciousness was the distinction of two heterogeneous realms of literature, the written and the oral. Folklore, when committed to paper, was radically transformed; therefore genuine Russian folk tales and songs of the seventeenth century could not reach us except through the whim of foreign travellers such as Collins and James.

From the seventeenth century on, both the development of the Russian secular book and the influence of folklore forms on written literature have continued. But the Russian eighteenth century launched new currents: it tended to create an aristocratic literature and to isolate and canonize the language of the elect. However, the narrowing of the social base of oral production, and the gradual change of folklore from a property of the whole people to that of the common folk, was not effected at once. Over a long period, folklore did not vanish from the household of the gentlefolk but continued to fill its nook there, while lofty poetry on the classic model reigned in the drawing-room. Even so, one of the most prominent among the initiators of the new literature, Vasilij Trediakovskij, more than once acknowledged that under the occidental, aristocratic make-up many native folklore traits were concealed.

As early as the twelfth century one may read in Russian sources that a rich man, suffering from sleeplessness, ordered his attendants to tickle the soles of his feet, to strum on the *gusli*, and to tell him fairy tales. Ivan the Terrible, who became one of the popular heroes of the Russian folk tale, was its most avid fancier, and three old blind men followed each other at his bedside, relating fairy tales before he slumbered. Skilful tellers of tales continued to enliven the leisure of tsar and tsarina, of princes and gentry, as late as the eighteenth century. Even at the close of that century we find in Russian newspapers advertisements of blind men applying for work in the homes of the gentry as tellers of tales. Lev Tolstoj, as a child, fell asleep to the tales of an old man who had once been bought by the count's grandfather because of his knowledge and masterly rendition of fairy tales.

Cheap coloured prints, intended for the common people, at times introduced the texts of folk tales. But in publications of a higher level the folk tale, for a long time, was inadmissible; and when, towards the end of the eighteenth century, an amateur of folklore, Čulkov, tried to regale his readers with three genuine folk tales, the critics protested 'because the simplest peasant could, without any trouble, invent some ten such tales and were they all put into print, it would be a waste of paper, quills, ink, printers' type, not to mention the labour of the gentle-man of letters'.

Later, in the same vein, contemporary critics reacted to Puškin's attempts at imitating the folk tale and resented the illicit intrusion of the *muzhik* into the society of nobles. If an imitation was to be sanctioned, all bluntness and vulgarity offensive to refined habits and tastes had to be erased. When the author, stylizing a folk tale, was ready and able to 'prettify' it and drain it of local colour, the critics declared with satis-faction: 'Obvious it is that this tale comes not from the *muzhik*'s hut but from the castle.' (Pletnev, discussing the tale of Ivan-Tsarevich adapted by Žukovskij.)

But it was Puškin who perceived to the full the artistic value of the folk tale. 'How fascinating are these stories!' he said. 'Each one is a poem.' Moreover, the poet, who felt more acutely than his contemporaries the needs and aspirations of native literature, understood that the modern Russian novel was only in bud and that the oral tradition still remained for the Russian prose writer an instructive and unequalled model. 'No-where but in the folk tale has it been possible to endow our language with such Russian breadth. But one must learn to speak Russian also out-side the fairy tale!'

Puškin could not confine himself to the remarkable achievements with which he crowned the century-old triumphal way of Russian poetry, and during the last period of his brief life-span (1799–1837) he tried to enrich modern Russian fiction by laying a foundation of native prose. From this quest emerges his interest in folk tales. He knew the folk tales thoroughly and recorded them, but, strange as it may seem, his own imitations of fairy tales are based, for the most part, on French translations of the Arabian Nights, the brothers Grimm or Washington Irving, rather than on Russian folklore. Likewise, it is curious that none of Puškin's fairy tales are composed in prose and that most of them are in a metre foreign to the Russian tale. Most surprising of all, he none the less succeeded in capturing the spirit and tone of the Russian folk tale. For instance, in his famous *Tale of the Golden Cockerel* Puškin simply retells Irving's *Legend of the Arabian Astrologer*, and he does it in trochaic tetra-meter, alien to Russian folk tales; yet both Russian and American readers, willy-nilly, associate this pastiche with Russian folklore.

In the structure of folk tales Puškin sought the answer to the question that tormented him: What is the essence of Russian prose? Thus arose his attempts to set genuine Russian folk tale motifs in free spoken verse –

that which is used by skilful jesters and which lies on the border between prose and poetry proper.

Puškin's experiments with the Russian folk tales, and Gogol's with the Ukrainian, exemplify the formative period of modern Russian prose. Likewise, it is not by chance that the later intensive recording and impassioned study of the true folk tales, and the appearance of such vast and magnificent collections as the books of Afanas'ev (1855–64),[2] Xudjakov and others,[3] coincide with the flowering of Russian literary prose. The Russian folk tale played a great role in the creative development of the classic masters of Russian prose – Tolstoj, Dostoevskij, Leskov, Ostrovskij. And the oral style, which is a constant and typical feature of Russian literature, finds its fountain-head in the folklore tradition.

Rarely are workers in the field of ethnography called upon to play such a many-sided role in the history of a national culture as was Aleksandr Nikolaevič Afanas'ev (1826–71). Without his tales a Russian child's bookshelf is incomplete. Generations of authors have drawn and still draw upon Afanas'ev's stock. Without it and without his three-volume work on the symbolism of the fairy tales and folk mythology,[4] there would never have been created the 'Snow Maiden' of Ostrovskij and Rimskij-Korsakov; there would have been less richness of protean imagery in the poetry of Esenin, who, after long searching in the hungry years of the civil war, procured a copy of Afanas'ev's study at the price of more than three bushels of wheat – and was jubilant over his luck.

In the quantity and diversity of its material, Afanas'ev's store of fairy tales remains unparalleled in Russian folklorism. Collectors and investigators of folk poetry and customs have learned and still learn from it. Around this collection there began heated and fertile discussions about the methods of recording, study and classification of popular narratives.

It is characteristic that Afanas'ev came to folklore as an outsider: by education he was a lawyer. Among the more than six hundred tales that he published, only some ten were recorded by him. For his publication he used mostly the rich stock of Vladimir Dal', the famous collector of lexical and folkloristic materials, and the remarkable collection of folk tales assembled by the Russian Geographical Society. Unfortunately, the place of the recording is noted in only two-thirds of the tales of Afanas'ev. He paid scant attention to questions of where and from whom this or that tale was heard. Here and there the editor did not refrain from some stylistic retouching of the texts, but in this respect he did not go so far as his principal model, the brothers Grimm.

It is true that the hypothetically reconstructed archetype of a tale interested Afanas'ev perhaps more than its actual, individual variants, but he did not follow the fanatic principle that the eminent historian of literature, A. Pypin, ascribed to him, namely that everything expressing the arbitrary manner of the individual should be weeded out from the presentation of the tale as 'twaddle that is only personal'.[5] However, in sundry cases, Afanas'ev artificially constructed a single text from several variants of a tale. Later, such an approach was naturally rejected, and as early as the 'sixties Xudjakov put forth the thesis that 'the text of folk tales must stand inviolable.' At the same time P. Rybnikov, who initiated the scientific recording of Russian epic folk songs (*byliny*), called for the study of 'all that characterizes and exemplifies the narrator and stamps not only the folk but also the individual'. And even in the review of the first issues of Afanas'ev's tales the leading critic, N. Dobroljubov, warned the collectors of folk poetry in the future not to confine their task to a simple textual recording of a tale or song, but to render the full social and psychological circumstances in which the song or tale was heard – above all to note the attitude of the teller to the tale and the reaction of the audience.[6]

These principles found a still more consistent application in the works of Russian collectors and students on tales and *byliny*. The focusing of attention on tellers and listeners became the concern of Russian folklorists.[7] From a mere laboratory preparation the recorded text tended to become a living organism. The present day shorthand or tape recording of a folk tale with its detailed background data and with its careful biography of the teller, or the further stage, the reproduction by sound film – all these are clearly brilliant technical achievements in comparison with the texts of Afanas'ev. But perhaps the unsophisticated approach of the editor of *Russian Folk Tales*, who culled his bits from all quarters, in fact enabled him to accomplish the enormous and imperative task of exhibiting the repertory of Russian tales in all its manifold wealth.

It is true that the further development of Russian research brought many essential corrections to the approach of Afanas'ev and was, in a certain way, an antithesis to this approach and to the romantic theories of language and lore that inspired him. But may one oppose this antithesis to the foregoing thesis, as if the former were a sober scientific conception and the latter an antiquated fallacy? No, a creative synthesis of both is necessary.

Afanas'ev and his teachers had overestimated the genetic originality of the folklore products, and they overlooked the constant interpenetration of written and oral literature. But the later opponents of this romantic viewpoint, conversely, overestimated the significance of such genetic links and missed the functional differences between folklore and belles-lettres; they did not take into account the autonomous structure of both these domains. Absorbed by the problem of the individual features in the repertory of a story-teller, some outstanding Russian folklorists of the recent past (as for instance Boris and Jurij Sokolov) have gone so far as to identify a tale variant with an individual literary work.[8] Meanwhile, the birth and life of folklore follow quite different laws than the birth and life of a literary work.[9]

A medieval author invents and writes down a tale: a literary work is born, without regard to how it will be received. Maybe it will be condemned by the community, and only generations or centuries later will descendants come across the manuscript, accept and imitate it. Or perhaps the community approves certain elements of the tale and rejects the rest. If the same author, however, invents a tale and begins to narrate it to the community, a work of oral poetry is conceived; but its entry into the folklore repertory depends entirely on whether or not the community accepts it. Only a work that gains the consensus of the collective body, and of this work only that part which the collective censorship passes, becomes an actual folklore entity. A writer may create in opposition to his milieu, but in folklore such an intention is inconceivable.

If Afanas'ev adopted from the Romanticists the thesis that the folk tale is a product of collective creation, we must now, in spite of obdurate attacks against this 'mystic survival', recognize that folklore as well as language really presupposes a collective creation, but this collective creation is not to be naively viewed as a kind of choral performance. Scientists of the Romantic school made a mistake, not in assuming that collective creation occurs, but in asserting that it gradually withers away and that the history of language and folklore is, therefore, a process of steady decadence and disintegration. In particular, the contemporary folk tale, no less than its antique archetype, represents a typically inter-personal, social value.

According to the experience of modern linguistics, language patterns exhibit a consistent regularity. The languages of the whole world manifest a paucity and relative simplicity of structural types, and at the base of all these types lie universal laws. This schematic and recurrent character of linguistic patterns finds its explanation first of all in the fact that language is a typical collective property. Similar phenomena of schematism and recurrence in the structure of folk tales throughout the world have long astonished and challenged investigators.

In folklore as well as in language, only a part of the similarities can be explained on the basis of common patrimony or of diffusion (migratory plots). And, since the fortuity of the other coincidences is impossible, there arises imperatively the question of structural laws that will explain all these striking coincidences – in particular, the repetitive tale plots of independent origins.

The remarkable studies of the Soviet folklorists, V. Propp and A. Nikiforov, on the morphology of the Russian folk tale have approached the solution.[10] Both of these scholars base their classification and analysis of the tale plots on the functions of the *dramatis personae*. By the concept of function, they mean the deed defined from the viewpoint of its signification for the plot.

The investigation of fairy tales through the Afanas'ev collection brought Propp to some suggestive conclusions. What are the constant and stable elements of the tale? The functions of the *dramatis personae*? By whom and how they are performed is irrelevant. These functions build the pivotal constituents of the tale. The number of functions occurring in fairy tales is very limited. The mutual connections and temporal sequences of these functions are regulated and restricted by certain laws. And, finally, there is his arresting conclusion, 'All fairy tales are uniform in their structure.'

The explanation that we have tried to develop in regard to corresponding linguistic phenomena suggests itself for the tale patterns as well. The folk tale is a typical collective property. The socialized sections of mental culture, as for instance language or folk tale, are subject to much stricter and more uniform laws than fields in which individual creation prevails.

Of course, in the composition of the folk tale there are, besides constants, also variables that the teller is free to alter; but these variations must not be overestimated. Afanas'ev avoided the danger of missing the tale itself behind its variants. 'The reflection of the personality of the teller in his tales' is indisputably an interesting problem, but, because in the folklore hierarchy the tale comes before the teller, it is necessary here to be doubly cautious.

Naturally, the profession, personal interests, and inclinations of a narrator find expression in the distribution of points of emphasis, in the choice of nomenclature and attributes of the *dramatis personae* – as when, for instance, a narrator employed as a postman expertly creates a twelve-headed dragon to send the king a threatening letter, first by post and then by wire. But attempts at biographical interpretation, when applied to the poetics of the tales, are unconvincing. It happens that a sensitive man likes to relate a sentimental tale; but the reverse is also possible, namely, a striking anti-biographism. In the district of Vereya, in the Moscow region, I met a teller renowned throughout the countryside, by profession a scavenger and by nature a gutter-mouthed ruffian: his tales were by contrast always full of virginal sentimentality and high-flown expressions.

The brothers Sokolov note that among the story-tellers there are dreamy fantasts obsessed by fairy tales, humorists addicted to tales of anecdotic tinge, and several other psychological types; and the mentality of a given teller manifests itself both in the selection of his repertory and in his manner of telling. Meanwhile, the question must be inverted. In the tale tradition there are different clear-cut genres – fairy tales, anecdotes, etc. – and a favourite manner of execution traditionally corresponds to each of these types. From this inventory the narrator obviously selects those parts which most nearly correspond to his individual likes or professional interests. But we may not discount the fact that he takes upon himself one of the roles that pre-exist in the folklore stock of conventional masks, whereas in written literature a creative personality can shape a completely new role.

For Afanas'ev the teller did not screen the tale, and this is quite natural: the basic problem had to be and was posed before the accessory problems. The same order of tasks confronts the reader who aims to acquaint himself with the world of Russian tales. Through Afanas'ev's collection he will meet the Russian tale in its most varied and striking examples.[11]

2. THEIR CHARACTERISTIC FEATURES

Oral poetry, we repeat, was for centuries the only verbal art that fulfilled the secular demands in Old Russia. During this period it had time to root itself deeply in Russian life. Is not this the main secret of the notable vitality of Russian folklore and particularly of the folk tale?

Among folklorists there reigned for a long time a romantic belief that the oral poetic tradition is richest in the remotest depths of the Russian land. These far-off areas drew the attention of the searchers, so that the Archangel *taiga* was better known to the ethnographer than the lore at hand in the villages close to Moscow. On the eve of the revolution, such villages were explored by a group of young field-workers, and it became evident that one or two hours by rail from the city, in the immediate neighbourhood of factories and warehouses, there was still an abundance of folklore, especially tales.

Up to the time of the revolution the tale continued to live a robust life among the peasants, rich and poor – cowherds, hunters, fishermen, workers and artisans, soldiers and coachmen, peddlars, innkeepers, vagabonds, beggars and thieves, haulers on the Volga, old men, women and children.[12] Intensive collecting in Soviet Russia indicates that the harvest among the Russian folk is not dwindling.[13] From a single person, the aged, illiterate, but rarely gifted peasant woman Kuprijanixa, in the Voronezh region, more than one hundred and twenty tales were recently recorded.[14] Neither in the *kolkhozes*, nor in the workers' settlements, nor in the Red Army, do the tales die out.

An outstanding expert, Jurij Sokolov, presents a balance-sheet in his textbook *Russian Folklore* (1938). 'In the principal printed collections of Russian tales there are more than three thousand items; there are just as many tales scattered about in various secondary publications. Almost as many, if not more, are still in unpublished manuscripts.' Recordings of Ukrainian and White Russian tales in books and manuscripts hardly yield place to the Russian.

Not only the quantity but also the quality of the tales was heightened by the exclusive, privileged place that, through many centuries, oral poetry occupied in all strata of Russian society. Students have noted striking traces of professionalism in the formal refinement of Russian tales.[15] The art of the tale was cultivated and handed down from generation to generation by Russian minstrels (*skomoroxi*). Masters of story-telling continue to be highly appreciated in the villages. For instance, in the Siberian associations (*artels*) of lumberers, fishermen, and hunters there are skilful tellers specially hired to beguile the hours of work and leisure.

'The song is beautiful through its harmony, and the tale through its narrative composition,' a popular Russian proverb says.[16] And how beloved is this mastery, another byword testifies, 'The narrative composition is better than the song.'[17]

The best connoisseur in the tales of all the Slavic peoples and their neighbours, the famous Czech investigator J. Polívka, in his synthetic study on the Eastern Slavic folk tales, comes to the conclusion that, in the peculiarity of its ritualized form and in its richness of narrative style, the tale of the Eastern Slavs occupies quite an exceptional place: in this regard it finds no parallel among the neighbouring peoples – neither in the West and South Slavic world, nor in the Germanic and Romance countries, nor in the Orient. In the Russian (Great Russian) tale these features manifest themselves, according to Polívka's observations, with a greater brightness and abundance than in the Byelo-Russian or Ukrainian tale. And on the western periphery of the Ukrainian area they disappear almost entirely.

Introductory and concluding formulas are specially cultivated in the Russian tales. The former frequently grow into elaborate jocular preludes, designed to focus and prepare the attention of the audience. They contrast strikingly with what is to come, for 'that's the flourish (*priskazka*), just for fun; the real tale (*skazka*) has not begun'. The introduction of a fairy tale may carry the listener away in advance to a certain kingdom, to a certain land, 'way beyond thrice nine lands'. Or it may parody this well-known formula and humorously localize the fantastic action in familiar Russian environment. 'In a certain kingdom, in a certain land, namely, in the land where we are living, there lived a tsar, the Giver-of-Peace (*mirotvorec* – official epithet of Alexander III), and after him, the Vendor-of-Liquor (*vinopolec* – Nicholas II, who instituted the State vodka monopoly)' – so began a picaresque fairy tale as told us by a sprightly narrator of the Dmitrov district, in the Moscow region, in 1916.

The conclusion, amusingly breaking into a solemn tone of the fairy tale, returns the audience to the everyday world and, in rhymed patter, shifts attention from the tale to the teller. The epilogue of a tale recorded by the Sokolovs from one of the best narrators in the White Sea country, in the Novgorod region, goes as follows:

> It's not to drink beer! It's not to brew wine!
> They were wedded and whirled away to love.
> Daily they lived and richer grew.
> I dropped in to visit, right welcome they made me –
> Wine runs on my lips, nary a drop in my mouth![18]

In other words, the still thirsty teller awaits his refreshment. Sometimes the allusions are more transparent: 'This is the end of my tale, and now I would not mind having a glass of vodka.'

The traditional departure of the epilogue from the utopian happy ending of the fairy tale may utilize also contemporary political topics. The foremost contemporary specialist in Russian folk tales, M. Azadovskij, quotes this concluding formula: 'Daily they lived and richer grew, until the Soviets came into power.'[19]

'The formal perfection of the Eastern Slavic (Russian, Byelo-Russian and Ukrainian) tales is not limited to preludes and epilogues, but almost every action and every situation are conveyed by manifold, typical formulas and idioms,' says Polívka. For these purposes the Russian tale efficiently draws upon other kinds of folklore, especially upon proverbs, riddles and incantations.[20]

Sometimes the tales include ditties, but it is noteworthy that the heroic epic songs (*byliny*), although belonging to a poetic category which is closest to the fairy tale, differ sharply from them in poetics. Where the tradition of the Russian heroic epos is still alive, this difference in types of folklore is clearly felt, and a true rhapsode of *byliny*, if he also tells tales, has recourse to quite other subjects and artistic devices; but where the heroic tradition ceases, many of the usual formulas and sometimes even entire plots are taken over from the epic song by the fairy tale. The favourite sovereign of the Russian heroic songs, Vladimir, the great prince who Christianized Russia at the end of the tenth century, moves from the *byliny* to the fairy tale. In his retinue we find the leading Russian valiant knight (*bogatyr'*, from the Persian *bagadur* 'athlete' borrowed through the Tatar medium), Il'ja Muromec, a peasant's son, and another popular hero, Alësa, son of a pope; his historical prototype, Aleksandr Popovič, was mentioned in the Russian Chronicle under the year 1223 as being among the knights killed by the Tatars. The epic tradition ascribes to Alësa the victory over the dragon Tugarin, a poetic reflection of the Polovcian chief Tugor-Kan, and the fairy tale recounts this story.

If the Russian fairy tales are striking by reason of their fanciful ornamentation and ceremonious style, other narrative types – the animal tales, novelettes, anecdotes – are based preponderantly on dialogue. The precipitous dialogue of the novelettes and anecdotes is sharply opposed to the devices of retardation used in the fairy tale. In the condensed and rich dialogue Löwis of Menar is inclined to see one of the most characteristic features of Russian narrative folklore.[21] The artistic significance of the dialogue is clearly felt by the tellers themselves. An eighty-year-old Siberian narrator assured Azadovskij that the talk in the tale is the most important and the most difficult, 'If any single word is wrong here, nothing will work out right. Everything has to be done quickly here.' The dialogue in the execution of the teller easily changes to scenic play. Here the tale, in its technique, borders closely on the folk drama.

Such varieties of the tale as the novelette and the anecdote show a tendency to become part of an actual dialogue. An excellent and well-tried story-teller of the Vereya district, a genuine master of anecdote, was unable to commence a tale without stimulation. 'But when,' he said to me, 'I come into an inn and people are arguing, and someone calls, "There is a God!" and I, to him, "You lie, son of a cur" – then I tell him a tale to prove it, until the *muzhiks* say: "You're right. There is no God." But again I have to fire back: "Nonsense!" And I tell them a tale about God. I can tell tales only to get back at folks (*voerečku*).'

The tales of anecdotal tinge manifest a disposition to verse form, which in the fairy tales occurs only in the preludes and epilogues. This form, a spoken free verse, based on a colloquial pitch and garnished with comical, conspicuous rhymes, is related to the free metres of buffoonery and wedding orations. Expert tellers possess such an abundant hoard of rhymes and syntactical clichés that they are often able to improvise such spoken verses on any given subject, much as experienced mourners are able to improvise long dirges in recitative verse.

To what extent is the repertory of Russian tale plots original? A Leningrad scholar, Andreev, tried to find an answer to this question. He followed the system of tale cataloguing used by Antti Aarne, and completed Aarne's European tale index with an inventory of Russian plots.[22] Statistical analysis of all these data[23] indicated that the plots common to the Russian and Western European tale represent only about one-third of the entire index; about one third are specifically Russian and do not occur in Western Europe; again, approximately one-third are present in the Western repertory and fail to appear in the Russian tales.

For all the popularity of the fairy tales in Russia, the number of their plots is relatively small. It embraces not more than one-fifth of the whole inventory of the Russian tale plots, and the set of Russian plots unknown to the Western fairy tale is very limited. The originality of the Russian fairy tale lies not in its plot, but, as has been mentioned before, in its stylistic peculiarities. The plots of Russian animal tales are even scarcer. They represent only one-tenth of the total of Russian tale plots. Most of the Western European animal tales are unknown in Russia, and the investigators link this fact to the absence of a developed animal epos in the Russian Middle Ages. The Russian animal tales are usually brief and dramatic; they are told to children and often also by children.[24]

The greater part of the Russian inventory of tale plots (more than sixty per cent) comprises novelettes and anecdotes, most of which are unfamiliar to the West European world. The milieu pictured in these tales is socially lower than that of the fairy tale. In the latter, a man of the people is confronted with the court background of high titles and exalted rank; in the novelettes and anecdotes, on the contrary, the background is popular and even the speech and behaviour of royalty are adapted to this environment. Azadovskij quotes a characteristic example: 'Do you know, sweetheart, what has come into my head?' the wife of the tsar says to her husband. 'Why do we have to spend money in a foreign hotel? 'Twere better to open our own.'

It would be extremely tempting to examine the plots current in the Russian folk tale but unknown in Western Europe, and vice versa. Are there common, unifying traits in each of these two groups? In what measure would the selection of plots and motifs, and particularly the choice of favourite motifs and plots, characterize the ideology of a certain ethnic milieu?

The tale of Ivan the Terrible quoted above was set down by Collins because he was collecting historical material about the famous tsar. But can this tale be used as an historical source? As Veselovskij showed, the same plot has been applied to the Emperor Hadrian, Tamerlane, Duke Othon and Wallenstein. It occurs both in the Talmud and in the Turkish folk book *Adventures of Nasr-Eddin*, as well as in a medieval Italian collection of short stories.[25] The role of the gentleman who unsuccessfully tried to imitate the good, honest bask-shoemaker is formally similar to the function of numerous fools and enviers in international folk anecdotes. Nevertheless, the application of this migratory plot to Ivan the Terrible is far from accidental. It illustrates how the Russian popular memory evaluated this tsar and his attitudes to the common people and to the gentlefolk. And the *lapti*, too, are characteristic of the Russian tale. They are here a symbol of poverty, and their confrontation with the person of the tsar is traditional. Compare the rhymed anecdote about Peter the Great, which I recorded several times in the Moscow region:

> Peter the First braided *lapti*
> and put a curse on them;
> 'To braid *lapti*', he said,

'is to eat once a day,
but to mend worn *lapti*,
is never to eat at all.'
And he cast away the awl.[26]

'The tale is an invention; the song, a truth,' declares a Russian proverb.[27] Even the demonology of the tales differs sharply from the Russian folk beliefs, which know neither Koscej the Deathless, Baba Jaga, the Sea King, the Firebird, nor other fantastic figures appearing in the native fairy tale. This pantheon still presents many enigmas. Oversimplified romantic interpretation of supernatural creatures in the folk tale as being relics of prehistoric myths about the forces of nature was rejected by later critics, but the question as to the genesis of the Russian magic world and its original peculiar traits still awaits further delving and resolution. Among these demonic names there are both common Slavic remainders and old Turkic borrowings. Thus, for instance, Baba Jaga together with the Polish *jedza baba* and such a Czech equivalent as *jazinka*, as well as the old Church Slavonic *jedza* and an old Serbian *jeza* 'illness, nightmare', originate in the Primitive Slavic form *enga*, related, for instance, to the Old English *inca* 'grudge, quarrel'. On the other hand the name of the chained and imprisoned demon *Koščej* signified in Old Russian, as did its Turkic prototype *košci*, simply prisoner. The intercourse and struggle of ancient Russia with the nomadic Turkic world bequeathed, in general, many names and attributes to the Russian tales.

A fairy tale fulfils the role of a social utopia. According to the definition of Boris Soklov, it is a type of dream compensation. It is a dream about the conquest of nature – about a magic world where 'at the pike's command, at my own request', all the pails will go up the hill by themselves, the axes will chop all alone, the unharnessed sleighs will glide to the forest, and the firewood will poke itself into the stove. It is a dream about the triumph of the wretched, about the metamorphosis of a hind into a tsar. Modern technical and social advances, therefore, easily give new attributes to the tale. In the latest tale records we find an aeroplane with levers 'to direct it to right and to left', instead of the wooden eagle on which the hero had travelled before. And the biography of the tsar dethroned by the hero has recently been enriched with a curious detail. The exiled monarch laments: 'I was once a tsar; now I am become the lowest hawker.' He is asked to give his identification, 'but the tsar had no papers to show'.[28]

It is not by chance that in the epoch when borders between Utopia and reality are being effaced, the question as to the ideology of the folk tale begins to come sharply into focus. The epoch of revolutionary storms inspired one of the most imaginative Russian poets, Velimir Xlebnikov, to revise the traditional images of the folk tale. The Russian fairy tale knows the magic carpet called Self-Flyer (*samolet*), and a magic tablecloth that lays itself to feed the hero and is named Self-Victualler (*samobranka*). The name Self-Flyer was appropriated by modern Russian for the aeroplane. 'Self-Flyer', writes Xlebnikov in a poem, 'walks through the sky. But where is Tablecloth, Self-Victualler – the wife of Self-Flyer? Is she by accident delayed, or cast into prison? I credit the fairy tales: they were just fairy tales, they will become truth.' During the same civil war, Lenin was fascinated by the Russian folk tales and noted that, if one were to examine them from a socio-political viewpoint, 'he could write from this material beautiful studies about the hopes and longings of our people.' At the same time, in the opposite camp, the philosopher and essayist Evgenij Trubetzkoy, meditating on Afanas'ev's tales, tried to define precisely these longings in a study of the 'other realm' and its seekers in the Russian folk tale.[29] In the particular emphatic stress on such quests the author discerned a striking feature of the Russian fairy tale. The outcasts wend their way to another realm to look for a 'better place' and 'easy bread'. In pursuit of this aim the good fellow has to master a 'cunning science', or, maybe, simply to 'follow his eyes'. And the hero declares: 'I will go I know not where; I will bring back I know not what.' He believes: 'It's three years by a crooked way, or three hours by the straight – only there is no thoroughfare.' But the dreamlike fantasy contracts the journey: 'Whether his way was long or short, he got in.' The tale paints this other realm in extremely earthy tones. The door of Paradise opens – 'And what a tidy room it is! It's large and clean. The bed is wide and the pillows are of down.'

There is in the Russian tradition a most characteristic tale about the peasant who contrives to climb to heaven and finds there, 'in the middle of a mansion, an oven; in the oven, a goose roasting, a suckling pig, and pies, pies, pies! ... In a word: There is all that the soul desires.' It is true that the peasant's expedition ends with his tumbling into a bog – a pitiful return to miserable reality, as E. Trubetzkoy points out mockingly. But the ryhmed epilogue of this tale catches far better the function of the fairy dream:

Not this is the miracle of miracles,
That the *muzhik* fell from heaven;
But that is the miracle of miracles:
That he had climbed into heaven.[30]

CHARLES BAUDELAIRE'S 'LES CHATS'*

Roman Jakobson and Claude Lévi-Strauss

It may come as a surprise that an anthropological review should publish a study devoted to a French poem of the nineteenth century; there is, however, a simple explanation. If a linguist and an ethnologist have seen fit to join forces in their efforts to try to understand what a Baudelaire sonnet is made of, it is because, independently, they have found themselves confronted with complementary problems. The linguist discerns structures in poetic works which are strikingly analogous to those which the analysis of myths reveals to the ethnologist. For his part, the latter cannot fail to recognize that myths do not consist simply of conceptual arrangements: they are also works of art which arouse in those who hear them (and in ethnologists themselves when they read them in transcription) profound aesthetic emotions. Is it possible that the two problems are but one and the same?

Admittedly, the author of this preliminary note has at one time described the myth as being in opposition to the poetic work (see C. Lévi-Strauss, *Anthropologie structurale*, p. 232), but those who have reproached him for this have not taken into account the fact that the very notion of opposition implies that the two forms were originally conceived of as complementary terms, belonging to the same category. The relationship outlined here does not in any way detract from the quality of discreteness which we first emphasized, that is, that each poetic work, considered in isolation, contains within itself its own variables which can be represented on a vertical axis, since it consists of superimposed levels: phonological, phonetic, syntactic, prosodic, semantic, etc. Whereas the myth, at least in the extreme, can be interpreted only on the semantic level, the system of variables (always an indispensable part of structural analysis) being supplied by the multiplicity of versions of the same myth, that is to say, a cross-section through a body of myths at the semantic level only. However, one should not lose sight of the fact that this

*' "Les Chats" de Charles Baudelaire,' *L'Homme,* II (Jan.–April, 1962), pp. 5–21; translated from the French by Katie Furness-Lane and edited, with Professor Jakobson's revisions, by Stephen Rudy.

distinction fulfils above all a particular practical need, in that it enables the structural analysis of myths to forge ahead even in the absence of a genuine linguistic base. Only by practising both methods, even if it means forcing oneself to change fields abruptly, can one begin to some extent to decide the initial wager: that if either method can be selected according to the circumstances, it is because, in the final analysis, they can be substituted one for the other, without necessarily being completely interchangeable.

C. L. S.

1. Les amoureux fervents et les savants austères
2. Aiment également, dans leur mûre saison,
3. Les chats puissants et doux, orgueil de la maison,
4. Qui comme eux sont frileux et comme eux sédentaires.

5. Amis de la science et de la volupté,
6. Ils cherchent le silence et l'horreur des ténèbres;
7. L'Érèbe les eût pris pour ses coursiers funèbres,
8. S'ils pouvaient au servage incliner leur fierté.

9. Ils prennent en songeant les nobles attitudes
10. Des grands sphinx allongés au fond des solitudes,
11. Qui semblent s'endormir dans un rêve sans fin;

12. Leurs reins féconds sont pleins d'étincelles magiques,
13. Et des parcelles d'or, ainsi qu'un sable fin,
14. Étoilent vaguement leurs prunelles mystiques.

If one can give credence to the feuilleton 'Le Chat Trott' by Champfleury, where this sonnet of Baudelaire was first published (*Le Corsaire,* November 14th, 1847), it must already have been written by March 1840, and — contrary to the claims of certain exegetes — the early text in *Le Corsaire* and that in *Les Fleurs du Mal* (1857) correspond word for word.

In the organization of the rhymes, the poet follows the scheme *aBBa CddC eeFgFg* (upper-case letters being used to denote the lines ending in masculine rhymes and lower-case letters being used for the lines ending in feminine rhymes). This chain of rhymes is divided into three strophic units, namely, two quatrains and one sestet composed of two tercets, which form a certain whole since the disposition of the rhymes within this sestet is controlled in sonnets, as Grammont has shown, 'by the same rules as in any strophe of six lines'.[1]

The rhyme-scheme of the sonnet in question is the corollary of three dissimilative rules:

1. Two plain (couplet) rhymes cannot follow one another;
2. If two contiguous lines belong to different rhymes, one of them must be feminine and the other masculine;
3. At the end of contiguous stanzas feminine lines and masculine lines alternate: [4]*sédentaires* – [8]*fierté* – [14]*mystiques.*

Following the classical pattern, the so-called feminine rhymes always end in a mute syllable and the masculine rhymes in a fully sounded syllable. The difference between the two classes of rhymes persists equally in the current pronunciation which suppresses the 'mute *e*' of the final syllable, the last fully sounded vowel being followed by consonants in all the feminine rhymes of the sonnet (*austères – sédentaires, ténèbres – funèbres, attitudes – solitudes, magiques – mystiques*), whereas all its masculine rhymes end in a vowel (*saison – maison, volupté – fierté, fin – fin*).

The relation between the classification of rhymes and the choice of grammatical categories emphasizes the importance of the role played by grammar as well as by rhyme in the structure of this sonnet.

All the lines end with nominal forms, either substantive (8), or adjectival (6). All the substantives are feminine. The final noun is plural in the eight lines with a feminine rhyme, which are all longer, either by a syllable in the traditional manner or by a post-vocalic consonant in present-day pronunciation, whereas the shorter lines, those with a masculine rhyme, end in all six cases with a singular noun.

In the two quatrains, the masculine rhymes are constituted by substantives and the feminine rhymes by adjectives, with the exception of the key-word [6]*ténèbres* which rhymes with [7]*funèbres*. We shall return later to the whole question of the relationship between these two particular lines. As far as the tercets are concerned, the three lines of the first tercet all end with substantives, and those of the second with adjectives. Thus, the rhyme which links the two tercets — the only instance in this poem of a homonymous rhyme ([11]*sans fin* – [13]*sable fin*) – places a masculine adjective in opposition to a feminine substantive; and it is the only adjective, and the only example of the masculine gender, among the masculine rhymes in the sonnet.

The sonnet is made up of three complex sentences delimited by full stops, i.e., each of the two quatrains and the sestet. These three sentences display an arithmetical progression according to the number of independent clauses and of the finite verbal forms:

1. One single finite (*aiment*);
2. Two finites (*cherchent, eût pris*);
3. Three finites (*prennent, sont, étoilent*).

On the other hand, the subordinate clause in each of the three sentences has but one finite: 1. *qui... sont*; 2. *s'ils pouvaient*; 3. *qui semblent*.

This ternary division of the sonnet implies an antinomy between both

two-rhyme sentences and the final three-rhyme sentence. It is counter-
balanced by a dichotomy which divides the work into two coupled
stanzas, that is, into two pairs of quatrains and two pairs of tercets. This
binary principle, supported in turn by the grammatical organization of the
text, also implies an antinomy, this time between the two initial subdivisions or stanzas of four lines and the two last stanzas of three lines. It is on
the tension between these two modes of arrangement and between their
symmetrical and dissymetrical constituents that the composition of the
whole work is based.

There is a clear-cut syntactical parallel between the pair of quatrains on
the one hand and the pair of tercets on the other. Both the first quatrain
and the first tercet consist of two clauses, of which the second is relative,
and introduced in both cases by the same pronoun, *qui*. This clause comprises the last line of its stanza and is dependent on a masculine plural
substantive, which serves as accessory in the principal clause ([3]*Les chats*,
[10]*Des ... sphinx*). The second quatrain (and equally the second tercet)
contains two coordinate clauses, of which the last, complex in its turn,
comprises the two final lines of the stanza (7-8 and 13-14) and includes
a subordinate clause which is linked to the main clause by a conjunction.
In the quatrain this clause is conditional ([8]*S'ils pouvaient*); that of the tercet
is comparative ([13]*ainsi qu'un*). The first is post-positive, whereas the
second, incomplete, is an interpolated clause.

In the 1847 *Le Corsaire* text, the punctuation of the sonnet corresponds
to this division. The first tercet ends with a full stop, as does the first
quatrain. In the second tercet and in the second quatrain, the last two lines
are preceded by a semicolon.

The semantic aspect of the grammatical subjects reinforces this parallelism between the two quatrains on the one hand and the two tercets
on the other:

I. Quatrains	II. Tercets
1. First	1. First
2. Second	2. Second

The subjects of the first quatrain and of the first tercet designate only
animate beings, whereas one of the two subjects of the second quatrain
and all the grammatical subjects of the second tercet are inanimate
substantives: [7]*L'Érèbe*, [12]*Leurs reins*, [13]*des parcelles*, [13]*un sable*. In addition

to these so-to-speak horizontal correspondences, there is a correspondence that could be called vertical, one which opposes the totality of the two quatrains to the totality of the two tercets. While all the direct objects in the two tercets are inanimate substantives ([9]*les nobles attitudes*, [14]*leurs prunelles*), the sole direct object of the first quatrain is an animate substantive ([3]*Les chats*). The objects of the second quatrain include, in addition to the inanimate substantives ([6]*le silence et l'horreur*), the pronoun *les* which refers to *Les chats* of the preceding sentence. If we look at the relationship between subject and object, the sonnet presents two correspondences which could be called diagonal. One descending diagonal links the two exterior stanzas (the first quatrain and the last tercet) and puts them in opposition to an ascending diagonal which links the two interior stanzas. In the exterior stanzas subject and object form part of the same semantic category: animate in the first quatrain (*amoureux, savants – chats*) and inanimate in the second tercet (*reins, parcelles – prunelles*). Conversely, in the interior stanzas, object and subject are in opposing categories: in the first tercet the inanimate object is opposed to the animate subject (*ils* [=*chats*] – *attitudes*), whereas in the second quatrain the same relationship (*ils* [= *chats*] – *silence, horreur*) alternates with that of the animate object and inanimate subject (*Érèbe – les* [=*chats*]).

Thus, each of the four stanzas retains its own individuality: the animate class, which is common to both subject and object in the first quatrain, is peculiar to the subject only in the first tercet; in the second quatrain this class characterizes either subject or object, whereas in the second tercet, neither the one nor the other.

There are several striking correspondences in the grammatical structure both of the beginning and of the end of the sonnet. At the end, as well as at the beginning, but nowhere else, there are two subjects with only one predicate and only one direct object. Each of these subjects, as well as their objects, has a modifier (*Les amoureux fervents, les savants austères – Les chats puissants et doux; des parcelles d'or, un sable fin – leurs prunelles mystiques*). The two predicates, the first and last in the sonnet, are the only ones accompanied by adverbs, both of them derived from adjectives and linked to one another by a deep rhyme: [2]*Aiment également* – [14]*Etoilent vaguement*. The second and penultimate predicates are the only ones that comprise a copula and a predicative adjective, the latter being emphasized in both cases by an internal rhyme: [4]*Qui comme eux sont frileux;* [12]*Leurs reins féconds sont pleins.* Generally speaking, only the two exterior stanzas are rich in adjectives: nine in the quatrain and five in the tercet; whereas the two interior stanzas have only three adjectives in all (*funèbres, nobles, grands*).

As we have already noted, it is only at the beginning and at the end of the poem that the subjects are of the same class as the objects: each one belongs to the animate class in the first quatrain and to the inanimate in the second tercet. Animate beings, their functions and their activities, dominate the initial stanza. The first line contains nothing but adjectives. Of these, the two substantival forms which act as subjects – *Les amoureux* and *les savants* – display verbal roots: the text is inaugurated by 'those who love' and by 'those who know'. In the last line of the poem, the opposite occurs: the transitive verb *Étoilent,* which serves as a predicate, is derived from a substantive. The latter is related to the series of inanimate and concrete appellatives which dominate this tercet and distinguish it from the three anterior stanzas. A clear homophony can be heard between this verb and the members of the series in question: /etɛsɛʃə/ – /e de parsɛʃə/ – /etwaʃə/. Finally, the subordinate clauses contained in the last lines of these two medial stanzas each include an adverbial infinitive, these two object-complements being the only infinitives in the entire poem: [8]*S'ils pouvaient ... incliner;* [11]*Qui semblent s'endormir.*

As we have seen, neither the dichotomous partition of the sonnet, nor the division into three stanzas, results in an equilibrium of the isometric constituents. But if one were to divide the fourteen lines into two equal parts, the seventh line would end the first half of the poem, and the eighth line would mark the beginning of the second half. It is, therefore, significant that just these two middle lines stand out most obviously by their grammatical make-up from the rest of the poem.

Actually, in more than one respect, the poem falls into three parts: in this case into the middle pair of lines and two isometric groups, that is to say, the six lines which precede this pair and the six which follow it. Hence there emerges a kind of couplet inserted between two sestets.

All personal verb-forms and pronouns and all the subjects of verbal clauses are plural throughout the sonnet, except in line seven, *L'Érèbe les eût pris pour ses coursiers funèbres,* which contains the only proper noun in the poem and is the only instance of both the finite verb and its subject being in the singular. Furthermore, it is the only line in which the possessive pronoun (*ses*) refers to a singular.

Only the third person is used in the sonnet. The only verbal tense used is the present, except in lines seven and eight, where the poet envisages an imaginary action ([7]*eût pris*) arising out of an unreal premise ([8]*S'ils pouvaient*).

The sonnet shows a pronounced tendency to provide every verb and every substantive with a modifier. Each verbal form is accompanied by a governed modifier (substantive, pronoun, infinitive) or by a predicative adjective. All transitive verbs govern only substantives (²⁻³*Aiment ... Les chats;* ⁶*cherchent le silence et l'horreur;* ⁹*prennent ... les ... attitudes;* ¹⁴*Étoilent ... leurs prunelles*). The pronoun which serves as the object in the seventh line is the sole deviation: *les eût pris.*

With the exception of adnominal adjuncts which are never accompanied by any modifier in the sonnet, the substantives (including the substantivized adjectives) are always modified by attributes (e.g. ³*chats puissants et doux*) or by adjuncts (⁵*Amis de la science et de la volupté*); line seven again provides the only exception: *L'Érèbe les eût pris.*

All five attributes in the first quatrain (¹*fervents,* ¹*austères,* ²*mûre,* ³*puissants,* ³*doux*) and all six in the two tercets (⁹*nobles,* ¹⁰*grands,* ¹²*féconds,* ¹²*magiques,* ¹³*fin,* ¹⁴*mystiques*) are qualitative epithets, whereas the second quatrain has no adjectives other than the determinative attribute in the seventh line (*coursiers funèbres*).

It is also this line which inverts the animate/inanimate order underlying the relation between subject and object in the other lines of this quatrain, and which is, in fact, the only one in the entire sonnet to adopt this inanimate/animate order.

Several striking peculiarities clearly distinguish line seven only, or the last two lines of the second quatrain, from the rest of the sonnet. However, it must be noted that the tendency for the medial distich to stand out agrees with the principle of an asymmetrical trichotomy, which puts the whole of the second quatrain in opposition to the first quatrain on the one hand and in opposition to the final sestet on the other, thus creating a kind of central strophe distinct in several respects from the marginal strophic units. We have already shown that only in the seventh line are subject and predicate in the singular, but this observation can be extended: only within the lines of the second quatrain do we find either subject or object in the singular and whereas in the seventh line the singularity of the subject (*L'Érèbe*) is opposed to the plurality of the object (*les*), the adjoining lines invert this relation, having a plural subject and a singular object (⁶*Ils cherchent le silence et l'horreur;* ⁸*S'ils pouvaient ... incliner leur fierté*).

In the other stanzas, both object and subject are plural (¹⁻³*Les amoureux ... et les savants ... Aiment ... Les chats;* ⁹*Ils prennent ... les attitudes;* ¹³⁻¹⁴*Et des parcelles ... Étoilent ... leurs prunelles*). It is notable that in the second quatrain singularity of subject and object coincides with the inanimate and plurality with the animate class. The importance of grammatical number to Baudelaire becomes particularly noteworthy by virtue of the role it plays in opposition-relations in the rhymes of the sonnet.

It must be added that the rhymes in the second quatrain are distinguishable by their structure from all other rhymes in the poem. The feminine rhyme *ténèbres – funèbres* in the second quatrain is the only one which brings together two different parts of speech. Moreover, all the rhymes in the sonnet, except those in the quatrain in question, comprise one or more identical phonemes, either immediately preceding or some distance in front of the stressed syllable, usually reinforced by a supportive consonant: [1]*savants austères* – [4]*sédentaires*, [2]*mûre saison* – [3]*maison*, [9]*attitudes – solitudes*, [11]*un rêve sans fin* – [13]*un sable fin*, [12]*étincelles magiques* – [14]*prunelles mystiques*. In the second quatrain, neither the pair [5]*volupté* – [8]*fierté*, nor [6]*ténèbres* – [7]*funèbres*, offer any correspondence in the syllable anterior to the rhyme itself. On the other hand, the final words in the seventh and eighth lines are alliterative, [7]*funèbres* – [8]*fierté*, and the sixth and fifth lines are linked by the repetition of the final syllable of [5]*volupté* in [6]*ténèbres* and by the internal rhyme [5]*science* – [6]*silence*, which reinforces the affinity between the two lines. Thus the rhymes themselves exhibit a certain relaxation of the ties between the two halves of the second quatrain.

A salient role in the phonic texture of the sonnet is played by the nasal vowels. These phonemes, 'as though veiled by nasality', as Grammont aptly puts it,[2] occur very frequently in the first quatrain (9 nasals, from 2 to 3 per line) but most particularly in the final sestet (22 nasals with increasing frequency throughout the first tercet, [9]3 – [10]4 – [11]6: *Qui semblent s'endormir dans un rêve sans fin* – and with a decreasing frequency throughout the second tercet, [12]5 – [13]3 – [14]1). In contrast, the second quatrain contains only 3: 1 per line, excepting the seventh, the sole line in the sonnet without a nasal vowel; this quatrain is also the only stanza where the masculine rhyme does not contain a nasal vowel. Then again, it is in the second quatrain that the role of phonic dominant passes from vowels to consonantal phonemes, in particular to liquids. The second quatrain is the only one which shows an excessive number of these liquid phonemes, 24 in all, as compared to 15 in the first quatrain, 11 in the first tercet and 14 in the second. The total number of /r/'s is slightly lower than the number of /l/'s (31 versus 33), but the seventh line, which has only two /l/'s, contains five /r/'s, that is to say, more than any other line in the sonnet – *L'Érèbe les eût pris pour ses coursiers funèbres*. According to Grammont, it is by opposition to / r / that / l / 'gives the impression of a sound that is neither grating, rasping, nor rough but, on the contrary, that glides and flows, that is limpid'.[3] The abrupt nature of every / r /, and particularly the French / r /, in comparison with the *glissando* of the / l / is clearly illustrated in Mlle Durand's recent acoustical analysis of the two liquids.[4] The agglomeration of the / r /'s eloquently echoes the delusive association of the cats with Erebus, followed by the antithetic ascent of the empirical felines to their miraculous transfigurations.

The first six lines of the sonnet are linked by a characteristic reiteration: a symmetrical pair of co-ordinate phrases linked by the same conjunction *et:* [1]*Les amoureux fervents et les savants austères;* [3]*Les chats puissants et doux;* [4]*Qui comme eux sont frileux et comme eux sédentaires;* [5]*Amis de la science et de la volupté.* The binarism of the determinants thus forms a chiasmus with the binarism of the determined in the next line – [6]*le silence et l'horreur des ténèbres* – which puts an end to these binary constructions. This construction, common to all the lines of this 'sestet', does not recur in the remainder of the poem. The juxtapositions without a conjunction are a variation of the same scheme: [2]*Aiment également, dans leur mûre saison* (parallel circumstantial complements); [3]*Les chats …, orgueil …* (a substantive in apposition to another).

These pairs of co-ordinate phrases and their rhymes (not only those which are exterior and underline the semantic links such as [1]*austères* – [4]*sédentaires,* [2]*saison* – [3]*maison,* but also and especially the internal rhymes) serve to draw the lines of this introduction closer together: [1]*amoureux* – [4]*comme eux* – [4]*frileux* – [4]*comme eux;* [1]*fervents* – [1]*savants* – [2]*également* – [2]*dans* – [3]*puissants;* [5]*science* – [6]*silence.* Thus all the adjectives characterizing the persons in the first quatrain are rhyme-words, with the one exception [3]*doux.* A double etymological figure links the openings of three of the lines: [1]*Les amoureux* – [3]*Aiment* – [5]*Amis,* in accordance with the unity of this crypto-stanza of six lines, which starts and ends with a couplet, each of whose first hemistiches rhyme: [1]*fervents* – [2]*également;* [5]*science* – [6]*silence.*

[3]*Les chats,* who are the direct object of the clause comprising the first three lines of the sonnet, become the implicit subject of the clauses in the following three lines ([4]*Qui comme eux sont frileux;* [6]*Ils cherchent le silence*), revealing the outline of a division of this quasi-sestet into two quasi-tercets. The middle 'distich' recapitulates the metamorphosis of the cats: from an implicit object ([7]*L'Érèbe les eût pris*) into an equally implicit grammatical subject ([8]*S'ils pouvaient*). In this respect the eighth line coin-

cides with the following sentence (⁹*Ils prennent*).

In general, the post-positive subordinate clauses form a kind of transition between the subordinating clause and the sentence which follows it. Thus, the implicit subject *chats* of the ninth and tenth lines changes into a reference to the metaphor *sphinx* in the relative clause of the eleventh line (*Qui semblent s'endormir dans un rêve sans fin*) and, as a result, links this line to the tropes serving as grammatical subjects in the final tercet. The indefinite article, entirely alien to the first ten lines with their fourteen definite articles, is the only one admitted in the four concluding lines of the sonnet.

Thus, thanks to the ambiguous references in the two relative clauses, in the eleventh and the fourth lines, the four concluding lines allow us to glimpse the contour of an imaginary quatrain which somehow corresponds to the initial quatrain of the sonnet. On the other hand, the final tercet has a formal structure which seems reflected in the first three lines of the sonnet.

Animate subjects are never expressed by substantives, but either by substantivized adjectives, in the first line of the sonnet (*Les amoureux, les savants*), or by personal and relative pronouns, in the further clauses. Human beings appear only in the first clause, in the form of a double subject supported by substantivized verbal adjectives.

The cats, named in the title of the sonnet, are called by name only once in the text, as the direct object in the first clause: ¹*Les amoureux ... et les savants ...* ²*Aiment ...* ³*Les chats*. Not only is the word *chats* avoided in the further lines of the poem, but even the initial hushing phoneme / ʃ / recurs only in a single word: ⁶ /il ʃɛrʃɛ /. It denotes, with reduplication, the first reported action of the felines. This voiceless sibilant, linked to the name of the poem's heroes, is carefully avoided throughout the remainder of the sonnet.

From the third line, the cats become an implicit subject, which proves to be the last animate subject in the sonnet. The substantive *chats*, in the roles of subject, object and adnominal adjunct, is replaced by the anaphoric pronouns ⁶, ⁸, ⁹*ils,* ⁷*les,* ⁸, ¹², ¹⁴*leur(s)*, and it is only to *les chats* that the substantive pronouns *ils* and *les* refer. These accessory (adverbial) forms occur solely in the two interior stanzas, i.e., in the second quatrain and in the first tercet. The corresponding autonomous form ⁴*eux* is used twice in the initial quatrain and refers only to the human characters of the sonnet, whereas no substantive pronouns occur in the final tercet.

The two subjects of the initial clause of the sonnet have one single predicate and one single object. Thus, [1]*Les amoureux fervents et les savants austères* end up [2]*dans leur mûre saison* by finding their identity in an intermediary being, an animal which encompasses the antinomic traits of two human but mutually opposed conditions. The two human categories, sensual /intellectual, oppose each other, and the mediation is achieved by means of the cats. Hence, the role of subject is latently assumed by the cats, who are at one and the same time scholars and lovers.

The two quatrains objectively present the personage of the cat, whereas the two tercets carry out his transfiguration. However, the second quatrain differs fundamentally from the first and, in general, from all the other stanzas. The equivocal formulation, *ils cherchent le silence et l'horreur des ténèbres*, gives rise to a misunderstanding summoned up in the seventh line of the sonnet and denounced in the following line. The aberrant character of this quatrain, especially the perplexity of its last half, and more particularly of the seventh line, is thoroughly marked by the peculiarities of its grammatical and phonic texture.

The semantic affinity between *L'Érèbe* ('dark region bordering on Hell', metonymic substitute for 'the powers of darkness' and particularly for Erebus, 'brother of Night') and the cats' predilection for *l'horreur des ténèbres*, corroborated by the phonic similarity between /tenɛbrə / and /erɛbə/ , all but harness the cats, heroes of the poem, to the grisly task of *coursiers funèbres*. Does the line which insinuates that *L'Érèbe les eût pris pour ses coursiers* raise a question of frustrated desire or one of false recognition? The meaning of this passage, long puzzled over by the critics,[5] remains purposely ambiguous.

Each of the quatrains, as well as each of the tercets, tries to give the cats a new identity. While the first quatrain linked the cats to two types of human condition, thanks to their pride they succeed in rejecting the new identity put forward in the second quatrain, which would associate them with an animal condition: that of coursers placed in a mythological context. It is the only identification that is rejected in the course of the whole poem. The grammatical composition of this passage, which contrasts expressly with that of the other stanzas, betrays its peculiar character: unreal conditional, lack of qualitative attributes, and an inanimate singular subject devoid of any modifier and governing an animate plural object.

Allusive oxymorons unite the stanzas. [8]*S'ils POUVAIENT au servage incliner leur fierté,* – but they *cannot* do so (*ils ne 'peuvent' pas*) because they are truly [3]*PUISSANTS*. They cannot be passively taken ([7]*PRIS*) to play an active role, and hence they themselves actively take ([9]*PREN-*

NENT) a passive role because they are obstinately *sédentaires*.

[8]*Leur fierté* predestines them for the [9]*nobles attitudes* [10]*Des grands sphinx*. The [10]*sphinx allongés* and the cats that mime them [9]*en songeant* are united by a paronomastic link between the only two participial forms in the sonnet: / ãsɔ̃ʒã / and /alɔ̃ʒe /. The cats seem to identify themselves with the sphinxes, who in their turn [11]*semblent s'endormir*, but the illusory comparison, assimilating the sedentary cats (and by implication all who are [4]*comme eux*,) to the immobility of the supernatural beings, achieves the status of a metamorphosis. The cats and the human beings who are identified with them are reunited in the mythical beasts with human heads and animal bodies. Thus, the rejected identification appears to be replaced by a new, equally mythological identification.

[9]*En songeant*, the cats manage to identify themselves with the [10]*grands sphinx*. A chain of paronomasias, linked to these key words and combining nasal vowels with continuant dentals and labials, reinforces the metamorphosis: [9]*en songeant* / ãsɔ̃ / ... / – [10]*grands sphinx* / ... / ãsfɛ̃ ... / – [10]*fond* /fɔ̃ / – [11]*semblent* /sã ... / – [11]*s'endormir* /sã ... / – [11]*dans un* / .ãzœ̃ / – [11]*sans fin* / sãfɛ̃/. The acute nasal / ɛ̃ / and the other phonemes of the word [10]*sphinx* /sfɛ̃ks / recur in the last tercet: [12]*reins*, /.ɛ̃ / – [12]*pleins* /..ɛ̃ / – [13]*étincelles* /..ɛ̃s ... / – [13]*ainsi* /ɛ̃s / – [13]*qu'un sable* /kõɛs ... / – [13]*fin* /fɛ̃ /.

We read in the first quatrain: [3]*Les chats puissants et doux, orgueil de la maison*. Does this mean that the cats, proud of their home, are the incarnation of that pride, or that the house, proud of its feline inhabitants, tries, like Erebus, to domesticate them? Whichever it may be, the [3]*maison* which circumscribes the cats in the first quatrain is transformed into a spacious desert, [10]*fond des solitudes*. And the fear of cold, bringing together the cats, [4]*frileux*, and the lovers, [1]*fervents* (note the paronomasia / fɛrvã / – /frilø /), is dispelled by the appropriate climate of the austere solitudes (as austere as the scholars) of the desert (torrid like the fervent lovers) which surrounds the sphinxes. On the temporal level, the [2]*mûre saison*, which rhymed with [3]*la maison* in the first quatrain and approached it in meaning, has a clear counterpart in the first tercet. These two visibly parallel groups of words ([2]*dans leur mûre saison* and [11]*dans un rêve sans fin*) mutually oppose each other, the one evoking numbered days and the other, eternity. No constructions with *dans* or with any other adverbal preposition occur elsewhere in the sonnet.

The miraculous quality of the cats pervades the two tercets. The metamorphosis unfolds right to the end of the sonnet. In the first tercet the image of the sphinxes stretched out in the desert already vacillates between the creature and its simulacrum, and in the following tercet the animate beings disappear behind particles of matter. Synecdoche substitutes for the cat-sphinxes various parts of their bodies: [12]*leur reins* (the loins of the cats), [14]*leur prunelles* (the pupils of their eyes). In the final tercet, the implicit subject of the interior stanzas again becomes an accessory part of the sentence. The cats appear first as an implicit adjunct of the subject – [12]*Leur reins féconds sont pleins* – then, in the poem's last clause, they function as a mere implicit adjunct of the object: [14]*Étoilent vaguement leurs prunelles*. Thus the cats appear to be linked to the object of the transitive verb in the last clause of the sonnet and to the subject in the penultimate, antecedent clause, thereby establishing a double correspondence on the one hand with the cats as direct object in the first clause of the sonnet, and on the other with the cats as subject of its second clause.

Whereas at the beginning of the sonnet both subject and object were of the animate class, the two similar parts of the final clause both belong to the inanimate class. In general, all the substantives in the last tercet are concrete nouns of the same class: [12]*reins*, [12]*étincelles*, [13]*parcelles*, [13]*or*, [13]*sable*, [14]*prunelles*, whilst in all previous stanzas the inanimate appellatives, except for the adnominal ones, were abstract nouns: [2]*saison*, [3]*orgueil*, [6]*silence*, [6]*horreur*, [8]*servage*, [8]*fierté*, [9]*attitudes*, [11]*rêve*. The inanimate feminine gender, common to the subject and to the object of the final clause – [13-16]*des parcelles d'or … Étoilent … leurs prunelles* – counterbalances the subject and object of the initial clause, which both belong to the animate masculine gender – [1-3] *Les amoureux … et les savants … Aiment … Les chats*. [13]*Parcelles* is the only feminine subject in the whole sonnet, and it contrasts with the masculine [13]*sable fin* at the end of the same line, which in turn is the only example of the masculine gender among the sonnet's masculine rhymes.

In the last tercet, the ultimate particles of matter serve in turns as object and subject. A new identification, the last within the sonnet, associates these incandescent particles with the [13]*sable fin* and transforms them into stars.

The remarkable rhyme which links the two tercets is the only homonymous rhyme in the whole sonnet and the only one among its masculine rhymes which juxtaposes different parts of speech. There is also a certain syntactic symmetry between the two rhyme-words, since both end subordinate clauses, of which one is complete and the other elliptical. The correspondence, far from being confined to the final syllable, closely brings the whole of both lines together: ¹¹*sãblə sadɔrmir dãnzœ̃ rɛvə sã ʃɛ̃/ – ¹³*parsɛlə dɔr ɛ̃si kœ̃ sablə ʃɛ̃/*. It is not by chance that precisely the rhyme that links the two tercets evokes *un sable fin*, thus taking the desert motif up again, in the same position as *un rêve sans fin* of the *grands sphinx* appears in the first tercet.

³*La maison*, which circumscribes the cats in the first quatrain, is abolished in the first tercet with its realm of desert solitudes, true unfolded house of the cat-sphinxes. In its turn, this 'non-house' yields to the cosmic innumerability of the cats (these, like all the personae of the sonnet, are treated as *pluralia tantum*). They become, so to speak, the house of the non-house, since within the irises of their eyes they enclose the sand of the deserts and the light of the stars.

The epilogue takes up again the initial theme of lovers and scholars united in *Les chats puissants et doux*. The first line of the second tercet seems to answer the first line of the second quatrain; the cats being ⁵*Amis ... de la volupté*, ¹²*Leurs reins féconds sont pleins*. One is tempted to believe that this has to do with the procreative force, but Baudelaire's works easily invite ambiguous solutions. Is it a matter of a power particular to the loins or of electric sparks in the animal's fur? Whatever it may be, it is a 'magic' power that is attributed to them. But the second quatrain opens with two collateral adjuncts: ⁵*Amis de la science et de la volupté*, and the final tercet alludes not only to the ²*amoureux fervents* but to the ¹*savants austères* as well.

In the last tercet, the rhyming suffixes emphasize the strong semantic link between the ¹²*étinCELLES*, ¹³*parCELLES d'or* and ¹⁴*prunELLES* of the cat-sphinxes on the one hand, and on the other, between the sparks ¹²*MagIQUES* emanating from the animal and its pupils ¹⁴*MystIQUES* illuminated by an inner light and open to a hidden meaning. This is the only rhyme in the sonnet which is stripped of its supporting consonant, as if to lay bare the equivalence of the morphemes, and the alliteration of the initial /m/'s ties the two adjectives even closer together. ⁶*L'horreur des ténèbres* vanishes before this double luminance, which is reflected on the phonic level by the predominance of phonemes of light timbre (acute tonality) among the nasal vowels of the final stanza (6 front versus 3 back vowels), whereas there was a far greater number of nasal vowels of grave tonality in the preceding stanzas (9 versus 0 in the first quatrain, 2 versus 1 in the second and 10 versus 3 in the first tercet).

Due to the preponderance of synecdochic tropes at the end of the sonnet, where parts of the animal are substituted for the whole and, on the other hand, the animal itself is substituted for the universe of which it is a part, the images seek, as if by design, to lose themselves in imprecision. The definite article gives way to the indefinite article and the adverb which accompanies the verbal metaphor – [14]*Étoilent vaguement* – brilliantly reflects the poetics of the epilogue. The conformity between the tercets and the corresponding quatrains (horizontal parallelism) is striking. The narrow limits of space ([3]*maison*) and of time ([2]*mûre saison*) imposed in the first quatrain are opposed in the first tercet by the removal or suppression of boundaries ([10]*fond des solitudes*, [11]*rêve sans fin*). Similarly, in the second tercet, the magic of the light radiating from the cats triumphs over [6]*l'horreur des ténèbres*, which nearly wrought such deception in the second quatrain.

Now, in drawing together the parts of our analysis, we shall try to show how the different levels on which we touched blend, complement each other or combine to give the poem the value of an absolute object.

To begin with, the divisions of the text: several can be distinguished which are perfectly clear, as much from the grammatical point of view as from the semantic relations between different parts of the poem.

As we have already pointed out, there is a primary division corresponding to the three parts, each of which ends with a period, namely, the two quatrains and the ensemble of the two tercets. The first quatrain presents, in the form of an objective and static picture, a factual situation or one that purports to be so. The second quatrain attributes to the cats a purpose which is interpreted by the powers of Erebus, and to the powers of Erebus a purpose in regard to the cats, which the latter reject. Thus, in these two sections, the cats are seen from without, first through the passivity to which lovers and scholars are especially susceptible, and secondly through the activity perceived by the powers of Erebus. By contrast, in the last part of the sonnet this opposition is overcome by acknowledging a passivity actively assumed by the cats, no longer interpreted from without but from within.

A second division enables us to oppose the ensemble of the two tercets to the ensemble of the two quatrains, at the same time revealing a close connection between the first quatrain and the first tercet, and between the second quatrain and the second tercet. As a matter of fact:

1. The ensemble of the two quatrains is opposed to the ensemble of the two tercets in the sense that the latter dispenses with the point of view of the observer (*amoureux, savants,* powers of Erebus) and

places the being of the cats outside all spatial and temporal limits.

2. The first quatrain introduces these spatio-temporal limits (*maison, saison*) and, the first tercet abolishes them (*au fond des solitudes, rêve sans fin*).

3. The second quatrain defines the cats in terms of the darkness in which they place themselves, the second tercet in terms of the light they radiate (*étincelles, étoiles*).

Finally, a third division is superimposed upon the preceding one by regrouping, this time in chiasmus, the initial quatrain and the final tercet, on the one hand, and on the other, the interior stanzas: the second quatrain and the first tercet. In the former couple, the independent clauses assign to the cats the role of syntactical modifiers, whereas from the outset the latter two stanzas assign to the cats the function of subject.

These phenomena of formal distribution obviously have a semantic foundation. The point of departure of the first quatrain is furnished by the proximity, within the same house, of the cats with the scholars or lovers. A double resemblance arises out of this contiguity (*comme eux, comme eux*). Similarly, a relation of contiguity in the final tercet also evolves to the point of resemblance, but whereas, in the first quatrain, the metonymical relation of the feline and human inhabitants of the house underlies their metaphorical relation, in the final tercet this situation is interiorized: the link of contiguity rests upon the synecdoche rather than upon the metonymy proper. The parts of the cat's body (*reins, prunelles*) provide a metaphorical evocation of the astral, cosmic cat, with a concomitant transition from precision to vagueness (*également – vaguement*). The analogy between the interior stanzas is based on connections of equivalence, the one turned down in the second quatrain (cats and *coursiers funèbres*), the other accepted in the first tercet (cats and *grands sphinx*). In the former case, this leads to a rejection of contiguity (between the cats and *L'Érèbe*) and, in the latter case, to the settlement of the cats *au fond des solitudes*. Contrary to the former case, the transition is made from a relation of equivalence, a reinforced form of resemblance (thus a metaphorical move), to relations of contiguity (thus metonymical), either negative or positive.

Up to this point, the poem has appeared to consist of systems of equivalences which fit inside one another and which offer, in their totality, the appearance of a closed system. There is, however, yet another way of looking at it, whereby the poem takes on the appearance of an open system in dynamic progression from beginning to end.

In the first part of this study we elucidated a division of the poem into two sestets separated by a distich whose structure contrasted vigorously with the rest. In the course of our recapitulation, we provisionally set this division to one side, because we felt that, unlike the others, it marks the stages of a progression from the order of the real (the first sestet) to that of the surreal (the second sestet). This transition operates via the distich, which by the accumulation of semantic and formal devices lures the reader for a brief moment into a doubly unreal universe, since, while sharing with the first sestet the standpoint of exteriority, it anticipates the mythological tone of the second sestet:

1 to 6	7 and 8	9 to 14
extrinsic		intrinsic
empirical	mythological	
real	*unreal*	*surreal*

By this sudden oscillation both of tone and of theme, the distich fulfils a function somewhat resembling that of modulation in a musical composition.

The purpose of this modulation is to resolve the opposition, implicit or explicit from the beginning of the poem, between the metaphorical and metonymical procedures. The solution provided by the final sestet is achieved by transferring this opposition to the very heart of the metonymy, while expressing it by metaphorical means. In effect, each of the tercets puts forward an inverse image of the cats. In the first tercet, the cats originally enclosed in the house are, so to speak, extravasated from it in order to expand spatially and temporally in the infinite deserts and the dream without end. The movement is from the inside to the outside, from cats in seclusion to cats at liberty. In the second tercet, the breaking down of barriers is interiorized by the cats attaining cosmic proportions, since they conceal in certain parts of their bodies (*reins* and *prunelles*) the sands of the desert and the stars of the sky. In both cases the transformation occurs via metaphorical devices, but there is no thorough equilibrium between the two transformations: the first still owes something to semblance (*prennent ... les ... attitudes ... qui semblent s'endormir*) and to dream (*en songeant ... dans un rêve ...*), whereas in the second case the transformation is declared and affirmed as truly achieved (*sont pleins ... Étoilent*). In the first, the cats close their eyes to sleep, in the second they keep them open.

Nevertheless, these ample metaphors of the final sestet simply transpose to the scale of the universe an opposition that was already implicitly formulated in the first line of the poem. Around the lovers and scholars terms are assembled which unite them respectively in a contracted or dilated relation: the man in love is joined to the woman as the scholar is to the universe: two types of conjunction, the one close and the other remote.[6] It is the same rapport that the final transfigurations evoke: dilation of the cats in time and space – constriction of time and space within the beings of the cats. But, here again, just as we noted earlier, the symmetry between the two formulae is not complete. The latter contains within it a collection of all the oppositions: the *reins féconds* recall the *volupté* of the *amoureux*, as do the *prunelles* the *science* of the *savants; magiques* refers to the active fervour of the one, *mystiques* to the contemplative attitude of the other.

Two final points:

The fact that all the grammatical subjects in the sonnet (with the exception of the proper noun *L'Érèbe*) are plural, and that all feminine rhymes are formed with plurals (including the substantive *solitudes*), is curiously illuminated by a few passages from Baudelaire's *Foules* which, moreover, seem to throw light upon the whole of the sonnet: 'Multitude, solitude: terms equal and interchangeable by the active and fertile poet ... The poet enjoys that incomparable privilege, that he can, at will, be both himself and another ... What men call love is very small, very restricted and very weak compared to that ineffable orgy, that blessed prostitution of the soul which gives itself in its entirety, its poetry and charity, to the unforeseen which emerges, to the unknown one who passes.'[7]

In the poet's sonnet, the cats are initially qualified as *puissants et doux* and in the final line their pupils are likened to the stars. Crépet and Blin[8] compare this to a line in Sainte-Beuve: "... l'astre puissant et doux"(1829) and find the same epithets in a poem by Brizeux (1832) in which women are thus apostrophized: "Êtres deux fois doués! Êtres puissants et doux!"

This would confirm, were there any need to do so, that for Baudelaire the image of the cat is closely linked to that of the woman, as is shown explicitly in two other poems entitled 'Le Chat' and pertaining to the same collection. Thus the sonnet "Viens, mon beau chat, sur mon cœur amoureux" contains the revealing line: 'Je vois ma femme en esprit ...' The second of these poems – 'Dans ma cervelle se promène ... Un beau chat, fort, doux ...' – squarely asks the question: 'est-il fée, est-il dieu?' This motif of vacillation between male and female is subjacent in 'Les Chats', where it shows through from beneath intentional ambiguities (*Les amoureux ... Aiment ... Les chats puissants et doux ...; Leurs reins féconds ...*) Michel Butor notes with reason that for Baudelaire 'these two aspects: femininity and supervirility, far from being mutually exclusive, are in fact bound together'.[9] All the characters in the sonnet are of masculine gender, but *les chats* and their alter ego, *les grands sphinx,* share an androgynous nature. This very ambiguity is emphasized throughout the sonnet by the paradoxical choice of feminine substantives for so-called masculine rhymes.[10] The cats, by their mediation, permit the removal of woman from the initial assemblage formed by lovers and scholars. 'Le poète des Chats', liberated from love 'bien petit, bien restreint', meets face to face and perhaps even blends with the universe, delivered from the scholars' austerity.

STRUCTURES OF EXCHANGE IN *CINNA*[*]

Jacques Ehrmann

At the exact centre of Corneille's *Cinna* (III, iii), we find Cinna soliloquizing. He is undecided as to whether he should continue to plot against Auguste in order to win Émilie's love or remain faithful to a ruler who not only has just given him permission to marry Émilie but also intends to give him a share of the power which Auguste now finds tiresome. I should like to paraphrase the three parts of his soliloquy as a prelude to examining more closely the second part which is at the centre of this particular centre. Cinna is questioning himself:

1. How, he asks, shall I label the act which I am about to commit (the murder of Auguste) except as a 'weakness'? I am doing it only in order to please a woman (Émilie) who has brought me to this weakness. What should my decision be? (v. 865–74).

2. Every solid reason which I latch on to (that I am sacrificing myself for love, revenging myself, performing a glorious and liberating act) does not seem sufficiently strong to justify an act which is no less than treason against the emperor who 'has overwhelmed me with honours', 'laden me with goods'. No, I cannot commit this crime (v. 875–93).

3. Still, I have an obligation to Émilie and so cannot withdraw: 'On you, Émilie, falls the decision about what I must do' (v. 893–905). But perhaps there is a chance that I can make her change her mind (v. 893–905).

Let us take a closer look at the second part of this scene:

> Qu'une âme généreuse a de peine à faillir!
> Quelque *fruit* que par là j'éspère de cueillir,
> Les douceurs de l'amour, celles de la vengeance,
> La gloire d'affranchir le lieu de ma naissance,
> N'ont point assez d'appas pour flatter ma raison,
> S'il les faut *acquérir* par une trahison,
> S'il faut percer le flanc d'un prince magnanime

[*] First appeared in *Les Temps modernes*, no. 246 (1966); English translation by Joseph H. McMahon reprinted from *Yale French Review*, vol. 36–7 (1966).

Qui du peu que je suis fait une telle estime,
Qui me *comble* d'honneurs, qui m'*accable* de biens,
Qui ne *prend* pour régner de conseils que les miens.

(v. 875–84)

Périsse mon amour, périsse mon espoir,
Plutôt que de ma main parte un crime si noir!
Quoi? ne m'*offre*-t-il pas tout ce que je souhaite,
Et qu'au *prix* de son sang ma passion *achète*?
Pour jouir de ses *dons* faut-il l'assassiner?
Et faut-il lui *ravir* ce qu'il me veut *donner*?

(v. 887–92)

The italic words establish with adequate clarity the nature of the relations which exist between the three main characters – Émilie, Cinna, and Auguste. These relations are based on a certain conception of exchange, so much so that it is not exaggerated to say that they are almost 'economic' by nature. I intend to follow this theme with each of the partners in the exchange and, in the process, show the play's organization, its internal arrangement, and the structures which make it coherent.

I should point out straight off that the malaise experienced by Cinna is an outgrowth of his hesitation between two systems of exchange: the one proposed by Émilie and the one which the emperor proposes. In his relations with Émilie, Cinna cannot cull benefits (Émilie herself, Rome's freedom, glory) except by *acquiring* them at the *price* of treason since the man he must assassinate in order to win Émilie is the same Auguste who *overwhelms* him with honours and *loads* him with goods. In terms of Émilie's system, the exchange is set up on the following links:

gather – acquire – overwhelm.

In his relations with Auguste, Cinna prefers to see his love *perish* rather than betray his emperor who is ready to *offer* him what he, Cinna, is about to *buy* – Émilie, Rome's freedom – by bringing about the death of the giver; such an action amounts in a way to *pillaging* the goods he is about to *be given*. In this second system (v. 887–93), the exchange is set up on the following links:

perish – offer – buy – prize – pillage – (– give, idem offer)

To understand the meaning of each of these acts and of each of the systems of exchange, we need only consider their double nature: to gather is to take, but it is also to receive freely; to acquire is at once to take and pay for what one has taken; to overwhelm is, for one person, to give and, for the other, to receive freely. A network of identities (=) or equations and of contraries (/) is thus set up. The first system looks schematically like this:

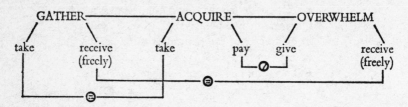

The second system looks like this:

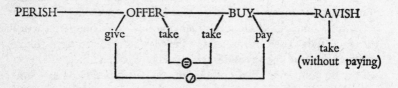

In the latter scheme we see that: (1) *to offer* and *to buy* are symmetrical; (2) *to perish* is the equivalent of *to lose*: 'May my love perish ... ' Cinna cries out, indicating that he prefers to lose Émilie rather than betray Auguste; (3) to pillage and to lose (to perish) are also symmetrical because both have the common property of being indivisible. Since they are verbs with only one meaning – and describe one-way actions – they cut the exchange off abruptly; but they are also opposites since, in the case of *to pillage*, the subject profits from his action; in the case of *to lose* he finds himself stripped of a possession.

Finally, if we set up the first system as a kind of mirror to the second, we notice the symmetry of the acts which compose them and which thereby serve to set off the difficulty in which Cinna finds himself.

This is a double symmetry which can be considered either along the vertical axis set up by Cinna (A A′) or else along the horizontal axis which passes from acquire to buy (B B′). There is, as we have already seen, only one point where the symmetry breaks down: with *pillage*, a word with a one-way meaning. Here the imbalance of the system shows itself and here, too, is the beginning of Cinna's disarray. For, as Cinna now sees, to kill

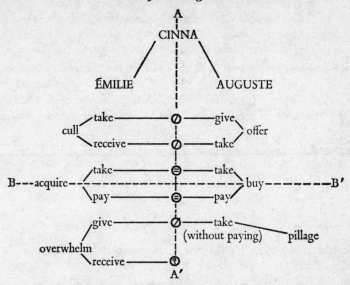

Auguste is an act with no counterpart and therefore an act with no justification. *To pillage* the life of Auguste is *to take, without payment,* the life of the individual who, as the other axis shows, is overwhelming his murderer with goods and honours. The only possible outcome, as Cinna indicated in the third part of his soliloquy, would be *to give back* what one intends to pillage. But how can Cinna give back that which, because of the fealty he has pledged to Émilie, he no longer possesses (v. 897–900):

> C'est à vous à régler ce qu'il faut que je fasse;
> C'est à vous, Émilie, à lui donner sa grâce;
> Vos seules volontés président à son sort,
> Et tiennent en mes mains et sa vie et sa mort.

The decision is no longer his because he is now no more than the hand which carries out Émilie's wishes. This leads to the important theme of the hand, the gift's agent, about which I shall have more to say presently.

The problem of exchange is complicated by the problem of the person. To give, to offer, to acquire, etc., are not adequate to give a proper account of the whole act. In order to give proper meaning to acts, we must also know who is giving what to whom. Cinna puts it this way (v. 250–4):

> Demain j'attends la haine ou la ferveur des hommes,
> Le nom de parricide ou de libérateur,

> César celui de prince ou d'un usurpateur.
> Du succès qu'on obtient contre la tyrannie
> Dépend ou notre gloire ou notre ignominie ...

There are two alternatives. The identity of the individual who deals death to another, like the identity of the individual who is murdered, will depend on the success or failure of the plot. If the plot succeeds, Cinna will be the Liberator; if it fails, he will be a parricide. If the plot succeeds, Auguste will be the tyrant; if it fails, he will be the ruler.

Reciprocally, the nature of the gift will be dependent on the person of the giver or the receiver. Schematically, it works out this way:

> Cinna brings death to Auguste
> Cinna brings freedom to Rome
> Cinna receives love from Émilie
> Cinna receives fame from Rome

Everything would be for the best if this schematization coincided with reality. But we must ask whether Auguste is still the tyrant whose portrait Cinna traced, first to the conspirators and, later, to Émilie (v. 163–243). Or is he the just monarch of the portrait which the same Cinna traces in the presence of Auguste himself (v. 405–42)? Reality has changed once Auguste informs Cinna of his intention to give Cinna both the empire and Émilie. The equation made between the death of Auguste and the freedom of Rome is false once Cinna becomes the first to recognize that Auguste is no longer a tyrant and once he is the first to profit from the transformation which has taken place in the emperor.

Since the identity of the recipient involves that of the giver, the giver's act boomerangs. And so we have the contradictory situation in which Cinna finds himself – 'basely working towards a noble goal' (v. 852). The contradiction is manifest in his anguish and indecision. As a result, his soliloquy is the pause between two decisions and corresponds to the character's need to evaluate the possibilities of the exchange, to weigh the probable gain and loss which will result from his commitment.

The other soliloquies in the play show similar characteristics. That is particularly true with Émilie's at the opening of the play; in that soliloquy she is trying to 'get things straight', to think over the conditions of the gamble and the stakes involved (v. 6–8):

> Durant quelques moments souffrez que je respire,
> Et que je considère, en l'état où je suis,
> Et ce que je *hasarde*, et ce que je *poursuis*.

What she is after is the death of her father's murderer, Auguste: 'A thousand deaths are his due for the murder he has done.' In other words, no price can be set on the death of a father. What she is endangering is the life of Cinna, the man she loves: 'I risk your blood in asking you for his.' In other words, she is gambling Cinna's life with Auguste as the stakes: 'If, in revenging myself, I lose you, then I have no revenge' (v. 36).

> Et l'on doit mettre au rang des plus cuisants malheurs
> La mort d'un ennemi qui *coûte* tant de pleurs.
> Mais peut-on en verser alors qu'on venge un père?
> Est-il *perte* à ce *prix* qui ne semble légère?
> Et quand son assassin tombe sous notre effort,
> Doit-on considérer ce que *coûte* sa mort?
>
> (v. 39–44)

This turnabout leads to a very Cornelian situation: love must be fame's servant and, in so being, increase fame's reserves. It isn't much different from getting better dividends through shrewd investment of capital (v. 48–52):

> Amour, sers mon devoir, et ne le combats plus:
> Lui céder, c'est ta gloire, et le vaincre, ta honte:
> Montre-toi généreux, souffrant qu'il te surmonte;
> Plus tu lui *donneras*, plus il te va *donner*,
> Et ne triomphera que pour te couronner.

But she has made up her mind. Once her confidante appears, Émilie can convey her decision in categorical terms (v. 53–6):

> Je l'ai juré, Fulvie, et je le jure encore,
> Quoique j'aime Cinna, quoique mon coeur l'adore,
> S'il veut me *posséder*, Auguste doit *périr*:
> Sa tête est le seul *prix* dont il peut m'*acquérir*.

The last verse is an amplification of the preceding, almost a translation of Émilie's thought into the economic language of the exchange. The roles she accepts can be seen in this kind of breakdown: (1) Émilie sells herself to Cinna for the price of Auguste; (2) Émilie buys Auguste from Cinna with herself as the prize. We should notice that the 'price' and the 'prize' are barter, not abstract or monetary. This gives them their double meaning. If the price which Cinna must pay in order to *obtain* Émilie is Auguste, the prize (the reward) that he will obtain for the murder of Auguste will be

Émilie since, at that point, he will be able to 'possess' her. Émilie's roles are thus reversible and contradictory since she is at once the buyer and the seller, the object sold and the purchase price.

The fact that the prices are fixed 'as barter' does not make them any more stable. Quite the contrary, as Fulvie knows when she questions the price that Émilie is demanding from Cinna. The prize is Auguste, the emperor who distributes benefices and favours, the emperor who, like Émilie, gives prizes. And these prizes, these rewards, are awards from which Émilie herself will profit – as Fulvie reminds her (v. 63–4):

> Auguste chaque jour, à force de bienfaits,
> Semble assez réparer les maux qu'il vous a faits ...

Émilie answers this argument (v. 69–74; 78–84):

> Toute cette faveur ne me *rend* pas mon père;
> Et de quelque façon que l'on me considère,
> Abondante en *richesse*, ou puissante en *crédit*,
> Je demeure toujours la fille d'un proscrit.
> Les *bienfaits* ne font pas toujours ce que tu penses;
> D'une main odieuse ils tiennent lieu d'offenses ...
> Je suis ce que j'étois, et je puis davantage,
> Et des mêmes *présents* qu'il verse dans mes mains
> J'*achète* contre lui les esprits des Romains;
> Je *recevrois* de lui la place de Livie
> Comme un moyen plus sûr d'attenter à sa vie.
> Pour qui venge son père il n'est point de forfaits,
> Et c'est *vendre* son sang que se *rendre* aux *bienfaits*.

Though Auguste may have changed, Émilie has stayed the same in spite of the gifts which have been tendered her. Why? Because all the material benefits, or even the prestige which Auguste might grant to Émilie, would not be enough to compensate for the death which he has 'given' to her father or, seen from another angle, the life he has 'taken' from him. No price, as we have seen, can be set on a father's life. Furthermore, the issue goes beyond the question of a father's death to touch on the question of every death and every life which no material offer can redeem. Émilie knows this: all the riches offered by Auguste, and transmitted to the conspirators, cannot make the plot succeed unless she gives herself almost as the booty which the leader of the plot will receive in exchange for the life of Auguste that she is demanding. Émilie is also aware of the importance of her person in the economy of vengeance and the coup d'état since she gambles with it in speaking to Cinna (v. 1035-6):

> Mille autres à l'envi *recevroient* cette *loi,*
> S'ils pouvoient m'*acquérir* à même *prix* que toi.

In addition she is fully aware that, whatever his power, Auguste cannot *give* her to anyone. Whatever goods he may control, Auguste does not yet possess mastery over hearts (v. 939-44). Since persons and goods are situated on two different planes, they constitute incomparable, unexchangeable gifts-in-kind. The person in Corneille's universe may be destructible; he cannot be trafficked in. Émilie begins her soliloquy by saying that 'all these favours do not bring my father back to me', and concludes by picking up the same idea again (v. 83-4):

> Pour qui venge son père il n'est point de forfaits,
> Et c'est *vendre* son sang que se rendre aux bienfaits.

If personal revenge has the prime place in Émilie's mind, it is reinforced and confirmed by the spirit of public vengeance (v. 107-12):

> Joignons à la douceur de venger nos parents,
> La gloire qu'on remporte à punir les tyrans,
> Et faisons publier par toute l'Italie:
> 'La liberté de Rome est l'oeuvre d'Émilie;
> On a touché son âme, et son coeur s'est épris;
> Mais elle n'a donné son amour qu'à ce *prix.*'

'Émilie's interest' comes before 'that of the Romans', for the fame that will be the *dividend* of her act is purely egocentric, 'interested', even though, in appearance at least, it goes against her own (amorous) *interest* – as Fulvie tries to make her understand (v. 113-14):

> Votre amour à ce *prix* n'est qu'un présent *funeste*
> Qui porte à votre amant sa *perte* manifeste.

It is unquestionably a sombre gift, not only because, in giving herself to Cinna, Émilie is at the same time handing him over to death but also because she is taking him away from herself by her own will. After wavering for a moment, she gets hold of herself (v. 133-4):

> Quoi qu'il en soit, qu'Auguste ou que Cinna périsse,
> Aux mânes paternels, je *dois* ce sacrifice.

Émilie's primary interest is the same as her family's. Within the terms of this interest – at least as far as she can see – one life is worth another. At this level of the exchange, lives become interchangeable:

Auguste: Cinna : : Émilie's father

What is important to Émilie is that there be a sacrifice of some kind; that there be some destruction equivalent to the destruction of her father.

Émilie's intransigence is not understandable unless we recognize that she does not claim the sacrifice as an individual but rather as a moral person, as the representative of her blood, her family, her household gods.[1] By sacrificing Auguste – and, if necessary, Cinna – to these demands she expects to earn an abundance of honour. The sacrifice, therefore, is positive for her. Auguste, for his part, is obeying a similar principle when he offers the empire and Émilie to Cinna. He, too, is counting on emerging from his sacrifice and gift as a greater man.

We have seen that Cinna has nothing to counterbalance these exercises in prestige – at least he can set up no alternative which will add to his prestige. If he *offers* Auguste to Émilie, he will betray Auguste and, in the bargain, *lose* his honour which amounts to no more nor less than *losing* himself; if he agrees to receive the empire and Émilie from Auguste's hands, he will also lose. As a result, neither the gift nor the sacrifice makes any sense unless they offer the promise, as a counterpart to the loss the sacrificing individual undergoes, of an immaterial gain in fame and honour which alone give the individual his amplitude and genuine identity. When applied to the three main characters this dialectic between sacrifice (or gift) and identity unveils the architecture and the rhythm of the play. Each character possesses a 'special space' which is properly his and to which he brings a particular mood. Émilie's special space corresponds to the beginning of the play where her mood is aggressive and set on conquest. Cinna's special space is at the play's centre when the mood is one of questioning and doubt. Auguste's special space corresponds to the denouement of the play; generosity and assurance are its dominant qualities.

As the play opens, Émilie declares, after some hesitation, that she is ready to sacrifice Auguste (or Cinna) to the demands of her household gods. Cinna also agrees with enthusiasm (I, iii) to sacrifice a tyrant to Rome and to Émilie, a tyrant who never hesitated to affirm his own power through countless sacrifices. But what will come to pass if the tyrant, at the height of his power (v. 357–9), worn out by ambition which no longer has any object (v. 365), instead of *taking* decides to *give*, instead of sacrificing others sacrifices himself? (v. 624–7):

> Je consens à me *perdre* afin de la [Rome] sauver.
> Pour ma tranquillité mon coeur en vain soupire:
> Cinna, par vos conseils je retiendrai l'empire;
> Mais je le retiendrai pour vous en *faire part*.

Not satisfied with leaving his empire to Cinna, he offers 'as a bonus', Émilie, the woman Cinna loves (v. 637; 643-5):

> Pour épouse, Cinna, je vous *donne* Émilie: ….
> Voyez-la de ma part, tâchez de la *gagner*:
> Vous n'êtes point pour elle un homme à dédaigner;
> De l'*offre* de vos vœux elle sera ravie.

The splendour of this double gift is enough to astonish the potential assassin, enough to make him do a literal turnabout. The murder which was supposed to free Rome from a tyrant and allow Cinna to marry Émilie no longer has a strict object once Auguste is no longer a tyrant and offers Émilie to Cinna.

The middle of the play, which I used as my point of departure – believing that we can only untie knots where we find them – corresponds to that balanced moment where *the meaning of the exchange changed*. The moment is one of paralysis, of breakdown, of *meaninglessness*, all of which prevent Cinna, the prisoner of two betrayals and two false understandings, from acting. His indecision in the third scene of Act III continues through the following scenes and even into Act IV. It affects Auguste as much as it does Cinna.

By starting with Cinna's case, we can see how this confusion about the person of the giver and the object given provokes this identity crisis. This is especially visible if we read Cinna's dialogue with Émilie which comes immediately after the soliloquy of scene iii. Here we see the degree to which gift and identity have become (or should become) synonymous, as I suggested at the outset (v. 911-16):

CINNA   Le désavouerez-vous, et du *don* qu'il me fait
            Voudriez-vous retarder le bienheureux effet?
ÉMILIE L'effet est en ta *main*.
CINNA   Mais plutôt en la *vôtre*.
ÉMILIE Je suis toujours moi-même, et mon coeur n'est point autre:
            Me *donner* à Cinna, c'est ne lui *donner* rien,
            C'est seulement lui faire un *présent* de son *bien*.

231

Émilie alone knows who she is because she alone knows what she is giving. Cinna has no similar certainty any more. He realizes that Émilie's present does not correspond to the identification, the equation, Émilie–Cinna (v. 915) which she claims to be establishing: 'But think at what price you are giving me your soul,' he exclaims. To which Émilie replies, not without reason, by setting up a distinction with regard to the nature of the gift (v. 936–9; 943):

> Et ton esprit crédule ose s'imaginer
> Qu'Auguste, pouvant tout, peut aussi me *donner*.
> Tu me veux de *sa main* plutôt que de la *mienne*;
> Mais ne crois pas qu'ainsi jamais je t'*appartienne*: ...
> Mais le coeur d'Émilie est hors de son pouvoir.

Further on she says (v. 957–60):

> et tu veux que moi-même
> Je retienne *ta main*! qu'il vive, et que je l'aime!
> Que je sois le *butin* de qui l'ose l'*épargner*,
> Et le *prix* du conseil qui le force à régner!

To consent to this, I might add, would be to lose possession of oneself and to agree to being treated as an object, as booty pillaged by the conqueror. This explains Émilie's anger and her rejection of her lover's offers of service once she has informed him that others would have been happy to do what he has refused (v. 1034–8):

> Et si pour me *gagner* il faut trahir ton maître,
> Mille autres à l'envi *recevroient* cette loi,
> S'ils pouvoient m'*acquérir* à même *prix* que toi,
> Mais n'appréhende pas qu'un autre ainsi m'*obtienne*.
> Vis pour ton cher tyran, tandis que je meure *tienne* ...

Immediately after, she claims she is ready to kill Auguste with her own hands and sacrifice herself through this deed.

In bypassing the possibility of an intermediary, she places the responsibility of her death on her lover and produces, quite literally, a short circuit which is likely to burn out the network of the exchange. Faced with this, Cinna begins indulging in a similar kind of blackmail (v. 1055–66). The sacrifice, since it has no counterpart, amounts to a genuine suicide: it is founded on an unreciprocated gift and is thus a pure loss. The short circuit, the break in the exchange, is thus not only a means whereby the individual denies himself, but also a way of denying the society in which he is one of the necessary links.[2] Auguste gives clear expression to the social meaning of suicide. When Euphorbe informs him of the supposed suicide of Maxime (v. 1113–14), Auguste answers (v. 1115–17):

> Sous ce pressant remords il a trop succombé,
> Et s'est à mes bontés lui-même *dérobé*;
> Il n'est crime envers moi qu'un repentir n'efface.

By removing himself from life, Maxime has deprived and cheated the emperor of the possibility of pardoning him and consequently of redeeming him.

Yet Auguste himself is tempted by suicide which he envisages as one of the possible solutions of the conspiracy which is being formed against him and about which he has learned. By taking his own life, he expects to be able to anticipate a similar design on Cinna's part and in so doing to deprive him of whatever fame might come to him from the assassination (v. 1170–6):

> Meurs et *dérobe*-lui la gloire de ta chute ...
> Meurs, puisque c'est un mal que tu ne peux guérir;
> Meurs enfin, puisqu'il faut ou tout *perdre*, ou mourir.

The alternative is simple: either the conspirators are doomed or he is. In either case there will be a sacrifice, a dead loss. Still, this is only one of the alternatives which Auguste envisages in his soliloquy (IV, ii). The lack of resolution which he evinces is the same as that shown by Cinna in his soliloquy. It is inspired by similar reasons which have to do with the ties that bind gift and identity together. If Auguste is forced to question his identity once again, it is because he has observed how the exchange has become impossible once the circulation of gifts is blocked. The question is no longer one of giving the empire to Cinna since Cinna's design is to take it from him by taking his life. He no longer knows either in whom he can confide his own interests nor to whom he can confide the empire (v. 1121–4):

> Ciel, à qui voulez-vous désormais que je fie
> Les secrets de mon âme et le soin de ma vie?
> Reprenez le pouvoir que vous m'avez commis,
> Si donnant des sujets il ôte les amis.

Asking heaven to accept the empire's burdens is a fairly frivolous way of giving up one's own responsibilities and of removing the problem of power from the political arena in order to place it in a very personal realm, or even in the care of eternity.

After this first movement – which reveals how far Auguste has yet to go – Auguste considers several solutions. In the first he adopts the conspirators' viewpoint and attempts to see the reasons behind their actions through their eyes. He reviews the history of bloodshed for which he was responsible while acquiring the empire and concludes that faithless blood will be infidelity's price.[3] Meditating on the conspirators' fraud, he stumbles across his own: for this blood, far from giving him the empire *in exchange*, is something he has *taken* from those who opposed him. Having made others *pay* for a good he possesses, he should in turn *pay* by giving his blood at this point in his life in order to *give* the empire *back*. The situation once again is symmetrical, albeit in a thoroughly negative way – the way of exchanges which are established on the reciprocity of a contradiction. On the one hand, it is a question of *taking* the blood of others in order to *purchase* the empire. On the other, it is a question of *giving* his blood in order to *pay* for the empire.

To this kind of solution, Auguste opposes another: destroy Cinna who seeks to destroy the empire in the person of its leader. But such a solution is no more possible than the other. Cinna's attempt cannot be compared to his predecessors', for they had sought to overturn a tyrant and Auguste was obliged to suppress them in order to affirm his power. Now that he has this power, Auguste is no longer a tyrant – and Cinna knows it. Thus an attack on Auguste's life is no more nor less than an attack on the 'state's good fortune'. What bothers Auguste is that punishment meted out to Cinna risks becoming a return to tyranny and thereby risks justifying a posteriori Cinna's attempt and those which may come in its aftermath. Auguste realizes that the loss of Cinna would be a dead loss because, as a result of it, he would fall back to the *status quo ante*: tyranny.

All the emperor's envisaged solutions – recourse to heaven, compliance in his own assassination, punishment for Cinna, suicide – are defective. Why? Because each of them, as I have tried to show, rests on a suppression which has no counterpart, on an annulment, since Auguste either steals or steals away. In other words, no one of the solutions is possible because all of them contradict all the rules governing the circuit of exchange.

At the end of his soliloquy Auguste has found no solution; his questions and exclamations are evidence of his indecision (v. 1187–92):

> O Romains, ô vengeance, ô pouvoir absolu
> Qui fuit en même temps ce qu'il se propose!
> D'un prince malheureux ordonnez quelque chose.
> Qui des deux dois-je suivre, et duquel m'éloigner?
> Ou laissez-moi périr, ou laissez-moi régner.

In the following scene Livie makes a proposal which would allow Auguste to open the circuit once again: 'Pardoning him can add to your renown' (v. 1214). It seems that there is still something else which Auguste can acquire; his empire and his fame are not yet at an end since, to his present possessions, Auguste can add something.

Still, Auguste's fatigue leads him to answer Livie's arguments with a desire to go away, to give up (v. 1237–40):

LIVIE   Quoi? vous voulez *quitter le fruit* de tant de peines?
AUGUSTE Quoi? vous voulez *garder* l'objet de tant de haines?
LIVIE   Seigneur, vous emporter à cette extrémité,
             C'est plutôt désespoir que génerosité.

Her head still clear, Livie points out that it is just this generosity (the *clémence* of the play's subtitle) which corresponds to self-possession. 'This', she tells him, 'is how one governs himself.' But Auguste does not *possess* himself precisely because he is letting himself go. He therefore is not ready to *give*, to be clement for once, not where goods are involved, but where a life is at stake.

Before discussing how Auguste finally achieves self-possesion and at the same time manifests his clemency, we should return to the beginning of the crisis – a crisis which is concerned simultaneously with power and identity.

At the beginning of the second act, Auguste asks his two close counsellors, Cinna and Maxime, if he should hold on to his power or give it up. In possession of everything, Auguste remains unsatisfied. He knows that this dissatisfaction is the result of desire's tendency to want what it does not yet possess. Since he already possesses everything, the only thing left to possess is himself (v. 365–70):

> L'ambition déplâit quand elle est assouvie,
> D'une contraire ardeur son ardeur est suivie;
> Et comme notre esprit, jusqu'au dernier soupir,
> Toujours vers quelque objet pousse quelque désir,
> Il se ramène en soi, n'ayant plus où se prendre,
> Et monté sur le faïte, il aspire à descendre.

Yet who is he? A tyrant cut from the same cruel cloth as Sulla and possessed of the hope that simply by giving up all power he will die peacefully? Or, like Caesar, a just sovereign risking assassination by the Roman senate? A circle emerges from such questions, for each question interminably sends him back to the following: What do I possess? And do I possess myself? How have I gained my possessions? What do I possess? etc ... Such questioning produces indecision in Auguste and leads him to do what precisely is impossible for one in his position: he asks his advisers to make up his mind for him (v. 393–6):

> Voilà, mes chers amis, ce qui me met en peine.
> Vous, qui me tenez lieu d'Agrippe et de Mécène,
> Pour résoudre ce point avec eux débattu,
> *Prenez* sur mon esprit le *pouvoir* qu'ils ont eu.

Cinna and Maxime reply in turn, Cinna urging Auguste to remain at the helm for the following reasons (v. 413–16):

> On ne *renonce* point aux grandeurs légitimes;
> On *garde* sans remords ce qu'on *acquiert* sans crimes;
> Et plus le *bien* qu'on *quitte* est noble, grand, exquis,
> Plus qui l'ose *quitter* le juge *mal acquis.*

On the basis of such arguments, Auguste is not a tyrant. His armed conquest of Rome was legitimate. If he disavows this, he disavows Caesar and, in so doing, identifies himself with Sulla (v. 424–32):

> Pour être usurpateurs [les conquérants] ne sont pas des tyrans
> Quand ils ont sous leurs lois asservis des provinces,
> Gouvernant justement, ils s'en font juste princes:
> C'est ce qui fit César; il vous faut aujourd'hui
> Condamner sa mémoire, ou faire comme lui.
> Si le pouvoir suprême est blâmé par Auguste,
> César fut un tyran, et son trépas fut juste,
> Et vous devez aux Dieux compte de tout le sang
> Dont vous l'avez vengé pour monter à son rang.

It is clear that this proposal anticipates those which Auguste will himself put forward in his fourth act soliloquy. Cinna pursues his point by offering an apologia of monarchy: the prince is the 'rightful possessor' of the kingdom and the sole dispenser of goods and honours (v. 505). The monarch, as a result, falls under the sign of the gift in contrast to the 'popular state' (the republic) which Cinna denounces by placing it under the venal sign of sale or theft: 'Honours are sold ... authority given up.' And again: 'Since they have little concern with the goods they control, they reap a rich harvest from the public field' (v. 517–18). As far as Cinna is concerned, returning Rome to freedom in order to give Rome her freedom back amounts to little more than returning Rome to the very disorder from which Auguste rescued the city; the profit which Rome has taken from Auguste's rise to power will be annulled; it is very much like a suicide on the political level, for the result of the exchange is *a dead loss* (v. 607–16):

> Considérez le *prix* que vous avez *coûté*:
> Non pas qu'elle vous croie avoir trop *acheté*;
> Des maux qu'elle a soufferts elle est trop bien *payée*;
> Mais une juste peur tient son âme effrayée;
> Si jaloux de son heure, et las de commander,
> Vous lui *rendez* un *bien* qu'elle ne peut *garder*,
> S'il lui faut à ce *prix* en *acheter* un autre,
> Si vous ne préférez son *intérêt* au vôtre,
> Si ce funeste *don* la met au désespoir,
> Je n'ose dire ici ce que j'ose prévoir.

For his part, but from a different position, Maxime reinforces Cinna's arguments in support of the legitimacy of the power Auguste holds (v. 445–6):

> Et qu'au *prix* de son sang, au péril de sa tête,
> Il a fait de l'État une juste conquête ...

He draws quite contrary conclusions, however (v. 451–8):

> Rome est à vous, Seigneur, l'empire est votre *bien*;
> Chacun en liberté peut disposer du sien:
> Il le peut à son choix *garder*, ou s'en *défaire*;
> Vous seul ne pourriez pas ce que peut le vulgaire,
> Et seriez devenu, pour avoir tout dompté,
> Esclave des grandeurs où vous êtes monté!
> *Possédez*-les, seigneur, sans qu'elles vous *possèdent*.
> Loin de vous captiver, souffrez qu'elles vous *cèdent* ...

In a curious and paradoxical way, Maxime shows himself to be much more perceptive than Cinna, much closer to the deepest preoccupations of Auguste. He is trying to disassociate power from the possession of goods. In his mind the capacity to bestow goods is a proof that a man is not enslaved and therefore is a proof that a man is in possession of himself. If Auguste gives the empire away, he will give away infinitely more than he will have received; he will thus – as in the potlatch – emerge from the test greater than ever (v. 469–72):

> Je veux bien avouer qu'une action si belle
> *Donne* à Rome bien plus que vous ne tenez d'elle;
> Mais commet-on un crime indigne de pardon,
> Quand la reconnoissance est au-dessus du *don*?

But the circuit of the exchange does not stop there. Auguste's gift is not entirely gratuitous since, in giving the empire away, Auguste will earn fame (v. 475–6):

> Et vous serez fameux chez la posterité,
> Moins pour l'avoir conquis que pour l'avoir quitté.

What is especially striking is that this argument, applied here to the empire, is the same as the one which later in the play, will allow Auguste to pardon the conspirators. Maxime already appears as Auguste's conscience which the emperor is not yet ready to heed. Unable to fulfil the first condition set up by Maxime – the possession of oneself – he can only as this point adopt a bastard solution (v. 626–7):

> Cinna, par vos conseils je *retiendrai* l'empire;
> Mais je le retiendrai pour vous en *faire part*.

Then, in a moment of irony, wanting to thank his counsellors for their 'disinterested' advice, he offers a reward to each: Cinna will have Émilie; Maxime will become governor of Sicily. Quite clearly, he deceives himself in the attribution of these gifts. Would it not have been more sensible for him to give a person to the individual who had advised himself to possess himself as a person, and political power to the individual who had spoken to him in terms of political power as the first step in preparing him for the succession?

The error stems, as I have already suggested, from the fact that Auguste, unable to possess himself, confuses the giving of power and gifts with the giving of persons. When Auguste leaves, Cinna and Maxime comment on his gesture (v. 691–4);

CINNA.   Et tout ce que la gloire a de vrais partisans
> Le hait trop puissamment pour aimer ses *présents*.
MAXIME.   Donc pour vous Émilie est un objet de haine?
CINNA.   La *recevoir* de lui me seroit une gêne.

(Cinna, incidentally, will change his mind later.) He finishes with this categorical statement (v. 698–700):

> Je veux ...
> L'épouser sur sa cendre, et qu'après notre effort
> Les *présents* du tyran soient le prix de sa mort.

In the very dense formulation of the last verse, Cinna confirms the dual and contradictory function of Émilie in the economy of the play: between Auguste and Cinna, Émilie is at once 'present' and 'prize'. Only later will Cinna become conscious of this contradiction.

Maxime, for his part, has discovered that he has been 'taken in' by Cinna:

> Et c'est pour l'acquérir qu'il nous fait conspirer. (v. 712)
> Je pense servir Rome, et je sers mon rival. (v. 720)
> Cependant par mes mains je vois qu'il me l'enlève. (v. 725)

Suddenly Maxime realizes that he has become the mediator of his own loss, at least to the extent that he helps his friend achieve what he himself wants: Émilie. The disturbance which he feels does not seem to be shared by Euphorbe, his freeman, who without any hesitation proposes a solution more in Maxime's interests (v. 730–4):

> L'issue en est aisée: agissez pour vous-même;
> D'un dessein qui vous *perd* rompez le coup fatal;
> *Gagnez* une maîtresse, accusant un rival.
> Auguste, à qui par là vous *sauverez* la vie,
> Ne vous pourra jamais *refuser* Émilie.

Thus, rather than help in giving Émilie to Cinna, he has only to give her to himself. How? Simply by giving Cinna to Auguste who, in turn, will give Émilie to Maxime. In moving from the first to the second situation, we notice a further interchange: the recipient of the gift is being transformed into the gift to be given.

	Phase I			Phase II	
Situation	Giver	Gift	Recipient & Giver	Gift	Recipient
I	Maxime	Émilie	Cinna	Auguste	Émilie
2	Maxime	Cinna	Auguste	Émilie	Maxime

If we now compare the nature of the 'gifts', we notice that the two situations present a perfect symmetry. In the first situation Maxime, in giving Émilie to Cinna, gives him a positive gift (+), and Cinna, in giving Auguste to Émilie, brings about an elimination (−); in the second situation, Maxime eliminates Cinna (−) by giving him to Auguste who offers a positive gift to Maxime by giving him Émilie (+):

	Givers	Gifts	Recipients
Situation 1	Maxime ⟶	Émilie (+) ⟶	Cinna
	Cinna ⟶	Auguste (−) ⟶	Émilie
Situation 2	Maxime ⟶	Cinna (−) ⟶	Auguste
	Auguste ⟶	Émilie (+) ⟶	Maxime

If we look only at the column which lists the gifts, the symmetry is perfect and we can thus rightfully wonder why Maxime experiences his scruples and sudden embarrassment. For Euphorbe, the problem is simple: where is there any wrong in betraying a traitor? No one, he says, is a criminal when he punishes a crime (v. 742). Maxime, enthusiastically, answers: 'A crime which will give Rome her freedom' (v. 743). Such a reply proves that Maxime is capable of distinguishing between a political crime and a crime of passion, which he places on another level. He has the right to give Cinna since Cinna has used political means in order to obtain personal ends. This is precisely what Maxime does not wish to do, for he wants to make a clean distinction between political conscience and personal conscience (v. 769–77):

> Nous disputons en vain, et ce n'est que folie
> De vouloir par sa *perte acquérir* Émilie:
> Ce n'est pas le moyen de plaire à ses beaux yeux
> Que de *priver* du jour ce qu'elle aime le mieux.
> Pour moi j'estime peu qu'Auguste me la *donne*:
> Je veux *gagner* son coeur plutôt que sa personne,
> Et ne fais point d'état de sa *possession*,
> Si je n'ai point de part à son affection.
> Puis-je la mériter par une triple offense?

To moral arguments of this kind Euphorbe opposes tactical fine points which are his contribution to Maxime's loss. We shall see why presently. For now, what we should notice is that Maxime's moral viewpoint is paradoxically loftier than Cinna's and certainly loftier than Émilie's. Cinna is beginning to feel remorse but, unwittingly, Maxime reproaches him for this (v. 838–41; 847–8):

> Et formez vos remords d'une plus juste cause,
> De vos lâches conseils, qui seuls ont arrêté
> Le bonheur renaissant de notre liberté.
> C'est vous seul aujourd'hui qui nous l'avez ôtée ...
> Mais entendez crier Rome à votre côté:
> '*Rends*-mois, rends-moi, Cinna, ce que tu m'as ôté ... '

By appointing himself as the spokesman of the Roman people, Maxime accuses his friend of having frustrated Rome's freedom, of having stolen it from her by pleading with Auguste to remain in power. He accuses him of misappropriating power. It matters little that, in his answer to this accusation, Cinna repeats his promise to assassinate Auguste (v. 854); his action is now being undertaken for another reason and cannot have the same value since it is inspired by personal interest.

Unfortunately, it is precisely the fault Maxime denounces in Cinna which Maxime himself, in a moment of aberration, will commit by revealing the plot to Auguste and in proposing to Émilie that she flee with him. For her the suggestion is both impossible and unthinkable since it proposes a shameful way of leaving the Game; it is even a kind of carica-ture of suicide. Émilie refuses because she sees that Maxime is trying to pass himself off as another Cinna (v. 1346–8):

> Ouvrez enfin les yeux, et connoissez Maxime:
> C'est un autre Cinna qu'en lui vous regardez;
> Le ciel vous *rend* en lui l'amant que vous *perdez* ...

But, as I have already said, one being cannot be replaced by another. Maxime, too, is brought to grief trying to do just that. It had to be this way: the most lucid individual, the person most capable of distinguishing personal motives from political motives becomes the person who even-tually makes the most radical confusion between them. Maxime becomes the traitor. Maxime becomes literally the one who gives – who gives his prince, his friend, the woman he loves. It is perverse and catastrophic conduct par excellence because these gifts, having no counterpart, are gratuitous gifts and therefore will never be allowed by social morality (v. 1401–6):

> Un même jour t'a vu, par une fausse adresse,
> Trahir ton souverain, ton ami, ta maîtresse,
> Sans que de tant de droits en un jour violés,
> Sans que de deux amants au tyran immolés,
> Il te reste aucun *fruit* que la honte et la rage
> Qu'un remords inutile allume en ton courage.

The *gratuitous* gift is a dead loss for society; it is a dead loss for the individual, too. Not only is the operation profitless, but it is also and quite literally of an inestimable cost to the individual since it robs him of life and renown: 'Il m'en *coûte* la vie, il m'en *coûte* la gloire' (v. 1417).

This is not Auguste's reaction to the situation. Having promised the greatest punishments for Émilie and Cinna, he greets Maxime in these words (v. 1667–9):

> Ne parlons de crime après ton repentir,
> Après que du péril tu m'as su garantir:
> C'est à toi que je *dois* et le jour et l'empire.

But Maxime explains straight away that his motives, far from being political, have to do only with passion. He ends his speech by accusing himself once again of treason and proposing suicide (v. 1689–92):

> J'ai trahi mon ami, ma maîtresse, mon maître,
> Ma gloire, mon pays, par l'avis de ce traître,
> Et croirai toutefois mon bonheur infini,
> Si je puis m'en punir après l'avoir puni.

By speaking in this way, Maxime delivers a final blow to Auguste who now knows that he can count on no one. Betrayed by Cinna, betrayed by Émilie, he now is betrayed by Maxime, by the very person towards whom he had hoped, in a last and futile effort, to be *indebted* for something. Auguste had believed that he possessed everything, persons as well as goods, and the goods were naught without the persons. Suddenly he finds that he has been thoroughly dispossessed. Yet it is because he no longer possesses (the confidence of) anyone that Auguste can look forward to possessing the only thing which remains to him, the only thing he has not yet possessed: himself. His about-face, his conversion must come to pass;

it leads to the triumph which shimmers through his celebrated declaration: 'I am the master of myself as I am of the world' (v. 1696).

The whole process leads to an equation: By giving others, Maxime has lost himself; by losing others, Auguste has found himself. Once he is in possession of himself, only he can save everything, recover everything to his advantage. He does this especially for those who have lost themselves. But he saves them not in order to have them in his care – which would be the same as subjugating them as though they were his goods – but rather in order to *give them back to themselves* (v. 1701–10):

> Soyons amis, Cinna, c'est moi qui t'en convie:
> Comme à mon ennemi je t'ai *donné* la vie,
> Et malgré la fureur de ton lâche destin,
> Je te la *donne* encore comme à mon assassin.
> Commençons un combat qui montre par l'issue
> Qui l'aura mieux de nous ou *donnée* ou *reçue*.
> Tu trahis mes bienfaits, je les veux *redoubler*;
> Je t'en avais *comblé*, je t'en veux *accabler*:
> Avec cette beauté que je t'avais *donnée*,
> *Reçois* le consulat pour la prochaine année.

To Émilie, he says (v. 1714):

> Te *rendant* un époux, je te *rends* plus qu'un père.

As Auguste was converted, so Émilie and Cinna find themselves converted – but because of and through Auguste.

Only Maxime remains to be saved. Auguste sets himself to this task by asking Cinna and Émilie to help him with it (v. 1734–8):

> Et tous deux avec moi faites grâce à Maxime:
> Il nous a trahis tous; mais ce qu'il a commis
> Vous *conserve* innocents, et me *rend* mes amis.
> (*A Maxime*)
> *Reprends* auprès de moi ta place accoutumée;
> Rentre dans ton *crédit* et dans ta renommée.

I have said that Maxime's conduct was catastrophic both for the individual and for society. And that is so, since in giving all the world away, he lost everything. Still, there now seems to be evidence that the wholly negative function of the traitor has a positive counterpart, at least to the extent that the hero needs the traitor in order to become a hero. Without Maxime, Octave could not become Auguste.

The circuit of gift-giving has not yet run its course. Once Auguste has given each person back to himself, each person can, in turn, give himself *freely* to Auguste and be prepared to sacrifice his life for the person who has restored that life. This is exactly what Cinna recognizes, and he speaks of it almost in accounting terms (v. 1749–52):

> Puisse le grand moteur des belles destinées
> Pour *prolonger* vos jours, *retrancher* nos années;
> Et moi, par un bonheur dont chacun soit jaloux,
> *Perdre* pour vous cent fois ce que je *tiens* de vous!

Moreover, in spite of – or more justly *because of* – this sublimated accounting system, an acounting system rooted in voluntary sacrifice, we now move in a realm of pure *generosity*.

This concept of 'generosity' – the glorious gift of a self which is in possession of itself – which is so vital to our understanding of Corneille and his contemporaries, is suddenly illuminated. We see plainly that gift and identity are inseparable and interchangeable. On their balance and fusion depends the fullness of the individual, the harmony of society – both and each being perfectly integrated.

One more observation must be made. Once each of these characters has given a demonstration of his generosity, the only act which remains for Auguste is to thank the gods by announcing that he will double the sacrifice he had intended to offer in their honour (v. 1777–8):

> Qu'on redouble demain les heureux sacrifices
> Que nous leur offrirons sous de meilleurs auspices.

It is not the result of chance that the emperor's last gift is destined not for men but rather for the gods. That fact underscores and confirms the religious nature of power to which I have made several allusions in these last pages. As God's representative on earth, the sovereign possesses everything. He provides the drive for the exchange; he is the centre from which all things set forth and to which they return.

The Auguste we see at the end,[4] betrayed but triumphing over betrayal by accepting it, can be considered the political equivalent of Christ, the Redeemer. In forgiving all, he redeems all and allows for the conversion both of those who were opposed to him (v. 1715–16) and those who, like Cinna, are now ready to sacrifice themselves for him. Finally, Livie's prophecy, which incorporates a heavenly revelation and which limns the immortal glory of Auguste, legitimates the comparison to Christ and allows us to believe that Corneille intended, probably indirectly, to be the apologist of the divine right of kings. This religious and political orientation of Cinna supplies the natural transition to the play which was to follow: *Polyeucte*.[5]

RETROSPECTION

This essay does not pretend to offer a total explanation of *Cinna* and I have not meant to give any such impression.

The method I have adopted, and the perspectives which that method opens on the play, do not contradict certain earlier approaches. On the contrary, in at least one instance they serve to complement and buttress; for, it seems to me, that my interpretation and Serge Doubrovsky's converge (*Corneille et la dialectique du héros*, Paris, 1963). I have been pleased to note this in re-reading, after I had finished my essay, the chapter of his book devoted to this play. The reader may decide. Doubrovsky, writing of Émilie, says, though he does not linger on the point: 'The rivalry is transformed into bargaining with her as the merchandise' (p. 191); of Cinna he writes: 'love's slavery leads Cinna to swindling' (p. 193); and of Auguste 'Auguste's problem has to do with possession' (p. 193). It seems therefore that the dialectic of the hero and the politics of the exchange are complementary in character.

Since the present essay takes as its points of departure the concepts of gift, exchange, and prize, juxtaposing them to the idea of the potlatch, a reader might be tempted to believe that my intention has been to delineate either an economy or an anthropology of literature as others have sought to establish a sociology, a psychoanalysis, or a history of literature. That would be a mistaken conception. Far from wanting to impose an alien language on the work, I have sought to base my analysis primarily on the metaphors found in the text. It was those metaphors, repeated insistently in the text, which formed the theme that struck me as the most prominent and also the most promising for any comment on the play – not that I put forward any claim to having exhausted its meaning.

By pursuing this thematic organization to its reasonable conclusion, using certain techniques borrowed from Lévi-Strauss and adapted to literary analysis, I have been able to show the internal structures of the work and, in so doing, comment on the behaviour of the characters and the general organization of the play from a literary point of view.

Furthermore, as I have indicated in my conclusion, this theme, along with its structures, is related to a reality (economic, religious, political, and even magical) which, while external to the work, none the less provides its historical and anthropological basis. Thus, while my appraisal remains primarily literary, it becomes anthropological to the extent that it goes beyond literature and touches on social facts and mental attitudes of an extraliterary nature. One would, of course, have to see if and how this method and these analyses can be applied to other works of Corneille and possibly to the whole of his work. On a broader scope, one would have to hunt out the themes of the exchange and the gift which are the most frequent and the most characteristic images found in the literary language of this whole era.

In this connection, it is well to draw attention to the fact that a critic who enlarged his investigation to include all the works, or the major works, of an era would see his goal metamorphosed. At that point, with the goal changed, the nature of his study would change. Instead of being literary, it would be either sociological or anthropological. The question is then raised of knowing at what moment the analysis of literary structures ceases to isolate the aesthetic or literary aspects of an object and moves on to isolate its anthropological and sociological aspects.

I should like to add a final remark which carries me one step further away from the present essay but which also justifies the essay by projecting it against an even more general context. I have said that I was not interested in looking upon literature as a form of economics. But that doesn't necessarily mean that the phenomenon of literature should be seen as unlike the phenomenon of economics. Using this perspective, it would be as much a question, with the one, of understanding the system established for the exchange of services, merchandise, and women which form the network of communications in ancient and modern collectivities as it would be, for the other, a question of understanding the system of word and image exchange in literary or artistic communication. The latter system of exchange is, in effect, readily comparable to the former: literary language, like the language of the other arts, has a metaphorical function in relation to everyday language, the language of reality, just as money has a metaphorical function in relation to the merchandise it is intended to represent.

Literary language is a guide-post to everyday language either by providing its 'value' (as classical and tragic language do) or in questioning its value (as modern language and the language of comedy do). A not illegitimate deduction could be made from this, namely that all literature constitutes an economics of language, that literature is language's economy. The laws of this economy vary. What formulates them is rhetoric. Every rhetorical structure is therefore an economic system (and could be a juridical, linguistic, or other system) which determines literary communication.

Still, the discovery of the ensemble of these laws for a given work would not exhaust the meanings of that work since the work does not remain vital, contemporary, and thereby communicable, unless each generation, each period finds a new meaning in it. And that meaning in some way escapes from the rules, either implicit or explicit, which governed at the moment of its creation and which its structures manifest.

How then is it possible not to see in literature, and in art in general, the exemplary and metaphorical mode of all other forms of communication which, each in its own way, attempt to reduce and to overcome the non-meaning of the world? How can we avoid thinking that literature and art are communication par excellence since this residue of meaning which constitutes their essence represents and actualizes infinitely that nugget – or that edge – of meaninglessness which brings about the necessity of all communication?

THE LEGITIMACY OF SOLOMON:
SOME STRUCTURAL ASPECTS OF OLD
TESTAMENT HISTORY*

Edmund Leach

I must start with a personal disavowal. This essay employs an explicitly Lévi-Straussian procedure but it is not intended as a guide to wider aspects of Lévi-Strauss's thought. Although I feel reasonably safe with Lévi-Strauss's concept of *structure*, I am quite out of my depth when it comes to the related but subtler notion of *esprit*. Lévi-Strauss's *esprit* appears in sundry guises. In 1952, originally in English, he/it was a personalized 'human mind', an uninvited guest who took his place around the conference table among a group of American linguists and anthropologists;[1] in the earlier chapters of *La Pensée sauvage* he is perhaps the *bricoleur* – handy man – who is busy contriving culture from the junk of history and anything else that comes to hand;[2] at the conclusion of *Le Cru et le cuit*,[3] in more abstract and more serious vein, *esprit* seems to be a kind of limiting characteristic of the human brain mechanism and appears as part of an extremely involved interchange relationship in which it (*esprit*) is the causal force producing myths of which its own structure is a precipitate. Elsewhere again[4] *esprit* seems to correspond to that very mysterious something which is a mediator between 'praxis et pratiques' and which is described as « le schème conceptuel par l'opération duquel une matière et une forme, dépourvues l'une et l'autre d'existence indépendante, s'accomplissent comme structures, c'est-à-dire comme êtres à la fois empiriques et intelligibles ». Now although I am entranced by the images which such verbal felicity calls to mind, I have to confess that, when it comes to the crunch, I have no clear idea of what it is that Lévi-Strauss is really talking about. This is my deficiency not his, but it may be relevant as an answer to potential critics of this essay. My subject-matter here is also the subject-matter of theology, but whereas a theologian can find in the Old Testament texts a mystical message which has hermeneutic import for the whole of humanity, my own analysis reveals only a patterning of arguments about endogamy and exogamy,

* Reprinted from *European Journal of Sociology*, vol. VII (1966).

legitimacy and illegitimacy as operative in the thought-processes of Palestinian Jews of the third century B.C. Perhaps if I had a better understanding of Lévi-Strauss's *esprit*, which manages to be both abstract and empirical, particular and universal, all at the same time, my conclusions might be less thin. It is the 'larger than life' elements in the schema which baffle me. If 'John Smith's mind' is only a 'ghost in a machine',[5] at least the machine itself is concrete and tangible; but 'the human mind' (*l'esprit humain*) seems to me to be all ghost and no machine, even when Lévi-Strauss himself expressly disclaims any metaphysical intention.

Of course the idea that there might be, that indeed there *must* be, some kind of 'mind' which is in some sense larger than, exterior to, and independent of any particular human individual is as old as philosophy itself. To this category of ideas belong not only Hegel's *Geist* and Durkheim's 'collective conscience' but even the basic idea of 'God' itself. All these are highly contentious terms. In particular, Durkheim's critics, interpreters and translators constantly dispute among themselves as to just how far he really intended to reify his concept of a collective personality.[6] Lévi-Strauss's *human mind* seems to me ambiguous in a precisely similar way.

The relevance of this difficulty for my present essay is this. I seek to demonstrate the creation of a myth as the precipitate of the development of an historical tradition. That myth has characteristics which Lévi-Strauss considers to be 'caused by' attributes of the human mind. I do not understand this proposition.

Having, I hope, made my deficiency of understanding clear, let me reaffirm that this essay is intended as a limited exercise in certain of Lévi-Strauss's methods; not as an exposition of his theoretical ideas.

Several recent commentators on the work of Lévi-Strauss have drawn attention to what appears to be an inconsistency between his theory and his practice. *La Pensée sauvage* is not presented as a peculiarity of savages but as a fundamental mode of ordering the world by means of verbal discriminations. There may be other modes of logic but 'structuralism' is postulated as a universal characteristic of the human psyche; it should thus manifest itself in every branch of culture, in all kinds of society, sophisticated as well as primitive. Yet when Lévi-Strauss comes to demonstrate his method in detail, as in *Les Structures élémentaires de la parenté* or more recently in *Le Cru et le cuit*, he confines his attention to ultra-primitive systems for which the ethnographic evidence is notably thin and the historical record virtually non-existent. The critics, Paul Ricœur in particular, have posed the question whether the apparent success of Lévi-Strauss's method has not depended upon the kinds of material to which it has been applied. Taking the particular case of myth interpretation, Ricœur has noted that although Lévi-Strauss first illustrated his technique by reference to the Oedipus myth he has never again committed himself to the interpretation of mythical materials derived from any of the historical societies of Western civilization. All his later and more detailed analyses have been concerned with the myths of a 'totemic' kind from very primitive sources, that is to say, mythologies in which there is a notable confusion between human beings and animals but which are characterized by the absence of any setting within an historical chronology, real or imaginary. Ricœur suggests that there may be a fundamental contrast between 'totemic' myths of this kind and the mythologies of civilized peoples. Thus, both in Judaism and in Christianity, the traditional hermeneutic has depended upon an assumption that the Bible constitutes a *sacred history*, the chronological axis of which is fundamental. The theologian sees the Bible as a record of the working out of the Divine Will through the processes of history; the significance of the mythological message (the *kerygma*) is inseparable from the recognition that the events occur in a particular historical sequence. Whatever may have been the origin of particular Biblical stories their synthesis has made them into a unity; they are not just a 'collection' of stories, they are stories constituting a sacred history and it is the historical element, the sense of ongoing destiny, that gives the Old Testament its value as a symbol of the unity of the Jewish people.[7] How then does this essential diachrony of the traditional hermeneutic relate to the synchrony of a structural analysis? This is a fair question. Myth proper lacks a chronology in any strict sense, for the beginning and the end must be apprehended simultaneously; significance is to be discerned only in the relations between the component parts of the story; sequence is simply a persistent rearrangement of elements which are present from the start. In this respect a Lévi-Straussian analysis of a myth sequence stands very close to a Freudian analysis of a dream sequence. Curiously enough the events recounted in the mythological tales of Australian Aborigines are explicitly described as occurring in 'dream time'; this would be an appropriate description for the temporal context of almost all the mythological stories to which Lévi-Strauss has so far devoted his attention.

In responding to Ricœur's challenge ('Structure et herméneutique', pp. 631 sq.) Lévi-Strauss has taken the line that prudence requires that we should proceed slowly. The fact that his method has so far been applied to very primitive contexts need not lead us to suppose that it cannot be applied to more sophisticated ones. He notes that, in the Biblical case, the present writer has already demonstrated the existence of Lévi-Straussian structures in the stories which make up the book of Genesis, but Lévi-Strauss himself remains extremely cautious.[8] He advances the rather curious proposition that Old Testament mythology has been 'deformed' by the intellectual operations of Biblical editors and he seems to imply that, on this account, a structural analysis of such materials must prove to be largely a waste of time.

I must confess that I do not fully understand the basis of this argument. Lévi-Strauss's view perhaps links up with his general assumption that a society is a totality of which the essence is embodied in a structure. This structure manifests itself in various forms – e.g. in myth, ritual, rules of marriage, law, etc. Structures of this kind vary both geographically through space and chronologically through time. One structure changes into an adjacent structure by dialectical variation of its component elements. These dialectical variations of a particular structural pattern will ordinarily be distributed through time and space in a random manner. If then the structure embodies a 'message' it is not a message consciously devised by any particular individual but rather a precipitate of the whole system. Conversely any decoding (or interpretation) of the structural pattern will (paradoxically) be dependent upon a random distribution of the more superficially meaningful elements in the system. This argument, which perhaps seems absurd when thus compressed, is in accordance with basic principles in communication theory which have long since been fully assimilated into the doctrines of general linguistics (see also pp. 262–3 below).

When Lévi-Strauss says that the Biblical texts have been 'deformed' he presumably means that the intellectual operations of the Biblical compilers have operated in conflict with the randomized non-intellectual workings of the structure of ancient Jewish culture, thus making the latter indecipherable.

But I think that Lévi-Strauss would also reject a structuralist interpretation of Biblical materials on other grounds. In structuralist analysis, the elements of a myth (the 'symbols') never have any intrinsic meaning. An element has significance only because of its position in the overall structure in relation to the other elements of the set. Thus we may compare one myth with another and note the varying positions and mutual relations of the various elements concerned but we cannot go further than this without referring back to the total ethnographic context to which the myth refers. In the case of ancient Judaism, Lévi-Strauss affirms that « le context ethnographique fait presque entièrement défaut. » This seems to me something of an exaggeration; Lévi-Strauss has shown no hesitation about applying structuralist analysis to the myths of the Tsimshian and the Bororo, peoples of whom our ethnographic knowledge is sketchy to say the least. No doubt our knowledge of Ancient Judaea is very unsatisfactory, but it is far from non-existent. In short, I consider Lévi-Strauss's attitude too cautious but it needs to be borne in mind that in the remainder of this essay I am engaged in an enterprise for which Lévi-Strauss himself has shown no enthusiasm.

What then is my theme? My purpose is to demonstrate that the Biblical story of the succession of Solomon to the throne of Israel is a myth which 'mediates' a major contradiction. The Old Testament as a whole asserts that the Jewish political title to the land of Palestine is a direct gift from God to the descendants of Israel (Jacob). This provides the fundamental basis for Jewish endogamy – the Jews should be a people of pure blood and pure religion, living in isolation in their Promised Land. But interwoven with this theological dogma there is a less idealized form of tradition which represents the population of ancient Palestine as a mixture of many peoples over whom the Jews have asserted political dominance by right of conquest. The Jews and their 'foreign' neighbours intermarry freely. The synthesis achieved by the story of Solomon is such that by a kind of dramatic trick the reader is persuaded that the second of these descriptions, which is morally bad, exemplifies the first description, which is morally good. My demonstration is a long and devious one, and the reader must be patient if I offer a number of minor distractions on the way.

First a word about method. My quotations come exclusively from the English-language Authorized Version of the Bible dated 1611. While purists may object to such a source it has the advantage of easy verification. I have cross-checked the quotations by reference to more recent English-language translations and also by following through the originals as glossed in a variety of standard Biblical commentaries. Since every word, indeed every letter, of the Hebrew text has provided occasion for scholarly dispute I cannot pretend to one hundred per cent accuracy but I do not think that this deficiency is of great significance. Only once or twice does my argument hang upon a point of linguistic detail. For the most part I am concerned with stories not with texts, and for this purpose the long-established English version is good enough.[9]

There is of course an enormous and vastly erudite critical literature which relies on the original Hebrew and purports to sift the historical facts from the legendary accretions and editorial glosses. I am fully aware that many histories of Ancient Israel have been written which treat of the matter as if the facts were as fully and precisely known as, say, the history of England since 1066. In the present essay I am not concerned to challenge the validity of any particular interpretation of this kind though I suspect that my anthropological experience does give me certain advantages over scholars of a more orthodox sort. The original authors and editors of the Biblical texts were obviously intensely interested in the 'history' of the Jewish people, but history is a malleable concept. We cannot know for certain just how the Palestinian Jews of the fourth century B.C. thought about their past but their historiography is more likely to have resembled that of modern tribal societies than that of nineteenth-century Europeans. Philo and Josephus, who were both orthodox Jews of sophisticated Hellenic culture living in the first century A.D., could both combine an intense respect for the Scriptures with a recognition that they were incredible. Philo interpreted the incredibility as 'allegory'; Josephus rewrote the texts in paraphrase so as to make the history seem more plausible, and on that account has been condemned by modern Christians for tampering with the 'true history' of the sacred texts! The real point is that Josephus understood very well that what Greek and Roman intellectuals of his time understood by 'true' history was something quite different from the history of the Scriptures. We too can safely accept this insight.

But in fact the usefulness or otherwise of my present paper does not depend at all upon whether any particular interpretation of the Old Testament is true or false considered as historiography, nor does it matter whether any particular interpretation is good or bad theology, Jewish or Christian. My concern is with patterns or structures in the record as we now have it, and this record has been substantially unchanged over a very long period. *Hamlet* remains the same play whatever kind of hash the critics choose to make of it, and the stories of the Old Testament retain the same structures despite all the changing fashions in theology. To assess these structures we do not need to know how particular stories came to assume their present form nor the dates at which they were written.

Nevertheless the structuralist does make certain special assumptions about the nature of his materials and these need to be emphasized.

Firstly, two points of agreement. All scholarly opinion recognizes that the present recension of the books of the Old Testament is an assemblage of very varied writings which was finally edited and made fully canonical only around 100 B.C.[10] Likewise all agree that the purportedly 'early' works in the collection contain numerous interpolations which have been inserted from time to time by later editors in the interests of consistency or with a view to providing traditional support for a disputed point of political or religious doctrine. But orthodox scholarship assumes that from the time of David onwards the individual characters in Biblical stories were 'real people', that is to say they had genuine flesh-and-blood historical existence and that even for earlier periods there is a substratum of genuine historical fact. In that case the historian's task is to distinguish this historical reality from the accretions of legend and editorial modification. Thus if two Biblical stories refer to individuals or places of the same name (or very similar names) in different contexts of time and place the *historian* will assume that two quite different 'real entities' are to be distinguished. For the *structuralist* on the other hand the fact that the same name crops up in two different places is of significance in itself in that it suggests a link between the two stories. He is then immediately led to consider whether or not the two stories are associated in other ways also. This is especially relevant in the present case since the duplication of Biblical names is relatively infrequent.

In this respect the structuralist anthropologist is much closer to the theologian than is the orthodox historian. For an historian, every event is unique in itself and two events which occur at different points in chronological time or at different places on the map can never in any sense be 'the same'. But in theological hermeneutic it is commonly assumed that an event reported as having occurred at time/place *A* can, in some sense, be predictive of another later event occurring at time/place *B*. Event *B* is felt to be somehow a *repetition* of Event *A*. Now this is a very 'mythological' way of treating reality and it is one to which the methods of structuralism are well adapted. Judged by nineteenth- and twentieth-century conventions a structuralist's approach to Biblical materials is unorthodox but it is not in fact a novelty. On the contrary, the general principle has been recognized for millennia. It could hardly be otherwise. After all, if it really be the case that the 'message' contained in a myth or in a set of myths is communicated through the structure, then it would be astonishing if two thousand years of intensive Biblical scholarship had not gained some inkling of this fact! If on the other hand structural analysis of Biblical materials were now to reveal 'messages' which are *not* in some degree already known, then we should have good grounds for supposing that the whole business is an accidental triviality. But this is not the case. For example, to start at the very beginning, the structure of the first chapter of Genesis is so obvious that it has been commented upon by Rabbinical authors from the earliest times. The pattern may be summarized as follows: the six days of the Creation form two separate sequences; the first three days are concerned with a static world devoid of life, and the second three days with a moving world of 'living' things; day four is paired with day one, five with two, and six with three.[11] The Rabbinical view has been that the structure of itself embodies a complex theological message. A version of this doctrine was quite recently propounded by Professor Leo Strauss (Chicago) in the following terms:

> It seems then that the sequence of creation in the first chapter of the Bible can be stated as follows: from the principle of separation, light; via something which separates, heaven; to something which is separated, earth and sea; to things which are productive of separated things, trees, for example; then things which can separate themselves from their courses, brutes; and finally a being which can separate itself from its way, the right way. I repeat, the clue to the first chapter seems to be the fact that the account of the creation consists of two main parts. This implies that the created world is conceived to be characterized by a fundamental dualism: things which are different from each other without having the capacity of local motion and things which in addition to being different from each other do have the capacity for local motion. This means the first chapter seems to be based on the assumption that the fundamental dualism is that of distinctness, otherness, as Plato would say, and of local motion.[12]

From this Professor Strauss goes on to argue that: 'The terrestial living things are created either not in the image of God – brutes; or in the image of God – man.' Nature versus Culture! Such arguments in work which has nothing to do with the school of Lévi-Strauss show that we should not regard structure and hermeneutic as intrinsically opposed.

Before I proceed further I must be sure that the reader fully understands the difference between comparison in terms of content and comparison in terms of structure. Comparison in terms of content is the orthodox and obvious technique of 'the comparative method in anthropology' as practised by Tylor, Frazer, Westermarck, Briffault and other scholars of the late nineteenth and early twentieth centuries. Frazer's three-volume *Folklore in the Old Testament* (1918–22) exhibits the method on a grand scale; but in the case of Biblical materials this type of exegesis dates back to the earliest times: when the author of Matthew i. 23 quotes a passage from Isaiah to validate the truth of his story of the Virgin Birth, he is simply comparing two stories of similar content. In general, the whole hermeneutic argument which represents the New Testament as a fulfilment of the Old, or the Books of Kings as a fulfilment of the warnings of Deuteronomy, depends upon such comparisons.

In contrast, structural analysis leads to the recognition of relationships of a more abstract kind which may associate bodies or material which have little or no similarity of content. A good example is provided by a comparison between the Biblical accounts of (*a*) the sacrifice of Jepthah's daughter and (*b*) the non-sacrifice of Abraham's son. Except that both stories are about 'sacrifice' the similarity of content is very slight.

The following is a summary of Judges xi. 30–40:

(*a*) Jepthah, the Gileadite, makes a vow to make a burnt offering to God if he is granted victory.

(*b*) God grants Jepthah victory.

(*c*) (By implication Jepthah plans to sacrifice an animal or a slave in fulfilment of his vow.)

(*d*) God, in the form of chance, imposes a substitution whereby Jepthah is made to sacrifice his only child, a virgin daughter.

Outcome

Jepthah has no descendants of any kind.

The following is a corresponding analysis of Genesis xxii. 1–18:

(*d*) God requires Abraham to sacrifice his only son Isaac as evidence of faith and obedience.

(*c*) As Abraham prepares to obey, God imposes a substitution whereby Abraham in fact sacrifices an animal in fulfilment of his duty.

(*b*) Abraham thus demonstrates his faith and obedience.

(*a*) God makes a vow that Abraham shall have countless descendants.

The Legitimacy of Solomon

Outcome

All the children of Israel claim descent from Abraham.

When presented in this way the two stories appear as mirror images of each other. 'God' is changed to 'father', 'father' is changed to 'God'; 'virgin daughter' is changed to 'virgin son'; the sequence represented by the clauses (a), (b), (c), (d) in the first story is exactly reversed in the second story. The mythical outcome of the first story 'the father has no descendants' is the exact opposite to the mythical outcome of the second 'the father has countless descendants'. It can thus be said that these two stories have an identical structure since the second can be produced from the first by the simplest possible transformation rule: 'Substitute for each element its binary opposite.'

One of the main arguments which Lévi-Strauss advances in his studies of myth proper is that the repetitions which are so characteristic of all forms of folklore are significant not so much because of their similarity as because of their differences. In Lévi-Strauss's view myths commonly focus around some irresolvable paradox of logic or of fact: e.g. 'How could there be a first man and a first woman who were not also brother and sister?', 'How can one fit a desire for immortality with a knowledge of the certainty of impending death?', 'How is it that human beings are on the one hand animals (natural) and on the other hand not-animals (cultural)?' The 'variations on a theme' which constantly recur in mythological systems serve to blur the edges of such 'contradictions' and thus to remove them from immediate consciousness.

If we treat the material selectively without reference to the chronological (historical) dimension then there are many sets of Biblical stories which conform to this principle of Lévi-Straussian analysis. I have cited some examples of this in earlier papers (see fn. 8). Another such set is provided by the stories of Dinah (Genesis xxxiv), Abimelech (Judges ix), Jepthah (Judges xi. 1–11), Samson (Judges xiii–xvi). Here the common theme is a 'contradiction' which is the historical torment of all religious sects which acquire political ambitions but which has been of particular significance in Jewish history from the earliest times right down to the present day. On the one hand the practice of sectarian endogamy is essential to maintain the purity of the faith, on the other hand exogamous marriages may be politically expedient if peaceful relations are to be maintained with hostile neighbours.

In a formal sense the Biblical texts consistently affirm the righteousness of endogamy and the sinfulness of exogamy, but the structural 'message' keeps harking back to the 'contradiction'. Thus:

(1) The Dinah story affirms unambiguously the sinfulness of allowing an Israelite girl to cohabit with a foreigner (in this case a Shechemite-Canaanite) even if the foreigner is prepared to adopt the Israelite faith. But the story points out that the enforcement of this principle must lead to political difficulties.

(2) Abimelech is a half-blood Israelite-Shechemite by a Shechemite mother. On the death of his father he joins his mother's people, kills all his pure-blooded half-brothers except one, and is himself killed.

(3) Jepthah is also a half-blood Israelite by a foreign mother. On the death of his father he is chased away by his father's people but eventually called back to be their leader. His pure-blooded relatives are thereby saved but his only daughter is sacrificed and he dies without descendants.

(4) Samson is a pure-blooded Israelite hero who has a series of sexual liaisons with foreign (Philistine) women interspersed with battles against Philistine men. The women are consistently treacherous and finally bring about his downfall. The treachery of the foreign women is here the counterpart of the dishonourableness of the foreign men in the Dinah story.

The stories form a 'set' but it is not a 'closed set'; they associate also with an indefinitely large number of other stories. It will be seen that the Dinah and Samson stories are 'opposites' and the Abimelech and Jepthah stories are 'opposites', but the Dinah and Abimelech stories are linked through the reference to Shechem. Both the latter imply that the 'King of Shechem' is a foreigner. But this is a very critical issue which leads much further afield, for Jeroboam was 'King of Shechem' and the foreignness or non-foreignness of Jeroboam is a matter of major import (see p. 266). The reader should take particular note of the way in which in these stories the moral issue of the legitimacy of sex-relations is intertwined with the political issue of 'How foreign is a foreigner?'

But what, it may be asked, is the merit of such structural comparison? Even if the similarity of pattern be conceded what does this tell us? To this question I can offer no simple answer. To some extent the pleasure which can be derived from structural analysis is aesthetic. Just as a mathematician feels that an elegant solution is 'better' than a clumsy solution to the same problem, so the merit of 'structuralism' cannot be narrowly judged by any such practical criterion as: 'Does this line of investigation lead to any useful result?' A demonstration of the elegance of the 'unconscious operations of the human mind' has merit in itself, even if some of us may feel uncertain as to just what kind of an operating agent this 'human mind' may be.

But if practical justification is needed, I would put it this way. At the very least the discovery of a consistent structural pattern in a set of ethnographic data leads us to compare what otherwise seems incomparable and invites further questions of a new kind at a different more concrete level of ethnography. I have not the space to develop this point but I can indicate what I mean. Jepthah's daughter is said to have been sacrificed at a place called Mizpah which was the locale for a four-day annual festival attended by unmarried girls (seeking husbands?) (Judges xi. 34–40). The non-sacrifice of Isaac took place on Mount Moriah which is the site of the temple at Jerusalem (Genesis xxii. 2; 2 Chronicles iii. 1). Strict attention to geographical detail suggests that there are at least two different places described as Mizpah in Old Testament texts but structural considerations would now lead us to consider whether they have anything in common and also whether they stand associated with Jerusalem in any other way than by a simple inversion of mythology.

But I must confine myself to a narrower theme, the structural analysis of chronological sequences. Let us return to the point made by Ricœur that the text of the Bible as we have it, is a chronological history and not a timeless myth. How does this affect the argument?

The facts are plain enough. Apart from the manuals of tribal law and custom and the sermons of the prophets, the main body of the Old Testament is presented as if it were a history of the Jewish people from the Creation down to the time of Ezra and Nehemiah. It is also plain that source materials of very different kinds have been brought together and synthesized, by skilful and perhaps repeated editing, into a single story. That in itself is not remarkable.

Much the same might be said of any kind of history book, whether the history in question be true, false or purely imaginary. An indefinitely large number of events have actually occurred in the past. Only a tiny selection of these events can ever come to be perpetuated as 'history'. The process by which the selection is made is a complex combination of pure accident and editorial interest but the net result is quite arbitrary. Political events get worked into the historical records because literate people everywhere seem to have a persistent belief in the 'importance' of politics. But this is only a value judgment and if the chroniclers of ancient kingdoms had happened to write about other matters we should not now find their stories less interesting. Of 'history' as of 'myth', it is quite sensible for the sociological enquirer to ask himself: 'Why does this particular incident (rather than some other) occur in the story in this particular form (rather than in some other)?' It is not sufficient to give the orthodox historian's answer which is: 'Well, that is what really happened,' for many other things also really happened which do not appear in the story at all.

The structuralist has a special kind of answer to this kind of question. He argues that the significance of individual items in any kind of story is to be found in their patterned arrangement. What attracts his attention is not the content of any particular story but the contrast of pattern as between one story and another. This principle should be just as applicable to stories which purport to be 'history' as to stories which are palpably 'myth'.

Any honest man who writes or edits a history believes that what he writes is true, and in the case of a religious history he may well believe that in displaying this truth he is inspired by God. But clearly he cannot believe that what he writes is the *whole* truth. What he records as the truth is only that part of the totality of things which *he* considers 'important', and it is plain that what constitutes historical importance can vary greatly both from place to place and from time to time. It is surely a commonplace that to understand any particular history book we first need to understand something about the particular interests and orientation of the latest editor. Editors are not authors. Most editors have a great respect for the texts with which they have to deal (and this perhaps is especially true of priestly editors of religious texts) but, even so, the rearrangements, glosses and emendations which any editor makes necessarily reflect the special attitudes of his own time rather than the attitudes and intentions of his predecessors.

Viewed in this rather special way, as a much edited history book, the Old Testament must be regarded as a compilation of ancient and modern documents finally brought together by editors who shared the general attitudes of the authors of the Books of Nehemiah and Ezra.[13] What this attitude may have been was perceptively assessed by S. A. Cook nearly forty years ago:

With Nehemiah and Ezra we enter upon the era of normative Judaism. Judah was a religious community whose representative was the high priest of Jerusalem. Instead of sacerdotal kings, there were royal priests anointed with oil, arrayed with kingly insignia, claiming the usual kingly dues in addition to the customary rights of priests. With his priests and Levites and with the chiefs and nobles of the Jewish families, the high priest directs this small state ... This hierarchical government can find no foundation in the Hebrew monarchy.[14]

It is in accord with the needs of such a society as this that the text of the Old Testament as a whole (as we now have it) sets the mark of approval on orderly government of a monarchical kind while disapproving of all individual monarchs. It is consistent that it should lay stress upon the unique importance of Jerusalem as the cult centre of the Jewish faith in which the tribe of Judah stands for the secular arm and that of Levi for the spiritual, and it is quite appropriate that the tone of Nehemiah and Ezra should be one of bigoted sectarianism which demands above all else that Jews shall separate themselves off sharply from all foreigners and that there shall be no intermarriage between Jew and Gentile. For Nehemiah and Ezra such intermarriage is the sin of sins. Yet this doctrine of exclusiveness leads to contradiction.

> Whatever the predominant party might think of foreign marriages, the tradition of the half-Moabite origin of David serves ... to emphasize the debt which Judah and Jerusalem owed to one of its neighbours ... Again, although some desired a self-contained community opposed to the heathen neighbours of Jerusalem the story of Jonah implicitly contends against the attempt of Judaism to close its doors. The conflicting tendencies were incompatible ... (Cook, op. cit.)

It is with precisely these incompatibilities that this essay is primarily concerned.

Here I must emphasize the very important distinction between structural contradiction (large scale incompatibility of implication) and content contradiction (inconsistencies in the small scale details of textual assertion). Contradictions of the latter kind abound. Mostly they are probably a by-product of editorial glosses originally introduced with the purposes of eliminating still more glaring contradictions. It is precisely the all-pervasiveness and random incidence of such inconsistency which makes these 'historical' texts appropriate material for structural analysis, for, under these randomized conditions, the underlying structure of the story ceases to be under the rational control of the editors and generates a momentum of its own.[15] At this point the story ceases to be simply a chronicle of events, it becomes a drama.

Ordinary modern readers are unlikely to pay close attention to Biblical genealogies or to recognize the variety of inconsistencies which these contain. The details are tedious, yet since I claim that it is the randomness of inconsistency which justifies the application of structural analysis I must at least exemplify what I mean.

In the remainder of this section I try to show how the editorial amendments of various hands have become woven into an involuted network which can convey a 'message' which was not necessarily consciously intended by any particular editor.

An explicit logical basis for the obsessional stress on endogamy which is so evident in Nehemiah and Ezra is provided by I Kings xi. 1–8. Solomon the wise, the great king, the builder of the temple, nevertheless is a sinner in that he 'loved many strange women, together with the daughter of Pharoah, women of the Moabites, Ammonites, Edomites, Zidonians and Hittites'. As a consequence 'did Solomon build an high place for Chemosh, the abomination of Moab, in the hill that is before Jerusalem and for Molech the abomination of the children of Ammon, and likewise did he for all his strange wives, which burnt incense and sacrificed unto their gods'. The inference is that if the Israelites would only keep to the rules and marry only with women of their own kind then they would not be led astray by their foreign wives! The practical difficulty is to decide just who is or who is not a foreign wife.

Taken at its face value, the text of the Old Testament represents the relation between the various tribal groups involved as one of binary segmentation of the most consistent kind. The skeleton genealogy of Fig. 1 is exactly comparable to dozens of diagrams discussed in contemporary works by British social anthropologists.[16] A traditional genealogy of this kind serves to discriminate very precisely to an exact 'degree of foreignness' which separates one group from another. Thus from the viewpoint of members of the tribe of Judah, the hierarchy of social distance should be: (1) Fellow members of the tribe (lineage) of Judah; (2) Other tribes descended from Leah; (3) Tribes descended from Zilpah; (4) The tribe of Benjamin; (5) Tribes descended from Joseph; (6) Tribes descended from Bilhah; (7) Edomites; (8) Ishmaelites; (9) Moabites and Ammonites; (10) Canaanites; (11) Other Gentiles; (12) Kenites. Biblical texts, notably Joshua xiv–xxii, also specify very precisely just which territorial areas

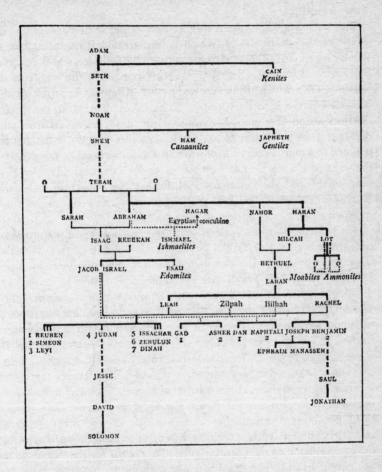

Fig. 1. – Skeleton Genealogy

NOTES: (i) Sarah, Abraham's half-sister, has the status of wife. Hagar the Egyptian is bond-servant to Sarah and concubine to Abraham.

(ii) Leah and Rachel are full sisters and kin to Jacob through both parents. Zilpah is bond-servant to Leah; Bilhah is bond-servant to Rachel.

(iii) Benjamin is the youngest child of Jacob-Israel. Rachel dies at his birth. He is the only one of the children to be born within the confines of the territory later allocated to his descendants (see Fig. 2). The name Benjamin means 'son of the right hand'.

(iv) Esau and Jacob are twins. Esau is the elder but he sells his birth-right to Jacob. In sharp contrast to Jacob, Esau's wives are all Canaanites (Genesis xxxvi).

within the Promised Land are to be regarded as the hereditary land of each tribal segment.

This territorial allocation is simpler than might at first appear, for the whole of the southern area, which is later treated as the 'Kingdom of Judah', is primarily allocated to Judah (with the Calebites and the tribe of Simeon as intrusive elements) while correspondingly the whole of the northern area, which is later treated as the 'Kingdom of Israel' (and is roughly equivalent to the historical Samaria), is allocated to the descendants of Joseph (Ephraim, Manasseh). Benjamin receives a narrow strip dividing these two main blocks while the other Israelite tribes are distributed in a ring around the North and East. The heart of the matter is thus treated as a segmentary opposition between the descendants of Leah (i.e. Judah) and the descendants of Rachel (i.e. Ephraim, Manasseh, Benjamin) but with Benjamin both territorially and genealogically in a somewhat equivocal position 'in the middle'[17] (see Fig. 2).

But squaring this ideal pattern with the practical realities must at all times have been very difficult. The tribal composition of the Palestinian population was not tidily distributed. Even in the capital city itself 'the Jebusites (Canaanites) dwell with the children of Judah at Jerusalem unto this day' (Joshua xv. 63). Hebron, the reputed site of Abraham's tomb where David ruled for seven years, is specified as the hereditary territory of Caleb the Kenazite (Edomite) with the gloss that it had formerly belonged to the children of Heth (Canaanites) (Joshua xv. 14; Genesis xxxvi. 9–11; Genesis xxiii. 17–20). Even the formal rule book (Deuteronomy xxiii) equivocates about just how foreign is a foreigner. Edomites (and more surprisingly Egyptians) are not to be abhorred. 'The children that are begotten of them shall enter into the congregation of the Lord in their third generation.' Ammonites and Moabites on the other hand are absolutely tainted; 'even to their tenth generation shall they not enter into the congregation of the Lord for ever.' Thus, even for the Patriarchs the distinction Israelite/Foreigner was not a clear-cut matter of black and white but a tapering off through various shades of grey. The reason for this must be sought in later circumstance. The Jewish sectarians of the late historical Jerusalem were surrounded not only by foreigners, who were unqualified heathen, but also by semi-foreigners, such as the Samaritans who claimed to be Israelites like themselves. How strictly should the rules of endogamy apply in such cases?

The same kind of ambiguity is to be found woven into seemingly quite straightforward historical traditions. 'History' tells us of two Israelite

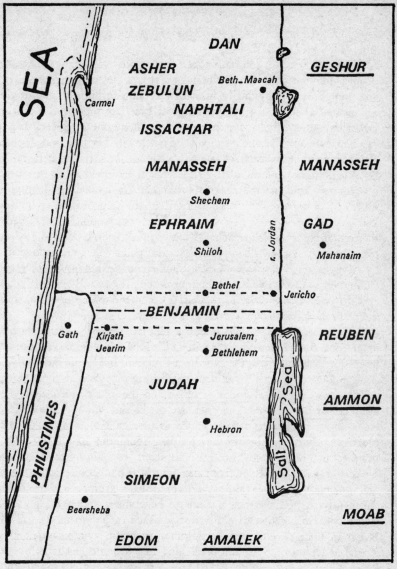

Frontier between Northern Kingdom of Jeroboam and Southern Kingdom of Rehoboam

Frontier of Tribal Territory of Benjamin

REUBEN .... Israelite Tribal Territories

AMMON .... Foreign Territories

Fig. 2. – *Schematic Map of Old Testament Palestine*

kingdoms, one in the South (the Kingdom of Judah), one in the North (the Kingdom of Israel).

This at once poses a contradiction. The children of Israel should be one people, not two. Are the Northerners real Israelites or foreigners? The text equivocates. Individually most of the kings in both kingdoms are represented as evil men, but the kings of Israel are more evil than the others and they are evil in a special way; with monotonous regularity they 'walk in the way of Jeroboam and his sin wherewith he made Israel to sin'. This particular sin is specified at 1 Kings xii. 25–35; it lies in the fact that he recognized holy places other than Jerusalem. Consistent with this there is a recurrent tendency to treat the Northerners as altogether heathen. This finds its purest expression in the story of Ahab, King of Israel, who is a 'bad guy' in every possible respect. To rub this point home Ahab is made the contemporary of Jehoshaphat, King of Judah, who is a 'good guy' in every possible respect. Then precisely at this point where the issue seems to have become clear-cut – Good Southerners (us)/Bad Northerners (foreigners) – the whole issue is compromised. The royal house of Judah and the royal house of Israel (Samaria) become allied by marriage and maintain the alliance over several generations.

These marriages are treated as legitimate marriages, which implies that in *this* context the Northerners are, after all, proper Israelites and legitimate members of the faith! So the Northern Kingdom is a legitimate foundation? But to admit this would contradict the doctrine of the unique legitimacy of the royal house of Judah and the unitary ascendancy of Solomon and Jerusalem. The existence of the dual kingdom is itself a paradox. Its foundation is represented as the result of a revolt by the Northerner JEROBOAM against the legitimate Southerner REHOBOAM. (The mythical nature of these 'historical' characters is shown by the fact that the former name is derived from the latter by a phonetic reversal of the first syllable.) However, although Jeroboam is a usurper, a secessionist and a heretic, he nevertheless seems to be granted a kind of spurious legitimacy. He is rather carefully distinguished as 'Jeroboam the son of Nebat an Ephrathite of Zereda, Solomon's servant, whose mother was Zeruah, a widow … Solomon made him ruler over all the charge of the house of Joseph' (1 Kings xi. 26–8). Observe that it is Solomon himself who sets up Jeroboam as ruler over the northern part of the Kingdom. Jeroboam stands to Solomon as Joseph to Pharoah. But this is ambiguous, for while Joseph was undeniably the servant of Pharoah it was Joseph not Pharoah who was favoured by God. Then again, the name of Jeroboam's mother reads like a pun. The word means 'leprous', which might be appropriate if the emphasis were on Jeroboam's illegitimate status. But perhaps we should also read Zeruiah[18] which would make Jeroboam a half-brother to Joab and a sister's son to King David (1 Chronicles ii. 16)! Jeroboam's status as a man of Zereda would imply that he was a metal-worker (2 Chronicles iv. 17) which in turn indicates a 'middle of the road' position (see below pp. 273–4). Finally Jeroboam is specified as one of the lineage of Ephrath, so the position of Ephrath in the genealogy should determine whether or not he can in any sense be of the blood royal. As it turns out the genealogies are strikingly inconsistent on precisely this point.

1 Chronicles ii alone contains several distinguishable doctrines. At v. 9 Caleb (Chelubai) is one of three sons of Hezron, a grandson of Judah. Salma (Salmon) and the line of Jesse to David descends from Caleb's brother Ram. However, at v. 19 Ephrath is Caleb's wife. From her descends a lineage which includes Salma and the men of Bethlehem. At v. 24 Caleb-Ephrath is a place. Genesis xxxv. 19 identifies this place as Bethlehem the birth-place of *Benjamin* and the burial-place of Rachel, but Ruth i. 2 with equal assurance identifies Ephrath as Bethlehem-*Judah* the ancestral home of Boaz and the House of Jesse. 1 Chronicles iv. 1–4 has Ephrath again the wife of Carmi (Chelubal : Caleb) who is a son of Hezron and ancestor of the men of Bethlehem, but vv. 11–16 go on to discuss the descendants of 'Caleb the son of Jephunneh', the Kenazite (Edomite) hero of Numbers xxxii. 12, and Joshua xv. 13.

Close pursuit of this jumble of alternatives merely leads to more and more confusion but in the end there is a kind of pattern to it: (*a*) the ancestral Caleb is simultaneously both a marginal foreigner (Edomite) and also an ultra-devout member of the faith who carries the principle of endogamy to its legal limits by marrying off his daughter to his own younger brother (Joshua xv. 13–17). (*b*) He is alternatively associated with Judah and with Benjamin, with Rehoboam through Jesse and with Jeroboam through Ephrath, or with both at once. (*c*) He is Lord of Hebron, which is David's city before the establishment of Jerusalem; but he is also not Lord of Hebron, since Hebron belongs to the Kohathites, a lineage of Levi (Joshua xxi. 10–12). But this too is a contradiction since the Levites received no inheritance (Joshua xiii. 14).

There is this much consistency at least: whatever is asserted about Caleb and/or Ephrath, the exact opposite is also asserted.

The reader need not try to digest all these details. The crux of the matter is quite simple; let me repeat: any attempt to synthesize into a unitary whole a set of stories which purport to provide historical justification for rival political positions must end up as a text full of paradoxical contradictions. The received text of the Old Testament abounds with such contradictions, and the final result is a 'history' of randomized incidents with the structure of 'myth'. What the myth then 'says' is not what the editors consciously intended to say but rather something which lies deeply embedded in Jewish traditional culture as a whole.

However we may choose to distinguish between Old Testament history and Old Testament myth, myth and history alike must serve mythical functions. Both must serve to justify the doctrine that the Israelites are the divinely ordained owners of the whole promised land from Dan to Beersheba, both must also justify the doctrine that the Israelites, a people of common descent, form an exclusive religious sect, and both doctrines need to be fitted in with the tradition of the dual monarchy and with the empirical fact that the land in question has a very mixed population in which the Israelites, narrowly defined, are a minority not in full political control. In any strictly logical sense the facts and the politico-religious theories are not mutually compatible as we can easily see if we transfer the argument to its modern setting: Jews cannot assimilate themselves fully into the nations of which they are a part while at the same time maintaining a narrow religious sectarianism which abhors every kind of social contact between Jew and non-Jew.

In the Biblical texts this fundamental contradiction is glossed over by offering repeated partial, yet contradictory, 'solutions'. The problem is not resolved because it is irresolvable, yet it seems to be resolved. Lévi-Strauss has made the same point in his studies of myth. Myths serve to provide an apparent resolution, or 'mediation', of problems which are by their very nature incapable of any final resolution. It will help to clarify later sections of this paper if we now reduce the foregoing Biblical contradiction to an elementary universalistic formula and if we also prejudge the issue of indicating where the analysis is going to lead to

(*a*) a taboo against incest coupled with a rule of exogamy provides a basis for forming marriage alliances between antagonistic groups within a single political community. Further, it is the nature of real political communities that they consist of self-discriminated groups which are at any point in time either mutually antagonistic or in alliance.

(*b*) a rule of endogamy provides a basis for expressing the unitary solidarity of a religious community, the chosen people of God. In real life religious communities and political communities seldom coincide. There is a near-incompatibility between a rule of endogamy and a taboo against incest. There is a total incompatibility between a rule of endogamy and the recognition that society consists of potentially antagonistic groups allied by marriage.

(c) The final editors of the Biblical texts were members of an established Jewish church whose members thought of themselves as the direct successors to the House of Judah (as manifested in David) and of the Kingdom of Judah (as governed by Rehoboam and his successors). In polar opposition to the Jewish church stands the world of the Gentiles. In polar opposition to David and Rehoboam stand Foreigners (as exemplified by e.g. Philistines). But just as in the real world there were intermediate categories such as Samaritans who were neither Jew nor Gentile, so also traditional 'history' provided intermediate categories, 'the descendants of Rachel', 'the House of Joseph', 'the tribe of Benjamin', 'the Kingdom of Jeroboam', 'the Calebites', 'the Edomites'. It is in the ambiguities of the relations between the Men of Judah and these other historical-legendary-mythical peoples that we see the 'resolution' of the endogamy/exogamy incompatibility described above.

A structural analysis requires us to distinguish a 'set' of stories and to display the structures which are common to the set. The Old Testament contains a very great number of distinguishable stories and since they are certainly, from one point of view, all members of a single set, a *full* structural analysis would need to tie *all* these stories together. My present objective is much more limited. I merely wish to show that the chronological sequence in Biblical history may itself have 'structural' relevance. For this purpose I need only to distinguish a suitable subset of stories which is likely to prove amenable to partial analysis. Where we start is somewhat arbitrary, so let me pose a problem:

What was the legal basis of Solomon's kingship over the whole land of Israel?

At first sight Solomon's title derives by right of military conquest backed by the strong arm of God. But closer inspection shows that, in the Biblical context, conquest does not provide a legitimate basis for lordship over land. The Israelites themselves are repeatedly the victims of conquest and deportation but this has no effect at all on their land title. Their title derives from God's promise to Abraham as specified in Genesis xvii. 8: 'And I will give unto thee, to thy seed after thee the land wherein

thou art a stranger, all the land of Canaan, for an everlasting possession.'

Here is the first inconsistency. Land which the Israelites conquer from
strangers can apparently become an inalienable everlasting possession:
land which strangers conquer from the Israelites remains the possession
of the Israelites. Some editors evidently thought that the graves of the
ancestors might provide a better title. In Genesis xxiii Abraham buys a
grave site[19] from the Hethites (Hittites). This is many generations before
there is any suggestion of conquest by force. And even after David had
conquered the Jebusites and taken Jersualem by force we find that he
purchases for cash an altar site which in due course becomes the site of the
Temple itself (2 Samuel xxiv. 24; 2 Chronicles iii. 1). But according to the
rules the *purchase* of land was not legitimate either. Leviticus xxv. 23–4 is
quite unambiguous. Land may be transferred by mortgage sale but the
ultimate title is unaffected. 'The land shall not be sold for ever: for the land
is mine; for ye are strangers and sojourners with me. And in all the land of
your possession ye shall grant a redemption of the land.'[20] But what is
good for an Israelite must be good for a Canaanite or a Hittite or an
Edomite as well. Why should not the Hittites 'ultimately' redeem the land
which they sold to Abraham? This is an awkward question around which
many Biblical stories seem to hinge.

The only fully legitimate mode of acquiring title to land is by inheritance (Exodus xxxii. 13). The rule of inheritance is embodied in the story
of the daughters of Zelophehad (Numbers xxvii. 7–11). Land is ordinarily
in the possession of men and is ordinarily inherited by the nearest male
patrilineal kin but, in the absence of sons, a man's daughters will inherit
before his brothers. It follows that, in ancient Judaea, title to land must
often have been held by women. The rule of endogamy, which was
probably more fiercely applied to women than to men (e.g. the story of
Dinah above), thus had the effect of preventing land from passing out to
strangers through the marriage of property-endowed women. On the
other hand, by declining to marry with strange women Jewish males were
prevented from gaining legitimate title to the land of strangers.

These legal details must constantly be borne in mind when considering
the significance of the stories which follow.

If legitimacy of title depends exclusively on inheritance then genealogies
assume paramount importance. What can we learn about the legitimacy
of Solomon's title from a consideration of his genealogy?

In the Old Testament the genealogy of the House of David emerges only piecemeal but in the New Testament Matthew and Luke both trace the descent of Jesus Christ in a patrilineal line from Abraham through David down to St Joseph. Matthew's list of fourteen generations from Abraham to Solomon is consistent with the Old Testament record but is peculiar in that, in addition to the fourteen men, it names four of their wives, each of whom is a prominent Old Testament personality. St Matthew's Gospel is addressed to Jewish Christians and it can hardly be doubted that the genealogy as there cited is in a form which would be generally acceptable to Hellenized Jews of the late first century A.D. We must infer therefore that the four women in question have something in common which makes them specially significant as ancestresses of Solomon. Christian commentators offer no convincing explanation. The four are Tamar, Rachab, Ruth and Bath-Sheba. Let us examine their stories one by one:

I. Tamar (Genesis xxxviii)

A. 1. Judah breaks the endogamy rule by taking a Canaanite woman, Shuah, as wife (Bath-Shuah in 1 Chronicles ii).

2. By her he has three sons Er, Onan, Shelah.

3. Judah arranges the marriage of Er to Tamar.

– Tamar's ancestry is unspecified but, by implication, it is pure not foreign.

4. Judah's son is punished by the death of Er.

5. Judah instructs Onan to fill the duties of a *levir* and raise up heirs to his dead brother's name. Onan refuses.

6. For this sin, Onan dies.

7. Judah promises Tamar that Shelah shall act as *levir* when he is grown up, but Judah fails to fulfil this obligation.

8. Tamar disguises herself as a harlot and seduces Judah.

9. Of this seduction are born the twins Pharez and Zarah.

10. Pharez is a patrilineal ancestor of Solomon.

Outcome

Tamar's deceit is treated as virtuous. Judah has 'pure-blooded' descendants through his pure-blooded daughter-in-law Tamar, whereas his own original sons were all of tainted blood through their mother Shuah. Appropriately when Shelah's descendants appear at 1 Chronicles iv. 21–3 they are palace craftsmen (potters and weavers) of servile status. Furthermore Shelah is the same as Shiloh, a place-name. This Shiloh is represented as the principal cult centre for all Israel until the establishment of the Kingdom when it is superseded by Solomon's temple at Jerusalem. Shiloh was located well to the north in the vicinity of Shechem and Samaria.

B. In 2 Samuel xiii we meet with another Tamar. She is the daughter of King David by a foreign wife and is seduced by her half-brother Amnon who is pure-blooded. Tamar's full brother Absolom later kills Amnon.

It will be observed that in the Genesis story it is Onan the *half-blood* son of Judah who is killed because he refuses to cohabit with his widowed *full-blooded* sister-in-law Tamar; in the Samuel story, it is Amnon the *full-blood* son of David (Judah) who is killed because he does cohabit with his virgin *half-blooded* half-sister Tamar. The outcome of the latter story moreover is the opposite to the first; none of the parties concerned have descendants and the succession passes to the line of Solomon, whose mother appropriately enough is called 'Daughter to Shuah' (see p. 274).

II. Rachab

Rachab the spouse of Salmon in St Matthew's list is traditionally identified as Rahab the harlot of Jericho whose adventures are recounted in Joshua ii and vi. Old Testament references do not name spouses for either Salmon or Rahab but the latter has always been treated as a Jewish saint. One Talmudic tradition makes her the wife of Joshua. Some quite orthodox textual critics recognize a possible link between this lady and Rechab, the presumptive ancestral founder of the Rechabites, a puritan sect mentioned in Jeremiah xxxv and elsewhere. It is structurally appropriate that they should be identical. The Rechabites are tent dwellers and referred to as 'Kenites', i.e. descendants of Cain, through Jabal who was 'the father of such as dwell in tents' (1 Chronicles ii. 55; Genesis iv. 20). A tortuous trail through Exodus iii. 1; Genesis xxv. 4; Judges i. 16 and iv. 11; Deuteronomy xxxiv. 3; Joshua vi. 25 then leads to the conclusion that 'the children of the Kenite Moses's father-in-law' who joined forces with the children of Judah after the destruction of Jericho are identical with the father's household of Rahab the harlot 'who dwelleth in Israel even unto this day'.

The appearance of Rahab as an ancestress of Solomon thus brings to mind a whole string of binary discriminations. Jericho 'the city of palm trees' is a city of the plain which was utterly destroyed save only for the virtuous harlot Rahab who has virtuous descendants, Rechabite-Kenites. Sodom, another city of the plain, was utterly destroyed save only for the virtuous Lot who then engaged in drunken incest with his daughters from whom are descended sinful foreigners, Ammonites and Moabites. Rahab's ascetic descendants live in tents and not cities and are contrasted favourably with their sinful neighbours 'the men of Judah and the inhabitants of Jerusalem' (Jeremiah xxxv). For their virtue it is promised that their stock shall endure for ever; in contrast, city-dwelling Kenites are promised certain disaster (Numbers xxiv. 21). Lot's virtue in Sodom turns to sin afterwards and the sin is that of ignoring endogamy altogether.

It will be seen that these stories mix together the following antitheses: Israelite/Foreigner, Endogamy/Exogamy, Tent-Dweller/City-Dweller, Virtue/Sin. This is a pattern which has been present from the beginning. Genesis iv. 12-22 contrasts Cain (a vagabond wanderer, a fratricide sinner, a saint protected by God) with his son Enoch (the first builder of a city). From Enoch are descended three lines: (i) the children of Jabal who are tent-dwelling pastoralists (ii) the children of Jubal who are musicians (iii) the children of Tubal-cain who are metal-workers. Metal-workers and travelling musicians would be almost the only categories of persons who would be equally welcome among nomadic Bedouin and settled agriculturalists. In structuralist jargon 'they mediate the opposition between Cain and Enoch.'[21]

Outcome

The implication of making Rahab the spouse of Salmon is that her harlotry, like that of Tamar, becomes a virtue. The adoption of her family into the Israelite congregation allows her child to be classed as legitimate, so Salmon has children who are classed as pure-blooded even though their mother is by birth a foreigner. Vowel signs apart, Hebrew Salmon is the same as Hebrew Solomon, so Rahab's virtue is the counterpart of the sin of Solomon's foreign wives.

III. Ruth

That the story of Ruth is in some sense a 'parallel' of the story of Tamar is expressly recognized in the text (Ruth iv. 12). The Ruth story runs as follows:

1. Elimelech of the tribe of Judah is married to an Israelite woman of pure descent, Naomi.

2. By her he has two sons.

3. Elimelech dies. The two sons break the endogamy rule and marry Moabite women, Orpah and Ruth.

4. (The sin is punished by the death of the two sons.)

5. Naomi and Ruth return home to Bethlehem. Naomi advises her daughter-in-law to go after Boaz, a kinsman of Elimelech, so that the latter shall act as *levir*.

6. The arrangement that Boaz shall act as *levir* is eventually formally agreed according to the proper legal form before witnesses.

7. Ruth is made pregnant and bears a son Obed who is pointedly described as the *son of Naomi*, i.e. the child is a replacement of the two dead sons of Elimelech whose line is thus continued through the impure blood of Ruth.

Outcome

Ruth's behaviour is entirely virtuous, even though her original approach to Boaz is pointedly made to resemble that of a harlot (Ruth iii. 7–8). Elimelech ends up with descendants who are treated as pure-blooded even though in a genetic sense they are, like Salmon's children, part foreigner.

IV. Bath-Sheba

In 1 Chronicles iii. 5 this lady's name is given as Bath-Shuah, which makes her the namesake of the Canaanite wife of Judah. Her lineage status is ambiguous. A patched-up genealogy makes her the granddaughter of Ahitophel the Gilonite, which would imply that she was of the tribe of Judah (2 Samuel xi. 3; xxiii. 34; Joshua xv. 51). But Bath-Sheba = 'daughter of Sheba' could imply that she came from Beersheba, a territory of the tribe of Simeon celebrated as being on the extreme southern frontier of Israelite territory. Sheba however is also the name of a Benjamite who leads an insurrection against King David (2 Samuel xx. 1). This Sheba took refuge, and was finally murdered at Beth-Maacah, a district on the extreme northern frontier of Israelite territory embracing Dan. It lies on the frontier of the land of Geshur. Absolom's mother, a daughter of the King of Geshur, is called Maacah.

These complexities serve to classify Bath-Sheba herself as 'a woman of Judah', a 'near foreigner' or 'a woman of Benjamin' according to choice; but they also offer an appropriate polarization of Bath-Sheba (Solomon) as 'a woman of the South (Judah)' against Maacah (Absolom) as 'a woman of the North (foreigner)'. Bath-Sheba was the wife of Uriah, the Hethite (Hittite), a foreigner serving in David's army. King David (Judah) lusts after her and seduces her: she conceives. David arranges that the virtuous Uriah shall be killed in battle; after which he takes Bath-Sheba to wife. The child is born but dies, as a punishment for David's sin. Bath-

Sheba bears another son who is Solomon. Solomon is David's specified heir in preference to other older and more legitimate-seeming sons. These older sons had been born in Hebron and not in Jerusalem.

Outcome

The son that dies was genetically David's but legally Uriah's. David's marriage to the widow ignores the levirate principle which has been emphasized in the Tamar and Ruth stories. Thus Solomon is very nearly, but not quite, 'a son of Heth' which would make him one of the original owners of Abraham's grave-site in Hebron. Note that if we accept the genealogy, David's ultimate alliance with Bath-Sheba is endogamous, she is of Judah, which makes Solomon a pure-blooded Jew. Contrast the original Judah's alliance with Bath-Sheba's namesake, who is explicitly a foreigner.

V. Abigail

A. The Bath-Sheba story is in certain respects the inverse of the Abigail story in 1 Samuel xxv:

David is not yet king. He encounters one Nabal, a sheep-owner of the house of Caleb. He seeks hospitality from Nabal which is refused. David plans to take revenge. Nabal's wife Abigail intercedes and David relents. Nabal dies ten days later, slain by God. David takes Abigail to wife. She has a son Chileab (Caleb) of whom nothing further is said.

Outcome

As in the Bath-Sheba story David's malevolence is responsible for the death of a husband of a beautiful woman whom David later takes to wife. Where Uriah is a 'good' man, Nabal is a 'bad' man. Uriah is a half-'outsider' – a Hethite fighting for David; Nabal is a half-'insider' – a Calebite of the tribe of Judah. Yet it is the child of Uriah's widow that is Solomon. It may be relevant that the claims of the 'sons of Heth' to Abraham's grave-site at Hebron are represented as antecedent to those of 'the sons of Caleb'.

B. The only other Biblical Abigail is also given as associate of King David. At 1 Chronicles ii. 16, Abigail and Zeruiah are sisters (or half-sisters) of David himself and their principal role is that they are respectively the mothers of Amasa and Joab, who are leading characters in a complex but highly structured story of feud and rebellion discussed below. Amasa's father is 'Jether (Jethro, Ithra) the Ishmaelite'. 2 Samuel xvii. 25 gives the father of Abigail and Zeruiah as Nahash[22] (i.e. the King of the Ammonites who had fought against both Saul and David (1 Samuel xi; 2 Samuel x)). 'Jether the Ishmaelite' is reminiscent of 'Jethro the Midianite' another great keeper of sheep who was father-in-law to Moses (Exodus iii). Indirectly this links Nabal the husband of Abigail I with Jether the husband of Abigail II. If the two Abigails were merged into one person it would imply that

either (*a*) David marries his own half-sister, a very kingly act which puts him in the same class as Abraham and Pharoah

or (*b*) David establishes by his marriage to Abigail a marriage-alliance with the archtype foreign enemy, the King of the Ammonites.

This latter alternative would fit with 2 Samuel x. 2, since David would then be mourning for his father-in-law. If the two alternatives are combined the impossible compromise between endogamy and exogamy is perfectly achieved! The fact that Zeruiah and Abigail are daughters of Nahash (a foreigner) *and* sisters of David likewise compromises the endogamy/exogamy principles.

All told, it must, I think, be agreed that these five stories (Tamar, Rahab, Ruth, Bath-Sheba, Abigail) do keep harping on a single theme which centres around the question of whether it is possible for a 'pure-blooded' Israelite to beget legitimate children from a woman who is not an Israelite, or conversely whether it is possible for an Israelite woman to bear an Israelite child after cohabitation with a man who is not a pure Israelite. In a narrow sense the answer to both these questions is 'No', but legal fictions such as that embodied in the levirate rule or the principle that 'the child of a harlot has no father' permit the issue to become obscured.

If then we ask: 'Why should these equivocal ladies be mixed up with the genealogy of King Solomon?', the answer must surely be that, in terms of later Palestinian politics as distinct from Jewish sectarian religion, a doctrine of narrowly defined endogamous exclusiveness makes no sense. Moreover, taken all together, these stories make it possible to argue that not only is Solomon 'directly descended' from Jacob the Israelite, but that he is also 'directly descended' from Esau the Edomite and even from Heth the Canaanite, so that he is the legitimate heir to all forms of land-title however derived!

Of course this is a quibble. But if Lévi-Strauss is right in his interpretations of myth, this is precisely the kind of quibble which a 'mythical history' is likely to contain. These same stories also illustrate another more general point, namely that, in mythology, 'sinfulness' is a very ambiguous quality which is close to 'godliness'. Cain the slayer of his brother became thereby a sanctified person protected by God,[23] and Biblical harlotry, though 'wrong', provides an easy road to sanctity through repentance. Tamar, Rahab, Ruth are all harlots after a fashion, but like Mary Magdalene they are also all saints. The converse can also be true. A zeal for fulfilment of ritual obligations can sometimes turn back on itself and mark out the actor as a sinner. Saul's villainies when you come to examine them closely are strikingly similar to David's virtues.

So much for the strictly genealogical aspects of Solomon's justification but I have still not demonstrated the existence of structural order in any specifically chronological sequences of events as recorded in Biblical history. This I shall now attempt.

My procedure will be as follows: I take the Biblical text from 1 Samuel iv to 2 Kings ii, and accept it at its face value, that is as a continuous history running from the death of Eli through the reigns of Saul and David to the succession of Solomon.[24] I provide an annotated precis, chapter by chapter, of the familiar story. Where my precis differs from the more usual type is that I pay attention to kinship status, and that I concentrate almost exclusively on the changing role positions of the principal *dramatis personae* and the relations between them. I assume as do structurally minded folklorists,[25] that there are really very few such 'principal roles' though, in the course of a sequence of stories, the same role may be filled by different individually named characters. Furthermore I start off with the basic assumption that the themes which we have already been discussing in this essay are likely to be constantly recurring, though that does not mean that these themes are the only ones which matter. In particular, I assume that the following antitheses, wherever they occur, have more than passing significance:

Israelite	– Foreigner (e.g. Philistine, Amalekite, Ammonite, Geshurite etc.)
House of Judah (as descendants of Leah)	– Houses of Joseph (Ephraim) and/or Benjamin (as descendants of Rachel)

Wives who are the daughters of Israelites	– Wives (and/or concubines) who are the daughters of foreigners
Fathers	– Sons
Full siblings (same father, same mother)	– Half-siblings (same father, different mother)
Legitimate king	– Usurper king
Priest (Levite)	– Non-priest

While the main purpose of the precis is simply to give the order of events in which they occur I also intersperse certain cross-references and commentary which are intended to draw attention to elements of 'structural' significance.

Let us then proceed:

1 Samuel

Chapter

iv–vi. The Ark is captured by the Philistines. Eli dies. The presence of the Ark causes disaster among the Philistines. [The true Faith and Foreigners cannot mix.]

vii. The Ark is returned by the Philistines and placed at Kirjath-Jearim [which lies precisely on the border of the territory of Judah and Benjamin (Joshua xviii. 14). 2 Samuel vi. 2–3 refers to the same place twice over, first as 'Baale of Judah' and then as 'Gibeah' the Benjamite city of Saul].

Samuel acts as Judge over the children of Israel in Mispah.

The Philistines are defeated.

viii. Samuel's sons act as Judges but they are failures (sinners).

The Israelites demand an hereditary king.

[The stage is thus set for a battle over the kingship between Judah and Benjamin.]

ix–x. Saul the Benjamite is selected by a process of randomized divination. Saul's destiny is shown by three omens, the first of which takes place at 'Rachel's sepulchre on the borders of Benjamin'. [At Genesis xxxv. 19 this place is described as 'in the way to Ephrath which is Bethlehem'. Bethlehem-Judah is the home town of the House of Jesse (cf. p. 267).] He is finally chosen by lot at Mispah.

[There is a direct duplication and inversion between x. 11 and

xix. 24. At the first reference, Saul's 'prophesying' indicates his regal potency; at the second it indicates his impotence and the regal potency of David.]

xi.   Nahash the Ammonite is defeated by Saul.

xii.   Prophet-judges are praised; Kings are deplored.

xiii.   Saul is defeated by the Philistines but his son Jonathan is victorious.

xiv.   Saul threatens to kill Jonathan (xiv. 44) [because of a ritual offence].

xv.   Saul defeats the Amalekites but fails to kill Agag. Ritual slaughter of Agag by Samuel. God withdraws support from Saul and instructs Samuel to start again.

[At xiii. 9, Saul offends by sacrificing when he should not.
At xiv. 24, Saul appears to be at fault for enforcing the ritual rules rather than for not doing so.
At xv. 22, Saul's specific fault is that he seeks to keep the ritual rules rather than listen to the instructions of God's prophet.]

xvi.   David is chosen. The selection is quite direct with no 'divination'. [Cf. xv. 23 which makes the surprising equation 'rebellion is as the sin of divination'. In fact it is David who rebels against Saul, but the contrast in selection procedures implies that it is Saul who is the rebel.]
David is now possessed by a 'good' spirit and Saul by an 'evil' spirit. David becomes Saul's servant.

xvii.   David kills Goliath the Philistine.

xviii.   Jonathan loves David. Michal (Jonathan's sister) loves David and marries him. [From here through to xxiii *every* reference to Jonathan serves to emphasize his role identification with David. This equation implies that David ultimately replaces Jonathan as Saul's 'rightful' successor.
David's relation with Michal is much more ambiguous. His marriage to Michal connotes an *alliance* between the House of David and the House of Saul and this is quite a different principle of solidarity from that denoted by the *identification* of David and Jonathan. The specific 'alliance' aspect of the marriage is emphasized by the fact that David pays a bride-price to Saul of 'two hundred foreskins of the Philistines'.]

xix.   Saul threatens to kill David [cf. xiv. 44 and xx]. Aided by Jonathan and Michal, David escapes. Saul's prophesying emphasizes his relative impotence. [Cf. x. 11.]

xx. David and Jonathan reaffirm their bond. Saul threatens to kill Jonathan. [Cf. xiv. 44 and xix.]

xxi. David is aided by the priest Ahimelech, who is betrayed by Doeg the Edomite.
David resides with Achish, King of Gath.
[This is the first of several incidents which serve to merge the antithesis Saul/David with the antithesis Saul/Foreigner, which is then (on the death of Saul) resolved as an antithesis David/Foreigner.]

xxii. David rejected by Achish. David places his parents in the care of the King of Moab. He himself returns to Judah. Ahimelech the priest, betrayed by Doeg the Edomite, is killed by Saul's order. [This marks off Saul as irredeemably evil.]

xxiii. David rescues a city of Judah (Keilah) from the Philistines. The people of Keilah betray David to Saul. David escapes to another city of Judah (Ziph). Jonathan reaffirms his solidarity with David. The people of Ziph betray David to Saul. David escapes. Saul fights with the Philistines. [The betrayal of David to Saul by his own people reaffirms the unity of the kingship despite the 'bad' cause of the King.]

xxiv. Saul resumes his pursuit of David. David finds Saul asleep but does not take vengeance. Saul and David make peace. Saul recognizes David as future king. David promises not to wipe out Saul's family. [Cf. xxvi.]

xxv. Samuel dies. The story of David and Abigail (p. 275 above).
David also marries Ahinoam of Jezreel [i.e. a woman of the House of Judah]. Michal, his wife from the House of Saul-Benjamin, is taken away from him and given elsewhere. [Judah and Benjamin are thus squarely ranged in opposition without any alliance between them.]

xxvi. Virtually a repetition of xxiv with the difference that this time Abishai and Joab the 'sons of Zeruiah' (i.e. David's sisters' sons) are mentioned as the champions on David's side and Abner (Saul's father's brother's son) as the champion on Saul's side. [As to the ambiguity of Zeruiah see pp. 266–7 above.]

xxvii. David, again in flight from Saul, again resides with Achish, King of Gath (see xxi). David pretends to Achish that he is his ally fighting against the Israelites, whereas actually he goes to fight against other foreigners, the Geshurites, the Gezrites and the

Amalekites. His relation with these foreigners is itself ambiguous since we are later told that he marries the daughter of the King of Geshur who is the mother of Absolom and Tamar.

xxviii. Saul at war with the Philistines consults the Witch of Endor. His doom is foretold.

xxix. The Philistines go to war against Saul with David as their ally. The Philistines themselves reject the alliance, and

xxx. David moves independently against the Amalekites and defeats them.

xxxi. The Philistines move against Saul and defeat him. 'Saul and his sons' are killed. [This includes Jonathan but the text at this point does *not* mention the name of Jonathan.] The bones of Saul and his sons are buried at Jabesh Gilead. [The significance of this is connected with Judges xxi.]

2 Samuel

i. David, still residing in Ziklag, a foreign town given to him by Achish (1 Samuel xxvii. 6), is told of Saul's death by an Amalekite who claims to have killed Saul. David executes the Amalekite (cf. vi below). He mourns for Saul.

ii. David returns to Hebron in Judah and is made King of Judah. [Hebron is in the centre to the west of Jordan.] Abner instals Ishbosheth a son of Saul as King of Israel in Mahanaim [which is in Gilead to the east of Jordan.]
The champions of both sides fight. Abner and the followers of Ishbosheth are defeated but Asahel, a brother of Joab (David's champion), is reluctantly killed by Abner in an unorthodox manner.

iii. Abner cohabits with Rizpah, a concubine of the deceased Saul [thus in effect usurping the throne of Ishbosheth (cf. xvi, 1 Kings ii).]
Abner now contracts a treaty of alliance with David. Michal is restored to the status of David's wife (cf. 1 Samuel xxv).
Joab treacherously kills Abner, thus avenging Asahel.
David mourns for Abner.

iv. Ishbosheth is treacherously assassinated by his own henchmen who are Beerothites (Beerothites are foreigners with the adopted status of Benjamites). David is told of this by the assassins and he has them executed (cf. i).

The more crucial of these events can be summarized as follows:

As at 1 Samuel xxix:

Saul (Benjamin) is opposed to David (Judah).

Israelite is opposed to Foreigner.

David (Judah) is allied to Foreigner.

Thereafter:

(i) Saul (Benjamin-Israel) is killed by a Foreigner who is killed by David (Judah-Israel). David mourns for Saul.

(ii) Abner (Benjamin-Israel) is killed by Joab (Judah-Israel) who is *not* killed by David (Judah-Israel). David mourns for Abner.

(iii) Ishbosheth (Benjamin-Israel) is killed by Foreigners-Benjamite-Israelites, who are killed by David (Judah-Israel).

Outcome:

David (Judah-Israel) is the sole survivor.

A very pure case of resolution through the mediation of opposites in the orthodox Lévi-Straussian manner. But let us proceed:

2 Samuel (*continued*)

v. David made King of all Israel in Hebron. He captures Zion (Jerusalem) from the Jebusites (Foreigners).

He twice defeats the Philistines.

vi. David brings the Ark from Kirjath-Jearim to Jerusalem (see 1 Samuel vii).

David behaves as a prophet (cf. 1 Samuel x).

Michal disapproves and is condemned to childlessness.

[This seems to emphasize that the 'alliance' of the houses of Saul and David is now irrelevant; from now on David's legitimacy is in his own right.]

vii. David plans to build the temple in Jerusalem.

Nathan's prophecy assures the succession to the House of David.

viii. David is victorious in further foreign wars. Foreign kings send tribute. [David is now established as an oriental despot of a unitary kingdom with a single sacred capital city.]

ix. Mephibosheth, a surviving son of Jonathan who has been lame from infancy [and is therefore incapacitated from the kingship?] is given a status in David's household somewhere between that of a son and a servant [i.e. the same status that David originally has in Saul's household].

x. Nahash the Ammonite dies (see 1 Samuel xi) and David offers mourning which is rejected. David's armies under Joab destroy the Ammonites and other foreigners.

xi–xii. The story of Bath-Sheba and Uriah the Hittite (see pp. 274–5 above).

[In this position, this story amounts to a mediation of the Israelite/Foreigner antithesis.]

xiii. Amnon, son of David and Ahinoam the Jezreelite, commits incest with his half-sister Tamar (cf. 1 Samuel xxv).

[For modern Christians, Amnon's sin is simply a grosser repetition of David's sexual offence of adultery. But in the actual text various kinds of offence are carefully discriminated. In the Bath-Sheba story we are explicitly told that Bath-Sheba was ritually clean when she cohabited with David and also that Uriah did not afterwards have sexual connection with his wife. David's offence is against the property rights of Uriah, it is not a 'sin' which entails ritual contamination. In sharp contrast, the real gravity of Amnon's offence is not that, as a royal prince, he cohabited with his royal sister, which borders on the legitimate, but that having cohabited, he then discards her, destroying her virginity without giving her the status of wife. The offence is one of ritual contamination. Absolom must avenge her not because his property rights have been infringed but because she has been dishonoured. Appropriately David's offence, which is a crime rather than a sin, ultimately results in the triumph of Solomon. Amnon's offence, which is a sin rather then a crime and the inverse of Onan's offence of refusing to act as *levir*, ultimately results in the total destruction of all concerned. David's offence amounts to giving greater weight to the moral principle of endogamy than to the civil law concerning a husband's property rights over his wife. Amnon's offence is that he carried the moral principle of endogamy to excess, to a point at which 'correct' behaviour becomes sinful (cf. Saul's sin noted at 1 Samuel xv above).]

Absolom, full brother to Tamar and son of David by Maacah, a foreign princess (see p. 274), kills Amnon. [Note that Amnon is pure-blooded but Absolom and Tamar are half-blooded.]

David mourns Amnon.

Absolom takes revenge with his mother's father, the king of Geshur (cf. 1 Samuel xxvii).

xiv. By Joab's intervention Absolom is brought home and forgiven (cf. xix).

xv. Absolom leads an insurrection.

David takes flight supported by his bodyguard of foreigners. The priests remove the Ark from Jerusalem but David sends it back. [David is once again in 'foreigner' status as at 1 Samuel xxvii.]

xvi. Mephibosheth (falsely) accused of treachery. Shimei, a Benjamite, calls for a renewal of the Judah-Benjamin feud.

David declines to take offence.

Absolom asserts his kingship by sleeping with David's concubines (cf. iii; 1 Kings ii).

xvii. The success of Absolom is attributed to his following the wise (i.e. Machiavellian) policies of Ahitophel the Gilonite. When Absolom changes his counsellor Ahitophel hangs himself. [By our reckoning Bath-Sheba is a granddaughter of Ahitophel (see p. 274). Observe that it is Absolom's failure to take Ahitophel's 'wise' advice which leads him to disaster. But later Adonijah's disaster results from his acceptance of Bath-Sheba's 'unwise' assistance (see 2 Kings ii).]

Amasa is made Absolom's champion. [Amasa is son of Abigail and mother's sister's son of Joab.]

David retreats to Mahanaim (cf. ii).

xviii. There is a battle between the two armies.

Despite David's instructions to the contrary Joab kills Absolom. David mourns Absolom.

xix. By Joab's persuasion King David is brought home to Jerusalem (cf. xiv). Mephibosheth and Shimei are forgiven (cf. xvi); but the Judah-Benjamin feud persists.

xx. Sheba, a Benjamite, leads an insurrection.

Amasa (not Joab) is David's champion.

Joab treacherously kills Amasa. Sheba takes flight and is killed by his own supporters at Beth Maacah.

Joab is again captain of David's army.

[Joab's killing of Amasa, his mother's sister's son, is 'close to' fratricide and comparable to Absolom's killing of Amnon at xiii.]

xxi. (i) As a sin-offering seven of 'Saul's sons' are, with David's consent, killed by the Gibeonites who are (like the Beerothites) foreigners with the adopted status of Israelites. The ambiguous text implies that five of the seven are sons born to Michal while she was separated from David.

(ii) David reburies the bones of Saul and Jonathan in their home sepulchre at Kish.

(iii) David's champions fight further successful battles against the Philistines. 'Jonathan the son of Shimei (Shimeah) the brother of David' kills a giant the son of Samson.

[In each of these three episodes the distinction between the House of Saul (Benjamin) and the House of David (Judah) is expressly repudiated. The blood-feud is paid off, the original blood-brotherhood of David and Jonathan is, by implication, reaffirmed.]

xxii. Praise psalm.

xxiii. A catalogue of David's glory.

xxiv. David having transgressed the law, famine ensues. He purchases a site [for the temple] from the Jebusites (see p. 270).

1 Kings

i. David is old. He takes a virgin (Abishag) as concubine: she remains a virgin.

Adonijah, David's son, leads an insurrection, challenging Solomon for the succession. He is supported by Joab. Solomon is supported by Benaiah, a priest.

[Adonijah's mother is given as Haggith without further elaboration. A very plausible textual emendation makes this 'woman of Gath' balancing Absolom's mother who was a 'woman of Geshur'. On this basis Adonijah, like Absolom, was a half-blood.]

Solomon, son of David and Bath-Sheba, is appointed legitimate successor. Adonijah and Joab take flight but are forgiven. [It may be significant that they do not take flight abroad; they seek sanctuary in a temple.]

ii. David dies.

Adonijah, with the aid of Bath-Sheba, seeks to obtain David's concubine Abishag (cf. 2 Samuel iii, xvi).

Solomon treats this as an act of treason and Adonijah and Joab are both executed by Benaiah.

Solomon the King, Benaiah the priest-captain and Zadok the high priest rule in their glory.

Shimei, the Benjamite (2 Samuel xvi, xix) disobeys Solomon's orders by visiting Achish, King of Gath (cf. 1 Samuel xxvii) and is executed. [Note that Bath-Sheba has a vicarious association with each of the insurrections. Her grandfather Ahitophel is Absolom's counsellor (2 Samuel xvii), Sheba (xx) bears her patronym, she intercedes for Adonijah with fatal results (1 Kings ii). This 'marginality' of her political role is fully consistent with her other attributes (see p. 274).]

I think that any reader who follows through the familiar story in the way I have presented it must recognize the existence of a pattern without perhaps being quite sure what the pattern is. The underlying structure becomes more obvious if we drastically reduce the number of *dramatis personae*, and think of the story, as a three-phase unit in which the same characters keep appearing on stage in different costumes.

Table A summarizes the principal sexual and homicidal incidents roughly in the order in which they occur in the narrative, and specifies the more notable relational attributes of the individuals concerned.

Table B reduces the whole thing to a 'pattern'. The story then appears as a three-act play.

Act I
Prologue: David-Abigail-Nabal (Adultery) [1 Samuel xxv (inserted)].
Scene I: David and Saul (Judah v. Benjamin) [1 Samuel iv–xxxi].
Scene II: David and Ishbosheth (Judah v. Benjamin, + adultery with former King's concubine) [2 Samuel i–x].

Act II
Prologue: (*a*) David-Bath-Sheba-Uriah (Adultery) [2 Samuel xi–xii].
          (*b*) Amnon-Tamar-Absolom (Half-sibling Incest) [2 Samuel xiii].
Scene I: Absolom and David (Son v. Father, + adultery with Father's concubine) [2 Samuel xiv–xix].
Scene II: Sheba and David (Benjamin v. Judah) [2 Samuel xx–xxiv].

Act III
Prologue: David-Abishag (Impotence) [1 Kings i. 1–4].
Scene: Adonijah and Solomon (Half-brother v. Half-brother, + attempted adultery with former Father-King's concubine) [1 Kings i. 5–ii. 46].

The 'play' develops two themes in parallel. The first is that of *sex relations*. The sections of the story which I have called 'prologues' ring the changes on sexual excess and sexual inadequacy. The second is a problem of *political relations*. In each 'scene' an anti-King (usurper) struggles for supremacy against a legitimate King. In each case anti-King and King are supported by champions. In the course of the story the opposition between rival lineages (Judah v. Benjamin) is replaced by a rivalry between father and son and then by a rivalry between half-brother and half-brother, a convergence which is paralleled on the sexual side by 'adultery with a rival's wife', 'adultery with a father's concubine' and 'incest with a half-sister'. David the original anti-King moves across the board to the position of King and the champions Amasa and Joab make corresponding moves in matching repetition.

The varying statuses of the women tie in both themes with the issue of endogamy/exogamy//Israelite/Foreigner. Each of the anti-Kings is tainted with Foreignness: David and Sheba both conduct their battles from frontier towns (Ziklag, Beth-Maacah); Absolom and Adonijah are half-bloods. But they are never classified outright as foreigners as are the Philistines, Amalekites, etc. The corresponding sexual puzzle implicit in the endogamy rule has already been discussed at length.

In 'Act III' the sexual and political themes are brought directly together in that the final bone of contention is *both* the Kingship *and* the sexual possession of Abishag. Notice here the role reversal of the mediator Bath-Sheba. At 1 Kings i. 17 she intercedes with David on behalf of Solomon *against* Adonijah, thus placing Adonijah in the status of usurper; at 1 Kings ii. 19 she intercedes with Solomon *on behalf* of Adonijah, and again puts Adonijah in the status of usurper. Destiny is destiny; all women are evil; the rebellious shall meet with their just deserts. When the rightful King (in the person of Solomon) is finally established his first acts are to wipe out (*a*) the surviving usurper (Adonijah), (*b*) the surviving champion of the House of David (Joab), (*c*) the surviving champion of the House of Saul (Shimei), thus bringing the story to a suitable 'clear stage' conclusion.

The view that 'history' in the Old Testament has more in common with drama than with history in an ordinary academic sense is not in itself at all new. This was indeed the favourite doctrine of the 'Myth and Ritual' school[26] and even the relatively orthodox von Rad points out that Saul's disasters seem to follow one upon another with the inevitability of Greek

TABLE A *Principal characters approximately in order of their elimination*

NAME	Relationship to David	Mother's Name	Mother's Lineage	Lineage of father (or step-father)	Fate
Nabal	wife's husband			Judah (Caleb) ambiguous (see p. 275)	dies of David's malevolence.
Abigail	wife/sister			Benjamin	
Saul	wife's father			Benjamin	dies in battle, killed by Amalekite.
Jonathan	wife's brother, adopted brother			Benjamin	dies in battle, killed by Amalekite.
Asahel	sister's son	Zeruiah	Foreigner (see pp. 275-6)	unspecified	killed by Abner, reluctantly.
Abner	wife's paternal uncle			Benjamin	murdered by Joab.
Ishbosheth	wife's brother			Benjamin	murdered by his own followers.
Michal	wife			Benjamin	dies childless (see p. 283).
Uriah	wife's husband			Cananite (Heth) (see p. 274)	dies of David's malevolence. Killed in battle.
Bath-Sheba	wife				survives.
Amnon	son	Ahinoam	Judah (Jezreel)	Judah	murdered by Absolom.
Tamar	daughter	Maacah	Foreigner	Judah	seduced and deserted by Amnon.
Absolom	son	Maacah	Foreigner (see p. 275)	Judah	killed in battle (near murder) by Joab.
Amasa	sister's son	Abigail		unspecified	murdered by Joab.
Sheba	none			Benjamin	murdered by his own followers.
Shimei	none			Benjamin	executed by Solomon.
Abishag	concubine			unspecified	remains a virgin.
Adonijah	son	Haggith	Foreigner	Judah	executed by Solomon.
Joab	sister's son	Zeruiah	Foreigner (see p. 275)	unspecified	executed by Solomon.
Benaiah	none			Levite	survives. Solomon's champion.
David	—			Judah	dies natural death.
Solomon	son	Bath-Sheba	(see p. 274)	Judah	survives as King.

TABLE B *Overall Dramatic Structure*

DRAMATIS PERSONAE	ACT I			ACT II				ACT III	
	Prologue	*Scene I*	*Scene II*	*Prologue (a)*	*Prologue (b)*	*Scene I*	*Scene II*	*Prologue*	*Scene*
Anti-King (Usurper)	David	David	David	David	Annnon	Absolom	Sheba		Adonijah
Anti-King's Champion		(Jonathan)	Asahel			Amasa	Shimei		Joab
Female Intermediary	Abigail	Michal	Michal	Bath-Sheba	Tanar			Abishag	Bath-Sheba Abishag
King's Champion	Jonathan	Jonathan	Abner			Joab	Amasa		Benaiah
King (Legitimate right-holder)	Nabal	Saul	Ishbosheth	Uriah	Absolom	David	David	David	Solomon

tragedy.[27] But it is one thing to sense the existence of a dramatic structure and another to show just what it is. I think that I have demonstrated the existence of a kind of patterning which was not previously suspected. Whether any particular reader considers this significant will be largely a matter of taste.

What then are the results of this exercise?

Firstly, the analysis shows that, in this case, the chronological sequence is itself of structural significance. This was not the case for most of the material examined earlier in this essay, where the variations-on-a-theme would be unaffected by the order in which they are cited.

Secondly, the analysis makes extended use of the genealogical and geographical detail which is so lavishly provided by the text. There are fashions in these matters. Modern theologians, Jewish and Christian alike, generally presume that these details have ceased to be relevant; nineteenth-century writers with their more reverent attitude to the infallible accuracy of 'gospel truth' felt it necessary to explain the genealogies away by postulating a folk memory of ancient tribal movements. But to the anthropologist the prolix details of 'who begat whom' seem all important. He takes it for granted that details of past kinship and affinal connections are 'remembered' only as justification for the assertion of rights. If, in a fieldwork situation, the investigator is gratuitously informed that '*A* was mother's brother to *B*' he should assume that this fact is socially significant. He should then consider 'Now just why should it be so important to remember that *A* was mother's brother to *B*?' And so also in the Biblical case. If the text informs us that *X* and *Y* were related in a certain way, then we should immediately assume that this information is of social significance, and needs to be related to everything else that the text may tell us about the mutual statuses of *X* and *Y*. If women are gratuitously added to a patrilineal genealogy the same argument applies.

The cases which I have analysed provide substantial support for this assumption. In demonstrating this I am also demonstrating that the thought processes of the Biblical compilers differed from our own in this special way. This seems to me to be a point with wide implications for the understanding of ancient history.

Thirdly, and distinctively, this kind of analysis rests on a presumption that the whole of the text as we now have it *regardless of the varying historical origins of its component parts* may properly be treated as a unity.

This contrasts very sharply with the method of orthodox scholarship. In the latter the occurrence of palpable duplication, inconsistency etc., is treated as evidence of a corrupt text. The task of the scholar is then to sift the true from the false, to distinguish one ancient version from another ancient version and so on. For orthodox scholarship, the present text is not a unity but an amalgamation of documents which are still capable of being distinguished. I do not for a moment wish to challenge this proposition but I greatly wonder whether the effort can be worthwhile. The unscrambling of omelettes is at best laborious and is not likely to improve the taste! If we treat the text as a unity then the ordinary distinction between myth and history disappears. The historical portions of the Old Testament constitute a unitary myth-history which functioned as a justification for the state of Jewish society at the time when this part of the Biblical text achieved approximate canonical stability. Scholarship cannot demonstrate precisely what this date was. It was earlier than A.D. 100 and probably later than 400 B.C. but it was certainly many centuries later than the purported date of the happenings which have been mentioned in this essay. So far as the mythical validity of these stories *at that date* is concerned the question of historical authenticity is irrelevant.

For ordinary men, as distinct from professional scholars, the significance of history lies in what is *believed* to have happened, not in what *actually* happened. And belief, by a process of selection, can fashion even the most incongruent stories into patterned (and therefore memorable) structures. For a contemporary English schoolboy, the really memorable facts about English sixteenth-century history are details such as the following:

(*a*) Henry VIII was a very successful masculine King who married many wives and murdered several of them.

(*b*) Edward VI was a very feeble masculine King who remained a virgin until his death.

(*c*) Mary Queen of Scots was a very unsuccessful female King who married many husbands and murdered several of them.

(*d*) Queen Elizabeth was a very successful female King who remained a virgin until her death.

(*e*) Henry VIII enhanced his prestige by divorcing the King of Spain's daughter on the grounds that she had previously been married to his elder brother who had died a virgin.

(*f*) Queen Elizabeth enhanced her prestige by going to war with Spain having previously declined to marry the King of Spain's son who had previously been married to her elder sister (Queen Mary of England).

It is not only in the pages of the Old Testament that the 'facts of history' come to be remembered as systems of patterned contradiction! This bears on the larger issue of the relation between history and hermeneutic (and/or that between history and dialectic). Patterned structures in the surviving historical record (or in the *remembered* historical record) do not embody *intrinsic* moral implications. The patterning is simply a logical ordering of the parts, in itself it is morally neutral. But as soon as moral judgments are injected into any part of the system – as soon as it is postulated that '*A* is a good man and *B* is a bad man' then, automatically, the logical ordering of the system causes the *whole* story to be permeated through and through with moral implication; the structure becomes 'dramatic'.

Furthermore, once an 'historical' text such as that of the Old Testament has become completely stabilized by a process of canonization the logical structure which it contains is also fixed. Thereafter, Jew and Christian and Muslim alike can use the same texts and derive different moral injunctions, even while relying on the same logical contrasts and mediations. The fact that the writers of sermons are unaware that this is how the process works does not alter the fact that this is what they do.

And I would like to add one final point about verifiability. Those professional anthropologists who remain sceptical about the *bona fides* of the Lévi-Straussian technique are wont to complain that the materials which Lévi-Strauss uses are so exotic and his principles of evidence selection so arbitrary that all verification is impossible. If only all the evidence were available then the defects of the analysis would be palpable. Well, in this Biblical case, all the evidence is very readily available and different types of analytical procedure can be directly compared. Robert H. Pfeiffer is a modern orthodox Biblical historian of the first rank, and he analyses at length precisely the same story of the succession of Solomon as I have done.[28] He uses a simpler more straightforward procedure and he finds in the story nothing more exciting than a prosaic account of a sequence of actual historical events. This procedure is essentially the same as that of Josephus in *Antiquities of the Jews*, Books VI and VII. If literalists prefer it that way, I am happy to leave it at that.

'THE HOUSE OF THE MIGHTY HERO' OR 'THE HOUSE OF ENOUGH PADDY'? SOME IMPLICATIONS OF A SINHALESE MYTH*

Marguerite S. Robinson

I. INTRODUCTION

The myth of King Dutthagamani of Ceylon offers an unusual opportunity to examine some of the fundamental concepts of myth-analysis.

The story of King Dutthagamani (c. 161–137 B.C.) is recorded in the ancient chronicles of Ceylon, especially the *Dipavamsa* (fourth century A.D.) and the *Mahavamsa* (latter part of the fifth century A.D.). The tale has been subjected to 'historical' speculation and commentary from that time until this; a modern example is S. Paranavitana, 'The Triumph of Dutthagamani', in the University of Ceylon's two-volume *History of Ceylon* (1959).

We must first indicate briefly the role of King Dutthagamani in the history of Ceylon. Buddhism was introduced to Ceylon during the reign of Devanampiya Tissa in the third century B.C.; the doctrine was brought to Ceylon by Mahinda Thera, who, according to Ceylon tradition, was the son of the great Indian emperor, Asoka.[1] Buddhism soon became widespread in Ceylon. After the death of Devanampiya Tissa in about 207 B.C., however, the northern half of the island was conquered by Tamil-speaking Hindus from South India.

Mahanaga, the younger brother of Devanampiya Tissa, then established a small kingdom in southern Ceylon; there he continued the support of Buddhism which had been suppressed in the North. Kavan Tissa, the father of Dutthagamani, is reputed to have been the son of the son of Mahanaga. And, as it is stated in the University of Ceylon's *History of Ceylon*,

in the course of time, a scion of the princely house that had found refuge in Rohana, as the southern part of the Island was anciently

* Reprinted from E. R. Leach (ed.), *Dialectic in Practical Religion* (Cambridge University Press, 1968).

named, summoned the people to the clarion call of religion and led
them to victory, so that the first Sinhalese dynasty recovered its
sovereignty over the whole Island, and raised Buddhism once again
to the pre-eminent position which it had temporarily lost ... [This
was] prince Dutthagamani who vanquished Elara (the Tamil King)
and has come to be regarded by the Sinhalese as their national hero
(vol. 1, part 1 (1959), p. 145).

The story of Dutthagamani is exceptionally well documented by
'historical' sources. We are fortunate in having available also what we
shall call 'quasi-historical' and 'mythical' sources.

The 'quasi-historical' sources consist of:

(a) the popular accounts of Dutthagamani found in Ceylonese newspapers and periodicals, and (b) the stories and poems about Dutthagamani
written by 'local historians' of the Kotmale Valley. In these accounts
assertions are made not as dogma but as 'good' history, i.e. probable
with regard to existing knowledge; however, the authors are not
scholarly historians.

By 'mythical' sources we refer more particularly to the accounts given
to us verbally in the course of our fieldwork by the villagers of
Morapitiya.[2] The word *myth* is here used in an operational sense suggested
by Dr Leach: 'A myth is a story about past or present events the truth
of which is asserted as a dogma' (unpublished notes).

We have collected twenty-eight 'historical', 'quasi-historical' and
'mythical' versions of the story of King Dutthagamani, representing a
time-span of sixteen hundred years. We shall use this corpus of material to
examine some anthropological problems concerning the analysis of myth.

The part of the story with which we are most concerned is that which
relates to the village of Morapitiya. The story goes that, while still a boy,
Dutthagamani fled from his father's palace and took refuge in the
Kotmale Valley in Central Ceylon in the village of Morapitiya. He
remained there, living in the house of Weerasuriya-gedara, until the
death of his father some years later; he then married one of the daughters
of this house.

Morapitiya today is a small, Kandyan (up-country), Sinhalese-speaking,
Buddhist, high-caste (Goyigama) village, whose residents claim that they
are 'descended from' Dutthagamani. The name Weerasuriya-gedara is
that of the most important *gedara* (house) in this present-day village.

In Central Ceylon persons who share a common *gedara* name are reputedly 'descended from' a common ancestor, but *descent* here is not a simple unilineal principle. *Gedara* names are ordinarily transmitted patrilineally but a woman who contracts a *binna* (uxorilocal) marriage may sometimes transmit the *gedara* name of her father to her sons, while the children of sons who move away from the ancestral home have a relatively weak claim on the ancestral name. A *gedara* name thus asserts relationship with a place – the home of the reputed ancestor – rather than lineage membership in a kinship sense (cf. Tambiah, 1958). As will appear in the course of this essay, the 'descent' which Morapitiyans claim from Dutthagamani is of a similar kind. The Morapitiyans, living in an isolated and relatively wealthy paddy-growing village, are held in respect by the people of the Kotmale Valley. They are deemed to be of higher status than the families of Goyigama caste in other Kotmale villages. This high status is attributed to their 'descent from' King Dutthagamani. Despite this difference of status, however, the Morapitiyans are closely intermarried with these Goyigama peoples in the surrounding villages. As might be expected, the Morapitiyans are vitally interested in perpetuating this link with Dutthagamani. Though aware, in varying degrees, of the 'historical' versions of the story, they say that their knowledge of Dutthagamani has been handed down within the village from one generation to the next; 'these things that we tell you are not found in books.'

Two kinds of myth-analysis are especially appropriate for our present purposes, the functional and the structural. The functionalist thesis was thus formulated by Malinowski:

> Myth serves principally to establish a sociological charter ... Myth, as a statement of primeval reality which still lives in present-day life and as a justification by precedent, supplies a retrospective pattern of moral values, sociological order, and magical belief ... The function of myth, briefly, is to strengthen tradition and endow it with a greater value and prestige by tracing it back to a higher, better, more supernatural reality of initial events ... Myth is a constant by-product of living faith, which demands precedent; of moral rule, which requires sanction ... (Malinowski, 1926: 144, 146).

Structural analysis of myth is a more recent approach developed principally by Lévi-Strauss. Applying concepts derived from structural linguistics to an analysis of myth, Lévi-Strauss considers a myth as a 'communication' in a language composed of 'units'.

Myth like the rest of language is made up of constituent units [each of which 'consists in a relation'] ... [However,] the true constituent units of a myth are not the isolated relations but *bundles of such relations* and it is only as *bundles* that these relations can be put to use, and combined so as to produce a meaning (Lévi-Strauss, 1958: 53; 1963: 210, 211).

The first-level units (or 'relations') of a myth are to be found by 'breaking down its story into the shortest possible sentences'. These units are then combined into 'bundles' analogous to the recurring themes of an orchestra score.

The myth will be treated as would be an orchestra score perversely presented as a unilinear series and where our task is to re-establish the correct disposition. As if, for instance, we were confronted with a sequence of the type: 1, 2, 4, 7, 8, 2, 3, 4, 6, 8, 1, 4, 5, 7, 8, 1, 2, 5, 7, 3, 4, 5, 6, 8 ... the assignment being to put all the 1's together, all the 2's, all the 3's etc. (1958: 54; 1963: 213).

When the content of the myth has been re-sorted in this way it is Lévi-Strauss's thesis that the whole will appear as a kind of 'theme and variations', the central theme being an inherent contradiction in the logic of morality. The ultimate 'meaning' of the myth lies in the resolution of such contradictions. In the case before us, for example, there is an inherent contradiction between the principle of caste endogamy and the fact that the Morapitiyans intermarry with persons whose caste status they consider inferior to their own. In the myth this is worked out in an equivocation as to the precise sense in which the Morapitiyans are to be deemed 'descended from' Dutthagamani, a being even more exalted than themselves. Likewise, there is an inherent contradiction in the requirement that a Buddhist hero who vanquishes the enemies of the true faith must be simultaneously a man of peace and a man of war.

We shall first analyse the Dutthagamani myth as a structure in accordance with Lévi-Strauss's theory. Here we draw attention to the contradiction between the virtue of non-violence and the need for violence, noted above, and also to the complementary opposition between spiritual (priestly) and temporal (kingly) authority which has been frequently discussed elsewhere (e.g. Hocart, 1927; Coomaraswamy, 1942; Needham, 1960). We shall at the same time demonstrate in some detail one particular axiom of Lévi-Strauss's theory, viz. that the basic pattern of themes (the structure) persists throughout all versions of a myth, regardless of the nature of their sources. The Dutthagamani myth, for which we have available twenty-eight versions, ranging from the fourth century A.D. to the present, provides an excellent test of this hypothesis.

Secondly we shall investigate the Dutthagamani myth as a sociological charter for the present-day Morapitiyans.

Although the Morapitiyans always spoke to us about their 'descent from King Dutthagamani', it turned out, on close investigation, that what they were actually claiming was descent from Dutthagamani's wife's sister. The full significance of this will become apparent only in the course of this essay but a preliminary explanation will be helpful. Orthodox marriage in modern Kandyan Ceylon is *diga* (virilocal); when *binna* (uxorilocal) residence is established there is commonly an implication that the status of the incoming husband is in some way inferior to that of his wife. This may be because the wife is an heiress or because the husband's caste status is in some way questionable. This explains why, in the case of *binna* marriage, the *gedara* name is commonly transmitted through the wife rather than the husband; indeed in such a case·the husband may come to be regarded as an assimilated member of his wife's *gedara*. It also explains why *binna* residence is proverbially considered dishonourable for high-caste men.[3] In following through the ramifications of the Dutthagamani myth the reader should remember these details. If Dutthagamani had established a *binna* marriage in Morapitiya he might without difficulty have been assimilated to the *gedara* in which he resided but this would imply loss of dignity for Dutthagamani. If on the other hand, as turns out to be the case, he marries a Morapitiyan girl and takes her away to live with him in *diga*, this preserves Dutthagamani's dignity but makes it difficult for the Morapitiyans to claim that he is their *gedara* ancestor.

It is highly relevant that caste distinction remains vitally important in Morapitiya. The traditional caste system of Kandyan Ceylon, though modelled on the Hindu scheme, is not identical with it. In the Hindu system, the caste of Priests (Brahmans) is contrasted with but superior to the caste of princes (Kshatriya). In Ceylon there is no special priestly caste; royalty and aristocrats and monks alike are all ordinarily members of the same high caste, the Cultivators (Goyigama). But within this single high caste there are, in practice, various sub-castes which compete with each other for high status, sometimes on grounds of nobility of birth and sometimes on grounds of religious orthodoxy, or perhaps on both grounds at once. As the Morapitiyans consider themselves to be of the highest possible caste status and of royal descent, they are particularly concerned about protecting their caste purity and extremely careful to maintain the traditional distances, both social and physical, between themselves and the people whom they consider to be of lower caste status.

The claim to 'descent' from King Dutthagamani is, in some sense, a series of concentric circles. It is recognized that the best claim of all is that of Weerasuriya-gedara Rambanda, a Morapitiyan who claims to be the eldest son of the eldest son of the eldest son of the eldest son of King Dutthagamani's wife's brother: a 'historical' time-span of two thousand two hundred years is thus collapsed into five generations. Weerasuriya-gedara Rambanda was the only Morapitiyan among my informants who credited Dutthagamani's wife with having had a brother, though a version of the story from another source (see p. 311 (20*a*)) has a similar implication. The Rambanda who thus presents himself as the senior member of the Weerasuriya-gedara according to principles of patrilineal descent and primogeniture is by far the wealthiest man in present-day Morapitiya. Other holders of the Weerasuriya-gedara house-name are granted a higher status than the rest of their fellow Morapitiyans, but all Morapitiyans are considered by the inhabitants of the rest of the Kotmale to be 'descendants' of King Dutthagamani. However, if no Morapitiyans are present, the people from other Kotmale Goyigama villages will tell an outsider that they also are 'descended' from King Dutthagamani ('after all, he stayed in Kotmale'). But their claim to 'descent' is relevant only in contrast to people from outside Kotmale, who have no claim at all.

In an otherwise completely factual account of the demography, climate, topography, etc. of the Kandyan area, the *Report of the Kandyan Peasantry Commission* (Govt. of Ceylon, 1951: 327–8) found it necessary to remark of Kotmale: 'It has historical associations with King Dutu Gemunu who is said to have spent his youth in the village of [Morapitiya] where it is recorded that he asweddumized (irrigated) paddy fields and spent his life as a peasant before he raised an army and reconquered Raja Rata (Pihiti) ... A few of these historical facts are set out here for the reason that they were mentioned with pride by inhabitants of this division in the course of our visits here.'

Evidently it is impossible to visit this area in any capacity without hearing about King Dutthagamani. Evidently, too, the ordinary Kotmale people are willing to grant the Morapitiyans a higher status because, by reflected glory, the Kotmale people are themselves thus asserting a claim to superiority over outsiders.

When the Morapitiyans understood that I really wanted to live in their village, I was taken immediately to what seemed a quite ordinary house. I could see no reason why it should be so obvious that I should live in this particular house. It was not the village headman's house and it was not the wealthiest or the biggest house in the village; nor, on the other hand, was it on the outskirts of the village or in some undesirable location. It was not until some time later that I came to understand that this was Weerasuriya-gedara, the house which was supposed to be located on the site where Prince Dutthagamani had lived. 'This', I was told, 'is the place where visitors live. First there was Prince Dutthagamani, and now you.'[4]

Finally, we shall examine the relationship between structure and charter, as exemplified in the myth of Dutthagamani. Lévi-Strauss and others following his theory of structural analysis have tended to separate completely the 'charter' aspects of a myth from its structural pattern. As Yalman comments before proceeding with his structural analysis of Sinhalese healing rituals, 'after all, to say that a myth is a charter for certain institutions, though no doubt true, does not tell us much about the intricacies of the myth itself' (Yalman, 1964: 116).

Are we justified in the assumption that the functionalist aspects of a myth are necessarily irrelevant to its symbolic structure, and vice versa? Or does the charter also have structure? We shall consider this question by examining the relationships between some of the themes of our structural analysis of the Dutthagamani myth, and some aspects of present-day Morapitiyan thought.

II. THE MYTH

A. Morapitiyan Version

What follows is a composite account of the myth of King Dutthagamani; it includes all the episodes mentioned in any of the sixteen accounts of the story related to me by Morapitiyans and their kinsmen from other Kotmale villages. Discrepancies and conflicting versions of the story will be discussed in the second part of this section.

Of the sixteen persons who told me the story of Dutthagamani, eight were Morapitiyans (six men and two women) and eight (seven men and one woman) were kinsmen of the Morapitiyans from other Kotmale villages. Of the eight Morapitiyans, four gave long and complete versions; all of these (three men and one woman) were elderly and important members of Weerasuriya-gedara. Of the other four Morapitiyans who gave shorter, more specialized accounts, one was another elderly Weerasuriya-gedara woman; two were very old men known for their knowledge of 'history'; the fourth was a young man inspired to talk about King Dutthagamani while on a trip to Monaragala Peak, where it is said that Dutthagamani spent his days herding buffalo while he lived in Morapitiya.

Of the eight non-Morapitiyans, two were priests, one (the woman) was a schoolteacher, one was a local historian who had written a pamphlet about Kotmale, and the other four were elderly men from near-by villages, who were reputed to know much about 'historical' matters (three of these were brought to me by Weerasuriya-gedaras; the fourth was in Morapitiya for a wedding). Two of the elderly men plus the schoolteacher and the local historian related long versions of the myth; the other four told parts of the tale.

1. In ancient times Ceylon was divided into three parts: Rohana in the south, Maya in the middle which included Kotmale, and Pihiti in the north around Anuradhapura. King Kalani Tissa ruled Maya and King Kavan Tissa ruled Rohana. Pihiti was in the hands of Tamil invaders.[5]

2. King Kalani Tissa of the Middle Kingdom had only one daughter, whose name was Viharamahadevi (meaning 'Great Goddess of the Buddhist Temple'). The king had a younger brother whose handwriting was very similar to the handwriting of a certain priest. The younger brother wrote a love-letter to the king's wife. The king found it and thought that the letter was written by the priest. He became very angry and had the priest boiled in oil. Those who do evil get *pao* (sin). Those who do good get *pin* (merit). The king got *pao*. A great flood covered Maya, and King Kalani Tissa was forced to send his daughter to sea in a golden boat. She drifted ashore in the Southern Kingdom of Rohana. King Kavan Tissa heard about this and came to the seashore. Viharamahadevi was very beautiful and therefore the king married her.

3. King Kavan Tissa and Viharamahadevi did not have any children for a long time. One day they took offerings (*dana*) to the priests at the temple. The king said, 'We have no children. After I die, who will rule the country?' He was advised to speak to a certain priest, who was seriously ill. The queen asked the sick priest to be born again in her

stomach after he died. The priest thought he would be able to help Buddhism in this way, and so he agreed.

4. The king and queen began their return to the palace. During the journey, the wheels of their carriage became stuck in the mud, and the horse could not pull them out. People said, 'Why did this happen? The priest must have died.' They turned back and found that the priest had died at the exact moment the carriage had stopped.

5. Ten months later Prince Gamani (meaning 'leader of crowds') was born. The priest's reason for being thus reborn was to send away the Tamils and to help Buddhism.

6. When Prince Gamani was born, he was given an elephant named Kadola.[6] Ten giants were born on the day the Prince was born.

7. Some years later another son, Prince Tissa (known as Prince Saddhatissa, the pious Tissa), was born to King Kavan Tissa and Viharamahadevi.

8. King Kavan Tissa believed he was not yet strong enough to challenge King Elara, the Tamil king of the North. He thought first he would increase his kingdom; secretly he sent colonists to clear the jungles and to settle in Kotmale, which had been hitherto unsettled. He sent a leader, Vira (*Vira* = mighty; heroic), and twenty families. Vira was Prince Gamani's *mama*.[7] It was on Viharamahadevi's suggestion that the king sent them to Kotmale.

9. When he arrived in Kotmale, Vira looked for a good place to settle and he found a place where pigs were living; he knew that pigs make their homes where no enemies can come and so he chose this place to live and called it Urupalase (*ūrā* = 'pigs'; *pälässa* = 'animal lair').

10. In the meanwhile, Prince Gamani was growing up and when he was twelve years old he asked his father to fight King Elara. King Kavan Tissa refused, saying that he was not yet ready for war with the Tamils. King Kavan Tissa became worried about the attitude of Prince Gamani, and he decided to make both his sons promise that they would never fight the Tamils without his permission.

11. He took three rice balls and called his two sons to him. 'I want you to make three promises,' he said. 'First, that you will never fight with each other.' The two princes agreed and the king took one rice ball and divided it, and both princes ate.

12. 'Secondly, that you will never harm a priest and that you will help Buddhism.' They agreed and ate the second rice ball.

13. 'And thirdly, that you will not fight King Elara without my

permission.' Prince Tissa agreed but Prince Gamani threw away his rice. He sent his father some female ornaments, saying that was all he was fit to wear. Then he went to his room, curled up into a ball, and slept. After this, Prince Gamani became known as Prince Dutthagamani ('the angry Gamani').

14. King Kavan Tissa was furious and ordered his son killed. Viharamahadevi was very unhappy when she heard this. She went quickly to her son's room and found him sleeping there. 'Why do you sleep curled up like this?' she asked. 'How can I sleep straight when the Tamils are at my head and the sea at my feet?' replied the prince.

15. Viharamahadevi packed some rice and curry for her son and told him to go quickly to Morapitiya, a small village of twenty huts, and to stay there until King Kavan Tissa died.

16. Prince Dutthagamani went alone, and when he arrived in Kotmale, he was tired. He sat down to have his lunch. He put part of his potato curry in the earth, and thought, 'If I am to become king, then this will become a potato plant.' That thing happened.

17. He travelled on and later stopped to eat some more from his food packet. He took some of his dry fish and put it in the water. He thought, 'If I am to become king, then this fish will swim.' That thing happened.

18. The prince travelled on further. He wanted to hide his sword. He saw a huge *nuga* tree; immediately it split in half and he hid his sword between the two halves. Afterwards, this place came to be called Kadadora (from *kadu dora*, 'sword door').

19. The next time he stopped, the prince ate some mango curry and put the seed in water. He thought, 'If I am to become king, then this will become a mango tree.' That thing happened.

20. Finally, Prince Dutthagamani came to Morapitiya. He saw the house called Urupalasegammahe.[8] The *Gamarala* ('village leader') was out in the fields. His wife was at home cooking. She asked Prince Dutthagamani where he came from. He said that he came from Rohana and that he was looking for a job. She asked him what kind of job he would like, and he said that he could work as a herdsman.

21. The wife gave separate rice and curry to Prince Dutthagamani and then took some to the farmers in the field. Her husband scolded her because she was late, but then she told him about the boy.

22. In the evening the farmer came back to the house and spoke to the boy. He said that he owned many buffaloes, and that the boy could live in his house and watch his buffaloes.

23. The next morning Prince Dutthagamani took a small stick and drove the buffaloes to the top of the mountain, Monaragala Peak. This is the mountain on which, many years earlier, the Lord Buddha wanted to leave the imprint of his foot. Because of the intervention of a peacock (monaragala) demon, he put his footprint on Adam's Peak instead.[9]

24. Prince Dutthagamani saw one small rock and then he saw another larger one. He took the large rock and put it on top of the small rock, and then he sat on it. This seat he called Galapitagala. After two or three days, Prince Dutthagamani went first and the buffaloes followed him. Whenever the Gammahe needed firewood, Dutthagamani would roll logs down the mountain. To this day, Morapitiyans never carry firewood but instead roll it down from Monaragala Mountain.

25. In the evenings, Prince Dutthagamani brought the buffaloes back to the field in front of Urupalasegammahe. He decided to build a fence around this field to keep the buffaloes in at night. He thought about it and a few minutes later the fence was built.

26. Nearby was a large, level, uncultivated field. Prince Dutthagamani wanted to cultivate it but he had no hoe. He went to the blacksmith and asked him to make one. But the blacksmith went to eat his lunch. Prince Dutthagamani took the iron, put it in the fire, bent it with his hands and made a hoe. When the blacksmith returned, he saw what had happened and he knew who Prince Dutthagamani must be. He fell on his knees and worshipped him. Prince Dutthagamani said, 'If you tell anyone who I am, I will kill you.'

27. The prince wanted water for his paddy field, but there was no water near by. He took a stick and drew a line from the nearest river to the field. Soon that line became water. Now that watercourse is called Raja Ela ('the King's stream'), and the paddy field is named Rajathalawa-ela ('the plain of the King's stream').

28. Prince Dutthagamani hoed his field. But he had no paddy seed. He asked the people to give him some seeds. But they thought he was only a poor shepherd and would not give him paddy seed. So he took some rice husks and planted them. His paddy grew better than any other in Kotmale.

29. Then it was time to harvest. He cut some paddy and in the other hand he took a stick. He drew a circle and made the outline of a threshing-floor (kamata). The next morning when he came back, the threshing-floor was dug and prepared.

30. Prince Dutthagamani then cut the harvest. He put wild buffaloes in the threshing-floor; they became tame and he got much paddy.

31. Other people heard what had happened and they too planted husks. But they got no paddy. A jackal came from the jungle. People asked the jackal what he was doing there. He said he was drinking bull's milk. 'How can a bull give milk?' they asked. The jackal laughed and ran into the threshing-floor. 'How can you get good paddy from husks?' he answered.

32. Prince Dutthagamani had no one to carry the paddy from the field to the house. He put a stick on the ground and pulled it along. The paddy followed. He continued until he arrived at Urupalasegammahe. The house filled with paddy and still it kept coming. The wife said, 'Enough paddy.' Prince Dutthagamani took a basket and put it sideways on the ground. Then the paddy stopped. From that time on this house was known as Weerasuriya-gedara, the 'house of enough paddy' (*vi*, paddy; *isuru*, enough; *gedara* house). This etymology and interpretation is given by the Morapitiyans. Elsewhere *isuru* usually means 'splendid'. A more orthodox interpretation of this name, is 'house of the mighty hero' (*vira*, strong; *suraya*, hero; *gedara*, house).

33. When Prince Dutthagamani had lived in Weerasuriya-gedara twelve years, King Kavan Tissa died.

34. Prince Tissa knew that if his brother returned, he would succeed to the throne. So he took the elephant Kadola and their mother, Viharamahadevi, and hid them far from the palace. But Viharamahadevi knew where Prince Dutthagamani was, and secretly she sent a giant to tell her son to come.

35. The people with whom Prince Dutthagamani had been living in Morapitiya had two daughters, Kalumenika and Rammenika. Kalumenika, the elder, was very proud and beautiful, but Rammenika, the younger, was plain. Prince Dutthagamani loved Kalumenika for her pride, and he asked her to come away with him, without telling her that he was to become king. She refused, saying that she did not want to marry a herdsman. Then he asked Rammenika. She accepted, and they left for the palace. They stopped first at Kadadora and the prince took his sword from the *nuga* tree.

36. Prince Dutthagamani sent a message to his brother, Prince Tissa, saying that he would fight him for the possession of his mother and his tusker, Kadola. Both brothers knew that whoever had the mother and the elephant would succeed to the throne. Many people on both sides were

killed in the battle and Prince Dutthagamani sent word to Prince Tissa that too many people were being killed and that there would not be enough left to fight King Elara. Dutthagamani said, 'We two will fight instead.' Tissa agreed because he had the tusker, Kadola and Dutthagamani had only a mare. They met in battle and Dutthagamani made his mare jump over the tusker and, while jumping, he drew the blunt edge of his sword across the back of Tissa's neck.

37. Kadola was so ashamed that a mare had jumped over him that he threw Tissa off his back and knelt before Prince Dutthagamani. Tissa ran away and hid in a temple. He told the priests what had happened and they made him a priest so that his brother would not kill him. Prince Dutthagamani went to the temple and said, 'If I had wanted to kill my brother, I would have killed him during the fight. I need Tissa to help the people to grow food while I fight King Elara.'

38. So the priests removed the robes from Tissa and gave him to his brother, who then became King Dutthagamani.

39. King Dutthagamani conquered King Elara, united Ceylon under his rule, and restored Buddhism to its rightful place in Ceylon.

40. He and Rammenika had only one child, a son, Sali Kumari.

41. A very beautiful girl named Asokamala went one day to offer flowers to the Buddha, but she forgot to put water on the flowers. Her mother said, 'You put no water on the flowers that you offered to the Lord Buddha; you are therefore a low-caste girl, a Rodiya.'

42. Sali Kumari saw her in the jungle one day and she was so beautiful that he followed her home. She said, 'You must go. I am a Rodiya.' But he stayed with her.

43. Because Sali Kumari married a low-caste woman, he could not inherit the throne from his father. King Dutthagamani died from the bite of a *naga* (cobra), after ruling for twenty-four years. His brother, Prince Tissa inherited the throne, and the sons and grandsons of Prince Tissa ruled after him.

B. The Variants

In listing the variant forms of the story, we have given each item a number which indicates some relationship between the variant form and a corresponding paragraph in the main story. This numbering, however, is somewhat arbitrary since some variants can be cross-referenced to several of the original paragraphs.

1. *The Morapitiyan variants*

The following are the conflicting versions of the myth told to me by Morapitiyans and their relatives.

22*a*. When Gamani first came to Urupalasegammahe he was told to sleep on the veranda, while the *Gamarala* and the rest of the family slept indoors.

35*a*. Kalumenika refused to marry Dutthagamani because he had no property (all others said it was because he was looking after cattle). The Morapitiyans say that in those days, which they compare favourably with the degenerate present, no one except high-caste farmers owned property.

35*b*. Dutthagamani kept Rammenika but did not marry her. One young boy commented, 'He just kept Rammenika for a joke.'

43*a*. When King Dutthagamani discovered that his son was married to a Rodiya woman, he called Sali Kumari and Asokamala to him and told them that he was not angry. He invited them to live in the palace with him, but they refused. Dutthagamani had a second palace built for them and sent them food there.

43*b*. After Dutthagamani became king, he saw a beautiful *naga* lady. She told him that her husband was a god and that he was watching her. She told Dutthagamani that he must not bathe for three years. If he did not obey, her husband would do something bad to him. Dutthagamani obeyed but he erred by one day. He thought the three years were over and he bathed, In reality, the three years were not over until the next day; therefore the *naga* bit his leg. In seven days he died.

2. *'Historical' variants*

The ancient chronicles of Ceylon, the *Dipavamsa* and the *Mahavamsa*, belong to

an inter-connected historical tradition which has to be considered in its entirety. It is a tradition of history writing that has its origin with the beginnings of Buddhism in India, and comes down to our own times, for the *Mahavamsa* and the *Dipavamsa* have both been continued down to our own day. It has been entirely the work of monks, and these traditions have come down to us because they were kept safe in the libraries attached to the *viharas* (temples).

(University of Ceylon, 1959: 47; cf. Geiger, 1908)

The earliest Sinhalese commentary, the *Atthakatha Mahavamsa*, at first ended with the *nirvana* of Mahinda, the missionary who brought Buddhism to Ceylon in the time of Devanampiya Tissa. Later, however, both pre-Buddhist legends of Ceylon and the history of the kings who succeeded Devanampiya Tissa were added.

> The whole took the form of a chronicle. There was finally a group of stories and legends which probably had their origin in the south, centring around the life and work of Dutthagamani. It was popular and secular in character at first. But to this was added a religious touch … According to accepted tradition, these records were first written down in the time of Vattagamani Abhaya, in the first century B.C. Though after this time the nucleus of the tradition was fixed, new stories, legends, traditions and anecdotes were being constantly added on, some from the hand of the narrator, and some after they had gained currency by repetition … The earliest extant record of this historical tradition is the *Dipavamsa* which, compiled by unknown authors, was completed about the middle of the fourth century A.D. … The best known chronicle is the *Mahavamsa* … The first part which consists of the first thirty-seven chapters is commonly known as the *Mahavamsa* … The rest of the chronicle is usually referred to as the *Culavamsa* (University of Ceylon, 1959: 47–9).

Authorship of the first part is attributed to Mahanama, a monk, who lived in the late fifth and early sixth centuries A.D. 'Scholars are generally of the opinion that Mahanama based his work mainly on the original *Atthakatha-Mahavamsa* which he followed very faithfully' (University of Ceylon, 1959: 50). The *Dipavamsa* has only eleven short verses on Dutthagamani, but of the thirty-seven chapters of the *Mahavamsa* eleven are concerned with the epic of Dutthagamani (chs. 22–32). The Dutthagamani story is also mentioned in later commentaries: most important are the *Mahavamsa-Tika*, written in Pali and placed between the seventh and tenth centuries, and the Cambodian *Mahavamsa*, of unknown date but placed after the *Mahavamsa-Tika*. We have consulted the *Mahavamsa-Tika* but have not had access to the Cambodian *Mahavamsa*. We have also consulted the *Rajavaliya*, a work which is thought to date from the eighteenth century (Law, 1947: 27–8).

Besides reference to the classical texts we have used the scholarly histories of Ceylon written in modern times. Of these, by far the most extensive and authoritative is the University of Ceylon's *History of*

Ceylon (1959). For purposes of comparison we have also used an earlier history, John M. Senaveratna's *The Story of the Sinhalese* (1923).

Thirdly, we have collected eight 'quasi-historical' versions of all or part of the Dutthagamani story. This material comes from a variety of sources: four articles from the *Ceylon Antiquary and Literary Register* (Bell, 1918; Mendis, 1916; Samarasekara, 1916; Anna P. Senaveratna, 1916); *A Gazetteer of the Central Province of Ceylon* (Lawrie, 1898); a long unpublished poem on Dutthagamani by Mallapalle Wettasinghe from Kotmale; *The Story of Kotmale*, a booklet by P. B. Kehelgama, a local historian who lives in the Kotmale Valley and who visited me in Morapitiya; and finally newspaper articles which ran in the press during my stay in Ceylon (in *Silumina* and in the *Ceylon Observer*).

How do these varying 'historical' and 'quasi-historical' versions of the Dutthagamani story compare with the Morapitiyan versions?

The *Dipavamsa* says of Dutthagamani:

> 6a. A prince, Abhaya by name, the son of Kakavanna, whom the ten warriors surrounded, whose elephant was Kandula, put thirty-two kings to death and alone continued the royal succession. This prince reigned twenty-four years ... Wise, enlightened Abhaya Dutthagamani, after having performed meritorius deeds, entered, after the dissolution of his body, the body of a Tusita god (*Dip.* xviii, 53–4; xix, 11).

The other *Dipavamsa* verses are concerned with the great Buddhist monuments built by King Dutthagamani.

Sections 1–7 and 10–12 of the Morapitiyan version agree, with minor variations,[10] with the *Mahavamsa* (i.e. with most of the story of the heritage, birth and early childhood of Dutthagamani). The *Mahavamsa* says nothing about Vira or about the settling of Kotmale.

The *Mahavamsa* records that Viharamahadevi, while pregnant with Gamani, had these longings of a pregnant woman:

> 5a. (This) did she crave: that while making a pillow for her head of a honeycomb one *usabha* long and resting on her left side in her beautiful bed, she should eat the honey that remained when she had given twelve thousand *bhikkhus* (priests) to eat of it; and then she longed to drink (the water) that had served to cleanse the sword with which the head of the first warrior among King Elara's warriors had been struck off, (and she longed to drink it) standing on this very head, and moreover (she longed) to adorn herself with garlands

of unfaded lotus-blossoms brought from the lotus-marshes of Anuradhapura.

The queen told this to the king, and the king asked the soothsayers. When the soothsayers heard it they said: 'The queen's son, when he has vanquished the Damilas and built up a united kingdom, will make the doctrine to shine forth brightly' (*Mahavamsa*, cf. *Rajavaliya*: 24).

Sections 13 and 14 of the Morapitiyan version agree with the *Mahavamsa*, with several important exceptions. In the *Mahavamsa*:

10a. King Kavan Tissa raises an army for Gamani but does not allow him to use if (cf. *Rajavaliya*: 24).

13a. Saddha Tissa as well as Gamani flings away his food when asked to swear not to fight the Tamils.

13b. Kavan Tissa does not attempt to have Gamani killed, but orders that he should be bound with a golden chain. This happens not at the time of the oath-swearing but four years later when Gamani feels himself ready to challenge the Tamils but his father refuses to allow him to do so. Dutthagamani then escapes to the 'Central Mountain Region in the interior of Ceylon'. The *Rajavaliya* version is similar but explicitly refers to Kotmale (*Rajavaliya*: 29).

Sections 15–35 of the Morapitiyan version (i.e. Dutthagamani's stay in Morapitiya) are not recorded in the *Mahavamsa*, nor are they described in any of the other chronicles.

Sections 36–8 (the fight of the brothers) agree with the *Mahavamsa* with minor variations; in the *Mahavamsa* these sections are greatly expanded.

Section 39, Dutthagamani's conquest of the Tamils, is a major theme of the *Mahavamsa*, which then devotes five chapters to description of the temples and monuments built by Dutthagamani.

39a. Here and in the last two chapters much is said about the good Buddhist works performed by Dutthagamani.

Sections 40 and 43 agree with the *Mahavamsa* except that in the *Mahavamsa* no cause is given for Dutthagamani's death other than 'a sickness that was to be mortal'. However, according to the *Mahavamsa*:

43c. Dutthagamani is stricken with illness immediately after enshrining relics of the Buddha in a magnificent relic chamber which he had caused to be built. These relics of the Buddha had first to be taken by force from the *Naga* king.

The *Mahavamsa* version of the union of Sali Kumari and Asokamala is somewhat different from the Morapitiyan version (sections 41 and 42) – according to the *Mahavamsa*, 'he (Sali Kumari) tenderly loved a Candala[11] woman of exceeding great beauty. Since he was greatly enamoured of Asokamaladevi, who already in a former birth had been his consort, he cared nothing for kingly rule' (*Mahavamsa*: 228). This episode is related at length in the *Mahavamsa-Tika*:

> 43*d*. The two had been husband and wife in an earlier existence. The husband received a pig from a hunter as payment for some smith's work he had done. He prepared it for food and expressed the wish that eight prominent *theras* (monks) might come and take part in the feast. The man was afterwards reborn as the son of Dutthagamani as a reward for his liberality.
>
> The virtuous wife was reborn as a Candala as punishment for an offence in another existence. Her mother scolded her for untidiness (she was youngest of seven daughters of a carpenter). She replied to her mother in abusive terms as had been used to her (quoted by Anna P. Senaveratna, 1916: 212–13).

John M. Senaveratna (1923), however, gives the same version as the Morapitiyans. It is relevant that in both versions Asokamala is de-casted by her mother, i.e. the purity of the caste is maintained through the female (see Yalman, 1963).

Carpenters and blacksmiths are low in the caste hierarchy and to offer pig-meat to monks would be impossibly insulting. That the smith should be *rewarded* by being born a prince is in the circumstances highly paradoxical and has the effect of casting a slur on Dutthagamani's own caste status. This also is the implication of 43*a* above.

The modern histories (University of Ceylon, 1959; Senaveratna, 1923) are, of course, based upon the chronicles and commentaries, but they tend to omit much of the Dutthagamani story as told in the *Mahavamsa* and to concentrate on the preparations for, and the actual conquest of, the Tamils. Nothing is said in either history of the life of the prince between the time of his escape from the palace and the death of his father, except that he found refuge in Kotmale (University of Ceylon, 1959: vol. 1, part 1, 151; J. M. Senaveratna, 1923: vol. 1, 139).

3. 'Quasi-historical' variants

We turn now to the eight 'quasi-historical' sources. Of these, five

(Samarasekera, Wettasinghe, Kehelgama, Lawrie and the newspaper articles) concern themselves with Dutthagamani's stay in Kotmale; in general, they agree with the composite Morapitiyan version. The following are the variants of the myth recounted in these eight sources.

20a. The prince arrived in Morapitiya and took up residence with a poor widow who had a son of his age. (From Samarasekera.)

20b. When Gamani arrived in Morapitiya, the *Gamarala*'s wife thought he was a prince. She told her daughter not to tell anyone else. The *Gamarala*'s wife helped the little boy very much. She gave him food on special plates. She did not tell her husband about this. (From Wettasinghe.)

21a. When Gamani arrived at Urupalasegammahe, the *Gammahe*'s daughter gave him separate rice and curry. He ate the rice but his bowl remained full. (From Wettasinghe.)

35c. Toward the end of his stay in Morapitiya, Dutthagamani became unhappy because he was unable to win Kalumenika's love. Gradually he moved out of their house to a hut which he built on Monaragala Peak.

Rammenika and her mother went every day to visit him there and while her mother went away to work on the fields, Rammenika stayed with Dutthagamani. They developed a very close and loving relationship.

26a. One day Rammenika stroked his head and Dutthagamani fell asleep. He dreamed and awakened suddenly, screaming. He went to the astrologer, who told him that it was a very good dream and that in three months he would become a king. Dutthagamani told the astrologer if he told anyone of this, he would kill him.

6b. One day Rammenika and Dutthagamani were making love and suddenly the prince rose, saying, 'Suranimala!' Suranimala, one of the giants born on the day Dutthagamani was born, had been sent by Viharamahadevi to see Dutthagamani. He asked about Dutthagamani's life in Morapitiya and said, 'More than your father, your mother worries about you always.' (From *Silumina*, 1963.)

35d. Dutthagamani tried to find a way to win Kalumenika's love. One day he found a beehive on Monaragala Peak. He brought it home and gave a piece to the *Gamarala* and one to the *Gammahe*, and he stretched forth to give a piece to Kalumenika, saying 'Take a piece and eat.' She said, 'I won't eat that,' and went inside. Then Rammenika ran forward and asked for it. When she took it, she gave Dutthagamani a pretty smile and ran into the house. (From *Silumina*, 1963.)

27a. There was a big stream which came from Monaragala Peak. In the stream was a large rock. Dutthagamani made a big hole in the middle of the rock. The water came up through the hole and made a good bathing-place. In the same way he made two other bathing-places in Morapitiya. Even today these bathing-places are always filled with water, even in the driest times. (From Wettasinghe.)

26*b*. Once while he was asleep on Monaragala, Dutthagamani saw his bowels go out from his mouth. Then they came into the body through the mouth. Dutthagamani was frightened. He asked the astrologer about it; the astrologer said, 'In seven days you will become the king of all Ceylon.' Dutthagamani said, 'If you tell anyone of this I will kill you.' (From Wettasinghe.)

6*c*. One day Ran Etana (Rammenika) sat with Dutthagamani and put her head on his lap. She dreamed that he and she became king and queen. She awoke and told him of her dream. At that moment a messenger arrived and said, 'The king is dead. The time has come for you to return to the Palace.' (From the *Ceylon Observer*, January 13th, 1963.)

35*e*. When King Kavan Tissa died and Dutthagamani was about to leave Morapitiya, he thanked the *Gamarala*'s wife for all the things she did. The *Gamarala*'s wife was very sorry to see him leave. Dutthagamani said to her, 'In the mornings you gave me cold rice; for that I give you a field of twelve *amunas*. In the evenings you gave me hot rice; for that I give you another field of twelve *amunas*.' (From Wettasinghe.)

38*a*. Dutthagamani invited all the Kotmale people to his coronation and gave them special treatment. (From Kehelgama.)

43*e*. Sali Kumari could not succeed to the throne because his mother was not of royal birth. (From Kehalgama.)

III. THE STRUCTURE OF THE MYTH[12]

Following Lévi-Strauss, we first isolate the constituent units of the myth, 'which are made up of relations' (Lévi-Strauss, 1963: 211). However, the 'true constituent units ... are not the isolated relations but *bundles of such relations* and it is only as bundles that such relations can be put to use and combined so as to produce a meaning' (ibid.). The meaning of the myth is thus to be found through analysis of the relations between the relations.

In Table 1 the vertical columns represent the 'bundles' of the Dutthagamani myth; each 'bundle' consists of several relations which exhibit a common feature. The plot of the myth is revealed by disregarding the columns and reading horizontally from left to right.

TABLE 1. Plot and structure in the myth of Dutthagamani

I	II	III	IV
Buddha driven away from Monaragala Peak by Peacock Demon (23)	—	—	—
Kalani Tissa kills Priest; gets *pao* (sin) (2)	—	—	—
—	—	—	Kavan Tissa takes offerings to priests (3)
—	—	—	Kavan Tissa refuses to fight Tamils (10)
—	—	—	Saddha Tissa ('the pious' Tissa) promises not to fight Tamils (13)
Gamani refuses to promise not to fight Tamils; becomes Duttha ('the angry, rebellious')-Gamani (13)	—	—	—
—	Dutthagamani given separate rice and curry by *Gammahe* (21)	—	—
—	Dutthagamani told to sleep on veranda (22a)	—	—
—	Dutthagamani watches buffaloes on Monaragala Peak (22)	—	—
—	—	Dutthagamani brings paddy to house until *Gammahe* says, 'Enough paddy'; house becomes known as Weerasuriya-gedara ('House of Enough Paddy') (32)	—
—	Dutthagamani moves to Monaragala Peak (35c)	—	—

313

TABLE I (*cont.*)

	II	III	IV
—	—	*Gamarala, Gammahe* and Rammenika eat food given them by Dutthagamani (35*d*)	—
—	Kalumenika refuses to take food from Dutthagamani (35*d*)	—	—
—	Kalumenika refuses to marry Dutthagamani (35)	—	—
—	—	Rammenika marries Dutthagamani (35)	—
—	—	Dutthagamani gives land to *Gammahe* (35*e*)	—
Dutthagamani and Saddha Tissa fight; Dutthagamani wins (36)	—	—	—
—	—	—	Saddha Tissa becomes priest (37)
—	—	—	Saddha Tissa grows food (37)
Dutthagamani slaughters Tamils (39)	—	—	—
—	Sali Kumari marries low-caste woman; becomes de-casted	—	—
—	—	—	Dutthagamani becomes a god (6*a*)
—	—	—	Saddha Tissa inherits throne (43)

All the entries in column I are acts of sinful violence, whereas all those in column IV are acts of pious non-violence. The problem posed by this classical part of the myth is thus seen to be: How can the hero (Dutthagamani), who must necessarily commit sinful violence in order to fulfil his predestined role, also be a pious Buddhist?

Dutthagamani's piety is in fact explicitly affirmed (6*a*), but the necessary paradoxical combination of piety and violence is also expressed in a number of other incidents, such as the dying priest who contemplates war against the Tamils (3) and the dream of Viharamahadevi (5a) which combines extreme bloodthirstiness with intentions of exaggerated piety. Indeed, when we examine the matter closely, we find that nearly all the individual items are in some degree self-contradictory. Thus Kavan Tissa, who is timid where Dutthagamani is aggressive (10, 13), nevertheless threatens aggression against Dutthagamani (14); Dutthagamani, whose name recalls his impious rebellion against a pious king (13), himself becomes a pious king (39, 39a); even Kadola, the male war elephant, the quintessential expression of the aggressiveness of kingship (6a, 34, 36), acts as a timid and devout worshipper when faced by Dutthagamani, but Dutthagamani's timid female steed turns into a military Pegasus.

Because of such internal inconsistency, the argument of the story can be viewed as a kind of dialectic between cross-cutting principles – the 'true constituent units' of the myth in Lévi-Strauss's terms. Many incidents in the story which at first appear arbitrary are then seen to be not only appropriate but essential.

The opposition between virtuous non-violence and sinful violence is a theme pervading the whole myth, but for the Morapitiyans there is an additional complication. In their case the myth must display the absolute superiority of their caste status on grounds of Buddhist piety and adherence to the taboos of caste with regard to commensality and sex relations, but it must also display their 'descent from Dutthagamani', a man of violence and therefore an impure sinner by definition. This contradiction is in fact resolved by implying that Kalumenika, the ancestress of the Morapitiyans, was a virgin impregnated by the divine Dutthagamani in some unspecified supernatural manner without resort to sexual relations. This special Morapitiyan problem and its solution are displayed in columns II and III of Table 1.

Thus the relations in column II exhibit the superior caste status of the Morapitiyans, while those in column III indicate the relationship of the Morapitiyans to Dutthagamani. The Morapitiyans derive their high status from Dutthagamani *because* he was a hero and a man of violence. At the same time, however, they cannot be 'descended' from him; nor are they 'descended' from Vira 'the strong', by implication another man of violence, nor from the *Gamarala*, nor the *Gammahe*, nor Rammenika, all three of whom accepted food from Dutthagamani (35d). On the contrary, the blood of the Morapitiyans is that of the proud and beautiful

Kalumenika, who would neither accept food from nor marry Dutthagamani. Dutthagamani's own issue becomes polluted. The reward of the virtuous is high-status descendants; the reward of the sinful is low-status descendants. In this context it becomes obvious why the Morapitiyans say that the meaning of Weerasuriya-gedara is 'the house of enough paddy' rather than 'the house of the mighty hero'.

The major antithesis of this myth, that between violence and non-violence, which is also that between *pao* and *pin*, appears as the implication of several sorts of oppositions:

1. *Explicitly, as the non-violence of the priesthood versus the violence of the kingship.* The story opens with a king killing a priest (1); piety in kings and princes is ineffective (8, 10, 7, 37); violence is triumphant. But violence is sinful (2). The opposition is resolved when Dutthagamani, a reincarnate priest (3–5), who achieves the kingship (38) and then triumphs through violence (39, 6a), becomes a pious king (39, 6a, 39a) but is succeeded by Saddha Tissa (43), a pious prince (7) who has been a priest (37). Dutthagamani's kingly violence is excused by the fact that his kingship is predestined and not a matter of personal choice (3, 16–19, 26, 5a, 26a, 26b, 6c). It is relevant that virtuous passivism is equated with female timidity while sinful violence is seen as a male quality (13) but the two actual females in this part of the story, Viharamahadevi and the mare, are both ambivalent with regard to passivity and violence (36, 5a).

2. *Theologically, as the opposition of the Buddha to Dutthagamani posing as the Peacock Demon, God of War.* This is resolved when Dutthagamani, turned virtuous king, is killed by the *naga*, who is well known in orthodox Buddhist tradition as an aggressive aspect of the Buddha himself (43). Dutthagamani then becomes a deity subordinate to the Buddha (6a). In Buddhist theology the Buddha is a man, not a god. His power is the power of sinlessness and merit and is contrasted not only with the sinful power of human violence but also with the supernatural power of gods and demons. The myth credits Dutthagamani with supernatural power (24–32, 36, 21a, 27a) which is lacking in all his more pious and more human opponents. However, the name of his mother Viharamahadevi indicates that she also is a goddess subservient to the Buddha (2). Variant 13b is relevant here and also the name Maya (1). Dutthagamani is both a magical king and a warrior-king. Now it has been shown by Dumézil (1939: 21 ff.; cf. also Eliade, 1961: ch. III) that ancient Indian mythology tends to polarize magical kingship represented by Varuna and warrior kingship represented by Indra. Varuna is a passive, inactive deity whose

power depends on his capacity to *bind* his opponents with magic (*maya*). In 13*b* Kavan Tissa stands to Dutthagamani as Varuna to Indra, but in the final resolution Dutthagamani combines the qualities of Varuna and Indra, yet is subordinate to the Buddha.

3. *In kinship terms, as the opposition between the helpful mother and mother's brother and the hostile father and brother.* The paradox here is that the relatives who are antagonistic in kinship terms are characterized by timidity while those who are collaborative in kinship terms are characterized by violence. The father and the brother are hostile but timid (13, 37); the mother's brother and the maternal grandfather are violent (2, 13, 14, 36, 37, 8). On the face of it, however, the contrast of the hostile father and collaborative mother's brother implies a patrilineal ideology. This opposition is resolved by a mythical transformation. The father is eliminated by death (33). The strong (i.e. active/violent) mother's brother residing in *diga* is dropped from the story and replaced by a passive, respectable figure, the rice-farming *Gamarala*, residing in *binna* (20, 21, 35*a*). The mediating role of the divine, yet violent, mother residing in *diga* (2, 15, 5*a*) is replaced by the mediating role of the very human *Gammahe*, residing in *binna* (20, 21). The residual hostility between the brothers is resolved by direct mediation. In breach of their oath the brothers fight (11), but do not harm one another (36, 37); Dutthagamani is victorious but Saddha Tissa ultimately succeeds (43). In the battle the passive brother is mounted on the war elephant Kadola, the aggressive symbol of kingship, but the aggressive brother is mounted on an unwarlike mare (36).[13]

4. *In caste and locality terms, as the opposition between the pure Morapitiyans and the impure stranger.* Dutthagamani in Morapitiya is repeatedly treated as if he were of different caste: his food is served separately (21, 20*b*, 21*a*); he is made to sleep separately (22*a*); Kalumenika refuses to take food from him (35*d*); the caste difference is asserted explicitly (43*e*); his sexual liaison with Rammenika produces only outcast offspring (43, 43*a*, 43*d*). Dutthagamani in Morapitiya engages in 'low' occupations – herding, smithing (2*c*, 26) – where the Morapitiyans themselves engage in 'high' occupations, rice-growing, property-owning (21, 35*a*). Nevertheless, the distinction gradually disappears. By the time he leaves Morapitiya, Dutthagamani has become a rice-farmer (27–32) and property-owner (35*e*), i.e. a man of high caste. The house itself which starts out as Urupalase ('Lair of Pigs') (9) becomes Weerasuriya-gedara, the 'House of Enough Paddy' (32).

5. *In terms of sex.* Sexual activity, a form of aggression, is inherently sinful. Lust leads to violence which flows from jealousy (2); lust leads to the breach of caste taboos and the procreation of polluted children (43). The conception of blessed children is a favour granted to pious parents (3), but it does not depend on sexual congress (4–5). The proud, pure-minded, beautiful Kalumenika is not credited with a husband, yet, residing in *binna*, she becomes the ancestress of the pure and royal Morapitiyans; the plain and lustful Rammenika marries in *diga* and bears a polluted child (43). The fact that Kalumenika's children are considered to be the 'descendants of Dutthagamani' seems to imply an asexual mode of conception through reincarnation as at (3). In this way the myth can slither over the difficulty that Dutthagamani cannot, in strict logic, be simultaneously *both* a stranger *and* a fully incorporate member of the 'House of Enough Paddy'.

TABLE 2.   Main structural oppositions and resolutions in the
myth of Dutthagamani

Abbreviations of proper names: KLT = Kalani Tissa; KVT = Kavan Tissa; ST = Saddha Tissa; Ga = Gamarala; Ge = Gammahe; V = Viharamahadevi; D = Dutthagamani; U = Urupalase; W = Weerasuriya-gedara; Mo. = Morapitiya; Mga = Monaragala Peak; K = Kalumenika; R = Rammenika.

NON-VIOLENCE	(Mediators)	VIOLENCE
	1. *Priesthood* v. *Kingship*	
Rohana		Maya
Pin (merit)		*Pao* (sin)
KVT shows respect to monks		KLT kills a monk (1)
	V mediates between:	
	(a) Rohana and Maya (1)	
	(b) *Pin* and *pao* (2)	
	(c) Priesthood and kingship (3)	
	(d) Piety and aggression (5a)	
ST as pious prince (7)		D as rebellious prince (13)
female timidity		male aggression
normal birth (7)		abnormal birth (3–6)
		coupled with:
		(a) indices of royal destiny (6, 3, 16–19, 26a)
		(b) recognition of supernatural quality by others (26, 37, 35, 20b)
		(c) worker of miracles (23–32)

Resolution: Dutthagamani, a reincarnate priest, becomes a virtuous king through violent action and then becomes a god. ST, a prince, becomes a priest before becoming a king without resort to violence. Kadola, symbol of kingship, is valiant in service of D, timid in service of ST.

TABLE 2 (cont.)

II. The Buddha v. Dutthagamani

The Buddha	Naga, aggressive guardian	Dutthagamani
Lord of Peace	of peaceful Buddha, kills	God of War (Peacock Demon)
Adam's Peak	warlike but now peaceful	Monaragala Peak
	D, who becomes a god	
	V also a deity subservient to	
	the Buddha	

III. Kinship Oppositions

Father (KVT) ⎫	Mother (V)	⎧ Maternal GF (KLT) 'Violent'
Pious, timid ⎬	protects son from father;	⎨ Mother's Brother (Vira)
Brother (ST) ⎭	links Rohana and Maya	⎩ Strong
living in Rohana	(Morapitiya)	Ga living diga in U
		('Lair of Pigs'), later
		called W ('House of
		Mighty Hero')

↓

IV. Caste and Locality

↓

————[modulates into]————

↓

Ga living binna in W	Ge mediates between:	D as stranger-hero and
('House of Enough Paddy')	(a) Ga and D (20, 21)	miracle-worker living apart
(20, 32)	(b) Own daughters and D	at Mga (23, 35c)
	(35c)	
	(c) Acquires property from	
(Alternative: Ge has son but	D which is transmitted	
no husband (20a))	to her Mo. progeny (35e)	
Daughters of Ga and Ge ←	stress on caste-difference →	D as stranger of doubtful
	(21, 20b, 21a, 22a, 35d,	status
	43e, etc.)	
High-caste occupations of Mo.		Low-status occupations of D
– rice-farming, property-		– herding, smithing, lack of
owning		property
	D ultimately claimed as	
	being of the highest caste,	
	an ancestor, land-owner,	
	rice-farmer, priest, king	
	(27–32, 35e, 3, 38)	

V. Sexual Distinctions

Asexual procreation		Sexual procreation
(meritorious)		(sinful)
Magical conception and		Normal conception of ST,
gestation of D, who is		who suffers defeat (7, 36)
victorious (3, 4, 36)		
K, the beautiful sister, who	D as (unrelated) stranger–	R, the plain sister, who
sticks firmly to caste	lover. His asexual relation	compromises her caste
principles and rejects D's	with K is virtuous; his	principles, accepts D's
advances, continues to reside	sexual relation with R is	advances, marries him in
binna and her children are	sinful	diga; and her son is
'descended from D'		caste-polluted (40–43)

Although the myth repudiates the idea of a sexually tainted *biological* continuity between Dutthagamani and the Morapitiyans, it offers the alternative of a property basis for *gedara* continuity (35e). The property which Dutthagamani presented to the *binna*-resident *Gammahe* would have passed to her descendants – *diga*-married sons or *binna*-married daughters, as the case might be. The interesting point, to which we shall return later, is that the majority of present-day Morapitiyans seem to imagine this succession as a line of *binna*-married ancestresses tracing back to the virtuous Kalumenika rather than as a line of *diga*-married ancestors tracing back to a son of the *Gammahe*.

It will be observed that the first three paragraphs of the myth, in its Morapitiyan form, spell out all the versions of the basic opposition which we have discussed: hostility of priests and kings, hostility between brothers, opposition between places (Rohana/Maya), the contrast between Sinhalese (Buddhists) and Tamils (worshippers of gods and demons), the contrast between the sin of lust and the virtue of asexual reincarnation. The resolution of these oppositions is concentrated into the final six paragraphs: the kingdoms are united, the brothers are united, priests and kings are merged, lust is punished, piety is rewarded.

Table 2 recapitulates this structural analysis in diagrammatic form. The items in the left-hand column are all characterized by the virtue of non-action, whereas those on the right are characterized by the sin of action. The individuals who are placed centrally – e.g. Viharamahadevi, the *Gammahe*, the *Naga* – are 'mediators' in that they very explicitly share qualities of sinful action and sinless inaction. Here the conflicts between the 'bundles' of Table 1 have become resolved by a process of mediation and synthesis.

Our conclusion that the main theme of the myth is the opposition of violence and non-violence is quite orthodox.

The *Mahavamsa* explicitly attempts to resolve the conflict between Dutthagamani's guilt for his slaughter of the Tamils and his good works in the spreading of Buddhism. Eight *arahants* (persons who have attained *nirvana*) were sent to the king after his great victory.

'We are sent by the brotherhood at Piyangudipa to comfort thee, O lord of men.' And thereon the king said again to them: 'How shall there be any comfort for me, O venerable sirs, since by me was caused the slaughter of a great host numbering millions?'
From this deed arises no hindrance in thy way to heaven. Only one

and a half human beings have been slain here by thee, O lord of men.
The one had come unto the (three) refuges, the other had taken on
himself the Five Precepts. Unbelievers and men of evil life were the
rest, not more to be esteemed than beasts. But as for thee, thou wilt
bring glory to the doctrines of the Buddha in manifold ways; therefore cast away care from thy heart, O ruler of men! (*Mahavamsa*,
p. 178).

From our structural analysis of the myth, it seems quite clear that
this resolution is far too simple. And the University of Ceylon's
History of Ceylon comments as follows:

Happily for the good name of Buddhism, [this] view has not been
taken seriously by later generations ... Whether the story that
Dutthagamani himself felt remorse and was reassured by such arguments is true or not, these accounts in the chronicle and the Pali
commentaries indicate that, in the early period, when the alliance
between the Buddhist Church and the Sinhalese State was being
forged, thinking men pondered on the inconsistencies brought
about by that alliance. But the people, as a whole, do not appear
to have been prepared to carry logical consistency to a point that
would endanger the life of the community, and only accepted so
much of Buddhism as was consistent with self-preservation. In later
ages, people were wise enough not to give thought to such incon-
venient questions (p. 162).

Perhaps we can use as a final variant a quotation from Gordon
Cumming's *Two Happy Years in Ceylon* (1892): 'It is said that in his last
hours the King (Dutthagamani) spoke somewhat bitterly of the state of
absolute slavery to the priests in which he had lived all his life' (Cumming:
vol. 1, 386). The inconsistency between the virtues of the priesthood
and the requirements of the kingship is fundamental.

It thus appears that Lévi-Strauss's hypothesis is fully borne out by the
Dutthagamani myth. The myth is composed of a series of motifs
organized in dialectic opposition. The same themes recur throughout
the twenty-eight versions we have collected, representing a time-span
of sixteen hundred years. We must now consider the implications of our
conclusion that a single basic structure underlies all the variants. Lévi-
Strauss says, 'Our method eliminates a problem which has been so far
one of the main obstacles to the progress of mythological studies, namely,

the quest for the *true* version, or the *earlier* one. On the contrary, we define the myth as consisting of all its versions; to put it otherwise: a myth remains the same as it is felt as such' (Lévi-Strauss, 1963: 216).

What then is the relationship between 'myth' and 'history', with regard to the story of Dutthagamani? The above statement carries with it the implication that the tale told by an elderly, uneducated, Morapitiyan woman is as 'true' as that which is recorded in the *Mahavamsa* – or in the University of Ceylon's *History of Ceylon*. Is the 'historical' (i.e. 'real') Dutthagamani any *truer* than the mythical (i.e. 'fictitious') Dutthagamani? The following viewpoint of Dr Leach is relevant here:

> In theory History and Myth stand opposed. History is what 'really happened'. Myth is a fictitious tale about the past cast in dogmatic form so as to justify some present belief. But in fact the history which appears in history books is not 'what actually happened' but only the idea of what actually happened as imagined by the historian ... Each body of ('historical') data has been the subject of drastic selection ... even contemporary documents do not report events 'as they actually happened'; they give us only a view of the facts as beheld by the reporter. 'Myths', which are wholly fantastic in their content, do no more nor less than that (Leach, unpublished notes).

An interesting parallel can be drawn between Dutthagamani and Tsoede, the culture-hero and mythical founder of the Nupe Kingdom (Nadel, 1942). Nadel, in his *A Black Byzantium*, considers in detail how far the stories about Tsoede are 'historical' and how far 'mythical'. His conclusion is that the stories refer more to the mythical Tsoede than to the 'historical' *Etsu* – but that the distinction is irrelevant.

The actions of both the 'mythical' Tsoede and the 'historical' *Etsu* serve in the same way as a charter for present-day activity. As Nadel says, 'We are not concerned here to determine what is and what is not historical truth in the rich cycle of traditions round the figure of Tsoede. The myth as it stands, and as it is treasured by the people of Nupe, is to us a sufficiently significant social reality' (Nadel, 1942: 75–6).

IV. STRUCTURE AND CHARTER

In its Kotmale Valley context the behaviour of the Morapitiyans is exceptional in several ways. Each of these distinctions is explicitly rationalized as being the proper style of action for the 'descendants' of

King Dutthagamani. The following are examples of such use of the Dutthagamani myth as a sociological charter:

(a) Morapitiyans will not work for money; this is the norm and it is virtual fact as well. An exception is made for prestige jobs; salaries which accrue to the village headman, teachers, and clerks are not considered to be in this category of 'working for money'. It is also permissible to engage in mercantile activities, as buying and selling are again categorized differently from rendering services for pay. 'Descendants of King Dutthagamani do not work for money.'

(b) The Morapitiyans work only their inherited lands. With very minor exceptions, no land is leased from the Crown and no one works on the tea estates or in the towns.

(c) The Morapitiyans use only the ancient *attam* (reciprocal labour) systems for their paddy work; hired labour, common elsewhere, is never used for paddy work in Morapitiya.

(d) In other Kotmale villages, the *Vel Vidane* (Irrigation Headman) is paid in kind by the villagers according to the amount of paddy they cultivate. In Morapitiya the *Vel Vidane* is not paid.

(e) The government of Ceylon has a rice-rationing system whereby a man who cultivates paddy may sell his rice to the government; he can then buy rice at a lower price with his ration card. Morapitiyans refuse to do this because they say that the government rice tastes bad. They sell rice only if they have more than they need for their households, or if they are desperately in need of money. 'Descendants of King Dutthagamani do not eat bad rice.'

(f) The schoolmaster of Morapitiya, appointed by the government, is a high-caste Kandyan Goyigama. He and his wife have lived in Morapitiya for six years but are still considered 'strangers' and not residents. The villagers say that although they are high-caste and Kandyan, they are not of the caste of the Morapitiyans because they are not descended from King Dutthagamani. The schoolmaster complained bitterly to me that neither he nor his wife had ever been inside any village house and that no one but the village headman and the priest had been to their house. They have one son whom they send away to school.

(g) Certain types of healing ceremonies, especially *pirit* chanting, are common throughout Ceylon. *Pirit* chanting is a generalized protection ceremony which may be used for many different occasions: at the completion of a new house or temple, at the start of a long voyage, at pregnancy, and to drive away *yakkuvas* (demons) from persons who have become possessed.[14] *Pirit* is usually chanted by Buddhist priests (*bhikkhus*) but is sometimes performed by lay singers. However, as Yalman says in his article on 'Sinhalese Healing Rituals', 'a *pirit* chanted by one or more *bhikkhus* is more effective than are those chanted by lay singers' (Yalman, 1964: 121). In Morapitiya, however, *pirit* chanted by Morapitiyans is equally as efficacious as *pirit* chanted by priests *because* the chanters are 'descended' from King Dutthagamani. The difference in the two types of chanting lies in another frame of reference: a man who invites priests to perform a *pirit* chanting gains merit (*pin*). But the protection gained from the chanting of *pirit* is the same whether it is performed by Morapitiyans or by priests. In this connection, it is significant that the Morapitiyan temple is named the Royal Temple of the Hills (Raja Giri Vihare) and the Morapitiyans say that only priests who are 'descended' from Dutthagamani may occupy the temple. This attitude was borne out in fact when, shortly before I left the village, the old priest of the Morapitiyan temple died and was succeeded by his senior student. The Morapitiyans said that the new priest was not 'descended' from Dutthagamani (i.e. he was a 'lower caste' Goyigama who was not a resident of Morapitiya); the Morapitiyans refused to accept this priest and were attempting to arrange matters so that he would have to vacate the temple. In the meantime, they brought in a priest from another village whenever they wanted a sermon (*bana*) chanted or a ceremony performed.

We can thus see some of the ways in which the myth of King Dutthagamani serves as a charter for the present-day norms of Morapitiyan society. The norms we have discussed, which are rather closely approximated by fact, are of course themselves interrelated and are partially dependent upon two other factors: the physical isolation of Morapitiya and its relative wealth. Under these circumstances, homogeneity is essential. Morapitiyans are 'descended' from King Dutthagamani; they are therefore, as they say, 'one people' (*eka minissu*) and are necessarily basically equal. Obvious distinctions in economic, political, educational and other statuses are considered 'temporary' differences. The maintenance of their 'royal descent' and their high-caste status depends upon their perpetuation as 'one people', where 'all are kinsmen' (*okkoma nada*), and thus upon their resistance to contamination and change from without, and to division from within.

It seems then that the elements of the myth which function most crucially as a sociological charter are:

(*a*) its emphasis on the caste-purity and caste-exclusiveness of the Morapitiyans;

(*b*) its emphasis on the fact that because of 'descent from Dutthagamani' this high, pure caste is also 'royal'.

As we have already seen in discussing the structure of the myth this second emphasis entails difficulty.

What is the Morapitiyan concept of 'descent' from Dutthagamani? It seems that what really constitutes 'descent' from King Dutthagamani is not kinship but residence, although the relationship is conceptualized in terms of kinship. People who live in Morapitiya are 'descended' from King Dutthagamani. People who do not live in Morapitiya are not so 'descended'. And we find that women who marry into the village say that they are 'descended' from the king. On the other hand, women who marry out and men who go to colonization schemes elsewhere gradulaly ose their claim to 'descent'; their children are not 'descended' from the king, unless they happened to return to Morapitiya to live. Even I had to be fitted into the scheme. When I had been living in the village for several weeks and the initial shock of my presence had worn off, it was declared that I was a reincarnated ancestor, and hence a 'descendant' of King Dutthagamani.

One crucial aspect of our structural analysis was that the Morapitiyans are not actually descended from Dutthagamani but, precisely, from the sister who refused to marry the prince. Highly significant, then, is our finding that in present-day Morapitiya the vital factor of 'descent' from King Dutthagamani is, in fact, a matter not of blood but of residence.

But difficulties remain. The Morapitiyans, as distinct from the people of Kotmale (see pp. 298–9), do not in fact argue: 'We are royal because Dutthagamani lived here'; they say 'We are royal because Dutthagamani was our ancestor.' However loosely the theory may be applied, a notion of genealogical connection seems to be involved. What sort of notion is this? In history we are dealing with a time-span of thousands of years; in Morapitiyan thought it is a matter of five generations. As we saw earlier, the wealthiest man in the community affirms his connection with the past as one of patrilineal primogeniture, but other ideas are also current. In Morapitiya today, as in other parts of Kandyan Ceylon, virilocal residence (*diga*) is the norm, but uxorilocal residence (*binna*) is not uncommon and it is asserted – at least by some – that 'in the old days' *binna* residence was the norm and was associated with the existence of four named exogamous matrilineal groups called *variga* which were spread through the whole Kotmale Valley. Very little is known about these *variga*[15] except their names and the fact that they were arranged into two ranked endogamous moieties with matrilineal descent.

Are we dealing here with another myth, or part of the same myth, or a detail of real social history? It does not in any case make it any easier to solve the problem of the descent of the Morapitiyans from Dutthagamani. In any form of unilineal system, patrilineal or matrilineal, Dutthagamani and Rammenika (and Kalumenika) must be in different lineages. So the *variga* system, whether real or imaginary, offers no simple explanation of how Kalumenika's descendants could have acquired a status of royalty from Dutthagamani. On the other hand, in Sinhalese social reality, as in the myth, the purity of any caste-group depends upon the purity of its women rather than that of its men (Yalman, 1963), and when Morapitiyans think of themselves as descended from Dutthagamani it may well be that they conceptualize a line of women, married in *binna*, who transmit their purity from mother to daughter.

Another way of discovering the relationship between the structural aspects and the charter aspects of the myth is to investigate the differential emphasis which Morapitiyans themselves place upon the various themes.

Table 3 shows the frequency-distribution of the ten episodes which were most often recounted by the Morapitiyans themselves and by the 'quasi-historical' sources (written mostly by people from, or with a special interest in, Kotmale). Of these, only episodes 6 and 7 are mentioned at all in the four 'historical' sources; each occurs twice but with some variation.

Items 1–5 seem to be the key themes for the Morapitiyans. They stress: (a) the high dignity of the name Weerasuriya-gedara (1), (b) the status of Dutthagamani as divine founder (2, 4), (c) the difference between Dutthagamani as the herdsman of Monaragala Peak and the Morapitiyan rice-farmers of the Kotmale Valley (3), (d) the kinship relation, however dubious in quality, between the Morapitiyans and Dutthagamani, and the royal status of the latter (5). Of the other items, 6, 7 and 9 emphasize Dutthagamani's aggressive virility and, by implication, the saintliness of passive femininity; 10 displays his supernatural power and shows that, despite his low-status role as herdsman, he could also adopt the high-status role of rice-farmer; 8 affirms the principle of descent through saintly women, but also, in view of Viharamahadevi's name, the assimilation of deities to the cult of orthodox Buddhism.

It thus appears that there is a relationship between the way in which a myth is used as a sociological charter and its structural patterning. Those

TABLE 3. Frequency-distribution of ten episodes most frequently recounted by Morapitiyans and their associates

	Morapitiyan (16 sources)	'Quasi-historical' (8 sources)	'Historical' (4 sources)
(1) Dutthagamani drew a line on the ground; the paddy followed. Because of this Urupalese-gammahe was named Weerasuriya-gedara, 'house of enough paddy'.	6	4	0
(2) Dutthagamani built a seat on Monaragala Peak by putting a big rock on top of a small one.	6	4	0
(3) Dutthagamani watched buffalo on Monaragala Peak every day.	6	4	0
(4) Dutthagamani named villages, bathing places, paddy fields, etc., in Kotmale.	5	4	0
(5) Rammenika married Dutthagamani and went with him to the palace.	5	2	0
(6) King Kavan Tissa asked his sons to promise not to fight the Tamils; Tissa agreed, Gamani refused.	4	4	2 (Both Tissa and Gamani refused to promise)
(7) Gamani sent a female ornament (or garment) to his father.	4	2	2
(8) Dutthagamani was sent to Morapitiya by his mother.	3	5	0
(9) Bending the iron with his hands, Dutthagamani made his hoe at the blacksmith's shop; the blacksmith recognized that he must be a prince. Dutthagamani said, 'If you tell anyone, I will kill you.'	3	5	0
(10) Dutthagamani sowed empty seeds in a Morapitiyan paddy field; they grew and he reaped much paddy.	3	4	0

aspects of the Dutthagamani myth which are most used as justification for modern Morapitiyan norms tend to be highly similar to the 'constituent units' of the myth discovered through structural analysis. Our findings indicate that the structural pattern of the Dutthagamani myth persists not only throughout all the twenty-eight oral and written versions of the myth but also in the Morapitiyan use of the myth as a sociological charter for the norms of the present-day social order.

ACKNOWLEDGMENTS

I should like to thank Dr Edmund R. Leach for his most stimulating and encouraging interest in my work in Ceylon and in particular for his substantial contributions to section III of this paper. I am grateful to Professor Cora Du Bois for her insightful comments and valuable advice in the preparation of this paper.

The fieldwork upon which this paper is based was carried out in Ceylon from December 1962 to August 1963, and was supported by a Public Health Service Fellowship (5 F1-MH-11, 859-04 (BEH)) and Research Grant (6353) from the National Institute of Mental Health. During the time this essay was written, I was a Postdoctoral Fellow of the National Institute of Mental Health (Fellowship 1F2 MH-11, 859-01 (BEH)) at the Peabody Museum, Harvard University, and an Associate Scholar of the Radcliffe Institute for Independent Study.

BIBLIOGRAPHY

Bell, H. C. P. (1918), 'Dutugemunu's Queen', *The Ceylon Antiquary and Literary Register*, 3, 3, 228.

Coomaraswamy, A. K. (1942), *Spiritual Authority and Temporal Power in the India Theory of Government* (New Haven: Yale University Press).

Geiger, W. (1908), *The Dipavamsa and Mahavamsa and their Historical Development in Ceylon* (Colombo: Govt. Printer).

Hocart, A. M. (1927), *Kingship* (London: Oxford University Press).

Law, B. C. (1947), *On The Chronicles of Ceylon* (Calcutta: Royal Asiatic Society of Bengal Monograph Series, vol. 3).

Lawrie, Sir A. C. (1898), *A Gazetteer of the Central Province of Ceylon.* 2 vols. (Colombo: J. A. Skeen, Govt. Printer).

Lévi-Strauss, C. (1958), *Anthropologie Structurale* (Paris: Librairie Plon).

—— (1963), Translation by Claire Jacobson and Brooke Grundfest Schoepf, *Structural Anthropology* (New York: Basic Books).

Malinowski, B. (1926), *Myth in Primitive Psychology*, reprinted (1955) in B. Malinowski, *Magic, Science and Religion and Other Essays*, pp. 93–148 (New York: Doubleday & Co.).

Mendis, G. C. (1916), 'Dutugemunu, a Lay of ancient Lanka', *The Ceylon Antiquary and Literary Register*, 2, 1, 29–35.

Nadel, S. F. (1942), *A Black Byzantium* (London: Oxford University Press).

Needham, R. (1960), 'The left hand of the Nugwe: an analytical note on the structure of Meru symbolism', *Africa*, XX, 20–33.

Samarasekera, G. P. (1916), 'The banishment of King Dutegumunu', *The Ceylon Antiquary and Literary Register*, 2, 2, 115–19.

Senaveratna, A. P. (1916), 'Some notable Sinhalese women in history', *The Ceylon Antiquary and Literary Register*, 1, 212–13.

Senaveratna, J. M. (1923), *The Story of the Sinhalese* (Colombo: *Times of Ceylon Co.*).

Tambiah, S. J. (1958), 'The structure of kinship and its relationships to land possession and residence in Pata Dubara, Central Ceylon', *J. R. Anthrop. Inst.* LXXXVIII, 1.

University of Ceylon (1959), *History of Ceylon*, I, 1 and 2 (Colombo: Ceylon University Press).

Yalman, N. (1964), 'The Structure of Sinhalese healing rituals' in *Religion in South Asia*, edited by E. B. Harper (Seattle: University of Washington Press).

THE SEX OF THE HEAVENLY BODIES*

Claude Lévi-Strauss

One of the first conversations I remember having with Roman Jakobson was about the way in which the opposition between the moon and the sun was marked in different languages and different mythologies. We wondered whether there was any pattern to be detected in the gender and/or the form of words designating the sun and the moon, or their relative size and luminosity in different languages or different myths of the same language. We very quickly realized that the problem was far from simple: that this opposition, whose binary nature seems too evident to the Western observer, could be expressed in other cultures in extraordinarily complex and, to our eyes, unexpected ways.

To mark the occasion of Roman Jakobson's sixty-second birthday which, as it happens, falls within a month or two of the twenty-fifth anniversary of our first meeting, I should like to present some data on the subject gathered from my general reading over the years, and remembered from those discussions. All the data are taken from various cultures of the North and South American continents. Notwithstanding this regional restriction, I hope that it may stimulate some further, wider research into a problem which greatly exercised the mythologists of the end of the nineteenth and beginning of the twentieth centuries, but which has been somewhat neglected since.

In both North and South America there are many languages which use the same word for the sun and the moon. Such is the case in the Iroquis language where the terms /gaä'gwā/ and /karakwa/ are used in the Onadaga and Mohawk dialects respectively, to denote the two bodies. To these terms may be added, if necessary, a determinor: /andá-kāgagwā/, 'day-time light-giver', and /soi-kāgagwā/, 'night-time light-giver'. A similar situation is found in the languages of the widespread Algonquin group. For example, in Blackfoot, /kèsúm/, 'sun, moon'; in Menomini, /kē'so/, 'sun'; /tipākē'so/, 'sun of the night, moon'; in

* First appeared in *To Honour Roman Jakobson* (Mouton, The Hague, 1956); translated from the French by Phillip Brew.

Montagnais, /čiseesk-pišum/ and /tepeskau-pišum/; in Arapaho, /hiuis/, 'celestial light-giver'; and in Gros-ventre, /hisös/.

The same word is used for the sun and the moon in Seminole, Hichiti, Choctaw and Cherokee. The Kutenai use the one word /natanek/ for the two heavenly bodies and the Klamath the one word /sábas/. For the moon the Quinauts use a word meaning nocturnal sun. There are many languages or dialects in California which use the same word for the sun and the moon: Achomawi, northern Maidu, Karik, Patwin, eastern and northern Pomo, Kato, Wailaki, Miwok, Lacustre and Wappo.

In South America there are languages such as Carib and Tupi which usually have two distinct terms. The use of one single term, on the other hand, is the general rule among tribes using the Tukano language: /muhi-pun/ in the dialect of the Uaupès, /avyá/ in Cubeo. The Uitoto call the sun /hitoma/, and the moon /hwibui/ or /manaide-hitoma/, 'the cold sun'. While the Chibcha of the Andean plateau use two distinct terms, /zuhé/ and /chia/ for the sun and the moon, which they make male and female respectively, the Cayapa, on the western slopes, say /pata/ and /popata/, both of which they make masculine, and the Waunana of the Chaco use one word, /edau/, meaning sun, daylight, moon.

Although in general they have a very rich vocabulary, about which we shall have more to say later, most of the Gé languages form their words for the sun and the moon from the same root, /put-/ or /pud-/. Several Arawak languages do the same. Thus the sun and the moon are respectively /kamoi/ and /kairi/ in Palikur, /kamu/ and /kaier/ in Vapidiana, /kxami/ and /kwataua/ in Kustenau, /kamai/ and /kaimaré/ in Paressi.

The use of a single term for the sun and the moon, or of terms formed from the same root, must not be interpreted as meaning that there is any objective confusion of the two bodies, or that they are thought of as being of the same sex. The Iroquis, for example, use the same word for the sun and the moon and depict them as coming from the head and the body respectively of a decapitated woman, or sometimes the other way round. And yet they depict the sun as male and the moon as female. This is on the basis of a different, traditional myth according to which the sun, as a *light*-source, comes from the decapitated head of a man, while the moon, as light-source, comes from the decapitated head of a woman, the two *bodies* from which these heads have been severed controlling the output of *heat* by day and by night respectively. Thus, whilst no distinction is made between the sun and the moon in the language, they are doubly distinguished in the mythology: once by the sex, male or female, and once by the part, upper or lower, of the human body from which they originally sprang – this double distinction corresponding to the two different functions, as light-source and as heat-source, which each of the two heavenly bodies fulfils.

In fact this distinction between the light-producing and heat-producing functions often seems to be more important than the distinction between the two bodies themselves, which is perhaps why the same word is used to denote them in their capacity as simple heavenly bodies. As we have seen, the Tukano languages of South America are the same in this respect as the Iroquis and Algonquin languages. The Cubeo, though, do not accord the same status to the sun and the moon. For them the sun is simply the moon emitting light and heat during the day. In its solar form the light-source, /avyá/, has no anthropomorphic connotations. The moon, on the other hand, is a male divinity and plays a role of considerable importance in the religious life of the tribe.

The Warrau of the Orinoco delta have two different words for the two heavenly bodies, and, like the Cubeo they accord them different status. It appears from the reports of observers that the word /okohi/ denotes the hottest period of the day and refers to the calorific properties of the sun as distinct from its luminosity. It is of course a fact that whereas both the moon and the sun are sources of light, only the latter possesses the property of emitting heat. The fact that it has a separate name, therefore, does not prevent the sun from being thought of as simply a rather special form of the moon. It is a concept which is wider in intension but narrower in extension. This is expressed in Warrau mythology by speaking of the moon as the 'receptacle' of the sun. Similarly the Sherente, who are members of the Gé group and live on the Central Plateau, have the words /bdu/ and /wa/ for the sun and moon respectively, but in place of the first word they prefer to use /sdakro/, which means 'light, solar heat'.

Despite the great distance which separates them, the Emok-Toba of the Chaco and the Cubeo have remarkably similar ideas. In both cases all the interest is centred in the moon, which is seen as a male divinity, a deflowerer of virgins and a cause of menstruation. The sun, /nála/, feminine in gender, has two qualities only, /lidàgá/, 'light-giving', and /n:táp/, 'heat-giving'. It plays only a minor role in the traditional mythology of the tribes. In general it is striking how often the same word is used to denote indifferently the sun as a heavenly body, daylight, and the season: for example, /kamu/, 'sun, daylight' in Vapidiana; /dě'i/, 'sun, daylight' in Chamacoco; /bari/, 'sun, daylight, summer' in Cashinawa; /antú/, 'sun, daylight, summer' in Araucan.

One could quote many other examples. The Wintu tribe of California, by way of contrast, see the moon as 'the silver underside of the sun's belly' – a double inversion of the Warrau conception.

The Surára Indians of Northern Brazil, to whom the moon is a demiurge, have an explanation for the lower ranking of the sun in their mythology. It is that the heavenly body which appears at night is accompanied by an infinite number of stars. The tops of the many hills which cover the region are seen, in their multiplicity, as a sort of terrestrial counterpart of the stars. These hills come immediately after the moon in the hierarchy of divinities, and as intercessors with the moon they are again placed ahead of the sun. The opposition between the plurality of the nocturnal light-sources and the singularity of the daytime light-source is fairly common in the tropical region ·of South America, and occurs as far away as the Southern Guaraní Indians, whose word for the stars, /yacitata/, is formed from /yaci/, 'moon', and /tata/, 'fire'.

Of course, the fact that we notice the plurality of the nocturnal light-sources is partly due to the fact that they stand out in much greater contrast to the blackness of the night than does the sun to the day. At night, the presence or the absence of the moon and stars makes the difference between a reasonable amount of light and a total lack of light, whereas the sun, which is seen as to some degree *identifiable with* the daylight rather than as forming a contrast to it, merely determines, by its presence or its absence behind the clouds, different degrees of light. This difference is of importance in the mythology of the Amazonian Mundurucu, who attribute it to the existence of two separate suns, a summer sun and a winter sun; significantly, they see the moon as the wife of the winter sun. The main opposition, then, is not the same as ours: it is not between two heavenly bodies, but between two sets of meteorological conditions. The opposition between darkness and light is brought out much more strongly at night by the moon shining or not shining than it is by the sun in the day-time; for when the sun shines it merely adds heat and light to a degree of light which is seen to be already quite considerable when thought of in the context of moonlight as opposed to pitch darkness. It is none the less true that though logically subordinate to the moon, the sun is empirically more powerful. These two oppositions can be expressed by the use of different genders. For the Déné-Peaux-de-Lièvre, the Dakotas, the Maidu, the central Algonquin, the Cherokees, the Seminole, the Chimila, the Mocovi, and the Tobas the sun is feminine and the moon masculine (though for the last-named the data available appear to be somewhat contradictory). The attribution of gender is the reverse for the Micmacs, the Menomini, the Blackfoot, the Chibcha, the ancient Peruvians, the Araucan, the Ona and the Yahgans. It should be noted, however, that in certain tribes the sex of the heavenly bodies will vary according to whether one looks at the language (in cases where the language distinguishes gender), the tribal rites, or the mythology; and, within mythology, according to whether one looks at popular mythology or 'classical' mythology. In the Arapaho tribe, for example, the myths which are of a more or less esoteric character have the sun as masculine but describe the moon sometimes as a man (the younger brother of the sun), and sometimes as a woman, in which case she may be the wife of the sun or the grandmother of a son conceived by the moon when she was of male sex.

In other cases the gender of the name varies according to whether it is sacred or profane. Within the same myth, the Thompson Indians distinguish the divine sun, who is male, from the visible sun, who is his daughter and who crosses the sky daily from east to west in search of him. It seems probable that a more detailed investigation would show that gender is rarely used as an absolute distinction between the sun and the moon. We have suggested other more fundamental oppositions which the sun and the moon can be used to express, such as light and darkness, stronger and weaker light, heat and cold, etc. And the sexes attributed to them appear to vary according to the role played within a particular mythological or ritual context.

Where the sun and the moon are of different sexes, they may or may not be related. If they are related, it may be as brother and sister or as husband and wife, or, as in the myth of the incest of the sun and the moon which is to be found throughout the New World, at once as brother and sister, and husband and wife. In this myth the moon is masculine, and the sun feminine, for the myth usually explains the dark patches on the surface of the moon as having been made by a young maiden on the face of her nocturnal and unknown lover in order to be able to recognize him later. The Peruvians appear to be the only ones to have legitimized this incest by reversing the sexes of the partners, although the myths of the Klamath and the Salish of the plateau, and those of several Southern Californian tribes, contain at least the hint of a similar solution.

Lehmann-Nitsche, who has investigated the matter on more than one occasion, has found that the distribution in South America of the myth in which a male sun is married to a female moon runs down the Andes from the Cumana of Venezuela through the Chibcha, the Inca and the Araucan down to Tierra del Fuego, with, according to some very old data on the mythology of the Toba, a branch out into the Chaco. He also mentions another, transversal axis running from east to west along which are distributed myths in which the sun and the moon are brothers, the sun being the elder of the two.

Leaving aside certain tribes of the Amazon and the Guyanas, such as the Tukuna and the Caribs, this latter mythological treatment presents a more or less continuous distribution from the Eastern and Central Gé of the Plateau, through the tribes of the Xingu, the Bakairi, the Bororo and the southern Tupi-Guaraní, to the Puelche of the Pampas, and it reappears in Colombia and in Ecuador on the western slopes of the Andes. The opposition between the sun and the moon in all these latter cases is expressed not by a difference in gender but by a difference in age, even when the two are twins, and above all by personality-differences: the sun is thoughtful, careful and capable; his brother the moon is rash, and commits all sorts of blunders, many of them fatal, which his elder brother has to try to rectify.

The multiplicity of terms for the sun and the moon in the Gé languages – some sacred, some profane, some referring to meteorological aspects, others being the names of divinities – might be thought to be due to their position at the intersection of the fraternal and conjugal axes, or, to be more precise, in the area of overlap between, on the one hand, the zone of the fraternal axis (which in principle requires distinct names for each of the two bodies) and, on the other, the north-west of the Amazon basin, where the same name is usually used for the sun and the moon, or where the sun is even seen as no more than a mere mode of the moon. Thus, while the tribes of the Xingu and the Bororo, who are near neighbours of the Gé, have distinct names: /kéri/ and /kamé/, /méri/ and /ari/, etc., the Gé often form them on the same radical: /pud/ and /pudléré/ in the Kraho language, /put/ and /puduvri/ in the Timbira, and /mbudti/ and /mbudvriré/ in the Apinayé language.

Were it not for this example, and that of the Cayapa, one would be tempted to say that neighbouring populations treat the opposition between the sun and the moon in one of two different ways: either they attribute to them different sexes or different degrees of reality, even when the words by which they refer to them are identical, or they give them the same sex but different names and different personalities. This analysis, however, would appear to be an over-simplification, for both to the north and to the south examples can be found which would seem to invalidate it, though one would like to be able to examine them in greater detail to see whether they are not in fact isolated exceptions. It is true that a fraternal axis can also be found in North America, where (if we ignore the classification traditionally given by specialists, who would no doubt deny the comparability of our examples) the distribution would appear to be approximately north-west–south-east, from the Salish of the plateau, through the Gros-Ventre, the Crow, the Hidatsa and the Cheyenne, down to the Arapaho.

Thus, as in the southern continent, the fraternal axis intercepts that along which the same word is used for the sun and the moon, and the position of the Cheyenne, the Gros-Ventre and the Arapaho, all of whom are central Algonquins, presents a certain formal analogy with that of the Gé. Thus in Arapaho we have /hicinicic/, 'the sun', and /bigucic/, 'the moon' – a contraction of /biga/, 'night' and /hicic/, 'light-source'. Since the Gé and the Algonquin see the sun and the moon as two brothers, linguistic and mythological requirements work in opposite directions, the one conflating what the other must distinguish.

It will by now have become clear that there is no necessary correspondence between linguistic oppositions and those which are expressed, for example, in religious beliefs, ritual, myths or folklore. The grammatical contrast of gender does not reflect a semantic contrast. The two may even be in contradiction. This is not all: it may well be that different types of *semantic* contrast are mutually contradictory. However, if we do not attempt the impossible task of providing a completely coherent explanation covering all aspects for each particular case, if we restrict ourselves to a very summary consideration of a number of initially unrelated facts, of which we have here considered only an infinitesimal number compared with the number one would need to examine in order to reach any sort of generalized conclusion, then at least the faint outline of a structure does begin to appear, sufficient at least to serve as a guide-line for some more detailed future investigation. According to this structure, the solutions adopted by each society (for there may well be several solutions for each society) are seen as responses to a series of binary alternatives. Either the sun and the moon are distinct or they are not. If they are not distinct, the sun is a mode of the moon, or vice versa. If they are distinct, the difference is sexual or non-sexual. If it is sexual, the sun may be male and the moon female or vice versa, and in either case the relationship may be that of husband and wife, brother and sister, or the two at once. If the difference is not one of sex, they may be two women or two men, and in this case there will be differences of character or strength. This latter opposition is sometimes weakened to the point where one of the two loses his individuality and becomes a sort of double of the first. In this case, the last alternative leads back to the first, showing that, potentially at least, the system is closed. This can be seen particularly clearly in the tribes of the Columbia River, and in others down as far as California. In different groups, and sometimes even in different myths within the same group, the sun and the moon may be two women or two men, the one a pale substitute for the other, or very strongly contrasted.

Of course, cases in intermediate positions will certainly occur. Far from invalidating the structure, however, they actually help to arrange its elements in series. Thus between the solution of the two brothers and that of the incestuous siblings falls the Apapocuva's solution of an abortive homosexual incest, a choice which leads the Southern Tupi-Guaraní, the group to which the Apapocuva belong, to divert the heterosexual tendencies of the moon towards a paternal aunt; this is how the Mbya, who are also Guaraní, explain the presence of the dark patches on the moon's surface. This would appear to be a point of intersection between the two axes occurring within a relatively limited area. Another point of intersection may be observed in the Columbia River basin. It is significant that in both cases the myths end with the exchange of roles between a sun which formerly appeared at night and a moon which formerly appeared by day but whose ardour threatened to consume the earth.

Elsewhere, the fraternal relationship becomes one of brothers-in-law (husband of sister and brother of wife), maternal uncle and nephew, and even father and son. What was a horizontal relationship now becomes a vertical one. Each system seems to exert an influence over its neighbour, which, under this influence, changes and evolves. In a sense each is a function of all the others. If one wishes to understand them, one must try to see them as a whole and in the interdependence of their relationships.

On account of its distribution throughout the two Americas and even beyond, it seems natural to choose as the referential axis the myth of the incestuous siblings. Furthermore, the geographical orientation of this axis and the logical structure of the myth make it more suitable for the generation, by modification in opposite directions, of the conjugal and fraternal myths than either of these two would be for the production of the other two. Throughout North and South American mythology is to be found the problem of the regular alternation of day and night, with its implication that the two heavenly bodies must keep at a reasonable distance from each other. Any appreciable movement towards or away from each other would result either in prolonged daylight or in prolonged night, the threat of which is evoked in other myths. In the myth of the incestuous siblings, the spacing of day and night is seen as the resultant of two opposite forces. The incestuous tendencies of the siblings pull them together, while fear of general reprobation holds them apart. The myth can move in either direction from this unstable position towards one of two positions of stability: either the contrast between the sexes disappears, which leads to the fraternal relationships, or the blood relationship disappears, which leads to the conjugal relationship. But in the first case the relationship of physical complementarity is replaced by one of moral superiority; and in the second the nodes of the physical complementarity are simply reversed. Thus both transformations of the myth resolve the contradiction on one axis only for it to reappear on another, and the number of parameters increases with each attempt at a solution.

It is now becoming clear that the binary model which we began to outline is in fact inadequate. It provides us with a means of defining in the abstract certain values of a limiting nature, but it does not enable us to interpret concrete properties or to measure the closeness of relationships. To do this we should need to work out an analogical model in which the initial and final positions of each myth would be plotted in a multi-dimensional space. Each of these dimensions would provide a parameter along which would be arranged, in the most appropriate fashion, all the variations of each semantic function. In terms of distance, the two bodies may be joined, close, at some distance, remote or completely unrelated. In terms of sex, they may be both male, man and woman, hermaphrodites, woman and man, or both female. They may be defined in other terms: concrete objects, animals, humans, meteorological phenomena, stars, heavenly bodies, demiurges, etc. In terms of family connections they may be blood relations, siblings, cousins, uncles, husbands and wives, related by marriage or quite unrelated. Since the two bodies are not always of the same kind at the outset, there will be a fifth parameter to express their relative homogeneity or heterogeneity, and a sixth will express variations in synchrony and diachrony according to whether each term retains its original nature throughout the myth or whether it changes.

Let us illustrate the method with an example. The Sherente myth of the bird-catcher, studied in *Le Cru et le cuit* (pp. 80–4), may be codified in solar and lunar terms since the heroes are drawn from complementary and opposite social units, each of which is associated with one of the two heavenly bodies. We should say then that in this myth the characters who embody the sun and the moon are (1) separate, (2) male, (3) related by marriage, (4) human. And, since they remain thus throughout the myth, they are homogeneous in synchrony. In contrast, in the myth of the incest between the sun and the moon, the protagonists are separate, man and woman, siblings and celestial. The brother and sister, who are human at the beginning of the myth, are both transformed simultaneously into celestial bodies; they are therefore homogeneous in diachrony. They would be heterogeneous in synchrony if the sun and the moon, as is sometimes the case, were different throughout.

If the model required three parameters only, each myth could be represented by a line, and the same number of co-ordinates would be sufficient to mark its initial position and the different stages of its development. It would then be possible to compare the semantic distances between these lines with those related to geography and history, in the hope of integrating these three aspects. But we have enumerated six parameters and further research will undoubtedly increase this number. Despite its complexity, which excludes the possibility of treating the problem diagrammatically, the method is at least of intuitive value. Even such a vague outline is enough to convince us that mythology does not treat the sex of the heavenly bodies as an isolated problem. Notions relating to it are closely bound up with many others in a way which completely ignores their empirical origins. We may say the same of the sun and the moon as we may say of the innumerable natural beings handled by mythology: mythology does not seek to give them a meaning; it expresses its own meaning through them.

SYSTEM, STRUCTURE AND CONTRADICTION IN *DAS KAPITAL*★

Maurice Godelier

Is it possible to analyse the relationship between an event and a structure, or to account for the origin and development of a structure, without being forced to abandon a structuralist point of view? These are two questions which are forcing themselves more and more on our attention, and some writers have already thought it possible to give an affirmative answer. One aspect of the recent interest in structuralism has been the revival of the dialogue between structuralism and Marxism. This will hardly seem surprising when it is remembered that over a century ago Marx was describing the whole of social life in terms of 'structures', differentiating different types of society on the basis of his hypothesis of the existence of necessary 'correspondances' between infrastructures and superstructures, and was claiming to be able to account for the evolution of different types of society by the appearance and growth of internal 'contradictions' between their structures.

It might seem, when one remembers the dialectic 'miracles' of Hegel and of certain Marxists, that with the appearance of the word 'contradiction' the structuralist-Marxist dialogue was doomed to be very short-lived. But is the matter to be so summarily dismissed? Is the Marxist dialectic the dialectic of Hegel? Marx himself is somewhat equivocal on this point when he says that Hegel's dialectic only needed to be 'put back on its feet' for it to lose all the mystification with which Hegelian idealism had encumbered it, and become a useful scientific instrument.

We have found it useful, in re-examining the problem, to take another look at the text of *Das Kapital* itself, and we hope to be able to demonstrate that, in its fundamental principles, Marx's dialectic has nothing at all in common with that of Hegel, because they are in fact referring to two quite different notions of contradiction. The traditional analysis of Marx's work is seen to be hopelessly wrong and in its place there emerges

★ First appeared in *Les Temps modernes*, no. 246 (1966); translated from the French by Phillip Brew.

a Marx who is largely unfamiliar to the average Marxist but who is capable of providing us with many unexpected and fruitful aids to the adoption of a scientific approach of the most modern kind.

I

FROM THE VISIBLE WORKING OF THE CAPITALIST SYSTEM TO ITS HIDDEN INTERNAL 'STRUCTURE'

Science would be superfluous if there were no difference between the appearance of things and their essence (Karl Marx, *Das Kapital*, book III, vol. III).

What does Marx mean by an economic 'system'? He means a certain combination of specific modes of production, distribution, sharing out and consumption of material goods. In this combination the mode of production of the goods plays the most important role. A mode of production is the combination of two mutually irreducible structures. They are, on the one hand, the productive forces and, on the other, the relationships of production. The notion of productive forces includes all the factors of production, including resources, equipment and men, which are to be found in a specific society at a specific time, and which must be combined in a specific way to produce the material goods which that society needs. The notion of relationships of production covers the functions fulfilled by individuals and groups in the process of production and in the control of the factors of production. The capitalist relationships of production, for example, are the relationships between a class of individuals who possess as their own private property the productive forces and the capital, and a class of individuals who possess neither of these and who must sell to the former class the use of their labour in exchange for a wage. Each class is complementary to the other and presupposes the existence of the other.

For Marx, a scientific investigation of the capitalist system consists in discovering the hidden internal structure beneath its visible functioning.

For Marx therefore, as for Claude Lévi-Strauss,[1] the structures are not to be confused with the visible social relationships. They constitute a *level of reality* which is invisible, but which is none the less present beneath the visible social relationships. The logic of these relationships, and, at a more general level, the laws of social practice derive from the operation of these hidden structures, and their discovery should enable us to account for all the observable facts.[2]

It will be helpful to consider a very brief summary of Marx's thesis. In the day-to-day working of the capitalist system everything conspires to make it *appear* as if the wages a worker received paid for his labour, and as if capital possessed the property of increasing of its own accord, providing its owner with a profit. In the day-to-day working of the system there is no *immediate* proof that the capitalist's profit represents unpaid labour provided by the worker. There is no *direct experience* of the exploitation of the worker by the capitalist.

For Marx the profit is a part of the exchange-value of the goods produced which is retained by the entrepreneur after deduction of the cost of production. The notion of an exchange-value of the goods presupposes the existence of some common unit of measure. This common measure cannot be the utility of the goods. There is clearly nothing in common between the utility of, for example, a cabbage and a fountain-pen ... The exchange-value of goods can only be based on their having in common the fact of being the product of labour. The substance of the value is therefore the work, the labour socially necessary for the production of the goods. The profit is that part of the value which is created through the use of the worker's labour but which is not paid for in the wages.[3] Profit is therefore unpaid work. But, in practice, both the capitalist and the worker have the impression that the wages pay for all the work done by the worker (wages here are taken to include bonuses, piece-work payments, overtime payments, etc.). So the payment of wages gives the unpaid work of the worker the appearance of being paid work:

> This form of wage, which is merely an expression of the false, visible appearance of paid labour, renders *invisible* the *real* relationship between capital and labour and gives an *impression* which is in fact the opposite of the truth; it is from these false appearances that all the legal notions of the wage-earner and the capitalist are derived, as are all the myths which surround capitalistic production.[4]

As soon as wages are thought of as the 'price' of labour, profit can no longer be seen as unpaid labour. It is necessarily seen as being produced by capital. Each side seems to be drawing from production the revenue to which it is entitled. There is no visible exploitation of one class by the other. The economic categories of wages, profits, interest, etc., express therefore the visible relations of the day-to-day practice of affairs, and as such they do have some *practical* use for us, but they are of no scientific value whatever. Any so-called economics based on these categories is no more than a 'systemization of the claims and pretensions of agents of production who are themselves prisoners of bourgeois relationships of production and merely constitutes an apology of these ideas ... it is therefore hardly surprising that popular notions of economics appear perfectly self-evident and that the relationships seem the more obvious for their internal structure remaining hidden'.[5] The appearance of intelligibility and coherence bestowed by this systemization of the way members of society normally see the system inevitably gives rise to a number of myths. 'To speak of the "price" of labour is as irrational as to speak of a yellow logarithm.' The myth here consists of a coherent theory of appearances, of what *seems* to be taking place in practice. It is clear then that a scientific description of the social reality cannot be based on the impressions which individuals have of it, even when these are the result of serious reflection. It is in fact the task of such a scientific description to show that these impressions *are* an illusion and to reveal the hidden internal logic of the life of the society. For Marx, then, the scientific model corresponds to a reality which is hidden beneath the visible reality. He in fact goes further, because for him this concealment is not due to the inability of the conscious mind to perceive the structure. It is implicit in the structure itself. If capital is not a thing but a social relationship, that is, an intangible reality, it must necessarily disappear from view when presented under the tangible forms of raw materials, equipment, money, etc. So it is not exactly the case that the individual is mistaken. It is rather that the reality is inaccessible to him. His impressions are based on the appearances beneath which the structure of the capitalist production process conceals itself. For Marx, to each real structure there corresponds a mode of appearance of this structure and this mode of appearance is the basis of a sort of spontaneous awareness of the structure for which neither the conscious mind nor the individual is responsible. Thus it is that a scientific description of the structure cannot ignore this spontaneous awareness of the structure. It will change the role of this spontaneous awareness and modify its effects on the behaviour of the individuals, but it will not eliminate it.[6]

Marx, then, in posing that the structure is not to be confused with the visible relationships, but that it explains their hidden logic, is clearly a forerunner of the modern structuralist movement. He can be most closely identified with this movement when he insists on the priority of the study of the structure over that of its origin and development. But before going on to talk about this let us compare the scientific practice of Lévi-Strauss to that of Marx by recalling the main features of the famous analysis of the kinship system of the Murngin tribe to be found in *Les Structures élémentaires de la parenté*.[7]

The kinship system of this Australian tribe used to be considered by the specialists to be 'abnormal' because they were unable to classify it in the typology of the so-called 'classical' Australian systems. These could be divided into three types, according to whether they contained two, four or eight matrimonial classes. It was observed that, in a two-class system, marriage was allowed between cross cousins but forbidden between parallel cousins. The same applied to the four-class Kariera system. Thus there was no difference between a two-class and a four-class system as far as the authorization or prohibition of marriage was concerned. In the Aranda system, however, which had eight subclasses, marriage between all first cousins, whether cross or parallel, was forbidden.

The Murngin system differs from both the Kariera and the Aranda systems. It contains eight subclasses like the Aranda system, yet it permits marriage with a matrilateral female cross cousin like the Kariera system. But, whereas the Kariera system permits marriage with both matrilateral and patrilateral female cross cousins, the Murngin system prohibits it with the patrilateral female cross cousin, thus introducing a dichotomy between matrilateral and patrilateral cross cousins. There are other peculiarities in the Murngin system. It recognizes seven genealogical lines of descent whereas the Aranda system makes do with four and the Kariera system with two; there are seventy-one different terms in its kinship nomenclature whereas the Aranda system has only forty-one and the Kariera system twenty-one.

An explanation was needed, then, to account for the dichotomy between cross cousins, the preference shown for marriage with a matrilateral female cross cousin, and also for the other peculiarities of the system. Lévi-Strauss has demonstrated that it is possible to account for all of these by supposing the existence and functioning beneath the *explicit* system of restricted exchange between eight subclasses, which is the *appearance* of the Murngin system, of an *implicit* four-class system of a totally different structure, of which even the Murngin themselves are unaware, and which ethnologists specializing in the field had not yet identified. Lévi-Strauss calls this a 'generalized exchange structure'.

Whereas in a restricted exchange system the rule for marriage is always symmetrical (that is, if a man from A marries a woman from B, a man from B can marry a woman from A) in a generalized exchange system if a man from A marries a woman from B, a man from B will marry a woman from C and a man from C a woman from A. A will therefore take a woman from B but will give up 'in exchange' a woman to C. Reciprocity in this case involves a certain number of partners and takes the form of the interplay of relationships in one particular and irreversible direction: $A \to B \to C \to A$. It can therefore be shown that in a four-class generalized exchange system the matrilateral female cross cousin is always in the class immediately following that of Ego, that is, the class into which he can marry, whereas the patrilateral female cross cousin is always in the preceding class, with whom marriage is therefore forbidden. The structure of such a system thus provides the theoretical formula for Murngin marriage rules and accounts for the law of the dichotomy of cross cousins.

It can then be easily demonstrated that if to a four-class generalized exchange system is added a matrilineal binary system, each class will be divided into two subclasses and the result is a system with eight subclasses which has the appearance of being a doubled-up restricted exchange system of the Aranda type. It is now easy to explain all the other peculiarities of the system such as the number of genealogical lines of descent, and the size of the nomenclature, which are seen as necessary consequences of the working of this implicit structure, as complementary facets of its internal logic.

It is not difficult to see the immense importance of Lévi-Strauss's demonstration. In seeking to account for a particular case which appeared to be abnormal and was unclassifiable in the traditional ethnological typology,[8] Lévi-Strauss had discovered the existence[9] and had accounted for the nature of a new family of structures, which were far more complex than those then known and far more difficult to identify because the cycle of exchanges which they determined was less immediately perceptible. A new classification of kinship systems became both necessary and possible, and into it was integrated the old typology of restricted exchange systems, the particularity of which was now obvious. At the practical level a new tool was made available which was to prove indispensable in the study of certain complex kinship systems in China, India, South-East Asia and Siberia which appeared to make no use of the notion of exchange.

Lévi-Strauss's methodological principles and conclusions are of no less importance epistemologically. Whether a structure is implicit,[10] as in the Murngin case, or explicit, as with the Kachin, it is never directly visible and accessible at the empirical level but has to be discovered through theoretical research, which will involve the setting up of hypotheses and models. In its very principle then Lévi-Strauss's structural analysis rejects the structural functionalism of Radcliffe-Brown,[11] and in general the whole of British and American empirical sociology in which the structure is seen as part of empirical reality.[12]

For Lévi-Strauss too, the structure is part of reality, but not part of empirical reality. One must not therefore try to equate the structure and the theoretical model set up to represent it. The structure does *not* exist only in and through the human mind, and this excludes the idealist and formalist structuralism which claims to be based on Lévi-Strauss's ideas.[13] His position is stated, far more explicitly than in *Anthropologie structurale*, in his reply to Maybury-Lewis, who had accused him of discovering pseudo-structures which were contradicted by the ethnographical facts:

> Of course only experiment can provide the final answer. But experiment which is suggested and guided by deductive reasoning will not be the same as the simple experiments with which the whole process began. The ultimate proof of the molecular structure of matter is provided by the electron microscope which enables us to see the actual molecules. But this does not alter the fact that in the future the molecule will have become no more visible to the naked eye than it was in the past. In the same way, one cannot hope to expect structural analysis to change the perception of the concrete social relationships. But it will account for them more satisfactorily.[14]

A subsidiary consequence of the structural method is the rejection of any form of psychologism or sociological finalism. From as early as his *Les Structures élémentaires de la parenté*, Lévi-Strauss has shown that the psychological approach of Warner provided only the illusion of an answer to the problem of the seven genealogical lines of descent of the Murngin tribe.[15] Warner's explanation was based on a supposed need to resolve the tensions which, without this large number of lines of descent, would arise in the group between Ego and the brother of the mother, that is, the father of the matrilateral female cross cousin, and therefore the potential future wife.[16] As we have seen, the real answer owes nothing to psychology but is found quite simply in the logic of the generalized exchange system, the existence of which Warner did not even suspect.

More fundamentally the analysis of the logic of a structure throws light on its potentialities and its capacity for evolution. Research into the origin and first appearance of a structure is, so to speak, guided by a proper knowledge of how that structure now works. In the case of the Murngin, Lévi-Strauss supposed that they had borrowed from elsewhere a system with eight subclasses which they had grafted on to their original matrimonial system.[17] He then showed that such a system would be unstable and that this would determine what form and types of evolution were possible. He showed that this instability was common to all generalized exchange systems, which are always 'harmonic' since the rules of filiation are the same as the rules of residence for determining the social status of an individual, whereas restricted exchange systems are always 'disharmonic and stable'.[18] He concluded that this was the basic reason for the unequal frequency of occurrence and capacity for evolution of the two families of structures.[19] These capacities therefore are the objective properties of the structures, which do not depend on the individual members of the society and of which the individual is, for the most part, unconscious. For example, if the Murngin system is the product of borrowing and an adaptation, it is to that extent the product of a conscious and deliberate act, but for the most part the Murngin remained unconscious of the logic of their new system and its capacity for evolution, and in any case these were not determined by their intentions. Seen in this perspective, social evolution ceases to be a series of meaningless accidents.[20]

This all-too-brief analysis of a fragment of one of the earliest works of Lévi-Strauss will none the less be sufficient to establish the validity of the comparison between Marx and modern structuralism. From it emerge two important principles of structural analysis as exemplified in the Lévi-Strauss approach: the first is that a structure is part of reality but not of visible relationships, the second is that the study of the internal functioning of a structure must precede and will throw light on the study of its coming into being and subsequent evolution. We have already shown that the first of these principles is to be found in Marx's work. We shall now show that it is impossible to understand the architecture of *Das Kapital* without the use of the second.

II

PRIORITY OF THE STUDY OF THE STRUCTURE ITSELF OVER THAT OF ITS ORIGIN AND SUBSEQUENT EVOLUTION

That this priority is observed in *Das Kapital* can easily be seen from a quick glance at its architecture. The work begins not with the theory of Capital, but with an exposition of the theory of Value, that is, with the definition of a number of categories necessary for the study of any system of mercantile production, whether based on the labour of a free peasant, a slave, a serf, or a wage-earning worker. This group of categories is developed from a definition of the exchange value of merchandise. Money next appears, as a special sort of merchandise, whose function is to express the exchange-value of other merchandise. Money ceases to be a simple means of exchange and begins to function as capital when it begins to earn money, when its initial value can be increased through its use. The general definition of capital whatever its form, whether commercial, financial or industrial capital, is that it is a value which can be put to use and thereby earns surplus value.

By the end of the second section of Volume I of *Das Kapital*, Marx has equipped himself with the theoretical instruments necessary to identify the specific structure of the capitalistic economic system and the relationship between capital and paid labour, and to set up the theory of capital. Before he could begin to elaborate this theory he needed the most precise definition of the notion of merchandise, since in the capital-labour relationship labour is seen as a merchandise. The analysis of the internal structure of the capitalist system then becomes possible, that is, the study of the mechanism of the production of surplus value through the capital-labour relationship. Book I contains a lengthy analysis of the two forms of surplus value: absolute surplus value (which is obtained by an increase in working hours without a corresponding increase in wages) and relative surplus value (which is obtained by a decrease in the cost of upkeep of the worker brought about by an increase in the productivity of labour in those branches of industry which produce the means of subsistence for the worker and his family).

It is not until the end of Book I that Marx approaches the problem of the origin of the relationships of production in the capitalist system through a discussion of what classical economists called 'the problem of primary Accumulation'. Marx then proceeds in a way which constitutes a complete break with the historicist approach. The study of the genesis of a structure can only be undertaken when it can be guided by a thorough and previously acquired knowledge of that structure. The study of the genesis of the specific structure of the capitalist system involves the identification of the particular historical circumstances in which individuals emerged who were free in their person but who were without means of production or money, and who were therefore forced to sell their labour to other individuals who were in possession of means of production and money, but who were forced to buy the labour of others in order to set these means of production to work and to set their money to earn profit. But Marx gives no more than a brief sketch of this in the course of a rapid summary of some of the conditions, forms and stages of the appearance of capitalism in Europe. He does not really give us a history of capitalism. Of these different stages we might note the disbandment of feudal retinues in England, the expropriation and partial expulsion of the peasants, the 'enclosure' movement, the transformation of merchants into merchant-manufacturers, colonial trade, and the development of protectionism. All these phenomena occurred in Portugal, Spain, Holland, France and England in the fifteenth, sixteenth, and seventeenth centuries and in general resulted in the appearance of a large number of producers without the means of production and of their use in a new structure of production.

   ... At the heart of the capitalist system, therefore, is the fundamental separation of the producer from the means of production. This separation reproduces itself, becoming more and more marked once the capitalist system has properly established itself. But since it is at the basis of the system, the system could not be established before it came into existence. Before the system could come into existence, therefore, the means of production must, partially at least, already have been wrested from the producers who had previously used them to carry out their own work, and been concentrated in the hands of the merchant-manufacturers who used them for the very different purpose of speculating on the work of others. The historical movement which had brought about the divorce of work done from its external conditions – this then is the ultimate origin of 'primary' accumulation, so-called because it belongs to a pre-historic age as far as the bourgeois world is concerned. The economic structure of

capitalism emerged from the very substance of the economic
structure of feudalism. The dissolution of one system threw up the
constituent elements of the other.[21]

The analysis of the birth of a new structure, then, means the analysis
of the historical conditions which surrounded the appearance of its
internal elements, and the relationships which grew up between them.
Economic history therefore rests on the prior identification of these
elements and their relationships, that is, on the prior elaboration of
economic theory. In Marx's text the dissolution of one system and the
birth of another are described at the same time and both are seen as being
due to the same process: the development of internal contradictions in
the old system (for which a theory must also be set up).

It might seem that the validity of this general approach, which proceeds
from the identification of the structure to the study of its origin, is
jeopardized by an obstacle which Marx himself set up. For how can the
hypothesis of the appearance of internal contradictions in a system be
reconciled with the thesis that the working of the system necessarily
reproduces the conditions under which it continues to work? For example,
the working of the capitalist system constantly reproduces the capital-
labour relationship upon which it is constructed. The working of the
mechanisms of profits and wages constantly enables the capitalist class
to accumulate new capital and to maintain itself in its position as the
dominant class, while at the same time it forces the working class constantly to offer its labour for sale and thus to maintain itself in its position
as the dominated class.[22] The capital-labour relationship, then, is seen as
the element of the economic structure of capitalism which remains
constant whatever other variations may occur, such as the movement
away from free-enterprise capitalism towards private- or state-monopoly
capitalism, the appearance of new productive forces, changes in the
composition of the working class or in the pattern of its trade-union or
its political organization, etc. The discovery and definition of this constant factor therefore constitutes the essential starting-point of any
scientific study of the system, and of its birth and evolution. This evolution is now seen as the study of those variations which are compatible
with the reproduction of the constant factor in the structure of the
system. Again at this level the question of a shift from political economics
to economic history arises. As well as synchronic analysis, diachronic
analysis becomes possible (that is, the analysis of various states of a

structure, corresponding to various moments in its evolution). But the diachronic analysis of those variations compatible with the reproduction of a constant relationship will not show up any structural incompatibility, or any condition likely to provoke structural change.[23]

But might it not be possible for incompatible variations to occur *within the functioning* of the system (since the very survival of the system would prove that they were not incompatible with its reproduction)? Before entering on a detailed analysis of the notion of contradiction in Marx, let us examine a little more closely the notion of 'structural compatibility', for it plays a capital and twofold role, an understanding of which will clarify the fundamental method and layout of *Das Kapital*. It enables Marx to account for the visible forms of the working of the capitalist system which he rejected at the beginning of the work. It also enables him to explain the new role and the new forms assumed by the 'antediluvian' forms of capital[24] (commercial capital and financial capital), when they function in the framework of modern capitalism. We shall briefly summarize these two points in order to draw out the methodological consequences. Marx, as we have seen, began by analysing the mechanism of the production of surplus value and he showed that it consisted of production provided by unpaid labour. He then shows how the internal and necessary connection between surplus value and labour disappears as soon as it is related not to the wages paid to the worker, but to the whole of the capital put forward by the capitalist – disappears, that is, as soon as the surplus value is seen as profit. The results of Book II enable him, in Volume I of Book III, to analyse the complex conditions necessary for the realization of maximum profit by the capitalist entrepreneur. For our present purposes we can safely leave aside the price-value and price-profit relationships, average profit and excess profit, the levels of profit in different branches of the national economy, etc. The essential point is Marx's conclusion. The capitalist has to deduct from his profit, which finally seems to have very little to do with the real exploitation of his own workers, a portion which is paid as ground rent to the owner of the factory site, another portion which he pays out as interest to a money-lender or to a bank, and another portion which he must pay to the state as taxes. The remainder constitutes his business profit. In showing that the mechanism of the production of surplus value is the common origin of the visible forms of capitalistic profit, even though certain types of capitalists seem to have no direct connection with the process of production, Marx successfully analyses the articulation of the internal structure of the system to the visible forms which at the beginning of his work he had set aside for reasons of principle.

When Marx returns to these visible forms he in each case defines their real function in the system and their internal compatibility with the essential structures already studied. In more modern terms his approach would be to describe the ideal birth of the various elements of a system on the basis of its internal laws of composition. Marx defines it himself in relation to money.

> There is one thing that everybody knows, even when he knows nothing else, and that is that merchandise can assume a particular value-form which contrasts in the most striking fashion with its natural forms: and this form is money. We must now do what the bourgeois economy has never tried to do: we must try to provide an explanation of the origin of the form money, that is to explain how the value contained in the relationship of value between different types of merchandise came to be expressed, from its simplest and least perceptible beginnings to this form – money – which is so striking to everyone. In doing this the enigma of money will be resolved once for all.[25]

We must first, however, clear up one misunderstanding which might arise over what we have called the ideal birth of economic categories. For although an object is classified as merchandise as soon as it is produced for exchange, this exchange in itself does not imply the existence of money, since it can be carried out by barter. For the exchange of merchandise to necessitate the specialization of one particular merchandise in the function of expressing and measuring the exchange-value of other types of merchandise (whether the special merchandise which fulfils this role be cocoa, shells, cattle or gold makes no difference to its function), certain precise conditions must exist. Other particular conditions must exist for the usual form of the means of exchange to be that of a precious metal. Marx then does not follow the Hegelian procedure of the deduction of one category from another. He first describes the functions of one element within a structure, or of one structure within a system, and explains the order of these functions. So there is no need to wait to discover where and how the first form of money was invented in order to resolve the 'enigma of money'. The object of economic theory is therefore to describe these functions and their order in any particular structure and thereby to define the categories of political economics and to relate them to each other in a sort of logical ideal genesis. But this genesis is not the real genesis and does not replace it. Once again economic theory points out the direction in which economic history should carry out its research, and itself uses the results of this research to make advances in its own field, the two subjects at all times retaining their separate identities. On this point Marx's rejection of any form of historical approach, or of any suggestion of an historical study of a system being given priority over its structural analysis, is total, and anticipates by more than half a century the radical rethinking in linguistics and sociology which led de Saussure and Lowie to reject the evolutionist approach of the nineteenth century.

One can understand capital independently of income from property. Capital is the economic force which dominates all others. We must therefore begin with it and end with it and it must be described and analysed before we describe and analyse the ownership of land. Once the two have been studied separately the relationship which exists between them must be studied. We cannot therefore range economic categories in the order of their historical importance. Their order must be determined by the relations which exist between them in modern bourgeois society, which is in fact exactly the opposite of what would seem to be their natural order, or the order in which they appeared in the historical evolution of the system. What is important is not the historical connection between economic relationships in the succession of different forms of society. Still less is it their order of succession 'in the mind' (Proudhon – a rather confused conception of the movement of history). What is important is their hierarchy in the framework of modern bourgeois society.[26]

This explains why the functioning of one structure must be compatible with the functioning of other structures in the same system. This also explains the place of the analysis of commercial capital and of financial capital in *Das Kapital*. For mercantile production is not an exclusive characteristic of modern capitalism. To the extent that exchange of merchandise existed in societies as different as, for example, those of the ancient oriental civilizations, the Greek and Roman slave societies, and the feudal societies of the Middle Ages, the functions of commerce and, to some extent, of credit must have existed. But in each case the forms and importance of these mercantile relationships changed. Marx shows for example that the very high rates of interest charged by money-lenders or the immense profits of the international trade in merchandise which prevailed in many pre-capitalist societies were incompatible with the development of industrial capitalism, which brought about the development of new forms of credit and brought rates of interest down to a far lower level, thereby radically altering the proportion of the value of the merchandise earned by commercial or financial capital. 'The development of credit came about as a reaction against usury. But one must be careful not to misunderstand the significance of this development ... What it means is the subordination of interest – producing capital to the conditions and needs of the capitalistic mode of production, and nothing more.'[27]

Thus the appearance of new structures brings about a modification of the older structures and of their role and conditions of existence. So our analysis throws up the notion of a limit to the functional compatibility of different structures. We are thus back with the problem of the birth of new structures and the notion of contradiction in Marx.

Let us consider this well-known passage from the preface to the *Contribution to the Critique of Political Economy*:

> The relationships of production correspond to a certain degree of development of the material productive forces. Together these various relationships of production constitute the economic structure of society, the concrete foundation on which is built the judicial and political superstructure and to which correspond certain forms of social consciousness ... the mode of physical production conditions the processes of social, political and intellectual life in general ... any change in the basic material economy will alter to a greater or lesser extent the whole enormous superstructure.[28]

The particular causality which Marx attributed to the economic factor in the overall interplay of all the interreacting causalities of the infrastructure and the superstructures has generally been misinterpreted. We have already seen that within any one infrastructure Marx distinguishes the relationships of production and the productive forces and that he never confuses the two. This irreducibility of the structures cannot apply to the economy alone, and we must remember that for Marx each social structure has its own content and mode of functioning and evolution. Recognition of this irreducibility immediately excludes two sorts of interpretation of the determining causality of the economy.

First, the non-economic structures cannot 'grow out of' the economic relationships and the 'causality of the economic factor' cannot be interpreted as 'the genesis of the superstructure from within the infrastructure'. Secondly, the non-economic structures are not simply 'phenomena' which accompany economic activity and which have only a passive role to play in social life, leaving the economic relationships alone with an active causality whose effects operate more or less automatically.[29] In either case it is difficult to see by what strange alchemy the economy could transform itself into, say, kinship relationships, or for what strange reason it should try to conceal itself, none too successfully at that, under the form of kinship relationships. The notion of a 'correspondance' between the structures then must be studied more closely, and its real meaning sought elsewhere.

Let us consider for example the process of production in our own capitalist society. The relationships of production between capitalist and worker, the obligation of the latter to work for the former, appear to be largely independent of any religious, political or even family links which might exist between them. Each social structure appears to be largely autonomous and the economist will tend to treat the non-economic structures as 'independent variables'. He will not look outside the economy in seeking to describe and explain it. The correspondence between structures therefore will be essentially 'external'. The situation may of course be different in a primitive society. For example, the Marxian economist will easily distinguish the productive forces of such a society (such as hunting, fishing, agriculture, etc.) but will not distinguish 'isolated' relationships of production. Or if he does he will distinguish them within the actual functioning of the relationships of kinship. These determine the rights of the individual in matters of the land and its products, his obligations to work for others, to receive and to give. They also determine the authority of certain individuals over others in society. Relationships of kinship dominate social life. How can we, from a Marxist point of view, reconcile the dominant role of kinship and the ultimately determining role of the economy?

This would seem to be impossible if the economy and kinship are seen as infrastructure and superstructure. But in a primitive society relationships of kinship function as relationships of production, just as they function as political relationships. Therefore the Marxist interpretation would be that relationships of kinship in this case are both infrastructure and superstructure.[30] And one may suppose that the complexity of kinship relationships in these primitive societies is proportional to the multiple functions which they have to assume.[31] One can also suppose that the dominant role of a complex structure of kinship relationships in primitive societies is related to the general structure of productive forces, and to the low level of economic development which necessitates the co-operation of individuals in the form of a group-based society, for the survival of the individual and for the race as a whole.[32]

From this abstract example the economy-kinship correspondence can now be seen not as an external relationship but as an internal correspondence, although this does not mean that the economic relationship between individuals related by kinship is ever to be confused with their political or sexual relationships, for example. Thus, to the extent that in this type of society kinship actually functions as relationships of production, the determining role of the economy will be seen not to contradict the dominant role of kinship but simply to express itself through it.[33]

We might see in this a potential contribution of Marx's theory to the scientific study of social structures and of their many different types of evolution which would be radically different from any which his usual interpreters have granted or refused him. For what is irreducible in fact are the functions and evolution of the structures and their differentiation is to be explained by the transformation and evolution of their functions. It may be supposed, for example, that the appearance of new conditions of production in primitive societies will modify their demography, will require new forms of authority and will bring into being new relationships of production. It may be supposed that beyond a certain point the old relationships of kinship will not be able to fulfil the new functions. These will develop outside the kinship relationship and will call into being distinct social, political and religious structures which will take over from the kinship relationship and begin to function in their turn as relationships of production. So it would not be a question of the kinship relationships being transformed into political relationships but rather that the political function of the old kinship relationships would evolve on the basis of the new problems thrown up by a new situation. There would be a shift of the kinship relationships towards a new role. They would carry a different social weight and the political and religious relationships, having assumed new functions, and, being both infrastructure and superstructure, would move into the central position now left vacant.

Thus to explain the determining role of the economy would be at the same time to explain the dominant role of non-economic structures in such-and-such a type of society, and societies distinct both in space and time can belong to the same type provided their overall structures are comparable, that is if the relationship between their social structures determined by the functions and importance of each of them was comparable. In this perspective, we can approach the familiar oppositions of structure-event (anthropology-history) and structure-individual (sociology-psychology) from a new angle.

An event, whether it originates from within a structure or from outside it, always affects the whole structure when it affects one of its elements. Between a cause and its ultimate effects there always lie the various known and unknown properties of one or more structures. This structural causality gives an event its full dimensions, whether or not they are understood, and explains its effects, whether or not they are intentional. We are therefore under no necessity to abandon the structuralist point of view. We do not need to come outside the structure to account for the event. When men by their acts create the conditions which bring about the appearance of new structures they in fact open up fields of objective possibilities of which they are largely unaware but which they discover through events, and whose limits they discover when the conditions in which these structures function change, with the result that the structures no longer play the same role and are thereby transformed. Thus behind the conscious rationality of the behaviour of the members of a society there always lies the more fundamental and unconscious rationality of the hierarchic structure of the social relationships which characterize that society. Rather than taking as our starting-point the individual and the hierarchy of his preferences and intentions, in order to explain the role and relationships of the structures of the society, we should in fact explain all the aspects of this role and relationship, including both those of which society is aware and those of which it is unaware, and seek in this hierarchy of structures the foundation of the hierarchy of 'values', that is, of the social norms of accepted behaviour. Then this hierarchy of values would account for the hierarchy of the needs of individuals playing particular roles and having particular status in society.

It is now seen to be impossible to challenge history with anthropology[34] or anthropology with history or to set up a sterile opposition between psychology and sociology, or sociology and history. Ultimately the possibility of developing the sciences of man depends on the possibility of discovering the laws governing the functioning, the evolution and the internal interacting correspondence of the social structures. One day these sciences of man will perhaps disprove Aristotle by also becoming sciences of the individual. The possibility of the development of these sciences of man thus depends on the structural method of analysis becoming widely used, once it has been developed sufficiently to describe the condition under which the structures and their functions change and evolve, the degree of acceptance and use of the structural method varying greatly at the present time from one field of study to another. We should hope that Marx's work, correctly interpreted, and uncluttered by that of his imitators, might help to hasten the process of acceptance.

THE STRUCTURAL BALANCE OF THE KINSHIP SYSTEMS OF SOME PRIMITIVE PEOPLES

Peter Abell

In this note I want to argue that it may be theoretically enlightening to consider some elementary kinship structures from the point of view of the *theory of structural balance*. The note is based on the now famous essay by Lévi-Strauss entitled *Structural Analysis in Linguistics and in Anthropology*.[1]

This essay, as the title suggests, is designed to draw some interesting parallels between the problems of linguistic and anthropological analysis. In the course of his argument, Lévi-Strauss, in order to illustrate his basic methodology, uses some ethnographic data from various sources concerning the avunculate kinship relation among some primitive peoples. It is upon this part of his work that I shall concentrate.

I shall first outline the theory of structural balance and then introduce Lévi-Strauss's argument; this completed, balance theory will be applied to Lévi-Strauss's material, and finally some possible lines for future inquiry will be indicated.

I. The Theory of Structural Balance

Only a very elementary introduction to the basic ideas of balance theory is given here. For a further account the reader is directed to my essay on 'Structural Balance in Dynamic Structures'.[2]

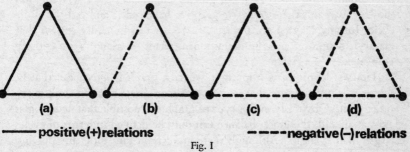

(a)　　　(b)　　　(c)　　　(d)

——— positive (+) relations　　　- - - - negative (−) relations

Fig. I

Consider three persons between any two of whom a positive (+) (friendly) or a negative (−) (unfriendly, enemy) relationship may hold. A *structure* like this may be represented by a graph, where points in a plane designate the persons and lines (arcs) joining the points indicate relations. Then, if we stipulate that the structure be *complete* (i.e. a relation holds between each pair of persons) in the case under consideration, the types of graph depicted in Fig. I exhaust the logical possibilities.

If we now adopt the following assumptions for a stable or *balanced* state of affairs:

(1) that the friend of my friend should be my friend;
(2) that the enemy of my friend should be my enemy;
(3) that the enemy of my enemy should be my friend;

then it is easy to see that the triangles (3-cycles) (a) and (c) are *balanced* but the triangles (b) and (d) are not.

Now, if the *sign* of an n-cycle is defined as the algebraic product of the signs of all its component arcs then triangles (a) and (c) are positive (+) and triangles (b) and (d) are negative (−). Thus positive triangles are balanced and negative triangles are unbalanced.

Consider next a graph consisting of more than three points (persons) and again stipulate that the graph be *complete*. In this case there will be a number of triangles and in accordance with the above notions some may well be positive and some negative. It would seem reasonable, therefore, to define a parameter, measuring the overall balance of the graph, as the ratio of the total number of positive triangles to the total number of triangles in the graph. This parameter will, of course, vary between zero and unity, taking the latter value at complete balance (all triangles positive) and the former value at complete imbalance (all triangles negative).

A little thought will reveal that *complete* graphs consisting of more than three points will possess cycles of greater length than three. Harary[3] has shown, however, that a *complete* graph is balanced if and only if all its cycles (of any length) are positive. In fact it can be easily shown that Harary's definition and the definition in terms of triangles are entirely equivalent.

Harary's definition is important where a graph is *incomplete*, that is, where it is not the case that every point is in direct relation with every other point. Obviously in this type of graph it is possible that *no* triangles exist at all and, therefore, balance can only be defined in terms of cycles larger than triangles. Although there are certain difficulties in applying

Harary's definition to incomplete graphs these need not detain us here.[4] For the purposes at hand we may state that: A graph is balanced if and only if all its cycles (of any length) are positive. The balance parameter may then be defined as the ratio of positive cycles of any length to the total number of cycles of any length in a given graph.

To conclude this section I shall state a theorem (without proof) which may well be of significance in kinship studies.[5]

Theorem I: If a complete graph is balanced then it is possible to define a bipartition of the points such that:

 (i) all the intra-class arcs are positive;
 (ii) all the inter-class arcs are negative.

(One class may be empty when all the arcs in the graph are positive.)

II. Lévi-Strauss's Analysis of the Maternal Uncle-Nephew Kinship Relation.

According to Lévi-Strauss, kinship relations, like that between maternal uncle and nephew, have been studied 'atomistically', i.e. they have been studied and described independently of the complete kinship system of which they are part. Lévi-Strauss pleads for a more systemic approach where the interrelationship between different relations is taken into consideration. Thus he says:

> When we consider societies ... it is not enough to study the correlation of attitudes between *father/son* and *uncle/sister's son*. This correlation is only one aspect of a global system containing four types of relationships which are organically linked, namely: *brother/sister*, *husband/wife*, *father/son* and *mother's brother/sister's son* ... if we know one pair of relations, it is always possible to infer the other.

It is not perfectly clear what Lévi-Strauss means by the phrase 'organically linked'. But I think we may assume that he is implying that the nature of any one binary relation in the kinship structure must be a function of the other binary relationships. Balance theory does precisely this; it suggests that the relationship that *ego* has with *alter* is a function of the relationship that they separately have with a third party and vice versa. That is, it postulates that only balanced 3-cycles are stable and unbalanced 3-cycles unstable and that the latter will change to the former if they happen to evolve. This 'organicism' also clearly stretches beyond 3-cycles if we include n-cycles (n > 3) in our analysis. Lévi-Strauss is thus correct (if we accept balance theory) when he says: 'If we know one pair of relations (i.e. two binary relations) it is possible to infer the other'; but only when this other relation completes a 3-cycle. However, the four relationships he considers do not constitute a 3-cycle and it is not correct that we can infer two relationships in a 4-cycle given two relationships. It seems, therefore, that a certain amount of clarification is called for.

To demonstrate his ideas Lévi-Strauss utilizes ethnographic data for the Trobriand Islanders of Melanesia,[6] the Cherkess of the Caucasus,[7] the Tonganese in Polynesia,[8] the natives of Lake Kubuta in New Guinea,[9, 10] and the Siuai of Bougainville.[11]

For each of these five cultures Lévi-Strauss concentrates upon four types of kinship relation – these are:

(1) husband–wife.
(2) wife–brother.
(3) father–son.
(4) nephew–maternal uncle.

TABLE I

Relation Type	Tribe				
	Trobriand	*Cherkess*	*Tonga*	*Lake Kubuta*	*Siuai*
Husband–Wife	+	−	+	−	−
Wife–Brother	−	+	−	+	+
Father–Son	+	−	−	+	+
Mat. Uncle–Nephew	−	+	+	−	−
Descent	M	P	P	P	M

M = matrilineal descent.
P = patrilineal descent.

The relations are designated, on the basis of ethnographic data, as either (+) – 'a free and familiar relationship' – or negative (−), characterized by 'hostility, antagonism or reserve'. Lévi-Strauss recognizes this to be an oversimplification. Classification according to this scheme leads to Table I.

The contents of this table seem to call into question Radcliffe-Brown's[12] hypothesis that in patrilineal societies the father's descent group represents traditional authority (Father–son relationship (−)) and the maternal uncle will then play the role of 'male mother' ((+) relationship), the natives of Kubuta being the exception to the hypothesis. But, on the other hand, the data seem to lend support to two other hypotheses:

(I) The wife/brother and wife/husband relationships are always different in sign.

(II) The father/son and maternal uncle/nephew relationships are always different in sign.

III. Lévi-Strauss's Model from the Point of View of Structural Balance.

The five kinship structures defined as in Table I may be represented graphically. In each case the graph is a 4-cycle and, further, *all the graphs are balanced*. There are 2^4 possible graphs of which eight are balanced and eight are imbalanced. The possible configurations are shown in Table II.

TABLE II

Relation Type	1	2	3	4	5	6	7	8	9	10	11	12	13	14	15	16
Husband–Wife	+	−	−	−	−	+	+	+	+	+	+	+	−	−	−	−
Wife–Brother	+	+	−	−	−	+	+	−	−	+	−	−	+	+	−	+
Father–Son	+	+	+	−	−	+	−	−	−	+	−	−	+	−	+	+
Mat. Uncle–Nephew	+	+	+	+	−	−	−	−	+	+	+	−	+	−	−	−
	B	Ø	B	Ø	B	Ø	B	Ø	Ø	Ø	B	B	B	B	Ø	Ø

B = Balanced.
Ø = Imbalanced.

From this table and Table I we can see that only four of the possible eight balanced stuctures appear empirically – four and not five because the Kubuta and the Siuai have the same structure. This means that there are four remaining balanced structures, namely 1, 3, 5 and 7 (Table II). But note that the two hypotheses at the end of section II effectively rule out these additional balanced structures. Thus the kinship systems in Table I could be neatly formalized as theorems in an axiomatic system containing the axioms of structural balance, the stipulation that only balanced (positive) structures exist, and hypotheses (I) and (II) in section II.

We should note that the effect of imposing these hypotheses on to the balance axioms is to preclude the possibility of the wife or son being a *structural isolate*. Since the kinship structures are balanced they are polarized (Theorem I). The Trobriand structure is polarized into a grouping of husband, wife and son, the maternal uncle being a structural isolate; the husband is structurally isolated in the Cherkess. The Siuai, Lake Kubuta and Tonga, on the other hand, do not have structural isolates; they exhibit, as it were, a pattern of 'two against two'. So we may say that the additional axioms (I) and (II) have the structural consequence of protecting the wife and son against structural isolation in the presence of the 'strains' towards balance in kinship structures. It is not hard to think of social and psychological reasons why such isolations are institutionally precluded.

So far we have concentrated upon the 4-cycles defined by Lévi-Strauss. But it is clear that we could create 3-cycles in the structures by including the husband/maternal uncle relationship and the wife (mother)/son relationship. As Lévi-Strauss comments, we can predict the nature of these relationships for if we assume that the resistant structures are balanced their sign is determined.[13] The completed structures are depicted in Fig. II. We see that in the Trobriand we have a 'positive grouping' of husband, wife and son. This family structure is thus emotionally something like that in our own society. But the Lake Kubuta and Siuai have a very different set-up. It appears that the union of wife and husband has the function of producing sons for the husband (father) but the emotional ties are between the wife and her brother. The structure appears in both a patrilineal and matrilineal descent system. The Cherkess, on the other hand, have strong positive bonds connecting the wife, her brother and her son, the husband being excluded. In a sense the husband has the function of producing children for this positive grouping, the incest taboo presumably precluding the obvious alternative. Finally, in the Tonga we have the rather strange situation (by our standards) that the son of a union does not

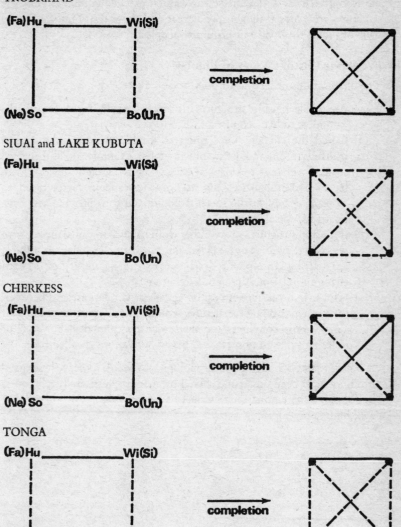

TROBRIAND

SIUAI and LAKE KUBUTA

CHERKESS

TONGA

Fa = Father; Hu = Husband; Wi = Wife; Si = Sister; Bo = Brother;
Un = Uncle; So = Son; Ne = Nephew.

Fig. II

365

have positive links with either of his natural parents. Presumably if these structures are 'correct' they imply a great deal about the organization and style of life of these various primitive peoples.

IV. Some Possible Lines of Inquiry

The observations in section III point to some interesting questions.

(1) Are stable kinship structures always balanced? If not, how is the 'strain' of imbalance managed?

(2) Could the change (over time) in kinship structures be studied fruitfully from this point of view? For example, do imbalanced structures change to balanced ones, and how? Could a change from balance to imbalance (due to some extraneous factor) lead to 'contradictions' in the social structure and thus provide a springboard for social change?

(3) If kinship structures move either from balance to imbalance or vice versa do they do it by: (a) changing the nature of the relationships; (b) deleting kinship units (decline of extended family!); or (c) both changing relationships and deleting units?

(4) If more than one *type* of positive and negative relation exists between the kin what type of structures would emerge? A close reading of Lévi-Strauss convinces me that some conceptual elaboration of different types of positive and negative relations is called for.

I have little knowledge of anthropology and for all I know these questions may have been posed and solved by more sophisticated techniques, but if not, it is my contention that the type of analyses outlined here could be extremely revealing.

ON THE MEANING OF THE WORD 'STRUCTURE' IN MATHEMATICS*

Marc Barbut

The words 'structure', 'structuralism' and the idea embodied in them have been the order of the day for a good ten years in the social sciences; at the present time every one of these possesses, to some degree, its own structuralist school.

This word 'structure' is also used in mathematics and, let it be remembered, in a sense which is capable of providing a precise and convenient framework for the researches of the human sciences when these need to be expressed in structural terms. Moreover, mathematics is here playing the role of humble servant of the other sciences, when its justification lies in refining the tools of analysis necessary to other disciplines.

The use of the word 'structure' in mathematics is a recent phenomenon, though at the same time predating its use in the social sciences. That is, in mathematics too, the idea was not imposed all at once, and a slow development was necessary which proceeded *grosso modo* from Evariste Galois to the Bourbaki, in order to attain the form in which it is known today by any undergraduate.

Of what does this idea consist; what is the meaning of the word? Rather than a lengthy discussion, let a simple example suffice for explanation.

Each of us has, at some time, learned 'the rule of signs': each number has an opposite, and to take the opposite of a number, x, written as $-x$, can also be explained as 'changing the sign of x'. To change the sign twice consecutively is to arrive back at x. We have the same situation if we associate with the number x (which is not equal to zero, though this is a technical detail) its inverse $\frac{1}{x}$: the inverse of the inverse is the number with which we began.

We can also combine the two operations: I have a number x, I take its opposite, $-x$, then the inverse of the opposite, $-\frac{1}{x}$; but we could go about

* First appeared in *Les Temps modernes*, no. 246 (1966); translated from the French by Susan Gray.

it another way and take first the inverse $\frac{1}{x}$, then the opposite of the inverse $-\left(\frac{1}{x}\right)$. And, as children are taught, whichever of the two orders we choose to perform the dual operation, the result is the same.

This whole discussion can be summarized by the following diagram,

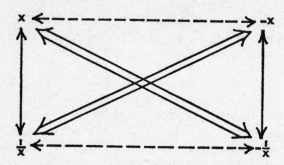

in which the dotted arrow ($\leftarrow$- - -$\rightarrow$) stands for the involutive operation (that is, an operation which, when repeated, has the effect of changing nothing) of 'taking the opposite': the opposite of x is $-x$, that of $-x$ is x; the opposite of $\frac{1}{x}$ is $-\frac{1}{x}$, that of $-\frac{1}{x}$ is $\frac{1}{x}$. Similarly the unbroken arrow ($\leftarrow$—$\rightarrow$) stands for the involutive operation of 'taking the inverse', and the thick unbroken arrow ($\Leftarrow$══$\Rightarrow$) the operation 'product' of the other two: that is, taking the inverse of the opposite (or equally well, the opposite of the inverse). We note that this last operation is itself involutive, as the diagram makes clear: one can go from $-\frac{1}{x}$ to x via $\frac{1}{x}$, that is to say, by passing along a dotted arrow, then an unbroken one. But an equivalent journey can take one from x to $-x$, then from $-x$ to $-\frac{1}{x}$, thus, in the end, from x to $-\frac{1}{x}$. And so in the same way we may go from $-\frac{1}{x}$ to x and from x to $-\frac{1}{x}$.

Now let us look at a little game: four letters *a*, *b*, *c*, *d* arranged in that order. The rule of the game: we can either leave the letters in the order *a b c d*, or change to a different arrangement, but only by changing them two at a time. For example, we can change the order to *b a d c*, which means exchanging *a* for *b* on the one side and *c* for *d* on the other, that is, making the exchanges within the first two letters and the last two. But, we can also make exchanges within the pairs made up of the first and third, and second and fourth letters; or again, within the first and fourth, and the second and third, thereby exhausting all the possibilities.

Starting from the *a b c d* order, and adding the first two permutations described above we have:

Note that these two permutations are involutive: each when repeated once more will bring one back to the original order. Furthermore, if we perform the first permutation (changing the first two letters with each other and doing the same with the last two) upon the *c d a b* arrangement, we obtain *d c b a*, that is, the order produced by the third permutation (first and fourth, second and third letters) when starting with *a b c d*, and this too is involutive.

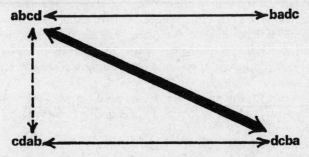

This is very close to the first diagram, of the links between a number, its opposite and its inverse; it can be shown that it is, in fact, the same, by examining what happens if we start with *a b c d* and apply the first permutation followed by the second:

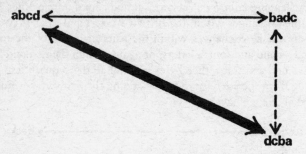

The final order is again *d c b a*, which was also given by the third permutation. This means that the arrangements *b a d c* and *c d a b* have a mutual correspondence. Thus we do indeed obtain the diagram:

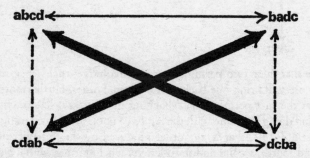

which is identical with that given in the first example. The objects to which the transformations, represented by the arrows, are applied and the nature of these transformations are all that have changed. However, the combination of transformations is the same, namely: two transformations, which we shall call α and β, that are subject to two rules of combination:

1. Each transformation is involutive: repeating it twice consecutively changes nothing.

In order to write this down properly we need a symbol that will mean 'no change', which is what we call an 'identical' transformation and we adopt the symbol I.

With this convention, we may write:

$$\alpha\alpha = I \quad (\alpha \text{ followed by } \alpha \text{ changes nothing})$$
$$\beta\beta = I$$

2. The first one followed by the second is the same transformation, γ, as the second followed by the first; this may be written:

$$\alpha\beta = \beta\alpha \; (= \gamma)$$

which is read as: α and β are commutative.

These two rules are sufficient to reconstruct the diagram. We shall write α and β as arrows pointing in two directions (rule (1)):

Now let us express rule (2) in diagram form: α followed by β;

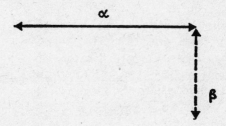

β followed by α;

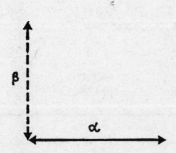

is the same transformation:

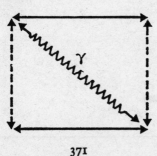

If we now go between $\alpha\beta$ and $\beta\alpha$ in every possible way on the diagram it is completed thus:

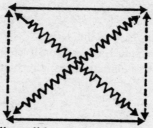

But we could equally well have expressed all that is contained in the two rules, not graphically, but by a written game: α followed by β and β followed by α is the same transformation, γ, according to rule (2). And γ followed by γ? Let us write:

$$\gamma\gamma = \alpha I \alpha.$$

αI is the same thing as α, since it stands for the transformation α followed by the identical transformation which changes nothing. Thus

$$\gamma\gamma = \alpha\alpha.$$

Now, $\alpha\alpha$ equals I (rule (1)). So

$$\gamma\gamma = I.$$

What is the result of γ followed by α?

$$\gamma\alpha = \beta\alpha\alpha = \beta I = \beta.$$

And α followed by γ?

$$\alpha\gamma = \alpha\alpha\beta = I\beta = \beta.$$

Thus we have another consequence of our rules:

$$\alpha\gamma = \gamma\alpha = \beta.$$

And similarly we could show that:

$$\beta\gamma = \gamma\beta = \alpha.$$

We can thus build up a table of the combinations between the four transformations I, α, β, γ:

	I	α	β	γ
I	I	α	β	γ
α	α	I	γ	β
β	β	γ	I	α
γ	γ	β	α	I

which is easily remembered: I combined with any transformation fails to change it; each transformation combined with itself gives I; combining two of the three transformations, other than I, gives the third one.

This table is of the Klein group, which is well-known in mathematics, and present in many human activities, as we shall demonstrate. But notice, first of all, that we have just examined two ways of obtaining it, and that these are in two distinct domains: elementary arithmetic and the permutations of four objects. We already have one abstraction in stating that these two domains have something in common at the operational level, the combination of operations.

The construction of the table and the reconstruction of the diagram were achieved regardless of the particular objects to which the transformations were applied, and keeping only to the specific rules of combination for these transformations; but we did know that the symbols α and β represented the transformations. Now we can forget even that, and pass to a second level of abstraction. We shall say: let there be an alphabet consisting of three letters I, α and β.

1. With this alphabet we can make words by putting the letters side by side:

$$\alpha \text{I} \alpha \alpha \beta, \ \beta \alpha \text{I} \alpha \beta \text{I} \text{ etc. are words.}$$

(Technically, this rule is known as the rule of 'associativity'.)

2. If we erase the letter I from a word, that word is unchanged (I is called the neutral element): $x\text{I}$, $\text{I}x$ and x are the same word, whatever the word x may be.

3. Each of the letters α and β followed by itself in a word may be replaced by the letter I (and therefore eventually eliminated).

4. If the formation $\alpha\beta$ appears in a word, it may be replaced by $\beta\alpha$, and vice versa, without altering the word.

Thus the word $\alpha \text{I} \alpha \alpha \beta$ will become, by successive application of the rules, $\alpha \alpha \alpha \beta$, $\text{I} \alpha \beta$, $\alpha \beta$.

The word $\beta \alpha \text{I} \alpha \beta \text{I}$ will become $\beta \alpha \alpha \beta \text{I}$, $\beta \text{I} \beta \text{I}$, $\beta \beta \text{I} \text{ II, I}$.

It is easily seen (we have performed the calculations above) that the language governed by the 'syntax' explained in the four rules consists of only four words: I, α, β and $\alpha\beta$ (or $\beta\alpha$); and that its 'grammar' is that of the Klein group table, with which we are familiar. What must be remembered is that we have had, in this presentation, to state two rules explicitly, that of associativity and that of the neutral element, which were tacitly understood at the time of our calculations, since we had given a meaning to α, β and I, namely, that they were transformations; in consequence, putting them side by side meant making combinations of transformations, and we know that this is associative, and that the identical transformation, I, changes nothing. Since we are not now giving them any meaning, our 'language' has no 'semantics'.

Now is the time to bring in the word 'structure'; or more precisely, 'algebraic structure'. An algebraic structure is a whole made up of any elements whatsoever, so long as they conform to one or more defined *laws of combination* or, synonymously, *operations* (in our example there is only one law). The way in which the elements combine may be given in the form of a table (or several tables if there is more than one operation) indicating the result of the combination of each pair of elements. (Our example was concerned with a binary law of combination, that is, of the elements in twos; such laws can also be ternary and quaternary, etc.) But this process is only applicable when the whole upon which the particular algebraic structure is defined is finite. If it is infinite the most one could do would be to give parts of the table, like the addition and multiplication tables for whole numbers (which form an infinite whole) that one finds on the back of children's exercise books. A more general and universally used method is to specify conditions and rules (in our example, the four rules set out above), which the operation or operations must satisfy, and which allow either for the reconstruction of the table (in the case of finite wholes) or, more usually, the unequivocal determination of the combinations between whatever elements are given. The collection of conditions which are satisfied by the operations constitutes what are often called the *axioms* of the structure.

When none of the conditions is redundant, that is, when none can be deduced from the others, these are together known as the axiomatic basis of the structure.

In other words, an axiomatic basis for an algebraic structure is that number of conditions which is both necessary and sufficient for reconstructing the table, if we confine ourselves to finite structures. Of course, one structure may have several axiomatic bases (various systems of conditions can produce the same table): as an example, another axiomatic basis for the Klein group, which we have taken as the prototype of an algebraic structure, would be as follows:

1. There are four elements I, α, β, γ, and a defined binary operation between them (written in juxtaposition, xy stands for the result of the operation between x as the first element and y as the second).

2. I is a neutral element: $Ix = xI = x$, whichever of the four elements x may be.

3. The operation is associative: $(xy)z = x(yz)$, whichever elements x, y and z may be.

4. For each element x there exists an 'inverse', that is, an element x', which when combined with x produces the neutral $xx' = x'x = I$.

5. Each element x has an 'order of repetition' less than 4; that is to say, there is a whole number n (not necessarily the same for two distinct elements, but always less than 4: $n = 1, 2$ or 3) such that x combined n consecutive times with itself gives the neutral I.

In actual fact, this system of rules is not a true axiomatic basis: it is redundant; the interested reader will, in any case, be able to amuse himself by constructing the table defined by these five rules, and will find that there is but one, namely the one with which he is already familiar: that of the Klein group.

The definition of an algebraic structure that was given above only brought one system into play; but the situation can be rather more complex, there may be several ... Let us quote from the Bourbaki (*Algèbre*, Chap. I, 'Structures Algébriques', 1951 edition, p. 41): 'The object of algebra is the study of structures which are determined by one or more given laws of combination, internal or external, between the elements of one or more systems.' It will be noted that in this sentence, which is the first in a paragraph entitled 'Definition of an Algebraic Structure', the word 'structure' is implicitly defined by its context. And the Bourbaki go on almost at once to notions which are inseparable from that of structure: the notions of isomorphism and representation.

First we shall explain what is meant by representation. The Klein group, when given by its table or by an appropriate axiomatic basis, but without specification of the elements (without semantics), is generally called the 'abstract' group. To obtain a representation of this group is to give a meaning to each element of the group, to make out of it 'concrete' objects, which are combined in the same way as the elements of the 'abstract' group. Thus, when we interpret the four elements of the Klein group, I, α, β, γ, as being the identical permutation plus α, β, γ as the following permutations of four letters:

$$\alpha: abcd \longrightarrow badc$$
$$\beta: abcd \longrightarrow cdab$$
$$\gamma: abcd \longrightarrow dcba$$

we provide ourselves with a representation of this group as a group of permutations (and here we have a particular case of a very general theorem, attributed to Cayley, according to which every finite group may be represented as a group of permutations).

Similarly, another representation is obtained from our second interpretation of the Klein group, in which I is the identical transformation and α, β, γ are the transformations:

$$\alpha = x \rightarrow -x$$

$$\beta = x \rightarrow \frac{1}{x}$$

$$\gamma = x \rightarrow -\frac{1}{x}$$

on a system of numbers (zero excepted).

Clearly, there is a constant double process in mathematics: from the 'concrete' to the 'abstract' (which is the structure, the syntax), and conversely from the 'abstract' to something 'concrete' (representation, semantics), which offers a strengthening of intuition, if this sense be familiar, by giving meaning to abstract objects, and permits greater efficiency in calculation. And it is a worth-while practice to attach equal importance to the results of the Klein group operations, whether read from the table (abstract group) or the diagram (concrete interpretation: the arrows stand for transformations):

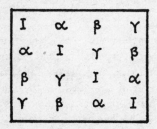
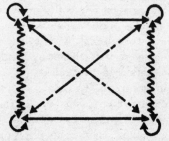

The two representations of the Klein group with which we are familiar constitute interpretations of it in two distinct languages (endowed with semantics), and therefore they allow a faithful translation from one to the other; the syntax is the same, only the meaning of the words has changed. And we may compile a dictionary, with the speech of the person who permutes objects on the left, and on the right that of him who carries out operations with numbers:

α	to change *abcd* to *badc*	to change the number x into its opposite $-x$
β	to change *abcd* to *cdab*	to change the number x into its inverse $\dfrac{1}{x}$
γ	to change *abcd* to *dcba*	to change the number x into the inverse of its opposite $-\dfrac{1}{x}$
I	to change nothing	to change nothing

It is these translations that are called *isomorphisms*: two groups (what we are saying here about groups may be said of any kind of structure whatsoever) are isomorphs if they are two representations of the same abstract group; further, one might add: if they have *the same structure*. This means that their elements may be placed in one-to-one correspondence, such that the image in the second group of the combination of any two elements from the first group is the same as the combination of the images of those two elements.

Isomorphism, the word itself, is plain enough: the form, the 'syntax', the 'structure' are the same; the differences lie, not only in the symbols used to write down the elements – this is trivial – but also in the meaning to be given to the elements; and one may equally well give them, provided one keeps to the rules, whichever of the possible meanings one wishes.

It is clear from this how mathematics is, as is often stated, a tool of communication: thanks to the three linked notions of structure, representation and isomorphism, men carrying on their activities in widely varying fields will be able, should the occasion arise, to understand one another, and realize that, from a certain point of view, what is most important in their activity – the combination of their acts, of their habits, of the operations they perform – is identical.

One is better able to grasp the richness and power of the process by examining some other derivations of our Klein group, which we have seen to be claimed equally well by anyone who knows only the four operations of elementary arithmetic, and anyone who knows only how to permute, to change the places of objects (pebbles, for example, as in ancient calculations).

Now here is a geometric figure. It is in the form of a tetrahedron: four points A, B, C, D, not in the same plane, the six lines joining them, the four triangular faces they generate. The lines AB and CD have no common vertex (see figure); we shall join their respective centre points (dotted axis —·—·—·—).

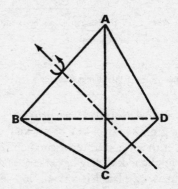

Half-turning the tetrahedron about this axis brings A to B and B to A, C to D and D to C. Thus, this half-turn permutates the vertices according to the permutation α: ABCD → BADC. And if we perform the half-turn twice consecutively each vertex returns to its original position; it is the identical permutation.

Similarly, by considering the half-turns about the axes joining the centre points of AC and BD, on the one hand, and of AD and BC on the other, we rediscover the permutations β and γ. Thus, the Klein group may just as easily be derived from the symmetrical properties of the tetrahedron.

Finally, let us pass on to the logician; he works with propositions which are linked to each other by the conjunctions 'and' and 'or', and he often operates with propositions by means of negation: if U is a proposition, NU will signify the negation of it. Let us consider for example:

$$U = (X \text{ and } Y) \text{ or } Z$$

in which X, Y and Z are propositions.

We know that

$$NU = (NX \text{ or } NY) \text{ and } NZ.$$

In other words, the negation of a complex proposition is obtained by taking the negation of the elementary propositions of which it is composed, and by changing the connectives 'and' and 'or'. But, equally, we may negate the elementary propositions without changing the connectives; this is a new operator, R, on the proposition:

$$RU = (NX \text{ and } NY) \text{ or } NZ.$$

We can also change the connectives without negating the elementary propositions: operator S gives

$$SU = (X \text{ or } Y) \text{ and } Z$$

and we see that

$$RS = SR = N.$$

(S followed by R, or R followed by S, gives the negation N.)

Moreover, it is plain that RR = SS = NN = I, where I represents no change; each operation is involutive, so that repeating it twice consecutively changes nothing.

This time we have rediscovered the Klein group, not by its representation as a group of permutations (as in the case of the tetrahedron), but by its axiomatic basis. It should be added that this representation of the Klein group, by the operations of rudimentary logic is sometimes called, by psychologists, the Piaget group.[1]

The experimental psychologists, for we are discussing them, often present their 'subjects' with the following situation: take an object, let us say a white disc, and modify one of its characteristics (shape or colour in our example). One may change either the shape, transforming the object into a white square, for example, or the colour, transforming it into a black disc. Lastly, one may change both shape and colour, turning it into a black square. If there are but two shapes (round and square), and two colours (black and white), our object has only four possible states, and these are linked by the elementary transformations summarized by the diagram:

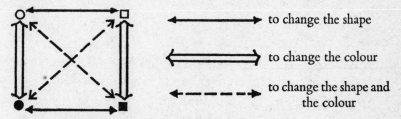

to change the shape

to change the colour

to change the shape and the colour

This is the diagram of the Klein group.

This leads us to another representation: each possible state of the object was characterized by two qualities (shape and colour), each of these having two possible values. We may write a change in the state of the object as xy, in which $x = 0$ if the shape does not change, otherwise $x = 1$; and $y = 0$ if the colour does not change, otherwise $y = 1$. All we have to remember for the game of transformations from one state to another is the rule for combination of the symbols 0 and 1, given by the table:

	0	1
0	0	1
1	1	0

If we write this law of combination as $+$ (it will be seen to be an addition), we shall have for example:

$$01 + 11 = 10$$

Adding the values of the first character we have:

$$0 + 1 = 1 \text{ from the table}$$

and this means: the shape is changed.

Proceeding in the same way with the second character:

$$1 + 1 = 0 \text{ from the table}$$

and this means: the colour changes twice.

Similarly: $01 + 01 = 00$ (shape unchanged, colour changed twice consecutively), and we may draw up a complete table:

	00	01	10	11
00	00	01	10	11
01	01	00	11	10
10	10	11	00	01
11	11	10	01	00

This is a table of the Klein group, almost an isomorphism:

$$I \text{ becomes } 00$$
$$\alpha \text{ becomes } 01$$
$$\beta \text{ becomes } 10$$
$$\gamma \text{ becomes } 11$$

The rule for combination of the symbols o and 1 is easily remembered, if one recalls that it is the same as that for the combination by addition of odd and even numbers:

even + even gives even
even + odd gives odd
odd + even gives odd
odd + odd gives even

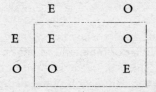

This is often said to concern binary arithmetic also.

The Klein group can thus be represented through the combination by addition, in binary arithmetic, of pairs of numbers; this may be generalized to triplets of numbers, xyz:

$$011 + 110 = 101$$

or to quadruplets, $xyzt$, etc. In the form of quadruplets this piece of arithmetic is, in fact, used in certain systems of geomantic divination.[2] The groups obtained with triplets and quadruplets, etc., yield analogies of the Klein group, of which they are generalizations; we shall return to this.

But since we are in the realm of ethnology or, more exactly, of an ethnological derivation of our group, let us give another example in the same discipline. We find in Claude Lévi-Strauss's *Les Structures élémentaires de la parenté* (P.U.F., Paris, 1949) a description of the Kariera system: there are four 'classes', such that each individual in the Kariera society may be placed in one class and one class only, and the class of a child is determined solely by those of its parents. To explain how classes are selected, Lévi-Strauss (op. cit., p. 208) makes use of an analogy, and tells us that it is the same as if there were

the Duponts from Paris
the Duponts from Bordeaux
the Durands from Paris
the Durands from Bordeaux

These are the four classes. The rules by which a child is placed in a class, according to that of its father and that of its mother, may be summarized by this diagram:

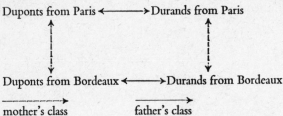

mother's class   father's class

The diagonal transformation, not drawn here, would represent the class of the father's mother or the mother's father.

Before leaving the subject of the derivations of the Klein group structure, let us cite one last very familiar one, since all Frenchmen, for example, use it daily; it concerns the combinations of certain grammatical categories in a language like French. An adjective, for example, is usually capable of having two genders (masculine or feminine) and two numbers (singular or plural). One may thus transform it by changing the gender, or the number, or both, as in the diagram:

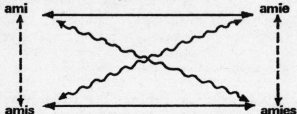

The reader will easily furnish other examples of the same type.

Up to now we have only considered the structure of one particular group, the Klein group, but there are other algebraic structures. To begin with, there are those of the group which constitute in their entirety a *kind* of structure, and which have in common the following definition: a system which has an associative binary operation, has a neutral element, and is such that each element may be inverted. Among the other kinds of algebraic structure we shall mention the most important: monoids (or semi-groups) and the quasi-groups, which are weaker forms of group structure (they have fewer axioms); rings, sets, algebras, vectorials, modules, which are stronger forms (more operations – two or three – and more axioms); matrices, Boolean algebra, which belong to another 'line' of structures.

Besides algebraic structures, we may distinguish, on the one hand, combinatory or relational structures, in which the links between the elements of the structure are given, not by means of operations, but by relations, generally binary (that is, linking the elements two by two), as are classificatory or hierarchic relations, etc.

On the other hand, there are the structures known as topological, which formalize the intuitive notions of juxtaposition, proximity, interior, exterior and boundaries, borrowed from our perception of space.

Further explanation of the nature of these diverse structures would not carry much weight in this paper. By contrast, it seems important to end by showing how one structure gives rise to smaller ones, and engenders a whole family (the technical term is category) of structures which are allied to it. We shall start, of course, from the structure which we have examined thoroughly, the Klein group. Let us consider its table:

	I	α	β	γ
I	I	α	β	γ
α	α	I	γ	β
β	β	γ	I	α
γ	γ	β	α	I

Now, let us confine our attention to the two elements I and α. Combined with each other, they reproduce I and α:

I	α	β	γ
α	I	γ	β
β	γ	I	α
γ	β	α	I

according to the table:

	I	α
I	I	α
α	α	I

with which we are already conversant; it is, in its notation, close to that of the addition of odd and even in binary arithmetic.

It is said that the whole generated by I and α is a stable part of the Klein group; moreover, as the restriction of the group operation to I and α produces a group, this is a *subgroup* of the Klein group.

The points made about I and α are equally valid for I and β, and for I and γ. And each time we obtain the same table of combinations between the two elements retained. Conversely, α and β combined give I and γ; so they do not constitute a stable part.

The reader can convince himself without difficulty that the only subgroups here are the three which have been stated, plus that generated by I above. One may visualize the system formed by the group and its subgroups by means of the following diagram:

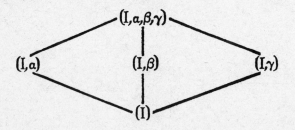

Thus, a given algebraic structure usually possesses subgroups. But the point made about I and α may be taken further; if we examine the table more closely, we can state that the whole (I, α, β, γ) may be divided into two classes: I and α on one hand and β and γ on the other;

	I	α	β	γ
I	I	α	β	γ
α	α	I	γ	β
β	β	γ	I	α
γ	γ	β	α	I

such that the classes combine again among themselves, following the rules of binary addition. In fact, let us consider the class (I, α) as unique, and denote it by the symbol 0; similarly the class (β, α) will be identified as a single object and called 1. The table becomes:

	0	1
0	0	1
1	1	0

Once the group is obtained, the result of the combination of the classes is called the *group-quotient* of the Klein group by its subgroup (I, α); in the same way we shall find a group-quotient associated with the subgroups (I, β) and (I, γ).

In this case the subgroup and group-quotient do not differ (they have the same structure); in general this is not the case, as a further example will show.

The link, the relationship, between a structure, a substructure and the structure quotient is made evident by the notion of *homomorphism*: these forms and structures resemble one another. But how, in what way exactly? To arrive at the group-quotient we made the subgroup (I, α) of the Klein group correspond to the element 0 of binary arithmetic; and we made (β, γ) correspond similarly to the element 1. Thus we defined a correspondence between the Klein group and a group from binary arithmetic, in which the images of each element of the Klein group are those indicated in the diagram below:

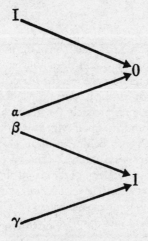

and this correspondence *relates to the structure* in the same sense as does the isomorphism defined above: the combination of the images of any two elements is the image of the combination of those elements. For example, α has for its image o, and β has I. The combination of α and β, in the original group from which we start, is γ. The image of γ is I, which is indeed the combination of o and I (images of α and β respectively) in the new group at which we arrive.

It is clear that a homomorphism is a generalization of the isomorphism, in the sense that the latter is a particular homomorphism, in which the correspondence between the two related structures is one to one. But it is another process that is used to build up homomorphic structures to a given structure, a process that is rather like a return to the one we have just examined, the derivation of the quotient. It is the construction of a *product* of structures (notice the duality of the terms employed: quotient, product).

Let us take the Klein group (I, α, β, γ) on the one hand, the group (o, I) on the other, and form their 'cartesian' product (a 'combinatory' product): it is a whole made up of the couples xy, where x may take the four values I, α, β and γ, while y may take the two values o and I. We thus obtain the eight ($8 = 4 \times 2$) couples Io, αo, βo, γo, II, αI, βI, γI. Now let us define an operation, written as Δ, between two couples in the following way: if xy and $x'y'$ are two couples, $xy \Delta x'y'$ is that couple in which the first element is the combination of x and x' in the Klein group (both x and x' belong to this group), and the second element the combination of y and y' in the group (o, I).

For example:

$$\alpha o \Delta \gamma I = \beta I$$

The process which served us at the time of the transition from the group (o, I) to the Klein group in the form of four couples, oo, oI, Io, II, is recognizable here; and thereby we see that the procedure for the product is indeed a return to that for the quotient, since the quotient of the Klein group by the group (o, I) is precisely the group (o, I).

To get back to the product, upon which we are presently engaged, its table in the operation Δ may be drawn up mechanically, by reading off the tables of the two groups combined. (Shown opposite.)

From this table, certain quotients of the group obtained become evident; the division into two classes, (Io, αo, βo, γo), which is a subgroup, and (II, αI, βI, γI), gives as quotient the group (o, I); the division into four classes, (Io, αo), which is a subgroup, (βo, γo), (II, αI) and (βI, γI), gives

I_0	α_0	β_0	γ_0	I_1	α_1	β_1	γ_1
α_0	I_0	γ_0	β_0	α_1	I_1	γ_1	β_1
β_0	γ_0	I_0	α_0	β_1	γ_1	I_1	α_1
γ_0	β_0	α_0	I_0	γ_1	β_1	α_1	I_1
I_1	α_1	β_1	γ_1	I_0	α_0	β_0	γ_0
α_1	I_1	γ_1	β_1	α_0	I_0	γ_0	β_0
β_1	γ_1	I_1	α_1	β_0	γ_0	I_0	α_0
γ_1	β_1	α_1	I_1	γ_0	β_0	α_0	I_0

as quotient the Klein group. So there is a homomorphism of the group obtained upon the Klein group.

Among the subgroups and quotients of this new group, we shall find only the groups which served for its construction; but we may now form more groups by generating its products with the groups that we already know, and so on ad infinitum; we shall thereby obtain a complete category to 2, 4, 6, 8, 16, 32, etc., elements, of which the elementary construction material is the group (0, 1), and which are such that there is always a homomorphic correspondence between any two of them.

Certainly, there exist other methods of generating structures, starting from a given one; those indicated here are the simplest and most usual. In any case, they will have given the reader a glimpse of the strength of the tools which mathematics can place at the disposition of other disciplines; but it would be a mistake to end on such an optimistic note, if we are considering the human sciences.

Mathematical structures offer a precise framework and convenient means of operation; but the reader will have been struck, in so far as the structure we have studied is concerned, by the poverty of its vocabulary, of its 'syntax', and this analogy was chosen intentionally: the complexity of syntax in the natural languages is a case which shows the extreme opposition between the richness of the structures in the human sciences and the general poverty of those in mathematics. This opposition points up the fact that the enormous efficiency of mathematical models achieves a simplicity rarely encountered among the human sciences, but at the expense of a reduction in phenomena to which those models may be applied. In order that mathematics in its present state may be applicable when reality is complex, as in the case of the physical sciences too, it must be viewed from a standpoint which only retains certain characteristics, those which matter; in general, we have not yet reached the point in the social sciences at which we know how to determine what these are.

SOME PROBLEMS IN THE THEORY OF STRUCTURAL BALANCE: TOWARDS A THEORY OF STRUCTURAL STRAIN

Peter Abell

Introduction

The theory of structural balance is relatively unique amongst theories in sociology in that it rests upon a set of clearly stated propositions from which flow some interesting theorems. The universal truth of these propositions[1] may, of course, be called into question – indeed I intend to do precisely this later on in the paper – yet, nevertheless, the theory warrants our close attention, not only because of its formal elegance but because of its logical proximity to a cluster of strategic concepts in social theory, namely strain, tension and polarization. It is, of course, all too easy to find counter-instances to the general theory and as a consequence reject it as a gross oversimplification. But such a course of action would seem to me to be unfortunate; the proper response to over-simply formulated models in sociology is elaboration by the introduction of additional complexity – not rejection. It is in this way that theoretical sociology has some chance of becoming a cumulative exercise. This essay is an attempt to do just that.

The concepts of strain and pattern-maintenance or tension-management have become of central importance in sociology with the growth of systems-theory. There have, however, been few attempts systematically to explore the actual 'operational' meaning of the terms. But one thing seems perfectly clear: they are in fact very complex conceptions and the strain or tension in a social system is rarely of one simple type. Strains can be generated in a variety of ways and presumably 'managed' likewise. In traditional social theory, the strain inherent in disequilibrated status systems has perhaps received most attention and Galtung[2] has brilliantly shown how a few simple ideas can be pushed a long way in the direction of a genuine social theory. Coser[3] in sorting out the seminal ideas of Simmel has suggested that a criss-crossing pattern of allegiances can be functionally important for the maintenance of a social structure (system). That is (if we equate strain with criss-cross), strain is functionally positive, though most authors have either implicitly or explicitly regarded strain as dysfunctional. In a recent paper[4] I have tried to show that strain (defined in terms of positive and negative affective relations in a social structure) is characteristic of social structures in 'normal conditions' but that in times of crisis there is a tendency for it to be minimized. It is still an open question how much strain a structure can accommodate without changing fundamentally. But it is perfectly clear that such a problem cannot be answered until we have some rudimentary theory and measurement techniques.

A further theoretical tradition – namely, Field Theory – that has proved insightful in matters of socio-structural strain is due to Lewin and his collaborator.[5] The central idea is one of 'social forces' of one kind or another impinging upon an actor; and, of course, if these forces are 'incompatible' this induces strain. Unfortunately neither the idea of a social force nor that of a social field has, as far as I know, ever been clearly articulated; there has been an over-easy use of the concepts without any real analysis of their nature. And one cannot help feeling that here we have a case of uncritical adoption of physical science concepts without prior attention to their precise structure. I have argued elsewhere that one of the most interesting interpretations of a 'socio-structural field' is in terms of a network of rules about behaviour, beliefs, etc., for in some sense rules backed by sanctions are the very stuff of social forces.[6] However, one of the endemic difficulties in using the concepts of force and field in the social sciences is in deciding how much algebraic and topological structure one can feed into the concepts. Force seems to imply a metric and field a continuum – both particularly alien to sociological data. We shall have to face these problems, albeit in a very preliminary manner, later in this essay, for we shall adopt the idea of an *affective field operating either at points or on relations in a social structure*. This conception will, I hope, arise quite naturally in the context of some critical remarks about structural balance theory.

I shall first of all review the theory of balance, then outline a series of problems and in some cases propose solutions, though not in all, since many of the problems require empirical evidence for their resolution.

The Theory of Structural Balance

The theory of structural balance as developed by Harary,[7] based upon ideas of Heider,[8] concerns positive (P) and negative (N), non-reflexive, symmetric relations defined on a set $\{X\}$ of points. The points usually represent members of a 'social group', though in the work of Abelson and Rosenberg they represent conceptual entities and in Heider's original work they correspond to both persons and objects. We shall see later that the nature of the points in set X necessitates certain differences in the theory, but for the moment it is perhaps best to think of them as individual persons. It is imperative to the theory that the relations P and N are 'defined' as positive and negative by the persons themselves.

Structures of this sort may be conveniently represented by an algebraic graph $G = (X; P, N)$, where points in a plane designate the persons, etc., and lines (*arcs*) connecting the points the relations.

If a structure has n points and all the $n(n-1)/2$ pairs of points are in either positive or negative symmetric relation then the structure (graph) is *complete*.

Now consider any three points, a, b and c. If this structure is complete it can be regarded as a triangle (3-cycle). 3-cycles are defined as *balanced* under the following conditions:

$$aPb \. bPc \rightarrow aPc \tag{1}$$
$$aPb \. bNc \rightarrow aNc \tag{2}$$
$$aNb \. bNc \rightarrow aPc \tag{3}$$

(for '.' read 'and', and for '$\rightarrow$' read 'if ... then ... ')

These three types of 3-cycle should be contrasted with the other two types that are logically possible:

$$aNb \. bNc \. aNc \tag{4}$$
$$aPb \. bPc \. aNc \tag{5}$$

The sociological motivation for the three 'axioms', statements (1), (2) and (3), may be illustrated in terms of normal 'friendship' and 'enmity' relations amongst people. The statements may be freely translated to read:

(1) the friend of my friend is my friend,
(2) the enemy of my friend is my enemy; and
(3) the enemy of my enemy is my friend.

If these three translations are contrasted with analogous translations of statements (4) and (5), the motivation becomes reasonably clear. Statement (4), for instance, reads: 'The enemy of my enemy is my enemy,' and statement (5) 'The friend of my friend is my enemy.' The theory of balance claims, given our normal understanding of friendship and enmity, that these situations are 'unstable' compared with the previous three. By definition they are unbalanced, which is meant to imply that they are 'strainful' for the individual participants, which in turn is supposed to be unstable. Balance theorists have found it very easy to switch between the concepts of balance and stability on the one hand and imbalance and instability on the other, but it is clear that some conceptual clarification is called for here. Furthermore, the reader may also feel that statement (4) does not necessarily represent an imbalanced (unstable!) state of affairs. For the moment, however, I shall use the words 'balanced' and 'stable' interchangeably and assume that (4) represents an unstable state of affairs.

The theory of balance requires, in addition to the above three axioms, that the *affective interaction* of the three actors *a*, *b* and *c* be *unsegmented*. It is quite evidently *not* an unstable state of affairs when a given person *a* has positive affective relations with both *b* and *c* and at the same time *b* and *c* are negatively related, if *a* interacts with *b* and *c* in completely different contexts and the interaction of *b* and *c* bears no relation to their separate interactions with *a*. Central to balance theory is the notion that the nature of the interaction of a given person *a* with two other actors *b* and *c* is a function of the interaction between these two. This idea which we may call the *assumption of unsegmented interaction* has not always been made explicit in balance theory but is essential to it. It has in fact been implicit in most studies and discussions, as these have, in the main, concentrated upon small face-to-face groups where it is not unreasonable to assume that the assumption holds. In larger social groupings, however, there is no a priori reason to suppose that affective interaction is unsegmented.

There is a further implicit assumption in the theory. This we will call the assumption of congruent perception; it states that the persons in a 3-cycle cognize the affective links in an identical manner. Balance theory is clearly concerned with the way in which the persons 'see' a structure, since strain and tension, etc., must ultimately relate to the individual perceptions and subjective mental states of the persons themselves.[9] So if there are differing estimations as to the nature of linkages in the structure the simple axioms may no longer be appropriate. For instance, if *a* has (as far as he is concerned) positive links with *b* and *c* and 'sees' the link between *b* and *c* as negative, he then, according to balance theory, finds himself in an imbalanced 3-cycle and is accordingly in a state of strain or tension. But if *b* and *c* see their link as positive and also agree with *a*'s estimate of his relationship with them, then, as far as they are concerned, the structure is balanced. Clearly then, one of the ways in which we may elaborate the theory is to take into account such situations.

There are thus four major conceptions at the foundation of balance theory:

(i) the relations P and N defined as positive and negative by the persons (actors) themselves;

(ii) the formal requirements of statements (1), (2) and (3);

(iii) the assumption of unsegmented interaction;

(iv) the assumption of congruent perception.

If the sign of a 3-cycle is defined as the algebraic product of the signs of all its component arcs (P is $+$, N is $-$), then according to statements (1), (2) and (3) 3-cycles are balanced if their sign is positive and imbalanced if it is negative.

A complete structure of n points will contain $\binom{n}{3}$ 3-cycles (Note: not the permutation $_nP_3$, as the cycles *abc*, *bca* and *cab* and their inverses are identical).

Thus a coefficient of 3-balance may be defined:

$$\beta(3) = C_3^+/C_3$$

where $C_3^+ = $ the total number of *positive* 3-cycles and $C_3 = $ the total number of 3-cycles (positive and negative) in a structure. The value of $\beta(3)$ will vary between zero when all the three cycles are negative (imbalanced) and unity when all the 3-cycles are positive (balanced). Thus a complete structure may be conveniently characterized by a balance parameter representing the extent to which the structure is balanced or imbalanced. I hope to show below, however, that the $\beta(3)$ parameter is in most cases altogether too crude an instrument for fruitful analysis.

The major substantive notion of balance theory is that if $\beta(3) < 1$ then it will tend towards 1. The sociological backing for this should be clear from the arguments presented earlier. An imbalanced structure is in a state of strain and unless this strain is resolved a permanent state of tension is created. So the idea of a structure moving towards balance is, on the face of it, synonymous with the idea of tension reduction.

We may, of course, ask the question, 'How do imbalanced structures come into being in the first place?' We can recognize at least two conditions under which this can happen. Firstly, in the initial phase of the growth of a structure, relationships tend to be specific in the sense that *a* and *b* will take up an affective orientation to one another independent of their relationships to *c*. In such a growth process, imbalanced structures can easily occur, and it is only with the lapse of time that the inherent strain of, for example, interacting with two persons in a friendly manner who are themselves hostile becomes evident. It is tempting to suggest that basic psychological variables play an entirely dominant role in the early phases which often lead to imbalanced structures (strain) and later the structural strains implicit in balance theory become operative, when there will be a tendency to resolve the strain either by a move towards balance (if this is compatible with the distribution of the psychological factors in the structure) or by segmentation of interaction or by complete withdrawal of affectivity. In this last case, relationships will become null or indifferent, and it becomes important to distinguish between, on the one hand, relationships that are cognized and affectively null, and, on the other, those that are non-cognized and *thus* affectively null. The second way in which we can obtain imbalanced structures is when some external factor influences the structure introducing imbalance – for example, when an economically expanding society induces social mobility and the breakdown of the traditional affective structure of the kinship system.

An obvious question to ask is, how do imbalanced structures move towards balance? Clearly by certain arcs changing their sign.[10] But, in general, a structure will be able to attain or approach balance in a variety of ways, by changing the signs of different combinations of arcs. It is tempting to postulate that a structure will attain balance through a process that involves the changing of sign of a minimum number of arcs. That is the process that involves the least amount of reorganization in the structure.

For instance, in Fig. I, structure (I) which is imbalanced may attain balance by changing to either structure (II) or structure (III). However, the change from (I) to (II) involves the change in sign of two arcs [(a,d) and (c,b)], whereas the change from (I) to (III) involves a change in sign of three arcs [(c,b), (c,d), and (d,b)]. Thus according to the conception of minimal reorganization we should predict the balancing process (I) → (II) rather than (I) → (III).

However, this argument is in effect based upon an assumption of equal importance of all the affective relations in the structure. That is, no allowance is made for the possible variation in intensity of these relations. If we revert once again to our previous example of sentiments of friendship and hostility between persons, it seems reasonably certain that intensity of friendship or hostility would be a factor we might have to take into consideration when analysing 'friendship' structures. For example, considering the structure in Fig. I once again, if the negative relation (a, d) is

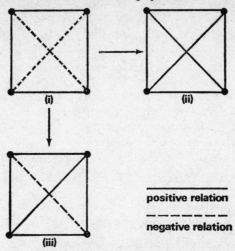

positive relation

negative relation

Fig. I. Alternative Balance Processes

extremely intense we may predict, in contradiction to what we said above, that the process (I) → (III) is more likely than (I) → (II). Thus, a more comprehensive theory of balance would most probably involve the notion of intensity of the affective relations.

A further problem also arises: it is logically possible to have two complete structures where one has a $\beta(3)$ value smaller in magnitude than the other but where both can attain balance by changing the sign of the same number of arcs. In the light of considerations like this the degree of imbalance of a structure has been defined as the minimum number of arcs that must change in sign in order for the structure to attain balance – the *line index*. But this idea is again based upon the assumption of equal importance of all arcs and consequently requires modification in the context of what was said above about intensities.

So far we have concentrated solely upon 3-cycles. However, we quite naturally want the theory of balance to apply to incomplete structures, i.e. where some of the points in the structure are not in either positive or negative relationship. Such structures present special problems, as it is logically possible that they contain no 3-cycles and so the balance 'axioms' do not apply in any straightforward manner. But since they may contain *n*-cycles ($n > 3$) the questions naturally arise, should we incorporate larger cycles into our analyses, and if so, how? It has been suggested that we apply the same algebraic law of multiplication to *n*-cycles as we did to

3-cycles, so that an n-cycle is balanced (positive) if and only if it contains an even number of negative arcs. Thus $\beta(n)$ may be defined as follows:

$$\beta(n) = \sum_{i=3}^{n} C_i^+/C_i \qquad (7)$$

where $C_i^+ =$ the number of positive cycles of length i and $C_i =$ the number of cycles (positive and negative) of length i. The sociological justification for this is, however, rather thin and we shall have occasion later on to question its theoretical utility.

One of the most attractive features of balance theory is the classic bi-polarization theorem, first proved by Harary; it states that:

Theorem 1 A complete symmetric affective structure is balanced if and only if there exists a unique bipartition of the point set such that:

(i) all the *intra*-class relations are positive; and
(ii) all the *inter*-class relations are negative (one class may be empty if all the relations in the structure are positive).

More recently it has been shown that this is a specific case of the more general theorem for incomplete structures:[11]

Theorem 2 An incomplete affective symmetric structure with θ components is balanced if and only if there are $2^{\theta-1}$ ways of bipartitioning the point set of the structure such that:

(i) all the *intra*-class relations are positive or unconnected
(ii) all the *inter*-class relations are negative or unconnected.

As we shall see, this theorem is much more useful, as, to some extent, it overcomes the more obvious objections to the simple bi-polarization theorem.

So far we have only considered the case where the affective relation between two structural units is symmetric. It is, of course, possible that symmetry does not occur in a given empirical situation. For instance, if we interpret aPb as 'a chooses b as a friend' and aNb as 'a chooses b as an enemy', then it is conceivable that, among other possibilities, aPb and bNa. Thinking in graphical terms, we are thus dealing with directed graphs and it becomes desirable to extend the theory of balance to include directed relations P and N. The first point to note is that we have to take into consideration 2-cycles.

Consider two points a and b and non-reflexive, directed relations P and N. Then four distinct types of 2-cycle are logically possible, namely:

$$(aPb \cdot bNa), (aNb \cdot bPa), (aNb \cdot bNa) \text{ and } (aPb \cdot bPa).$$

2-cycles are defined as balanced under either of the following conditions:

$$aPb \longrightarrow bPa \tag{8}$$
$$aNb \longrightarrow bNa \tag{9}$$

and 3-cycles are defined as balanced under any of the following conditions:

$$[(aPb \cdot bPc) \text{ v } (aPb \cdot cPb) \text{ v } (bPa \cdot bPc)] \longrightarrow [(aPc \text{ v } cPa)] \tag{10}$$
$$[(aPb \cdot bNc) \text{ v } (aPb \cdot cNb) \text{ v } (bPa \cdot bNc)] \longrightarrow [(aNc \text{ v } cNa)] \tag{11}$$
$$[(aNb \cdot bNc) \text{ v } (aNb \cdot cNb) \text{ v } (bNa \cdot bNc)] \longrightarrow [(aPc \text{ v } cPa)] \tag{12}$$

(for 'v' read 'or')

If the relations P and N are interpreted as 'chooses friend' and 'chooses enemy' respectively, the reader may satisfy himself that statements (8) to (12) correspond reasonably well with our intuitive notions about 'stable' or balanced states.

If we apply the same algebraic law of multiplication as before, a balance parameter involving 2- and 3-cycles may be defined:

$$\beta_d (2, 3) = C_3^+ + C_2^+/C_3 + C_2 \tag{13}$$

where $C_3^+ =$ the total number of positive 3-cycles, $C_2^+ =$ the total number of positive 2-cycles, C_3 the total number of 3-cycles and C_2 the total number of 2-cycles in a structure.

Since every pair of points in a complete balanced directed structure must satisfy one of the conditions:

$$aPb \longleftrightarrow bPa \tag{14}$$
$$aNb \longleftrightarrow bNa \tag{15}$$

the analogies of Theorems 1 and 2 apply to these structures also. So the introduction of directed relations does not, in any appreciable sense, complicate the theory.

Having given this rather cursory review of the theory we are now in a position to consider some criticisms.

The Postulates of Balance Theory

If we accept the truth of the balance 'axioms', this necessitates our acceptance of the partitioning Theorems 1 and 2. Furthermore, if we concentrate upon complete structures, then we are bound to accept the idea that affective structures tend towards bi-polarization (Theorem 1). But is this in accordance with our experience? The answer to this question depends to a large degree upon our interpretation of the phrase 'tends towards'.

In a previous paper[12] I tried to interpret this idea in a probablistic manner. This turns out, however, to be only of limited applicability, being particularly inappropriate when structures are near completion. Nevertheless we do find affective structures which do not polarize as balance theory would predict. Indeed, if we take a liberal interpretation of Coser, social structures are rendered stable precisely because they do not polarize perfectly, so that at least some structural entities are in a position to provide 'bridges' between opposing groups. Coser is, in fact, concerned with structures where people have differing allegiances. But if we think in terms of positive allegiances and negative sentiments it is not difficult to draw the connections between this theory and balance theory. There are, I believe, close interconnections between balance theory, criss-cross theory and cross pressure theory (see note 4).

If we find a continuing non-polarized situation, then this implies that imbalanced cycles persist. In terms of 3-cycles this means that at least one of the following types of cycle is present in the structure:

$$aNb \, . \, bNc \, . \, aNc$$
$$aPb \, . \, bPc \, . \, aNc$$

The continued occurrence of such cycles could, of course, be due to either or both of the assumptions of unsegmented interaction and congruent perception not holding; and if this is the case, then the simple theory may be preserved. In fact at the risk of preserving the theory against falsification we may suggest that if such cycles do persist in a structure then we may search for independent evidence for segmentation or differing perceptions. However, we can make a more direct criticism: why should we regard all negative 3-cycles ($aNb \, . \, bNc \, . \, cNa$) as imbalanced, i.e. 'unstable'? Surely, for example, a situation where three persons have mutual feelings of hostility towards each other is not necessarily unstable?

James Davis,[13] in response to this question, has recently introduced what he calls the *theory of clustering*. The essence of this theory is to regard only cycles with one negative arc as unstable. Davis's central theorem is that an affective structure has a *clustering* if and only if it contains no cycles having exactly one negative arc. A clustering on a structure is a partition of its point set into subsets (called plus-sets) such that each positive arc joins two points in the same subset and each negative arc joins two points from different subsets. If the plus-sets are unique then they are called *clusters.* He shows that for a complete graph the plus-sets are clusters. Thus, by relaxing the assumption that all negative 3-cycles are unstable Davis obtains a theory in which the stable state of affairs may be one with more than two positive groupings, i.e. *n*-polarization[14] rather than bi-polarization. Davis's theory is of extreme interest as it overcomes two of the standard criticisms of balance theory at once; it rejects the idea that an all-negative 3-cycle is unstable, and does not necessarily imply a movement to structural bi-polarization. The question as to whether all-negative 3-cycles are stable or not is of course an empirical one, but it does seem that our normal everyday knowledge tells us that if they are, then they are not unstable in the same way as (*aPc . bPc . aNc*) 3-cycles are. For this type of cycle is postulated as unstable because it is in a state of *endogenous strain,* but it is difficult to see how an all-negative 3-cycle is in a state of strain. Nevertheless, such 3-cycles are probably peculiarly vulnerable to *exogenous* factors in the sense that a state of tripartite mutual hostility is unlikely to be stable in the face of *external pressures to conflict,* etc. This distinction between endogenous strain and exogenous factors is of crucial importance, and failure to recognize it has lead to many ill-founded criticisms of balance theory. *Perhaps changes in affective structures, in the absence of exogenous factors, operate according to the ideas of clustering theory (i.e. any all-negative 3-cycles may persist) but in their presence according to the balance axioms.* I have considered these problems in much more detail elsewhere.[15]

These ideas are summarized in Table I.

Endogenous strain operating only	Conflict inducing exogenous factors operating also

unstable 3-cycles:
    aNb . bPc . cPa
	unstable 3-cycles:
	    aNb . bPc . cPa
	    aNb . bNc . cNa

stable 3-cycles:
    aPb . bPc . cPa
    aNb . bNc . cNa
    aNb . bNc . cPa
	stable 3-cycles:
	    aPb . bPc . cPa
	    aNb . bNc . cPa

Complete structures tend to cluster (Cluster theorem). Incomplete structures tend to plus-sets.	Complete structures tend to polarize (Theorem 1). Incomplete structures tend to a series of positive groupings (Theorem 2).

TABLE I

We may now turn to a much more difficult problem – the assumption of congruent perception. This states that all the relationships in a 3-cycle must be perceived in the same way (i.e. have the same sign) by the three persons in the cycle. Clearly if this is not the case then the cycle may be balanced as far as one individual is concerned, but not the other. Since the idea of strain is central to balance theory and strain must be a function of the perceived situation, then we cannot but take this into consideration. So it is possible that any 3-cycle could be 'viewed' in three different ways. This introduces a complexity into balance theory which at the present it cannot handle.

Analytically we can distinguish four possible conditions:

(i) All perceptions are in agreement, i.e. the assumption of congruent perception holds.

(ii) The perceptions differ, but all agree that the 3-cycle is balanced in one way or another. For example, in Fig. II the three 3-cycles correspond to the three differing perceptions but all are balanced. (I shall adopt the convention that cycles are depicted with one bold point to indicate that the cycle is this 'person's' perception.)

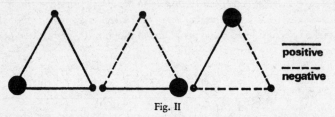

Fig. II

(iii) Some perceptions are of balanced 3-cycles and some of imbalanced ones. For example, Fig. III depicts such a situation.

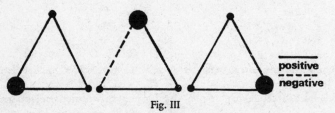

Fig. III

(iv) There are differing perceptions, but all are of imbalanced cycles. For example, the situation depicted in Fig. IV.

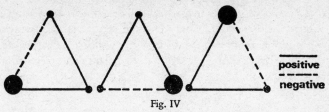

positive
negative

Fig. IV

It seems clear that the summary parameters $\beta(3)$ or $\beta(n)$ are of little utility when situations like (iii) and (iv) arise. We have, in effect, to compute the balance in the structure from each participant's point of view. Although a comparison of the values of, say, $\beta(3)$ for each participant in a structure would give some idea of who perceived the structure as most balanced or imbalanced, such information is only of marginal interest. In the next section we shall develop a theory of point strain that seems more appropriate for these situations. It might seem that we could simplify the issues by postulating that participants in a 3-cycle 'agree' on the nature of the relationships they have with each other, the locus of differing perceptions being the relationships of 'other' participants. For example, it is unlikely that two people a and b would disagree about whether their relationship was positive or negative, but it is much more likely that a could be 'mistaken' about the relationship that b has with c. But even if we make this assumption it is logically possible that the three participants in a 3-cycle perceive the structure differently, but all the perceptions are balanced or all imbalanced. So such a postulation does not appreciably simplify our problems of analysis.

Measures of Balance and the Problem of *n*-cycles

The elementary ideas behind balance theory really rest upon the analysis of 3-cycles, though as we have seen it is convenient, particularly in incomplete structures, to incorporate larger cycles into our analysis. If this is done, cycles with an uneven number of negative arcs are taken to be imbalanced, and we can define $\beta(n)$ as in expression (7).

Now the sociological motivation for the statements about balanced 3-cycles is reasonably clear and well founded in our common-sense experience. But that for *n*-cycles $(n > 3)$ is not. A large cycle with only one negative arc would contribute, according to expression (7), to the imbalance of a given structure. Furthermore, such a cycle would be accorded the same 'importance' as a negative 3-cycle. This seems sociologically dubious. It would be more consonant with our understanding to give it a lower weighting than a 3-cycle, as a contributor to imbalance. Or putting it the other way round, we would expect a large cycle with one negative arc to be more stable than a 3-cycle with one negative arc. As a consequence it has been suggested[16] that the balance parameter should be defined as follows:

$$\beta^\star(n) = \sum_{i=3}^{n} f(i) C_i^+ / C_i \qquad (16)$$

where $f(i)$ is a decreasing function. On the face of it this is an attractive proposal. The difficulty arises, however, in specifying the function $f(i)$. The form of the function will probably be specific to a particular structure and, what is more, it may well not be homogeneous throughout the structure. In an organization, for example, certain n-cycles $(n > 3)$ may be of greater functional importance than others, and if the cycle were imbalanced at a particular instant, one would expect a disproportionately strong tendency to balance compared with a less functional cycle of the same length. The usefulness of expression (16) is, however, something that can be settled not in the context of a priori theorizing, but rather in the context of particular empirical investigations.

I believe, however, that balance theory is perhaps best confined to 3-cycles and possibly 4-cycles and thus affective structures containing no such cycles are not subject to the instability or stability implied by balance theory. So for the rest of the paper I shall concentrate purely upon 3-cycles.

There is a further point concerning summary measures of balance. If we consider the structures depicted in Fig. V, $\beta(3)$ of $S_1 < \beta(3)$ of S_2.

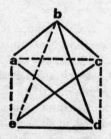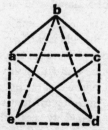

Fig. V

Nevertheless, it is only necessary to change the sign of two arcs of S_1 $((b,c)$ and $(d,e))$ and S_2 $((b,c)$ and $(b,d))$ in order to obtain a balanced structure. It is in the light of considerations like this that the degree of imbalance of a structure has been defined as the minimum number of arcs that must change in order for the structure to attain balance (line index). But we may still ask which is the best measure of balance in a structure – a line index or the $\beta(3)$ value? To say that a structure's imbalance should be measured in terms of a line index seems to imply that a structure will attain balance or tend towards balance by changing or attempting to change the sign of these arcs. But this can in turn imply an omniscience on behalf of the structural units that is hardly credible; it seems to suggest a sort of general consensus on how to reduce strain. But we must remember that strain is 'felt' individually by the structural units and presumably each structural unit tries to minimize the strain that it feels. *There is no reason to suppose that a set of strain-minimizing entities will reduce strain in a manner that is, from a global standpoint, the most efficient.* Consider point *a* in S_1 (Fig. V), for instance. It finds itself in an imbalanced 3-cycle (*abc*) but is supposed to maintain its positive link with *b* and its negative link with *c* on 'the understanding that' *b* and *c* will change their positive linkage to a negative one. Likewise *e* and *d*. Clearly there is embedded here a 'rationality' assumption that requires much further substantiation before we can possibly accept it. But I think we may call into question the whole practice of using summary parameters like $\beta(3)$ or $\beta(n)$ to characterize a structure. They are so insensitive to the precise nature and location of imbalance (strain) that they have little diagnostic value. What we really want is a measure of the strain in the various 'parts' of the structure, rather in the same way as an engineer has for the various components of a structure such as a bridge. We can then detect the 'weak spots' (those under the greatest strain) and quite reasonably predict that these are the places where change is likely to take place.

The Concept of Structural Strain

There are two entities making up an affective structure, the structural units (points) and the affective relations themselves. So we can distinguish between:

(i) the strain at a point in an affective structure – *Point Strain*;
(ii) the strain on an affective link in a structure – *Arc Strain*.

Let us first consider point strain. In general a point may be in balanced 3-cycles and imbalanced 3-cycles. Clearly if it is in only balanced 3-cycles it does not experience any strain and if it is only in imbalanced 3-cycles it experiences a great deal of strain. If it is in an equal number of balanced and imbalanced 3-cycles then we may envisage that in some way these cancel each other out. It is thus important to distinguish between points of this latter sort which are not in an aggregate state of strain and points of the first sort that are, as it were, strongly stabilized in the structure. To revert to our example of a bridge once again – we may draw the parallel with the components that are under tension and those that are under compression, though the parallel should not be pursued too far, as extreme compression can lead to rupture but strongly stabilized points are unlikely to suffer any catastrophic change – indeed, they are likely to be the most stable points in the structure.

The *point strain coefficient* of the i'th point, θ_i, may be defined as follows:

$$\theta_i = \frac{C_3^- - C_3^+}{C_3^- + C_3^+} \tag{17}$$

where $C_3^- =$ the number of imbalanced 3-cycles in which point i is involved and $C_3^+ =$ the number of balanced 3-cycles in which point i is involved. θ_i takes on a value of -1 when all the 3-cycles 'on point' i are balanced, $+1$ when they are all imbalanced, and zero when it is on an equal number of positive and negative 3-cycles. We can thus calculate a point strain coefficient for each point in a structure. Point strain measures are clearly relevant to the situations outlined in the previous section of this paper, where we encounter differing perceptions. The θ_i values can be calculated according to i's perceptions; thus the greater the positive value of θ_i the greater the 'felt' strain of point i.

Let us turn to what is perhaps a more useful measure, arc strain. Arcs may also be involved in balanced and imbalanced cycles, so we can define the strain on an arc in an entirely analogous manner to the strain at a point. The *arc strain coefficient* of the ij'th affective arc, θ_{ij}, may be defined as follows:

$$\theta_{ij} = \frac{C_3^- - C_3^+}{C_3^- + C_3^+} \tag{18}$$

where $C_3^- =$ the total number of imbalanced 3-cycles in which a particular affective link is involved and $C_3^+ =$ the total number of balanced 3-cycles in which it is involved. Thus if a link is involved in negative 3-cycles only, it will be under maximum strain ($\theta_{ij} = 1$).

We can, for any affective structure, define a symmetric matrix of θ_{ij} values which will give us some indication of the arcs which are under strain. The matrix for structures S_1 (Fig. V) is:[17]

	a	b	c	d	e
a	—	$\frac{1}{3}$	$-\frac{1}{3}$	$-\frac{1}{3}$	$\frac{1}{3}$
b		—	1	$\frac{1}{3}$	$\frac{1}{3}$
c			—	$\frac{1}{3}$	$\frac{1}{3}$
d				—	1
e					—

We see that arcs (b,c) and (d,e) are under maximum strain, that is, they are both involved in negative 3-cycles only. Interestingly, according to the line-index measure, it is (b,c) and (d,e) that change sign for S_1 to move to balance. Of course if $\theta_{ij} = 1$ then a change of sign of the arc ij will render all the cycles in which the arc is involved positive (balanced). But if $\theta_{ij} < 1$ then a change in sign of ij will render balanced some cycles that were imbalanced and vice versa. Only if $\theta_{ij} > 0$ will there be a net reduction of strain in the structure if the arc changes sign. If we look at the strain matrix for structures S_2 (Fig. V), it has the following entries:

	a	b	c	d	e
a	—	$\frac{1}{3}$	$-\frac{1}{3}$	$-\frac{1}{3}$	-1
b		—	$\frac{1}{3}$	$\frac{1}{3}$	$\frac{1}{3}$
c			—	-1	$-\frac{1}{3}$
d				—	$-\frac{1}{3}$
e					—

There are no $\theta_{ij} = 1$ entries; so any change of sign in arcs will necessarily be a 'cost benefit' exercise. S_2 can attain balance by changing the sign of the arcs (b,c) and (b,d) as both these arcs have a θ_{ij} value of $\frac{1}{3}$ (but notice that (a,b) and (b,c) have this also). So it is not in general possible, by a simple inspection of the strain coefficients, to predict which arcs will change their sign in a balancing process.

The line index predicts that (b,c) and (b,d) will change sign. But, as we have pointed out, this prediction assumes a level of rationality that is unrealistic. Strain theory would predict that (a,b) and (b,c) are equally likely to change sign. If this does happen, of course, S_2 will not move to balance. In fact the $\beta(3)$ value of the structure so generated is less than for S_1, thus demonstrating how a structure can move away from global balance by attempting to resolve local strains. Of course this process introduces further strains which in turn must be resolved, and we may even postulate an eventual state of perfect balance. But the point stands that structures may move away from global balance in their attempt to resolve strains and attain stability.

Finally, in this section, we may state the following almost trivial theorems:

Theorem 3 If and only if $\theta_i = -1$ in a complete symmetric affective structure then *all* the values of $\theta_{ij} = -1$.

Theorem 4 If and only if $\theta_i = +1$ in a complete symmetric affective structure then *all* the values $\theta_{ij} = +1$.

Proof of Theorem 3 If $\theta_i = -1$ then all the 3-cycles involving point i are balanced. Therefore all the arcs incident out of point i are in balanced 3-cycles. Therefore all the θ_{ij} values are equal to -1.

And if all the θ_{ij} values are -1 all the arcs incident out of i are in balanced cycles only. Since every cycle involving point i must involve one of these arcs, θ_i must equal -1 also.

The proof of Theorem 4 is entirely parallel.

The Problem of Intensity of Affective Relations

In the course of this essay I have repeatedly emphasized that, as it stands at present, balance theory is analytically weak as it does not take into account the intensity of affective relations. In fact we might go so far as to suggest that the theory is of little use at all without the incorporation of intensity measures. Our common sense tells us, for instance, that we cannot under-stand a friendship structure without considering degrees of friendship.

Attempts to incorporate intensity measures have been made. It has been assumed that real-number measures of affectivity can be obtained and the 'strength' of a balanced or imbalanced cycle is then defined as the arith-metical product of its component arcs. There is, however, little or no sociological justification for the implicit weightings in such a multiplica-tion process. Flament[18] has suggested that the major problem of incorpora-ting affective intensities into the theory is not mathematical but sociological; we have no theories of how affective strengths effect behaviour. In the following paragraphs, however, I shall make some tentative proposals for measuring strain in affective structures, whilst recognizing that the ideas are very much in need of empirical support. It is perhaps sociologically wise to ask, first of all, what type of measures of affectivity we can expect to obtain. It seems clear that the likelihood of obtaining metric measures is very remote. So we will start to develop the theory in terms of ordinal measures. This means that we are dealing with what I have termed elsewhere *Ordinal Structures* (*Graphs*).[19]

We assume that we can obtain:

(i) a linear order of positive affectivity $\phi_1^P < \phi_2^P \dots \phi_m^P \dots \phi_\alpha^P$

and (ii) a linear order of negative affectivity $\phi_1^N < \phi_2^N \dots \phi_m^N \dots \phi_\gamma^N$.

Note that we do not assume $\alpha = \gamma$ so it is logically possible that there are a different number of negative and positive categories of affectivity.[20]

So an ordinal valued affective structure may be depicted as either an ordinal algebraic graph[21] or as a matrix $//A//$ where $a_{ij} =$ the appropriate measure of positive or negative affectivity.

Now consider any arc ij in a valued structure. In general there will be three 'affective force fields' acting on the arc:

(i) *Conservative forces* (F_c) of the 'balanced' 3-cycles of which ij is a component arc.
(ii) *Non-Conservative forces* (F_d) of the imbalanced 3-cycles of which ij is a component arc.
(iii) *The Inertial force* (F_i) of the ij'th arc itself. We will assume that the more intense the arc the greater its inertia.[22]

So the arc is under net strain if:

$$F_d > F_i \oplus F_c \tag{19}$$

where $\oplus$ reads something like 'the combined effect of'.

If we are able to obtain metric measures of F_d, F_c and F_i then $\oplus$ becomes the ordinary addition of arithmetic and the inequality a simple inequality on the number system.

If

$$F_d < F_i \oplus F_c \tag{20}$$

the arc is *stabilized* in the structure.
Further if

$$F_d = F_i \oplus F_c \tag{21}$$

then the arc is neither under strain nor stabilized.
The outstanding problem is then to compute F_c, F_d and F_i.

We may define F_i for the ij'th arc as equal to its valuation on either the positive or negative linear ordering. This seems eminently reasonable, for, in effect, it states that the greater the intensity of an affective link (positive or negative) the greater its inertia. That is, the stronger the link the greater the force that must act upon it to change its sign.

F_d and F_c are more difficult to deal with as in both cases we have the problem of aggregating arc strengths in the 3-cycles. Let us define a general aggregation relation o. Consider the ij'th arc in an imbalanced 3-cycle (i,j,k) then let f_d^{ij} be the force acting on this arc. Then

$$f_d{}^{ij} = \phi^{ik} \text{ o } \phi^{jk} \tag{22}$$

where ϕ^{ik} = the intensity (positive or negative) of the ik'th arc and ϕ^{jk} = the intensity (positive or negative) of the jk'th arc.

Likewise, we may define $f_c{}^{ij}$, the force acting on the ij'th arc, as a consequence of its being in a balanced 3-cycle (i, j, l). Then

$$f_c{}^{ij} = \phi^{il} \text{ o } \phi^{jl} \tag{23}$$

If the ij'th arc is in s imbalanced and balanced 3-cycles then

$$F_d = \overset{k=s}{\underset{k=1}{Z}} \ (\phi^{ik} \text{ o } \phi^{jk}) \tag{24}$$

where Z is an aggregating operation over s imbalanced 3-cycles. And

$$F_c = \overset{k=t}{\underset{=1}{Z}} \ (\phi^{il} \text{ o } \phi^{jl}) \tag{25}$$

where Z is an aggregating operation over t balanced 3-cycles.

So $t + s$ equals the number of 3-cycles in which the arc ij is involved.

So we have three major problems: what sort of algebraic structure should we build into the aggregating operations $\oplus$, o and Z? The answer to this question is in part an empirical one, and rests upon observations of how the participants in a structure themselves aggregate affectivity.

The simplest model is to assume integer values for both linear orders of ϕ so that $\oplus$, o becomes the normal addition of arithmetic and Z becomes R (summation).

Then we may define a strain coefficient $\theta^v{}_{ij}$ for the ij'th arc.

$$\theta^v{}_{ij} = \frac{F_d - F_c - F_i}{F_d + F_c + F_i} \tag{26}$$

So if $\quad\quad\quad F_d > F_i + F_c, \ \theta^v{}_{ij}$ is positive $\tag{27}$

if $\quad\quad\quad F_d < F_i + F_c, \ \theta^v{}_{ij}$ is negative $\tag{28}$

and if $\quad\quad\quad F_d = F_i + F_c, \ \theta^v{}_{ij} = 0.$ $\tag{29}$

If $\quad\quad F_c + F_i = 0, \ \theta^v{}_{ij} = 1$ (i.e. maximum strain) $\tag{30}$

and if $\quad F_d = 0, \ \theta^v{}_{ij} = -1$ (i.e. maximum stabilization). $\tag{31}$

We are, however, having a certain amount of empirical success with a rather different assumption. We assume that the 'strongest' arc in a 3-cycle 'dominates'. That is, if we apply counting 1, 2 ... α and 1, 2 ... γ to the linear orders we assume that the force acting on a link is equal to the arc with the greatest value in any particular 3-cycle in which it is involved. So the strongest arc (positive or negative) dominates in either a balanced or imbalanced 3-cycle. Now since α does not necessarily equal γ – indeed in friendship structures it is generally true that $\alpha > \gamma$ – this means that in some sense friendship can dominate hostility in such structures. It is probably the case that 'integrative' social systems in general possess more categories of positive affectivity than negative and 'coercive systems' the reverse. So in the latter hostility can dominate strain relations. The way in which cultures change their positive and negative affective discriminations may be a very good guide to the likelihood of conflict behaviour.

There is, however, much need for empirical work in this field.

Concluding Remarks

I have attempted to show that, in concentrating on summary parameters such as $\beta(3)$, balance theory loses much of its analytical power. The most important feature of the theory is its formalization of at least one sociological conception of strain and so it is most revealing to locate actual points of strain in a complex structure. To this end a rudimentary theory of strain has been elaborated.

SCIENCE VERSUS LITERATURE*

Roland Barthes

French university departments keep an official list of the social and human sciences recognized as being taught, and are thus restricted to awarding degrees in specific subjects; it is possible to become a doctor of aesthetics, psychology or sociology, but not of heraldry, semantics or victimology. It is thus the institution which directly determines the nature of human knowledge, by imposing its own modes of division and classification on it, in exactly the same way that a language, with its 'compulsory headings' (and not only its exclusions), obliges us to think in a certain way. In other words, science (this word will henceforth be taken here to mean the social and human sciences as a whole) is defined not by its content (often ill-determined and labile) nor by its method (this varies from science to science: what do historical science and experimental psychology have in common?) nor by its ethic (science is not alone in being serious-minded and rigorous) nor by its mode of communication (science is printed in books, like everything else), but simply by its *status*, that is its determination by society; the subject-matter of science is everything that society deems worthy of being handed on. In short, science is what is taught.

Literature has all the secondary characteristics of science, that is, all those attributes which do not define it. Its contents are exactly the same as those of science; there is certainly not a single scientific topic that has not been dealt with at some point in the world's literature. The world of the literary work is a total one, in which all knowledge, social, psychological or historical, has a place, with the result that for us literature has that great cosmogonic unity which the ancient Greeks enjoyed but which we are denied today by the fragmented state of our sciences. Moreover, like science, literature has its methods; it has its programmes of research, which vary from school to school and age to age (again like those of science), its rules of investigation and sometimes even its pretensions to experiment. Like science, literature also has its ethic, a certain way of extracting the rules governing its practice from the view it takes of its own nature and, consequently, of submitting its projects to a certain sense of the absolute.

* Reprinted from *The Times Literary Supplement* (September 28th, 1967).

There is one last feature which not only unites science and literature but also divides them more surely than any other of their differences: they are both discursive (the ancient idea of the *logos* expressed this very well). But science and literature do not assume or, if one prefers, profess the language which constitutes both of them in the same way. As far as science is concerned language is simply an instrument, which it profits it to make as transparent and neutral as possible: it is subordinate to the matter of science (workings, hypotheses, results) which, so it is said, exists outside language and precedes it. On the one hand and *first* there is the content of the scientific message, which is everything; on the other hand and *next*, the verbal form responsible for expressing that content, which is nothing. It is no coincidence that, from the sixteenth century onwards, the corporate blossoming of empiricism, rationalism and an evidential religion (with the Reformation), that is, of the scientific spirit in the widest sense of the term, should have been accompanied by a regression in the autonomy of language, henceforth relegated to the rank of instrument or 'fine style', whereas in the Middle Ages human culture had shared out the secrets of speech and nature almost equally, under the headings of the Seven Liberal Arts.

For literature, on the other hand, or at any rate that literature which has freed itself from classicism and humanism, language can no longer be the convenient instrument or the superfluous backcloth of a social, emotional or poetic 'reality' which pre-exists it, and which it is language's subsidiary responsibility to express, by means of submitting itself to a number of stylistic rules. Language is literature's Being, its very world; the whole of literature is contained in the act of writing, and no longer in those of 'thinking', 'portraying', 'telling' or 'feeling'. Technically, as Roman Jakobson has defined it, the 'poetic' (i.e., the literary) refers to that type of message which takes as its object not its content but its own form. Ethically, it is only by its passage through language that literature can continue to shake loose the essential concepts of our culture, one of the chief among which is the 'real'. Politically, it is by professing and illustrating that no language is innocent, by practising what might be called 'integral language' that literature is revolutionary. Thus today literature finds itself bearing unaided the entire responsibility for language, for although science has a certain need of language it is not, like literature, *in* language. The one is taught, that is, expressed and exhibited, the other is fulfilled rather than transmitted (only its history being taught). Science is spoken, literature written, the one is led by the voice, the other follows the hand; they do not both have the same physical body and hence the same desire behind them.

Since it turns essentially on a certain way of taking language, conjured away into thin air in one case and assumed in the other, the opposition between science and literature is of particular importance for structuralism. Agreed that this word, most often imposed from outside, is today applied to projects that are very diverse, sometimes divergent and sometimes even antagonistic, and no one can arrogate the right to speak in its name. The present writer does not claim to be doing so, but retains contemporary 'structuralism' only in its most specialized and consequently most relevant version, using it to mean a certain mode of analysis of cultural artefacts, in so far as this mode originates in the methods of contemporary linguistics. This is to say that structuralism, itself developed from a linguistic model, finds in literature, which is the work of language, an object that has much more than an affinity with it; the two are homogeneous. Their coincidence does not exclude a certain confusion or even cleavage, according to whether structuralism sets out to maintain a scientific distance between itself and its object or whether, on the other hand, it agrees to compromise and abandon the analysis of which it is the bearer in that infinitude of language that today passes through literature; in short, whether it elects to be science or writing.

As a science, structuralism can be said to 'find itself' at each level of the literary work. First, at the level of the content or, to be more exact, of the form of the content, since it seeks to establish the 'language' of the stories that are told, their articulation, their units and the logic which links these together; in short, the general mythology in which each literary work shares. Secondly, at the level of the forms of discourse. By virtue of its method structuralism gives special attention to classification, hierarchies and arrangements; its essential object is the taxonomy or distributive model which every human creation, be it institution or book, inevitably establishes, since there can be no culture without classification. Now the discourse, or the complex of words superior to the phrase, has its own forms of organization; it too is a classification and a classification which signifies. In this respect structuralism has an august forebear whose historical role has generally been underestimated or discredited for ideological reasons: Rhetoric, that impressive attempt by a whole culture to analyse and classify the forms of speech, and to make the world of language intelligible. And, finally, at the level of the words. The phrase does not only have a literal or indicative sense, it is crammed with additional meanings.

The literary word is at once a cultural reference, a rhetorical model, a deliberately ambiguous utterance and a simple indicative unit; it has three dimensions, within which lies the field of structural analysis, whose aims are much wider than those of the old stylistics, based as they were on an erroneous idea of 'expressivity'. At every level, therefore, be it that of the argument, the discourse or the words, the literary work offers structuralism the picture of a structure perfectly homological (present-day research is tending to prove this) with that of language itself. Structuralism has emerged from linguistics and in literature it finds an object which has itself emerged from language. We can understand then why structuralism should want to found a science of literature or, to be more exact, a linguistics of discourse, whose object is the 'language' of literary forms, grasped on many levels. This aim is a comparatively new one, since until now literature has only been approached 'scientifically' in a very marginal way, through the history of literary works, their authors, the schools they belong to, or the texts themselves (philology).

But although it may be a new aim it is not a satisfactory, or at least not a sufficient, one. It does nothing to solve the dilemma we spoke of at the beginning and which is suggested allegorically by the opposition between science and literature, in so far as the latter assumes its language under the name of writing, whereas the former evades it, by pretending to believe that this language is merely instrumental. In short, structuralism will be just one more 'science' (several are born each century, some of them only ephemeral) if it does not manage to place the actual subversion of scientific language at the centre of its programme, that is, to 'write itself'. How could it fail to question the very language it uses in order to know language? The logical continuation of structuralism can only be to rejoin literature, no longer as an 'object' of analysis but as the activity of writing, to do away with the distinction derived from logic which turns the work itself into a language-object and science into a meta-language, and thus to forgo that illusory privilege which science attaches to the possession of a captive language.

It remains therefore for the structuralist to turn himself into a 'writer', certainly not in order to profess or practise 'fine style', but in order to rediscover the crucial problems involved in every utterance, once it is no longer wrapped in the beneficent cloud of strictly *realist* illusions, which see language simply as the medium of thought. This transformation, still pretty theoretical it must be admitted, requires that certain things should be made clear or recognized. In the first place, the relationship between subjectivity and objectivity or, if one prefers, the place of the subject in his own work, can no longer be thought of as in the halcyon days of positivist science. Objectivity and rigour, those attributes of the scientist which are still used as a stick to beat us with, are essentially preparatory qualities necessary at the time of starting out on the work, and as such there is no cause to suspect or abandon them. But they are not qualities that can be transferred to the discourse itself, except by a sort of sleight-of-hand, a purely metonymical procedure which confuses *precaution* with its end-product in discourse. Every utterance implies its own subject, whether this subject be expressed in an apparently direct fashion, by the use of 'I', or indirectly, by being referred to as 'he', or avoided altogether by means of impersonal constructions. These are purely grammatical decoys, which do no more than vary the way in which the subject is constituted within the discourse, that is, the way he gives himself to others, theatrically or as a phantasm; they all refer therefore to forms of the imaginary. The most specious of these forms is the privative, the very one normally practised in scientific discourse, from which the scientist excludes himself because of his concern for objectivity. What is excluded, however, is always only the 'person', psychological, emotional or biographical, certainly not the subject. It could be said moreover that this subject is heavy with the spectacular exclusion it has imposed on its person, so that, on the discursive level – one, be it remembered, which cannot be avoided – objectivity is as imaginary as anything else. In point of fact, only an integral formalization of scientific discourse (that of the human sciences, of course, since this has largely been achieved in the others) can preserve science from the risks of the imaginary, unless, naturally, it agrees to practise that imaginary *in the full awareness of what it is doing*, a knowledge that can only be attained by writing; only writing has a hope of removing the bad faith attaching to any language which is ignorant of itself.

Only writing, again, and this is a first step towards defining it, can practise language in its totality. To resort to scientific discourse as if to an instrument of thought is to postulate that there exists a neutral state of language, from which a certain number of specialized languages, the literary or poetic languages for example, have derived, as so many deviants or embellishments. It is held that this neutral state would be the referential code for all the 'ex-centric' languages, which themselves would be merely its subcodes. By identifying itself with this referential code, as the basis of all normality, scientific discourse is arrogating to itself a right which it is writing's duty precisely to contest. The notion of 'writing' implies indeed that language is a vast system, none of whose codes is privileged or, if one prefers, central, and whose various departments are related in a 'fluctuating hierarchy'. Scientific discourse believes itself to be a superior code; writing aims at being a total code, including its own forces of destruction. It follows that writing alone can smash the theological idol set up by a paternalistic science, refuse to be terror-stricken by what is wrongly thought of as the 'truth' of the content and of reasoning, and open up all three dimensions of language to research, with its subversions of logic, its mixing of codes, its shifts of meaning, dialogues and parodies. Only writing can oppose the self-assurance of the scientist, in so far as he 'expresses' his science, with what Lautréamont called the 'modesty' of the writer.

There is, finally, between science and literature, a third margin which science must reconquer, that of pleasure. In a civilization entirely brought up by monotheism to the idea of sin, where every value is attained through suffering, the word 'pleasure' has an unfortunate ring; there is something frivolous, trivial and incomplete about it. Coleridge said: 'A poem is that species of composition which is opposed to works of science by purposing for its immediate object, pleasure, not truth'; an ambiguous statement, for although it assumes the nature of the poem (or of literature) to be in some degree erotic, our civilization continues to assign it to a special reserve where it can keep an eye on it, so to speak, distinct from the more important territory of truth. Yet 'pleasure', as we are readier to admit these days, implies an experience much vaster and more meaningful than the mere satisfaction of a 'taste'. Now the pleasure of language has never been seriously measured, although, in its way, the ancient Rhetoric had the right idea when it established a special class of discourse, devoted to spectacle and admiration, the epideictic. But classical art wrapped the 'pleasurable', which it claimed to have made its law (Racine: 'La première règle est de plaire ...') in all the constraints of the 'natural'. Only the baroque, a literary experiment which has never been more than tolerated by our society, at least in France, has dared to explore to some extent what might be called the Eros of language. Scientific discourse is far from doing so, for if it accepted this idea it would have to give up all those privileges with which society as instituted surrounds it, and agree to return to that 'literary life' which, Baudelaire tells us in connection with Edgar Allan Poe, is 'le seul élément où puissent respirer certains êtres déclassés'.

What we must perhaps ask for today is a mutation in the consciousness, the structure and the objectives of scientific discourse, at a time, however, when the human sciences, now firmly established and flourishing, seem to be leaving less and less room for a literature commonly charged with being unreal and inhuman. To be precise: the role of literature is actively to *represent* to the scientific establishment what the latter denies, to wit the sovereignty of language. And structuralism ought to be in a strong position to cause such a scandal because, being acutely aware of the linguistic nature of human artefacts, it alone today can reopen the question of the linguistic status of science. Its subject-matter being language – all languages – it has come to define itself very quickly as the meta-language of our culture. But this stage must be transcended, because the opposition of language-objects and their meta-languages is still subject in the end to the paternalistic model of a science without a language. The task confronting structuralist discourse is to make itself entirely homogeneous with its object. There are two ways in which this task can be successfully tackled, both equally radical: by an exhaustive formalization or else by 'integral writing'. In the second of these hypotheses, the one we are defending here, science will become literature, to the same extent as literature, growingly subject as it is to an overturning of the traditional genres of poetry, narrative, criticism and essay, already is and always has been a science. What the human sciences are discovering today, in whatever field it may be, sociological, psychological, psychiatric, linguistic, etc., literature has always known. The only difference is that literature has not *said* it, but *written* it. In contrast to the integral truth of literature, the human sciences, belatedly formulated in the wake of bourgeois positivism, appear as the technical alibis proffered by our society in order to maintain within itself the faction of a theological truth proudly, and improperly, freed from language.

SELECT BIBLIOGRAPHY

For the newcomer to structuralism who finds the complete bibliography somewhat daunting I have selected certain books to provide further reading. Fuller
details of them will be found in the complete bibliography.

Bachelard, G., *The Psychoanalysis of Fire*
   Some would deny that Bachelard is a structuralist, but he provides an essential
   link in the chain between the Freudian writers of the inter-war years and the
   contemporary school of Lacan.

Barthes, R., *Writing Degree Zero; Sur Racine; Système de la Mode*
   Barthes is the doyen of structuralist literary criticism and literary semiology.
   It is a pity that, of his most important works, only *Writing Degree Zero* has
   been translated into English. *Sur Racine* is probably the best book on Racine
   in any language or of any methodological persuasion.

Chomsky, N., *Language and Mind*
   Chomsky's theories of language have aroused enormous controversies among
   philosophers, psychologists and linguists. The intellectual demands and returns
   made by his works are equally high. *Language and Mind*, whilst it makes no
   concessions to the non-professional, is the most readily intellectually accessible.

Goldmann, L., *The Hidden God*
   Somewhat apart from the mainstream of structuralism, Goldmann draws on
   an older Marxist tradition established by Lukács. *The Hidden God* is a seminal
   and brilliant study of the relationship between literature, ideas and the social
   order in seventeenth-century France.

Leach, E., *Political Systems of Highland Burma*
   Leach's contribution to new ways of thinking about the raw data of social
   anthropology is best demonstrated in this study. Its appeal and interest are far
   wider than the title suggest. I would also recommend a volume of essays he
   edited, *The Structural Study of Myth and Totemism*, in which a number of
   English-speaking social anthropologists examine the contribution of Lévi-
   Strauss to a central problem of the discipline.

Lévi-Strauss, C., *The Elementary Structures of Kinship; Structural Anthropology*
   Until the translations of the three volumes of *Mythologiques* appear, the reader
   who has no French will have to make do with these two books. Either one
   would have been a lifetime's work for a lesser figure, but the full flavour of
   the method only emerges in his truly monumental study of the myths of
   Amerindia.

Needham, R., *Structure and Sentiment*

> An extremely technical and polemical defence of Lévi-Strauss's ideas in *The Elementary Structures of Kinship* that the master himself has rejected. An intellectual tour de force that, despite its difficulty, does make clear what the professionals are fighting about.

Saussure, F. de, *Course in General Linguistics*

> The author and the book that started it all. Over half a century later the ideas are still fresh and the lode far from worked out.

Vygotsky, L. S., *Thought and Language*

> There is an enormous amount of Russian and East European work on and associated with structuralism, most of which is inaccessible. *Thought and Language* deals with two fundamental human phenomena and deserves a wider audience than simply professionals.

A BIBLIOGRAPHY OF STRUCTURALISM

I

Abraham, S. and Kiefer, F. 1965. 'Some remarks on linguistic theory'. *Acta linguistica Academiae scientiarum hungaricae* 15, 3–4

Allard, M., Elzière, M., Gardin, J. C. and Hours, F. 1963. *Analyse conceptuelle du Coran sur cartes perforées* (Vol. I, Code; Vol. II, Commentary) (Mouton & Co., Paris/The Hague)

Apter, D. E. 1966. 'An experiment in structural theory'. *Documento de Trabajo*, No. 18 (Instituto Torcuato di Tella, Centro de Sociologia Comparada, Buenos Aires) (mimeo)

Aron, R. 1962. 'Note sur la structure en science politique'. In Bastide, R. (ed.), 1962

Bach, E. 1965. 'Linguistique structurelle et philosophie des sciences'. *Diogène* 51

Bachelard, G. 1934. *Le Nouvel Esprit scientifique* (Alcan, Paris)

—— 1938. *La Psychanalyse du feu* (Nouvelle Revue Française, Paris. Coll. Psychologie, 7). English trans. *The Psychoanalysis of Fire* by Alan C. M. Ross (Routledge, London, 1964)

—— 1939. *Lautréamont* (José Corti)

—— 1948a. *La Terre et les rêveries de la volonté* (José Corti)

—— 1948b. *La Terre et les rêveries du repos* (José Corti)

—— 1957. *La Poétique de l'espace* (P.U.F., Paris)

—— 1959. *La Poétique de la rêverie* (P.U.F., Paris)

—— 1961. *La Flamme d'une chandelle* (P.U.F., Paris)

Barbut, M. 1966. 'Sur le sens du mot structure en mathématiques'. *Les Temps Modernes*, No. 246

Barthes, R. 1953. *Le Degré zéro de l'écriture* (Seuil, Paris). English trans. *Writing Degree Zero* by A. Lavers and C. Smith (Cape Editions, London, 1967)

—— 1954. *Michelet par lui-même* (Seuil, Paris. Coll. Ecrivains de Toujours, 19)

—— 1957. *Mythologies* (Seuil, Paris)

—— 1961. 'La littérature aujourd'hui'. *Tel Quel*, No. 7, Autumn

—— 1962. 'A propos de deux ouvrages récents de Claude Lévi-Strauss: Sociologie et Socio-Logique'. *Information sur les Sciences Sociales*, Vol. I, No. 4

—— 1963a. *Sur Racine* (Seuil, Paris)

—— 1963b. 'L'activité structuraliste'. *Les Lettres Nouvelles*, No. 32, Feb.

—— 1963c. 'Le message photographique'. *Communications*, No. 1

—— 1963d. 'Criticism as language'. *The Times Literary Supplement*, Sept. 27th

—— 1964a. *Essais critiques* (Seuil, Paris)

Barthes, R. 1964b. *Éléments de sémiologie* (Seuil, Paris. Coll. Communications, 4). English trans. *Elements of Semiology* (Cape Editions, London, 1967)

—— 1964c. 'Rhétorique de l'image'. *Communications*, No. 4

—— 1964d. 'Les sciences humaines et l'œuvre de Lévi-Strauss'. *Annales*, 19th yr, No. 6

—— 1966a. *Critique et vérité* (Seuil, Paris)

—— 1966b. 'Introduction à l'analyse structurale des récits'. *Communications*, No. 8

—— 1967a. *Système de la mode* (Seuil, Paris)

—— 1967b. 'Le discours de l'histoire'. *Social Science Information*, Vol. VI, 4

—— 1967c. 'Science versus literature'. *The Times Literary Supplement*, Sept. 28th

Bastide, R. (ed.). 1962. *Sens et usage du terme 'structure' dans les sciences humaines* (Mouton & Co., The Hague)

—— 1965 (with L.-J. Delpech). 'Théories sociologiques: actionnalisme et structuralisme'. *L'Année Sociologique*, 3rd series

Beneveniste, E. 1946. 'Structure des relations de personnes dans le verbe'. *Bulletin de la Société de Linguistique*

—— 1962. ' "Structure" en linguistique'. In Bastide, R. (ed.), 1962

Bense, M. 1956. 'Information über Strukturen'. In *Aesthetische Information* (Agis Verlag, Baden Baden)

Bersani, L. 1967. 'Criticism, French style'. *Partisan Review*, Spring ·

Blanchot, M. 1949a. *Lautréamont et Sade* (Éditions de Minuit, Paris)

—— 1949b. *Le Part du feu* (Gallimard, Paris)

—— 1955. *L'Espace littéraire* (Gallimard, Paris)

—— 1959. *Le Livre à venir* (Gallimard, Paris)

—— 1962. *L'Attente, l'oubli* (Gallimard, Paris)

Boons, J.-P. 1967. 'L'importance du jugement d'importance dans le langage des sciences sociales'. *Social Science Information*, Vol. VI, 2–3

Boucourechliev, A. 1963. *Beethoven* 'Solfèges' (Seuil, Paris)

Boulez, P. 1963. *Penser la musique aujourd'hui* (Gonthier, Paris)

Bouligand, G. 1958. *Aspects de la mathématisation* (Paris. Conférences du Palais de la Découverte)

Bourdieu, P. 1966. 'Champ intellectuel et projet créateur'. *Les Temps Modernes*, No. 246

Brelet, G. 1965. 'Musique et structure'. *Revue Internationale de Philosophie*, No. 73–4, fasc. 3/4

Bremond, C. 1964. 'Le message narratif'. *Communications*, No. 4

—— 1966a. 'L'analyse conceptuelle du Coran'. *Communications*, No. 7

—— 1966b. 'La logique des possibles narratifs'. *Communications*, No. 8

Brøndal, V. 1943. *Essais de linguistique générale* (Munksgaard, Copenhagen), XII

Burridge, K. O. L. 1967. 'Lévi-Strauss and myth'. In Leach, E. R. (ed.), 1967a

Buyssens, E. 1943. *Les Langages et le discours, essai de linguistique fonctionnelle dans le cadre de la sémiologie* (Office de Publicité, Brussels)

A Bibliography of Structuralism

Carbonnier, J. 1962. 'Les structures en droit privé'. In Bastide, R. (ed.), 1962

Caruso, P. 1965. 'Il crudo e il cotto'. *Automazione e Automatismi*, 88

Castel, R. 1964. 'Méthode structurale et idéologies structuralistes'. *Critique*, Vol. XX, No. 210

Charbonnier, G. 1961. 'Entretiens avec Claude Lévi-Strauss'. *Les Lettres Nouvelles*, No. 10. English trans. by J. and D. Weightman (Cape Editions, London, 1969)

Chatman, S. 1967. 'The semantics of style'. *Social Science Information*, Vol. VI, 4

Cherry, C. 1957. *On Human Communication* (M.I.T. Press, Cambridge, Mass.)

Chomsky, N. 1957. *Syntactic Structures* (Mouton & Co., The Hague)

—— 1964. *Current Issues in Linguistic Theory* (Mouton & Co., The Hague)

—— 1965. *Aspects of the Theory of Syntax* (M.I.T. Press, Cambridge, Mass.)

—— 1966a. *Cartesian Linguistics* (Harper & Row, New York)

—— 1966b. *Topics in the Theory of Generative Grammar* (Mouton & Co., The Hague)

—— 1968a (with M. Halle). *The Sound Pattern of English* (Harper & Row, New York)

—— 1968b. *Language and Mind* (Harcourt Brace & World, New York)

Cluny, C.-M. 1964. 'Qui a peur de Jean Racine?' *La Nouvelle Revue Française*, 12, No. 134

Cohen, M. 1958. 'Linguistique moderne et idéalisme'. *Recherches Internationales*, No. 7, May

Concept d'information dans la science contemporaine. 1965. (Éditions de Minuit, Paris)

Courtenay, B. de. 1895. *Versuch einer Theorie Alternationen* (Strasbourg)

Cuisenir, J. 1963. 'Formes de la parenté et formes de la pensée'. *L'Esprit*, No. 322, Nov.

Dagognet, F. 1965. *Gaston Bachelard* (Sa vie, son œuvre, avec un exposé de sa philosophie) (P.U.F., Paris)

Dalcq, A. 'Structure germinale et morphogenèse animale'. *Revue Internationale de Philosophie*, No. 73-4, fasc. 3/4

Damisch, H. 1963. 'L'horizon ethnologique'. *Les Lettres Nouvelles*, No. 32, Feb.

Davie, D. *et al.* (eds.). 1961. *Poetics*, Vol. I (Mouton & Co., The Hague)

Deliege, C. 1965. 'La musicologie devant le structuralisme'. *L'Arc*, 26

Derrida, J. 1967. *L'écriture et la différence* (Seuil, Paris)

—— 1968. *De la grammatologie* (Éditions de Minuit, Paris)

Dorfles, G. 1962. *Simbola comunicazione consumo* (Einaudi, Turin)

—— 1965. 'Pour ou contre une esthétique structuraliste?' *Revue Internationale de Philosophie*, No. 73-4, fasc. 3/4

Doroszewski, W. 1930. 'Langue et parole'. *Odbitka z Prac Fílogisznych*, XLV (Warsaw)

Doubrovsky, S. 1966. *Pourquoi la nouvelle critique* (Mercure de France)

Douglas, M. 1967. 'The meaning of myth, with special reference to "La Geste d'Asdiwal" '. In Leach, E. R. (ed.), 1967a

Dubois, J. 1965. *Grammaire structurale du français* (Larousse, Paris)

—— 1967. 'Pourquoi des dictionnaires?' *Social Science Information*, Vol. VI, 4

Dumazedier, J. 1964. 'Structures lexicales et significations complexes'. *Revue Française de Sociologie*, 5, 1

Dumézil, G. 1940. *Mitra varuna: essai sur deux représentations Indo-Européennes de la souveraineté* (Paris, Bibliothèque de l'École des Hautes Études: Sciences Religieuses, Vol. 56)

Durand, G. 1960. *Les Structures anthropologiques de l'imaginaire* (P.U.F., Paris)

Ebeling, L. 1960. *Linguistic units* (Mouton & Co., The Hague)

Eco, U. 1964a. 'Lettura di "Steve Canyon" '. In *Apocalittici e integrati* (Bompiani, Milan)

—— 1964b. 'Il mito di superman'. In *Apocalittici e integrati* (Bompiani, Milan)

—— 1966. 'James Bond: une combinatoire narratif'. *Communications*, No. 8

—— 1967. 'Sociology and the novel'. *The Times Literary Supplement*, Sept. 28th

Ehrmann, J. 1966. 'Les structures de l'échange dans "Cinna" '. *Les Temps Modernes*, No. 246. English trans. in *Yale French Review*, Vol. 36–7, 1966

Erlich, V. 1955. *Russian formalism* (Mouton & Co., The Hague)

Études phonologiques dédiées à la mémoire de M. le Prince N. S. Trubetzkoy. 1964. (Univ. of Alabama Press)

Explorations in cultural anthropology (Essays in honour of George Peter Murdock). 1964. (McGraw-Hill, New York)

Faye, J.-P. 1964. *Analogues* (Seuil, Paris. Coll. Tei Quel)

—— 1967. *Le Récit hunique* (Seuil, Paris)

Fodor, J. A. and Katz, J. J. (eds.). 1964. *The Structure of Language: Readings in the Philosophy of Language* (Prentice Hall, New Jersey)

For Roman Jakobson on the Occasion of his Sixtieth Birthday. 1956. (Mouton & Co., The Hague)

Forge, A. 1967. 'Lévi-Strauss'. *New Society*, Nov. 2nd

Fox, R. 1967. '*Totem and Taboo* reconsidered'. In Leach, E. R. (ed.), 1967a

Foucault, M. 1961. *Histoire de la folie à l'âge classique* (Plon, Paris)

—— 1963a. *Raymond Roussel* (Gallimard, Paris. Coll. Le Chemin)

—— 1963b. *Naissance de la clinique* (P.U.F., Paris)

—— 1963c. 'Le langage à l'infini'. *Tel Quel*, No. 15, Autumn

—— 1966. *Les Mots et les choses* (Gallimard, Paris)

Francastel, P. 1962. 'Note sur l'emploi du mot "structure" en l'histoire de l'art'. In Bastide, R. (ed.), 1962.

—— 1965a. *La Réalité figurative, éléments structurels de sociologie de l'art* (Gonthier, Paris)

—— 1965b. 'Art, forme, structure'. *Revue Internationale de Philosophie*, No. 73–4, fasc. 3/4

Friedmann, G. 1966. 'Une rhétorique des symboles'. *Communications*, No. 7

Furtado, C. 1965. 'Développement et stagnation en Amérique Latine: une approche structuraliste'. *Annales*, No. 3

Gaboriau, M. 1963. 'Anthropologie structurale et histoire'. *L'Esprit*, No. 322, Nov.

Gandillac, M. de, Goldmann, L. and Piaget, J. 1965. *Entretiens sur les notions de genèse et de structure* (Mouton & Co., Paris/The Hague)

Geertz, C. 1967. 'The cerebral savage'. *Encounter*, April

Genette, G. 1963. 'Réponse à une enquête sur la critique'. *Tel Quel*, No. 14, Summer

—— 1965a. 'L'homme et les signes'. *Critique*, 16, No. 2

—— 1965b. 'Structuralisme et critique littéraire'. *L'Arc*, 26

—— 1966a. *Figures* (Seuil, Paris. Coll. Tel Quel)

—— 1966b. 'Enseignement et rhétorique au XXe siècle'. *Annales*, March–April

—— 1966c. 'Frontières du récit'. *Communications*, No. 8

Glucksmann, A. 1965. 'La déduction de la cuisine et les cuisines de la déduction'. *Information sur les Sciences Sociales*, Vol. IV, 2

Goddard, D. 1965. 'Conceptions of structure in Lévi-Strauss in British anthropology'. *Social Research*, 32, No. 4

Godel, R. 1957. *Les sources manuscrites du cours de linguistique générale de F. de Saussure* (Droz, Geneva; Minard, Paris)

Godelier, M. 1966. 'Système, structure et contradiction dans "Le Capital"'. *Les Temps Modernes*, No. 246

Goldman, M. 1962. 'Le concept de structure significative en histoire de la culture'. In Bastide, R. (ed.), 1962

Goldmann, L. 1955. *Le Dieu caché* (Gallimard, Paris)

—— 1959. *Recherches dialectique* (Gallimard, Paris)

—— 1964. *Pour une sociologie du roman* (Gallimard, Paris)

—— 1966. *Sciences humaines et philosophie* (Gonthier, Paris)

—— 1967a. 'Entretien sur le structuralisme'. *L'Homme et la Société*, Jan.

—— 1967b. 'Ideology and writing'. *The Times Literary Supplement*, Sept. 28th

Gorny, W. 1961. 'Text structure against the background of language structure'. In Davie, D. *et al.* (eds.), 1961

Granger, G. 1957. 'Événement et structure dans les sciences de l'homme'. *Cahiers de l'Institut de science économique appliquée*, No. 55, May

—— 1960. *Pensée formelle et sciences de l'homme*, ed. Montaigne (Aubier, Paris)

—— 1965. 'Objets, structures et significations'. *Revue Internationale de Philosophie*, No. 73–4, fasc. 3/4

Greene, J. C. 1967. 'Les Mots et les Choses'. *Social Science Information*, Vol. VI, 4

Greimas, A. J. 1964. 'La structure élémentaire de la signification en linguistique'. *L'Homme*, IV, 3

—— 1966a. *Sémantique structurale* (Larousse, Paris)

—— 1966b. 'Éléments pour une théorie de l'interprétation du récit mythique'. *Communications*, No. 8

—— 1966c. 'Structure et histoire'. *Les Temps Modernes*, No. 246

Greimas, A. J. 1966d. Introduction to *Le Langage, une introduction* by L. Hjelmslev (Éditions de Minuit, Paris)

Gritti, J. 1966. 'Un récit de presse: les derniers jours d'un "grand homme"'. *Communications*, No. 8

—— 1967. 'Le centre d'études des communications de masse'. *Annales*, Sept.–Oct.

Guaraldi, A. 1965. 'Per une surrealisme logico'. *Revue Internationale de Philosophie*, No. 73–4, fasc. 3/4

Guirand, P. 1963. 'Structure aléatoire de la double articulation'. *Bulletin de la Société Linguistique de Paris*, 58, fasc. 1

Guyonnet, J. 1963. 'Structures et communication'. In *La Musique et ses problèmes contemporains, Cahiers Renaud-Barrault*, No. 41, Dec.

Harris, Z. S. 1951. *Methods in Structural Linguistics* (Univ. of Chicago Press)

Hartman, G. 1966. 'Structuralism: The Anglo-American adventure'. *Yale French Review*, Vol. 36–7

Hjelmslev, L. 1953. *Prolegomena to a theory of Language*. Indiana Univ. Publications in Anthropology and Linguistics, Memoir 7 (Waverly Press, Baltimore)

—— 1959. *Essais linguistiques* (Nordisk Sprog -og Kulturforlag, Copenhagen)

—— 1966. *Le Langage, une introduction* (Éditions de Minuit, Paris)

Hoijer, H. (ed.). 1963. *Language in Culture* (Univ. of Chicago Press)

Horalek, K. 1965. 'Sprachfunktion und funktionelle Stilistik' (Linguistic function and functional stylistics). *Linguistics*, 14

Hrusovsky, J. 1965. 'Struktura a dialektika' (Structure and dialectic). *Filosoficky Casopis*, 20, No. 2

Ingarden, R. 1961. 'Poetics and linguistics'. In Davie, D. *et al.* (eds.), 1961

Ivanov, V. V. and Toporov, V. N. 1965. *Slavjanskie jazykovye modelirujuscie semioticeskie sistemy* (The semiotic systems shaping the Slavs) (Izd. Nauka, Moscow)

Jakobson, R. 1948 (with Gregoire, H. and Szeflel, M.). *La geste du Prince Igor*. Annuaire de l'Institute de Philologie et d'Histoire Orientales et Slaves, University Library of Brussels, VIII, New York

—— 1956 (with M. Halle). *Fundamentals of Language* (Mouton & Co., The Hague)

—— 1961. 'Poetry of Grammar and grammar of Poetry'. In Davie, D. *et al.* (eds.), 1961

—— 1962 (with C. Lévi-Strauss). ' "Les Chats" de Charles Baudelaire'. *L'Homme*, 2

—— 1963. *Essais de linguistique générale* (Éditions de Minuit, Paris)

—— 1966a (with others). *Poetics*, Vol. II (Mouton & Co., The Hague)

—— 1966b (with J. Tynyanov). 'Problems of literary and linguistic studies'. *New Left Review*, No. 37

—— 1967. *Selected Writings* (Vol. I, Phonological Studies; Vol. II, Slav Epic Studies) (Mouton & Co., The Hague)

Kanters, R. 1966. 'La querelle des critiques'. *La Revue de Paris*, Jan.

Krausova, N. 1965. 'Rozpravac v proze' (Problems of prose). *Slovenska Literatura,* 12, No. 2

Lacan, J. 1966a. *Écrits* (Seuil, Paris)

—— 1966b. 'The insistence of the letter in the unconscious'. *Yale French Review,* Vol. 36-7

Lagache, D. 1962a. 'Structure en psychologie'. In Bastide, R. (ed.), 1962

—— 1962b. 'Structure en psychopathologie'. Ibid.

—— 1962c. 'Structure en psychanalyse'. Ibid.

Lanteri-Laurap, G. 1967. 'Histoire et structure dans la connaissance de l'homme'. *Annales,* July-Aug.

Laplanche, J. and Leclaire, S. 1961. 'L'inconscient'. *Les Temps Modernes,* No. 183

Leach, E. R. 1954. *Political Systems of Highland Burma* (Bell & Sons, London, for L.S.E.)

—— 1958. 'Magical hair'. *Journal of the Royal Anthropological Institute,* No. 88, pt. II

—— 1961a. *Rethinking Anthropology* (Athlone Press, London)

—— 1961b. *Pul Eliya: a Village in Ceylon* (Cambridge Univ. Press, London)

—— 1961c. 'Lévi-Strauss in the Garden of Eden: An examination of some recent developments in the analysis of myth'. Transactions of the New York Academy of Sciences, Series 2

—— 1962. 'Genesis as myth'. *Discovery,* May

—— 1964a. 'Anthropological aspects of language: animal categories and verbal abuse'. In E. H. Lenneberg (ed.), *New Directions in the Study of Language* (M.I.T. Press, Cambridge, Mass.)

—— 1964b. 'Telstar et les aborigènes ou *La Pensée sauvage'. Annales,* Nov.-Dec.

—— 1965. 'Claude Lévi-Strauss: Anthropologist and philosopher'. *New Left Review,* No. 34

—— 1966. 'The legitimacy of Solomon: Some structural aspects of Old Testament History'. *European Journal of Sociology,* 7

—— 1967a. (ed.) *The Structural Study of Myth and Totemism* (Tavistock, London)

—— 1967b. 'Brain-twister'. *New York Review of Books,* Vol. IX, No. 6

Lefebvre, H. 1962. 'Le concept de structure chez Marx'. In Bastide, R. (ed.), 1962

—— 1963. 'Réflexions sur le structuralisme et l'histoire'. *Cahiers internationales de Sociologie,* XXXV

—— 1965. *Métaphilosophie. Prolégomes* (Éditions de Minuit, Paris, Coll. Arguments, 26)

—— 1966. *Le Langage et la société* (Gallimard, Paris)

—— 1967. 'Claude Lévi-Strauss et le nouvel éléatisme'. *L'Homme et la Société,* Jan.

Lepschy, G. 1966. *La Linguistica Struturale* (Einaudi, Turin)

Lesage, L. 1967. *The New French Criticism* (Pennsylvania State Univ. Press)

Leska, O. and Novak, P. 1965. 'K voprosu o strukturnom analize jazyka' (On the problem of the structural analysis of language). *Slovo a Slovesnost,* 26, No. 2

Lévi-Strauss, C. 1945. 'L'analyse structurale en linguistique et en anthropologie'. *Word, Journal of the Linguistic Circle of New York*, No. 1

—— 1947. 'Le serpent au corps rempli de poissons'. Actes du XXVIIIe Congrès International des Américanistes

—— 1948. *La Vie familiale et sociale des Indiens Nambikwara*. Société des Américanistes (Paris)

—— 1949a. *Les Structures élémentaires de la parenté* (P.U.F., Paris)

—— 1949b. 'Le sorcier et sa magie'. *Les Temps Modernes*, No. 41

—— 1949c. 'L'efficacité symbolique'. *Revue de l'Histoire des Religions*, No. 85

—— 1949d. 'Histoire et ethnologie'. *Revue de Metaphysique et de Morale*, 54th yr.

—— 1950. Introduction à l'œuvre de Marcel Mauss, in *Sociologie et anthropologie* by Marcel Mauss (P.U.F., Paris)

—— 1951. 'Language and the analysis of social laws'. *American Anthropology*, 53, No. 2

—— 1952a. *Race et histoire*. UNESCO. English trans., *Race and History* (UNESCO, 1952)

—— 1952b. 'Towards a general theory of communication'. Paper submitted to the International Conferences of Linguists and Anthropologists, Univ. of Indiana

—— 1953. 'Social Structure'. In A. L. Kroeber (ed.), *Anthropology Today* (Univ. of Chicago Press)

—— 1955a. *Tristes tropiques* (Plon, Paris). English trans. – minus several chapters – by J. Russell, published as *World on the Wane* (Hutchinson, London, 1961)

—— 1955b. 'Les mathématiques de l'homme'. *Bulletin International des Sciences Sociales*, No. 4

—— 1955c. 'The Structural study of myth'. *Journal of American Folklore*, 68

—— 1955d. 'Diogène couché'. *Les Temps Modernes*, No. 110

—— 1956a. 'The family'. In H. L. Shapiro (ed.), *Man, Culture and Society* (Oxford University Press, London)

—— 1956b. 'Les organisations dualistes existent-elles?' *Bijdragen tot de Taal- Land- en Volkenkunde*, 112

—— 1956c. 'Structure et dialectique'. In *For Roman Jakobson* (Mouton & Co., The Hague)

—— 1957. 'Le symbolisme cosmique dans la structure sociale et l'organisation cérémonielle des tribes américaines'. *Série Orientale Roma*, No. 14

—— 1958a. *Anthropologie structurale* (Plon, Paris). English trans. by C. Jacobson and B. Grundfest Schoepf, *Structural Anthropology* (Basic Books, New York, 1963; The Penguin Press, London, 1968)

—— 1958b. 'Le dualisme dans l'organisation sociale et les représentations religieuses'. In Annuaire de l'École Pratique des Hautes Études (Sciences religieuses)

—— 1960a. *La Geste d'asdiwal*. In Annuaire de l'École Pratique des Hautes Études (Sciences religieuses, 1958–9)

—— 1960b. 'Four Winnebago myths. A structural sketch'. In S. Diamond (ed.), *Culture in History* (Univ. of Columbia Press, New York)

—— 1960c. 'La structure et la forme: Réflexions sur un ouvrage de Vladimir Propp'. *Cahiers de l'Institut de Science Économique Appliquée*, No. 99, March. Série M. No. 7

—— 1960d. 'L'anthropologie sociale devant l'histoire'. *Annales*, July–Aug.

—— 1960e. 'Leçon Inaugurale'. English trans., *The Scope of Anthropology* (Cape Editions, London, 1967)

—— 1961 (with G. Charbonnier). *Entretiens avec Claude Lévi-Strauss*. English trans. by J. and D. Weightman (Cape Editions, London, 1969)

—— 1962a. *La Pensée sauvage* (Plon, Paris). English trans., *The Savage Mind* (Weidenfeld & Nicolson, London, 1967)

—— 1962b. *Le Totemisme aujourd'hui* (P.U.F., Paris). English trans. by R. Needham, *Totemism* (Beason Press, Boston, 1963; Merlin Press, London, 1964)

—— 1962c. 'Les limites de la notion de structure en ethnologie'. In Bastide, R. (ed.), 1962

—— 1962d. 'Jean-Jacques Rousseau, fondateur des sciences de l'homme'. In *Jean-Jacques Rousseau* (Neufchatel)

—— 1962e. 'Comptes rendus divers'. *L'Homme*, Vol. 2

—— 1963a. 'The bear and the barber'. *Journal of the Royal Anthropological Institute*, No. 93, Part I

—— 1963b. 'Réponses à quelques questions'. *L'Esprit*, No. 322, Nov.

—— 1964. *Mythologiques: le cru et le cuit* (Plon, Paris). English trans., *The Raw and the Cooked* (Harper & Row, New York, 1970).

—— 1965. 'Riposte a un questionario sullo strutturalismo'. *Paragone*, 16 (182)

—— 1966a. *Mythologiques: du miel aux cendres* (Plon, Paris)

—— 1966b. 'Anthropology: Its achievements and future'. *Current Anthropology*, Vol. VII, No. 2

—— 1966c. 'The Culinary Triangle'. *Partisan Review*, Vol. XXXIII

—— 1967. 'A contre-courant'. *Le Nouvel Observateur*, No. 115

—— 1968a. 'La grande aventure de l'ethnologie'. *Le Nouvel Observateur*, No. 166

—— 1968b. *Mythologiques: l'origine des manières de table* (Plon, Paris, 1968). (N.B. For a Bibliography of the published works of Claude Lévi-Strauss, 1936–64, see *Current Anthropology*, Vol. VII, No. 2)

Lewis, P. E. 1966. 'Merleau-Ponty and the phenomenology of language'. *Yale French Review*, Vol. 36–7

Lotman, J. 1964a. *Lekcii po struktural'noj poetike* (Lecture on structuralist poetics) (Trudy po znakovym sistemam I). Tartu, Transactions of the Tartu State University

—— 1964b. 'Sur la délimitation linguistique et littéraire de la notion de structure'. *Linguistics*, No. 6

Lotman, J. 1967. 'Problèmes de la typologie des cultures'. *Social Science Information*, Vol. VI, No. 2–3

Lounsbury, F. G. 1964. 'The structural analysis of kinship semantics'. In H. G. Lunt (ed.), *Proceedings* of the IXth International Congress of Linguistics (Mouton & Co., The Hague)

Lyotard, J. F. 1965. 'Les indiens ne cueillent pas les fleurs: À propos de Lévi-Strauss'. *Annales*, 20 (1)

Macherey, P. 1966. 'L'analyse littéraire, tombeau des structures'. *Les Temps Modernes*, No. 246

Marchal, A. 1962. 'L'attitude structuraliste et le concept de structure en économie politique'. In Bastide, R. (ed.), 1962

Martinet, A. 1960. *Éléments de linguistique générale* (Armand Colin, Paris). English trans. by E. Palmer (Faber, London, 1964)

—— 1962. *A Functional View of Language* (Clarendon Press, Oxford)

—— 1965. 'Structure et langue'. *Revue Internationale de Philosophie*, No. 73–4, fasc. 3/4. Reprinted in English in *Yale French Review*, Vol. 36–7, 1966

Materna, P. 1965. *Operative auffassung der methode, ein beitrag zur strukturellen Methodologie* (The operative conception of the method, a contribution to structural methodology) (N.C.A.V., Prague)

Mathiot, A. 1962. 'Le mot "structure" en droit public'. In Bastide, R. (ed.), 1962

Mauron, C. 1950. *L'introduction à la psychanalyse de Mallarmé* (Neufchatel). English trans. published by Univ. of Calif. Press and Cambridge Univ. Press

—— 1957. *L'inconscient dans l'œuvre et la vie de Racine* (Ophrys, Gap)

—— 1963. *Des métaphores obsédantes au mythe personnel* (José Corti)

—— 1964a. *Psychocritique du genre comique* (José Corti)

—— 1964b. *Mallarmé par lui-même* (Seuil, Paris)

—— 1966. *Le dernier Baudelaire* (José Corti)

Mayenowa, M. R. 1967. 'Semiotics today: reflections on the 2nd International Conference on Semiotics'. *Social Science Information*, Vol. VI, No. 2–3

Mendelson, E. M. 1967. 'The "Uninvited Guest": Ancilla to Lévi-Strauss on Totemism and Primitive thought'. In Leach, E. R. (ed.), 1967a

Metz, C. 1964. 'Le cinéma: langue ou langage?' *Communications*, No. 4

—— 1966a. 'Les sémiotiques ou sémies'. *Communications*, No. 7

—— 1966b. 'La grande syntagmatique du film narratif'. *Communications*, No. 8

Miel, J. 1966. 'Jacques Lacan and the structure of the unconscious'. *Yale French Review*, Vol. 36–7

Miller, J. H. 1966. 'The Geneva School'. *Critical Quarterly*, Vol. 8, 4

Moles, A. 1961. 'The analysis of structures of the poetic message at different levels of sensibility'. In Davie, D. *et al.* (eds.), 1961

Moraze, M. 1962. 'Structures temporelles'. In Bastide, R. (ed.), 1962

Morin, V. 1963 (with J. Majault). *Un mythe moderne: l'érotisme* (Castermann, Paris)

—— 1966. 'L'histoire drôle'. *Communications*, No. 8

Morris, C. W. 1938. 'Foundations of the theory of signs'. In O. Neurath, R. Carnap and C. W. Morris (eds.), *International Encyclopedia of Unified Science* (Univ. of Chicago Press)

—— 1946. *Signs, Language and Behaviour* (Prentice-Hall, New Jersey)

—— 1964. *Signification and Significance, a Study of the Relations of Signs and Values* (M.I.T. Press, Cambridge, Mass.)

Mouloud, N. 1965a. 'Réflexions sur le problème des structures'. *Revue Philosophique de la France et de l'étranger*, Jan.–Mar.

—— 1965b. 'La logique des structures et l'épistémologie'. *Revue Internationale de Philosophie*, No. 73–4, fasc. 3/4

Mounin, G. 1962. 'Les analyses sémantiques'. *Cahiers de l'Isea*, suppl. no. 113, Mar., series M, No. 13

—— 1963. *Les problèmes théoriques de la traduction* (Gallimard, Paris)

—— 1965. 'Les structurations sémantiques'. *Diogène*, 49

Mrazek, R. 1965. 'K metodologii strukturniho popisu syntaxe rustiny' (Methodological questions in the structural description of Russian syntax). *Československa rusistika*, 10, No. 3

Mukarovsky, J. 1948. 'Strukturalismus v estetice ave vede o literature'. *Kapitoly z české poetiky* dil I: Obecne veci basnictvi 20, Nakladatelstvi Svodada, Prague

Murphy, R. F. 1963. 'On Zen Marxism: filiation and alliance'. *Man*, Feb.

Needham, R. 1962. *Structure and Sentiment* (Univ. of Chicago Press)

—— 1967. Review of *The Savage Mind*. *Man*, Vol. II, No. 2

Nettl, P. 1966. 'Lévi-Strauss'. *New Statesman*, 72, Dec. 9th

Nodelman, S. 1966. 'Structural analysis in art and anthropology'. *Yale French Review*, Vol. 36–7.

Notion de structure et structure de la connaissance. Centre International de Synthèse, Paris. Semaine de Synthèse, 20, Apr. 18th–27th, 1957 (Michel, Paris)

Nutini, H. G. 1965. 'Some considerations on the nature of social structure and model building'. *American Anthropologist*, 67, No. 3

Ortigues, R. 1962. *Le Discours et le symbole* (Aubier, Paris)

—— 1964. 'Nature et culture dans l'œuvre de Claude Lévi-Strauss'. *Critique*, 19, 189

Paci, E. 1965a. 'Il senso delle strutture in Lévi-Strauss' (The meaning of structure in Lévi-Strauss). *Revue Internationale de Philosophie*, No. 73–4, fasc. 3/4

—— 1965b. 'Anthropologia strutturale e fenomenologie'. *Automazione e Automatismi*, 88

Pages, R. 1962. 'Le vocable "structure" et la psychologie sociale'. In Bastide, R. (ed.), 1962

Papp, E. 1964. 'Mathematische und strukturelle Methoden in der sowjetischen Sprachwissenschaft' (Mathematical and structural methods in Soviet linguistics). *Acta linguistica Academiae scientiarum hungaricae*, 14, No. 1–2

Perroux, F. 1962. 'Structures économiques'. In Bastide, R. (ed.), 1962

Piaget, J. 1968. *Le Structuralisme* (P.U.F., Paris). English trans., *Structuralism* (Basic Books, New York, 1970).

Picard, R. 1965. *Nouvelle critique ou nouvelle imposture?* (Pauvert, Paris)

—— 1966. 'Un nihilisme confortable'. *Le Nouvel Observateur*, No. 74

Piguet, J.-C. 1965. 'Les conflits de l'analyse et de la dialectique'. *Annales*, No. 3

Pividal, R. 1964. 'Signification et position de l'œuvre de Lévi-Strauss'. *Annales*, Nov.–Dec.

—— 1965. 'Peut-on acclimater *La Pensée sauvage?*' *Annales*, No. 3

Planck, M. 1963. *L'image du monde dans la physique moderne* (Gonthier, Paris)

Poetics. Poetyka. Poetika. 1961 (Mouton & Co., The Hague)

Pontalis, J.-B. 1967. 'Les mots du psychanalyste'. *Social Science Information*, Vol. VI, 2–3

Poole, R. C. 1966. 'Indirect communication. 2. Merleau-Ponty and Lévi-Strauss'. *New Blackfriars*, 47, Aug.

Postal, P. 1964. 'Underlying and superficial linguistic structure'. *Harvard Educational Review*, 34, No. 2

Pouillon, J. 1966. '(Structuralisme) Présentation: un essai de définition'. *Les Temps Modernes*, No. 246

Poulet, G. 1961. *Les Métamorphoses du cercle* (Plon, Paris)

—— 1963. *L'espace proustien* (Gallimard, Paris)

—— 1964. *Études sur le temps humain*. Vol. III (Plon, Paris)

—— 1967. *Trois essais de mythologie* (José Corti)

Prigogine, I. 1965. 'Quelques remarques sur la structure de la physique'. *Revue Internationale de Philosophie*, No. 73–4, fasc. 3/4

Propp, V. 1958. 'Morphology of the Folk Tale' (English trans. from the Russian). Part II. *International Journal of American Linguistics*, 24: 4

Renzi, E. 1965. 'Sulla nozione di inconscio in Lévi-Strauss'. *Automazione e Automatismi*, 88

Revzin, I. I. 1965. 'O celjax strukturnogo izucenija hudozestvennogo tvorcestva' (The goals of a structural study of literary works). *Voprosy Literatury*, 6, No. 6

Reznikov, L. O. 1964. *Gnoseologiceskie Voprosy Semiotiki* (The epistemological problems of semiotics) (Izd. LGU, Leningrad)

Rice, F. and Guss, A. (eds.). 1965. *Information Sources in Linguistics: a Bibliographical Handbook* (Center of Applied Linguistics, Washington, D.C.)

Richard, J.-P. 1955. *Poésie et profondeur* (Seuil, Paris)

—— 1962. *L'univers imaginaire de Mallarmé* (Seuil, Paris)

—— 1963. 'Quelques aspects nouveaux de la critique littéraire en France'. *Le Français dans le Monde*, March

—— 1964. *Onze études sur la poésie moderne* (Seuil, Paris)

—— 1967. *Paysage de Chateaubriand* (Seuil, Paris)

Ricœur, P. 1963. 'Structure et herméneutique'. *L'Esprit*, No. 322, Nov.

—— 1964. 'Le symbolisme et l'explication structurale'. *Cahiers Internationaux de Symbolisme*, 4

Riffaterre, M. 1966. 'Describing poetic structures: Two approaches to Baudelaire's "Les Chats"'. *Yale French Review*, Vol. 36-7

Rigby, P. 1967. 'The structural context of girls' puberty rites'. *Man*, Vol. II, 3

Rippere, V. L. 1966. 'Towards an anthropology of literature'. *Yale French Review*, Vol. 36-7

Rosiello, L. 1965. *Struttura, uso e funzioni della lingua* (Structure, usage and functions of language) (Vallecchi, Florence)

Rossi, A. 1964. 'Strutturalismo e analisi letteraria' (Structuralism and literary analysis). *Paragone*, 15: 180

Ruwet, N. 1963a. 'Linguistique et sciences de l'homme'. *L'Esprit*, No. 322, Nov.
—— 1963b. 'L'analyse structurale de la poésie'. *Linguistics*, 2

Saussure, F. de. 1879. *Mémoire sur le système primitif des voyelles dans les langues Indo-Européennes* (Leipzig)
—— 1916. *Cours de linguistique générale*. 1st edition published posthumously; 4th edn. 1949 (Payot, Paris). English trans. by W. Baskin, 1960 (New York, Philosophical Library; Peter Owen, London)

Scheffler, H. W. 1966. 'Structuralism in anthropology'. *Yale French Review*, Vol. 36-7

Scheflen, A. E. 1967. 'Psychoanalytic terms and some problems of semiotics'. *Social Science Information*, Vol. VI, 4

Sebag, L. 1964. *Marxisme et structuralisme* (Payot, Paris)
—— 1965. 'Le myth, code et message'. *Les Temps Modernes*, 226

Sebeok, T. A. 1953. 'The structure and content of Cheremis Charms'. *Anthropos*, 48
—— 1966. (ed.) *Current trends in linguistics*, Vol. III, Theoretical Foundations. (Mouton & Co., The Hague)

Segal, D. 1966. 'The semantics of a text and its formal structure'. In Jakobson, R. *et al.* (eds.), 1966a

Seglov, J. K. 1964. 'Pour la construction d'un modèle structural des nouvelles de Sherlock Holmes'. *Marcatre*, 8–9–10

Segre, C. (ed.). 1965. 'Strutturalismo e critica'. In *Catalogo Generale del Saggiatore* (1958/65) (Saggiatore, Milan)

Simpozium po strukturnomo Izucheni Ju Zuakovyh sistem. 1962. Academy of Science of the USSR, Moscow

Sommerfelt, A. 1965. 'Structures linguistiques et structures des groupes sociaux'. *Diogène*, 51

Starobinski, J. 1964. *L'invention de la liberté 1700-1789* (Skira, Geneva)
—— 1965. 'Les directions nouvelles de la recherche critique'. *Preuves*, June

Steiner, G. 1966. 'A conversation with Claude Lévi-Strauss'. *Encounter*, 26, April

Stender-Petersen, A. 1949. 'Esquisse d'une théorie structurale de la littérature'. *Recherches Structurales*, TCLC, 5, Copenhagen

Stepankova, J. 1965. 'Geneticky strukturalismus v sociologii literatury: nad knihou L. Goldmanna *za sociologii romanu*' (Genetic structuralism in the sociology of literature: on Goldmann's *Pour une sociologie du roman*). *Česka Literature*, 13, No. 3

Tarn, N. 1967. 'Pansies for thoughts: reflections on the work of Claude Lévi-Strauss'. *Listener*, 77, May 11th

Thompson, J. 1961. 'Linguistic structure and the Poetic line'. In Davie, D. *et al.* (eds.), 1961

Todorov, T. 1964. 'La description de la signification en littérature'. *Communications*, No. 4

—— 1965a. 'L'héritage méthodologique du formalisme'. *L'Homme*, 5, 1

—— 1965b. 'Note sur les théories stylistiques de V. V. Vinogradov'. *Annales*, No. 3

—— 1965c. 'Procédés mathématiques dans les études littéraires'. *Annales*, No. 3

—— 1966a. (ed.) *Théorie de la littérature* (Textes des formalistes russes réunis et présentés par Todorov) (Seuil, Paris)

—— 1966b. 'Perspectives sémiologiques'. *Communications*, No. 7

—— 1966c. 'Les catégories du récit littéraire'. *Communications*, No. 8

—— 1967a. 'Le structuralisme dans les revues'. *Social Science Information*, VI, 4

—— 1967b. 'De la sémiologie à la rhétorique'. *Annales*, No. 6, Nov.–Dec.

—— 1967c. *Littérature et signification* (Larousse, Paris)

Trubetzkoy, N. S. 1957. *Principes de phonologie* (trans. by Cantineau, J.) (Klincksiek, Paris)

Turnell, M. 1966. 'Criticism of Roland Barthes'. *Encounter*, Feb.

Vachek, J. (ed.). 1964. *A Prague School Reader in Linguistics* (Indiana Univ. Press)

Venclova, T. 1967. 'Le colloque sémiotique de Tartu'. *Social Science Information*, VI, 4

Verguin, J. 1967. *Essai d'analyse fonctionnelle et structurale* (Mouton, Paris)

Verstraeten, P. 1963. 'Lévi-Strauss ou la tentation du néant'. *Les Temps Modernes*, pt. I, No. 206; pt. II, No. 207–8

—— 1964. *Esquisse pour une critique de la raison structuraliste* (doctoral dissertation) (University of Brussels)

Viet, J. 1965. *Les méthodes structuralistes dans les sciences sociales* (Mouton, Paris)

Vilar, P. 1962. 'La notion de structure en histoire'. In Bastide, R. (ed.), 1962

Vogt, E. Z. 1965. 'Structural and conceptual replication in Zinacantan culture'. *American Anthropologist*, 67, No. 2

Von Neumann, J. 1958. *The Computer and the Brain* (Yale Univ. Press)

Vygotsky, L. S. 1962. *Thought and Language*, edited and trans. by E. Hanfmann and G. Vankar (M.I.T. Press, Cambridge, Mass.)

Wachtel, N. 1966. 'Structuralisme et histoire: À propos de l'organisation sociale de Cuzco'. *Annales*, No. 1, Jan.–Feb.

Warnock, M. 1966. 'Anthropological omnivore'. *New Society*, Oct. 13th

Weber, J.-P. 1958. *La Psychologie de l'art* (P.U.F., Paris)

—— 1960. *Genèse de l'œuvre poétique* (Gallimard, Paris)

—— 1963. *Domaines thématiques* (Gallimard, Paris)

—— 1966. *Néo-critique et paléo-critique, ou contra Picard* (Pauvert, Paris)

Weiller, J. 1962. 'Les préférences de structure'. In Bastide, R. (ed.), 1962

West, F. 1968. 'Semiology and the Cinema'. Paper for discussion at B.F.I. Education Dept. seminar on 18.1.68 (mimeo)

Wierzbicka, A. 1965. 'Rosyjska szkola poetyki lingwistycznej a jezykoznawstwo strukturalne'. *Pamietnik Literacki*, 56, No. 2

Willis, R. G. 1967. 'The head and the loins: Lévi-Strauss and beyond'. *Man*, II, 4

Wold, H. and Jureen, L. 1953. 'Structural systems'. In *Demand Analysis* (Wiley, 1953)

Wolff, E. 1962. 'Le sens et l'emploi du mot "structure" en biologie'. In Bastide, R. (ed.), 1962

Worsley, P. 1967. 'Groote Eylandt Totemism and *Le Totemisme aujourd'hui*'. In Leach, E. R. (ed.), 1967a

Yaiman, N. 1967. 'The Raw: the Cooked: : Nature: Culture'. In Leach, E. R. (ed.), 1967a

Zeraffa, M. 1964. 'Aspects structuraux de l'absurde dans la littérature contemporaine'. *Journal de Psychologie normale et pathologique*, Oct.–Dec.

II. RELATED WORKS

Berger, P. and Pullberg, S. 1966. 'The concept of reification'. *New Left Review*, No. 35

Bloomfield, L. 1957. *Language* (Allen & Unwin, London)

Ceccato, S. 1965. 'Operational linguistics'. *Foundations of Language*, 1 (3)

Dolezel, L. 1965. 'Prazska skola a statisticka teorie basnickeho jazyka' (The Prague school and the statistical theory of Poetic language). *Česka Literatura*, 13, No. 1

Durkheim, E. and Mauss, M. 1903. 'De quelques formes primitives de classification: contribution à l'étude des représentations collectives'. *L'Année sociologique*, 6. English trans. *Primitive Classification* (Cohen & West, London, 1963)

Evans-Pritchard, E. E. 1934. 'Levy-Bruhl's theory of primitive mentality' (Extract from the *Bulletin of the Faculty of Arts*, 2, Pt. 1). Imprimerie de l'Institut Français d'Archéologie Orientale, Cairo

Greenberg, J. H. (ed.). 1963. *Universals of Language* (M.I.T. Press, Cambridge, Mass.)

Hiorth, F. 1964. 'Some reflexions on grammaticality'. *Inquiry*, 7, No. 2

Homans, G. C. and Schneider, D. M. 1955. *Marriage, Authority, and Final Causes: A Study of Unilateral Cross-cousin Marriage* (Free Press, New York)

Humbalek, R. P. 1966. 'Ku skumaniu vseobecnej problematiky systemov' (An approach to the general problems of systems). *Filozofia*, 21, No. 1

Katz, J. J. 1964. 'Mentalism in linguistics'. *Language*, 40, No. 2

Kroeber, A. L. 1953. *Anthropology Today* (Univ. of Chicago Press)

Mauss, M. 1950. 'Essai sur le don: forme et raison de l'échange dans les sociétés archaïques'. In *Sociologie et Anthropologie* by M. Mauss (P.U.F., Paris). English trans. *The Gift, Forms and Functions of Exchange in Archaic Societies* (Free Press, New York, 1954. Cohen & West, London, 1966)

Merleau-Ponty, M. 1945. *La Phénoménologie de la perception* (Gallimard, Paris). English trans. *The Phenomenology of Perception*, by C. Smith (Routledge and Humanities Press, London, 1962)

Peirce, C. S. 1940. *Selected Writings*, ed. by J. Buchlev (Harcourt Brace, New York)

Picard, R. 1963. 'Critical trends in France'. *The Times Literary Supplement*, Sept. 27th

Pierson, J. L. 1964. 'Langue-parole? signifiant-signifié-signe?' *Studia Linguistica*, 17, No. 1

Radcliffe-Brown, A. R. 1931. *The Social Organisation of Australian Tribes* (Macmillan, Melbourne)

—— 1952. *Structure and Function in Primitive Society* (Cohen & West, London)

—— 1958. *Method in Social Anthropology* (Univ. of Chicago Press)

Rousseau, J.-J. 1755. *Discours sur l'origine et les fondements de l'inégalité parmi les hommes* (Amsterdam)

Ruwet, N. 1964. 'Le linguistique générale aujourd'hui'. *Arch. europ. de Soc.*, V

Sapir, E. 1921. *Language* (Harcourt Brace, New York)

Sartre, J.-P. 1948. *Qu'est-ce que la littérature?* (Gallimard, Paris)

—— 1960. *Critique de la raison dialectique* (Gallimard, Paris)

Souriau, E. 1950. *Les Deux cent mille situations dramatiques* (Flammarion, Paris)

Ziff, P. 1964. 'About grammaticalness'. *Mind*, 73 (290)

III. JOURNAL ISSUES DEVOTED TO STRUCTURALISM AND SEMIOTICS

Aletheia, No. 4, May 1966

Annales, No. 6, Nov.–Dec. 1964

L'Arc, No. 26, 1965

Communications, No. 4, 1964 and No. 8, 1966

L'Esprit, No. 322, Nov. 1963

Revue Internationale de Philosophie, No. 73–4, fasc. 3/4, 1965

Social Science Information, Vol. VI, 2–3 and Vol. VI, 4

Les Temps Modernes, No. 246, Nov. 1966

The Times Literary Supplement, 1965: April 29th, pp. 320–23 and Sept. 30th, pp. 863–5; 1966, June 23rd, pp. 545–6; 1967, June 15th, pp. 521–2

Yale French Review, Vol. 36–7, 1966

NOTES

INTRODUCTION

1. R. Bastide (ed.), *Sens et usage du terme 'structure' dans les sciences humaines* (Mouton, The Hague, 1962), includes extended essays on the history and variations in the meaning of structure in a variety of disciplines.

2. Jean Pouillon, 'Présentation: un essai de définition', *Les Temps Modernes*, no. 246 (November, 1966), pp. 769–90.

3. Music, too, in so far as any composition may be expressed in terms of operations and relations, shares this characteristic of possessing structure.

4. E.g. by Ernest Nagel, *The Structure of Science* (Routledge & Kegan Paul, London, 1961). See particularly chaps. 13 and 14.

5. Ibid., p. 447.

6. Ibid., p. 448.

7. Ibid., p. 450.

8. See particularly, A. Schutz, *Collected Papers* (Mouton, The Hague, 1962), vol. I, pt. 1 and pt. III, 5 (pp. 218–22). 'Any theoretical analysis... would have to start from the face-to-face relation as a basic structure of the world of daily life.'

9. See M. Merleau-Ponty, *Signs* (Northwestern Univ. Press, Evanston, 1964), chap. 4.

10. Prigogine's statement (in 'Quelques remarques sur la structure de la physique', *Revue Internationale de Philosophie*, no. 73–4, 1965, pp. 335–41): 'Définir la structure de la physique est en ce moment une tâche particulièrement malaisée', is true relative to physics at other times rather than to other disciplines now.

11. Cf. Aristotle's injunction (*Poetics*, chap. 24) that a probable impossibility is to be preferred to an improbable possibility.

12. J. Piaget, *Le Structuralisme* (P.U.F., Paris, 1968).

13. M. Foucault, *Les Mots et les choses* (Gallimard, Paris, 1966).

14. See, for example, *Principles of Topological Psychology* (McGraw-Hill, New York, 1936).

15. Some experiments showing this are discussed in J. Piaget, *Les Mécanismes perceptifs* (P.U.F., Paris, 1961).

16. A formal exposition of the group, together with its axioms, theorems, and their proofs, is to be found in J. A. Green, *Sets and Groups* (Routledge & Kegan Paul, London, 1965).

17. Where $\otimes$ throughout stands for the binary operation.

18. The notion of 'greater than' in the set of integers is a simple example of a relation.

19. A detailed consideration of topological space and topological structures is to be found in G. F. Simmons, *Introduction to Topology and Modern Analysis* (McGraw-Hill, New York, 1963).

20. G. G. Granger, 'Objets, structures et significations', *Revue Internationale de Philosophie*, no. 73–4 (1965), pp. 251–90.

21. Since all operations may be rewritten as relations.

22. A. R. Radcliffe-Brown, 'On Social Structure', in *Structure and Function in Primitive Society* (Cohen & West, London, 1952).

23. Quoted by Pouillon in 'Présentation'; see note 2 above.

24. My three types of structure are derived in part from Carl Hempel's discussion in 'Typological Methods in the Social Sciences', reprinted in M. Natanson (ed.), *Philosophy of the Social Sciences* (Random House, New York, 1963).

25. Max Weber, *The Methodology of the Social Sciences* (Free Press, Glencoe, Illinois, 1949), p. 90.

26. Max Weber, *Theory of Social and Economic Organisation* (Free Press, Glencoe, Illinois, 1964), pp. 329–36.

27. Hempel, op. cit., p. 212.

28. Classification, it should be noted, may be on the basis of the qualities either of the elements or of the relations between elements. The majority tend to be of the former type but some (e.g. E. Bott, *Family and Social Network* (Tavistock, London, 1957)) are of the latter.

29. *The authoritarian personality* studied by Adorno *et al.* (Harper, New York, 1950), is one of the best examples, in both senses, of this approach.

30. See Hempel, op. cit., pp. 213–14.

31. But see below.

32. See below.

33. Martin Joos (ed.), *Readings in Linguistics* (American Council of Learned Societies, New York, 1963), p. 18.

34. As Piaget (in *Le Structuralisme*) has pointed out, this notion has been modified by Jespersen and recently somewhat put in doubt by Jakobson. Ferdinand de Saussure has answered such critics in advance by distinguishing between the 'relatively arbitrary' and the 'radically arbitrary'.

35. N. Chomsky, *Syntactic Structures* (Mouton, The Hague, 1957).

36. Z. S. Harris, *Methods in Structural Linguistics* (University of Chicago Press, 1951).

37. Propp discovered that, in all the Russian tales he studied, there were certain elements that were constant even where the stories themselves changed; he further suggested that a study of this kind could be fruitfully made of all the stories imagined by man throughout time. A second, revised edition of *Morphology of the Folktale* was published for the American Folklore Society and the Indiana University Research Center for the Language Sciences by the University of Texas Press in 1968.

38. See below.

39. N. Chomsky, *Current Issues in Linguistic Theory* (Mouton, The Hague, 1964).

40. Ibid., 'De quelques constantes de la théorie linguistique', *Diogène*, no. 51 (1965), p. 14 (my translation).

41. This is a highly simplified version of Chomsky's *Syntactic Structures*.

42. See below.

43. Chomsky, 'De quelques constantes'.

44. M. Mauss, *Sociologie et anthropologie*, preceded by an introduction to Mauss's works by C. Lévi-Strauss (P.U.F., Paris, 1950).

45. 'Essai sur le don: forme et raison de l'échange dans les sociétés archaïques', in *Sociologie et anthropologie*. (English translation, *The Gift, Forms and Functions of Exchange in Archaic Societies* (Cohen & West, London, 1966).)

46. Op. cit., p. xxxiii (my translation).

47. C. Lévi-Strauss, *Tristes Tropiques* (Plon, Paris, 1955).

48. G. Balandier, 'Grandeur et servitude de l'ethnologue', *Cahiers du Sud*, 43 (337) (1956), p. 451.

49. J. Viet, *Les Méthodes structuralistes dans les sciences sociales* (Mouton, The Hague, 1965), p. 69.

50. Balandier, op. cit., p. 451.

51. Viet, op. cit., p. 69.

52. Demonstrated in the three volumes of *Mythologiques* (*Le Cru et le cuit* (Plon, Paris, 1964); *Du Miel aux cendres* (Plon, Paris, 1967); *L'Origine des manières de table* (Plon, Paris, 1968) and discussed in E. R. Leach (ed.), *The Structural Study of Myth and Totemism* (Tavistock, London, 1967).

53. In *Tristes Tropiques*.

54. '*Esprit*' is generally rendered as 'mind' by Jakobson and Schoepf; I have translated it as 'reason' since I believe this conveys the Cartesian nuance better.

Notes

55. C. Lévi-Strauss, 'Histoire et ethnologie', in *Anthropologie structurale* (Plon, Paris, 1958), 3–33, p. 28 (my translation). (This has since been published in *Revue de Métaphysique et de Morale*, 54 (3–4) (1959), 363–91.)

56. See above, p. 24.

57. C. Lévi-Strauss, 'Structure sociale', *Bulletin de Psychologie*, 6 (May 5th, 1953), pp. 358–90 (my translation); cited in Viet, *Méthodes structuralistes*.

58. C. Lévi-Strauss, 'La structure et la forme. Réflexions sur un ouvrage de Vladimir Propp', *Cahiers de l'I.S.E.A.*, 99, Série M, no. 7 (March, 1960), 3–36, p. 3 (my translation; author's italics).

59. P. 19 (my translation and italics).

60. Introduction to Mauss, *Sociologie et Anthropologie*, p. 24 (my translation).

61. *Le Cru et le cuit*, Overture, p. 19 (my translation).

62. C. Lévi-Strauss, 'La notion de structure en ethnologie', in *Anthropologie structurale*, 303–52, p. 307.

63. C. Lévi-Strauss, *La Pensée sauvage* (Plon, Paris, 1962), p. 190.

64. Ibid., pp. 191–7.

65. See footnote 57.

66. This is condensed from the much more extended analysis in *Du Miel aux cendres*, pp. 311–26 (my translation).

67. *Du Miel aux cendres*, p. 139.

68. See below.

69. See below.

70. 'A Conceptual Introduction to Latent Structure Analysis', in P. F. Lazarsfeld (ed.), *Mathematical Thinking in the Social Sciences* (Free Press, New York, 1954), chap. 7, pp. 347–87; 'Latent Structure Analysis', in S. Koch (ed.), *Psychology: A Study of a Science, Conceptual and Systematic* (McGraw-Hill, New York, 1959), vol. 3, pp. 476–543.

71. H. M. Blalock, *Causal Inferences in Nonexperimental Research* (University of N. Carolina Press, Chapel Hill, 1961).

72. F. Harary, 'Structural Duality', *Behavioral Science* 2(4) (October, 1957), pp. 255–65; 'On the measurement of structural balance', *Behavioral Science* 4(4) (October, 1959), pp. 316–23: (with R. Z. Norman), *Graph Theory as a Mathematical Model in Social Science* (Institute for Social Research, Ann Arbor, 1953).

73. See below.

74. Notably by C. Lefort in his objections to Lévi-Strauss ('L'échange et la lutte des hommes', *Les Temps Modernes*, 6(64) (February, 1951), pp. 1400–17).

75. Alasdair MacIntyre in private discussion has indicated that he finds Lévi-Strauss's classification by binary oppositions somewhat unsatisfactory, since though logically all classifications may be reduced to terms of binary opposition there is no evidence, rather the reverse, that lived experience has this quality. His objections seem to me analogous to those of Lefort, and analogously refutable, though I appreciate that this does not exhaust the problem raised by the apparent hiatus or disjuncture between experience and the reality signified by the structure.

76. P.U.F., Paris, 1949: new edition (revised and corrected), Mouton, The Hague/Paris, 1967.

77. G. T. Guilbaud, 'Les structures de parenté de l'Île d'Ambrym', in *Comptes-rendus du Séminaire sur les modèles mathématiques dans les sciences sociales*, Année 1960–1, Fascicule II, 2è trimestre (Groupe de mathématique sociale et de statistique, Paris, 1961), pp. 5–10.

78. H. Hoffmann, 'Symbolic logic and the analysis of social organization', *Behavioral Science*, 4(4) (October, 1959), pp. 288–98.

79. 'Compte-rendu du colloque sur le mot "structure"', in Bastide (ed.), *Sens et usages du terme* 'structure', pp. 139–65.

80. Lévi-Strauss, *Anthropologie structurale*, p. 356 (my translation).

81. Pouillon, 'Présentation'.

82. 'Charles Baudelaire's "Les Chats"' (translated by Katie Furness-Lane), see below.

83. Even studies such as William Empson's *Seven Types of Ambiguity* (Chatto & Windus, London, 1930) suggest implicitly that there is a finite, if ambiguous, set of ambiguities, which, once laid bare, reveal the (ambiguous) truth.

84. Roland Barthes, *Essais Critiques* (Seuil, Paris, 1964), pp. 255, 270 (my translation, author's italics).

85. Ibid.

86. Roland Barthes, *Sur Racine* (Seuil, Paris, 1963). The book was attacked by Raymond Picard in *Nouvelle Critique ou nouvelle imposture* (Pauvert, Paris, 1966). Barthes replied with *Critique et vérité*; several polemical articles and at least one book (Serge Doubrovsky, *Pourquoi la nouvelle critique?* (Mercure de France, Paris, 1966)) have since appeared. The whole affair, as Doubrovsky himself has indicated, bears a striking resemblance to the 'querelle des Anciens et des Modernes'. Plus ça change, plus c'est la même chose.

87. Barthes, *Sur Racine*, p. 9.

88. Ibid., pp. 15–16.

89. Ibid., pp. 34–5.

90. See below.

91. T. Todorov, 'Le structuralisme dans les revues', *Social Science Information* VI, 4 (1967).

92. R. Barthes, 'Introduction à l'analyse structurale des récits', *Communications* 8 (1966).

93. Umberto Eco, 'Il mito di Superman' and 'Lettura di "Steve Canyon"', in *Apocalittici e Integrati* (Bompiani, Milan, 1964).

94. J. K. Seglov, 'Pour la construction d'un modèle structurel des nouvelles de Sherlock Holmes', *Marcatre*, nos 8–10 (1964).

95. See below.

96. As Barthes has explicitly recognized (*Essais Critiques*, p. 256).

97. Jean Starobinski, 'Remarques sur le structuralisme', in F. Schalk (ed.), *Ideen und Formen: Festschrift für Hugo Friedrich* (V. Klostermann, Frankfurt-am-Main, 1965).

98. Doubrovsky, *Pourquoi la Nouvelle Critique?* p. 90 (my translation).

99. Todorov, 'Le structuralisme dans les revues'.

IMITATION AND STRUCTURAL CHANGE IN CHILDREN'S LANGUAGE

1. A. N. Gvozdev, *Voprosy izucheniia detskoi rechi* (Problems in the language development of the child) (Academy of Pedagogical Science, Moscow, 1961).

2. 'Control of grammar in imitation, comprehension, and production'. *J. verb. Learn. verb. Behav.*, 1963, 2, 121–35.

3. Conducted with the support of a grant from the National Institute of Mental Health and the facilities of the Institute for Human Development and the Institute for Human Learning at the University of California, Berkeley. The work was done in collaboration with Wick Miller, now Assistant Professor of Anthropology at the University of Utah.

4. Martin D. S. Braine, 'The ontogeny of English phrase structure: the first phase', *Language* (1963), 39, pp. 1–13.

5. R. Brown and C. Fraser, 'The acquisition of syntax', in C. N. Cofer and Barbara Musgrave (eds.), *Verbal Behavior and Learning* (McGraw-Hill, New York, 1963).

6. W. Miller and S. Ervin, 'The development of grammar in child language', in U. Bellugi and R. Brown (eds.), *The Acquisition of Language* (Child Development Monograph, 1964), 29, pp. 9–34.

7. R. Brown, 'Linguistic determination and the part of speech', *J. abnorm. soc. Psychol.*, 1957, 55, pp. 1–5.

Notes

8. R. H. Weir, *Language in the Crib* (Mouton, The Hague, 1962).
9. N. Chomsky, *Syntactic Structures* (Mouton, The Hague, 1957).

DE SAUSSURE'S SYSTEM OF LINGUISTICS

1. By Ferdinand de Saussure (1857–1913), edited posthumously by two disciples, Charles Bally and Albert Sechehaye, first edition, 1916, second 1922. Our page references are to the second edition. A letter after a page number indicates the paragraph, the letter *a* being assigned to the beginning of the page even when the paragraph is continued from the preceding page. – A study and research fellowship from the American Council of Learned Societies has greatly encouraged and aided our work. We thank two eminent admirers of de Saussure, Professors Leonard Bloomfield and Roman Jakobson, for reading and commenting upon an earlier version of this article.
2. L. Bloomfield, review of Sapir's Language in the *Classical Weekly* (1922), 15, pp. 142–3.
3. 'La physiologie des sons (all. Laut- ou Sprachphysiologie) est souvent appelée "phonétique" (all. Phonetik, angl. phonetics). Ce terme nous semble impropre; nous le remplaçons par celui de *phonologie*. Car *phonétique* a d'abord désigné et doit continuer à désigner l'étude des évolutions des sons … ' (55–6). This argument has not prevailed; and standard English terminology will be best preserved by translating *phonologie* as *phonetics* and *phonétique* as *historical phonetics*.
4. We adopt *langue* and *parole* as technical terms in English.
5. 'Es ist eingewendet, dass es noch eine andere wissenschaftliche Betrachtung der Sprache gäbe, als die geschichtliche. Ich muss das in Abrede stellen' (*Prinzipien*, 3te Aufl., Einl.§10).

THE SEMANTICS OF STYLE

1. 'Style', in *Dictionary of World Literature*, J. Shipley (ed.) (N. J. Paterson, rev. ed., 1960), p. 399.
2. Middleton Murry, *The Problem of Style* (London, 1922 and reprinted, London, 1960. All page references are to the latter). After distinguishing several senses of the term, Murry proceeds unwittingly to illustrate its dangers by getting entrapped in the very polysemy he warns of.
3. See entry I under 'style' in the *Shorter Oxford English Dictionary* (*S.O.E.D.*).
4. Tenney, op. cit., p. 397.
5. The ultimate confusion is clearly evident in the fact that entry II, 2 in the *S.O.E.D.* does not end here, but, after the minor halt of a semi-colon, hastens back to a normative sense: the full entry is 'The manner of expression characteristic of a particular writer (hence of an orator), or of a literary group or period; a writer's mode of expression considered in regard to clearness, effectiveness, beauty, and the like.'
6. See Murry's first as opposed to his second and third definitions, pp. 5–9. The difference between the latter two seems simply a matter of degree: the second is ordinary excellence, the 'lucid exposition of a series of intellectual ideas', while the third is 'the highest achievement of literature'. The second is usually called 'effective prose style' in English.
7. Again, the *S.O.E.D.* does not end entry II, 3 without an evaluative touch ' … often used for: Good or fine style'.
8. According to C. Brooks and R. P. Warren, *Understanding Poetry* (New York, 1950), p. 640, 'Style, in its larger sense, is essentially the same thing as form.'
9. The book by G. Puttenham, *The Art of English Poetry* (1589), is the most famous of these handbooks in English. The section on 'Ornament' is in Book III.
10. See J. Arthos, 'Trope', in *Encyclopedia of Poetry and Poetics*, A. Preminger (ed.) (Princeton, 1965).
11. See J. W. H. Atkins, *English Literary Criticism: The Renascence* (London, 1947), p. 172.

12. See M. Halliday, A. McIntosh and P. Strevens, *The linguistic Sciences and Language Teaching* (Bloomington, 1964), p. 92. Style in the sense of 'relations among the [language] participants' is called 'style of discourse' and is separated from 'individual style' (style B), p. 97.

13. N. Enkvist, 'On Defining Style', in J. Spencer and M. Gregory (eds.), *Linguistics and Style* (London, 1964), esp. chap. III.

14. W. V. Harris, 'Style and the Twentieth-century Novel', *Western Humanities Review* 18 (1964), p. 128. F. L. Lucas, *Style* (New York, 1962), p. 18: 'Our subject, then is simply the effective use of languages, especially in prose.'

15. We are doubtless in for a flood of textbooks, with titles like *Elements of Style* and *The Practical Stylist*.

16. As quoted in Tenney, op. cit., p. 398.

17. From 'The Art of Writing', in *The Dance of Life* (London, 1933), p. 163, as quoted in Enkvist, op. cit., p. 11.

18. Ibid., p. 12. He cites Stendhal, Burke, Goodman, De Quincey, Bally and Seidler as holders of this view.

19. 'Elocutio', in *Dictionary of World Literature*.

20. As quoted in Sister Miriam Joseph, *Rhetoric in Shakespeare's Time* (New York, 1962), p. 33.

21. G. Saintsbury, 'Modern English Prose', *Miscellaneous Essays* (London, 1892), p. 84.

22. W. K. Wimsatt traces the reaction from the seventeenth century, in the writings of Thomas Sprat, Pascal, Swift, Buffon, Cardinal Newman, Coleridge, Wackernogel, De Quincey, Schopenhauer, Lewes, Pater, Brunetière, Joubert, Boeckh and Murry (*The Prose Style of Samuel Johnson* (New Haven, 1963), pp. 1–2).

23. A. C. Bradley, 'Poetry for Poetry's Sake', *Oxford Lectures on Poetry* (London, 1909), p. 9.

24. Wimsatt, loc. cit.

25. Ibid., pp. 12–13.

26. Ibid., p. 11.

27. M. Beardsley, *Aesthetics* (New York, 1958), chaps. III–V. I am very much indebted to Beardsley for extended personal communications on this work and the concept of style. If this critique seems severe, the reader is asked to remember that it would not even exist if it did not have Beardsley's formulation as a point of departure. A popularization for teachers, with many additional and interesting examples, is M. Beardsley, 'Style and Good Style', in G. Tate (ed.), *Reflections on High School English* (Tulsa, Okla., 1966), pp. 91–105.

28. Following Beardsley (*Aesthetics*, p. 125) we can use 'designation' to refer to characteristics *necessary* to a thing for it to be what it is, that is, for a term to *hold* in respect to its referent; these apply regardless of the context (a sea must have a lot of water by definition). 'Connotations' are not necessarily but varyingly applicable characteristics, widely assumed by speakers to be properties of a thing ('calm' and 'stormy' are both attributed to the sea, but unlike 'containing much water', which is always and necessarily a component of 'sea', the context may rule one or another out; e.g., 'The sea rose up and sank the ship' eliminates 'calm'). Borrowing terms from current linguistics, we might describe *designation* as 'context-free' and *connotation* as 'context-sensitive'. (Designation, of course, *is* context-sensitive if the word has more than one sense; the proper *sense* holds regardless of context.)

29. Ibid., p. 221. Enkvist, 'On Defining Style' p. 17, also has some difficulty in accounting for the reasons for calling the distinction between 'drizzling' and 'pouring' non-stylistic and that between 'fine man' and 'nice chap' stylistic. What *is* 'roughly the same' as opposed to 'different' in meaning?

30. Beardsley, 'Style and Good Style', p. 96.

31. Beardsley, *Aesthetics*, p. 225.

32. Note that the sense of 'express' and 'expressive' is clearly different from that intended

by stylists like Bally, namely conveying 'affective' or 'emotive' meanings. This sense will be discussed below.

33. Collected in W. K. Wimsatt, *The Verbal Icon* (New York, 1958): see particularly Section 3, 'The Substantive Level' and 'Verbal Style: Logical and Counterlogical'. Quotations and discussions below are on pp. xii and 201–3.

34. Beardsley, *Aesthetics*, pp. 116–19.

35. L. T. Milic, 'Unconscious Ordering in the Prose of Swift', in J. Leed (ed.), *The Computer and Literary Style* (Kent, Ohio, 1966), argues that the most important features of style are unconscious: It seems to me that 'unconscious' is an unfortunate term for what Milic has in mind. Obviously, a writer is not usually 'conscious' of stylistic selection in the sense that he literally says to himself: 'Now I will introduce a balance' or 'now an alliteration', or 'now a series', or 'what have you?' (although in stylistic eras more heavily influenced by the handbooks such mental processes may have been not uncommon). But saying that the words 'balance' and so on did not actually pass through his mind is not the same thing as saying that he was 'unconscious' of introducing a balance at a given point, or, indeed, of using balance so frequently as to allow it to earmark his style. Milic finds that the accumulation of terms in series – usually *long* series – is one of Swift's most important stylistica; for example: ' ... vast Numbers of our People are compelled to seek their Livelihood by Begging, Robbing, Stealing, Cheating, Pimping, Forswearing, Flattering, Subborning, Forging, Gaming, Lying, Fawning, Hectoring, Voting, Scribbling, Star-gazing, Poysoning, Whoring, Canting, Libelling, Free-Thinking, and the like occupations' (pp. 84–5). The use of series 'argues a well-stocked mind' (p. 104). But in what sense can we say that Swift was 'unconscious' of creating this series, with its highly deliberate and ironic positioning of otherwise innocuous terms like 'voting', 'scribbling', 'star-gazing' and 'free-thinking'? Furthermore, even if a predilection for series *is* unconscious, it is still context-determined to the extent that the subject under discussion must be conducive to serial thinking and exemplification, so that it is not a good instance of a stylistic decision 'less likely to be affected by the occasional and temporary character of a given composition (its subject-matter)'. Milic asserts that unless style characteristics 'appear regardless of the subject-matter of the composition, they must be of very low usefulness'. This notion seems needlessly restrictive (it excludes not only imagery and metrics, but even vocabulary selection). But an author is characterized not only by what is constant in his style from one piece to another, from one genre or subject to another, but also by his selections *with respect to* that genre or subject: we are interested not merely in Milton's style but in Milton's epic style as opposed to his pastoral style. Compare the following observations of Spitzer and Guiraud: 'Das Wort "Stil" ist hierbei im allgemeinen im gebräuchlichen Sinn der *bewussten* Verwendung sprachlicher Mittel zu irgendwendlichen Ausdruckszielen verwandt' (L. Spitzer, *Stilstudien* (München, 1928), I, ix); 'La *conscience* dans le choix ne me semble pas non plus entrer dans la définition du style, et c'est précisément un des buts de la stylistique de déterminer les forces profondes qui informent et choisissent le langage dans l'opacité de notre expérience et de notre durée' (P. Guiraud, 'Stylistiques', *Neophilologus* 38 (1954), pp. 1–11 (my italics)).

36. See R. Posner, 'The Use and Abuse of Stylistic Statistics', *Archivum Linguisticum* 15 (1963), pp. 111–39; Milic, op. cit., p. 82, uses the terms 'attributive' for 'stylometric', and 'interpretive' for 'stylistic'. The attributive task is 'to identify a given work as the product of a given writer by means of the individual fingerprints of his style'; while the interpretive task is 'to obtain a deeper understanding of the writer, his mind, his work, his personality'.

37. 'It may be sufficient, if evidence of authorship is all that is required, to use a computer to determine quantitatively the density in a given text of one or two specific linguistic features; but this is diagnosis, not description. And the features chosen for this purpose may not, indeed probably will not, be features which are stylistically significant in terms of literary response and artistic effect.' J. Spencer and M. Gregory, 'An approach to the study of style', *Linguistics and Style*, p. 91.

38. Milic, op. cit., pp. 79–80.

39. R. Ohmann, *Shaw: the Style and the Man* (Middletown, Conn., 1962), pp. xi-xiii.

40. A. Rodway, 'By Algebra to Augustanism', in R. Fowler (ed.), *Essays on Style and Language* (New York, 1966), p. 61.

41. R. P. Draper, 'Style and Matter', *Journal des Langues vivantes* 27 (1961), pp. 15-23.

42. Ibid., p. 21.

43. Beardsley, *Aesthetics*, p. 224. 'Secondary meaning' is 'connotation', reference to properties of a thing which are usually or widely felt to be characteristic of it, but not essential to it (see n. 28). But why style features should be limited to secondary meaning is not explained. And Beardsley does not seem to be restricting 'meaning' to 'secondary meaning' when he discusses the example from Johnson quoted above: ' ... the Johnsonian syntax ... has both meaning and general purport' (p. 224).

44. Ibid., p. 172.

45. Ibid., p. 222.

46. Milic, op. cit., p. 83.

47. C. K. Ogden and I. A. Richards, *The Meaning of Meaning* (6th ed., New York, 1943), p. 22. Cf. J. Bruner, J. Goodnow and G. Austin, *A Study of Thinking* (New York, 1956).

48. W. J. Entwistle, *Aspects of Language* (London, 1953), pp. 94-5. Bally called the expressive features 'stylistics' and reserved 'style' for 'the individual sum of characteristics of a particular speaker, writer or poet' (Entwistle, p. 273). Cf. S. Ullmann's definition (*Language and Style* (New York, 1964), p. 101): 'Everything that transcends the purely referential and communicative side of language ... emotive overtones, emphasis, rhythm, symmetry, euphony, and evocative elements' ... as well as milieu (historical, foreign, provincial, professional, etc.).

49. As quoted in Enkvist, 'On Defining Style', p. 16, n.

50. Quoted in R. A. Sayce, 'The Definition of the Term "Style" ', *Proceedings of the Third Congress of the International Comparative Literature Association* (The Hague, 1962), p. 158.

51. C. Osgood, 'Some Effects of Motivation of Style of Encoding', in T. Sebeok, ed., *Style in Language* (New York, 1958), p. 293. Cf. Guiraud, op. cit., p. 3; Bruneau, 'La Stylistique', *Romance Philology* 5 (1951), pp. 1-14.

52. Ohmann, *Shaw*, p. 185. The replacement of linguistic norm by contextualist theories proposed by M. Riffaterre ('Criteria for Style Analysis', *Word* 15 (April, 1959), and 'Stylistic Context', *Word* 16 (August, 1960)), and subscribed to by Enkvist (op. cit., pp. 29 sq.) is very useful; the context, of course, is not equivalent to style, nor are the coincidences and deviations, but are the means of recognizing it.

53. Sayce, op cit., p. 159. Cf. D. Hymes, 'Phonological Aspects of Style: some English Sonnets', in *Style in Language*, p. 109.

54. W. Winter, 'Styles as Dialects', *Ninth Congress of Linguists*, as quoted in Enkvist, op. cit., p. 35. The definition of R. Wellek and A. Warren: ' ... the individual linguistic system of a work, or a group of works' (*Theory of Literature* (New York, 1955), p. 169) is not completely satisfactory because of the ambiguity of the phrase 'linguistic system'.

55. A miscellany of definitions can be dismissed because they take 'style' so far from etymological and reasonable theoretical bases, for example, calling 'style' any 'aesthetic use of language', etc.

56. 'Casual and non-casual utterances within unified structure', in *Style in Language*, pp. 57-68.

57. Beardsley, *Aesthetics*, p. 173.

58. Consider another of Beardsley' omparisons: 'Would you join me for lunch?' v. 'How about a sandwich?' These differ not only to the extent that they characterize (a) the first message and its situation as being more formal than the second, and (b) the speaker as being for the moment more, rather than less, formal, and more generally, *capable* of such formality, but also to the extent that (c) 'lunch' is, in the real world, slightly different from 'a sandwich'. But (c) is not, in my view, the stylistic fact; it is simply a detail of meaning. Connections with semantic *structure* are also present: some occasions – say, speaking at a

business meeting or a trial – demand greater adherence to 'logical consistency and progression' than others (like courting or speaking at a testimonial dinner).

HISTORICAL DISCOURSE

1. R. Jakobson, *Essais de linguistique générale* (Éditions de Minuit, Paris, 1963), ch. 9 [a translation of *Shifters, Verbal Categories, and the Russian Verb* (Department of Slavic Languages and Literatures, Harvard, 1957)].

2. The term is derived from de Saussure's Anagrams, and we take it from J. Kristeva, 'Bakhtine, le mot, le dialogue et le roman', *Critique*, no. 239 (April, 1967), pp. 438–65. It designates the kind of writing at two levels which carries on a dialogue between the text and other texts and so postulates a new logic.

3. In any type of discourse the exordium poses one of the most interesting problems of rhetoric, in that it codifies breaches of silence and combats aphasia.

4. 'Before taking up my pen I have looked into my heart; and, finding neither selfish affection nor implacable hatred for any creature, I believe I am able to judge of men and affairs without violating the requirements of justice and truth.' (L. Blanc, *Histoire de dix ans*, 1842).

5. Cf. E. Raimondi, *Opere di Niccolo Macchiavelli* (Ugo Mursia editore, Milan, 1966).

6. E.g. 'the innocence and wisdom of the young Joseph ... his mysterious dreams ... his jealous brothers ... the selling into slavery of this great man ... his fidelity to his master ... his admirable chastity; the persecutions which this draws upon his head; his imprisonment and steadfastness ... ' (Bossuet, *Discours sur l'histoire universelle*, in *Œuvres* (Bibliothèque de la Pléiade, Paris, 1961), p. 674).

7. L. Irigaray, 'Négation et transformation négative dans le langage des schizophrènes', *Langages*, no. 5 (March, 1967), pp. 84–98.

8. Cf. 'Introduction à l'analyse structurale du récit', *Communications*, no. 8, November, 1966.

9. A passage from Michelet (*Histoire du moyen âge*, vol. III, book vi, ch. 1) has the following syllogistic structure: (i) to divert a threat of rebellion the attention of the populace must be distracted; (ii) the best way to do this is to give them a scapegoat; (iii) the princes therefore chose Aubriot, etc.

10. This referential illusion, or confusion of meaning and referent, is expressed with extreme clarity in Thiers's naïve statement of the historian's ideal: 'To be simply true, to be what things are, neither more, nor less, nor otherwise, nor other.' (Quoted by C. Jullian *Historiens français du XIXe siècle* (Hachette, Paris, n.d.), p. lxiii.)

11. Cf. 'La rhétorique de l'image', *Communications*, no. 4 (November, 1964).

12. This (and not merely religious subversion) is the meaning of the Red Guards' profanation of the temple marking Confucius' birthplace (January, 1967); we may note incidentally that the phrase 'cultural revolution' is another way, though a poor one, of saying 'destruction of the foundations of civilization'.

13. 'It has been said that the aim of the historian is to relate, not to prove; I do not know if this is so, but I am certain that, in history, the best proof, the one most likely to impress and convince, the one that leaves least room for distrust and doubt, is complete narration ... ' (A. Thierry, *Récits des temps mérovingiens* (1851), vol. II, p. 227).

STRUCTURAL ANTHROPOLOGY AND HISTORY

1. C. Lévi-Strauss, *Leçon inaugurale* (Paris, 1960); tr. *The Scope of Anthropology* (Cape Editions, London, 1967).

2. C. Lévi-Strauss, *La Pensée sauvage* (Plon, Paris, 1962); tr. *The Savage Mind* (Weidenfeld, London, 1962).

3. C. Lévi-Strauss, *Race et histoire* (tr. *Race and History*) (UNESCO, Paris, 1952).

4. C. Lévi-Strauss, *Anthropologie structurale* (Plon, Paris, 1958), p. 19; tr. *Structural Anthropology* (Basic Books, London, 1963).

5. Ibid., p. 23.

6. Ibid., p. 6.

7. Ibid., p. 6.

8. Ibid., p. 8.

9. Ibid., p. 6.

10. *Race et histoire*, p. 252.

11. Ibid., p. 248.

12. *Anthropologie structurale*, p. 28.

13. C. Lévi-Strauss, Introduction to M. Mauss, *Sociologie et anthropologie* (P.U.F., Paris, 1950).

14. C. Lévi-Strauss, *Tristes Tropiques* (Plon, Paris, 1955), chap. XX; tr. *World on the Wane* (Hutchinson, London, 1961).

15. C. Lévi-Strauss, *Les Structures élémentaires de la parenté* (P.U.F., Paris, 1949), p. 120; tr. *Elementary Structures of Kinship* (Eyre & Spottiswoode, London, 1969).

16. *La Pensée sauvage*, p. 339.

17. *Leçon inaugurale*, p. 23.

18. *Anthropologie structurale*, p. 266.

19. Ibid., p. 346.

20. *La Pensée sauvage*, p. 307.

21. *Anthropologie structurale*, p. 342.

22. *Préface à Mauss*, p. XIX.

23. *Anthropologie structurale*, p. 343.

24. Ibid., p. 344.

25. *Préface à Mauss*, p. XX.

26. *Anthropologie structurale*, p. 266.

27. *Préface à Mauss*, p. XLIX.

28. *Leçon inaugurale*, p. 25.

29. *Préface à Mauss*, p. XIX.

30. *La Pensée sauvage*, p. 92.

31. *Tristes Tropiques*, chap. V.

32. *Anthropologie structurale*, p. 8.

THE MYTHICAL STRUCTURE OF THE ANCIENT SCANDINAVIANS: SOME THOUGHTS ON READING DUMÉZIL

1. Littleton (1964), p. 147.

2. For Dumézil's contributions to Scandinavian mythology see the bibliography of this article. A testimony to an awakening interest for his work in Scandinavia is the appearance of a Swedish translation of his *Les Dieux des Germains* in 1962: *De Nordiska Gudarna*, tr. Åke Ohlmarks (Bonniers, Stockholm, 1962).

3. Most recently in the autumn term of 1965 a Harvard, where discussions with his students have proved highly stimulating.

4. See bibliography in *Hommages à Georges Dumézil*, pp. XI–XXIII.

5. In his 1960 article Lévi-Strauss writes: 'On définira ainsi progressivement un "univers du conte" analysable en paires d'oppositions, diversement combinées au sein de chaque personnage, lequel, loin de constituer une entité, est, à la manière du phonème, tel que le conçoit Roman Jakobson, un "faisceau d'éléments différentiels".

6. Lévi-Strauss (1955, reprinted 1965).

7. Betz (1957), col. 2475: 'Der Gegensatz von Helm und Dumézil ist z.T. der Gegensatz von Historikern auf der einen und Strukturisten und Komparatisten auf der andern Seite.'

8. Dumézil (1952), p. 23.

9. Dumézil (1952), p. 54.

10. E.g., Martinet (1964), pp. 37–8.

11. De Vries (1956–7), vol. II, p. 25.

12. Dumézil, *L'idéologie* (1958), p. 56.

13. Lévi-Strauss (1955, reprinted 1965), p. 99.

14. *The Younger Edda*, ch. 20 (35).

15. De Vries (1956–7), vol. II, p. 162.

16. Turville-Petre (1964), p. 144.

17. *The Younger Edda*, ch. 33 (46). Holtsmark (1964), p. 67, points out that these descriptions probably stem from Snorri's conceptions of the devil.

18. De Vries (1956–7), vol. I, pp. 257–61; Holtsmark (1964), p. 37.

19. *The Younger Edda*, Skaldskaparmál, ch. 26 (132).

20. *Egils Saga*, 25.

21. Turville-Petre (1964), p. 200.

22. Ibid., p. 190.

23. *The Elder Edda*, 172.

24. *The Younger Edda*, 2. Holtsmark (1964), 14 and 17, comments on the problem of spiritual enlightenment.

25. *The Younger Edda*, 2.

26. *The Younger Edda*, ch. 15 (28).

27. On Yggdrasill as the mediator of the universe see Dumézil, *Les Dieux des Indo-Européens* (1952), p. 104.

ON RUSSIAN FAIRY TALES

1. *Lapti*: Russian peasant shoes woven of bast.

2. The best edition (by Azadovskij, Andreev and Jurij Sokolov) is *Narodnye russkie skazki*, I–III (Moscow-Leningrad, 1936–40). Besides his main collection, Afanas'ev published *Russkie narodnye legendy* (Moscow, 1860), and *Russkie zavetnye skazki* (Geneva, 1865).

3. I. Xudjakov, *Velikorusskie skazki*, I–III (St Petersburg, 1860–2); A. Èrlenvejn, *Narodnye skazki, sobrannye sel'skimi učiteljami* (Moscow, 1863); E. Čudinskij, *Russkie narodnye skazki pribautki i pobasenki* (Moscow, 1864).

4. A. Afanas'ev, *Poètičeskie vozzrenija slavjan na prirodu*, I–III (Moscow, 1865–9).

5. A. Pypin, 'Russkie narodnye skazki', *Otečestvennye zapiski*, 1856.

6. *Sovremennik*, LXXI (1858).

7. See B. Sokolov, *Skaziteli* (Moscow, 1924); M. Azadovskij, 'Eine sibirische Märchenerzählerin', *Folklore Fellows Communications*, no. 68 (Helsinki, 1926); E. Gofman, 'K voprosu ob individual'nom stile skazoenika', *Xudozestvennyi fol'klor*, IV–V (1929).

8. B. Sokolov, *Russkij fol'klor*, I–II (Moscow, 1929–30); Ju. Sokolov, 'Fol'kloristika literaturovedenie', *Pamjati P. N. Sakulina* (Moscow, 1931), and *Russkij fol'klor*, Moscow 1938 (a detailed survey of the research in Russian folklore).

9. P. Bogatyrev and R. Jakobson, 'Die Folklore als besondere Form des Schaffens', *Donum natalicium Schrijnen* (Nijmegen-Utrecht, 1929). (See Jakobson, *Selected Writings*, IV, p. 1 ff.)

10. A. Nikiforov, 'K voprosu o morfologičeskom izučenii narodnoj skazki', *Sbornik Otd. rus. jaz. i slov. Akademii nauk*, CI (1928); V. Propp, *Morfologija skazki* (Leningrad, 1928), and 'Transformacii volšebnyx skazok', *Poètika*, IV (1928).

11. An excellent anthology of Russian tales from different collections is that of M. Azadovskij, *Russkaja skazka*, I–II (Leningrad, 1931–2).

12. The most important collections of folk tales recorded in pre-revolutionary Russia are:

Notes

D. Sadovnikov, *Skazki i predanija Samarskogo kraja* (St Petersburg, 1884); V. Dobrovol'skij, *Smolenskij ètnografičeskij sbornik*, 2 vols. (1891–1903); N. Ončukov, *Severnye skazki* (St Petersburg, 1909); D. Zelenin, *Velikorusskie skazki Permskoj gubernii* (St Petersburg, 1914); *Velikorusskie skazki Vjatskoj gubernii* (St Petersburg, 1915); B. and Ju. Sokolov, *Skazki i pesni Belozerskogo kraja* (Moscow, 1915); A. Smirnov, *Sbornik velikorusskix skazok arxiva Russkogo geografičeskogo obščestva*, I–II (St Petersburg, 1917). The most detailed history of collection and investigation of Russian tales up to the First World War is that of S. Savčenko, *Russkaja narodnaja skazka* (Kiev, 1914).

13. The most important collections of Russian tales made after the revolution are: M. Serova, *Novgorodskie skazki* (Leningrad, 1924); M. Azadovskij, *Skazki iz raznyx mest Sibiri* (Irkutsk, 1928), *Verxnelenskie skazki* (Irkutsk, 1938), *Skazki Magaja* (Leningrad, 1940); O. Ozarovskaja, *Pjatireč'e* (Leningrad, 1931); I. Karnauxova, *Skazki i predanija Severnogo kraja* (Moscow, 1934); V. Sidel'nikov & V. Krupjanskaja, *Volzskijfol'klor* (Moscow, 1937); T. Akimova & P. Stepanov, *Skazki Saratovskoj oblasti* (Saratov, 1937); A. Nečaev, *Belomorskie skazki, rasskazannye M. M. Korguevym* (Leningrad, 1938); M. Krasnozenova, *Skazki Krasnojarskogo kraja* (Leningrad, 1938).

14. N. Grinkova, 'Skazki Kuprijanixi', *Xudozestvennyj fol'klor*, I, 1926; I. Plotnikov, *Skazki Kuprijanixi* (Voronež, 1937).

15. N. Brodskij, 'Sledy professional'nyx skazocnikov v russkix skazkax', *Ètnografičeskoe obozrenie*, 1904; R. Volkov, *Skazka* (Odessa, 1924); J. Polívka, *Slovanské pohádky*, I (Prague, 1932).

16. 'Krasna pesnjal adom, a skazka skladom .

17. 'Sklad lučše pesni.'

18. *Ne pivo pit' – ne vino kurit',*
Povenčali – i žit' pomcali,
Stali žit' poživat' – i dobra naživat'.
Ja zaxodil v gosti, – ugostili xorošo
Po gubam teklo, – a v rot ne popalo.

19. M. Azadovskij, *Literatura i fol'klor* (Moscow, 1938).

20. E. Eleonskaja, 'Nekotorye zamečanija o roli zagadki v skazke', *Ètnografičeskoe obozrenie* (1907); 'Nekotorye zamečanija po povodu složenija skazok', ibid. (1912).

21. Löwis of Menar, *Russische Volksmärchen* (Jena, 1914); M. Gabel', *Dialog v skazke* (Kharkov, 1929).

22. A. Aarne and S. Thompson, 'The Types of the Folk-Tale', *Folklore Fellows Communications*, no. 74 (1928); N. Andreev, *Ukazatel' skazočnyx sjuzetov po sisteme Aarne* (Leningrad, 1929).

23. N. Andreev, 'K obzoru russkix skazočnyx sjužetov', *Xudožestvennyj f ol'klor*, II–III (Moscow, 1927).

24. L. Kolmačevskij, *Životnyj èpos na zapade i u slavjan* (Kazan, 1882); V. Bobrov, *Russkie narodnye skazki o životnyx* (Warsaw, 1908); A. Nikiforov, 'Narodnaja detskaja skazka dramatičeskogo zanra', *Skazočnaja komissija v 1927 g.* (Leningrad, 1928).

25. A. Veselovskij, 'Skazki ob Ivane Groznom', *Sobranie socinenij*, XVI (Leningrad, 1938).

26. *Pëtr Pervyj lapti plël,*
da ix za eto i proklël.
I skazal: 'lapti plest' –
odnova na den' est',
a starye kovyrjat':
ni odnova ne valjat'!'
I koeedyk zabrosil.

27. 'Skazka – skladka, pesnja – byl'.

28. M. Schlauch, 'Folklore in the Soviet Union', *Science and Society*, VIII (1944).

Notes

29. E. Trubetzkoy, ' "Inoe carstvo" i ego iskateli v russkoj narodnoj skazke', *Russkaja myel'* (Prague, 1923).
30. *Ne to čudo iz čudes,*
    čto mužik upal s nebes,
    a to čudo iz čudes,
    kak tuda on vlez.

CHARLES BAUDELAIRE'S 'LES CHATS'

1. M. Grammont, *Petit traité de versification française* (Paris, 1908), p. 86.
2. M. Grammont, *Traité de phonétique* (Paris, 1930), p. 384.
3. M. Grammont, *Traité de phonétique*, p. 388.
4. M. Durand, "La Spécificité du phonème. Application au cas de R/L", *Journal de Psychologie*, LVII (1960), pp. 405-19.
5. Cf. *L'Intermédiaire des chercheurs et des curieux*, LXVII, cols. 338 and 509.
6. M. E. Benveniste, who was kind enough to read this study in manuscript, pointed out to us that between *les amoureux fervents* and *les savants austères*, *la mûre saison* also plays the role of intermediary: it is, in effect, in *leur mûre saison* that they reunite to identify themselves *également* with the cats. For, continues M. Benveniste, to remain *amoureux fervents* in *leur mûre saison* already signifies that one is outside the common fold, as are *les savants austères* by their vocation. The initial situation of the sonnet is that of a life outside this world (nevertheless life in the underworld is rejected) and, transferred to the cats, this situation develops from chilly seclusion to vast starry solitudes where *science et volupté* are a dream without end.

In support of these comments, for which we thank their author, we could cite another poem in *Les Fleurs du Mal*: 'Le savant amour ... fruit d'automne aux saveurs souveraines' ('L'Amour du mensonge').

7. Ch. Baudelaire, *Œuvres*, II (Bibliothèque de la Pléiade, Paris, 1961), pp. 243ff.
8. Ch. Baudelaire, *Les Fleurs du Mal* (Edition critique établie par J. Crépet et G. Blin, Paris, 1942), p. 413.
9. M. Butor, *Histoire extraordinaire, essai sur un rêve de Baudelaire* (Paris, 1961), p. 85.
10. In L. Rudrauf's study, *Rime et sexe* (Tartu, 1936), the exposition of 'A theory of the alternation of masculine and feminine rhymes in French poetry' is followed by a 'controversy' with Maurice Grammont (pp. 47ff). According to the latter, 'for alternation as established in the XVIth century based upon the presence or absence of an unstressed *e* at the end of the word, we have availed ourselves of the terms "feminine" and "masculine" because the unstressed *e* at the end of a word was, in the majority of cases, indicative of the feminine gender: *un petie chat/une petite chatte*, or rather one could say that the specific termination of the feminine, in contradistinction to the masculine, always contained an unstressed *e*. 'However, Rudrauf expressed certain doubts: 'But was it purely the grammatical consideration that guided the poets of the XVIth century in their establishment of this rule of alternation and in their choice of the epithets "masculine" and "feminine" to designate the two kinds of rhymes? Let us not forget that the poets of the Pléiade wrote their stanzas with an eye to song, and that song underscores, much more than does the spoken word, the alternation of a strong (masculine) syllable and of a weak (feminine) syllable. Consciously or unconsciously, the musical point of view and the sexual point of view must have played a role along with the grammatical analogy (p. 49).

Inasmuch as this alternation of rhymes based upon the presence or absence of an unstressed *e* at the ends of lines is no longer realized, in Grammont's view it has been replaced by an alternation of rhymes ending either with a consonant or with a stressed vowel. While fully prepared to acknowledge that 'the final syllables ending with a vowel are all masculine' (p. 46), Rudrauf is at the same time tempted to establish a scale of twenty-four degrees for the consonantal rhymes, 'ranging from the most brusque and virile end syllables to the most femininely suave' (pp. 12ff). The rhymes with a voiceless stop at their end form the extreme masculine pole (1°) and the rhymes with a voiced spirant are viewed as the feminine pole (24°) of Rudrauf's scale. If one applies this tentative classification to the consonantal rhymes of 'Les Chats', one is conscious of a gradual movement towards the masculine pole, which results in an attenuation of the contrast between the two kinds of rhymes: [1]*austères* – [4]*sédentaires* (liquid: 19°); [6]*ténèbres* – [7]*funèbres* (voiced stop followed by a liquid: 15°); [9]*attitudes* – [10]*solitudes* (voiced stop: 13°); [12]*magiques* – [14]*mystiques* (voiceless stop: 1°).

STRUCTURES OF EXCHANGE IN 'CINNA'

1. There are certain resemblances visible between this and the system of *potlatch* analysed by Marcel Mauss in his now classic 'Essai sur le don' (*Sociologie et Anthropologie*, P.U.F., Paris, 1950). In the potlatch—a form of gift exchange which is at once freely willed and performed under constraint, gratuitous and yet done with a purpose, that is practised in Polynesia, Melanesia, and elsewhere—individuals do not find themselves in confrontation as individuals so much as in their capacity as representatives of the 'mind of their ancestors'. With them, as with Corneille's characters, it is a question of honour. 'This', Mauss writes, 'is noble commerce, full of politeness and generosity; in any case, whenever it is done in some other spirit, with an eye to immediate gain, it is the object of clearly manifested scorn' (pp. 201–2). Elsewhere, Mauss writes: 'Polynesian *mana* itself symbolizes not only the magical force of each being but also his honour; some of the best translations of this word would be: authority, richness' (p. 203). As can be seen, the economy of relationships as it appears in Corneille is partially based, as in the potlatch, on a system of 'generous' gifts which is at once free and obligatory. But the honour of the characters—like *mana* Mauss speaks of—is also involved in this exchange; it is stronger than the individuals who practise it and without it they could not properly be said to exist. Though I do not wish to push the comparison any further, I hope that these few similarities will have allowed us to get a surer hold on the economic elements which are an essential part of the Corneillian individual's constitution.

2. For a discussion of the social value attributed to suicide in the literature of the first half of the seventeenth century, see my *Un Paradis désespéré* ... (P.U.F., Paris, 1962).

3. This is the argument which Livie will answer later in maintaining that state crimes cannot be compared to individual crimes (v. 1609–10).

4. I am making a deliberate distinction; the Auguste we encounter at the end is quite different from the Auguste we meet at the beginning of the play. There is, after all, a world of difference between a man who is seeking to abandon his power and one who grants pardon to his intended assassin.

There is a greater relationship between the two words, abandon and pardon, than might meet the eye at a casual glance. Etymologically the two words have an identical and contradictory meaning. The verb *abandon* comes from the Old French *mettre à bandon* which meant 'to put under someone else's ban, i.e. to relinquish oneself to another's authority' (*O.E.D.*). To abandon, then, is to divest oneself of a properly possessed power. By another token, to pardon is to excuse from a debt. We see an example of this in an Old French text where it is written: 'Quant Rolles vit qu'ele ot tele amour viers son segnor, si li *pardonna* la moitie de sa raencon.' Thus, to pardon is also to strip oneself of something; but, in contradistinction to abandon, it is to do so in a way which leads to rendering something which the other does not yet possess (since he is to receive it from me) and which therefore clearly belongs to me. From the juridical and economic point of view, the process of pardoning is thus much more complex than the process of abandoning, for it implies a dual debt, a debt which can only be paid by currency which, while immaterial, is none the less essential to every society to the extent that such currency is the very basis of 'credit'. It is a matter of the recognition which brings glory and honour to the person who is its object. Pardon, by the very complexity of the ties which it binds, tends to tighten up the social fabric—which is what we are seeing at the end of *Cinna*—whereas any process of abandonment slackens them. The anthropological ramifications of these remarks bring us back to Marcel Mauss's 'Essai sur le don'.

Notes

5. See Michel Beaujour, 'Polyeucte et la monarchie de droit divi...
(April, 1963).

THE LEGITIMACY OF SOLOMON:
SOME STRUCTURAL ASPECTS OF OLD TESTAMENT HIST...

1. C. Lévi-Strauss, Anthropologie structurale (Plon, Paris, 1958), p. 81.
2. C. Lévi-Strauss, La Pensée sauvage (Plon, Paris, 1962).
3. C. Lévi-Strauss, Mythologiques: Le Cru et le cuit (Plon, Paris, 1964), p. 346.
4. Lévi-Strauss, La Pensée sauvage, p. 173.
5. G. Ryle, The Concept of Mind (Hutchinson, London, 1949), pp. 15 sqq. 'The dogma of the Ghost in the Machine' is Professor Ryle's label for what he calls 'the Official Doctrine', deriving from Descartes, which treats mind and body as separate entities. Ryle's book is designed to demonstrate that this dogma 'is entirely false'.
6. Morris Ginsberg, On the Diversity of Morals (Heinemann, London, 1956), p. 239, has translated a passage from Durkheim's Sociologie et philosophie (Presses univ. de France, Paris, 1924), pp. 74-5, as follows: 'Kant postulates God because without this hypothesis morality would be unintelligible. I postulate a personality, specifically distinct from individuals, because otherwise morality would have no object and duty, no point of attachment.'

D. F. Pocock in his translation of Sociology and Philosophy (Cohen & West, London, 1953), pp. 51-2, substitutes for the word 'personality' the word 'society', thus quite altering the degree of reification implied.

7. These comments are a free interpretation of part of what is argued at length by Paul Ricœur in 'Structure et herméneutique' in Esprit (November, 1963), pp. 596-628. Ricœur makes extensive references to Gerhard von Rad, Theologie des Alten Testaments Bd. I, Die Theologie der geschichtlichen Überlieferungen Israels (Chr. Kaiser Verlag, Munich, 1957) which has been translated into English as Old Testament Theology vol. I, The Theology of Israel's Historical Tradition (Oliver and Boyd, London, 1962). Von Rad, like all orthodox Biblical scholars, takes it for granted that a fundamental core of 'real history' underlies the narrative at least from the time of David onwards. My own scepticism is far more radical: King David and King Solomon are no more likely to be historical than are King Agamemnon and King Menelaus.

On the other hand, I share M. I. Finley's view (e.g. 'Myth, Memory and History', History and Theory, IV (1965), pp. 281-302) that the distinction between myth and hystory is not necessarily clear-cut. It need not be inconsistent to affirm that an historical record has mythical characteristics and functions. In point of fact von Rad's historical assumptions, when modified by his refined techniques of textual criticism, often lead to conclusions which are entirely in accord with the implications of the 'structuralist' procedures exemplified in this essay.

8. E. R. Leach, 'Lévi-Strauss in the Garden of Eden', Transactions of the New York Academy of Sciences, 1961, 23-4, pp. 386-96. E. R. Leach, 'Genesis as Myth', Discovery, XXIII (1962), pp. 30-5.

Lévi-Strauss seems to regard ethnology and history as complementary but quite distinct forms of inquiry (La Pensée sauvage, p. 39). This may explain why he uses a narrow definition of myth which makes it appear that the myths of contemporary Amerindians are cultural products of an entirely different kind from the mythical-historical traditions of the Jewish people in the first century B.C. My own view is that this distinction is quite artificial and that the structural analysis of myth should be equally applicable to both the time of men and the time of gods. (Cf. Finley, op. cit., p. 288.)

9. Apart from the sources mentioned in the text, the commentaries which I have found most useful are:

James Hastings, A Dictionary of the Bible, 5 volumes (T. and T. Clark, New York, 1898–1904).

opaedia Biblica, 4 volumes (A. & C. Black, London,

lance of the Bible (Hodder & Stoughton, London, 1894).

ational Critical Commentary (T. and T. Clark, London,

of a different kind are: G. Widengren, 'Early Hebrew
. H. Hooke, *Myth, Ritual and Kingship* (Clarendon Press,

Myths: The Book of Genesis (Cassell, London, 1964).

on of the evidence see Aage Bentzen, *Introduction to the Old
. Gad, Copenhagen, 1958). It is probable that a substantially
ed by 400 B.C. but modifications were still being introduced
in the first cen.... re was more than one canonical orthodoxy.

11. Graves and Patai, o.... t. (p. 25), take note of the antiquity of this style of analysis.
They are plainly scornful: 'This scheme and others like it prove the Rabbis' desire to credit
God with systematic thought.' As my citation from Leo Strauss shows, there is more to it
than that.

12. Leo Strauss, 'Interpretation of Genesis' (typescript of a lecture delivered at University
College, University of Chicago, January 25th, 1957).

13. If Nehemiah was a flesh-and-blood historical character then he lived about 400 B.C.

14. S. A. Cook, Article 'Jews', *Encyclopaedia Britannica*, 14th edition.

15. From the point of view of general communication theory randomly distributed minor
textual inconsistencies may be looked upon as *Gaussian noise*. For a non-technical explanation
of this point see C. Cherry, *On Human Communication* (M.I.T. Press and John Wiley and
Sons Inc., Cambridge, Massachusetts, 1957), p. 198.

16. E.g. Evans-Pritchard, *The Nuer* (Clarendon Press, Oxford, 1940). E. Peters, 'The
Proliferation of Segments in the Lineage of the Bedouin of Cyrenaica', *Journal of the Royal
Anthropological Institute*, xc (1960), pp. 23–53. M. Fortes, *The Dynamics of Clanship among the
Tallensi* (Oxford University Press, London, 1946).

17. It deserves note that the fully historical Kingdom of Judaea of Simon Maccabaeus
(second century B.C.) consisted of territory which, in the traditional narrative, was allocated
to Judah, Benjamin and Ephraim. Samaria was at that time a separate province to the north.
Ahab, the prototype 'bad' northern king in the traditional history, is specifically described as
King of Samaria (1 Kings xvi. 29–30; xxi. 1).

In the genealogy, the tribe of Benjamin is linked with the tribes of Ephraim and Manasseh
in that all are descended from Rachel, but Ephraim and Manasseh are the descendants of
Joseph who becomes a foreigner. Joseph is the first of Jacob-Israel's sons to become separated
from his father and the land of Israel. He becomes ruler of Egypt and marries an Egyptian.
In contrast, Benjamin is the last of Jacob-Israel's sons to become separated from his father and
his homeland (Genesis xliii, xlvii. 20).

18. In Hebrew as in English the phonemic difference between Zeruah and Zeruiah is slight,
indeed in the lexicon of Biblical Hebrew the two words appear as adjacent entries. Some
ancient texts imply that Zeruah was a harlot, but in Biblical contexts this too has ambiguous
implications (see p. 277).

19. There is a flat contradiction between Genesis xxiii and L. 13 on the one hand, and
Genesis xxxiii. 18–20 and Acts vii. 16 on the other. The first reference makes Abraham
purchase a grave-site from the Hethites (Hittites) at Hebron; the second reference makes
Abraham purchase a grave-site from the Shechemites at Shechem. David was first crowned
king at Hebron; the secessionist Jeroboam was crowned king at Shechem. This contradiction,
like the Calebite inconsistencies, must be a residue of editorial attempts to justify simultaneously two rival claims to the same title of ancestral right. As will be seen from the map Hebron
and Shechem are symmetrically located north and south of the east–west frontier.

Notes

In the story of Naboth's vineyard Naboth's virtue lies in the fact that he denies the right of King Ahab to buy out his inheritance with money (1 Kings xxi. 2, 3).

21. Cf. von Rad, *Theologie des Alten Testaments*, p. 64, also G. von Rad, *Genesis* (S.C.M. Press, London, 1961), p. 107.

22. Orthodox scholarship here presumes a corrupt text and would substitute 'Jesse' for 'Nahash'.

23. Cf. I. Schapera, 'The Sin of Cain', *Journal of the Royal Anthropological Institute*, LXXXV (1955), part I, Jan.–Dec., pp. 33–43, discusses sociological explanations of the fact that blood revenge cannot be taken against a fratricide.

24. Modern Biblical scholarship recognizes this material as having a distinct and unitary core referred to by von Rad and others as 'The Succession Document'.

25. Cf. V. Propp, *The Morphology of the Folktale* (Indiana University Research Center in Anthropology and Linguistics, Bloomington, 1958).

26. Cf. Hooke, op. cit.; also Lord Raglan, *The Hero* (Methuen, London, 1936).

27. Von Rad, *Theologie des Alten Testaments*, p. 325.

28. Robert H. Pfeiffer, *Introduction to the Old Testament* (A. and C. Black, London, 1952), pp. 342–59.

'THE HOUSE OF THE MIGHTY HERO' OR 'THE HOUSE OF ENOUGH PADDY'? SOME IMPLICATIONS OF A SINHALESE MYTH

1. According to Northern Buddhist tradition, Mahinda (Mahendra) was a brother of Asoka.

2. The name Morapitiya is fictitious. Readers who are aware of the real name of this community are asked to respect the anonymity of the villagers concerned.

3. 'The proverb is that the *binna* husband should take care to have constantly ready at the door of his wife's room a walking stick, a *talpat* and a torch, that he may be prepared at any hour of the day or night, and whatever may be the state of the weather or his own health, to quit the house on being ordered' (D'Oyly, 1835: 129).

4. [The personal incidents recorded at pp. 299 and 325 are more revealing than the author suggests. The Morapitiyans placed Mrs Robinson in the category of 'distinguished strangers who, though not of our caste, can nevertheless be assimilated nto our caste by the fiction of reincarnation' (Editor).]

5. [In the classical version of the story Kalani appears as Kalyani. The kings of Kalyani were *nagas* and it is implied that Kalyani Tissa (Kalani Tissa) is descended from the *naga* king Maniakkhika, who was mother's brother to the *naga* Mahodara, the guardian protector of the Buddha. Likewise, in the classical story, Māyā (meaning 'magic') is replaced by Malaya (meaning 'mountain'), which is represented as the homeland of the barbarous descendants of the children born to Vijaya from his relations with the *yakkhini* (*Mahavamsa* i. 63–76; vii. 59–68; xxiv. 7; xxii. 12–13; Kavan). Tissa = Kakavannatissa in the *Mahavamsa* xxii. 11 (Editor).]

6. Kadola = Kandula n the *Mahavamsa* xxii. 61, a magical elephant with six tusks, cf. *Rajavaliya*: 29–30.

7. *Māmā* is a classificatory kinship term meaning 'mother's brother', 'father's sister's husband', 'father-in-law', etc. A Sinhalese should properly only marry a girl of his own sub-caste (i.e. a known relative) who is in the classificatory standing of *nāna*, that is the daughter of a *māmā*. A man's father-in-law is therefore in the standing of *māmā* even before the relevant marriage. In the myth, Vira's status towards Dutthagāmani seems to be that of 'mother's brother'.

8. The Dictionary gives *Gammahē* as 'Village Headman among the Veddas', cf. Pieris (1956: 294) who has *Gammahē* = *Gamarāla* but *māhālla* = 'old woman', and the Morapitiyans

insist that *Gammähē* means *Gamarāla*'s wife. They infer from this that the *Gamarāla* was living in *binna* (uxorilocally). The logic of the story is that the *Gamarāla* = Vira, but the myth itself does not make this equation.

9. [The Peacock is the vehicle of Kataragama Deviyo (Skanda), the Ceylonese God of War, a deity whose cult is very ancient but certainly of Hindu origin. A virtuous Sinhalese Buddhist can gain almost as much merit by making a pilgrimage to the shrine of the Kataragama Deviyo as from ascending Adam's Peak to pay reverence to the Buddha's footprint. The cult of Kataragama is markedly phallic, whereas that of the Buddha is sexually ascetic (Editor).]

10. For example, according to the *Mahavamsa* xxii. 19, the monk of paragraph 2 was thrown into the sea instead of being boiled in oil.

11. Candala are reputedly the ancestors of the Rodiya, the lowest and most polluted of all present-day Sinhalese castes. Rodiya women are renowned for their beauty and for their professional activities as prostitutes.

12. The numbers in parentheses throughout this section indicate cross-references to the corresponding numbered incidents in the myth in section 11.

13. In the *Rajavaliya* version this opposition is quite explicit. 'Then the Kadol elephant being wroth thought within himself, "On my back was a woman, on the horse rode a man" ' (*Rajavaliya*: 30).

14. In light of the importance of the roles played by Dutthagāmani's mother and his elephant in the myth, it is interesting to note that the last time a Morapitiyan was severely possessed by a *yakkuva* (demon) was the day that the wife of the Koralemahatmaya died and the time before that was on the day that his elephant died. (The Koralemahatmaya is the head-man of the Korale, an administrative unit composed of several villages; he was a Morapitiyan.)

15. The term *variga* (*varga*, *waruge*, etc.) appears frequently in the sociological literature of Ceylon. The Seligmans, writing of the Veddas in 1911, interpret the word as meaning 'matri-lineal clan'. Perera (1910), writing of Sinhalese, translates it as 'caste'. Leach (1961b), with reference to North Central Province Sinhalese material, translates it as 'sub-caste'. Leach (1963) has further pointed out that the Vedda 'clans' described by the Seligmans do not appear to have the characteristics of matrilineal descent groups and has suggested that the Seligmans mis-understood their evidence. However, with numerous qualifications, it might appear that the Vedda *waruge* encountered by the Seligmans were in certain respects (a) matrilineal, (b) exogamous, (c) ranked. It should be noted that these are characteristics claimed for the Kotmale Valley *variga* also.

SYSTEM, STRUCTURE AND CONTRADICTION IN *DAS KAPITAL*

1. C. Lévi-Strauss, 'La notion de structure en ethnologie', *Anthropologie structurale* (Plon Paris, 1958), ch. xv, p. 305.

2. Ibid., p. 306.

3. We have deliberately simplified the exposition. In fact the profit may or may not correspond to the surplus value actually produced by a firm.

4. Marx, *Das Kapital*, book i, vol. ii.

5. Ibid., book iii, vol. ii.

6. Similarly for Spinoza the second, mathematical type of knowledge does not eliminate the first, everyday kind.

7. C. Lévi-Strauss, *Les Structures élémentaires de la parenté* (P.U.F., Paris, 1949), ch. xiv, pp. 216–46. See also A. Weil's algebraic study, ch. xiv, pp. 278–87.

8. This is similar to the results of the 'black body' radiation experiment – a 'small detail' (cf. Bachelard, *La Psychanalyse du Feu*) which upset the whole nineteenth-century Newtonian approach to physics.

This is not quite correct. Lévi-Strauss credits Hodson with the discovery of the correlation between the law of marriage with the matrilateral female cross cousin and the existence of a specific social structure. But Hodson believed that this structure must always be tripartite and patrilinear, whereas in fact it can contain any number of classes and need only be harmonic. See Lévi-Strauss, *Structures élémentaires*, pp. 292–3; T. C. Hodson, *Primitive Culture of India* (Royal Asiatic Society, London, 1922).

10. Its discovery was made all the more difficult in this case by the fact that the appearance of the system suggested a structure of the Aranda type but 'instead of the true symmetry of the Kariera and Aranda systems we find a pseudo-symmetry which turns out in fact to be two asymmetric structures superimposed' (*Structures élémentaires*, p. 242).

11. A. R. Radcliffe-Brown, *Structure and Function in Primitive Society* (Cohen & West, London, 1952).

12. See C. Lévi-Strauss, *On manipulated sociological models*, Bijdragen (1960).

13. Hence Lévi-Strauss's repeated criticisms of the idealism and formalism which have in fact become the main opponents of scientific structuralism, cf. 'La Structure et la forme' (*Cahiers de l'I.S.É.A.*, March, 1960), and the preface to *Le Cru et le cuit* (Plon, Paris, 1964).

14. Lévi-Strauss, *On manipulated sociological models*, p. 53.

15. Lévi-Strauss, *Structures élémentaires*, p. 235.

16. W. Lloyd Warner, 'Morphology and Function of the Australian Murngin type of Kinship', *American Anthropologist*, vol. 32–3, 1931, pp. 179–82.

17. Cases of borrowings of all or part of social institutions such as kinship, mythology, dance, etc., are quite common in Australia. Stanner was able to observe a case of the borrowing of the institution of kinship in the Nangiomeri tribe (see *Structures élémentaires*, p. 227).

18. The Kariera system, for example, is matrilinear and patrilocal.

19. 'This characteristic (that of being a harmonic regime) explains why the appearance of a class system is so rare whenever marriage is determined by a law of generalized exchange' (*Structures élémentaires*, p. 272).

20. Hence Lévi-Strauss's criticism of the associationist evolutionism of the nineteenth century (see *Structures élémentaires*, pp. 129, 185).

21. Marx, *Das Kapital*, book I, vol. III.

22. This is not invalidated by the phenomena of social mobility by which some workers may become capitalists or which are due to the effects of competition leading to the ruin of some capitalists or a particular category of business.

23. This diachrony always seems to resolve itself in the synchronic or at least to be only a manifestation of the many different modes of existence that the same structure can assume in different local conditions. Cf. Marx: 'The same economic base, the same that is in its fundamental conditions, can, under the effect of the large number of different empirical conditions, such as natural conditions, racial relationships, exterior historical influences etc., appear with an infinite number of variations which only the analysis of these empirical conditions will elucidate' (*Das Kapital*, book III, vol. III).

24. Marx, *Das Kapital*, book III, vol. II.

25. Ibid., book I, vol. I.

26. Karl Marx, *Contribution to the Critique of Political Economy* (Foreign Languages Publishing House, Moscow, 1961), p. 171.

27. Marx, *Das Kapital*, book III, vol. II.

28. Marx, *Contribution*, p. 28.

29. Engels: *Lettre à Starkenberg*, January 25th, 1894 (Foreign Languages Publishing House, Moscow, 1961).

30. Engels's declaration in *L'Origine de la famille de la propriété privée de l'État* (Foreign Languages Publishing House, Moscow, 1961, p. 15 of the preface) that 'The determining factor, in the final, historical, analysis, is the production and reproduction of day-to-day life' might lead one to suppose that kinship plays a determining role alongside the economy, whereas it is in fact, in this type of society, an element of the economic infra-structure.

31. Because of this plurality of the function of kinship Beatty and other anthropologists have claimed that kinship has no content of its own but is simply a symbolic form through which the content of social life, economic, political, religious and other relationships is expressed, so that kinship is no more than a language or means of expression. Without denying that kinship does function as a symbolic language of social life Schneider objects to this that kinship also has a content of its own which can be discovered by separating off the economic, political and religious aspects of its functioning. This reveals all the blood relationships and relationships through marriage which act as a means of expression of social life, and are the terms of the symbolic language of kinship. Kinship here, then, is one of the contents of social life and also serves as a mode of appearance and expression of all other contents. But in thus trying to restore some content to kinship Schneider runs a grave risk of falling into the very biologism which he condemns in Gellner. It is well known that the complex of blood relationships and relationships through marriage is not kinship, since a system of kinship is always a particular group of these relationships within which social rules are set up governing descent and marriage, and it is because only certain relationships are selected and retained as important that real kinship is not a biological but a social fact.

The mistake which both Beatty and Schneider make is to seek the content of this type of kinship outside the economic, political and religious relationships, since kinship is neither an external form nor a residual content but functions directly, internally as economic or political relationships, etc., and thus functions as a mode of expression of the social life and as a symbolic form of this life.

The scientific problem then is to determine why this should be the case in different types of society, and methodologically the only conclusion would seem to be that binary oppositions of concepts of the form-content type are inappropriate in trying to account for the functioning of the social structures. See Gellner, 'Ideal Language and Kinship Structure', *Philosophy of Science*, vol. XXIV (1957); Needham, 'Descent Systems and Ideal Language', Ibid., vol. XXVII (1960); Gellner, 'The Concept of Kinship', Ibid., vol. XXVII (1960); Barnes, 'Physical and Social Kinship', Ibid., vol. XXVIII (1961); Gellner, 'Nature and Society in Social Anthropology', Ibid., vol. XXX (1963); Schneider, 'The Nature of Kinship', *American Anthropologist*, vol. 66, Nov.–Dec., 1964.

32. On this point, see Lévi-Strauss: 'The situation is quite different in groups where the satisfaction of economic needs depends entirely on the conjugal partnership and on the division of labour between the sexes. Not only do men and women have different technical specializations and are thus mutually dependent for the manufacture of the essential objects of everyday life, they also specialize in the production of different types of food. A complete and, above all, a regular diet therefore really depends on the couple operating as a co-operative for production, especially at the more primitive levels where very hard physical surroundings combined with a rudimentary degree of technical development will make life precarious, whether based on hunting, horticulture or simply the gathering of food in the wild. It would be almost impossible for an individual to survive if left abandoned to his own devices.' (*Structures élémentaires*, p. 48.)

33. Writing about the rank and importance of social structures in a society with a particular type of production, Marx says in the introduction to the *Contribution to the Critique of Political Economy*: 'It is like a sort of background lighting against which the colours appear and by which their individual tints are altered. It is like a particular type of atmosphere which determines the specific gravity of everything which exists in it' (p. 171).

34. Cf. Roland Barthes, 'Les Sciences humaines et l'œuvre de Lévi-Strauss', *Annales* (Nov.–Dec., 1964), p. 1086.

Notes

THE STRUCTURAL BALANCE OF THE KINSHIP SYSTEMS OF SOME PRIMITIVE PEOPLES

1. C. Lévi-Strauss, *Anthropologie structurale* (Plon, Paris, 1958); Eng. tr. by Jakobson and Schoepf, *Structural Anthropology* (Penguin, Harmondsworth, 1968).

2. P. Abell, 'Structural Balance in Dynamic Structures', *Sociology*, vol. 2 (1968).

3. F. Harary, 'On the Measurement of Structural Latence', *Behav. Sci.*, vol. 4 (1959).

4. See Abell, op. cit.

5. For a proof of this theorem see Harary, op. cit. This theorem is a special case of a more general theorem, a proof of which can be found in Abell, op. cit.

6. B. Malinowski, *The Sexual Life of Savages in North-Western Melanesia* (London, 1929).

7. Dubois de Minpereux, cited in M. Kivalevski, 'La Famille ¦matriarcale au Caucuse', *L'Anthropologie*, vol. IV (1893).

8. E. N. Gifford, 'Tonga Society', *Bernice P. Bishop Bulletin*, no. 61 (Honolulu, 1929).

9. F. E. Williams, 'Group Sentiment and Primitive Justice', *American Anthropologist*, A.S., vol. XLIII, no. 4, pt. 1 (1941).

10. F. E. Williams, 'Natives of Lake Kubuta, Papua', *Oceana*, vol. XI (1940–1).

11. D. L. Oliver, *A Solomon Island Society: Kinship and Leadership among the Siuai of Bougainville* (Camb. Mass., 1955).

12. A. R. Radcliffe-Brown, 'The Mother's Brother in South Africa', *South African Journal of Science*, vol. XXI (1924).

13. The reader might suggest that we should have included these from the beginning, especially the mother/son relationship. I agree, but I am trying to follow Lévi-Strauss, who was concerned with the four relationships so far dealt with. In terms of balance theory this prediction might equally have been carried out the other way round. For instance, if mother/son is positive and mother/husband negative, then father/son must be negative.

ON THE MEANING OF THE WORD 'STRUCTURE' IN MATHEMATICS

1. See, for example: J. Piaget, *Traité de Logique* (P.U.F., Paris, 1949).

2. See R. Jaulin, 'La Géomancie; Essai d'analyse formelle' (to appear in *Cahiers de l'Homme*).

SOME PROBLEMS IN THE THEORY OF STRUCTURAL BALANCE

1. We shall see later in the paper that Balance Theory must be carefully circumscribed by a *ceteris paribus* clause.

2. J. Galtung, 'Rank and Social Integration: A Multidimensional Approach', in *Sociological Theories in Progress*, ed. Berger, Zelditch and Anderson (Houghton Mifflin Company, Boston, 1966).

3. L. Coser, *The Functions of Social Conflict* (Routledge & Kegan Paul, London, 1956).

4. P. Abell, 'Towards a Theory of Polarization' (mimeo), University of Essex (1968).

5. K. Lewin, *Topological Psychology* (McGraw-Hill, New York, 1936).

6. P. Abell, 'Towards a Model of Social Role' (mimeo), University of Essex (1968).

7. F. Harary, 'On the Measurement of Structural Balance', *Behavioral Science*, vol. 4 (1959).

8. F. Heider, 'Attitudes and Cognitive Organisation', *Journal of Psychology*, vol. 21 (1946).

9. This argument is complicated if we view the affective links in a structure as institutionalized. Then the problem reduces to one of whether or not a role incumbent cognizes 'correctly' the relationship between his role and other related roles. If he does not do so, then in some sense he is imperfectly socialized into his role. We shall, in this paper, however, ignore the problems of institutionalization of affective links.

10. It is also possible for a structure to attain balance by expelling points. We shall not, however, consider this option here.

11. P. Abell, 'Structural Balance in Dynamic Structures', *Sociology*, vol. 2 (1968).

12. Ibid.

13. J. Davis, 'Clustering and Structural Balance in Graphs', *Human Relations*, vol. 20 (1967).

14. Abell, 'Towards a Theory of Polarization'.

15. Ibid.

16. C. Flament, *Applications of Graph Theory to Group Structure* (Prentice-Hall, 1963).

17. The point coefficient can be entered down the diagonal of the arc-strain matrix, giving a full summary of the strain parameters.

18. Flament, op. cit.

19. P. Abell, 'Measurement in Sociology: I', *Sociology*, vol. 2 (1968).

20. We have a certain amount of empirical evidence that people tend to make more positive discriminations than negative ones.

21. An ordinal graph is exactly like an ordinary graph, except that a valuation from the linear orders is attached to each arc.

22. I shall concentrate upon arc strain in the following paragraphs, but the ideas are very readily applicable to point strain, except that the concept of Inertia is inappropriate.